The Quest of the Historical

A Critical Study of its Progress From Reimarus to Wrede

By

Albert Schweitzer

Privatdocent in New Testament Studies in the University of Strassburg

Translated By

W. Montgomery

With a Preface by

F. C. Burkitt

Norrisian Professor of Divinity in the University of Cambridge

Second English Edition

London

Adam and Charles Black

1911

Note: Pagination from the original version can be found throughout this document in brackets.

Contents

- Preface
- I. The Problem
- II. Hermann Samuel Reimarus
- III. The Lives Of Jesus Of The Earlier Rationalism
- IV. The Earliest Fictitious Lives Of Jesus
- V. Fully Developed Rationalism—Paulus
- VI. The Last Phase Of Rationalism—Hase And Schleiermacher
- VII. David Friedrich Strauss—The Man And His Fate
- VIII. Strauss's First "Life Of Jesus"
- IX. Strauss's Opponents And Supporters
- X. The Marcan Hypothesis
- XI. Bruno Bauer. The First Sceptical Life Of Jesus
- XII. Further Imaginative Lives Of Jesus
- XIII. Renan
- XIV. The "Liberal" Lives Of Jesus
- XV. The Eschatological Question
- XVI. The Struggle Against Eschatology
- XVII. Questions Regarding The Aramaic Language, Rabbinic Parallels, And Buddhistic Influence
- XVIII. The Position Of The Subject At The Close Of The Nineteenth Century
- XIX. Thoroughgoing Scepticism And Thoroughgoing Eschatology
- XX. Results
- Index Of Authors And Works
- Footnotes

First Edition published March 1910

Preface

The book here translated is offered to the English-speaking public in the belief that it sets before them, as no other book has ever done, the history of the struggle which the best-equipped intellects of the modern world have gone through in endeavouring to realise for themselves the historical personality of our Lord.

Every one nowadays is aware that traditional Christian doctrine about Jesus Christ is encompassed with difficulties, and that many of the statements in the Gospels appear incredible in the light of modern views of history and nature. But when the alternative of "Jesus or Christ" is put forward, as it has been in a recent publication, or when we are bidden to choose between the Jesus of history and the Christ of dogma, few except professed students know what a protean and kaleidoscopic figure the "Jesus of history" is. Like the Christ in the Apocryphal Acts of John, He has appeared in different forms to different minds. "We know Him right well," says Professor Weinel.[1] What a claim!

Among the many bold paradoxes enunciated in this history of the Quest, there is one that meets us at the outset, about which a few words may be said here, if only to encourage those to persevere to the end who might otherwise be repelled halfway—the paradox that the greatest attempts to write a Life of Jesus have been written with hate.[2] It is in full accordance with this faith that Dr. Schweitzer gives, in paragraph after paragraph, the undiluted expression of the views of men who agree only in their unflinching desire to attain historical truth. We are not accustomed to be so ruthless in England. We sometimes tend to forget that the Gospel has moved the world, and we think our faith and devotion to it so tender and delicate a thing that it will break, if it be not handled with the utmost circumspection. So we become dominated [pg vi] by phrases and afraid of them. Dr. Schweitzer is not afraid of phrases, if only they have been beaten out by real contact with facts. And those who read to the end will see that the crude sarcasm of Reimarus and the unflinching scepticism of Bruno Bauer are not introduced merely to shock and by way of contrast. Each in his own way made a real contribution to our understanding of the greatest historical problem in the history of our race. We see now that the object of attack was not the historical Jesus after all, but a temporary idea of Him, inadequate because it did not truly represent Him or the world in which He lived. And by hearing the writers' characteristic phrases, uncompromising as they may be, by looking at things for a moment from their own point of view, different as it may be from ours, we are able to be more just, not only to these men of a past age, but also to the great Problem that occupied them, as it also occupies us.

For, as Father Tyrrell has been pointing out in his last most impressive message to us all, Christianity is at the Cross Roads. If the Figure of our Lord is to mean anything for us we must realise it for ourselves. Most English readers of the New Testament have been too long content with the rough and ready Harmony of the Four Gospels that they unconsciously construct. This kind of "Harmony" is not a very convincing picture when looked into, if only because it almost always conflicts with inconvenient statements of the Gospels themselves, statements that have been omitted from the "Harmony", not on any reasoned theory, but simply from inadvertence or the difficulty of fitting them in. We treat the Life of our Lord too much as it is treated in the Liturgical "Gospels", as a simple series of disconnected anecdotes.

Dr. Schweitzer's book does not pretend to be an impartial survey. He has his own solution of the problems, and it is not to be expected that English students will endorse the whole of his view of the Gospel History, any more than his German fellow-workers have done. But valuable and suggestive as I believe his constructive work to be in its main outlines, I venture to think his grasp of the nature and complexity of the great Quest is even more remarkable, and his exposition of it cannot fail to stimulate us in England. Whatever we may think of Dr. Schweitzer's solution or that of his opponents, we too have to reckon with the Son of Man who was expected to come before the apostles had gone over the cities of Israel, the Son of Man who would come in His Kingdom before some that heard our Lord speak should taste death, the Son of Man who came to give His life a ransom for many, whom [pg vii]they would see hereafter coming with the clouds of heaven. "Who is this Son of Man?" Dr. Schweitzer's book is an attempt to give the full historical value and the true historical setting to these fundamental words of the Gospel of Jesus.

Our first duty, with the Gospel as with every other ancient document, is to interpret it with reference to its own time. The true view of the Gospel will be that which explains the course of events in the first century and the second century, rather than that which seems to have spiritual and imaginative value for the twentieth century. Yet I cannot refrain from pointing out here one feature of the theory of thoroughgoing eschatology, which may appeal to those who are accustomed to the venerable forms of ancient Christian aspiration and worship. It may well be that absolute truth cannot be embodied in human thought and that its expression must always be clothed in symbols. It may be that we have to translate the hopes and fears of our spiritual ancestors into the language of our new world. We have to learn, as the Church in the second century had to learn, that the End is not yet, that New Jerusalem, like all other objects of sense, is an image of the truth rather than the truth itself. But at least we are beginning to see that the apocalyptic vision, the New Age which God is to bring in, is no mere embroidery of Christianity, but the heart of its enthusiasm. And therefore the expectations of vindication and judgment to come, the imagery of the Messianic Feast, the "other-worldliness" against which so many eloquent words were said in the nineteenth century, are not to be regarded as regrettable accretions foisted on by superstition to the pure morality of the original Gospel. These ideas are the Christian Hope, to be allegorised and "spiritualised" by us for our own use whenever necessary, but not to be given up so long as we remain Christians at all. Books which teach us boldly to trust the evidence of our documents, and to accept the eschatology of the Christian Gospel as being historically the eschatology of Jesus, help us at the same time to retain a real meaning and use for the ancient phrases of the Te Deum, and for the mediaeval strain of "Jerusalem the Golden."

F. C. Burkitt.

Cambridge, 1910.
[pg 001]

I. The Problem

When, at some future day, our period of civilisation shall lie, closed and completed, before the eyes of later generations, German theology will stand out as a great, a unique phenomenon in the mental and spiritual life of our time. For nowhere save in the German temperament can there be found in the same perfection the living complex of conditions and factors—of philosophic thought, critical acumen, historical insight, and religious feeling—without which no deep theology is possible.

And the greatest achievement of German theology is the critical investigation of the life of Jesus. What it has accomplished here has laid down the conditions and determined the course of the religious thinking of the future.

In the history of doctrine its work has been negative; it has, so to speak, cleared the site for a new edifice of religious thought. In describing how the ideas of Jesus were taken possession of by the Greek spirit, it was tracing the growth of that which must necessarily become strange to us, and, as a matter of fact, has become strange to us.

Of its efforts to create a new dogmatic we scarcely need to have the history written; it is alive within us. It is no doubt interesting to trace how modern thoughts have found their way into the ancient dogmatic system, there to combine with eternal ideas to form new constructions; it is interesting to penetrate into the mind of the thinker in which this process is at work; but the real truth of that which here meets us as history we experience within ourselves. As in the monad of Leibnitz the whole universe is reflected, so we intuitively experience within us, even apart from any clear historical knowledge, the successive stages of the progress of modern dogma, from rationalism to Ritschl. This experience is true knowledge, all the truer because we are conscious of the whole [pg 002] as something indefinite, a slow and difficult movement towards a goal which is still shrouded in obscurity. We have not yet arrived at any reconciliation between history and modern thought—only between half-way history and half-way thought. What the ultimate goal towards which we are moving will be, what this something is which shall bring new life and new regulative principles to coming centuries, we do not know. We can only dimly divine that it will be the mighty deed of some mighty original genius, whose truth and rightness will be proved by the fact that we, working at our poor half thing, will oppose him might and main—we who imagine we long for nothing more eagerly than a genius powerful enough to open up with authority a new path for the world, seeing that we cannot succeed in moving it forward along the track which we have so laboriously prepared.

For this reason the history of the critical study of the life of Jesus is of higher intrinsic value than the history of the study of ancient dogma or of the attempts to create a new one. It has to describe the most tremendous thing which the religious consciousness has ever dared and done. In the study of the history of dogma German theology settled its account with the past; in its attempt to create a new dogmatic, it was endeavouring to keep a place for the religious life in the thought of the present; in the study of the life of Jesus it was working for the future—in pure faith in the truth, not seeing whereunto it wrought.

Moreover, we are here dealing with the most vital thing in the world's history. There came a Man to rule over the world; He ruled it for good and for ill, as history testifies; He destroyed the world into which He was born; the spiritual life of our own time seems like to perish at His hands, for He leads to battle against our thought a host of dead ideas, a ghostly army upon which death has no power, and Himself destroys again the truth and goodness which His Spirit creates in us, so that it cannot rule the world. That He continues, notwithstanding, to reign as the alone Great and alone True in a world of which He denied the continuance, is the prime example of that antithesis between spiritual and natural truth which underlies all life and all events, and in Him emerges into the field of history.

It is only at first sight that the absolute indifference of early Christianity towards the life of the historical Jesus is disconcerting. When Paul, representing those who recognise the signs of the times, did not desire to know Christ after the flesh, that was the first expression of the impulse of self-preservation by which Christianity continued to be guided for centuries. It felt that with the introduction of the historic Jesus into its faith, there would arise something new, something which had not been foreseen in the thoughts of the Master Himself, and that thereby a contradiction [pg 003] would be brought to light, the solution of which would constitute one of the great problems of the world.

Primitive Christianity was therefore right to live wholly in the future with the Christ who was to come, and to preserve of the historic Jesus only detached sayings, a few miracles, His death and resurrection. By abolishing both the world and the historical Jesus it escaped the inner division described above, and remained consistent in its point of view. We, on our part, have reason to be grateful to the early Christians that, in consequence of this attitude they have handed down to us, not biographies of Jesus but only Gospels, and that therefore we possess the Idea and the Person with the minimum of historical and contemporary limitations.

But the world continued to exist, and its continuance brought this one-sided view to an end. The supra-mundane Christ and the historical Jesus of Nazareth had to be brought together into a single personality at once historical and raised above time. That was accomplished by Gnosticism and the Logos Christology. Both, from opposite standpoints, because they were seeking the same goal, agreed in sublimating the historical Jesus into the supra-mundane Idea. The result of this development, which followed on the discrediting of eschatology, was that the historical Jesus was again introduced into the field of view of Christianity, but in such a way that all justification for, and interest in, the investigation of His life and historical personality were done away with.

Greek theology was as indifferent in regard to the historical Jesus who lives concealed in the Gospels as was the early eschatological theology. More than that, it was dangerous to Him; for it created a new supernatural-historical Gospel, and we may consider it fortunate that the Synoptics were already so firmly established that the Fourth Gospel could not oust them; instead, the Church, as though from the inner necessity of the antitheses which now began to be a constructive element in her thought, was obliged to set up two antithetic Gospels alongside of one another.

When at Chalcedon the West overcame the East, its doctrine of the two natures dissolved the unity of the Person, and thereby cut off the last possibility of a return to the historical Jesus. The self-contradiction was elevated into a law. But the Manhood was so far admitted as to preserve, in appearance, the rights of history. Thus by a deception the formula kept the Life prisoner and prevented the leading spirits of the Reformation from grasping the idea of a return to the historical Jesus.

This dogma had first to be shattered before men could once more go out in quest of the historical Jesus, before they could even grasp the thought of His existence. That the historic Jesus is something [pg 004] different from the Jesus Christ of the doctrine of the Two Natures seems to us now self-evident. We can, at the present day, scarcely imagine the long agony in which the historical view of the life of Jesus came to birth. And even when He was once more recalled to life, He was still, like Lazarus of old, bound hand and foot with grave-clothes—the grave-clothes of the dogma of the Dual Nature. Hase relates, in the preface to his first Life of Jesus (1829), that a worthy old gentleman, hearing of his project, advised him to treat in the first part of the human, in the second of the divine Nature. There was a fine simplicity about that. But does not the simplicity cover a presentiment of the revolution of thought for which the historical method of study was preparing the way—a presentiment which those who were engaged in the work did not share in the same measure? It was fortunate that they did not; for otherwise how could they have had the courage to go on?

The historical investigation of the life of Jesus did not take its rise from a purely historical interest; it turned to the Jesus of history as an ally in the struggle against the tyranny of dogma. Afterwards when it was freed from this πάθος it sought to present the historic Jesus in a form intelligible to its own time. For Bahrdt and Venturini He was the tool of a secret order. They wrote under the impression of the immense influence exercised by the Order of the Illuminati[3] at the end of the eighteenth century. For Reinhard, Hess, Paulus, and the rest of the rationalistic writers He is the admirable revealer of true virtue, which is coincident with right reason. Thus each successive epoch of theology found its own thoughts in Jesus; that was, indeed, the only way in which it could make Him live.

But it was not only each epoch that found its reflection in Jesus; each individual created Him in accordance with his own character. There is no historical task which so reveals a man's true self as the writing of a Life of Jesus. No vital force comes into the figure unless a man breathes into it all the hate or all the love of which he is capable. The stronger the love, or the stronger the hate, the more life-like is the figure which is produced. For hate as well as love can write a Life of Jesus, and the greatest of them are written with hate: that of Reimarus, the Wolfenbüttel Fragmentist, and that of David Friedrich Strauss. It was not so much hate of the Person of Jesus as of the supernatural nimbus with which it was so easy to surround Him, and with which He had in fact been surrounded. They were eager to picture Him as truly and purely human, to strip from Him the robes of splendour with which He [pg 005] had been apparelled, and clothe Him once more with the coarse garments in which He had walked in Galilee.

And their hate sharpened their historical insight. They advanced the study of the subject more than all the others put together. But for the offence which they gave, the science of historical theology would not have stood where it does to-day. "It must needs be that offences come; but woe to that man by whom the offence cometh." Reimarus evaded that woe by keeping the offence to himself and preserving silence during his lifetime—his work, "The Aims of Jesus and

His Disciples," was only published after his death, by Lessing. But in the case of Strauss, who, as a young man of twenty-seven, cast the offence openly in the face of the world, the woe fulfilled itself. His "Life of Jesus" was his ruin. But he did not cease to be proud of it in spite of all the misfortune that it brought him. "I might well bear a grudge against my book," he writes twenty-five years later in the preface to the "Conversations of Ulrich von Hutten,"[4] "for it has done me much evil ('And rightly so!' the pious will exclaim). It has excluded me from public teaching in which I took pleasure and for which I had perhaps some talent; it has torn me from natural relationships and driven me into unnatural ones; it has made my life a lonely one. And yet when I consider what it would have meant if I had refused to utter the word which lay upon my soul, if I had suppressed the doubts which were at work in my mind—then I bless the book which has doubtless done me grievous harm outwardly, but which preserved the inward health of my mind and heart, and, I doubt not, has done the same for many others also."

Before him, Bahrdt had his career broken in consequence of revealing his beliefs concerning the Life of Jesus; and after him, Bruno Bauer.

It was easy for them, resolved as they were to open the way even with seeming blasphemy. But the others, those who tried to bring Jesus to life at the call of love, found it a cruel task to be honest. The critical study of the life of Jesus has been for theology a school of honesty. The world had never seen before, and will never see again, a struggle for truth so full of pain and renunciation as that of which the Lives of Jesus of the last hundred years contain the cryptic record. One must read the successive Lives of Jesus with which Hase followed the course of the study from the 'twenties to the 'seventies of the nineteenth century to get an inkling of what it must have cost the men who lived through that decisive period really to maintain that "courageous freedom of investigation" which the great Jena professor, in the preface to his first Life of Jesus, claims for his researches. One sees in him the marks of the struggle with which he gives up, bit by bit, things [pg 006] which, when he wrote that preface, he never dreamed he would have to surrender. It was fortunate for these men that their sympathies sometimes obscured their critical vision, so that, without becoming insincere, they were able to take white clouds for distant mountains. That was the kindly fate of Hase and Beyschlag.

The personal character of the study is not only due, however, to the fact that a personality can only be awakened to life by the touch of a personality; it lies in the essential nature of the problem itself. For the problem of the life of Jesus has no analogue in the field of history. No historical school has ever laid down canons for the investigation of this problem, no professional historian has ever lent his aid to theology in dealing with it. Every ordinary method of historical investigation proves inadequate to the complexity of the conditions. The standards of ordinary historical science are here inadequate, its methods not immediately applicable. The historical study of the life of Jesus has had to create its own methods for itself. In the constant succession of unsuccessful attempts, five or six problems have emerged side by side which together constitute the fundamental problem. There is, however, no direct method of solving the problem in its complexity; all that can be done is to experiment continuously, starting from definite assumptions; and in this experimentation the guiding principle must ultimately rest upon historical intuition.

The cause of this lies in the nature of the sources of the life of Jesus, and in the character of our knowledge of the contemporary religious world of thought. It is not that the sources are in themselves bad. When we have once made up our minds that we have not the materials for a complete Life of Jesus, but only for a picture of His public ministry, it must be admitted that there are few characters of antiquity about whom we possess so much indubitably historical information, of whom we have so many authentic discourses. The position is much more favourable, for instance, than in the case of Socrates; for he is pictured to us by literary men who exercised their creative ability upon the portrait. Jesus stands much more immediately before us, because He was depicted by simple Christians without literary gift.

But at this point there arises a twofold difficulty. There is first the fact that what has just been said applies only to the first three Gospels, while the fourth, as regards its character, historical data, and discourse material, forms a world of its own. It is written from the Greek standpoint, while the first three are written from the Jewish. And even if one could get over this, and regard, as has often been done, the Synoptics and the Fourth Gospel as standing in something of the same relation to one another as Xenophon does to Plato as sources for the life of Socrates, yet the complete irreconcilability of the historical data would compel the critical [pg 007] investigator to decide from the first in favour of one source or the other. Once more it is found true that "No man can serve two masters." This stringent dilemma was not recognised from the beginning; its emergence is one of the results of the whole course of experiment.

The second difficulty regarding the sources is the want of any thread of connexion in the material which they offer us. While the Synoptics are only collections of anecdotes (in the best, historical sense of the word), the Gospel of John—as stands on record in its closing words—only professes to give a selection of the events and discourses.

From these materials we can only get a Life of Jesus with yawning gaps. How are these gaps to be filled? At the worst with phrases, at the best with historical imagination. There is really no other means of arriving at the order and inner connexion of the facts of the life of Jesus than the making and testing of hypotheses. If the tradition preserved by the Synoptists really includes all that happened during the time that Jesus was with His disciples, the attempt to discover the connexion must succeed sooner or later. It becomes more and more clear that this presupposition is indispensable to the investigation. If it is merely a fortuitous series of episodes that the Evangelists have handed down to us, we may give up the attempt to arrive at a critical reconstruction of the life of Jesus as hopeless.

But it is not only the events which lack historical connexion; we are without any indication of a thread of connexion in the actions and discourses of Jesus, because the sources give no hint of the character of His self-consciousness. They confine themselves to outward facts. We only begin to understand these historically when we can mentally place them in an intelligible connexion and conceive them as the acts of a clearly defined personality. All that we know of the development of Jesus and of His Messianic self-consciousness has been arrived at by a series of working hypotheses. Our conclusions can only be considered valid so long as they are not found incompatible with the recorded facts as a whole.

It may be maintained by the aid of arguments drawn from the sources that the self-consciousness of Jesus underwent a development during the course of His public ministry; it may, with equally good grounds, be denied. For in both cases the arguments are based upon little details in the narrative in regard to which we do not know whether they are purely accidental, or whether they belong to the essence of the facts. In each case, moreover, the experimental working out of the hypothesis leads to a conclusion which compels the rejection of some of the actual data of the sources. Each view equally involves a violent treatment of the text.

Furthermore, the sources exhibit, each within itself, a striking [pg 008] contradiction. They assert that Jesus felt Himself to be the Messiah; and yet from their presentation of His life it does not appear that He ever publicly claimed to be so. They attribute to Him, that is, an attitude which has absolutely no connexion with the consciousness which they assume that He possessed. But once admit that the outward acts are not the natural expression of the self-consciousness and all exact historical knowledge is at an end; we have to do with an isolated fact which is not referable to any law.

This being so, the only way of arriving at a conclusion of any value is to experiment, to test, by working them out, the two hypotheses—that Jesus felt Himself to be the Messiah, as the sources assert, or that He did not feel Himself to be so, as His conduct implies; or else to try to conjecture what kind of Messianic consciousness His must have been, if it left His conduct and His discourses unaffected. For one thing is certain: the whole account of the last days at Jerusalem would be unintelligible, if we had to suppose that the mass of the people had a shadow of a suspicion that Jesus held Himself to be the Messiah.

Again, whereas in general a personality is to some extent defined by the world of thought which it shares with its contemporaries, in the case of Jesus this source of information is as unsatisfactory as the documents.

What was the nature of the contemporary Jewish world of thought? To that question no clear answer can be given. We do not know whether the expectation of the Messiah was generally current or whether it was the faith of a mere sect. With the Mosaic religion as such it had nothing to do. There was no organic connexion between the religion of legal observance and the future hope. Further, if the eschatological hope was generally current, was it the prophetic or the apocalyptic form of that hope? We know the Messianic expectations of the prophets; we know the apocalyptic picture as drawn by Daniel, and, following him, by Enoch and the Psalms of Solomon before the coming of Jesus, and by the Apocalypses of Ezra and Baruch about the time of the destruction of Jerusalem. But we do not know which was the popular form; nor, supposing that both were combined into one picture, what this picture really looked like. We know only the form of eschatology which meets us in the Gospels and in the Pauline epistles; that is to say, the form which it took in the Christian community in consequence of the coming of Jesus. And to combine these three—the prophetic, the Late-Jewish apocalyptic, and the Christian—has not proved possible.

Even supposing we could obtain more exact information regarding the popular Messianic expectations at the time of Jesus, we should still not know what form they assumed in the self-consciousness [pg 009] of One who knew Himself to be the Messiah but held that the time was not yet come for Him to reveal Himself as such. We only know their aspect from without, as a waiting for the Messiah and the Messianic Age; we have no clue to their aspect from within as factors in the Messianic self-consciousness. We possess no psychology of the Messiah. The Evangelists have nothing to tell us about it, because Jesus told them nothing about it; the sources for the contemporary spiritual life inform us only concerning the eschatological expectation. For the form of the Messianic self-consciousness of Jesus we have to fall back upon conjecture.

Such is the character of the problem, and, as a consequence, historical experiment must here take the place of historical research. That being so, it is easy to understand that to take a survey of the study of the life of Jesus is to be confronted, at first sight, with a scene of the most boundless confusion. A series of experiments are repeated with constantly varying modifications suggested by the results furnished by the subsidiary sciences. Most of the writers, however, have no suspicion that they are merely repeating an experiment which has often been made before. Some of them discover this in the course of their work to their own great astonishment—it is so, for instance, with Wrede, who recognises that he is working out, though doubtless with a clearer consciousness of his aim, an idea of Bruno Bauer's.5 If old Reimarus were to come back again, he might confidently give himself out to be the latest of the moderns, for his work rests upon a recognition of the exclusive importance of eschatology, such as only recurs again in Johannes Weiss.

Progress, too, is curiously fitful, with long intervals of marking time between the advances. From Strauss down to the 'nineties there was no real progress, if one takes into consideration only the complete Lives of Jesus which appeared. But a number of separate problems took a more clearly defined form, so that in the end the general problem suddenly moved forward, as it seemed, with a jerk.

There is really no common standard by which to judge the works with which we have to do. It is not the most orderly narratives, those which weave in conscientiously every detail of the text, which have advanced the study of the subject, but precisely the eccentric ones, those that take the greatest liberties with the text. It is not by the mass of facts that a writer sets down alongside of one another as possible—because he writes easily and there is no one there to contradict him, and because facts on paper do not come into collision so sharply as they do in reality—it is not in that way that he shows his power of reconstructing history, but by that which he recognises as impossible. The constructions [pg 010] of Reimarus and Bruno Bauer have no solidity; they are mere products of the imagination. But there is much more historical power in their clear grasp of a single definite problem, which has blinded them to all else, than there is in the circumstantial works of Beyschlag and Bernard Weiss.

But once one has accustomed oneself to look for certain definite landmarks amid this apparent welter of confusion one begins at last to discover in vague outline the course followed, and the progress made, by the critical study of the life of Jesus.

It falls, immediately, into two periods, that before Strauss and that after Strauss. The dominant interest in the first is the question of miracle. What terms are possible between a historical treatment and the acceptance of supernatural events? With the advent of Strauss this problem found a solution, viz., that these events have no rightful place in the history, but are simply mythical elements in the sources. The way was thus thrown open. Meanwhile, alongside of the problem of the supernatural, other problems had been dimly apprehended. Reimarus had drawn attention to the contemporary eschatological views; Hase, in his first Life of Jesus (1829), had sought to trace a development in the self-consciousness of Jesus.

But on this point a clear view was impossible, because all the students of the subject were still basing their operations upon the harmony of the Synoptics and the Fourth Gospel; which means that they had not so far felt the need of a historically intelligible outline of the life of Jesus. Here, too, Strauss was the light-bringer. But the transient illumination was destined to be obscured by the Marcan hypothesis,⁶ which now came to the front. The necessity of choosing between John and the Synoptists was first fully established by the Tübingen school; and the right relation of this question to the Marcan hypothesis was subsequently shown by Holtzmann.

While these discussions of the preliminary literary questions were in progress the main historical problem of the life of Jesus was slowly rising into view. The question began to be mooted: what was the significance of eschatology for the mind of Jesus? With this problem was associated, in virtue of an inner connexion which was not at first suspected, the problem of the self-consciousness of Jesus. At the beginning of the 'nineties it was generally felt that, in the solution given to this dual problem, an in some measure assured knowledge of the outward and inward course of the life of Jesus had been reached. At this point Johannes Weiss revived the comprehensive claim of Reimarus on behalf of [pg 011] eschatology; and scarcely had criticism adjusted its attitude to this question when Wrede renewed the attempt of Bauer and Volkmar to eliminate altogether the Messianic element from the life of Jesus.

We are now once more in the midst of a period of great activity in the study of the subject. On the one side we are offered a historical solution, on the other a literary. The question at issue is: Is it possible to explain the contradiction between the Messianic consciousness of Jesus and His non-Messianic discourses and actions by means of a conception of His Messianic consciousness which will make it appear that He could not have acted otherwise than as the Evangelists describe; or must we endeavour to explain the contradiction by taking the non-Messianic discourses and actions as our fixed point, denying the reality of His Messianic self-consciousness and regarding it as a later interpolation of the beliefs of the Christian community into the life of Jesus? In the latter case the Evangelists are supposed to have attributed these Messianic claims to Jesus because the early Church held Him to be the Messiah, but to have contradicted themselves by describing His life as it actually was, viz., as the life of a prophet, not of one who held Himself to be the Messiah. To put it briefly: Does the difficulty of explaining the historical personality of Jesus lie in the history itself, or only in the way in which it is represented in the sources?

This alternative will be discussed in all the critical studies of the next few years. Once clearly posed it compels a decision. But no one can really understand the problem who has not a clear notion of the way in which it has shaped itself in the course of the investigation; no one can justly criticise, or appraise the value of, new contributions to the study of this subject unless he knows in what forms they have been presented before.

The history of the study of the life of Jesus has hitherto received surprisingly little attention. Hase, in his Life of Jesus of 1829, briefly records the previous attempts to deal with the subject. Friedrich von Ammon, himself one of the most distinguished students in this department, in his "Progress of Christianity,"⁷ gives some information "regarding the most notable biographies of Jesus of the last fifty years." In the year 1865 Uhlhorn treated together the Lives of Jesus of Renan, Schenkel, and Strauss; in 1876 Hase, in his "History of Jesus," gave the only complete literary history of the subject;⁸ in 1892 Uhlhorn extended his former lecture to include the works of Keim, Delff, Beyschlag, and Weiss;⁹ in 1898 [pg 012] Frantzen described, in a short essay, the progress of the study since Strauss;¹⁰ in 1899 and 1900 Baldensperger gave, in the *Theologische Rundschau*, a survey of the most recent publications;¹¹ Weinel's book, "Jesus in the Nineteenth Century," naturally only gives an analysis of a few classical works; Otto Schmiedel's lecture on the "Main Problems of the Critical Study of the Life of Jesus" (1902) merely sketches the history of the subject in broad outline.[12]

Apart from scattered notices in histories of theology this is practically all the literature of the subject. There is room for an attempt to bring order into the chaos of the Lives of Jesus. Hase made ingenious comparisons between them, but he was unable to group them according to inner principles, or to judge them justly. Weisse is for him a feebler descendant of Strauss, Bruno Bauer is the victim of a fantastic imagination. It would indeed have been difficult for Hase to discover in the works of his time any principle of division. But now, when the literary and eschatological methods of solution have led to complementary results, when the post-Straussian period of investigation seems to have reached a provisional close, and the goal to which it has been tending has become clear, the time seems ripe for the attempt to trace genetically in the successive works the shaping of the problem as it now confronts us, and to give a systematic historical account of the critical study of the life of Jesus. Our endeavour will be to furnish a graphic description of all the attempts to deal with the subject; and not to dismiss them with stock phrases or traditional labels, but to show clearly what they really did to advance the formulation of the problem, whether their contemporaries recognised it or not. In accordance with this principle many famous Lives of Jesus which have prolonged an honoured existence through many successive editions, will make but a poor figure, while others, which have received scant notice, will appear great. Behind Success comes Truth, and her reward is with her.
[pg 013]

II. Hermann Samuel Reimarus

"Von dem Zwecke Jesu und seiner Jünger." Noch ein Fragment des Wolfenbüttelschen Ungenannten. Herausgegeben von Gotthold Ephraim Lessing. Braunschweig, 1778, 276 pp. (The Aims of Jesus and His Disciples. A further Instalment of the anonymous Wolfenbüttel Fragments. Published by Gotthold Ephraim Lessing. Brunswick, 1778.)

Johann Salomo Semler. Beantwortung der Fragmente eines Ungenannten insbesondere vom Zwecke Jesu und seiner Jünger. (Reply to the anonymous Fragments, especially to that entitled "The Aims of Jesus and His Disciples.") Halle, 1779, 432 pp.

Before Reimarus, no one had attempted to form a historical conception of the life of Jesus. Luther had not so much as felt that he cared to gain a clear idea of the order of the recorded events. Speaking of the chronology of the cleansing of the Temple, which in John falls at the beginning, in the Synoptists near the close, of Jesus' public life, he remarks: "The Gospels follow no order in recording the acts and miracles of Jesus, and the matter is not, after all, of much importance. If a difficulty arises in regard to the Holy Scripture and we cannot solve it, we must just let it alone." When the Lutheran theologians began to consider the question of harmonising the events, things were still worse. Osiander (1498-1552), in his "Harmony of the Gospels," maintained the principle that if an event is recorded more than once in the Gospels, in different connexions, it happened more than once and in different connexions. The daughter of Jairus was therefore raised from the dead several times; on one occasion Jesus allowed the devils whom He cast out of a single demoniac to enter into a herd of swine, on another occasion, those whom He cast out of two demoniacs; there were two cleansings of the Temple, and so forth.[13] The correct view of the Synoptic Gospels as being interdependent was first formulated by Griesbach.

The only Life of Jesus written prior to the time of Reimarus which has any interest for us, was composed by a Jesuit in the [pg 014] Persian language. The author was the Indian missionary Hieronymus Xavier, nephew of Francis Xavier, and it was designed for the use of Akbar, the Moghul Emperor, who, in the latter part of the sixteenth century, had become the most powerful potentate in Hindustan. In the seventeenth century the Persian text was brought to Europe by a merchant, and was translated into Latin by Louis de Dieu, a theologian of the Reformed Church, whose intention in publishing it was to discredit Catholicism.[14] It is a skilful falsification of the life of Jesus in which the omissions, and the additions taken from the Apocrypha, are inspired by the sole purpose of presenting to the open-minded ruler a glorious Jesus, in whom there should be nothing to offend him.

Thus there had been nothing to prepare the world for a work of such power as that of Reimarus. It is true, there had appeared earlier, in 1768, a Life of Jesus by Johann Jakob Hess[15] (1741-1828), written from the standpoint of the older rationalism, but it retains so much supernaturalism and follows so much the lines of a paraphrase of the Gospels, that there was nothing to indicate to the world what a master-stroke the spirit of the time was preparing.

Not much is known about Reimarus. For his contemporaries he had no existence, and it was Strauss who first made his name known in literature.[16] He was born in Hamburg on the 22nd of December, 1694, and spent his life there as a professor of Oriental Languages. He died in 1768. Several of his writings appeared during his lifetime, all of them asserting the claims of rational religion as against the faith of the Church; one of them, for example, being an essay on "The Leading Truths of Natural Religion." His *magnum opus*, however, which laid the historic basis of his attacks, was only circulated, during his lifetime, among his acquaintances, as an anonymous manuscript. In 1774 Lessing began to publish the most important portions of it, and up to 1778 had published seven fragments, thereby involving himself in a quarrel with Goetze, the Chief Pastor of Hamburg. The manuscript of the whole, which runs to 4000 pages, is preserved in the Hamburg municipal library.

The following are the titles of Fragments which he published:

The Toleration of the Deists.

The Decrying of Reason in the Pulpit.

The impossibility of a Revelation which all men should have good grounds for believing.

[pg 015]

The Passing of the Israelites through the Red Sea.

Showing that the books of the Old Testament were not written to reveal a Religion.

Concerning the story of the Resurrection.

The Aims of Jesus and His disciples.

The monograph on the passing of the Israelites through the Red Sea is one of the ablest, wittiest, and most acute which has ever been written. It exposes all the impossibilities of the narrative in the Priestly Codex, and all the inconsistencies which arise from the combination of various sources; although Reimarus has not the slightest inkling that the separation of these sources would afford the real solution of the problem.

To say that the fragment on "The Aims of Jesus and His Disciples" is a magnificent piece of work is barely to do it justice. This essay is not only one of the greatest events in the history of criticism, it is also a masterpiece of general literature. The language is as a rule crisp and terse, pointed and epigrammatic—the language of a man who is not "engaged in literary composition" but is wholly concerned with the facts. At times, however, it rises to heights of passionate feeling, and then it is as though the fires of a volcano were painting lurid pictures upon dark clouds. Seldom has there been a hate so eloquent, so lofty a scorn; but then it is seldom that a work has been written in the just consciousness of so absolute a superiority to contemporary opinion. And withal, there is dignity and serious purpose; Reimarus's work is no pamphlet.

Lessing could not, of course, accept its standpoint. His idea of revelation, and his conception of the Person of Jesus, were much deeper than those of the Fragmentist. He was a thinker; Reimarus only a historian. But this was the first time that a really historical mind, thoroughly conversant with the sources, had undertaken the criticism of the tradition. It was Lessing's greatness that he grasped the significance of this criticism, and felt that it must lead either to the destruction or to the re-casting of the idea of revelation. He recognised that the introduction of the historical element would transform and deepen rationalism. Convinced that the fateful moment had arrived, he disregarded the scruples of Reimarus's family and the objections of Nicolai and Mendelssohn, and, though inwardly trembling for that which he himself held sacred, he flung the torch with his own hand.

Semler, at the close of his refutation of the fragment, ridicules its editor in the following apologue. "A prisoner was once brought before the Lord Mayor of London on a charge of arson. He had been seen coming down from the upper story of the burning house. 'Yesterday,' so ran his defence, 'about four o'clock I went into my neighbour's store-room and saw there a burning candle which the servants had carelessly forgotten. In [pg 016] the course of the night it would have burned down, and set fire to the stairs. To make sure that the fire should break out in the day-time, I threw some straw upon it. The flames burst out at the sky-light, the fire-engines came hurrying up, and the fire, which in the night might have been dangerous, was promptly extinguished.' 'Why did you not yourself pick up the candle and put it out?' asked the Lord Mayor. 'If I had put out the candle the servants would not have learned to be more careful; now that there has been such a fuss about it, they will not be so careless in future.' 'Odd, very odd,' said the Lord Mayor, 'he is not a criminal, only a little weak in the head.' So he had him shut up in the mad-house, and there he lies to this day."

The story is extraordinarily apposite—only that Lessing was not mad; he knew quite well what he was doing. His object was to show how an unseen enemy had pushed his parallels up to the very walls, and to summon to the defence "some one who should be as nearly the ideal defender of religion as the Fragmentist was the ideal assailant." Once, with prophetic insight into the future, he says: "The Christian traditions must be explained by the inner truth of Christianity, and no written traditions can give it that inner truth, if it does not itself possess it."

Reimarus takes as his starting-point the question regarding the content of the preaching of Jesus. "We are justified," he says, "in drawing an absolute distinction between the teaching of the Apostles in their writings and what Jesus Himself in His own lifetime proclaimed and taught." What belongs to the preaching of Jesus is clearly to be recognised. It is contained in two phrases of identical meaning, "Repent, and believe the Gospel," or, as it is put elsewhere, "Repent, for the Kingdom of Heaven is at hand."

The Kingdom of Heaven must however be understood "according to Jewish ways of thought." Neither Jesus nor the Baptist ever explain this expression; therefore they must have been content to have it understood in its known and customary sense. That means that Jesus took His stand within the Jewish religion, and accepted its Messianic expectations without in any way correcting them. If He gives a new development to this religion it is only in so far that He proclaims as near at hand the realisation of ideals and hopes which were alive in thousands of hearts.

There was thus no need for detailed instruction regarding the nature of the Kingdom of Heaven; the catechism and confession of the Church at its commencement consisted of a single phrase. Belief was not difficult: "they need only believe the Gospel, namely that Jesus was about to bring in the Kingdom of God."[17]

[pg 017]

As there were many among the Jews who were already waiting for the Kingdom of God, it was no wonder that in a few days, nay in a few hours, some thousands believed, although they had been told only that Jesus was the promised prophet.

This was the sum total of what the disciples knew about the Kingdom of God when they were sent out by their Master to proclaim its coming. Their hearers would naturally think of the customary meaning of the term and the hopes which attached themselves to it. "The purpose of sending out such propagandists could only be that the Jews who groaned under the Roman yoke and had long cherished the hope of deliverance should be stirred up all over Judaea and assemble themselves in their thousands."

Jesus must have known, too, that if the people believed His messengers they would look about for an earthly deliverer and turn to Him for this purpose. The Gospel, therefore, meant nothing more or less to all who heard it than that, under the leadership of Jesus, the Kingdom of Messiah was about to be brought in. For them there was no difficulty in accepting the belief that He was the Messiah, the Son of God, for this belief did not involve anything metaphysical. The nation was the Son of God; the kings of the covenant-people were Sons of God; the Messiah was in a pre-eminent sense the Son of God. Thus even in His Messianic claims Jesus remained "within the limits of humanity."

The fact that He did not need to explain to His contemporaries what He meant by the Kingdom of God constitutes a difficulty for us. The parables do not enlighten us, for they presuppose a knowledge of the conception. "If we could not gather from the writings of the Jews some further information as to what was understood at that time by the Messiah and the Kingdom of God, these points of primary importance would be very obscure and incomprehensible."

"If, therefore, we desire to gain a historical understanding of Jesus' teaching, we must leave behind what we learned in our catechism regarding the metaphysical Divine Sonship, the Trinity, and similar dogmatic conceptions, and go out into a wholly Jewish world of thought. Only those who carry the teachings of the catechism back into the preaching of the Jewish Messiah will arrive at the idea that He was the founder of a new religion. To all unprejudiced persons it is manifest that Jesus had not the slightest intention of doing away with the Jewish religion and putting another in its place."

From Matt. v. 18 it is evident that Jesus did not break with the Law, but took His stand upon it unreservedly. If there was anything at all new in His preaching, it was the righteousness which was requisite for the Kingdom of God. The righteousness of the Law will no longer suffice in the time of the coming Kingdom; a [pg 018] new and deeper morality must come into being. This demand is the only point in which the preaching of Jesus went beyond the ideas of His contemporaries. But this new morality does not do away with the Law, for He explains it as a fulfilment of the old commandments. His followers, no doubt, broke with the Law later on. They did so, however, not in pursuance of a command of Jesus, but under the pressure of circumstances, at the time when they were forced out of Judaism and obliged to found a new religion.

Jesus shared the Jewish racial exclusiveness wholly and unreservedly. According to Matt. x. 5 He forbade His disciples to declare to the Gentiles the coming of the Kingdom of God. Evidently, therefore, His purpose did not embrace them. Had it been otherwise, the hesitation of Peter in Acts x. and xi., and the necessity of justifying the conversion of Cornelius, would be incomprehensible.

Baptism and the Lord's Supper are no evidence that Jesus intended to found a new religion. In the first place the genuineness of the command to baptize in Matt. xxviii. 19 is questionable, not only as a saying ascribed to the risen Jesus, but also because it is universalistic in outlook, and because it implies the doctrine of the Trinity and, consequently, the metaphysical Divine Sonship of Jesus. In this it is inconsistent with the earliest traditions regarding the practice of baptism in the Christian community, for in the earliest times, as we learn from the Acts and from Paul, it was the custom to baptize, not in the name of the Trinity, but in the name of Jesus, the Messiah.

But, furthermore, it is questionable whether Baptism really goes back to Jesus at all. He Himself baptized no one in His own lifetime, and never commanded any of His converts to be baptized. So we cannot be sure about the origin of Baptism, though we can be sure of its meaning. Baptism in the name of Jesus signified only that Jesus was the Messiah. "For the only change which the teaching of Jesus made in their religion was that whereas they had formerly believed in a Deliverer of Israel who was to come in the future, they now believed in a Deliverer who was already present."

The "Lord's Supper," again, was no new institution, but merely an episode at the last Paschal Meal of the Kingdom which was passing away, and was intended "as an anticipatory celebration of the Passover of the New Kingdom." A Lord's Supper in our sense, "cut loose from the Passover," would have been inconceivable to Jesus, and not less so to His disciples.

It is useless to appeal to the miracles, any more than to the "Sacraments," as evidence for the founding of a new religion. In the first place, we have to remember what happens in the case of miracles handed down by tradition. That Jesus effected cures, [pg 019] which in the eyes of His contemporaries were miraculous, is not to be denied. Their purpose was to prove Him to be the Messiah. He forbade these miracles to be made known, even in cases where they could not possibly be kept hidden, "with the sole purpose of making people more eager to talk of them." Other miracles, however, have no basis in fact, but owe their place in the narrative to the feeling that the miracle-stories of the Old Testament must be repeated in the case of Jesus, but on a grander scale. He did no really miraculous works; otherwise, the demands for a sign would be incomprehensible. In Jerusalem when all the people were looking eagerly for an overwhelming manifestation of His Messiahship, what a tremendous effect a miracle would have produced! If only a single miracle had been publicly, convincingly, undeniably, performed by Jesus before all the people on one of the great days of the Feast, such is human nature that all the people would at once have flocked to His standard.

For this popular uprising, however, He waited in vain. Twice He believed that it was near at hand. The first time was when He was sending out the disciples and said to them: "Ye shall not have gone over the cities of Israel before the Son of Man comes" (Matt. x. 23). He thought that, at the preaching of the disciples, the people would flock to Him from every quarter and immediately proclaim Him Messiah; but His expectation was disappointed.

The second time, He thought to bring about the decisive issue in Jerusalem. He made His entry riding on an ass's colt, that the Messianic prophecy of Zechariah might be fulfilled. And the people actually did cry "Hosanna to the Son of David!" Relying on the support of His followers He might now, He thought, bid defiance to the authorities. In the temple He arrogates to Himself supreme power, and in glowing words calls for an open revolt against the Sanhedrin and the Pharisees, on the ground that they have shut the doors of the Kingdom of Heaven and forbidden others to go in. There is no doubt, now, that He will carry the people with Him! Confident in the success of His cause, He closes the great incendiary harangue in Matt. xxiii. with the words "Truly from henceforth ye shall not see me again until ye shall say Blessed is he that cometh in the name of the Lord"; that is, until they should hail Him as Messiah.

But the people in Jerusalem refused to rise, as the Galilaeans had refused at the time when the disciples were sent out to rouse them. The Council prepared for vigorous action. The voluntary concealment by which Jesus had thought to whet the eagerness of the people became involuntary. Before His arrest He was overwhelmed with dread, and on the cross He closed His life with the words "My God! my God! why hast Thou forsaken me?" "This avowal cannot, without violence, be interpreted otherwise than as [pg 020] meaning that God had not aided Him in His aim and purpose as He had hoped. That shows that it had not been His purpose to suffer and die, but to establish an earthly kingdom and deliver the Jews from political oppression—and in that God's help had failed Him."

For the disciples this turn of affairs meant the destruction of all the dreams for the sake of which they had followed Jesus. For if they had given up anything on His account, it was only in order to receive it again an hundredfold when they should openly take their places in the eyes of all the world as the friends and ministers of the Messiah, as the rulers of the twelve tribes of Israel. Jesus never disabused them of this sensuous hope, but, on the contrary, confirmed them in it. When He put an end to the quarrel about pre-eminence, and when He answered the request of the sons of Zebedee, He did not attack the assumption that there were to be thrones and power, but only addressed Himself to the question how men were in the present to establish their claims to that position of authority.

All this implies that the time of the fulfilment of these hopes was not thought of by Jesus and His disciples as at all remote. In Matt. xvi. 28, for example, He says: "Truly I say unto you there are some standing here who shall not taste of death, till they see the Son of man coming in his kingdom." There is no justification for twisting this about or explaining it away. It simply means that Jesus promises the fulfilment of all Messianic hopes before the end of the existing generation.

Thus the disciples were prepared for anything rather than that which actually happened. Jesus had never said a word to them about His dying and rising again, otherwise they would not have so played the coward at His death, nor have been so astonished at His "resurrection." The three or four sayings referring to these events must therefore have been put into His mouth later, in order to make it appear that He had foreseen these events in His original plan.

How, then, did they get over this apparently annihilating blow? By falling back upon the second form of the Jewish Messianic hope. Hitherto their thoughts, like those of their Master, had been dominated by the political ideal of the prophets—the scion of David's line who should appear as the political deliverer of the nation. But alongside of that there existed another Messianic expectation which transferred everything to the supernatural sphere. Appearing first in Daniel, this expectation can still be traced in the Apocalypses, in Justin's "Dialogue with Trypho," and in certain Rabbinic sayings. According to these—Reimarus makes use especially of the statements of Trypho—the Messiah is to appear twice; once in human lowliness, the second time upon the clouds of heaven. When the first [pg 021] *systema*, as Reimarus calls it, was annihilated by the death of Jesus, the disciples brought forward the second, and gathered followers who shared their expectation of a second coming of Jesus the Messiah. In order to get rid of the difficulty of the death of Jesus, they gave it the significance of a spiritual redemption—which had not previously entered their field of vision or that of Jesus Himself.

But this spiritual interpretation of His death would not have helped them if they had not also invented the resurrection. Immediately after the death of Jesus, indeed, such an idea was far from their thoughts. They were in deadly fear and kept close within doors. "Soon, however, one and another ventures to slip out. They learn that no judicial search is being made for them." Then they consider what is to be done. They did not take kindly to the idea of returning to their old haunts; on their journeyings the companions of the Messiah had forgotten how to work. They had seen that the preaching of the Kingdom of God will keep a man. Even when they had been sent out without wallet or money they had not lacked. The women who are mentioned in Luke viii. 2, 3, had made it their business to make good provision for the Messiah and His future ministers.

Why not, then, continue this mode of life? They would surely find a sufficient number of faithful souls who would join them in directing their hopes towards a second coming of the Messiah, and while awaiting the future glory, would share their possessions with them. So they stole the body of Jesus and hid it, and proclaimed to all the world that He would soon return. They prudently waited, however, for fifty days before making this announcement, in order that the body, if it should be found, might be unrecognisable.

What was much in their favour was the complete disorganisation of the Jewish state. Had there been an efficient police administration the disciples would not have been able to plan this fraud and organise their communistic fellowship. But, as it was, the new society was not even subjected to any annoyance in consequence of the remarkable death of a married couple who were buried from the apostles' house, and the brotherhood was even allowed to confiscate their property to its own uses.

It appears, then, that the hope of the Parousia was the fundamental thing in primitive Christianity, which was a product of that hope much more than of the teaching of Jesus. Accordingly, the main problem of primitive dogmatics was the delay of the Parousia. Already in Paul's time the problem was pressing, and he had to set to work in 2 Thessalonians to discover all possible and impossible reasons why the Second Coming should be delayed. Reimarus mercilessly exposes the position of the apostle, who was obliged to fob people off somehow or other. The author of 2 Peter [pg 022] has a much clearer notion of what he would be at, and undertakes to restore the confidence of Christendom once for all with the sophism of the thousand years which are in the sight of God as one day, ignoring the fact that in the promise the reckoning was by man's years, not by God's. "Nevertheless it served the turn of the Apostles so well with those simple early Christians, that after the first believers had been bemused with it, and the period originally fixed had elapsed, the Christians of later generations, including Fathers of the Church, could continue ever after to feed themselves with empty hopes." The saying of Christ about the generation which should not die out before His return clearly fixes this event at no very distant date. But since Jesus has not yet appeared upon the clouds of heaven "these words must be strained into meaning, not that generation, but the Jewish people. Thus by exegetical art they are saved for ever, for the Jewish race will never die out."

In general, however, "the theologians of the present day skim lightly over the eschatological material in the Gospels because it does not chime in with their views, and assign to the coming of Christ upon the clouds quite a different purpose from that which it bears in the teaching of Christ and His apostles." Inasmuch as the non-fulfilment of its eschatology is not admitted, our Christianity rests upon a fraud. In view of this fact, what is the evidential value of any miracle, even if it could be held to be authentic? "No miracle would prove that two and two make five, or that a circle has four angles; and no miracles, however numerous, could remove a contradiction which lies on the surface of the teachings and records of Christianity." Nor is there any weight in the appeal to the fulfilment of prophecy, for the cases in which Matthew countersigns it with the words "that the Scripture might be fulfilled" are all artificial and unreal; and for many incidents the stage was set by Jesus, or His disciples, or the Evangelists, with the deliberate purpose of presenting to the people a scene from the fulfilment of prophecy.

The sole argument which could save the credit of Christianity would be a proof that the Parousia had really taken place at the time for which it was announced; and obviously no such proof can be produced.

Such is Reimarus' reconstruction of the history. We can well understand that his work must have given offence when it appeared, for it is a polemic, not an objective historical study. But we have no right simply to dismiss it in a word, as a Deistic production, as Otto Schmiedel, for example, does;[18] it is time that Reimarus came to his own, and that we should recognise a historical performance of no mean order in this piece of Deistic polemics. [pg 023] His work is perhaps the most splendid achievement in the whole course of the historical investigation of the life of Jesus, for he was the first to grasp the fact that the world of thought in which Jesus moved was essentially eschatological. There is some justification for the animosity which flames up in his writing. This historical truth had taken possession of his mind with such overwhelming force that he could no longer understand his contemporaries, and could not away with their profession that their beliefs were, as they professed to be, directly derived from the preaching of Jesus.

What added to the offence was that he saw the eschatology in a wrong perspective. He held that the Messianic ideal which dominated the preaching of Jesus was that of the political ruler, the son of David. All his other mistakes are the consequence of this fundamental error. It was, of course, a mere makeshift hypothesis to derive the beginnings of Christianity from an imposture. Historical science was not at that time sufficiently advanced to lead even the man who had divined the fundamentally eschatological character of the preaching of Jesus onward to the historical solution of the problem; it needed more than a hundred and twenty years to fill in the chasm which Reimarus had been forced to bridge with that makeshift hypothesis of his.

In the light of the clear perception of the elements of the problem which Reimarus had attained, the whole movement of theology, down to Johannes Weiss, appears retrograde. In all its work the thesis is ignored or obscured that Jesus, as a historical personality, is to be regarded, not as the founder of a new religion, but as the final product of the eschatological and apocalyptic thought of Late Judaism. Every sentence of Johannes Weiss's *Die Predigt Jesu vom Reiche Gottes* (1892) is a vindication, a rehabilitation, of Reimarus as a historical thinker.

Even so the traveller on the plain sees from afar the distant range of mountains. Then he loses sight of them again. His way winds slowly upwards through the valleys, drawing ever nearer to the peaks, until at last, at a turn of the path, they stand before him, not in the shapes which they had seemed to take from the distant plain, but in their actual forms. Reimarus was the first, after eighteen centuries of misconception, to have an inkling of what eschatology really was. Then theology lost sight of it again, and it was not until after the lapse of more than a hundred years that it came in view of eschatology once more, now in its true form, so far as that can be historically determined, and only after it had been led astray, almost to the last, in all its historical researches by the sole mistake of Reimarus—the assumption that the eschatology was earthly and political in character. Thus theology shared at least the error of the man whom it knew only as a Deist, not as an [pg 024] historian, and whose true greatness was not recognised even by Strauss, though he raised a literary monument to him.

The solution offered by Reimarus may be wrong; the data of observation from which he starts out are, beyond question, right, because the primary datum of all is genuinely historical. He recognised that two systems of Messianic expectation were present side by side in Late Judaism. He endeavoured to bring them into mutual relations in order to represent the actual movement of the history. In so doing he made the mistake of placing them in consecutive order, ascribing to Jesus the political Son-of-David conception, and to the Apostles, after His death, the apocalyptic system based on Daniel, instead of superimposing one upon the other in such a way that the Messianic King might coincide with the Son of Man, and the ancient prophetic conception might be inscribed within the circumference of the Daniel-descended apocalyptic, and raised along with it to the supersensuous plane. But what matters the mistake in comparison with the fact that the problem was really grasped?

Reimarus felt that the absence in the preaching of Jesus of any definition of the principal term (the Kingdom of God), in conjunction with the great and rapid success of His preaching constituted a problem, and he formulated the conception that Jesus was not a religious founder and teacher, but purely a preacher.

He brought the Synoptic and Johannine narratives into harmony by practically leaving the latter out of account. The attitude of Jesus towards the law, and the process by which the disciples came to take up a freer attitude, was grasped and explained by him so accurately that modern historical science does not need to add a word, but would be well pleased if at least half the theologians of the present day had got as far.

Further, he recognised that primitive Christianity was not something which grew, so to speak, out of the teaching of Jesus, but that it came into being as a new creation, in consequence of events and circumstances which added something to that preaching which it did not previously contain; and that Baptism and the Lord's Supper, in the historical sense of these terms, were not instituted by Jesus, but created by the early Church on the basis of certain historical assumptions.

Again, Reimarus felt that the fact that the "event of Easter" was first proclaimed at Pentecost constituted a problem, and he sought a solution for it. He recognised, further, that the solution of the problem of the life of Jesus calls for a combination of the methods of historical and literary criticism. He felt that merely to emphasise the part played by eschatology would not suffice, but that it was necessary to assume a creative element in the tradition, to which he ascribed the miracles, the stories which turn on the [pg 025] fulfilment of Messianic prophecy, the universalistic traits and the predictions of the passion and the resurrection. Like Wrede, too, he feels that the prescription of silence in the case of miracles of healing and of certain communications to the disciples constitutes a problem which demands solution.

Still more remarkable is his eye for exegetical detail. He has an unfailing instinct for pregnant passages like Matt. x. 23, xvi. 28, which are crucial for the interpretation of large masses of the history. The fact is there are some who are historians by the grace of God, who from their mother's womb have an instinctive feeling for the real. They follow through all the intricacy and confusion of reported fact the pathway of reality, like a stream which, despite the rocks that encumber its course and the windings of its valley, finds its way inevitably to the sea. No erudition can supply the place of this historical instinct, but erudition sometimes serves a useful purpose, inasmuch as it produces in its possessors the pleasing belief that they are historians, and thus secures their services for the cause of history. In truth they are at best merely doing the preliminary spade-work of history, collecting for a future historian the dry bones of fact, from which, with the aid of his natural gift, he can recall the past to life. More often, however, the way in which erudition seeks to serve history is by suppressing historical discoveries as long as possible, and leading out into the field to oppose the one true view an army of possibilities. By arraying these in support of one another it finally imagines that it has created out of possibilities a living reality.

This obstructive erudition is the special prerogative of theology, in which, even at the present day, a truly marvellous scholarship often serves only to blind the eyes to elementary truths, and to cause the artificial to be preferred to the natural. And this happens not only with those who deliberately shut their minds against new impressions, but also with those whose purpose is to go forward, and to whom their contemporaries look up as leaders. It was a typical illustration of this fact when Semler rose up and slew Reimarus in the name of scientific theology.[19]

Reimarus had discredited progressive theology. Students—so Semler tells us in his preface—became unsettled and sought other callings. The great Halle theologian—born in 1725—the pioneer of the historical view of the Canon, the precursor of Baur in the reconstruction of primitive Christianity, was urged to do away with the offence. As Origen of yore with Celsus, so Semler takes Reimarus sentence by sentence, in such a way that if his work were lost it could be recovered from the refutation. The fact was that Semler had nothing in the nature of a complete or well-articulated [pg 026] argument to oppose to him; therefore he inaugurated in his reply the "Yes, but" theology, which thereafter, for more than three generations, while it took, itself, the most various modifications, imagined that it had finally got rid of Reimarus and his discovery.

Reimarus—so ran the watchword of the guerrilla warfare which Semler waged against him—cannot be right, for he is one-sided. Jesus and His disciples employed two methods of teaching: one sensuous, pictorial, drawn from the sphere of Jewish ideas, by which they adapted their meaning to the understanding of the multitude, and endeavoured to raise them to a higher way of thinking; and alongside of that a purely spiritual teaching which was independent of that kind of imagery. Both methods of teaching continued to be used side by side, because there were always contemporary representatives of the two degrees of capability and the two kinds of temperament. "This is historically so certain that the Fragmentist's attack must inevitably be defeated at this point, because he takes account only of the sensuous representation." But his attack was not defeated. What happened was that, owing to the respect in which Semler was held, and the absolute incapacity of contemporary theology to overtake the long stride forward made by Reimarus, his work was neglected, and the stimulus which it was capable of imparting failed to take effect. He had no predecessors; neither had he any disciples. His work is one of those supremely great works which pass and leave no trace, because they are before their time; to which later generations pay a just tribute of admiration, but owe no gratitude. Indeed it would be truer to say that Reimarus hung a mill-stone about the neck of the rising theological science of his time. He avenged himself on Semler by shaking his faith in historical theology and even in the freedom of science in general. By the end of the eighth decade of the century the Halle professor was beginning to retrace his steps, was becoming more and more disloyal to the cause which he had formerly served; and he finally went so far as to give his approval to Wöllner's edict for the regulation of religion (1788). His friends attributed this change of front to senility—he died 1791.

Thus the magnificent overture in which are announced all the *motifs* of the future historical treatment of the life of Jesus breaks off with a sudden discord, remains isolated and incomplete, and leads to nothing further.
[pg 027]

III. The Lives Of Jesus Of The Earlier Rationalism

Johann Jakob Hess. Geschichte der drei letzten Lebensjahre Jesu. (History of the Last Three Years of the Life of Jesus.) 3 vols., 1400 pp. Leipzig-Zurich, 1768-1772; 3rd ed., 1774 ff.; 7th ed., 1823 ff.

Franz Volkmar Reinhard. Versuch über den Plan, welchen der Stifter der christlichen Religion zum Besten der Menschheit entwarf. (Essay upon the Plan which the Founder of the Christian Religion adopted for the Benefit of Mankind.) 500 pp. 1781; 4th ed., 1798; 5th ed., 1830. Our account is based on the 4th ed. The 5th contains supplementary matter by Heubner.

Ernst August Opitz. Preacher at Zscheppelin. Geschichte und Characterzüge Jesu. (History of Jesus, with a Delineation of His Character.) Jena and Leipzig, 1812. 488 pp.

Johann Adolph Jakobi. Superintendent at Waltershausen. Die Geschichte Jesu für denkende und gemütvolle Leser, 1816. (The History of Jesus for thoughtful and sympathetic readers.) A second volume, containing the history of the apostolic age, followed in 1818.

Johann Gottfried Herder. Vom Erlöser der Menschen. Nach unsern drei ersten Evangelien. (The Redeemer of men, as portrayed in our first three Gospels.) 1796. Von Gottes Sohn, der Welt Heiland. Nach Johannes Evangelium. (The Son of God, the Saviour of the World, as portrayed by John's Gospel.) Accompanied by a rule for the harmonisation of our Gospels on the basis of their origin and order. Riga, published by Hartknoch, 1797. See Herder's complete works, ed. Suphan, vol. xix.

That thorough-going theological rationalism which accepts only so much of religion as can justify itself at the bar of reason, and which conceives and represents the origin of religion in accordance with this principle, was preceded by a rationalism less complete, as yet not wholly dissociated from a simple-minded supernaturalism. Its point of view is one at which it is almost impossible for the modern man to place himself. Here, in a single consciousness, orthodoxy and rationalism lie stratified in successive layers. Here, to change the metaphor, rationalism surrounds religion without touching it, and, like a lake surrounding some ancient castle, mirrors its image with curious refractions.

This half-developed rationalism was conscious of an impulse—it is the first time in the history of theology that this impulse [pg 028] manifests itself—to write the Life of Jesus; at first without any suspicion whither this undertaking would lead it. No rude hands were to be laid upon the doctrinal conception of Jesus; at least these writers had no intention of laying hands upon it. Their purpose was simply to gain a clearer view of the course of our Lord's earthly and human life. The theologians who undertook this task thought of themselves as merely writing an historical supplement to the life of the God-Man Jesus. These "Lives" are, therefore, composed according to the prescription of the "good old gentleman" who in 1829 advised the young Hase to treat first of the divine, and then of the human side of the life of Jesus.

The battle about miracle had not yet begun. But miracle no longer plays a part of any importance; it is a firmly established principle that the teaching of Jesus, and religion in general, hold their place solely in virtue of their inner reasonableness, not by the support of outward evidence.

The only thing that is really rationalistic in these older works is the treatment of the teaching of Jesus. Even those that retain the largest share of supernaturalism are as completely undogmatic as the more advanced in their reproduction of the discourses of the Great Teacher. All of them make it a principle to lose no opportunity of reducing the number of miracles; where they can explain a miracle by natural causes, they do not hesitate for a moment. But the deliberate rejection of all miracles, the elimination of everything supernatural which intrudes itself into the life of Jesus, is still to seek. That principle was first consistently carried through by Paulus. With these earlier writers it depends on the degree of enlightenment of the individual whether the irreducible minimum of the supernatural is larger or smaller.

Moreover, the period of this older rationalism, like every period when human thought has been strong and vigorous, is wholly unhistorical. What it is looking for is not the past, but itself in the past. For it, the problem of the life of Jesus is solved the moment it succeeds in bringing Jesus near to its own time, in portraying Him as the great teacher of virtue, and showing that His teaching is identical with the intellectual truth which rationalism deifies.

The temporal limits of this half-and-half rationalism are difficult to define. For the historical study of the life of Jesus the first landmark which it offers is the work of Hess, which appeared in 1768. But it held its ground for a long time side by side with rationalism proper, which failed to drive it from the field. A seventh edition of Hess's Life of Jesus appeared as late as 1823; while a fifth edition of Reinhard's work saw the light in 1830. And when Strauss struck the death-blow of out-and-out rationalism, the half-and-half rationalism did not perish with it, but allied itself [pg 029] with the neo-supernaturalism which Strauss's treatment of the life of Jesus had called into being; and it still prolongs an obscure existence in a certain section of conservative literature, though it has lost its best characteristics, its simple-mindedness and honesty.

These older rationalistic Lives of Jesus are, from the aesthetic point of view, among the least pleasing of all theological productions. The sentimentality of the portraiture is boundless. Boundless, also, and still more objectionable, is the want of respect for the language of Jesus. He must speak in a rational and modern fashion, and accordingly all His utterances are reproduced in a style of the most polite modernity. None of the speeches are allowed to stand as they were spoken; they are taken to pieces, paraphrased, and expanded, and sometimes, with the view of making them really lively, they are recast in the mould of a freely invented dialogue. In all these Lives of Jesus, not a single one of His sayings retains its authentic form.

And yet we must not be unjust to these writers. What they aimed at was to bring Jesus near to their own time, and in so doing they became the pioneers of the historical study of His life. The defects of their work in regard to aesthetic feeling and historical grasp are outweighed by the attractiveness of the purposeful, unprejudiced thinking which here awakens, stretches itself, and begins to move with freedom.

Johann Jakob Hess was born in 1741 and died in 1828. After working as a curate for seventeen years he became one of the assistant clergy at the Frauminster at Zurich, and later "Antistes," president, of the cantonal synod. In this capacity he guided the destinies of the Church in Zurich safely through the troublous times of the Revolution. He was not a deep thinker, but was well read and not without ability. As a man, he did splendid work.

His Life of Jesus still keeps largely to the lines of a paraphrase of the Gospels; indeed, he calls it a paraphrasing history. It is based upon a harmonizing combination of the four Gospels. The matter of the Synoptic narratives is, as in all the Lives of Jesus prior to Strauss—with the sole exception of Herder's—fitted more or less arbitrarily into the intervals between the Passovers in the fourth Gospel.

In regard to miracles, he admits that these are a stumbling-block. But they are essential to the Gospel narrative and to revelation; had Jesus been only a moral teacher and not the Son of God they would not have been necessary. We must be careful, however, not to prize miracles for their own sake, but to look primarily to their ethical teaching. It was, he remarks, the mistake of the Jews to regard all the acts of Jesus solely from the point of view of their strange and miraculous character, and to forget their moral teaching; whereas we, from distaste for miracle as such, run the risk of [pg 030] excluding from the Gospel history events which are bound up with the Gospel revelation.

Above all, we must retain the supernatural birth and the bodily resurrection, because on the former depends the sinlessness of Jesus, on the latter the certainty of the general resurrection of the dead. The temptation of Jesus in the wilderness was a stratagem of Satan by which he hoped to discover "whether Jesus of Nazareth was really so extraordinary a person that he would have cause to fear Him." The resurrection of Lazarus is authentic.

But the Gospel narrative is rationalised whenever it can be done. It was not the demons, but the Gadarene demoniacs themselves, who rushed among the swine. Alarmed by their fury the whole herd plunged over the precipice into the lake and were drowned; while by this accommodation to the fixed idea of the demoniacs, Jesus effected their cure. Perhaps, too, Hess conjectures, the Lord desired to test the Gadarenes, and to see whether they would attach greater importance to the good deed done to two of their number than to the loss of their swine. This explanation, reinforced by its moral, held its ground in theology for some sixty years and passed over into a round dozen Lives of Jesus.

This plan of "presenting each occurrence in such a way that what is valuable and instructive in it immediately strikes the eye" is followed out by Hess so faithfully that all clearness of impression is destroyed. The parables are barely recognisable, swathed, as they are, in the mummy-wrappings of his paraphrase; and in most cases their meaning is completely travestied by the ethical or historical allusions which he finds in them. The parable of the pounds is explained as referring to a man who went, like Archelaus, to Rome to obtain the kingship, while his subjects intrigued behind his back.

Of the peculiar beauty of the speech of Jesus not a trace remains. The parable of the Sower, for instance, begins: "A countryman went to sow his field, which lay beside a country-road, and was here and there rather rocky, and in some places weedy, but in general was well cultivated, and had a good sort of soil." The beatitude upon the mourners appears in the following guise: "Happy are they who amid the adversities of the present make the best of things and submit themselves with patience; for such men, if they do not see better times here, shall certainly elsewhere receive comfort and consolation." The question addressed by the Pharisees to John the Baptist, and his answer, are given dialogue-wise, in fustian of this kind:—*The Pharisees*: "We are directed to enquire of you, in the name of our president, who you profess to be? As people are at present expecting the Messiah, and seem not indisposed to accept you in that capacity, we are the more anxious that you should declare yourself with regard to your vocation and person." [pg 031] John: "The conclusion might have been drawn from my discourses that I was not the Messiah. Why should people attribute such lofty pretensions to me?" etc. In order to give the Gospels the true literary flavour, a characterisation is tacked on to each of the persons of the narrative. In the case of the disciples, for instance, this runs: "They had sound common sense, but very limited insight; the capacity to receive teaching, but an incapacity for reflective thought; a knowledge of their own weakness, but a difficulty in getting rid of old prejudices; sensibility to right feeling, but weakness in following out a pre-determined moral plan."

The simplest occurrences give occasion for sentimental portraiture. The saying "Except ye become as little children" is introduced in the following fashion: "Jesus called a boy who was standing near. The boy came. Jesus took his hand and told him to stand beside Him, nearer than any of His disciples, so that he had the foremost place among them. Then Jesus threw His arm round the boy and pressed him tenderly to His breast. The disciples looked on in astonishment, wondering what this meant. Then He explained to them," etc. In these expansions Hess does not always escape the ludicrous. The saying of Jesus in John x. 9, "I am the door," takes on the following form: "No one, whether he be sheep or shepherd, can come into the fold (if, that is to say, he follows the right way) except in so far as he knows me and is admitted by me, and included among the flock."

Reinhard's work is on a distinctly higher level. The author was born in 1753. In 1792, after he had worked for fourteen years as Docent in Wittenberg, he was appointed Senior Court Chaplain at Dresden. He died in 1812.

"I am, as you know, a very prosaic person," writes Reinhard to a friend, and in these words he has given an admirable characterisation of himself. The writers who chiefly appeal to him are the ancient moralists; he acknowledges that he has learned more from them than from a "collegium homileticum." In his celebrated "System of Christian Ethics" (5 vols., 1788-1815) he makes copious use of them. His sermons—they fill thirty-five volumes, and in their day were regarded as models—show some power and depth of thought, but are all cast in the same mould. He seems to have been haunted by a fear that it might some time befall him to admit into his mind a thought which was mystical or visionary, not justifiable by the laws of logic and the canons of the critical reason. With all his philosophising and rationalising, however, certain pillars of the supernaturalistic view of history remain for him immovable.

At first sight one might be inclined to suppose that he frankly shared the belief in miracle. He mentions the raising of the [pg 032] widow's son, and of Lazarus, and accepts as an authentic saying the command of the risen Jesus to baptize all nations. But if we look more closely, we find that he deliberately brings very few miracles into his narrative, and the definition by which he disintegrates the conception of miracle from within leaves no doubt as to his own position. What he says is this: "All that which we call miraculous and supernatural is to be understood as only relatively so, and implies nothing further than an obvious exception to what can be brought about by natural causes, so far as we know them and have experience of their capacity. A cautious thinker will not venture in any single instance to pronounce an event to be so extraordinary that God could not have brought it about by the use of secondary causes, but must have intervened directly."

The case stands similarly with regard to the divinity of Christ. Reinhard assumes it, but his "Life" is not directed to prove it; it leads only to the conclusion that the Founder of Christianity is to be regarded as a wonderful "divine" teacher. In order to prove His uniqueness, Reinhard has to show that His plan for the welfare of mankind was something incomparably higher than anything which hero or sage has ever striven for. Reinhard makes the first attempt to give an account of the teaching of Jesus which should be historical in the sense that all dogmatic considerations should be excluded. "Above all things, let us collect and examine the indications which we find in the writings of His companions regarding the designs which He had in view."

The plan of Jesus shows its greatness above all in its universality. Reinhard is well aware of the difficulty raised in this connexion by those sayings which assert the prerogative of Israel, and he discusses them at length. He finds the solution in the assumption that Jesus in His own lifetime naturally confined Himself to working among His own people, and was content to indicate the future universal development of His plan.

With the intention "of introducing a universal change, tending to the benefit of the whole human race," Jesus attaches His teaching to the Jewish eschatology. It is only the form of His teaching, however, which is affected by this, since He gives an entirely different significance to the terms Kingdom of Heaven and Kingdom of God, referring them to a universal ethical reorganisation of mankind. But His plan was entirely independent of politics. He never based His claims upon His Davidic descent. This was, indeed, the reason why He held aloof from His family. Even the entry into Jerusalem had no Messianic significance. His plan was so entirely non-political that He would, on the contrary, have welcomed the severance of all connexion between the state and religion, in order to avoid the risk of a conflict between these two powers. Reinhard explains the voluntary death of Jesus as due to [pg 033] this endeavour. "He quitted the stage of the world by so early and shameful a death because He wished to destroy at once and for ever the mistaken impression that He was aiming at the foundation of an earthly kingdom, and to turn the thoughts, wishes, and efforts of His disciples and companions into another channel."

In order to make the Kingdom of God a practical reality, it was necessary for Him to dissociate it from all the forces of this world, and to bring morality and religion into the closest connexion. "The law of love was the indissoluble bond by which Jesus for ever united morality with religion." "Moral instruction was the principal content and the very essence of all His discourses." His efforts "were directed to the establishment of a purely ethical organisation."

It was important, therefore, to overthrow superstition and to bring religion within the domain of reason. First of all the priesthood must be deprived for ever of its influence. Then an improvement of the social condition of mankind must be introduced, since the level of morality depends upon social conditions. Jesus was a social reformer. Through the attainment of "the highest perfection of which Society is capable, universal peace" was "gradually to be brought about."

But the point of primary importance for Him was the alliance of religion with reason. Reason was to maintain its freedom by the aid of religion, and religion was not to be withdrawn from the critical judgment of reason: all things were to be tested, and only the best retained.

"From these data it is easy to determine the characteristics of a religion which is to be the religion of all mankind: it must be ethical, intelligible, and spiritual."

After the plan of Jesus has been expounded on these lines, Reinhard shows, in the second part of his work, that, prior to Jesus, no great man of antiquity had devised a plan of beneficence of a scope commensurate with the whole human race. In the third part the conclusion is drawn that Jesus is the uniquely divine Teacher.

But before the author can venture to draw this conclusion, he feels it necessary first to show that the plan of Jesus was no chimera. If we were obliged to admit its impracticability Jesus would have to be ranked with the visionaries and enthusiasts; and these, however noble and virtuous, can only injure the cause of rational religion. "Visionary enthusiasm and enlightened reason—who that knows anything of the human mind can conceive these two as united in a single soul?" But Jesus was no visionary enthusiast. "With what calmness, self-mastery, and cool determination does He think out and pursue His divine purpose?" By the truths which He revealed and declared to be divine communications He [pg 034] did not desire to put pressure upon the human mind, but only to guide it. "It would be impossible to show a more conscientious respect and a more delicate consideration for the rights of human reason than is shown by Jesus. He will conquer only by convincing." "He is willing to bear with contradiction, and condescends to meet the most irrational objections and the most ill-natured misrepresentations with the most incredible patience."

It was well for Reinhard that he had no suspicion how full of enthusiasm Jesus was, and how He trod reason under His feet!

But what kind of relation was there between this rational religion taught by Jesus and the Christian theology which Reinhard accepted? How does he harmonise the symbolical view of Baptism and the Lord's Supper which he here expounds with ecclesiastical doctrine? How does he pass from the conception of the divine teacher to that of the Son of God?

This is a question which he does not feel himself obliged to answer. For him the one circle of thought revolves freely within the other, but they never come into contact with each other.

So far as concerns the presentation of the teaching, the Life of Jesus by Opitz follows the same lines as that of Reinhard. It is disfigured, however, by a number of lapses of taste, and by a crass supernaturalism in the description of the miracles and experiences of the Great Teacher.

Jakobi writes "for thoughtful and sympathetic readers." He recognises that much of the miraculous is a later addition to the facts, but he has a rooted distrust of thoroughgoing rationalism, "whose would-be helpful explanations are often stranger than the miracles themselves." A certain amount of miracle must be maintained, but not for the purpose of founding belief upon it: "the miracles were not intended to authenticate the teaching of Jesus, but to surround His life with a guard of honour."[20]

Whether Herder, in his two Lives of Jesus, is to be classed with the older rationalists is a question to which the answer must be "Yes, and No," as in the case of every attempt to classify those men of lonely greatness who stand apart from their contemporaries, but who nevertheless are not in all points in advance of them.

Properly speaking, he has really nothing to do with the rationalists, since he is distinguished from them by the depth of his insight and his power of artistic apprehension, and he is far from sharing their lack of taste. Further, his horizon embraces problems of which rationalism, even in its developed form, never [pg 035] came in sight. He recognises that all attempts to harmonise the Synoptists with John are unavailing; a conclusion which he had avowed earlier in his "Letters referring to the Study of Theology."[21] He grasps this incompatibility, it is true, rather by the aid of poetic, than of critical insight. "Since they cannot be united," he writes in his "Life of Jesus according to John," "they must be left standing independently, each evangelist with his own special merit. Man, Ox, Lion, and Eagle, they advance together, supporting the throne of glory, but they refuse to coalesce into a single form, to unite into a Diatessaron." But to him belongs the honour of being the first and the only scholar, prior to Strauss, to recognise that the life of Jesus can be construed either according to the Synoptists, or according to John, but that a Life of Jesus based on the four Gospels is a monstrosity. In view of this intuitive historical grasp, it is not surprising that the commentaries of the theologians were an abomination to him.

The fourth Gospel is, in his view, not a primitive historical source, but a protest against the narrowness of the "Palestinian Gospels." It gives free play, as the circumstances of the time demanded, to Greek ideas. "There was need, in addition to those earlier, purely historical Gospels, of a Gospel at once theological and historical, like that of John," in which Jesus should be presented, not as the Jewish Messiah, "but as the Saviour of the World."

The additions and omissions of this Gospel are alike skilfully planned. It retains only those miracles which are symbols of a continuous permanent miracle, through which the Saviour of the World works constantly, uninterruptedly, among men. The Johannine miracles are not there for their own sakes. The cures of demoniacs are not even represented among them. These had no interest for the Graeco-Roman world, and the Evangelist was unwilling "that this Palestinian superstition should become a permanent feature of Christianity, to be a reproach of scoffers or a belief of the foolish." His recording of the raising of Lazarus is, in spite of the silence of the Synoptists, easily explicable. The latter could not yet tell the story "without exposing a family which was still living near Jerusalem to the fury of that hatred which had sworn with an oath to put Lazarus to death." John, however, could recount it without scruple, "for by this time Jerusalem was probably in ruins, and the hospitable family of Bethany were perhaps already with their Friend in the other world." This most naïve of explanations is reproduced in a whole series of Lives of Jesus.

In dealing with the Synoptists, Herder grasps the problem with [pg 036] the same intuitive insight. Mark is no epitomist, but the creator of the archetype of the Synoptic representation.

"The Gospel of Mark is not an epitome; it is an original Gospel. What the others have, and he has not, has been added by them, not omitted by him. Consequently Mark is a witness to an original, shorter Gospel-scheme, to which the additional matter of the others ought properly to be regarded as a supplement."

Mark is the "unornamented central column, or plain foundation stone, on which the others rest." The birth-stories of Matthew and Luke are "a new growth to meet new needs." The different tendencies, also, point to a later period. Mark is still comparatively friendly towards the Jews, because Christianity had not yet separated itself from Judaism. Matthew is more hostile towards them because his Gospel was written at a time when Christians had given up the hope of maintaining amicable relations with the Jews and were groaning under the pressure of persecution. It is for that reason that the Jesus of the Matthaean discourses lays so much stress upon His second coming, and presupposes the rejection of the Jewish nation as something already in being, a sign of the approaching end.

Pure history, however, is as little to be looked for in the first three Gospels as in the fourth. They are the sacred epic of Jesus the Messiah, and model the history of their hero upon the prophetic words of the Old Testament. In this view, also, Herder is a precursor of Strauss.

In essence, however, Herder represents a protest of art against theology. The Gospels, if we are to find the life of Jesus in them, must be read, not with pedantic learning, but with taste. From this point of view, miracles cease to offend. Neither Old Testament prophecies, nor predictions of Jesus, nor miracles, can be adduced as evidence for the Gospel; the Gospel is its own evidence. The miracles stand outside the possibility of proof, and belong to mere "Church belief," which ought to lose itself more and more in the pure Gospel. Yet miracles, in a limited sense, are to be accepted on the ground of the historic evidence. To refuse to admit this is to be like the Indian king who denied the existence of ice because he had never seen anything like it. Jesus, in order to help His miracle-loving age, reconciled Himself to the necessity of performing miracles. But, in any case, the reality of a miracle is of small moment in comparison with its symbolic value.

In this, therefore, Herder, though in his grasp of many problems he was more than a generation in advance of his time, belongs to the primitive rationalists. He allows the supernatural to intrude into the events of the life of Jesus, and does not feel that the adoption of the historical standpoint involves the necessity of doing away with miracle. He contributed much to the clearing up of [pg 037] ideas, but by evading the question of miracle he slurred over a difficulty which needed to be faced and solved before it should be possible to entertain the hope of forming a really historical conception of the life of Jesus. In reading Herder one is apt to fancy that it would be possible to pass straight on to Strauss. In reality, it was necessary that a very prosaic spirit, Paulus, should intervene, and should attack the question of miracle from a purely historical standpoint, before Strauss could give expression to the ideas of Herder in an effectual way, *i.e.* in such a way as to produce offence. The fact is that in theology the most revolutionary ideas are swallowed quite readily so long as they smooth their passage by a few small concessions. It is only when a spicule of bone stands out obstinately and causes choking that theology begins to take note of dangerous ideas. Strauss is Herder with just that little bone sticking out—the absolute denial of miracle on historical grounds. That is to say, Strauss is a Herder who has behind him the uncompromising rationalism of Paulus.
[pg 038]

IV. The Earliest Fictitious Lives Of Jesus

Karl Friedrich Bahrdt. Briefe über die Bibel im Volkston. Eine Wochenschrift von einem Prediger auf dem Lande. (Popular Letters about the Bible. A weekly paper by a country clergyman.) J. Fr. Dost, Halle, 1782. 816 pp.

Ausführung des Plans und Zwecks Jesu. In Briefen an Wahrheit suchende Leser. (An Explanation of the Plans and Aims of Jesus. In letters addressed to readers who seek the truth.) 11 vols., embracing 3000 pp. August Mylius, Berlin, 1784-1792. This work is a sequel to the Popular Letters about the Bible.

Die sämtlichen Reden Jesu aus den Evangelisten ausgezogen. (The Whole of the Discourses of Jesus, extracted from the Gospels.) Berlin, 1786.

Karl Heinrich Venturini. Natürliche Geschichte des grossen Propheten von Nazareth. (A Non-supernatural History of the Great Prophet of Nazareth.) Bethlehem (Copenhagen), 1st ed., 1800-1802; 2nd ed., 1806. 4 vols., embracing 2700 pp. The work appeared anonymously. The description given below is based on the 2nd ed., which shows dependence, in some of the exegetical details, upon the then recently published commentaries of Paulus.

It is strange to notice how often in the history of our subject a few imperfectly equipped free-lances have attacked and attempted to carry the decisive positions before the ordered ranks of professional theology have pushed their advance to these decisive points.

Thus, it was the fictitious "Lives" of Bahrdt and Venturini which, at the end of the eighteenth and beginning of the nineteenth centuries, first attempted to apply, with logical consistency, a non-supernatural interpretation to the miracle stories of the Gospel. Further, these writers were the first who, instead of contenting themselves with the simple reproduction of the successive sections of the Gospel narrative, endeavoured to grasp the inner connexion of cause and effect in the events and experiences of the life of Jesus. Since they found no such connexion indicated in the Gospels, they had to supply it for themselves. The particular form which their explanation takes—the hypothesis of a secret society of which Jesus is the tool—is, it is true, rather a sorry makeshift. Yet, in a sense, these Lives of Jesus, for all their colouring of fiction, are the first which deserve the name. The rationalists, and even Paulus, confine themselves to describing the teaching of Jesus; Bahrdt and Venturini make a bold attempt to paint the portrait of Jesus Himself. It is [pg 039] not surprising that their portraiture is at once crude and fantastic, like the earliest attempts of art to represent the human figure in living movement.

Karl Friedrich Bahrdt was born in 1741 at Bischofswerda. Endowed with brilliant abilities, he made, owing to a bad upbringing and an undisciplined sensuous nature, a miserable failure. After being first Catechist and afterwards Professor Extraordinary of Sacred Philology at Leipzig, he was, in 1766, requested to resign on account of scandalous life. After various adventures, and after holding for a time a professorship at Giessen, he received under Frederick's minister Zedlitz authorisation to lecture at Halle. There he lectured to nearly nine hundred students who were attracted by his inspiring eloquence. The government upheld him, in spite of his serious failings, with the double motive of annoying the faculty and maintaining the freedom of learning. After the death of Frederick the Great, Bahrdt had to resign his post, and took to keeping an inn at a vineyard near Halle. By ridiculing Wöllner's edict (1788), he brought on himself a year of confinement in a fortress. He died in disrepute, in 1792.

Bahrdt had begun as an orthodox cleric. In Halle he gave up his belief in revelation, and endeavoured to explain religion on the ground of reason. To this period belong the "Popular Letters about the Bible," which were afterwards continued in the further series, "An Explanation of the Plans and Aims of Jesus."

His treatment of the life of Jesus has been too severely censured. The work is not without passages which show a real depth of feeling, especially in the continually recurring explanations regarding the relation of belief in miracle to true faith, in which the actual description of the life of Jesus lies embedded. And the remarks about the teaching of Jesus are not always commonplace. But the paraphernalia of dialogues of portentous length make it, as a whole, formless and inartistic. The introduction of a galaxy of imaginary characters—Haram, Schimah, Avel, Limmah, and the like—is nothing less than bewildering.

Bahrdt finds the key to the explanation of the life of Jesus in the appearance in the Gospel narrative of Nicodemus and Joseph of Arimathea. They are not disciples of Jesus, but belong to the upper classes; what rôle, then, can they have played in the life of Jesus, and how came they to intercede on His behalf? They were Essenes. This Order had secret members in all ranks of society, even in the Sanhedrin. It had set itself the task of detaching the nation from its sensuous Messianic hopes and leading it to a higher knowledge of spiritual truths. It had the most widespread ramifications, extending to Babylon and to Egypt. In order to deliver the people from the limitations of the national faith, which could only lead to disturbance and insurrection, they must find a [pg 040] Messiah who would destroy these false Messianic expectations. They were therefore on the look-out for a claimant of the Messiahship whom they could make subservient to their aims.

Jesus came under the notice of the Order immediately after His birth. As a child He was watched over at every step by the Brethren. At the feasts at Jerusalem Alexandrian Jews, secret members of the Essene Order, put themselves into communication with Him, explained to Him the falsity of the priests, inspired Him with a horror of the bloody sacrifices of the Temple, and made him acquainted with Socrates and Plato. This is set forth in dialogues of a hundred pages long. At the story of the death of Socrates, the boy bursts into a tempest of sobs which His friends are unable to calm. He longs to emulate the martyr-death of the great Athenian.

On the market-place at Nazareth a mysterious Persian gives Him two sovereign remedies—one for affections of the eye, the other for nervous disorders.

His father does his best for Him, teaching Him, along with His cousin John, afterwards the Baptist, about virtue and immortality. A priest belonging to the Essene Order, who makes their acquaintance disguised as a shepherd, and takes part in their conversations, leads the lads deeper into the knowledge of wisdom. At twelve years old, Jesus is already so far advanced that

He argues with the Scribes in the Temple concerning miracles, maintaining the thesis that they are impossible.

When they feel themselves ready to appear in public the two cousins take counsel together how they can best help the people. They agree to open the eyes of the people regarding the tyranny and hypocrisy of the priests. Through Haram, a prominent member of the Essene Order, Luke the physician is introduced to Jesus and places all his science at His disposal.

In order to produce any effect they were obliged to practise accommodation to the superstitions of the people, and introduce their wisdom to them under the garb of folly, in the hope that, beguiled by its attractive exterior, the people would admit into their minds the revelation of rational truth, and after a time be able to emancipate themselves from superstition. Jesus, therefore, sees Himself obliged to appear in the rôle of the Messiah of popular expectation, and to make up His mind to work by means of miracles and illusions. About this He felt the gravest scruples. He was obliged, however, to obey the Order; and His scruples were quieted by the reminder of the lofty end which was to be reached by these means. At last, when it is pointed out to Him that even Moses had followed the same plan, He submits to the necessity. The influential Order undertakes the duty of stage-managing the miracles, and that of maintaining His father. On the reception of Jesus into the number of the Brethren of the First [pg 041] Degree of the Order it is made known to Him that these Brethren are bound to face death in the cause of the Order; but that the Order, on its part, undertakes so to use the machinery and influence at its disposal that the last extremity shall always be avoided and the Brother mysteriously preserved from death.

Then begins the cleverly staged drama by means of which the people are to be converted to rational religion. The members of the Order are divided into three classes: The Baptized, The Disciples, The Chosen Ones. The Baptized receive only the usual popular teaching; the Disciples are admitted to further knowledge, but are not entrusted with the highest mysteries; the Chosen Ones, who in the Gospels are also spoken of as "Angels," are admitted into all wisdom. As the Apostles were only members of the Second Degree, they had not the smallest suspicion of the secret machinery which was at work. Their part in the drama of the Life of Jesus was that of zealous "supers." The Gospels which they composed therefore report, in perfect good faith, miracles which were really clever illusions produced by the Essenes, and they depict the life of Jesus only as seen by the populace from the outside.

It is therefore not always possible for us to discover how the events which they record as miracles actually came about. But whether they took place in one way or another—and as to this we can sometimes get a clue from a hint in the text—it is certain that in all cases the process was natural. With reference to the feeding of the five thousand, Bahrdt remarks: "It is more reasonable here to think of a thousand ways by which Jesus might have had sufficient supplies of bread at hand, and by the distribution of it have shamed the disciples' lack of courage, than to believe in a miracle." The explanation which he himself prefers is that the Order had collected a great quantity of bread in a cave and this was gradually handed out to Jesus, who stood at the concealed entrance and took some every time the apostles were occupied in distributing the former supply to the multitude. The walking on the sea is to be explained by supposing that Jesus walked towards the disciples over the surface of a great floating raft; while they, not being able to see the raft, must needs suppose a miracle. When Peter tried to walk on the water he failed miserably. The miracles of healing are to be attributed to the art of Luke. He also called the attention of Jesus to remarkable cases of apparent death, which He then took in hand, and restored the apparently dead to their sorrowing friends. In such cases, however, the Lord never failed expressly to inform the disciples that the persons were not really dead. They, however, did not permit this assurance to deprive them of their faith in the miracle which they felt they had themselves witnessed.

[pg 042]

In teaching, Jesus had two methods: one, exoteric, simple, for the world; the other, esoteric, mystic, for the initiate. "No attentive reader of the Bible," says Bahrdt, "can fail to notice that Jesus made use of two different styles of speech. Sometimes He spoke so plainly and in such universally intelligible language, and declared truths so simple and so well adapted to the general comprehension of mankind that even the simplest could follow Him. At other times he spoke so mystically, so obscurely, and in so veiled a fashion that words and thoughts alike baffled the understandings of ordinary people, and even by more practised minds were not to be grasped without close reflection, so that we are told in John vi. 60 that 'many of His disciples, when they heard this, said, This is an hard saying; who can hear it?' And Jesus Himself did not deny it, but only told them that the reason of their not understanding His sayings lay in their prejudices, which made them interpret everything literally and materially, and overlook the ethical meaning which underlay His figurative language." Most of these mystical discourses are to be found in John, who seems to have preserved for us the greater part of the secret teaching imparted to the initiate. The key to the understanding of this esoteric teaching is to be found, therefore, in the prologue to John's Gospel, and in the sayings about the new birth. "To be born again" is identical with the degree of perfection which was attained in the highest class of the Brotherhood.

The members of the Order met on appointed days in caves among the hills. When we are told in the Gospels that Jesus went alone into a mountain to pray, this means that He repaired to one of these secret gatherings, but the disciples, of course, knew nothing about that. The Order had its hidden caves everywhere; in Galilee as well as in the neighbourhood of Jerusalem.

"Only by sensuous means can sensuous ideas be overcome." The Jewish Messiah must die and rise again, in order that the false conceptions of the Messiah which were cherished by the multitude might be destroyed in the moment of their fulfilment—that is, might be spiritualised. Nicodemus, Haram, and Luke met in a cave in order to take counsel how they might bring about the death of Jesus in a way favourable to their plans. Luke guaranteed that by the aid of powerful drugs which he would give Him the Lord should be enabled to endure the utmost pain and suffering and yet resist death for a long time. Nicodemus undertook so to work matters in the Sanhedrin that the execution should follow immediately upon the sentence, and the crucified remain only a short time upon the cross. At this moment Jesus rushed into the cave. He had scarcely had time to replace the stone which concealed the entrance, so closely had He been pursued over the rocks by hired assassins. He Himself is firmly resolved [pg 043] to die, but care must be taken that He shall not be simply assassinated, or the whole plan fails. If He falls by the assassin's knife, no resurrection will be possible.

In the end, the piece is staged to perfection. Jesus provokes the authorities by His triumphal Messianic entry. The unsuspected Essenes in the council urge on His arrest and secure His condemnation—though Pilate almost frustrates all their plans by acquitting Him. Jesus, by uttering a loud cry and immediately afterwards bowing His head, shows every appearance of a sudden death. The centurion has been bribed not to allow any of His bones to be broken. Then comes Joseph of Ramath, as Bahrdt prefers to call Joseph of Arimathea, and removes the body to the cave of the Essenes, where he immediately commences measures of resuscitation. As Luke had prepared the body of the Messiah by means of strengthening medicines to resist the fearful ill-usage which He had gone through—the being dragged about and beaten and finally crucified—these efforts were crowned with success. In the cave the most strengthening nutriment was supplied to Him. "Since the humours of the body were in a thoroughly healthy condition, His wounds healed very readily, and by the third day He was able to walk, in spite of the fact that the wounds made by the nails were still open."

On the morning of the third day they forced away the stone which closed the mouth of the grave. As Jesus was descending the rocky slopes the watch awakened and took to flight in alarm. One of the Essenes appeared, in the garb of an angel, to the women and announced to them the resurrection of Jesus. Shortly afterwards the Lord appeared to Mary. At the sound of His voice she recognises Him. "Thereupon Jesus tells her that He is going to His Father (to heaven—in the mystic sense of the word—that is to say, to the Chosen Ones in their peaceful dwellings of truth and blessedness—to the circle of His faithful friends, among whom He continued to live, unseen by the world, but still working for the advancement of His purpose). He bade her tell His disciples that He was alive."

From His place of concealment He appeared several times to His disciples. Finally He bade them meet Him at the Mount of Olives, near Bethany, and there took leave of them. After exhorting them, and embracing each of them in turn, He tore Himself away from them and walked away up the mountain. "There stood those poor men, amazed—beside themselves with sorrow—and looked after Him as long as they could. But as He mounted higher, He entered ever deeper into the cloud which lay upon the hill-top, until finally He was no longer to be seen. The cloud received Him out of their sight."

From the mountain He returned to the chief lodge of the [pg 044] Brotherhood. Only at rare intervals did He again intervene in active life—as on the occasion when He appeared to Paul upon the road to Damascus. But, though unseen, He continued to direct the destinies of the community until His death.

Venturini's "Non-supernatural History of the Great Prophet of Nazareth" is related to Bahrdt's work as the finished picture to the sketch.

Karl Heinrich Venturini was born at Brunswick in 1768. On the completion of his theological studies he vainly endeavoured to secure a post as Docent in the theological faculty at Helmstadt, or as Librarian at Wolfenbüttel.

His life was blameless and his personal piety beyond reproach, but he was considered to be too free in his ideas. The Duke of Brunswick was personally well disposed towards him, but did not venture to give him a post on the teaching staff in face of the opposition of the consistories. He was reduced to earning a bare pittance by literary work, and finally in 1806 was thankful to accept a small living in Hordorf near Brunswick. He then abandoned theological writing and devoted his energies to recording the events of contemporary history, of which he published a yearly chronicle—a proceeding which under the Napoleonic *régime* was not always unattended with risk, as he more than once had occasion to experience. He continued this undertaking till 1841. In 1849 death released him from his tasks.

Venturini's fundamental assumption is that it was impossible, even for the noblest spirit of mankind, to make Himself understood by the Judaism of His time except by clothing His spiritual teaching in a sensuous garb calculated to please the oriental imagination, "and, in general, by bringing His higher spiritual world into such relations with the lower sensuous world of those whom He wished to teach as was necessary to the accomplishment of His aims." "God's Messenger was morally bound to perform miracles for the Jews. These miracles had an ethical purpose, and were especially designed to counteract the impression made by the supposed miracles of the deceivers of the people, and thus to hasten the overthrow of the kingdom of Satan."

For modern medical science the miracles are not miraculous. He never healed without medicaments and always carried His "portable medicine chest" with Him. In the case of the Syro-phoenician woman's daughter, for example, we can still detect in the narrative a hint of the actual course of events. The mother explains the case to Jesus. After enquiring where her dwelling was he made a sign to John, and continued to hold her in conversation. The disciple went to the daughter and gave her a sedative, and when the mother returned she found her child cured.

[pg 045]

The raisings from the dead were cases of coma. The nature-miracles were due to a profound acquaintance with the powers of Nature and the order of her processes. They involve fore-knowledge rather than control.

Many miracle stories rest on obvious misunderstandings. Nothing could be simpler than the explanation of the miracle at Cana. Jesus had brought with Him as a wedding-gift some jars of good wine and had put them aside in another room. When the wine was finished and His mother became anxious, He still allowed the guests to wait a little, as the stone vessels for purification had not yet been filled with water. When that had been done He ordered the servants to pour out some of his wine, but to tell no one whence it came. When John, as an old man, wrote his Gospel, he got all this rather mixed up—had not indeed observed it very closely at the time, "had perhaps been the least thing merry himself," says Venturini, and had believed in the miracle with the rest. Perhaps, too, he had not ventured to ask Jesus for an explanation, for he had only become His disciple a few days before.

The members of the Essene Order had watched over the child Jesus even in Egypt. As He grew older they took charge of His education along with that of His cousin, John, and trained them both for their work as deliverers of the people. Whereas the nation as a whole looked to an insurrection as the means of its deliverance, they knew that freedom could only be achieved by means of a spiritual renewal. Once Jesus and John met a band of insurgents: Jesus worked on them so powerfully by His fervid speech that they recognised the impiousness of their purpose. One of them sprang towards Him and laid down his arms; it was Simon, who afterwards became His disciple.

When Jesus was about thirty years old, and, owing to the deep experiences of His inner life, had really far outgrown the aims of the Essene Order, He entered upon His office by demanding baptism from John. Just as this was taking place a thunderstorm broke, and a dove, frightened by the lightning, fluttered round the head of Jesus. Both Jesus and John took this as a sign that the hour appointed by God had come.

The temptations in the wilderness, and upon the pinnacle of the Temple, were due to the machinations of the Pharisee Zadok, who pretended to enter into the plans of Jesus and feigned admiration for Him in order the more surely to entrap Him. It was Zadok, too, who stirred up opposition to Him in the Sanhedrin.

But Jesus did not succeed in destroying the old Messianic belief with its earthly aims. The hatred of the leading circles against Him grew, although He avoided everything "that could offend their prejudices." It was for this reason that He even forbade His disciples to preach the Gospel beyond the borders of Jewish [pg 046] territory. He paid the temple-tax, also, although he had no fixed abode. When the collector went to Peter about it, the following dialogue took place.

Tax-collector (*drawing Peter aside*). Tell me, Simon, does the Rabbi pay the didrachma to the Temple treasury, or should we not trouble Him about it?

Peter. Why shouldn't He pay it? Why do you ask?

Tax-collector. It's been owing from both of you since last Nisan, as our books show. We did not like to remind your Master, out of reverence.

Peter. I'll tell Him at once. He will certainly pay the tax. You need have no fear about that.

Tax-collector. That's good. That will put everything straight, and we shall have no trouble over our accounts. Good-bye!

When Jesus hears of it He commands Peter to go and catch a fish, and to take care, in removing the hook, not to tear its mouth, that it may be fit for salting (!) In that case it will doubtless be worth a *stater*.

The time arrived when an important move must be made. In full conclave of the Secret Society it was resolved that Jesus should go up to Jerusalem and there publicly proclaim Himself as the Messiah. Then He was to endeavour to disabuse the people of their earthly Messianic expectations.

The triumphal entry succeeded. The whole people hailed Him with acclamations. But when He tried to substitute for their picture of the Messiah one of a different character, and spoke of times of severe trial which should come upon all, when He showed Himself but seldom in the Temple, instead of taking His place at the head of the people, they began to doubt Him.

Jesus was suddenly arrested and put to death. Here, then, the death is not, as in Bahrdt, a piece of play-acting, stage-managed by the Secret Society. Jesus really expected to die, and only to meet His disciples again in the eternal life of the other world. But when He so soon gave up the ghost, Joseph of Arimathea was moved by some vague premonition to hasten at once to Pontius Pilate and make request for His body. He offers the Procurator money. *Pilate* (*sternly and emphatically*): "Dost thou also mistake me? Am I, then, such an insatiable miser? Still, thou art a Jew—how could this people do me justice? Know, then, that a Roman can honour true nobility wherever he may find it. (*He sits down and writes some words on a strip of parchment.*) Give this to the captain of the guard. Thou shall be permitted to remove the body. I ask nothing for this. It is granted to thee freely."

"A tender embrace from his wife rewarded the noble deed of the Roman, while Joseph left the Praetorium, and with Nicodemus, who was impatiently awaiting him, hastened to Golgotha." There [pg 047] he received the body; he washed it, anointed it with spices, and laid it on a bed of moss in the rock-hewn grave. From the blood which was still flowing from the wound in the side, he ventured to draw a hopeful augury, and sent word to the Essene Brethren. They had a hold close by, and promised to watch over the body. In the first four-and-twenty hours no movement of life showed itself. Then came the earthquake. In the midst of the terrible commotion a Brother, in the white robes of the Order, was making his way to the grave by a secret path. When he, illumined by a flash of lightning, suddenly appeared above the grave, and at the same moment the earth shook violently, panic seized the watch, and they fled. In the morning the Brother hears a sound from the grave: Jesus is moving. The whole Order hastens to the spot, and Jesus is removed to their Lodge. Two brethren remain at the grave—these were the "angels" whom the women saw later. Jesus, in the dress of a gardener, is afterwards recognised by Mary Magdalene. Later, He comes out at intervals from the hiding-place, where He is kept by the Brethren, and appears to the disciples. After forty days He took His leave of them: His strength was exhausted. The farewell scene gave rise to the mistaken impression of His Ascension.

From the historical point of view these lives are not such contemptible performances as might be supposed. There is much penetrating observation in them. Bahrdt and Venturini are right in feeling that the connexion of events in the life of Jesus has to be discovered; the Gospels give only a series of occurrences, and offer no explanation why they happened just as they did. And if, in making Jesus subservient to the plans of a secret society, they represented Him as not acting with perfect freedom, but as showing a certain passivity, this assumption of theirs was to be brilliantly vindicated, a hundred years later, by the eschatological school, which asserts the same remarkable passivity on the part of Jesus, in that He allows His actions to be determined, not indeed by a secret society, but by the eschatological plan of God. Bahrdt and Venturini were the first to see that, of all Jesus' acts, His death was most distinctively His own, because it was by this that He purposed to found the kingdom.

Venturini's "Non-supernatural History of the Great Prophet of Nazareth" may almost be said to be reissued annually down to the present day, for all the fictitious "Lives" go back directly or indirectly to the type which he created. It is plagiarised more freely than any other Life of Jesus, although practically unknown by name.
[pg 048]

V. Fully Developed Rationalism—Paulus

Heinrich Eberhard Gottlob Paulus. Das Leben Jesu als Grundlage einer reinen Geschichte des Urchristentums. Heidelberg, C. F. Winter. (The Life of Jesus as the Basis of a purely Historical Account of Early Christianity.) 1828. 2 vols., 1192 pp.
Freut euch mit Gottesandacht, wenn es gewährt euch ist,
Dem, so kurz er war, weltumschaffenden Lebensgang
Nach Jahrhunderten fern zu folgen,
Denket, glaubet, folget des Vorbildes Spur!
(Closing words of vol. ii.)
(Rejoice with grateful devotion, if unto you 'tis permitted,
After the lapse of centuries, still to follow afar off
That Life which, short as it was, changed the course of the ages;
Think ye well, and believe; follow the path of our Pattern.)

Paulus was not the mere dry-as-dust rationalist that he is usually represented to have been, but a man of very versatile abilities. His limitation was that, like Reinhard, he had an unconquerable distrust of anything that went outside the boundaries of logical thought. That was due in part to the experiences of his youth. His father, a deacon in Leonberg, half-mystic, half-rationalist, had secret difficulties about the doctrine of immortality, and made his wife promise on her death-bed that, if it were possible, she would appear to him after her death in bodily form. After she was dead he thought he saw her raise herself to a sitting posture, and again sink down. From that time onwards he firmly believed himself to be in communication with departed spirits, and he became so dominated by this idea that in 1771 he had to be removed from his office. His children suffered sorely from a *régime* of compulsory spiritualism, which pressed hardest upon Heinrich Eberhard Gottlob, born in 1761, who, for the sake of peace, was obliged to pretend to his father that he was in communication with his mother's spirit.

He himself had inherited only the rationalistic side of his father's temperament. As a student at the Tübingen Stift (theological institute) he formed his views on the writings of [pg 049] Semler and Michaelis. In 1789 he was called to Jena as Professor of Oriental Languages, and succeeded in 1793 to the third ordinary professorship of theology. The naturalistic interpretation of miracles which he upheld in his commentary on the Synoptic Gospels, published in 1800-1802, aroused the indignation of the consistories of Meiningen and Eisenach. But their petition for his removal from the professorship was unsuccessful, since Herder, who was president of the consistorium, used his influence to protect him. In 1799 Paulus, as Pro-rector, used his influence on behalf of his colleague Fichte, who was attacked on the ground of atheism; but in vain, owing to the passionate conduct of the accused.

With Goethe, Schiller, and Wieland, Paulus and his wife, a lively lady of some literary talents, stood in the most friendly relations.

When the Jena circle began to break up, he accepted, in 1803, an invitation from the Elector of Bavaria, Maximilian Joseph II., to go to Würzburg as Konsistorialrat and professor. There the liberal minister, Montgelas, was desirous of establishing a university founded on the principles of illuminism—Schelling, Hufeland, and Schleiermacher were among those whom he contemplated appointing as Docents. Here the Catholic theological students were obliged to attend the lectures of the Protestant professor of theology, as there were no Protestants to form an audience. His first course was on "Encyclopädie" (*i.e.* introduction to the literature of theology).

The plan failed. Paulus resigned his professorship and became in 1807 a member of the Bavarian educational council (*Schulrat*). In this capacity he worked at the reorganisation of the Bavarian school system at the time when Hegel was similarly engaged. He gave four years to this task, which he felt to be laid upon him as a duty. Then, in 1811, he went to Heidelberg as professor of theology; and he remained there until his death, in 1851, at the age of ninety. One of his last sayings, a few hours before he died, was, "I am justified before God, through my desire to do right." His last words were, "There is another world."

The forty years of his Heidelberg period were remarkably productive; there was no department of knowledge on which he did not write. He expressed his views about homoeopathy, about the freedom of the Press, about academic freedom, and about the duelling nuisance. In 1831, he wrote upon the Jewish Question; and there the veteran rationalist showed himself a bitter anti-Semite, and brought upon himself the scorn of Heine. On politics and constitutional questions he fought for his opinions so openly and manfully that he had to be warned to be more discreet. In philosophy he took an especially keen interest. When in Jena he had, in conjunction with Schiller, busied himself in the study [pg 050] of Kant. He did a particularly meritorious service in preparing an edition of Spinoza's writings, with a biography of that thinker, in 1803, at the time when neo-Spinozism was making its influence felt in German philosophy. He constituted himself the special guardian of philosophy, and the moment he detected the slightest hint of mysticism, he sounded the alarm. His pet aversion was Schelling, who was born fourteen years later than he, in the very same house at Leonberg, and whom he had met as colleague at Jena and at Würzburg. The works, avowed and anonymous, which he directed against this "charlatan, juggler, swindler, and obscurantist," as he designated him, fill an entire library.

In 1841, Schelling was called to the chair of philosophy in Berlin, and in the winter of 1841-1842 he gave his lectures on "The Philosophy of Revelation" which caused the Berlin reactionaries to hail him as their great ally. The veteran rationalist—he was eighty years old—was transported with rage. He had had the lectures taken down for him, and he published them with critical remarks under the title "The Philosophy of Revelation at length Revealed, and set forth for General Examination, by Dr. H. E. G. Paulus" (Darmstadt, 1842). Schelling was furious, and dragged "the impudent scoundrel" into a court of law on the charge of illicit publication. In Prussia the book was suppressed. But the courts decided in favour of Paulus, who coolly explained that "the philosophy of Schelling appeared to him an insidious attack upon sound reason, the unmasking of which by every possible means was a work of public utility, nay, even a duty." He also secured the result at which he aimed; Schelling resigned his lectureship.

In his last days the veteran rationalist was an isolated survival from an earlier age into a period which no longer understood him. The new men reproached him for standing in the old ways; he accused them of a want of honesty. It was just in his immobility and his one-sidedness that his significance lay. By his consistent carrying through of the rationalistic explanation he performed a service to theology more valuable than those who think themselves so vastly his superiors are willing to acknowledge.

His Life of Jesus is awkwardly arranged. The first part gives a historical exposition of the Gospels, section by section. The second part is a synopsis interspersed with supplementary matter. There is no attempt to grasp the life of Jesus as a connected whole. In that respect he is far inferior to Venturini. Strictly regarded, his work is only a harmony of the gospels with explanatory comments, the ground plan of which is taken from the Fourth Gospel.[22]

[pg 051]

The main interest centres in the explanations of the miracles, though the author, it must be admitted, endeavoured to guard against this. "It is my chief desire," he writes in his preface, "that my views regarding the miracle stories should not be taken as by any means the principal thing. How empty would devotion or religion be if one's spiritual well-being depended on whether one believed in miracles or no!" "The truly miraculous thing about Jesus is Himself, the purity and serene holiness of His character, which is, notwithstanding, genuinely human, and adapted to the imitation and emulation of mankind."

The question of miracle is therefore a subsidiary question. Two points of primary importance are certain from the outset: (1) that unexplained alterations of the course of nature can neither overthrow nor attest a spiritual truth, (2) that everything which happens in nature emanates from the omnipotence of God.

The Evangelists intended to relate miracles; of that there can be no doubt. Nor can any one deny that in their time miracles entered into the plan of God, in the sense that the minds of men were to be astounded and subdued by inexplicable facts. This effect, however, is past. In periods to which the miraculous makes less appeal, in view of the advance in intellectual culture of the nations which have been led to accept Christianity, the understanding must be satisfied if the success of the cause is to be maintained.

Since that which is produced by the laws of nature is really produced by God, the Biblical miracles consist merely in the fact that eyewitnesses report events of which they did not know the secondary causes. Their knowledge of the laws of nature was insufficient to enable them to understand what actually happened. For one who has discovered the secondary causes, the fact remains, as such, but not the miracle.

The question of miracle, therefore, does not really exist, or exists only for those "who are under the influence of the sceptical delusion that it is possible really to think any kind of natural powers as existing apart from God, or to think the Being of God apart from the primal potentialities which unfold themselves in the never-ceasing process of Becoming." The difficulty arises from the "original sin" of dissolving the inner unity of God and nature, of denying the equivalence implied by Spinoza in his "Deus sive Natura."

For the normal intelligence the only problem is to discover the secondary causes of the "miracles" of Jesus. It is true there is one miracle which Paulus retains—the miracle of the birth, or at least the possibility of it; in the sense that it is through holy [pg 052] inspiration that Mary receives the hope and the power of conceiving her exalted Son, in whom the spirit of the Messiah takes up its dwelling. Here he indirectly denies the natural generation, and regards the conception as an act of the self-consciousness of the mother.

With the miracles of healing, however, the case is very simple. Sometimes Jesus worked through His spiritual power upon the nervous system of the sufferer; sometimes He used medicines known to Him alone. The latter applies, for instance, to the cures of the blind. The disciples, too, as appears from Mark vi. 7 and 13, were not sent out without medicaments, for the oil with which they were to anoint the sick was, of course, of a medicinal character; and the casting out of evil spirits was effected partly by means of sedatives.

Diet and after-treatment played a great part, though the Evangelists say little about this because directions on these points would not be given publicly. Thus, the saying, "This kind goeth not out save by prayer and fasting," is interpreted as an instruction to the father as to the way in which he could make the sudden cure of the epileptic into a permanent one, viz. by keeping him to a strict diet and strengthening his character by devotional exercises.

The nature miracles suggest their own explanation. The walking on the water was an illusion of the disciples. Jesus walked along the shore, and in the mist was taken for a ghost by the alarmed and excited occupants of the boat. When Jesus called to them, Peter threw himself into the water, and was drawn to shore by Jesus just as he was sinking. Immediately after taking Jesus into the boat they doubled a headland and drew clear of the storm centre; they therefore supposed that He had calmed the sea by His command. It was the same in the case where He was asleep during the storm. When they waked Him He spoke to them about the wind and the weather. At that moment they gained the shelter of a hill which protected them from the wind that swept down the valley; and they marvelled among themselves that even the winds and the sea obeyed their Messiah.

The feeding of the five thousand is explained in the following way. When Jesus saw the multitude all hungered, He said to His disciples, "We will set the rich people among them a good example, that they may share their supplies with the others," and he began to distribute His own provisions, and those of the disciples, to the people who were sitting near them. The example had its effect, and soon there was plenty for every one.

The explanation of the transfiguration is somewhat more complicated. While Jesus was lingering with a few followers in this mountainous district He had an interview upon a high mountain at night with two dignified-looking men whom His three companions took for Moses and Elias. These unknown persons, [pg 053] as we learn from Luke ix. 31, informed Him of the fate which awaited Him at Jerusalem. In the early morning, as the sun was rising, the three disciples, only half awake, looked upwards from the hollow in which they had been sleeping and saw Jesus with the two strangers upon the higher part of the mountain, illuminated by the beams of the rising sun, and heard them speak, now of the fate which threatened Him in the capital, now of the duty of steadfastness and the hopes attached thereto, and finally heard an exhortation addressed to themselves, bidding them ever to hold Jesus to be the beloved Son of the Deity, whom they must obey.... Their drowsiness, and the clouds which in an autumnal sunrise float to and fro over those mountains,[23] left them no clear recollection of what had happened. This only added to the wonder of the vague undefined impression of having been in contact with apparitions from a higher sphere. The three who had been with Him on the mount never arrived at any more definite knowledge of the facts, because Jesus forbade them to speak of what they had seen until the end should come.

In dealing with the raisings from the dead the author is in his element. Here he is ready with the unfailing explanation taken over from Bahrdt that they were only cases of coma. These narratives should not be headed "raisings from the dead," but "deliverances from premature burial." In Judaea, interment took place three hours after death. How many seemingly dead people may have returned to consciousness in their graves, and then have perished miserably! Thus Jesus, owing to a presentiment suggested to Him by the father's story, saves the daughter of Jairus from being buried while in a cataleptic trance. A similar presentiment led Him to remove the covering of the bier which He met at the gate of Nain, and to discover traces of life in the widow's son. A similar instinct moved Him to ask to be taken to the grave of Lazarus. When the stone is rolled away He sees His friend standing upright and calls to him joyfully, "Come forth!"

The Jewish love of miracle "caused everything to be ascribed immediately to the Deity, and secondary causes to be overlooked; consequently no thought was unfortunately given to the question of how to prevent these horrible cases of premature burial from taking place!" But why does it not appear strange to Paulus that Jesus did not enlighten His countrymen as to the criminal character of over-hasty burial, instead of allowing even his closest followers to believe in miracle? Here the hypothesis condemns itself, although it has a foundation of fact, in so far as cases of premature burial are abnormally frequent in the East.

[pg 054]

The resurrection of Jesus must be brought under the same category if we are to hold fast to the facts that the disciples saw Him in His natural body with the print of the nails in His hands, and that He took food in their presence. Death from crucifixion was in fact due to a condition of rigor, which extended gradually inwards. It was the slowest of all deaths. Josephus mentions in his *Contra Apionem* that it was granted to him as a favour by Titus, at Tekoa, that he might have three crucified men whom he knew taken down from the cross. Two of them died, but one recovered. Jesus, however, "died" surprisingly quickly. The loud cry which he uttered immediately before His head sank shows that His strength was far from being exhausted, and that what supervened was only a death-like trance. In such trances the process of dying continues until corruption sets in. "This alone proves that the process is complete and that death has actually taken place."

In the case of Jesus, as in that of others, the vital spark would have been gradually extinguished, had not Providence mysteriously effected on behalf of its favourite that which in the case of others was sometimes effected in more obvious ways by human skill and care. The lance-thrust, which we are to think of rather as a mere surface wound, served the purpose of a phlebotomy. The cool grave and the aromatic unguents continued the process of resuscitation, until finally the storm and the earthquake aroused Jesus to full consciousness. Fortunately the earthquake also had the effect of rolling away the stone from the mouth of the grave. The Lord stripped off the grave-clothes and put on a gardener's dress which He managed to procure. That was what made Mary, as we are told in John xx. 15, take Him for the gardener. Through the women, He sends a message to His disciples bidding them meet Him in Galilee, and Himself sets out to go thither. At Emmaus, as the dusk was falling, He met two of His followers, who at first failed to recognise Him because His countenance was so disfigured by His sufferings. But His manner of giving thanks at the breaking of bread, and the nail-prints in His uplifted hands, revealed to them who He was. From them He learns where His disciples are, returns to Jerusalem, and appears unexpectedly among them. This is the explanation of the apparent contradiction between the message pointing to Galilee and the appearances in Jerusalem. Thomas was not present at this first appearance, and at a later interview was suffered to put his hand into the marks of the wounds. It is a misunderstanding to see a reproach in the words which Jesus addresses to him. What, then, is the meaning of "Blessed are they that have not seen and have believed"? It is a benediction upon Thomas for what he has done in the interests of later generations. "Now," Jesus says, "thou, Thomas, art convinced because thou hast so unmistakably seen Me. It is [pg 055] well for those who now or in the future shall not see Me; for after this they can feel a firm conviction, because thou hast convinced thyself so completely that to thee, whose hands have touched Me, no possible doubt can remain of My corporeal reanimation." Had it not been for Thomas's peculiar mental constitution we should not have known whether what was seen was a phantom or a real appearance of the reanimated Jesus.

In this way Jesus lived with them for forty days, spending part of that time with them in Galilee. In consequence of the ill-treatment which He had undergone, He was not capable of continuous exertion. He lived quietly and gathered strength for the brief moments in which He appeared among His own followers and taught them. When He felt his end drawing near He returned to Jerusalem. On the Mount of Olives, in the early sunlight, He assembled His followers for the last time. He lifted up His hands to bless them, and with hands still raised in benediction He moved away from them. A cloud interposes itself between them and Him, so that their eyes cannot follow Him. As he disappeared there stood before them, clothed in white, the two dignified figures whom the three disciples who were present at the transfiguration had taken for Moses and Elias, but who were really among the secret adherents of Jesus in Jerusalem. These men exhorted them not to stand waiting there but to be up and doing.

Where Jesus really died they never knew, and so they came to describe His departure as an ascension.

This Life of Jesus is not written without feeling. At times, in moments of exaltation, the writer even dashes into verse. If only the lack of all natural aesthetic feeling did not ruin everything! Paulus constantly falls into a style that sets the teeth on edge. The episode of the death of the Baptist is headed "Court-and-Priest intrigues enhance themselves to a judicial murder." Much is spoiled by a kind of banality. Instead of "disciples," he always says "pupils," instead of "faith," "sincerity of conviction." The appeal which the father of the lunatic boy addresses to Jesus, "Lord, I believe, help thou my unbelief," runs "I am sincerely convinced; help me, even if there is anything lacking in the sincerity of my conviction."

The beautiful saying in the story of Martha and Mary, "One thing is needful," is interpreted as meaning that a single course will be sufficient for the meal.[24] The scene in the home at Bethany rejoices in the heading, "Geniality of Jesus among sympathetic friends in a hospitable family circle at Bethany. A Messiah with no stiff solemnity about Him." The following is the explanation [pg 056] which Paulus discovers for the saying about the tribute-money: "So long as you need the Romans to maintain some sort of order among you," says Jesus, "you must provide the means thereto. If you were fit to be independent you would not need to serve any one but God."

Among the historical problems, Paulus is especially interested in the idea of the Messiahship, and in the motives of the betrayal. His sixty-five pages on the history of the conception of the Messiah are a real contribution to the subject. The Messianic idea, he explains, goes back to the Davidic kingdom; the prophets raised it to a higher religious plane; in the times of the Maccabees the ideal of the kingly Messiah perished and its place was taken by that of the super-earthly deliverer. The only mistake which Paulus makes is in supposing that the post-Maccabean period went back to the political ideal of the Davidic king. On the other hand, he rightly interprets the death of Jesus as the deed by which He thought to win the Messiahship proper to the Son of Man.

With reference to the question of the High Priest at the trial, he remarks that it does not refer to the metaphysical Divine Sonship, but to the Messiahship in the ancient Jewish sense, and accordingly Jesus answers by pointing to the coming of the Son of Man.

The importance of eschatology in the preaching of Jesus is clearly recognised, but Paulus proceeds to nullify this recognition by making the risen Lord cut short all the questions of the disciples in regard to this subject with the admonition "that in whatever way all this should come about, and whether soon or late, their business was to see that they had done their own part."

How did Judas come to play the traitor? He believed in the Messiahship of Jesus and wanted to force Him to declare Himself. To bring about His arrest seemed to Judas the best means of rousing the people to take His side openly. But the course of events was too rapid for him. Owing to the Feast the news of the arrest spread but slowly. In the night "when people were sleeping off the effects of the Passover supper," Jesus was condemned; in the morning, before they were well awake, He was hurried away to be crucified. Then Judas was overcome with despair, and went and hanged himself. "Judas stands before us in the history of the Passion as a warning example of those who allow their cleverness to degenerate into cunning, and persuade themselves that it is permissible to do evil that good may come—to seek good objects, which they really value, by intrigue and chicanery. And the underlying cause of their errors is that they have failed to overcome their passionate desire for self-advancement."

Such was the consistently rationalistic Life of Jesus, which evoked so much opposition at the time of its appearance, and [pg 057] seven years later received its death-blow at the hands of Strauss. The method is doomed to failure because the author only saves his own sincerity at the expense of that of his characters. He makes the disciples of Jesus see miracles where they could not possibly have seen them; and makes Jesus Himself allow miracles to be imagined where He must necessarily have protested against such a delusion. His exegesis, too, is sometimes violent. But in this, who has the right to judge him? If the theologians dragged him before the Lord, He would command, as of old, "Let him that is without sin among you cast the first stone at him," and Paulus would go forth unharmed.

Moreover, a number of his explanations are right in principle. The feeding of the multitudes and the walking on the sea must be explained somehow or other as misunderstandings of something that actually happened. And how many of Paulus' ideas are still going about in all sorts of disguises, and crop up again and again in commentaries and Lives of Jesus, especially in those of the "anti-rationalists"! Nowadays it belongs to the complete duty of the well-trained theologian to renounce the rationalists and all their works; and yet how poor our time is in comparison with theirs—how poor in strong men capable of loyalty to an ideal, how poor, so far as theology is concerned, in simple commonplace sincerity!

VI. The Last Phase Of Rationalism—Hase And Schleiermacher

Karl August Hase. Das Leben Jesu zunächst für akademische Studien. (The Life of Jesus, primarily for the use of students.) 1829. 205 pp. This work contains a bibliography of the earliest literature of the subject. 5th ed., 1865.

Friedrich Ernst Daniel Schleiermacher. Das Leben Jesu. 1864. Edited by Rütenik. The edition is based upon a student's note-book of a course of lectures delivered in 1832.

David Friedrich Strauss. Der Christus des Glaubens und der Jesus der Geschichte. Eine Kritik des Schleiermacher'schen Lebens Jesu. (The Christ of Faith and the Jesus of History. A criticism of Schleiermacher's Life of Jesus.) 1865.

In their treatment of the life of Jesus, Hase and Schleiermacher are in one respect still wholly dominated by rationalism. They still cling to the rationalistic explanation of miracle; although they have no longer the same ingenuous confidence in it as their predecessors, and although at the decisive cases they are content to leave a question-mark instead of offering a solution. They might, in fact, be described as the sceptics of rationalism. In another respect, however, they aim at something beyond the range of rationalism, inasmuch as they endeavour to grasp the inner connexion of the events of Jesus' ministry, which in Paulus had entirely fallen out of sight. Their Lives of Jesus are transitional, in the good sense of the word as well as in the bad. In respect of progress, Hase shows himself the greater of the two.

Scarcely thirteen years have elapsed since the death of the great Jena professor, his Excellency von Hase, and already we think of him as a man of the past. Theology has voted to inscribe his name upon its records in letters of gold—and has passed on to the order of the day. He was no pioneer like Baur, and he does not meet the present age on the footing of a contemporary, offering it problems raised by him and still unsolved. Even his "Church History," with its twelve editions, has already had its day, although it is still the most brilliantly written work in this department, and conceals beneath its elegance of form a massive erudition. He [pg 059] was more than a theologian; he was one of the finest monuments of German culture, the living embodiment of a period which for us lies under the sunset glow of the past, in the land of "once upon a time."

His path in life was unembarrassed; he knew toil, but not disappointment. Born in 1800, he finished his studies at Tübingen, where he qualified as a Privat-Docent in 1823. In 1824-1825 he spent eleven months in the fortress of Hohenasperg, where he was confined for taking the part of the Burschenschaften,[25] and had leisure for meditation and literary plans. In 1830 he went to Jena, where, with a yearly visit to Italy to lay in a store of sunshine and renewed strength, he worked until 1890.

Not without a certain reverence does one take this little text-book of 205 pages into one's hands. This is the first attempt by a fully equipped scholar to reconstruct the life of Jesus on a purely historical basis. There is more creative power in it than in almost any of his later works. It manifests already the brilliant qualities of style for which he was distinguished—clearness, terseness, elegance. What a contrast with that of Bahrdt, Venturini, or Paulus!

And yet the keynote of the work is rationalistic, since Hase has recourse to the rationalistic explanation of miracles wherever that appears possible. He seeks to make the circumstances of the baptism intelligible by supposing the appearance of a meteor. In the story of the transfiguration, the fact which is to be retained is that Jesus, in the company of two unknown persons, appeared to the disciples in unaccustomed splendour. Their identification of His companions as Moses and Elias is a conclusion which is not confirmed by Jesus, and owing to the position of the eyewitnesses, is not sufficiently guaranteed by their testimony. The abrupt breaking off of the interview by the Master, and the injunction of silence, point to some secret circumstance in His history. By this hint Hase seems to leave room for the "secret society" of Bahrdt and Venturini.

He makes no difficulty about the explanation of the story of the *stater*. It is only intended to show "how the Messiah avoided offence in submitting Himself to the financial burdens of the community." In regard to the stilling of the storm, it seems uncertain whether Jesus through His knowledge of nature was enabled to predict the end of the storm or whether He brought it about by the possession of power over nature. The "sceptic of rationalism" thus leaves open the possibility of miracle. He proceeds somewhat similarly in explaining the raisings from the dead. They can be made intelligible by supposing that they were cases of coma, but it is also possible to look upon them as [pg 060] supernatural. For the two great Johannine miracles, the change of the water into wine and the increase of the loaves, no naturalistic explanation can be admitted. But how unsuccessful is his attempt to make the increase of the bread intelligible! "Why should not the bread have been increased?" he asks. "If nature every year in the period between seed-time and harvest performs a similar miracle, nature might also, by unknown laws, bring it about in a moment." Here crops up the dangerous anti-rationalistic intellectual supernaturalism which sometimes brings Hase and Schleiermacher very close to the frontiers of the territory occupied by the disingenuous reactionaries.

The crucial point is the explanation of the resurrection of Jesus. A stringent proof that death had actually taken place cannot, according to Hase, be given, since there is no evidence that corruption had set in, and that is the only infallible sign of death. It is possible, therefore, that the resurrection was only a return to consciousness after a trance. But the direct impression made by the sources points rather to a supernatural event. Either view is compatible with the Christian faith. "Both the historically possible views—either that the Creator gave new life to a body which was really dead, or that the latent life reawakened in a body which was only seemingly dead—recognise in the resurrection a manifest proof of the care of Providence for the cause of Jesus, and are therefore both to be recognised as Christian, whereas a third view—that Jesus gave Himself up to his enemies in order to defeat them by the bold stroke of a seeming death and a skilfully prepared resurrection—is as contrary to historical criticism as to Christian faith."

Hase, however, quietly lightens the difficulty of the miracle question in a way which must not be overlooked. For the rationalists all miracles stood on the same footing, and all must equally be abolished by a naturalistic explanation. If we study Hase carefully, we find that he accepts only the Johannine miracles as authentic, whereas those of the Synoptists may be regarded as resting upon a misunderstanding on the part of the authors, because they are not reported at first hand, but from tradition. Thus the discrimination of the two lines of Gospel tradition comes to the aid of the anti-rationalists, and enables them to get rid of some of the greatest difficulties. Half playfully, it might almost be said, they sketch out the ideas of Strauss, without ever suspecting what desperate earnest the game will become, if the authenticity of the Fourth Gospel has to be given up.

Hase surrenders the birth-story and the "legends of the Childhood"—the expression is his own—almost without striking a blow. The same fate befalls all the incidents in which angels figure, and the miracles at the time of the death of Jesus. He [pg 061] describes these as "mythical touches." The ascension is merely "a mythical version of His departure to the Father."

Hase's conception even of the non-miraculous portion of the history of Jesus is not free from rationalistic traits. He indulges in the following speculations with regard to the celibacy of the Lord. "If the true grounds of the celibacy of Jesus do not lie hidden in the special circumstances of His youth, the conjecture may be permitted that He from whose religion was to go forth the ideal view of marriage, so foreign to the ideas of antiquity, found in His own time no heart worthy to enter into this covenant with Him." It is on rationalistic lines also that Hase explains the betrayal by Judas. "A purely intellectual, worldly, and unscrupulous character, he desired to compel the hesitating Messiah to found His Kingdom upon popular violence.... It is possible that Judas in his terrible blindness took that last word addressed to him by Jesus, 'What thou doest, do quickly,' as giving consent to his plan."

But Hase again rises superior to this rationalistic conception of the history when he refuses to explain away the Jewish elements in the plan and preaching of Jesus as due to mere accommodation, and maintains the view that the Lord really, to a certain extent, shared this Jewish system of ideas. According to Hase there are two periods in the Messianic activity of Jesus. In the first He accepted almost without reservation the popular ideas regarding the Messianic age. In consequence, however, of His experience of the practical results of these ideas, He was led to abandon this error, and in the second period He developed His own distinctive views. Here we meet for the first time the idea of two different periods in the life of Jesus, which, especially through the influence of Holtzmann and Keim, became the prevailing view, and down to Johannes Weiss, determined the plan of all Lives of Jesus. Hase created the modern historico-psychological picture of Jesus. The introduction of this more penetrating psychology would alone suffice to place him in advance of the rationalists.

Another interesting point is the thorough way in which he traces out the historical and literary consequences of this idea of development. The apostles, he thinks, did not understand this progress of thought on the part of Jesus, and did not distinguish between the sayings of the first and second periods. They remained wedded to the eschatological view. After the death of Jesus this view prevailed so strongly in the primitive community of disciples that they interpolated their expectations into the last discourses of Jesus. According to Hase, the apocalyptic discourse in Matt. xxiv. was originally only a prediction of the judgment upon and destruction of Jerusalem, but this was obscured later by the influx of the eschatological views of the apostolic community. Only John remained free from this error. Therefore the non-eschatological [pg 062] Fourth Gospel preserves in their pure form the ideas of Jesus in His second period.

Hase rightly observes that the Messiahship of Jesus plays next to no part in His preaching, at any rate at first, and that, before the incident at Caesarea Philippi, it was only in moments of enthusiastic admiration, rather than with settled conviction, that even the disciples looked on Him as the Messiah. This indication of the central importance of the declaration of the Messiahship at Caesarea Philippi is another sign-post pointing out the direction which the future study of the life of Jesus was to follow.

Schleiermacher's Life of Jesus introduces us to quite a different order of transitional ideas. Its value lies in the sphere of dogmatics, not of history. Nowhere, indeed, is it so clear that the great dialectician had not really a historical mind than precisely in his treatment of the history of Jesus.

From the first it was no favourable star which presided over this undertaking. It is true that in 1819 Schleiermacher was the first theologian who had ever lectured upon this subject. But his Life of Jesus did not appear until 1864. Its publication had been so long delayed, partly because it had to be reconstructed from students' note-books, partly because immediately after Schleiermacher, in 1832, had delivered the course for the last time, it was rendered obsolete by the work of Strauss. For the questions raised by the latter's Life of Jesus, published in 1835, Schleiermacher had no answer, and for the wounds which it made, no healing. When, in 1864, Schleiermacher's work was brought forth to view like an embalmed corse, Strauss accorded to the dead work of the great theologian a dignified and striking funeral oration.

Schleiermacher is not in search of the historical Jesus, but of the Jesus Christ of his own system of theology; that is to say, of the historic figure which seems to him appropriate to the self-consciousness of the Redeemer as he represents it. For him the empirical has simply no existence. A natural psychology is scarcely attempted. He comes to the facts with a ready-made dialectic apparatus and sets his puppets in lively action. Schleiermacher's dialectic is not a dialectic which generates reality, like that of Hegel, of which Strauss availed himself, but merely a dialectic of exposition. In this literary dialectic he is the greatest master that ever lived.

The limitations of the historical Jesus both in an upward and downward direction are those only which apply equally to the Jesus of dogma. The uniqueness of His Divine self-consciousness is not to be tampered with. It is equally necessary to avoid Ebionism which does away with the Divine in Him, and Docetism [pg 063] which destroys His humanity. Schleiermacher loves to make his hearers shudder by pointing out to them that the least false step entails precipitation into one or other of these abysses; or at least would entail it for any one who was not under the guidance of his infallible dialectic.

In the course of this dialectic treatment, all the historical questions involved in the life of Jesus come into view one after another, but none of them is posed or solved from the point of view of the historian; they are "moments" in his argument.

He is like a spider at work. The spider lets itself down from aloft, and after making fast some supporting threads to points below, it runs back to the centre and there keeps spinning away. You look on fascinated, and before you know it, you are entangled in the web. It is difficult even for a reader who is strong in the consciousness of possessing a sounder grasp of the history than Schleiermacher to avoid being caught in the toils of that magical dialectic.

And how loftily superior the dialectician is! Paulus had shown that, in view of the use of the title Son of Man, the Messianic self-consciousness of Jesus must be interpreted in accordance with the passage in Daniel. On this Schleiermacher remarks: "I have already said that it is inherently improbable that such a predilection (*sc.* for the Book of Daniel) would have been manifested by Christ, because the Book of Daniel does not belong to the prophetic writings properly so-called, but to the third division of the Old Testament literature."

In his estimate of the importance to be attached to the story of the baptism, too, he falls behind the historical knowledge of his day. "To lay such great stress upon the baptism," he says, "leads either to the Gnostic view that it was only there that the λόγος united itself with Jesus, or to the rationalistic view that it was only at the baptism that He became conscious of His vocation." But what does history care whether a view is gnostic or rationalistic if only it is historical!

This dialectic, so fatal often to sound historical views, might have been expressly created to deal with the question of miracle. Compared with Schleiermacher's discussions all that has been written since upon this subject is mere honest—or dishonest—bungling. Nothing new has been added to what he says, and no one else has succeeded in saying it with the same amazing subtlety. It is true, also, that no one else has shown the same skill in concealing how much in the way of miracle he ultimately retains and how much he rejects. His solution of the problem is, in fact, not historical, but dialectical, an attempt to transcend the necessity for a rationalistic explanation of miracle which does not really succeed in getting rid of it.

[pg 064]

Schleiermacher arranges the miracles in an ascending scale of probability according to the degree in which they can be seen to depend on the known influence of spirit upon organic matter. The most easily explained are the miracles of healing "because we are not without analogies to show that pathological conditions of a purely functional nature can be removed by mental influence." But where, on the other hand, the effect produced by Christ lies outside the sphere of human life, the difficulties involved become insoluble. To get rid, in some measure, of these difficulties he makes use of two expedients. In the first place, he admits that in particular cases the rationalistic method may have a certain limited application; in the second place he, like Hase, recognises a difference between the miracle stories themselves, retaining the Johannine miracles, but surrendering, more or less completely, the Synoptic miracles as not resting on evidence of the same certainty and exactness.

That he is still largely under the sway of rationalism can be seen in the fact that he admits on an equal footing, as conceptions of the resurrection of Jesus, a return to consciousness from a trance-state, or a supernatural restoration to life, thought of as a resurrection. He goes so far as to say that the decision of this question has very little interest for him. He fully accepts the principle of Paulus that apart from corruption there is no certain indication of death.

"All that we can say on this point," he concludes, "is that even to those whose business it was to ensure the immediate death of the crucified, in order that the bodies might at once be taken down, Christ appeared to be really dead, and this, moreover, although it was contrary to their expectations, for it was a subject of astonishment. It is no use going any further into the matter, since nothing can be ascertained in regard to it."

What is certain is that Jesus in His real body lived on for a time among His followers; that the Fourth Gospel requires us to believe. The reports of the resurrection are not based upon "apparitions." Schleiermacher's own opinion is what really happened was reanimation after apparent death. "If Christ had only eaten to show that He could eat, while He really had no need of nourishment, it would have been a pretence—something docetic. This gives us a clue to all the rest, teaching us to hold firmly to the way in which Christ intends Himself to be represented, and to put down all that is miraculous in the accounts of the appearances to the prepossessions of the disciples."

When He revealed himself to Mary Magdalene He had no certainty that He would frequently see her again. "He was conscious that His present condition was that of genuine human life, but He had no confidence in its continuance." He bade His [pg 065] disciples meet Him in Galilee because He could there enjoy greater privacy and freedom from observation in His intercourse with them. The difference between the present and the past was only that He no longer showed Himself to the world. "It was possible that a movement in favour of an earthly Messianic Kingdom might break out, and we need only take this possibility into account in order to explain completely why Jesus remained in such close retirement." "It was the premonition of the approaching end of this second life which led Him to return from Galilee to Jerusalem."

Of the ascension he says: "Here, therefore, something happened, but what was seen was incomplete, and has been conjecturally supplemented." The underlying rationalistic explanation shows through!

But if the condition in which Jesus lived on after His crucifixion was "a condition of reanimation," by what right does Schleiermacher constantly speak of it as a "resurrection," as if resurrection and reanimation were synonymous terms? Further, is it really true that faith has no interest whatever in the question whether it was as risen from the dead, or merely as recovered from a state of suspended animation, that Jesus showed Himself to His disciples? In regard to this, it might seem, the rationalists were more straightforward.

The moment one tries to take hold of this dialectic it breaks in one's fingers. Schleiermacher would not indeed have ventured to play so risky a game if he had not had a second position to retire to, based on the distinction between the Synoptic and the Johannine miracle stories. In this respect he simplified matters for himself, as compared with the rationalists, even more than Hase. The miracle at the baptism is only intelligible in the narrative of the Fourth Gospel, where it is not a question of an external occurrence, but of a purely subjective experience of John, with which we have nothing to do. The Synoptic story of the temptation has no intelligible meaning.

"To change stones into bread, if there were need for it, would not have been a sin." "A leap from the Temple could have had no attraction for any one."

The miracles of the birth and childhood are given up without hesitation; they do not belong to the story of the life of Jesus; and it is the same with the miracles at His death. One might fancy it was Strauss speaking when Schleiermacher says: "If we give due consideration to the fact that we have certainly found in these for the most part simple narratives of the last moments of Christ two incidents, such as the rending of the veil of the Temple and the opening of the graves, in reference to which we cannot possibly suppose that they are literal descriptions of actual facts, then we are bound to ask the question whether the same does not apply to many other points. Certainly the mention of [pg 066] the sun's light failing and the consequent great darkness looks very much as if it had been imported by poetic imagination into the simple narrative."

A rebuke could have no possible effect upon the wind and sea. Here we must suppose either an alteration of the facts or a different causal connexion.

In this way Schleiermacher—and it was for this reason that these lectures on the life of Jesus became so celebrated—enabled dogmatics, though not indeed history, to take a flying leap over the miracle question.

What is chiefly fatal to a sound historical view is his one-sided preference for the Fourth Gospel. It is, according to him, only in this Gospel that the consciousness of Jesus is truly reflected. In this connexion he expressly remarks that of a progress in the teaching of Jesus, and of any "development" in Him, there can be no question. His development is the unimpeded organic unfolding of the idea of the Divine Sonship.

For the outline of the life of Jesus, also, the Fourth Gospel is alone authoritative. "The Johannine representation of the way in which the crisis of His fate was brought about is the only clear one." The same applies to the narrative of the resurrection in this Gospel. "Accordingly, on this point also," so he concludes his discussion, "I take it as established that the Gospel of John is the narrative of an eyewitness and forms an organic whole. The first three Gospels are compilations formed out of various narratives which had arisen independently; their discourses are composite structures, and their presentation of the history is such that one can form no idea of the grouping of events." The "crowded days," such as that of the sermon on the mount and the day of the parables, exist only in the imagination of the Evangelists. In reality there were no such days. Luke is the only one of them who has some semblance of historical order. His Gospel is compiled with much insight and critical tact out of a number of independent documents, as Schleiermacher believed himself to have shown convincingly in his critical study of Luke's Gospel, published in 1817.

It is only on the ground of such a valuation of the sources that we can arrive at a just estimate of the different representations of the locality of the life of Jesus. "The contradictions," Schleiermacher proceeds, "could not be explained if all our Gospels stood equally close to Jesus. But if John stands closer than the others, we may perhaps find the key in the fact that John, too, mentions it as a prevailing opinion in Jerusalem that Jesus was a Galilaean, and that Luke, when he has got to the end of the sections which show skilful arrangement and are united by similarity of subject, gathers all the rest into the framework of a journey to Jerusalem. Following this analogy, and not remembering that Jesus had occasion to go [pg 067] several times a year to Jerusalem, the other two gathered into one mass all that happened there on various occasions. This could only have been done by Hellenists."[26]

Schleiermacher is quite insensible to the graphic realism of the description of the last days at Jerusalem in Mark and Matthew, and has no suspicion that if only a single one of the Jerusalem sayings in the Synoptists is true Jesus had never before spoken in Jerusalem.

The ground of Schleiermacher's antipathy to the Synoptists lies deeper than a mere critical view as to their composition. The fact is that their "picture of Christ" does not agree with that which he wishes to insert into the history. When it serves his purpose, he does not shrink from the most arbitrary violence. He abolishes the scene in Gethsemane because he infers from the silence of John that it cannot have taken place. "The other Evangelists," he explains, "give us an account of a sudden depression and deep distress of spirit which fell upon Jesus, and which He admitted to His disciples, and they tell us how He sought relief from it in prayer, and afterwards recovered His serenity and resolution. John passes over this in silence, and his narrative of what immediately precedes is not consistent with it." It is evidently a symbolical story, as the thrice-repeated petition shows. "If they speak of such a depression of spirit, they have given the story that form in order that the example of Christ might be the more applicable to others in similar circumstances."

On these premises it is possible to write a Life of Christ; it is not possible to write a Life of Jesus. It is, therefore, not by accident that Schleiermacher regularly speaks, not of Jesus, but of Christ. [pg 068]

VII. David Friedrich Strauss—The Man And His Fate

In order to understand Strauss one must love him. He was not the greatest, and not the deepest, of theologians, but he was the most absolutely sincere. His insight and his errors were alike the insight and the errors of a prophet. And he had a prophet's fate. Disappointment and suffering gave his life its consecration. It unrolls itself before us like a tragedy, in which, in the end, the gloom is lightened by the mild radiance which shines forth from the nobility of the sufferer.

Strauss was born in 1808 at Ludwigsburg. His father was a merchant, whose business, however, was unsuccessful, so that his means steadily declined. The boy took his ability from his mother, a good, self-controlled, sensible, pious woman, to whom he raised a monument in his "Memorial of a Good Mother" written in 1858, to be given to his daughter on her confirmation-day.

From 1821 to 1825 he was a pupil at the "lower seminary" at Blaubeuren, along with Friedrich Vischer, Pfizer, Zimmermann, Märklin, and Binder. Among their teachers was Ferdinand Christian Baur, whom they were to meet with again at the university.

His first year at the university was uninteresting, as it was only in the following year that the reorganisation of the theological faculty took place, in consequence of the appointment of Baur. The instruction in the philosophical faculty was almost equally unsatisfactory, so that the friends would have gained little from the two years of philosophical propaedeutic which formed part of the course prescribed for theological students, if they had not combined to prosecute their philosophical studies for themselves. The writings of Hegel began to exercise a powerful influence upon them. For the philosophical faculty, Hegel's philosophy was as yet non-existent.

These student friends were much addicted to poetry. Two [pg 069] journeys which Strauss made along with his fellow-student Binder to Weinsberg to see Justinus Kerner made a deep impression upon him. He had to make a deliberate effort to escape from the dream-world of the "Prophetess of Prevorst." Some years later, in a Latin note to Binder, he speaks of Weinsberg as "Mecca nostra."[27]

According to Vischer's picture of him, the tall stripling made an impression of great charm, though he was rather shy except with intimates. He attended lectures with pedantic regularity.

Baur was at that time still immersed in the prolegomena to his system; but Strauss already suspected the direction which the thoughts of his young teacher were to take.

When Strauss and his student friends entered on their duties as clergymen, the others found great difficulty in bringing their theological views into line with the popular beliefs which they were expected to preach. Strauss alone remained free from inner struggles. In a letter to Binder[28] of the year 1831, he explains that in his sermons—he was then assistant at Klein-Ingersheim near Ludwigsburg—he did not use "representative notions" (Vorstellungen, used as a philosophical technicality) such as that of the Devil, which the people were already prepared to dispense with; but others which still appeared to be indispensable, such as those of an eschatological character, he merely endeavoured to present in such a way that the "intellectual concept" (Begriff) which lay behind, might so far as possible shine through. "When I consider," he continues, "how far even in intellectual preaching the expression is inadequate to the true essence of the concept, it does not seem to me to matter much if one goes even a step further. I at least go about the matter without the least scruple, and cannot ascribe this to a mere want of sincerity in myself."

That is Hegelian logic.

After being for a short time Deputy-professor at Maulbronn, he took his doctor's degree with a dissertation on the ἀποκατάστασις πάντων (restoration of all things, Acts iii. 21). This work is lost. From his letters it appears that he treated the subject chiefly from the religious-historical point of view.[29]

When Binder took his doctorate with a philosophical thesis on the immortality of the soul, Strauss, in 1832, wrote to him expressing the opinion that the belief in personal immortality could not properly be regarded as a consequence of the Hegelian system, since according [pg 070] to Hegel, it was not the subjective spirit of the individual person, but only the objective Spirit, the self-realising Idea which constantly embodies itself in new creations, to which immortality belongs.[30]

In October 1831 he went to Berlin to hear Hegel and Schleiermacher. On the 14th of November Hegel, whom he had visited shortly before, was carried off by cholera. Strauss heard the news in Schleiermacher's house, from Schleiermacher himself, and is said to have exclaimed, with a certain want of tact, considering who his informant was: "And it was to hear him that I came to Berlin!"

There was no satisfactory basis for a relationship between Schleiermacher and Strauss. They had nothing in common. That did not prevent Strauss's Life of Jesus being sometimes described by opponents of Schleiermacher as a product of the latter's philosophy of religion. Indeed, as late as the 'sixties, Tholuck thought it necessary to defend the memory of the great theologian against this reproach.

As a matter of fact, the plan of the Life of Jesus arose during Strauss's intercourse with Vatke, to whom he felt himself strongly drawn. Moreover, what was first sketched out was not primarily the plan of a Life of Jesus, but that of a history of the ideas of primitive Christianity, intended to serve as a standard by which to judge ecclesiastical dogma. The Life of Jesus was originally designed, it might almost be said, as a mere prologue to this work, the plan of which was subsequently carried out under the title, "Christian Theology in its Historical Development and in its Antagonism with Modern Scientific Knowledge" (published in 1840-1841).

When in the spring of 1832 he returned to Tübingen to take up the position of "Repetent"[31] in the theological college (*Stift*), these plans were laid on the shelf in consequence of his pre-occupation with philosophy, and if things had gone according to Strauss's wishes, they would perhaps never have come to fulfilment. The "Repetents" had the right to lecture upon philosophy. Strauss felt himself called upon to come forward as an apostle of Hegel, and lectured upon Hegel's logic with tremendous success. Zeller, who attended these lectures, records the unforgettable impression which they made on him. Besides championing Hegel, Strauss also lectured upon Plato, and upon the history of modern philosophy. These were three happy semesters.

"In my theology," he writes in a letter of 1833,[32] "philosophy occupies such a predominant position that my theological views can only be worked out to completeness by means of a more thorough study of philosophy, and this course of study I am now [pg 071] going to prosecute uninterruptedly and without concerning myself whether it leads me back to theology or not." Further on he says: "If I know myself rightly, my position in regard to theology is that what interests me in theology causes offence, and what does not cause offence is indifferent to me. For this reason I have refrained from delivering lectures on theology."

The philosophical faculty was not altogether pleased at the success of the apostle of Hegel, and wished to have the right of the "Repetents" to lecture on philosophy curtailed. The latter, however, took their stand upon the tradition. Strauss was desired to intermit his lectures until the matter should be settled. He would have liked best to end the situation by entering the philosophical faculty. The other "Repetents," however, begged him not to do so, but to continue to champion their rights. It is possible also that obstacles were placed in the way of his plan by the philosophical faculty. However that may be, it was in any case not carried through. Strauss was forced back upon theology.

According to Hase,[33] Strauss began his studies for the Life of Jesus by writing a detailed critical review of his (Hase's) text-book. He sent this to Berlin to the *Jahrbücher für wissenschaftliche Kritik*, which, however, refused it. His resolve to publish first, instead of the general work on the genesis of Christian doctrine, a critical study on the life of Jesus was doubtless determined by Schleiermacher's lectures on this subject. When in Berlin he had procured a copy of a lecture note-book, and the reading of it incited him to opposition.

Considering its character, the work was rapidly produced. He wrote it sitting at the window of the Repetents' room, which looks out upon the gateway-arch. When its two volumes appeared in 1835 the name of the author was wholly unknown, except for some critical studies upon the Gospels. This book, into which he had poured his youthful enthusiasm, rendered him famous in a moment—and utterly destroyed his prospects. Among his opponents the most prominent was Steudel, a member of the theological faculty, who, as president of the *Stift*, made representations against him to the Ministry, and succeeded in securing his removal from the post of "Repetent." The hopes which Strauss had placed upon his friends were disappointed. Only two or three at most dared to publish anything in his defence.

He first accepted a transfer to the post of Deputy-professor at Ludwigsburg, but in less than a year he was glad to give it up, and he then returned to Stuttgart. There he lived for several years, busying himself in the preparation of new editions [pg 072] of the Life of Jesus, and in writing answers to the attacks which were made upon him.

Towards the end of the 'thirties he became conscious of a growing impulse towards more positive views. The criticisms of his opponents had made some impression upon him. The second volume of polemics was laid aside. In its place appeared the third edition of the Life of Jesus, 1838-1839, containing a series of amazing concessions. Strauss explains that in consequence of reading de Wette's commentary and Neander's Life of Jesus he had begun to feel some hesitation about his former doubts regarding the genuineness and credibility of the Fourth Gospel. The historic personality of Jesus again began to take on intelligible outlines for him. These inconsistencies he removed in the next edition, acknowledging that he did not know how he could so have temporarily vacillated in his point of view. The matter admits, however, of a psychological explanation. He longed for peace, for he had suffered more than his enemies suspected or his friends knew. The ban of the outlaw lay heavy upon his soul. In this spirit he composed in 1839 the monologues entitled *Vergängliches und Bleibendes im Christentum* ("Transient and Permanent Elements in Christianity"), which appeared again in the following year under the title *Friedliche Blätter* ("Leaves of Peace").

For a moment it seemed as though his rehabilitation would be accomplished. In January 1839 the noble-minded Hitzig succeeded in getting him appointed to the vacant chair of dogmatics in Zurich. But the orthodox and pietist parties protested so vehemently that the Government was obliged to revoke the appointment. Strauss was pensioned off, without ever entering on his office.

About that time his mother died. In 1841 he lost his father. When the estate came to be settled up, it was found that his affairs were in a less unsatisfactory condition than had been feared. Strauss was secure against want. The success of his second great work, his "Christian Theology" (published in 1840-41), compensated him for his disappointment at Zurich. In conception it is perhaps even greater than the Life of Jesus; and in depth of thought it is to be classed with the most important contributions to theology. In spite of that it never attracted so much attention as the earlier work. Strauss continued to be known as the author of the Life of Jesus. Any further ground of offence which he might give was regarded as quite subsidiary.

And the book contains matter for offence in no common degree. The point to which Strauss applies his criticism is the way in which the Christian theology which grew out of the ideas of the ancient world has been brought into harmony with [pg 073] the Christianity of rationalism and of speculative philosophy. Either, to use his own expression, both are so finely pulverised in the process—as in the case of Schleiermacher's combination of Spinozism with Christianity—that it needs a sharp eye to rediscover the elements of the mixture; or the two are shaken together like water and oil, in which case the semblance of combination is only maintained so long as the shaking continues. For this crude procedure he desires to substitute a better method, based upon a preliminary historical criticism of dogma, in order that thought may no longer have to deal with the present form of Church theology, but with the ideas which worked as living forces in its formation.

This is brilliantly worked out in detail. The result is not a positive, but a negative Hegelian theology. Religion is not concerned with supra-mundane beings and a divinely glorious future, but with present spiritual realities which appear as "moments" in the eternal being and becoming of Absolute Spirit. At the end of the second volume, where battle is joined on the issue of personal immortality, all these ideas play their part in the struggle. Personal immortality is finally rejected in every form, for the critical reasons which Strauss had already set forth in the letters of 1832. Immortality is not something which stretches out into the future, but simply and solely the present quality of the spirit, its inner universality, its power of rising above everything finite to the Idea. Here the thought of Hegel coincides with that of Schleiermacher. "The saying of Schleiermacher, 'In the midst of finitude to be one with the Infinite, and to be eternal in a moment,' is all that modern thought can say about immortality." But neither Schleiermacher nor Hegel was willing to draw the natural inferences from their ultimate position, or at least they did not give them any prominence.

It is not the application of the mythological explanation to the Gospel history which irrevocably divides Strauss from the theologians, but the question of personal immortality. It would be well for them if they had only to deal with the Strauss of the Life of Jesus, and not with the thinker who posed this question with inexorable trenchancy. They might then face the future more calmly, relieved of the anxiety lest once more Hegel and Schleiermacher might rise up in some pious but critical spirit, not to speak smooth things, but to ask the ultimate questions, and might force theology to fight its battle with Strauss all over again.

At the very time when Strauss was beginning to breathe freely once more, had turned his back upon all attempts at compromise, and reconciled himself to giving up teaching; and when, after settling his father's affairs, he had the certainty of being secure [pg 074] against penury; at that very time he sowed for himself the seeds of a new, immitigable suffering by his marriage with Agnese Schebest, the famous singer.

They were not made for one another. He could not look to her for any sympathy with his plans, and she on her part was repelled by the pedantry of his disposition. Housekeeping difficulties and the trials of a limited income added another element of discord. They removed to Sontheim near Heilbronn with the idea of learning to adapt themselves to one another far from the distractions of the town; but that did not better matters. They lived apart for a time, and after some years they procured a divorce, custody of the children being assigned to the father. The lady took up her residence in Stuttgart, and Strauss paid her an allowance up to her death in 1870.

What he suffered may be read between the lines in the passage in "The Old Faith and the New" where he speaks of the sacredness of marriage and the admissibility of divorce. The wound bled inwardly. His mental powers were disabled. At this time he wrote little. Only in the apologue "Julian the Apostate, or the Romanticist on the throne of the Caesars"—that brilliant satire upon Frederic William IV., written in 1847—is there a flash of the old spirit.

But in spite of his antipathy to the romantic disposition of the King of Prussia he entered the lists in 1848 on behalf of the efforts of the smaller German states to form a united Germany, apart from Austria, under the hegemony of Prussia. He did not suffer his political acumen to be blunted either by personal antipathies or by particularism. The citizens of Ludwigsburg wished to have him as their representative in the Frankfort parliament, but the rural population, who were pietistic in sympathies, defeated his candidature. Instead, his native town sent him to the Würtemberg Chamber of Deputies. But here his philistinism came to the fore again. The phrase-mongering revolutionary party in the chamber disgusted him. He saw himself more and more forced to the "right," and was obliged to act politically with men whose reactionary sympathies he was far from sharing. His constituents, meanwhile, were thoroughly discontented with his attitude. In the end the position became intolerable. It was also painful to him to have to reside in Stuttgart, where he could not avoid meeting the woman who had brought so much misery into his life. Further—he himself mentions this point in his memoirs—he had no practice in speaking without manuscript, and cut a poor figure as a debater. Then came the "Blum Case." Robert Blum, a revolutionary, had been shot by court martial in Vienna. The Würtemberg Chamber desired to vote a public celebration of his funeral. [pg 075] Strauss did not think there was any ground for making a hero of this agitator, merely because he had been shot, and was not inclined to blame the Austrian Government very severely for meting out summary justice to a disturber of the peace. His attitude brought on him a vote of censure from his constituents. When, subsequently, the President of the Chamber called him to order for asserting that a previous speaker had "concealed by sleight of hand" (*wegeskamotiert*, "juggled away") an important point in the debate, he refused to accept the vote of censure, resigned his membership, and ceased to attend the diets. As he himself put it, he "jumped out of the boat." Then began a period of restless wandering, during which he beguiled his time with literary work. He wrote, *inter alia*, upon Lessing, Hutten, and Reimarus, rediscovering the last-named for his fellow-countrymen.

At the end of the 'sixties he returned once more to theology. His "Life of Jesus adapted for the German People" appeared in 1864. In the preface he refers to Renan, and freely acknowledges the great merits of his work.

The Prusso-Austrian war placed him in a difficult position. His historical insight made it impossible for him to share the particularism of his friends; on the contrary, he recognised that the way was now being prepared for the realisation of his dream of 1848—an alliance of the smaller German States under the hegemony of Prussia. As he made no secret of his opinions, he had the bitter experience of receiving the cold shoulder from men who had hitherto loyally stood by him.

In the year 1870 it was granted to him to become the spokesman of the German people; through a publication on Voltaire which had appeared not long before he had become acquainted with Renan. In a letter to Strauss, written after the first battles, Renan made a passing allusion to these great events. Strauss seized the opportunity to explain to him, in a vigorous "open letter" of the 12th of August, Germany's reason and justification for going to war. Receiving an answer from Renan, he then, in a second letter, of the 29th of September, took occasion to defend Germany's right to demand the cession of Alsace, not on the ground of its having formerly been German territory, but for the defence of her natural frontiers. The resounding echo evoked by these words, inspired, as they were, by the enthusiasm of the moment, compensated him for much of the obloquy which he had had to bear.

His last work, "The Old Faith and the New," appeared in 1872. Once more, as in the work on theology published in 1840-1841, he puts to himself the question, What is there of permanence in this artificial compound of theology and philosophy, faith and thought? [pg 076] But he puts the question with a certain bitterness, and shows himself too much under the influence of Darwinism, by which his mind was at that time dominated. The Hegelian system of thought, which served as a firm basis for the work of 1840, has fallen in ruins. Strauss is alone with his own thoughts, endeavouring to raise himself above the new scientific world-view. His powers of thought, never, for all his critical acumen, strong on the creative side, and now impaired by age, were unequal to the task. There is no force and no greatness in the book.

To the question, "Are we still Christians?" he answers, "No." But to his second question, "Have we still a religion?" he is prepared to give an affirmative answer, if the assumption is granted that the feeling of dependence, of self-surrender, of inner freedom, which has sprung from the pantheistic world-view, can be called religion. But instead of developing the idea of this deep inner freedom, and presenting religion in the form in which he had experienced it, he believes himself obliged to offer some new construction based upon Darwinism, and sets himself to answer the two questions, "How are we to understand the world?" and "How are we to regulate our lives?"—the form of the latter is somewhat lacking in distinction—in a quite impersonal way. It is only the schoolmaster and pedant in him—who was always at the elbow of the thinker even in his greatest works—that finds expression here.

It was a dead book, in spite of the many editions which it went through, and the battle which raged over it was, like the fiercest of the Homeric battles, a combat over the dead.

The theologians declared Strauss bankrupt, and felt themselves rich because they had made sure of not being ruined by a similar unimaginative honesty. Friedrich Nietzsche, from the height of his would-be Schopenhauerian pessimism, mocked at the fallen hero.

Before the year was out Strauss began to suffer from an internal ulcer. For many months he bore his sufferings with quiet resignation and inner serenity, until on the 8th of February 1874, in his native town of Ludwigsburg, death set him free.

A few weeks earlier, on the 29th of December 1873, his sufferings and his thoughts received illuminating expression in the following poignant verses:—

Wem ich dieses klage,
Weiss, ich klage nicht;
Der ich dieses sage,
Fühlt, ich zage nicht.
Heute heisst's verglimmen,
Wie ein Licht verglimmt,
In die Luft verschwimmen,
Wie ein Ton verschwimmt.
[pg 077]
Möge schwach wie immer,
Aber hell und rein,
Dieser letzte Schimmer
Dieser Ton nur sein.[34]

He was buried on a stormy February day.
[pg 078]

VIII. Strauss's First "Life Of Jesus"

First edition, 1835 and 1836. 2 vols. 1480 pp.
The second edition was unaltered.
Third edition, with alterations, 1838-1839.
Fourth edition, agreeing with the first, 1840.

Considered as a literary work, Strauss's first Life of Jesus is one of the most perfect things in the whole range of learned literature. In over fourteen hundred pages he has not a superfluous phrase; his analysis descends to the minutest details, but he does not lose his way among them; the style is simple and picturesque, sometimes ironical, but always dignified and distinguished.

In regard to the application of the mythological explanation to Holy Scripture, Strauss points out that De Wette, Eichhorn, Gabler, and others of his predecessors had long ago freely applied it to the Old Testament, and that various attempts had been made to portray the life of Jesus in accordance with the critical assumptions upon which his undertaking was based. He mentions especially Usteri as one who had helped to prepare the way for him. The distinction between Strauss and those who had preceded him upon this path consists only in this, that prior to him the conception of myth was neither truly grasped nor consistently applied. Its application was confined to the account of Jesus' coming into the world and of His departure from it, while the real kernel of the evangelical tradition—the sections from the Baptism to the Resurrection—was left outside the field of its application. Myth formed, to use Strauss's illustration, the lofty gateways at the entrance to, and at the exit from, the Gospel history; between these two lofty gateways lay the narrow and crooked streets of the naturalistic explanation.

The principal obstacle, Strauss continues, which barred the way to a comprehensive application of myth, consisted in the supposition that two of our Gospels, Matthew and John, were reports of eyewitnesses; and a further difficulty was the offence caused by [pg 079] the word myth, owing to its associations with the heathen mythology. But that any of our Evangelists was an eyewitness, or stood in such relations with eyewitnesses as to make the intrusion of myth unthinkable, is a thesis which there is no extant evidence sufficient to prove. Even though the earthly life of the Lord falls within historic times, and even if only a generation be assumed to have elapsed between His death and the composition of the Gospels; such a period would be sufficient to allow the historical material to become intermixed with myth. No sooner is a great man dead than legend is busy with his life.

Then, too, the offence of the word myth disappears for any one who has gained an insight into the essential character of religious myth. It is nothing else than the clothing in historic form of religious ideas, shaped by the unconsciously inventive power of legend, and embodied in a historic personality. Even on a priori grounds we are almost compelled to assume that the historic Jesus will meet us in the garb of old Testament Messianic ideas and primitive Christian expectations.

The main distinction between Strauss and his predecessors consisted in the fact that they asked themselves anxiously how much of the historical life of Jesus would remain as a foundation for religion if they dared to apply the conception of myth consistently, while for him this question had no terrors. He claims in his preface that he possessed one advantage over all the critical and learned theologians of his time without which nothing can be accomplished in the domain of history—the inner emancipation of thought and feeling in regard to certain religious and dogmatic prepossessions which he had early attained as a result of his philosophic studies. Hegel's philosophy had set him free, giving him a clear conception of the relationship of idea and reality, leading him to a higher plane of Christological speculation, and opening his eyes to the mystic interpenetration of finitude and infinity, God and man.

God-manhood, the highest idea conceived by human thought, is actually realised in the historic personality of Jesus. But while conventional thinking supposes that this phenomenal realisation must be perfect, true thought, which has attained by genuine critical reasoning to a higher freedom, knows that no idea can realise itself perfectly on the historic plane, and that its truth does not depend on the proof of its having received perfect external representation, but that its perfection comes about through that which the idea carries into history, or through the way in which history is sublimated into idea. For this reason it is in the last analysis indifferent to what extent God-manhood has been realised in the person of Jesus; the important thing is that the idea is now alive in the common consciousness of those who have been [pg 080] prepared to receive it by its manifestation in sensible form, and of whose thought and imagination that historical personality took such complete possession, that for them the unity of Godhood and manhood assumed in Him enters into the common consciousness, and the "moments" which constitute the outward course of His life reproduce themselves in them in a spiritual fashion.

A purely historical presentation of the life of Jesus was in that first period wholly impossible; what was operative was a creative reminiscence acting under the impulse of the idea which the personality of Jesus had called to life among mankind. And this idea of God-manhood, the realisation of which in every personality is the ultimate goal of humanity, is the eternal reality in the Person of Jesus, which no criticism can destroy.

However far criticism may go in proving the reaction of the idea upon the presentment of the historical course of the life of Jesus, the fact that Jesus represented that idea and called it to life among mankind is something real, something that no criticism can annul. It is alive thenceforward—to this day, and for ever more.

It is in this emancipation of spirit, and in the consciousness that Jesus as the creator of the religion of humanity is beyond the reach of criticism, that Strauss goes to work, and batters down the rubble, assured that his pick can make no impression on the stone. He sees evidence that the time has come for this undertaking in the condition of exhaustion which characterised contemporary theology. The supernaturalistic explanation of the events of the life of Jesus had been followed by the rationalistic, the one making everything supernatural, the other setting itself to make all the events intelligible as natural occurrences. Each had said all that it had to say. From their opposition now arises a new solution—the mythological interpretation. This is a characteristic example of the Hegelian method—the *synthesis* of a *thesis* represented by the supernaturalistic explanation with an *antithesis* represented by the rationalistic interpretation.

Strauss's Life of Jesus is, therefore, like Schleiermacher's, the product of antithetic conceptions. But whereas in the latter the antitheses Docetism and Ebionism are simply limiting conceptions, between which his view is statically suspended, the synthesis with which Strauss operates represents a composition of forces, of which his view is the dynamic resultant. The dialectic is in the one case descriptive, in the other creative. This Hegelian dialectic determines the method of the work. Each incident of the life of Jesus is considered separately; first as supernaturally explained, and then as rationalistically explained, and the one explanation is refuted by the other. "By this means," says Strauss in his preface, "the incidental advantage is secured that [pg 081] the work is fitted to serve as a repertory of the leading views and discussions of all parts of the Gospel history."

In every case the whole range of representative opinions is reviewed. Finally the forced interpretations necessitated by the naturalistic explanation of the narrative under discussion drives the reader back upon the supernaturalistic. That had been recognised by Hase and Schleiermacher, and they had felt themselves obliged to make a place for inexplicable supernatural elements alongside of the historic elements of the life of Jesus. Contemporaneously there had sprung up in all directions new attempts to return by the aid of a mystical philosophy to the supernaturalistic point of view of our forefathers. But in these Strauss recognises only the last desperate efforts to make the past present and to conceive the inconceivable; and in direct opposition to the reactionary ineptitudes by means of which critical theology was endeavouring to work its way out of rationalism, he sets up the hypothesis that these inexplicable elements are mythical.

In the stories prior to the baptism, everything is myth. The narratives are woven on the pattern of Old Testament prototypes, with modifications due to Messianic or messianically interpreted passages. Since Jesus and the Baptist came into contact with one another later, it is felt necessary to represent their parents as having been connected. The attempts to construct Davidic genealogies for Jesus, show us that there was a period in the formation of the Gospel History during which the Lord was simply regarded as the son of Joseph and Mary, otherwise genealogical studies of this kind would not have been undertaken. Even in the story of the twelve-year-old Jesus in the temple, there is scarcely more than a trace of historical material.

In the narrative of the baptism we may take it as certainly unhistorical that the Baptist received a revelation of the Messianic dignity of Jesus, otherwise he could not later have come to doubt this. Whether his message to Jesus is historical must be left an open question; its possibility depends on whether the nature of his confinement admitted of such communication with the outer world. Might not a natural reluctance to allow the Baptist to depart this life without at least a dawning recognition of the Messiahship of Jesus have here led to the insertion of a legendary trait into the tradition? If so, the historical residuum would be that Jesus was for a time one of the adherents of the Baptist, and was baptized by him, and that He soon afterwards appeared in Galilee with the same message which John had proclaimed, and even when He had outgrown his influence, never ceased to hold John in high esteem, as is shown by the eulogy which He pronounced upon him. But if the baptism of John was a baptism of [pg 082] repentance with a view to "him who was to come," Jesus cannot have held Himself to be sinless when He submitted to it. Otherwise we should have to suppose that He did it merely for appearance' sake. Whether it was in the moment of the baptism that the consciousness of His Messiahship dawned upon Him, we cannot tell. This only is certain, that the conception of Jesus as having been endowed with the Spirit at His baptism, was independent of, and earlier than, that other conception which held Him to have been supernaturally born of the Spirit. We have, therefore, in the Synoptists several different strata of legend and narrative, which in some cases intersect and in some are superimposed one upon the other.

The story of the temptation is equally unsatisfactory, whether it be interpreted as supernatural, or as symbolical either of an inward struggle or of external events (as for example in Venturini's interpretation of it, where the part of the Tempter is played by a Pharisee); it is simply primitive Christian legend, woven together out of Old Testament suggestions.

The call of the first disciples cannot have happened as it is narrated, without their having known anything of Jesus beforehand; the manner of the call is modelled upon the call of Elisha by Elijah. The further legend attached to it—Peter's miraculous draught of fishes—has arisen out of the saying about "fishers of men," and the same idea is reflected, at a different angle of refraction, in John xxi. The mission of the seventy is unhistorical.

Whether the cleansing of the temple is historical, or whether it arose out of a Messianic application of the text, "My house shall be called a house of prayer," cannot be determined. The difficulty of forming a clear idea of the circumstances is not easily to be removed. How freely the historical material has been worked up, is seen in the groups of stories which have grown out of a single incident; as, for example, the anointing of Jesus at Bethany by an unknown woman, out of which Luke has made an anointing by a penitent sinner, and John an anointing by Mary of Bethany.

As regards the healings, some of them are certainly historical, but not in the form in which tradition has preserved them. The recognition of Jesus as Messiah by the demons immediately arouses suspicion. It is doubtless rather to be ascribed to the tendency which grew up later to represent Him as receiving, in His Messianic character, homage even from the world of evil spirits, than to any advantage in respect of clearness of insight which distinguished the mentally deranged, in comparison with their contemporaries. The cure of the demoniac in the synagogue at Capernaum may well be historical, but, in other cases, the procedure is so often raised into the region of the miraculous that a psychical influence of Jesus upon the sufferer no longer suffices [pg 083] to explain it; the creative activity of legend must have come in to confuse the account of what really happened.

One cure has sometimes given rise to three or four narratives. Sometimes we can still recognise the influences which have contributed to mould a story. When, for example, the disciples are unable to heal the lunatic boy during Jesus' absence on the Mount of Transfiguration, we are reminded of 2 Kings iv., where Elisha's servant Gehazi tries in vain to bring the dead boy to life by using the staff of the prophet. The immediate healing of leprosy has its prototype in the story of Naaman the Syrian. The story of the ten lepers shows so clearly a didactic tendency that its historic value is thereby rendered doubtful.

The cures of blindness all go back to the case of the blind man at Jericho. But who can say how far this is itself historical? The cures of paralytics, too, belong rather to the equipment of the Messiah than to history. The cures through touching clothes, and the healings at a distance, have myth written on their foreheads. The fact is, the Messiah must equal, nay, surpass, the deeds of the prophets. That is why raisings from the dead figure among His miracles.

The nature miracles, over a collection of which Strauss puts the heading "Sea-Stories and Fish-Stories," have a much larger admixture of the mythical. His opponents took him severely to task for this irreverent superscription.

The repetition of the story of the feeding of the multitude arouses suspicion regarding the credibility of what is narrated, and at once invalidates the hypothesis of the apostolic authorship of the Gospel of Matthew. Moreover, the incident was so naturally suggested by Old Testament examples that it would have been a miracle if such a story had not found its way into the Life of Jesus. An explanation on the analogy of an expedited process of nature, is here, as in the case of the miracle at Cana also, to be absolutely rejected. Strauss allows it to be laughed out of court. The cursing of the fig-tree and its fulfilment go back in some way or other to a parable of Jesus, which was afterwards made into history.

More important than the miracles heretofore mentioned are those which have to do with Jesus Himself and mark the crises of His history. The transfiguration had to find a place in the life of Jesus, because of the shining of Moses' countenance. In dealing with the narratives of the resurrection it is evident that we must distinguish two different strata of legend, an older one, represented by Matthew, which knew only of appearances in Galilee, and a later, in which the Galilaean appearances are excluded in favour of appearances in Jerusalem. In both cases, however, the narratives are mythical. In any attempt to explain [pg 084] them we are forced on one horn of the dilemma or the other—if the resurrection was real, the death was not real, and vice versa. That the ascension is a myth is self-evident.

Such, and so radical, are the results at which Strauss's criticism of the supernaturalistic and the rationalistic explanations of the life of Jesus ultimately arrives.

In reading Strauss's discussions one is not so much struck with their radical character, because of the admirable dialectic skill with which he shows the total impossibility of any explanation which does not take account of myth. On the whole, the supernaturalistic explanation, which at least represents the plain sense of the narratives, comes off much better than the rationalistic, the artificiality of which is everywhere remorselessly exposed.

The sections which we have summarised are far from having lost their significance at the present day. They marked out the ground which is now occupied by modern critical study. And they filled in the death-certificates of a whole series of explanations which, at first sight, have all the air of being alive, but are not really so. If these continue to haunt present-day theology, it is only as ghosts, which can be put to flight by simply pronouncing the name of David Friedrich Strauss, and which would long ago have ceased to "walk," if the theologians who regard Strauss's book as obsolete would only take the trouble to read it.

The results so far considered do not represent the elements of the life of Jesus which Strauss was prepared to accept as historical. He sought to make the boundaries of the mythical embrace the widest possible area; and it is clear that he extended them too far.

For one thing, he overestimates the importance of the Old Testament motives in reference to the creative activity of the legend. He does not see that while in many cases he has shown clearly enough the source of the *form* of the narrative in question, this does not suffice to explain its *origin*. Doubtless, there is mythical material in the story of the feeding of the multitude. But the existence of the story is not explained by referring to the manna in the desert, or the miraculous feeding of a multitude by Elisha.[35] The story in the Gospel has far too much individuality for that, and stands, moreover, in much too closely articulated an historical connexion. It must have as its basis some historical fact. It is not a myth, though there is myth in it. Similarly with the account of the transfiguration. The substratum of historical fact in the life of Jesus is much more extensive than Strauss is prepared to admit. Sometimes he fails to see the foundations, because he proceeds like an explorer who, in working on the ruins of an Assyrian city, should cover up the most valuable [pg 085] evidence with the rubbish thrown out from another portion of the excavations.

Again, he sometimes rules out statements by assuming their impossibility on purely dialectical grounds, or by playing off the narratives one against another. The Baptist's message to Jesus is a case in point. This is connected with the fact that he often fails to realise the strong confirmation which the narratives derive from their connexion with the preceding and following context.

That, however, was only to be expected. Who ever discovered a true principle without pressing its application too far?

What really alarmed his contemporaries was not so much the comprehensive application of the mythical theory, as the general mining and sapping operations which they were obliged to see brought to bear upon the Gospels.

In section after section Strauss cross-examines the reports on every point, down to the minutest detail, and then pronounces in what proportion an alloy of myth enters into each of them. In every case the decision is unfavourable to the Gospel of John. Strauss was the first to take this view. It is true that, at the end of the eighteenth century, many doubts as to the authenticity of this Gospel had been expressed, and Bretschneider, the famous General Superintendent at Gotha (1776-1848), had made a tentative collection of them in his *Probabilia*.[36] The essay made some stir at the time. But Schleiermacher threw the aegis of his authority over the authenticity of the Gospel, and it was the favourite Gospel of the rationalists because it contained fewer miracles than the others. Bretschneider himself declared that he had been brought to a better opinion through the controversy.

After this episode the Johannine question had been shelved for fifteen years. The excitement was, therefore, all the greater when Strauss reopened the discussion. He was opposing a dogma of critical theology, which, even at the present day, is wont to defend its dogmas with a tenacity beyond that of the Church itself.

The luminous haze of apparent circumstantiality which had hitherto prevented men from recognising the true character of this Gospel is completely dissipated. Strauss shows that the Johannine representation of the life of Jesus is dominated by a theory, and that its portraiture shows the further development of the tendencies which are perceptible even in the Synoptists. He shows this, for example, in the case of the Johannine narrative of the baptism of Jesus, in which critics had hitherto seen the most credible account of what occurred, pointing out that it is just in this pseudo-simplicity that the process of bringing Jesus and the Baptist into the closest possible relations reaches its limit. [pg 086] Similarly, in regard to the call of the first disciples, it is, according to Strauss, a later postulate that they came from the Baptist's following and were brought by him to the Lord. Strauss does not scruple even to assert that John introduces imaginary characters. If this Gospel relates fewer miracles, the miracles which it retains are proportionately greater; so great, indeed, that their absolutely miraculous character is beyond the shadow of doubt; and, moreover, a moral or symbolical significance is added.

Here, therefore, it is no longer the unconscious action of legend which selects, creates, or groups the incidents, but a clearly-determined apologetic and dogmatic purpose.

The question regarding the different representations of the locality and chronology of the life of Jesus, had always been decided, prior to Strauss, in favour of the Fourth Gospel. De Wette makes it an argument against the genuineness of Matthew's Gospel that it mistakenly confines the ministry of Jesus to Galilee. Strauss refuses to decide the question by simply weighing the chronological and geographical statements one against the other, lest he should be as one-sided in his own way as the defenders of the authenticity of the Fourth Gospel were in theirs. On this point, he contents himself with remarking that if Jesus had really taught in Jerusalem on several occasions, it is absolutely unintelligible how all knowledge of this could have so completely disappeared from the Synoptic tradition; for His going up to the Passover at which He met His death is there represented as His sole journey to Jerusalem. On the other hand, it is quite conceivable that if Jesus had only once been in Jerusalem there would be a tendency for legend gradually to make several journeys out of this one, on the natural assumption that He regularly went up to the Feasts, and that He would proclaim His Gospel not merely in the remote province, but also in the capital.

From the triumphal entry to the resurrection, the difference between the Synoptic and Johannine narratives is so great that all attempts to harmonise them are to be rejected. How are we to reconcile the statement of the Synoptists that the ovation at the triumphal entry was offered by Galilaeans who accompanied him, with that of John, according to which it was offered by a multitude from Jerusalem which came out to welcome Jesus—who, moreover, according to John, was not coming from Galilee and Jericho—and escorted Him into the city. To suppose that there were two different triumphal entries is absurd.

But the decision between John and the Synoptists is not based solely upon their representation of the facts; the decisive consideration is found in the ideas by which they are respectively dominated. John represents a more advanced stage of the mythopoeic process, inasmuch as he has substituted for the Jewish Messianic conception, [pg 087] the Greek metaphysical conception of the Divine Sonship, and, on the basis of his acquaintance with the Alexandrian Logos doctrine, even makes Jesus apply to Himself the Greek speculative conception of pre-existence. The writer is aware of an already existing danger from the side of a Gnostic docetism, and has himself an apologetic Christology to propound, thus fighting the Gnostics as a Gnostic of another kind. That he is free from eschatological conceptions is not, from the historical point of view, an advantage, but very much the reverse. He is not unacquainted with eschatology, but deliberately transforms it, endeavouring to substitute for the expectation of the Second Coming of Christ, as an external event of the future, the thought of His inward presence.

The most decisive evidence of all is found in the farewell discourses and in the absence of all mention of the spiritual struggle in Gethsemane. The intention here is to show that Jesus not only had a foreknowledge of His death, but had long overcome it in anticipation, and went to meet His tragic fate with perfect inward serenity. That, however, is no historical narrative, but the final stage of reverent idealisation.

The question is decided. The Gospel of John is inferior to the Synoptics as a historical source just in proportion as it is more strongly dominated than they by theological and apologetic interests. It is true that the assignment of the dominant motives is for Strauss's criticism mainly a matter of conjecture. He cannot define in detail the attitude and tendency of this Gospel, because the development of dogma in the second century was still to a great extent obscure. He himself admits that it was only subsequently, through the labours of Baur, that the positions which he had taken up in 1835 were rendered impregnable. And yet it is true to say that Johannine study has added in principle nothing new to what was said by Strauss. He recognised the decisive point. With critical acumen he resigned the attempt to base a decision on a comparison of the historical data, and allowed the theological character of the two lines of tradition to determine the question. Unless this is done the debate is endless, for an able man who has sworn allegiance to John will always find a thousand ways in which the Johannine data can be reconciled with those of the Synoptists, and is finally prepared to stake his life upon the exact point at which the missing account of the institution of the Lord's Supper must be inserted into the narrative.

This changed estimate of John carries with it a reversal of the order in which the Gospels are supposed to have originated. Instead of John, Luke, Matthew, we have Matthew, Luke, and John—the first is last, and the last first. Strauss's unsophisticated instinct freed Matthew from the humiliating vassalage to which [pg 088] Schleiermacher's aesthetic had consigned him. The practice of differentiating between John and the Synoptists, which in the hands of Schleiermacher and Hase had been an elegant amusement, now received unexpected support, and it at last became possible for the study of the life of Jesus to go forward.

But no sooner had Strauss opened up the way than he closed it again, by refusing to admit the priority of Mark. His attitude towards this Gospel at once provokes opposition. For him Mark is an epitomising narrator, a mere satellite of Matthew with no independent light. His terse and graphic style makes on Strauss an impression of artificiality. He refuses to believe this Evangelist when he says that on the first day at Capernaum "the whole town" (Mark i. 33) came together before Peter's door, and that, on other occasions (Mark iii. 20, vi. 31), the press was so great that Jesus and His disciples had no leisure so much as to eat. "All very improbable traits," he remarks, "the absence of which in Matthew is entirely to his advantage, for what else are they than legendary exaggerations?" In this criticism he is at one with Schleiermacher, who in his essay on Luke[37] speaks of the unreal vividness of Mark "which often gives his Gospel an almost apocryphal aspect."

This prejudice against Mark has a twofold cause. In the first place, this Gospel with its graphic details had rendered great service to the rationalistic explanation of miracle. Its description of the cure of the blind man at Bethsaida (Mark viii. 22-26)—whose eyes Jesus first anointed with spittle, whereupon he at first saw things dimly, and then, after he had felt the touch of the Lord's hand upon his eyes a second time, saw more clearly—was a veritable treasure-trove for rationalism. As Strauss is disposed to deal much more peremptorily with the rationalists than with the supernaturalists, he puts Mark upon his trial, as their accessory before the fact, and pronounces upon him a judgment which is not entirely unprejudiced. Moreover, it is not until the Gospels are looked at from the point of view of the plan of the history and the inner connexion of events that the superiority of Mark is clearly realised. But this way of looking at the matter does not enter into Strauss's purview. On the contrary, he denies that there is any traceable connexion of events at all, and confines his attention to determining the proportion of myth in the content of each separate narrative.

Of the Synoptic question he does not, strictly speaking, take any account. That was partly due to the fact that when he wrote it was in a thoroughly unsatisfactory position. There was a confused welter of the most various hypotheses. The priority of Mark, [pg 089] which had had earlier champions in Koppe,[38] Storr,[39] Gratz,[40] and Herder,[41] was now maintained by Credner and Lachmann, who saw in Matthew a combination of the logia-document with Mark. The "primitive Gospel" hypothesis of Eichhorn, according to which the first three Gospels went back to a common source, not identical with any of them, had become somewhat discredited. There had been much discussion and various modifications of Griesbach's "dependence theory," according to which Mark was pieced together out of Matthew and Luke, and Schleiermacher's *Diegesentheorie*,[42] which saw the primary material not in a gospel, but in unconnected notes; from these, collections of narrative passages were afterwards formed, which in the post-apostolic period coalesced into continuous descriptions of the life of Jesus such as the three which have been preserved in our Synoptic Gospels.

In this matter Strauss is a sceptical eclectic. In the main he may be said to combine Griesbach's theory of the secondary origin of Mark with Schleiermacher's *Diegesentheorie*, the latter answering to his method of treating the sections separately. But whereas Schleiermacher had used the plan of John's Gospel as a framework into which to fit the independent narratives, Strauss's rejection of the Fourth Gospel left him without any means of connecting the sections. He makes a point, indeed, of sharply emphasising this want of connexion; and it was just this that made his work appear so extreme.

The Synoptic discourses, like the Johannine, are composite structures, created by later tradition out of sayings which originally belonged to different times and circumstances, arranged under certain leading ideas so as to form connected discourses. The sermon on the mount, the discourse at the sending forth of the twelve, the great parable-discourse, the polemic against the Pharisees, have all been gradually formed like geological deposits. So far as the original juxtaposition may be supposed to have been here and there preserved, Matthew is doubtless the most trustworthy authority for it. "From the comparison which we have been making," says Strauss in one passage, "we can already see that the hard grit of these sayings of Jesus (*die körnigen Reden Jesu*) has not indeed been dissolved by the flood of oral tradition, but they have often been washed away from their original position and like rolling pebbles (*Gerölle*) have been deposited in places to which [pg 090] they do not properly belong."[43] And, moreover, we find this distinction between the first three Evangelists, viz. that Matthew is a skilful collector who, while he is far from having been able always to give the original connexion, has at least known how to bring related passages aptly together, whereas in the other two many fragmentary sayings have been left exactly where chance had deposited them, which was generally in the interstices between the larger masses of discourse. Luke, indeed, has in some cases made an effort to give them an artistic setting, which is, however, by no means a satisfactory substitute for the natural connexion.

It is in his criticism of the parables that Strauss is most extreme. He starts out from the assumption that they have mutually influenced one another, and that those which may possibly be genuine have only been preserved in a secondary form. In the parable of the marriage supper of the king's son, for example, he confidently assumes that the conduct of the invited guests, who finally ill-treated and slew the messengers, and the question why the guest is not wearing a wedding-garment are secondary features.

How external he supposes the connexion of the narratives to be is clear from the way in which he explains the juxtaposition of the story of the transfiguration with the "discourse while descending the mountain." They have, he says, really nothing to do with one another. The disciples on one occasion asked Jesus about the coming of Elijah as forerunner; Elijah also appears in the story of the transfiguration: accordingly tradition simply grouped the transfiguration and the discourse together under the heading "Elijah," and, later on, manufactured a connexion between them.

The tendency of the work to purely critical analysis, the ostentatious avoidance of any positive expression of opinion, and not least, the manner of regarding the Synoptists as mere bundles of narratives and discourses, make it difficult—indeed, strictly speaking, impossible—to determine Strauss's own distinctive conception of the life of Jesus, to discover what he really thinks is moving behind the curtain of myth. According to the view taken in regard to this point his work becomes either a negative or a positive life of Jesus. There are, for instance, a number of incidental remarks which contain the suggestion of a positive construction of the life of Jesus. If they were taken out of their context and brought together they would yield a picture which would have points of contact with the latest eschatological view. Strauss, however, deliberately restricts his positive suggestions to these few detached remarks. He follows out no line to its conclusion. Each separate problem is indeed considered, and light is thrown upon it from various quarters with much critical [pg 091] skill. But he will not venture on a solution of any of them. Sometimes, when he thinks he has gone too far in the way of positive suggestion, he deliberately wipes it all out again with some expression of scepticism.

As to the duration of the ministry he will not even offer a vague conjecture. As to the connexion of certain events, nothing can, according to him, be known, since the Johannine outline cannot be accepted and the Synoptists arrange everything with an eye to analogies and association of ideas, though they flattered themselves that they were giving a chronologically arranged narrative. From the contents of the narratives, however, and from the monotonous recurrence of certain formulae of connexion, it is evident that no clear view of an organically connected whole can be assumed to be present in their work. We have no fixed points to enable us to reconstruct even in a measure the chronological order.

Especially interesting is his discussion of the title "Son of Man." In the saying "the Son of Man is Lord also of the Sabbath day" (Matt. xii. 8), the expression might, according to Strauss, simply denote "man." In other passages one gets the impression that Jesus spoke of the Son of Man as a supernatural person, quite distinct from Himself, but identified with the Messiah. This is the most natural explanation of the passage in Matt. x. 23, where he promises the disciples, in sending them forth, that they shall not have gone over the cities of Israel before the Son of Man shall come. Here Jesus speaks of the Messiah as if He Himself were his forerunner. These sayings would, therefore, fall in the first period, before He knew Himself to be the Messiah. Strauss does not suspect the significance of this incidental remark; it contains the germ of the solution of the problem of the Son of Man on the lines of Johannes Weiss. But immediately scepticism triumphs again. How can we tell, asks Strauss, where the title Son of Man is genuine in the sayings of Jesus, and where it has been inserted without special significance, merely from habit?

Not less insoluble, in his opinion, is the question regarding the point of time at which Jesus claimed the Messianic dignity for Himself. "Whereas in John," Strauss remarks, "Jesus remains constant in His avowal, his disciples and followers constant in their conviction, that He is the Messiah; in the Synoptics, on the other hand, there are, so to speak, relapses to be observed; so that, in the case of the disciples and the people generally, the conviction of Jesus' Messiahship expressed on earlier occasions, sometimes, in the course of the narrative, disappears again and gives place to a much lower view of Him; and even Jesus Himself, in comparison with His earlier unambiguous declaration, is more reserved on later occasions." The account of the confession of the Messiahship at Caesarea Philippi, where Jesus pronounces Peter blessed because of [pg 092] his confession, and at the same time forbids the Twelve to speak of it, is unintelligible, since according to this same Gospel His Messiahship had been mooted by the disciples on several previous occasions, and had been acknowledged by the demoniacs. The Synoptists, therefore, contradict themselves. Then there are the further cases in which Jesus forbids the making known of His Messiahship, without any reason whatever. It would, no doubt, be historically possible to assume that it only gradually dawned upon Him that He was the Messiah—in any case not until after His baptism by John, as otherwise He would have to be supposed to have made a pretence upon that occasion—and that as often as the thought that He might be the Messiah was aroused in others by something that occurred, and was suggested to Him from without, He was immediately alarmed at hearing spoken, aloud and definitely, that which He Himself had scarcely dared to cherish as a possibility, or in regard to which He had only lately attained to a clear conviction.

From these suggestions one thing is evident, namely, that for Strauss the Messianic consciousness of Jesus was an historical fact, and is not to be referred, as has sometimes been supposed, to myth. To assert that Strauss dissolved the life of Jesus into myth is, in fact, an absurdity which, however often it may be repeated by people who have not read his book, or have read it only superficially, does not become any the less absurd by repetition.

To come to detail, Jesus thought of His Messiahship, according to Strauss, in the form that He, although of human parentage, should after His earthly life be taken up into heaven, and thence should come again to bring in His Kingdom. "As, moreover, in the higher Jewish theology, immediately after the time of Jesus, the idea of the pre-existence of the Messiah was present, the conjecture naturally suggests itself that it was also present at the time when Jesus' thoughts were being formed, and that consequently, if He once began to think of Himself as the Messiah, He might also have referred to Himself this feature of the Messianic conception. Whether Jesus had been initiated, as Paul was, into the wisdom of the schools in such a way that He could draw this conception from it, is no doubt open to question."

In his treatment of the eschatology Strauss makes a valiant effort to escape from the dilemma "*either* spiritual *or* political" in regard to the Messianic plans of Jesus, and to make the eschatological expectation intelligible as one which did not set its hopes upon human aid, but on Divine intervention. This is one of the most important contributions to a real understanding of the eschatological problem. Sometimes one almost seems to be reading Johannes Weiss; as, for example, when Strauss explains that Jesus could promise His followers that they should sit on thrones without [pg 093] thinking of a political revolution, because He expected a reversal of present conditions to be brought about by God, and referred this judicial authority and kingly rule to the time of the παλιγγενεσία. "Jesus, therefore, certainly expected to restore the throne of David, and, with His disciples, to rule over a people freed from political bondage, but in this expectation He did not set His hopes on the sword of human followers (Luke xxii. 38, Matt. xxvi. 52), but upon the legions of angels which His heavenly Father could give Him (Matt. xxvi. 53). When He speaks of the coming of His Messianic glory, it is with angels and heavenly powers that He surrounds Himself (Matt. xvi. 27, xxiv. 30 ff., xxv. 31). Before the majesty of the Son of Man coming in the clouds of heaven the nations will submit without striking a blow, and at the sound of the angel's trumpet-blast will, with the dead who shall then arise, range themselves before Him and His disciples for judgment. All this Jesus did not purpose to bring about by any arbitrary action of His own, but left it to His heavenly Father, who alone knew the right moment for this catastrophic change (Mark xiii. 32), to give Him the signal of its coming; and He did not waver in His faith even when death came upon Him before its realisation. Any one who shrinks from adopting this view of the Messianic background of Jesus' plans, because he fears by so doing to make Jesus a visionary enthusiast, must remember how exactly these hopes corresponded to the long-cherished Messianic expectation of the Jews; and how easily, on the supernaturalistic assumptions of the period and among a people which preserved so strict an isolation as the Jews, an ideal which was in itself fantastic, if it were the national ideal and had some true and good features, could take possession of the mind even of one who was not inclined to fanaticism."

One of the principal proofs that the preaching of Jesus was eschatologically conditioned is the Last Supper. "When," says Strauss, "He concluded the celebration with the saying, 'I will not drink henceforth of the fruit of the vine until I drink it new with you in my Father's kingdom,' He would seem to have expected that in the Messianic kingdom the Passover would be celebrated with peculiar solemnity. Therefore, in assuring them that they shall next partake of the Feast, not in the present age, but in the new era, He evidently expects that within a year's time the pre-Messianic dispensation will have come to an end and the Messianic age will have begun." But it must be admitted, Strauss immediately adds, that the definite assurance which the Evangelists put into His mouth may after all only have been in reality an expression of pious hope. In a similar way he qualifies his other statements regarding the eschatological ideas of Jesus by recalling that we cannot determine the part which the expectations of primitive Christianity may have had in moulding these sayings.

[pg 094]

Thus, for example, the opinions which he expresses on the great Parousia discourse in Matt. xxiv. are extremely cautious. The detailed prophecies regarding the Second Coming which the Synoptists put into the mouth of Jesus cannot be derived from Jesus Himself. The question suggests itself, however, whether He did not cherish the hope, and make the promise, that He would one day appear in glory as the Messiah? "If in any period of His life He held Himself to be the Messiah—and that there was a period when He did so there can be no doubt—and if He described Himself as the Son of Man, He must have expected the coming in the clouds which Daniel had ascribed to the Son of Man; but it may be questioned whether He thought of this as an exaltation which should take place even in His lifetime, or as something which was only to take place after His death. Utterances like Matt. x. 23, xvi. 28 rather suggest the former, but the possibility remains that later, when he had begun to feel that His death was certain, his conception took the latter form, and that Matt. xxvi. 64 was spoken with this in view." Thus, even for Strauss, the problem of the Son of Man is already the central problem in which are focused all the questions regarding the Messiahship and eschatology.

From all this it may be seen how strongly he had been influenced by Reimarus, whom, indeed, he frequently mentions. It would be still more evident if he had not obscured his historical views by constantly bringing the mythological explanation into play.

The thought of the supernatural realisation of the Kingdom of God must also, according to Strauss, be the starting-point of any attempt to understand Jesus' attitude towards the Law and the Gentiles, so far as that is possible in view of the conflicting data. The conservative passages must carry most weight. They need not necessarily fall at the beginning of His ministry, because it is questionable whether the hypothesis of a later period of increasing liberality in regard to the law and the Gentiles can be made probable. There would be more chance of proving that the conservative sayings are the only authentic ones, for unless all the indications are misleading the *terminus a quo* for this change of attitude is the death of Jesus. He no doubt looked forward to the abolition of the Law and the removal of the barriers between Jew and Gentile, but only in the future Kingdom. "If that be so," remarks Strauss, "the difference between the views of Jesus and of Paul consisted only in this, that while Jesus expected these limitations to fall away when, at His second coming, the earth should be renewed, Paul believed himself justified in doing away with them in consequence of the first coming of the Messiah, upon the still unregenerated earth."

The eschatological passages are therefore the most authentic of all. If there is anything historic about Jesus, it is His assertion [pg 095] of the claim that in the coming kingdom He would be manifested as the Son of Man.

On the other hand, in the predictions of the passion and resurrection we are on quite uncertain ground. The detailed statements regarding the manner of the catastrophe place it beyond doubt that we have here *vaticinia ex eventu*. Otherwise the despair of the disciples when the events occurred could not be explained. Yet it is possible that Jesus had a prevision of His death. Perhaps the resolve to die was essential to His conception of the Messiahship and He was not forced thereto by circumstances. This we might be able to determine with certainty if we had more exact information regarding the conception of the suffering Messiah in contemporary Jewish theology; which is, however, not available. We do not even know whether the conception had ever existed in Judaism. "In the New Testament it almost looks as if no one among the Jews had ever thought of a suffering or dying Messiah." The conception can, however, certainly be found in later passages of Rabbinic literature.

The question is therefore insoluble. We must be content to work with possibilities. The result of a full discussion of the resolve to suffer and the significance attached to the suffering is summed up by Strauss in the following sentences. "In view of these considerations it is possible that Jesus might, by a natural process of thought, have come to see how greatly such a catastrophe would contribute to the spiritual development of His disciples, and in accordance with national conceptions, interpreted in the light of some Old Testament passages, might have arrived at the idea of an atoning power in His Messianic death. At the same time the explicit utterance which the Synoptists attribute to Jesus describing His death as an atoning sacrifice, might well belong rather to the system of thought which grew up after the death of Jesus, and the saying which the Fourth Gospel puts into His mouth regarding the relation of His death to the coming of the Paraclete might seem to be prophecy after the event. So that even in these sayings of Jesus regarding the purpose of His death, it is necessary to distinguish between the particular and the general."

Strauss's "Life of Jesus" has a different significance for modern theology from that which it had for his contemporaries. For them it was the work which made an end of miracle as a matter of historical belief, and gave the mythological explanation its due.

We, however, find in it also an historical aspect of a positive character, inasmuch as the historic Personality which emerges from the mist of myth is a Jewish claimant of the Messiahship, whose world of thought is purely eschatological. Strauss is, therefore, no mere destroyer of untenable solutions, but also the prophet of a coming advance in knowledge.

[pg 096]

It was, however, his own fault that his merit in this respect was not recognised in the nineteenth century, because in his "Life of Jesus for the German People" (1864), where he undertook to draw a positive historic picture of Jesus, he renounced his better opinions of 1835, eliminated eschatology, and, instead of the historic Jesus, portrayed the Jesus of liberal theology.
[pg 097]

IX. Strauss's Opponents And Supporters

David Friedrich Strauss. Streitschriften zur Verteidigung meiner Schrift über das Leben-Jesu und zur Charakteristik der gegenwärtigen Theologie. (Replies to criticisms of my work on the Life of Jesus; with an estimate of present-day theology.) Tübingen, 1837.

Das Leben-Jesu, 3te verbesserte Auflage (3rd revised edition). 1838-1839, Tübingen.

August Tholuck. Die Glaubwürdigkeit der evangelischen Geschichte, zugleich eine Kritik des Lebens Jesu von Strauss. (The Credibility of the Gospel History, with an incidental criticism of Strauss's "Leben-Jesu.") Hamburg, 1837.

Aug. Wilh. Neander. Das Leben Jesu-Christi. Hamburg, 1837.

Dr. Neanders auf höhere Veranlassung abgefasstes Gutachten über das Buch des Dr. Strauss' "Leben-Jesu" und das in Beziehung auf die Verbreitung desselben zu beachtende Verfahren. (Dr. Neander's report, drawn up at the request of the authorities, upon Dr. Strauss's "Leben-Jesu" and the measures to be adopted in regard to its circulation.) 1836.

Leonhard Hug. Gutachten über das Leben-Jesu, kritisch bearbeitet von D. Fr. Strauss. (Report on D. Fr. Strauss's critical work upon the Life of Jesus.) Freiburg, 1840.

Christian Gottlob Wilke. Tradition und Mythe. Ein Beitrag zur historischen Kritik der kanonischen Evangelien überhaupt, wie insbesondere zur Würdigung des mythischen Idealismus im Leben-Jesu von Strauss. (Tradition and Myth. A Contribution to the General Historical Criticism of the Gospels; with special reference to the mythical idealism of Strauss's "Leben-Jesu.") Leipzig, 1837.

August Ebrard. Wissenschaftliche Kritik der evangelischen Geschichte. (Scientific Criticism of the Gospel History.) Frankfort, 1842.

Georg Heinr. Aug. Ewald. Geschichte Christus' und seiner Zeit. (History of Christ and His Times.) 1855. Fifth volume of the "Geschichte des Volkes Israel."

Christoph Friedrich von Ammon. Die Geschichte des Lebens Jesu mit steter Rücksicht auf die vorhandenen Quellen. (History of the Life of Jesus with constant reference to the extant sources.) 3 vols. 1842-1847.

Scarcely ever has a book let loose such a storm of controversy; and scarcely ever has a controversy been so barren of immediate result. The fertilising rain brought up a crop of toadstools. Of the forty or fifty essays on the subject which appeared in the next [pg 098] five years, there are only four or five which are of any value, and even of these the value is very small.

Strauss's first idea was to deal with each of his opponents separately, and he published in 1837 three successive *Streitschriften*.[44] In the preface to the first of these he states that he has kept silence for two years from a rooted objection to anything in the nature of reply or counter-criticism, and because he had little expectation of any good results from such controversy. These essays are able, and are often written with biting scorn, especially that directed against his inveterate enemy, Steudel of Tübingen, the representative of intellectual supernaturalism, and that against Eschenmayer, a pastor, also of Tübingen. To a work of the latter, "The Iscariotism of our Days" (1835), he had referred in the preface to the second volume of his Life of Jesus in the following remark: "This offspring of the legitimate marriage between theological ignorance and religious intolerance, blessed by a sleep-walking philosophy, succeeds in making itself so completely ridiculous that it renders any serious reply unnecessary."

But for all his sarcasm Strauss does not show himself an adroit debater in this controversy, any more than in later times in the Diet.

It is indeed remarkable how unskilled in polemics is this man who had produced a critical work of the first importance with almost playful ease. If his opponents made no effort to understand him rightly—and many of them certainly wrote without having carefully studied the fourteen hundred pages of his two volumes—Strauss on his part seemed to be stricken with a kind of uncertainty, lost himself in a maze of detail, and failed to keep continually re-formulating the main problems which he had set up for discussion, and so compelling his adversaries to face them fairly.

Of these problems there were three. The first was composed of the related questions regarding miracle and myth; the second concerned the connexion of the Christ of faith with the Jesus of [pg 099] history; the third referred to the relation of the Gospel of John to the Synoptists.

It was the first that attracted most attention; more than half the critics devoted themselves to it alone. Even so they failed to get a thorough grasp of it. The only thing that they clearly see is that Strauss altogether denies the miracles; the full scope of the mythological explanation as applied to the traditional records of the life of Jesus, and the extent of the historical material which Strauss is prepared to accept, is still a riddle to them. That is in some measure due, it must in fairness be said, to the arrangement of Strauss's own work, in which the unconnected series of separate investigations makes the subject unnecessarily difficult even for one who wishes to do the author justice.

The attitude towards miracle assumed in the anti-Strauss literature shows how far the anti-rationalistic reaction had carried professedly scientific theology in the direction of supernaturalism. Some significant symptoms had begun to show themselves even in Hase and Schleiermacher of a tendency towards the overcoming of rationalism by a kind of intellectual gymnastic which ran some risk of falling into insincerity. The essential character of this new kind of historical theology first came to light when Strauss put it to the question, and forced it to substitute a plain yes or no for the ambiguous phrases with which this school had only too quickly accustomed itself to evade the difficulties of the problem of miracle. The mottoes with which this new school of theology adorned the works which it sent forth against the untimely troubler of their peace manifest its complete perplexity, and display the coquettish resignation with which the sacred learning of the time essayed to cover its nakedness, after it had succumbed to the temptation of the serpent insincerity. Adolf Harless of Erlangen chose the

melancholy saying of Pascal: "Tout tourne bien pour les élus, jusqu'aux obscurités de l'écriture, car ils les honorent à cause des clartés divines qu'ils y voient; et tout tourne en mal aux reprouvés, jusqu'aux clartés, car ils les blasphèment à cause des obscurités qu'ils n'entendent pas."[45]

Herr Wilhelm Hoffmann,[46] deacon at Winnenden, selected Bacon's aphorism: "Animus ad amplitudinem mysteriorum pro modulo suo dilatetur, non mysteria ad angustias animi constringantur." (Let the mind, so far as possible, be expanded to the greatness of the mysteries, not the mysteries contracted to the compass of the mind.)

[pg 100]

Professor Ernst Osiander,[47] of the seminary at Maulbronn, appeals to Cicero: "O magna vis veritatis, quae contra hominum ingenia, calliditatem, sollertiam facillime se per ipsam defendit." (O mighty power of truth, which against all the ingenious devices, the craft and subtlety, of men, easily defends itself by its own strength!)

Franz Baader, of Munich,[48] ornaments his work with the reflection: "Il faut que les hommes soient bien loin de toi, ô Vérité! puisque tu supporte (*sic!*) leur ignorance, leurs erreurs, et leurs crimes." (Men must indeed be far from thee, O Truth, since thou art able to bear with their ignorance, their errors, and their crimes!)

Tholuck[49] girds himself with the Catholic maxim of Vincent of Lerins: "Teneamus quod semper, quod ubique, quod ab omnibus creditum est." (Let us hold that which has been believed always, everywhere, by all.)

The fear of Strauss had, indeed, a tendency to inspire Protestant theologians with catholicising ideas. One of the most competent reviewers of his book, Dr. Ullmann in the *Studien und Kritiken*, had expressed the wish that it had been written in Latin to prevent its doing harm among the people.[50] An anonymous dialogue of the period shows us the schoolmaster coming in distress to the clergyman. He has allowed himself to be persuaded into reading the book by his acquaintance the Major, and he is now anxious to get rid of the doubts which it has aroused in him. When his cure has been safely accomplished, the reverend gentleman dismisses him with the following exhortation: "Now I hope that after the experience which you have had you will for the future refrain from reading books of this kind, which are not written for you, and of which there is no necessity for you to take any notice; and for the refutation of which, should that be needful, you have no [pg 101] equipment. You may be quite sure that anything useful or profitable for you which such books may contain will reach you in due course through the proper channel and in the right way, and, that being so, you are under no necessity to jeopardise any part of your peace of mind."

Tholuck's work professedly aims only at presenting a "historical argument for the credibility of the miracle stories of the Gospels." "Even if we admit," he says in one place, "the scientific position that no act can have proceeded from Christ which transcends the laws of nature, there is still room for the mediating view of Christ's miracle-working activity. This leads us to think of mysterious powers of nature as operating in the history of Christ—powers such as we have some partial knowledge of, as, for example, those magnetic powers which have survived down to our own time, like ghosts lingering on after the coming of day." From the standpoint of this spurious rationalism he proceeds to take Strauss to task for rejecting the miracles. "Had this latest critic been able to approach the Gospel miracles without prejudice, in the Spirit of Augustine's declaration, 'dandum est deo, eum aliquid facere posse quod nos investigare non possumus,' he would certainly—since he is a man who in addition to the acumen of the scholar possesses sound common sense—have come to a different conclusion in regard to these difficulties. As it is, however, he has approached the Gospels with the conviction that miracles are impossible; and on that assumption, it was certain before the argument began that the Evangelists were either deceivers or deceived."

Neander, in his Life of Jesus,[51] handles the question with more delicacy of touch, rather in the style of Schleiermacher. "Christ's miracles," he explains, "are to be understood as an influencing of nature, human or material." He does not, however, give so much [pg 102] prominence as Schleiermacher had done to the difficulty involved in the supposition of an influence exercised upon material nature. He repeats Schleiermacher's assertions, but without the imposing dialectic which in Schleiermacher's hands almost commands assent. In regard to the miracle at Cana he remarks: "We cannot indeed form any clear conception of an effect brought about by the introduction of a higher creative principle into the natural order, since we have no experience on which to base such a conception, but we are by no means compelled to take this extreme view as to what happened; we may quite well suppose that Christ by an immediate influence upon the water communicated to it a higher potency which enabled it to produce the effects of strong wine." In the case of all the miracles he makes a point of seeking not only the explanation, but the higher symbolical significance. The miracle of the fig-tree—which is *sui generis*—has only this symbolical significance, seeing that it is not beneficent and creative but destructive. "It can only be thought of as a vivid illustration of a prediction of the Divine judgment, after the manner of the symbolic actions of the Old Testament prophets."

With reference to the ascension and the resurrection he writes: "Even though we can form no clear idea of the exact way in which the exaltation of Christ from the earth took place—and indeed there is much that is obscure in regard to the earthly life of Christ after His resurrection—yet, in its place in the organic unity of the Christian faith, it is as certain as the resurrection, which apart from it cannot be recognised in its true significance."

That extract is typical of Neander's Life of Jesus, which in its time was hailed as a great achievement, calculated to provide a learned refutation of Strauss's criticism, and of which a seventh edition appeared as late as 1872. The real piety of heart with which it is imbued cannot conceal the fact that it is a patchwork of unsatisfactory compromises. It is the child of despair, and has perplexity for godfather. One cannot read it without pain.

Neander, however, may fairly claim to be judged, not by this work, but by his personal attitude in the Strauss controversy. And here he appears as a magnanimous and dignified representative of theological science. Immediately after the appearance of Strauss's book, which, it was at once seen, would cause much offence, the Prussian Government asked Neander to report upon it, with a view to prohibiting the circulation, should there appear to be grounds for doing so. He presented his report on the 15th of November 1835, and, an inaccurate account of it having appeared in the *Allgemeine Zeitung*, subsequently published it.[52] In it he censures the work as being written from a too purely rationalistic point of view, but strongly urges the Government not to suppress it by an edict. He [pg 103] describes it as "a book which, it must be admitted, constitutes a danger to the sacred interests of the Church, but which follows the method of endeavouring to produce a reasoned conviction by means of argument. Hence any other method of dealing with it than by meeting argument with argument will appear in the unfavourable light of an arbitrary interference with the freedom of science."

In holding that scientific theology will be able by its own strength to overthrow whatever in Strauss's Life of Jesus deserves to be overthrown, Neander is at one with the anonymous writer of "Aphorisms in Defence of Dr. Strauss and his Work,"[53] who consoles himself with Goethe's saying—

Das Tüchtige, auch wenn es falsch ist,
Wirkt Tag für Tag, von Haus zu Haus;
Das Tüchtige, wenn's wahrhaftig ist,
Wirkt über alle Zeiten hinaus.[54]
(Strive hard, and though your aim be wrong,
Your work shall live its little day;
Strive hard, and for the truth be strong,
Your work shall live and grow for aye.)

"Dr. Strauss," says this anonymous writer, "does not represent the author's views, and he on his part cannot undertake to defend Dr. Strauss's conclusions. But it is clear to him that Dr. Strauss's work considered as a scientific production is more scientific than the works opposed to it from the side of religion are religious. Otherwise why are they so passionate, so apprehensive, so unjust?"

This confidence in pure critical science was not shared by Herr Privat-Docent Daniel Schenkel of Basle, afterwards Professor at Heidelberg. In a dreary work dedicated to his Göttingen teacher Lücke, on "Historical Science and the Church,"[55] he looks for future salvation towards that middle region where faith and science interpenetrate, and hails the new supernaturalism which approximates to a scientific treatment of these subjects "as a hopeful phenomenon." He rejoices in the violent opposition at Zurich which led to the cancelling of Strauss's appointment, regarding it as likely to exercise an elevating influence. A similarly lofty position is taken up by the anonymous author of "Dr. Strauss and the Zurich Church,"[56] to which De Wette contributed a preface. [pg 104] Though professing great esteem for Strauss, and admitting that from the purely historical point of view he is in the right, the author feels bound to congratulate the Zurichers on having refused to admit him to the office of teacher.

The pure rationalists found it much more difficult than did the mediating theologians, whether of the older or younger school, to adjust their attitude to the new solution of the miracle question. Strauss himself had made it difficult for them by remorselessly exposing the absurd and ridiculous aspects of their method, and by refusing to recognise them as allies in the battle for truth, as they really were. Paulus would have been justified in bearing him a grudge. But the inner greatness of that man of hard exterior comes out in the fact that he put his personal feelings in the background, and when Strauss became the central figure in the battle for the purity and freedom of historical science he ignored his attacks on rationalism and came to his defence. In a very remarkable letter to the Free Canton of Zurich, on "Freedom in Theological Teaching and in the Choice of Teachers for Colleges,"[57] he urges the council and the people to appoint Strauss because of the principle at stake, and in order to avoid giving any encouragement to the retrograde movement in historical science. It is as though he felt that the end of rationalism had come, but that, in the person of the enemy who had defeated it, the pure love of truth, which was the only thing that really mattered, would triumph over all the forces of reaction.

It would not, however, be true to say that Strauss had beaten rationalism from the field. In Ammon's famous Life of Jesus,[58] in which the author takes up a very respectful attitude towards Strauss, there is a vigorous survival of a peculiar kind of rationalism inspired by Kant. For Ammon, a miraculous event can only exist when its natural causes have been discovered. "The sacred history is subject to the same laws as all other narratives of antiquity." Lücke, in dealing with the raising of Lazarus, had thrown out the question whether Biblical miracles could be thought of historically at all, and in so doing supposed that he was putting their absolute character on a firmer basis. "We," says Ammon, "give the opposite answer from that which is expected; only historically conceivable miracles can be admitted." He cannot away with the constant confusion of faith and knowledge found in [pg 105] so many writers "who swim in an ocean of ideas in which the real and the illusory are as inseparable as salt and sea-water in the actual ocean." In every natural process, he explains, we have to suppose, according to Kant, an interpenetration of natural and supernatural. For that very reason the purely supernatural does not exist for our experience. "It is no doubt certain," so he lays it down on the lines of Kant's *Kritik der reinen Vernunft*, "that every act of causation which goes forth from God must be immediate, universal, and eternal, because it is thought as an effect of His will, which is exalted above space and time and interpenetrates both of them, but without abolishing them, leaving them undisturbed in their continuity and succession. For us men, therefore, all action of God is mediate, because we are completely surrounded by time and space, as the fish is by the sea or the bird by the air, and apart from these relations we should be incapable of apperception, and therefore of any real experience. As free beings we can, indeed, think of miracle as immediately Divine, but we cannot perceive it as such, because that would be impossible without seeing God, which for wise reasons is forbidden to us." "In accordance with these principles, we shall hold it to be our duty in what follows to call attention to the natural side even of the miracles of Jesus, since apart from this no fact can become an object of belief."

It is only in this intelligible sense that the cures of Jesus are to be thought of as "miracles." The magnetic force, with which the mediating theology makes play, is to be rejected. "The cure of psychical diseases by the power of the word and of faith is the only kind of cure in which the student of natural science can find any basis for a conjecture regarding the way in which the cures of Jesus were effected."

In the case of the other miracles Ammon assumes a kind of Occasionalism, in the sense that it may have pleased the Divine Providence "to fulfil in fact the confidently spoken promises of Jesus, and in that way to confirm His personal authority, which was necessary to the establishment of His doctrine of the Divine salvation."

In most cases, however, he is content to repeat the rationalistic explanation, and portrays a Jesus who makes use of medicines, allows the demoniac himself to rush upon the herd of swine, helps a leper, whom he sees to be suffering only from one of the milder forms of the disease, to secure the public recognition of his being legally clean, and who exerts himself to prevent by word and act the premature burial of persons in a state of trance. The story of the feeding of the multitude is based on some occasion when there was "a bountiful display of hospitality, a generous sharing of provisions, inspired by Jesus' prayer of thanksgiving and the [pg 106] example which He set when the disciples were inclined selfishly to hold back their own supply." The story of the miracle at Cana rests on a mere misunderstanding, those who report it not having known that the wine which Jesus caused to be secretly brought forth was the wedding-gift which he was presenting in the name of the family. As a disciple of Kant, however, Ammon feels obliged to refute the imputation that Jesus could have done anything to promote excess, and calculates that the present of wine which Jesus had intended to give the bridal pair may be estimated as equivalent to not more than eighteen bottles.[59] He explains the walking on the sea by claiming for Jesus an acquaintance with "the art of treading water."

Only in regard to the explanation of the resurrection does Ammon break away from rationalism. He decides that the reality of the death of Jesus is historically proved. But he does not venture to suppose a real reawakening to life, and remains at the standpoint of Herder.

But the way in which, in spite of the deeper view of the conception of miracle which he owes to Kant, he constantly falls back upon the most pedestrian naturalistic explanations, and his failure to rid himself of the prejudice that an actual, even if not a miraculous fact must underlie all the recorded miracles, is in itself sufficient to prove that we have here to do with a mere revival of rationalism: that is, with an untenable theory which Strauss's refutation of Paulus had already relegated to the past.

It was an easier task for pure supernaturalism than for pure rationalism to come to terms with Strauss. For the former Strauss was only the enemy of the mediating theology—there was nothing to fear from him and much to gain. Accordingly Hengstenberg's *Evangelische Kirchenzeitung* hailed Strauss's book as "one of the most gratifying phenomena in the domain of recent theological literature," and praises the author for having carried out with logical consistency the application of the mythical theory which had formerly been restricted to the Old Testament and certain parts only of the Gospel tradition. "All that Strauss has done is to bring the spirit of the age to a clear consciousness of itself and of the necessary consequences which flow from its essential [pg 107] character. He has taught it how to get rid of foreign elements which were still present in it, and which marked an imperfect stage of its development."

He has been the most influential factor in the necessary process of separation. There is no one with whom Hengstenberg feels himself more in agreement than with the Tübingen scholar. Had he not shown with the greatest precision how the results of the Hegelian philosophy, one may say, of philosophy in general, reacted upon Christian faith? "The relation of speculation to faith has now come clearly to light."

"Two nations," writes Hengstenberg in 1836, "are struggling in the womb of our time, and two only. They will be ever more definitely opposed to one another. Unbelief will more and more cast off the elements of faith to which it still clings, and faith will cast off its elements of unbelief. That will be an inestimable advantage. Had the Time-spirit continued to make concessions, concessions would constantly have been made to it in return." Therefore the man who "calmly and deliberately laid hands upon the Lord's anointed, undeterred by the vision of the millions who have bowed the knee, and still bow the knee, before His appearing," has in his own way done a service.

Strauss on his part escaped with relief from the musty atmosphere of the study—beloved by theology in carpet-slippers—to the bracing air of Hengstenberg's *Kirchenzeitung*. In his "Replies" he devotes to it some fifty-four pages. "I must admit," he says, "that it is a satisfaction to me to have to do with the *Evangelische Kirchenzeitung*. In dealing with it one knows where one is and what one has to expect. If Herr Hengstenberg condemns, he knows why he condemns, and even one against whom he launches his anathema must admit that the attitude becomes him. Any one who, like the editor of the *Evangelische Kirchenzeitung*, has taken upon him the yoke of confessional doctrine with all its implications, has paid a price which entitles him to the privilege of condemning those who differ from his opinions."[60]

Hengstenberg's only complaint against Strauss is that he does not go far enough. He would have liked to force upon him the rôle of the Wolfenbüttel Fragmentist, and considers that if Strauss did not, like the latter, go so far as to suppose the apostles guilty of deliberate deceit, that is not so much from any regard for the historical kernel of Christianity as in order to mask his attack.

Even in Catholic theology Strauss's work caused a great sensation. Catholic theology in general did not at that time take up an attitude of absolute isolation from Protestant scholarship; [pg 108] it had adopted from the latter numerous rationalistic ideas, and had been especially influenced by Schleiermacher. Thus, Catholic scholars were almost prepared to regard Strauss as a common enemy, against whom it was possible to make common cause with Protestants. In 1837 Joseph Mack, one of the Professors of the Catholic faculty at Tübingen, published his "Report on Herr Dr. Strauss's Historical Study of the Life of Jesus."[61] In 1839 appeared "Dr. Strauss's Life of Jesus, considered from the Catholic point of view,"[62] by Dr. Maurus Hagel, Professor of Theology at the Lyceum at Dillingen; in 1840 that lover of hypotheses and doughty fighter, Johann Leonhard Hug,[63] presented his report upon the work.[64]

Even French Catholicism gave some attention to Strauss's work. This marks an epoch—the introduction of the knowledge of German critical theology into the intellectual world of the Latin nations. In the *Revue des deux mondes* for December 1838, Edgar Quinet gave a clear and accurate account of the influence of the Hegelian philosophy upon the religious ideas of cultured Germany.[65] In an eloquent peroration he lays bare the danger which was menacing the Church from the nation of Strauss and Hegel. His countrymen need not think that it could be charmed away by some ingenious formula; a mighty effort of the Catholic spirit was necessary, if it was to be successfully opposed. "A new barbarian invasion was rolling up against sacred Rome. The barbarians were streaming from every quarter of the horizon, bringing their strange gods with them and preparing to beleaguer the holy city. As, of yore, Leo went forth to meet Attila, so now let the Papacy put on its purple and come forth, while yet there is time, to wave back with an authoritative gesture the devastating hordes into that moral wilderness which is their native home."

Quinet might have done better still if he had advised the Pope to issue, as a counterblast to the unbelieving critical work of [pg 109] Strauss, the Life of Jesus which had been *revealed* to the faith of the blessed Anna Katharina Emmerich.[66] How thoroughly this refuted Strauss can be seen from the fragment issued in 1834, "The Bitter Sufferings of Our Lord Jesus Christ," where even the age of Jesus on the day of His death is exactly given. On that Maundy Thursday the 13th Nisan, it was exactly thirty-three years and eighteen weeks less one day. The "pilgrim" Clement Brentano would certainly have consented, had he been asked, to allow his note-books to be used in the sacred cause, and to have given to the world the Life of Jesus as it was revealed to him by this visionary from the end of July 1820 day by day for three years, instead of allowing this treasure to remain hidden for more than twenty years longer. He himself ascribed to these visions the most strictly historical character, and insisted on considering them not merely as reflections on what had happened, but as the immediate reflex of the facts themselves, so that the picture of the life of Jesus is given in them as in a mirror. Hug, it may be mentioned, in his lectures, called attention to the exact agreement of the topography of the passion story in Katharina's vision with the description of the locality in Josephus. If he had known her complete Life of Jesus he would doubtless have expressed his admiration for the way in which she harmonises John and the Synoptists; and with justice, for the harmony is really ingenious and skilfully planned.

Apart from these merits, too, this Life of Jesus, written, it should be observed, earlier than Strauss's, contains a wealth of interesting information. John at first baptized at Aenon, but later was directed to remove to Jericho. The baptisms took place in "baptismal springs."

Peter owned three boats, of which one was fitted up especially [pg 110] for the use of Jesus, and carried a complement of ten persons. Forward and aft there were covered-in spaces where all kinds of gear could be kept, and where also they could wash their feet; along the sides of the boat were hung receptacles for the fish.

When Judas Iscariot became a disciple of Jesus he was twenty-five years old. He had black hair and a red beard, but could not be called really ugly. He had had a stormy past. His mother had been a dancing-woman, and Judas had been born out of wedlock, his father being a military tribune in Damascus. As an infant he had been exposed, but had been saved, and later had been taken charge of by his uncle, a tanner at Iscariot. At the time when he joined the company of Jesus' disciples he had squandered all his possessions. The disciples at first liked him well enough because of his readiness to make himself useful; he even cleaned the shoes.

The fish with the *stater* in its mouth was so large that it made a full meal for the whole company.

A work to which Jesus devoted special attention—though this is not mentioned in the Gospels—was the reconciliation of unhappy married couples. Another matter which is not mentioned in the Gospels is the voyage of Jesus to Cyprus, upon which He entered after a farewell meal with His disciples at the house of the Canaanitish woman. This voyage took place during the war between Herod and Aretas while the disciples were making their missionary journey in Palestine. As they could not give an eyewitness report of it they were silent; nor did they make any mention of the feast to which the Proconsul at Salamis invited the Saviour. In regard to another journey, also, which Jesus made to the land of the wise men of the East, the "pilgrim's" oracle has the advantage of knowing more than the Evangelists.

In spite of these additional traits a certain monotony is caused by the fact that the visionary, in order to fill in the tale of days in the three years, makes the persons known to us from the Gospel history meet with the Saviour on several occasions previous to the meeting narrated in the Gospels. Here the artificial character of the composition comes out too clearly, though in general a lively imagination tends to conceal this. And yet these naïve embellishments and inventions have something rather attractive about them; one cannot handle the book without a certain reverence when one thinks amid what pains these revelations were received. If Brentano had published his notes at the time of the excitement produced by Strauss's Life of Jesus, the work would have had a tremendous success. As it was, when the first two volumes appeared at the end of the 'fifties, there were sold in one year three thousand and several hundred copies, without reckoning the French edition which appeared contemporaneously.

[pg 111]

In the end, however, all the efforts of the mediating theology, of rationalism and supernaturalism, could do nothing to shake Strauss's conclusion that it was all over with supernaturalism as a factor to be reckoned with in the historical study of the Life of Jesus, and that scientific theology, instead of turning back from rationalism to supernaturalism, must move straight onward between the two and seek out a new path for itself. The Hegelian method had proved itself to be the logic of reality. With Strauss begins the period of the non-miraculous view of the Life of Jesus; all other views exhausted themselves in the struggle against him, and subsequently abandoned position after position without waiting to be attacked. The separation which Hengstenberg had hailed with such rejoicing was really accomplished; but in the form that supernaturalism practically separated itself from the serious study of history. It is not possible to date the stages of this process. After the first outburst of excitement everything seems to go on as quietly as before; the only difference is that the question of miracle constantly falls more and more into the background. In the modern period of the study of the Life of Jesus, which begins about the middle of the 'sixties, it has lost all importance.

That does not mean that the problem of miracle is solved. From the historical point of view it is really impossible to solve it, since we are not able to reconstruct the process by which a series of miracle stories arose, or a series of historical occurrences were transformed into miracle stories, and these narratives must simply be left with a question mark standing against them. What has been gained is only that the exclusion of miracle from our view of history has been universally recognised as a principle of criticism, so that miracle no longer concerns the historian either positively or negatively. Scientific theologians of the present day who desire to show their "sensibility," ask no more than that two or three little miracles may be left to them—in the stories of the childhood, perhaps, or in the narratives of the resurrection. And these miracles are, moreover, so far scientific that they have at least no relation to those in the text, but are merely spiritless, miserable little toy-dogs of criticism, flea-bitten by rationalism, too insignificant to do historical science any harm, especially as their owners honestly pay the tax upon them by the way in which they speak, write, and are silent about Strauss.

But even that is better than the delusive fashion in which some writers of the present day succeed in discussing the narratives of the resurrection "as pure historians" without betraying by a single word whether they themselves believe it to be possible or not. But the reason modern theology can allow itself these liberties is that the foundation laid by Strauss is unshakable.

Compared with the problem of miracle, the question regarding [pg 112] the mythical explanation of the history takes a very subordinate place in the controversy. Few understood what Strauss's real meaning was; the general impression was that he entirely dissolved the life of Jesus into myth.

There appeared, indeed, three satires ridiculing his method. One showed how, for the historical science of the future, the life of Luther would also become a mere myth,[67] the second treated the life of Napoleon in the same way;[68] in the third, Strauss himself becomes a myth.[69]

M. Eugène Mussard, "candidat au saint ministère," made it his business to set at rest the minds of the premier faculty at Geneva by his thesis, *Du système mythique appliqué à l'histoire de la vie de Jésus*, 1838, which bears the ingenious motto οὐ σεσοφισμένοις μύθοις (not ... in cunningly devised myths, 2 Peter i. 16). He certainly did not exaggerate the difficulties of his task, but complacently followed up an "Exposition of the Mythical Theory," with a "Refutation of the Mythical Theory as applied to the Life of Jesus."

The only writer who really faced the problem in the form in which it had been raised by Strauss was Wilke in his work "Tradition and Myth."[70] He recognises that Strauss had given an exceedingly valuable impulse towards the overcoming of rationalism and supernaturalism and to the rejection of the abortive [pg 113] mediating theology. "A keener criticism will only establish the truth of the Gospel, putting what is tenable on a firmer basis, sifting out what is untenable, and showing up in all its nakedness the counterfeit theology of the new evangelicalism with its utter lack of understanding and sincerity." Again, "the approval which Strauss has met with, and the excitement which he has aroused, sufficiently show what an advantage rationalistic speculation possesses over the theological second-childishness of the new evangelicals." The time has come for a rational mysticism, which shall preserve undiminished the honesty of the old rationalism, making no concessions to supernaturalism, but, on the other hand, overcoming the "truculent rationalism of the Kantian criticism" by means of a religious conception in which there is more warmth and more pious feeling.

This rational mysticism makes it a reproach against the "mythical idealism" of Strauss that in it philosophy does violence to history, and the historic Christ only retains His significance as a mere ideal. A new examination of the sources is necessary to decide upon the extent of the mythical element.

The Gospel of Matthew cannot, Wilke agrees, have been the work of an eyewitness. "The principal argument against its authenticity is the absence of the characteristic marks of an eyewitness, which must necessarily have been present in a gospel actually composed by a disciple of the Lord, and which are not present here. The narrative is lacking in precision, fragmentary and legendary, tradition everywhere manifest in its very form." There are discrepancies in the legends of the first and second chapters, as well as elsewhere, *e.g.* the stories of the baptism, the temptation, and the transfiguration. In other cases, where there is a basis of historic fact, there is an admixture of legendary material, as in the narratives of the death and resurrection of Jesus.

In the Gospel of Mark, Wilke recognises the pictorial vividness of many of the descriptions, and conjectures that in some way or other it goes back to the Petrine tradition. The author of the Fourth Gospel is not an eyewitness; the κατά (according to) only indicates the origin of the tradition; the author received it, either directly or indirectly, from the Apostle, but he gave to it the gnosticising dialectical form of the Alexandrian theology.

As against the *Diegesentheorie*[71] Wilke defends the independence and originality of the individual Gospels. "No one of the Evangelists knew the writing of any of the others, each produced an independent work drawn from a separate source."

In the remarks on points of detail in this work of Wilke's there is evidence of a remarkable grasp of the critical data; we already get a hint of the "mathematician" of the Synoptic problem, [pg

114] who, two years later, was to work out convincingly the literary argument for the priority of Mark. But the historian is quite subordinated to the literary critic, and, when all is said, Wilke takes up no clearly defined position in regard to Strauss's main problem, as is evident from his seeking to retain, on more or less plausible grounds, a whole series of miracles, among them the miracle of Cana and the resurrection.

For most thinkers of that period, however, the question "myth or history" yielded in interest to the philosophical question of the relation of the historical Jesus to the ideal Christ. That was the second problem raised by Strauss. Some thought to refute him by showing that his exposition of the relation of the Jesus of history to the ideal Christ was not justified even from the point of view of the Hegelian philosophy, arguing that the edifice which he had raised was not in harmony with the ground-plan of the Hegelian speculative system. He therefore felt it necessary, in his reply to the review in the *Jahrbücher für wissenschaftliche Kritik*, to expound "the general relationship of the Hegelian philosophy to theological criticism,"[72] and to express in more precise form the thoughts upon speculative and historical Christology which he had suggested at the close of the second volume of his "Life of Jesus."

He admits that Hegel's philosophy is ambiguous in this matter, since it is not clear "whether the evangelical fact as such, not indeed in its isolation, but together with the whole series of manifestations of the idea (of God-manhood) in the history of the world, is the truth; or whether the embodiment of the idea in that single fact is only a formula of which consciousness makes use in forming its concept." The Hegelian "right," he says, represented by Marheineke and Göschel, emphasises the positive side of the master's religious philosophy, implying that in Jesus the idea of God-manhood was perfectly fulfilled and in a certain sense intelligibly realised. "If these men," Strauss explains, "appeal to Hegel and declare that he would not have recognised my book as an expression of his meaning, they say nothing which is not in accordance with my own convictions. Hegel was personally no friend to historical criticism. It annoyed him, as it annoyed Goethe, to see the historic figures of antiquity, on which their thoughts were accustomed lovingly to dwell, assailed by critical doubts. Even if it was in some cases wreaths of mist which they took for pinnacles of rock, they did not want to have this forced upon their attention, nor to [pg 115] be disturbed in the illusion from which they were conscious of receiving an elevating influence."

But though prepared to admit that he had added to the edifice of Hegel's religious philosophy an annexe of historical criticism, of which the master would hardly have approved, Strauss is convinced that he is the only logical representative of Hegel's essential view. "The question which can be decided from the standpoint of the philosophy of religion is not whether what is narrated in the Gospels actually happened or not, but whether in view of the truth of certain conceptions it must necessarily have happened. And in regard to this, what I assert is that from the general system of the Hegelian philosophy it by no means necessarily follows that such an event must have happened, but that from the standpoint of the system the truth of that history from which actually the conception arose is reduced to a matter of indifference; it may have happened, but it may just as well not have happened, and the task of deciding on this point may be calmly handed over to historical criticism."

Strauss reminds us that, even according to Hegel, the belief in Jesus as God-made-man is not immediately given with His appearing in the world of sense, but only arose after His death and the removal of His sensible presence. The master himself had acknowledged the existence of mythical elements in the Life of Jesus; in regard to miracle he had expressed the opinion that the true miracle was "Spirit." The conception of the resurrection and ascension as outward facts of sense was not recognised by him as true.

Hegel's authority may, no doubt, fairly be appealed to by those who believe, not only in an incarnation of God in a general sense, "but also that this manifestation of God in flesh has taken place in this man (Jesus) at this definite time and place."... "In making the assertion," concludes Strauss, "that the truth of the Gospel narrative cannot be proved, whether in whole or in part, from philosophical considerations, but that the task of inquiring into its truth must be left to historical criticism, I should like to associate myself with the 'left wing' of the Hegelian school, were it not that the Hegelians prefer to exclude me altogether from their borders, and to throw me into the arms of other systems of thought—only, it must be admitted, to have me tossed back to them like a ball."

In regard to the third problem which Strauss had offered for discussion, the relation of the Synoptists to John, there was practically no response. The only one of his critics who understood what was at stake was Hengstenberg. He alone perceived the significance of the fact that critical theology, having admitted mythical elements first in the Old Testament, and then in the beginning and [pg 116] end of the Gospel history, and having, in consequence of the latter admission, felt obliged to give up the first three Gospels, retaining only the fourth, was now being besieged by Strauss in its last stronghold. "They withdrew," says the *Evangelische Kirchenzeitung*, "into the Gospel of John as into a fortress, and boasted that they were safe there, though they could not suppress a secret consciousness that they only held it at the enemy's pleasure; now the enemy has appeared before it; he is using the same weapons with which he was formerly victorious; the Gospel of John is in as desperate case as formerly the Synoptists. The time has come to make a bold resolve, a decisive choice; either they must give up everything, or else they must successively re-occupy the more advanced positions which at an earlier date they had successively abandoned." It would be impossible to give a more accurate picture of the desperate position into which Hase and Schleiermacher had brought the mediating theology by their ingenious expedient of giving up the Synoptics in favour of the Gospel of John. Before any danger threatened, they had abandoned the outworks and withdrawn into the citadel, oblivious of the fact that they thereby exposed themselves to the danger of having their own guns turned upon them from the positions they had abandoned, and being obliged to surrender without striking a blow the position of which they had boasted as impregnable. It is impossible to emphasise strongly enough the fact that it was not Strauss, but Hase and Schleiermacher, who had brought the mediating theology into this hopeless position, in which the fall of the Fourth Gospel carried with it the surrender of the historical tradition as a whole.

But there is no position so desperate that theology cannot find a way out of it. The mediating theologians simply ignored the problem which Strauss had raised. As they had been accustomed to do before, so they continued to do after, taking the Gospel of John as the authentic framework, and fitting into it the sections of the Synoptic narrative wherever place could best be found for them. The difference between the Johannine and Synoptic representations of Jesus' method of teaching, says Neander, is only apparently irreconcilable, and he calls out in support of this assertion all the reserves of old worn-out expedients and artifices, among others the argument that the Pauline Christology is only explicable as a combination of the Synoptic and Johannine views. Other writers who belong to the same apologetic school, such as Tholuck,

Ebrard,[73] [pg 117] Wieseler,[74] Lange,[75] and Ewald,[76] maintain the same point of view, only that their defence is usually much less skilful.

The only writer who really in some measure enters into the difficulties is Ammon. He, indeed, is fully conscious of the difference, and thinks we cannot rest content with merely recognising it, but must find a solution, even if rather a forced one, "by subordinating the indefinite chronological data of the Synoptists, of whom, after all, only one was, or could have been, an eyewitness, to the ordered narrative of John." The fourth Evangelist makes so brief a reference to the Galilaean period because it was in accordance with his plan to give more prominence to the discourses of Jesus in the Temple and His dialogues with the Scribes as compared to the parables and teaching given to the people. The cleansing of the Temple falls at the outset of Jesus' ministry; Jesus begins His Messianic work in Jerusalem by this action of making an end of the unseemly chaffering in the court of the Temple. The question regarding the relative authenticity of the reports is decisively settled by a comparison of the two accounts of [pg 118] the triumphal entry, because there it is quite evident that "Matthew, the chief authority among the Synoptists, adapts his narrative to his special Jewish-Messianic standpoint." According to Ammon's rationalistic view, the work of Jesus consisted precisely in the transformation of this Jewish-Messianic idea into the conception of a "Saviour of the world." In this lies the explanation of the fate of Jesus: "The mass of the Jewish people were not prepared to receive a Christ so spiritual as Jesus was, since they were not ripe for so lofty a view of religion."

Ammon here turns his Kantian philosophy to account. It serves especially to explain to him the consciousness of pre-existence avowed by the Jesus of the Johannine narrative as something purely human. We, too, he explains, can "after the spirit" claim an ideal existence prior to the spatial creation without indulging any delusion, and without, on the other hand, thinking of a real existence. In this way Jesus is for Himself a Biblical idea, with which He has become identified. "The purer and deeper a man's self-consciousness is, the keener may his consciousness of God become, until time disappears for him, and his partaking in the Divine nature fills his whole soul."

But Ammon's support of the authenticity of John's Gospel is, even from a purely literary point of view, not so unreserved as in the case of the other opponents of Strauss. In the background stands the hypothesis that our Gospel is only a working-over of the authentic John, a suggestion in regard to which Ammon can claim priority, since he had made it as early as 1811,[77] nine years before the appearance of Bretschneider's *Probabilia*. Were it not for the ingenuous fashion in which he works the Synoptic material into the Johannine plan, we might class him with Alexander Schweizer and Weisse, who in a similar way seek to meet the objections of Strauss by an elaborate theory of editing.[78]

The first stage of the discussion regarding the relation of John to the Synoptists passed without result. The mediating theology continued to hold its positions undisturbed—and, strangest of all, Strauss himself was eager for a suspension of hostilities.

It is as though history took the trouble to countersign the [pg 119] genuineness of the great critical discoveries by letting the discoverers themselves attempt to cancel them. As Kant disfigures his critical idealism by making inconsistent additions in order to refute a reviewer who had put him in the same category with Berkeley, so Strauss inserts additions and retractations in the third edition of his Life of Jesus in deference to the uncritical works of Tholuck and Neander!

Wilke, the only one of his critics from whom he might have learned something, he ignores. "From the lofty vantage ground of Tholuck's many-sided knowledge I have sometimes, in spite of a slight tendency to vertigo, gained a juster point of view from which to look at one matter or another," is the avowal which he makes in the preface to this ill-starred edition.

It would, indeed, have done no harm if he had confined himself to stating more exactly here and there the extent of the mythical element, had increased the number of possible cures, had inclined a little less to the negative side in examining the claims of reported facts to rank as historical, and had been a little more circumspect in pointing out the factors which produced the myths; the serious thing was that he now began to hesitate in his denial of the historical character of the Fourth Gospel—the very foundation of his critical view.

A renewed study of it, aided by De Wette's commentary and Neander's Life of Jesus, had made him "doubtful about his doubts regarding the genuineness and credibility of this Gospel." "Not that I am convinced of its genuineness," he admits, "but I am no longer convinced that it is not genuine."

He feels bound, therefore, to state whatever makes in its favour, and to leave open a number of possibilities which formerly he had not recognised. The adhesion of the first disciples may, he now thinks, have happened essentially in the form in which it is reported in the Fourth Gospel; in transferring the cleansing of the Temple to the first period of Jesus' ministry, John may be right as against the Synoptic tradition "which has no decisive evidence in its favour"; in regard to the question whether Jesus had been only once, or several times, in Jerusalem, his opinion now is that "on this point the superior circumstantiality of the Fourth Gospel cannot be contested."

As regards the prominence allowed to the eschatology also all is toned down and softened. Everywhere feeble compromises! But what led Strauss to place his foot upon this shelving path was the essentially just perception that the Synoptists gave him no clearly ordered plan to set against that of the Fourth Gospel; consequently he felt obliged to make some concessions to its strength in this respect.

Yet he recognised almost immediately that the result was a mere patchwork. Even in the summer of 1839 he complained [pg 120] to Hase in conversation that he had been deafened by the clamour of his opponents, and had conceded too much to them.[79] In the fourth edition he retracted all his concessions. "The Babel of voices of opponents, critics, and supporters," he says in his preface, "to which I had felt it my duty to listen, had confused me in regard to the idea of my work; in my diligent comparison of various views I had lost sight of the thing itself. In this way I was led to make alterations which, when I came to consider the matter calmly, surprised myself; and in making which it was obvious that I had done myself an injustice. In all these passages the earlier text has been restored, and my work has therefore consisted, it might be said, in removing from my good sword the notches which had not so much been hewn in it by the enemy as ground into it by myself."

Strauss's vacillation had, therefore, not even been of any indirect advantage to him. Instead of endeavouring to find a purposeful connexion in the Synoptic Gospels by means of which he might test the plan of the Fourth Gospel, he simply restores his former view unaltered, thereby showing that in the decisive point it was incapable of development. In the very year in which he prepared his improved edition, Weisse, in his *Evangelische Geschichte*, had set up the hypothesis that Mark is the ground-document, and had thus carried criticism past the "dead-point" which Strauss had never been able to overcome. Upon Strauss, however, the new suggestion made no impression. He does, it is true, mention Weisse's book in the preface to his third edition, and describes it as "in many respects a very satisfactory piece of work." It had appeared too late for him to make use of it in his first volume; but he did not use it in his second volume either. He had, indeed, a distinct antipathy to the Marcan hypothesis.

It was unfortunate that in this controversy the highly important suggestions in regard to various historical problems which had been made incidentally in the course of Strauss's work were never discussed at all. The impulse in the direction of progress which might have been given by his treatment of the relation of Jesus to the law, of the question regarding His particularism, of the eschatological conception, the Son of Man, and the Messiahship of Jesus, wholly failed to take effect, and it was only after long and circuitous wanderings that theology again came in sight of these problems from an equally favourable point of view. In this respect Strauss shared the fate of Reimarus; the positive solutions of which the outlines were visible behind their negative criticism escaped observation in consequence of the offence caused by the negative side of their work; and even the authors themselves failed to realise their full significance.
[pg 121]

X. The Marcan Hypothesis

Christian Hermann Weisse. Die evangelische Geschichte kritisch und philosophisch bearbeitet. (A Critical and Philosophical Study of the Gospel History.) 2 vols. Leipzig, Breitkopf and Härtel, 1838. Vol. i. 614 pp. Vol. ii. 543 pp.

Christian Gottlob Wilke. Der Urevangelist. (The Earliest Evangelist.) 1838. Dresden and Leipzig. 694 pp.

Christian Hermann Weisse. Die Evangelienfrage in ihrem gegenwärtigen Stadium. (The Present Position of the Problem of the Gospels.) Leipzig, 1856.

The "Gospel History" of Weisse was written, like Strauss's Life of Jesus, by a philosopher who had been driven out of philosophy and forced back upon theology. Weisse was born in 1801 at Leipzig, and became Professor Extraordinary of Philosophy in the university there in 1828. In 1837, finding his advance to the Ordinary Professorship barred by the Herbartians, he withdrew from academic teaching and gave himself to the preparation of this work, the plan of which he had had in mind for some time. Having brought it to a satisfactory completion, he began again in 1841 as a Privat-Docent in Philosophy, and became Ordinary Professor in 1845. From 1848 onwards he lectured on Theology also. His work on "Philosophical Dogmatics, or the Philosophy of Christianity,"[80] is well known. He died in 1866, of cholera. Lotze and Lipsius were both much influenced by him.

Weisse admired Strauss and hailed his Life of Jesus as a forward step towards the reconciliation of religion and philosophy. He expresses his gratitude to him for clearing the ground of the primeval forest of theology, thus rendering it possible for him (Weisse) to develop his views without wasting time upon polemics, "since most of the views which have hitherto prevailed may be regarded as having received the *coup de grâce* from Strauss." He is at one with Strauss also in his general view of the relations of philosophy and religion, holding that it is only if philosophy, by following its own path, attains independently to the conviction of the truth of Christianity that its alliance with theology and religion [pg 122] can be welcomed as advantageous.[81] His work, therefore, like that of Strauss, leads up finally to a philosophical exposition in which he shows how for us the Jesus of history becomes the Christ of faith.[82]

Weisse is the direct continuator of Strauss. Standing outside the limitations of the Hegelian formulae, he begins at the point where Strauss leaves off. His aim is to discover, if possible, some thread of general connexion in the narratives of the Gospel tradition, which, if present, would represent a historically certain element in the Life of Jesus, and thus serve as a better standard by which to determine the extent of myth than can possibly be found in the subjective impression upon which Strauss relies. Strauss, by way of gratitude, called him a dilettante. This was most unjust, for if any one deserved to share Strauss's place of honour, it was certainly Weisse.

The idea that Mark's Gospel might be the earliest of the four, first occurred to Weisse during the progress of his work. In March 1837, when he reviewed Tholuck's "Credibility of the Gospel

History," he was as innocent of this discovery as Wilke was at the same period. But when once he had observed that the graphic details of Mark, which had hitherto been regarded as due to an attempt to embellish an epitomising narrative, were too insignificant to have been inserted with this purpose, it became clear to him that only one other possibility remained open, viz., that their absence in Matthew and Luke was due to omission. He illustrates this from the description of the first day of Jesus' ministry at Capernaum. "The relation of the first Evangelist to Mark," he avers, "in those portions of the Gospel which are common to both is, with few exceptions, mainly that of an epitomiser."

The decisive argument for the priority of Mark is, even more than his graphic detail, the composition and arrangement of the whole. "It is true, the Gospel of Mark shows very distinct traces of having arisen out of spoken discourses, which themselves were by no means ordered and connected, but disconnected and fragmentary"—being, he means, in its original form based on notes of the incidents related by Peter. "It is not the work of an eyewitness, nor even of one who had had an opportunity of questioning eyewitnesses thoroughly and carefully; nor even of deriving assistance from inquirers who, on their part, had made a connected [pg 123] study of the subject, with a view to filling up the gaps and placing each individual part in its right position, and so articulating the whole into an organic unity which should be neither merely inward, nor on the other hand merely external." Nevertheless the Evangelist was guided in his work by a just recollection of the general course of the life of Jesus. "It is precisely in Mark," Weisse explains, "that a closer study unmistakably reveals that the incidental remarks (referring for the most part to the way in which the fame of Jesus gradually extended, the way the people began to gather round Him and the sick to besiege Him), far from shutting off and separating the different narratives, tend rather to unite them with each other, and so give the impression not of a series of anecdotes fortuitously thrown together, but of a connected history. By means of these remarks, and by many other connecting links which he works into the narration of the individual stories, Mark has succeeded in conveying a vivid impression of the stir which Jesus made in Galilee, and from Galilee to Jerusalem, of the gradual gathering of the multitudes to Him, of the growing intensity of loyalty in the inner circle of disciples, and as the counterpart of all this, of the growing enmity of the Pharisees and Scribes—an impression which mere isolated narratives, strung together without any living connexion, would not have sufficed to produce." A connexion of this kind is less clearly present in the other Synoptists, and is wholly lacking in John. The Fourth Gospel, by itself, would give us a completely false conception of the relation of Jesus to the people. From the content of its narratives the reader would form the impression that the attitude of the people towards Jesus was hostile from the very first, and that it was only in isolated occasions, for a brief moment, that Jesus by His miraculous acts inspired the people with astonishment rather than admiration; that, surrounded by a little company of disciples he contrived for a time to defy the enmity of the multitude, and that, having repeatedly provoked it by intemperate invective, he finally succumbed to it.

The simplicity of the plan of Mark is, in Weisse's opinion, a stronger argument for his priority than the most elaborate demonstration; one only needs to compare it with the perverse design of Luke, who makes Jesus undertake a journey through Samaria. "How," asks Weisse, "in the case of a writer who does things of this kind can it be possible at this time of day to speak seriously of historical exactitude in the use of his sources?"

To come down to detail, Weisse's argument for the priority of Mark rests mainly on the following propositions:—

1. In the first and third Gospels, traces of a common plan are found only in those parts which they have in common [pg 124] with Mark, not in those which are common to them, but not to Mark also.

2. In those parts which the three Gospels have in common, the "agreement" of the other two is mediated through Mark.

3. In those sections which the First and Third Gospels have, but Mark has not, the agreement consists in the language and incidents, not in the order. Their common source, therefore, the "Logia" of Matthew, did not contain any type of tradition which gave an order of narration different from that of Mark.

4. The divergences of wording between the two other Synoptists is in general greater in the parts where both have drawn on the Logia document than where Mark is their source.

5. The first Evangelist reproduces this Logia-document more faithfully than Luke does; but his Gospel seems to have been of later origin.

This historical argument for the priority of Mark was confirmed in the year in which it appeared by Wilke's work, "The Earliest Gospel,"[83] which treated the problem more from the literary side, and, to take an illustration from astronomy, supplied the mathematical confirmation of the hypothesis.

[pg 125]

In regard to the Gospel of John, Weisse fully shared the negative views of Strauss. What is the use, he asks, of keeping on talking about the plan of this Gospel, seeing that no one has yet succeeded in showing what that plan is? And for a very good reason: there is none. One would never guess from the Gospel of John that Jesus, until His departure from Galilee, had experienced almost unbroken success. It is no good trying to explain the want of plan by saying that John wrote with the purpose of supplementing and correcting his predecessors, and that his omissions and additions were determined by this purpose. Such a purpose is betrayed by no single word in the whole Gospel.

The want of plan lies in the very plan itself. "It is a fixed idea, one may say, with the author of this Gospel, who had heard that Jesus had fallen a victim in Jerusalem to the hatred of the Jewish rulers, especially the Scribes, that he must represent Jesus as engaged, from His first appearance onward, in an unceasing struggle with 'the Jews'—whereas we know that the mass of the people, even to the last, in Jerusalem itself, were on the side of Jesus; so much so, indeed, that His enemies were only able to get Him into their power by means of a secret betrayal."

In regard to the graphic descriptions in John, of which so much has been made, the case is no better. It is the graphic detail of a writer who desires to work up a vivid picture, not the natural touches of an eyewitness, and there are, moreover, actual inconsistencies, as in the case of the healing at the pool of Bethesda. The circumstantiality is due to the care of the author not to assume an acquaintance, on the part of his readers, with Jewish usages or the topography of Palestine. "A considerable proportion of the details are of such a character as inevitably to suggest that the narrator inserts them because of the trouble which it has cost him to orientate himself in regard to the scene of the action and the dramatis personae, his object being to spare his readers a similar difficulty; though he does not always go about it in the way best calculated to effect his purpose."

The impossibility also that the historic Jesus can have preached the doctrine of the Johannine Christ, is as clear to Weisse as to Strauss. "It is not so much a picture of Christ that John sets forth, as a conception of Christ; his Christ does not speak *in* His own Person, but *of* His own Person."

On the other hand, however, "the authority of the whole Christian Church from the second century to the nineteenth" carries too much weight with Weisse for him to venture altogether to deny the Johannine origin of the Gospel; and he seeks a [pg 126] middle path. He assumes that the didactic portions really, for the most part, go back to John the Apostle. "John," he explains, "drawn on by the interest of a system of doctrine which had formed itself in his mind, not so much as a direct reflex of the teaching of his Master, as on the basis of suggestions offered by that teaching in combination with a certain creative activity of his own, endeavoured to find this system also in the teaching of his Master."

Accordingly, with this purpose, and originally for himself alone, not with the object of communicating it to others, he made an effort to exhibit, in the light of this system of thought, what his memory still retained of the discourses of the Lord. "The Johannine discourses, therefore, were recalled by a laborious effort of memory on the part of the disciple. When he found that his memory-image of his Master was threatening to dissolve into a mist-wraith, he endeavoured to impress the picture more firmly in his recollection, to connect and define its rapidly disappearing features, reconstructing it by the aid of a theory evolved by himself or drawn from elsewhere regarding the Person and work of the Master." For the portrait of Christ in the Synoptic Gospels the mind of the disciples who describe Him is a neutral medium; for the portrait in John it is a factor which contributes to the production of the picture. The same portrait is outlined by the apostle in the first epistle which bears his name.

These tentative "essays," not originally intended for publication, came, after the death of the apostle, into the hands of his adherents and disciples, and they chose the form of a complete Life of Jesus as that in which to give them to the world. They, therefore, added narrative portions, which they distributed here and there among the speeches, often doing some violence to the latter in the process. Such was the origin of the Fourth Gospel.

Weisse is not blind to the fact that this hypothesis of a Johannine basis in the Gospel is beset with the gravest—one might almost say with insuperable—difficulties. Here is a man who was an immediate disciple of the Lord, one who, in the Synoptic Gospels, in Acts, and in the Pauline letters, appears in a character which gives no hint of a coming spiritual metamorphosis, one, moreover, who at a relatively late period, when it might well have been supposed that his development was in all essentials closed (at the time of Paul's visit to Jerusalem, which falls at least fourteen years after Paul's conversion), was chosen, along with James and Peter, and in contrast with the apostles of the Gentiles, Paul and Barnabas, as an apostle of the Jews—"how is it possible," asks Weisse, "to explain and make it intelligible, that a man of these antecedents displays in his thought and speech, in fact in his whole mental attitude, a thoroughly Hellenistic stamp? How came he, the beloved disciple, who, according to this very Gospel which [pg 127] bears his name, was admitted more intimately than any other into the confidence of Jesus, how came he to clothe his Master in this foreign garb of Hellenistic speculation, and to attribute to Him this alien manner of speech? But, however difficult the explanation may be, whatever extreme of improbability may seem to us to be involved in the assumption of the Johannine authorship of the Epistle and of these essential elements of the Gospel, it is better to assent to the improbability, to submit to the burden of being forced to explain the inexplicable, than to set ourselves obstinately against the weight of testimony, against the authority of the whole Christian Church from the second century to the present day."

There could be no better argument against the genuineness of the Fourth Gospel than just such a defence of its genuineness as this. In this form the hypothesis may well be destined to lead a harmless and never-ending life. What matters for the historical study of the Life of Jesus is simply that the Fourth Gospel should be ruled out. And that Weisse does so thoroughly that it is impossible to imagine its being done more thoroughly. The speeches, in spite of their apostolic authority, are unhistorical, and need not be taken into account in describing Jesus' system of thought. As for the unhappy redactor, who by adding the narrative pictures created the Gospel, all possibility of his reports being accurate is roundly denied, and as if that was not enough, he must put up with being called a bungler into the bargain. "I have, to tell the truth, no very high opinion of the literary art of the editor of the Johannine Gospel-document," says Weisse in his "Problem of the Gospels" of 1856, which is the best commentary upon his earlier work.

His treatment of the Fourth Gospel reminds us of the story that Frederic the Great once appointed an importunate office-seeker to the post of "Privy Councillor for War," on condition that he would never presume to offer a syllable of advice!

The hypothesis which was brought forward about the same time by Alexander Schweizer,[84] with the intention of saving the genuineness of the Gospel of John, did not make any real contribution to the subject. The reading of the facts which form his starting-point is almost the exact converse of that of Weisse, since he regards, not the speeches, but certain parts of the narrative as Johannine. That which it is possible, in his opinion, to refer [pg 128] to the apostle is an account, not involving any miracles, of the ministry of Jesus at Jerusalem, and the discourses which He delivered there. The more or less miraculous events which occur in the course of it— such as, that Jesus had seen Nathanael under the fig-tree, knew the past life of the Samaritan woman, and healed the sick man at the Pool of Bethesda—are of a simple character, and contrast markedly with those which are represented to have occurred in Galilee, where Jesus turned water into wine and fed a multitude with a few crusts of bread. We must, therefore, suppose that this short, authentic, spiritual Jerusalem-Gospel has had a Galilaean Life of Jesus worked into it, and this explains the inconsistencies of the representation and the oscillation between a sensuous and a spiritual point of view.

This distinction, however, cannot be made good. Schweizer was obliged to ascribe the reports of a material resurrection to the Galilaean source, whereas these, since they exclude the Galilaean appearances of Jesus, must belong to the Jerusalem Gospel; and accordingly, the whole distinction between a spiritual and material Gospel falls to the ground. Thus this hypothesis at best preserves the nominal authenticity of the Fourth Gospel, only to deprive it immediately of all value as a historical source.

Had Strauss calmly examined the bearing of Weisse's hypothesis, he would have seen that it fully confirmed the line he had taken in leaving the Fourth Gospel out of account, and he might have been less unjust towards the hypothesis of the priority of Mark, for which he cherished a blind hatred, because, in its fully developed form, it first met him in conjunction with seemingly reactionary tendencies towards the rehabilitation of John. He never in the whole course of his life got rid of the prejudice that the recognition of the priority of Mark was identical with a retrograde movement towards an uncritical orthodoxy.

This is certainly not true as regards Weisse. He is far from having used Mark unreservedly as a historical source. On the contrary, he says expressly that the picture which this Gospel gives of Jesus is drawn by an imaginative disciple of the faith, filled with the glory of his subject, whose enthusiasm is consequently sometimes stronger than his judgment. Even in Mark the mythopoeic tendency is already actively at work, so that often the task of historical criticism is to explain how such myths could have been accepted by a reporter who stands as near the facts as Mark does.

Of the *miracula*[85]—so Weisse denominates the "non-genuine" miracles, in contradistinction to the "genuine"—the feeding of [pg 129] the multitude is that which, above all others, cries aloud for an explanation. Its historical strength lies in its being firmly interwoven with the preceding and following context; and this applies to both the Marcan narratives. It is therefore impossible to regard the story, as Strauss proposes to do, as pure myth; it is necessary to show how, growing out of some incident belonging to that context, it assumed its present literary form. The authentic saying about the leaven of the Pharisees, which, in Mark viii. 14 and 15, is connected with the two miracles of feeding the multitude, gives ground for supposing that they rest upon a parabolic discourse repeated on two occasions, in which Jesus spoke, perhaps with allusion to the manna, of a miraculous food given through Him. These discourses were later transformed by tradition into an actual miraculous giving of food. Here, therefore, Weisse endeavours to substitute for Strauss's "unhistorical" conception of myth a different conception, which in each case seeks to discover a sufficient historical cause.

The miracles at the baptism of Jesus are based upon His account of a vision which He experienced in that moment. The present form of the story of the transfiguration has a twofold origin. In the first place, it is partly based on a real experience shared by the three disciples. That there is an historical fact here is evident from the way in which it is connected with the context by a definite indication of time. The six days of Mark ix. 2 cannot really be connected, as Strauss would have us suppose, with Ex. xxiv. 16;[86] the meaning is simply that between the previously reported discourse of Jesus and the event described there was an interval of six days. The three disciples had a waking, spiritual vision, not a dream-vision, and what was revealed in this vision was the Messiahship of Jesus. But at this point comes in the second, the mythico-symbolical element. The disciples see Jesus accompanied, according to the Jewish Messianic expectations, by those whom the people thought of as His forerunners. He, however, turns away from them, and Moses and Elias, for whom the disciples were about to build tabernacles, for them to abide in, disappear. The mythical element is a reflection of the teaching which Jesus imparted to them on that occasion, in consequence of which there dawned on them the spiritual "significance of those expectations and predictions, which they were to recognise as no longer pointing forward to a future fulfilment, but as already fulfilled." The high mountain upon which, according to

Mark, the event took place is not to be understood in a literal sense, but as symbolical of the sublimity of the revelation; it is to be sought not on the map of Palestine, but in the recesses of the spirit.

[pg 130]

The most striking case of the formation of myth is the story of the resurrection. Here, too, myth must have attached itself to an historical fact. The fact in question is not, however, the empty grave. This only came into the story later, when the Jews, in order to counteract the Christian belief in the resurrection, had spread abroad the report that the body had been stolen from the grave. In consequence of this report the empty grave had necessarily to be taken up into the story, the Christian account now making use of the fact that the body of Jesus was not found as a proof of His bodily resurrection. The emphasis laid on the identity of the body which was buried with that which rose again, of which the Fourth Evangelist makes so much, belongs to a time when the Church had to oppose the Gnostic conception of a spiritual, incorporeal immortality. The reaction against Gnosticism is, as Weisse rightly remarks, one of the most potent factors in the development of myth in the Gospel history. As an additional instance of this he might have cited the anti-gnostic form of the Johannine account of the baptism of Jesus.

What, then, is the historical fact in the resurrection? "The historical fact," replies Weisse, "is only the existence of a belief—not the belief of the later Christian Church in the myth of the bodily resurrection of the Lord—but the personal belief of the Apostles and their companions in the miraculous presence of the risen Christ in the visions and appearances which they experienced." "The question whether those extraordinary phenomena which, soon after the death of the Lord, actually and undeniably took place within the community of His disciples, rest upon fact or illusion—that is, whether in them the departed spirit of the Lord, of whose presence the disciples supposed themselves to be conscious, was really present, or whether the phenomena were produced by natural causes of a different kind, spiritual and psychical, is a question which cannot be answered without going beyond the confines of purely historical criticism." The only thing which is certain is "that the resurrection of Jesus is a fact which belongs to the domain of the spiritual and psychic life, and which is not related to outward corporeal existence in such a way that the body which was laid in the grave could have shared therein." When the disciples of Jesus had their first vision of the glorified body of their Lord, they were far from Jerusalem, far from the grave, and had no thought of bringing that spiritual corporeity into any kind of relation with the dead body of the Crucified. That the earliest appearances took place in Galilee is indicated by the genuine conclusion of Mark, according to which the angel charges the women with the message that the disciples were to await Jesus in Galilee.

Strauss's conception of myth, which failed to give it any point [pg 131] of vital connexion with the history, had not provided any escape from the dilemma offered by the rationalistic and supernaturalistic views of the resurrection. Weisse prepared a new historical basis for a solution. He was the first to handle the problem from a point of view which combined historical with psychological considerations, and he is fully conscious of the novelty and the far-reaching consequences of his attempt. Theological science did not overtake him for sixty years; and though it did not for the most part share his one-sidedness in recognising only the Galilaean appearances, that does not count for much, since it was unable to solve the problem of the double tradition regarding the appearances. His discussion of the question is, both from the religious and from the historical point of view, the most satisfying treatment of it with which we are acquainted; the pompous and circumspect utterances of the very latest theology in regard to the "empty grave" look very poor in comparison. Weisse's psychology requires only one correction—the insertion into it of the eschatological premise.

It is not only the admixture of myth, but the whole character of the Marcan representation, which forbids us to use it without reserve as a source for the life of Jesus. The inventor of the Marcan hypothesis never wearies of repeating that even in the Second Gospel it is only the main outline of the Life of Jesus, not the way in which the various sections are joined together, which is historical. He does not, therefore, venture to write a Life of Jesus, but begins with a "General Sketch of the Gospel History" in which he gives the main outlines of the Life of Jesus according to Mark, and then proceeds to explain the incidents and discourses in each several Gospel in the order in which they occur.[87]

He avoids the professedly historical forced interpretation of detail, which later representatives of the Marcan hypothesis, Schenkel in particular, employ in such distressing fashion that Wrede's book, by making an end of this inquisitorial method of extracting the Evangelist's testimony, may be said to have released the Marcan hypothesis from the torture-chamber. Weisse is free from these over-refinements. He refuses to divide the Galilaean ministry of Jesus into a period of success and a period of failure and gradual falling off of adherents, divided by the controversy [pg 132] about legal purity in Mark vii.; he does not allow this episode to counterbalance the general evidence that Jesus' public work was accompanied by a constantly growing success. Nor does it occur to him to conceive the sojourn of the Lord in Phoenician territory, and His journey to the neighbourhood of Caesarea Philippi, as a compulsory withdrawal from Galilee, an abandonment of His cause in that district, and to head the chapter, as was usual in the second period of the exegesis of Mark, "Flights and Retirements." He is content simply to state that Jesus once visited those regions, and explicitly remarks that while the Synoptists speak of the Pharisees and Scribes as working actively against Him, there is nowhere any hint of a hostile movement on the part of the people, but that, on the contrary, in spite of the Scribes and Pharisees the people are always ready to approve Him and take His part; so much so that His enemies can only hope to get Him into their power by a secret betrayal.

Weisse does not admit any failure in Jesus' work, nor that death came upon Him from without as an inevitable necessity. He cannot, therefore, regard the thought of suffering as forced upon Jesus by outward events. Later interpreters of Mark have often held that the essential thing in the Lord's resolve to die was that by His voluntary acceptance of a fate which was more and more clearly revealing itself as inevitable, He raised it into the sphere of ethico-religious freedom: this was not Weisse's view. Jesus, according to him, was not moved by any outward circumstances when He set out for Jerusalem in order to die there. He did it in obedience to a supra-rational higher necessity. We can at most venture to conjecture that a cessation of His miracle-working power, of which He had become aware, revealed to Him that the hour appointed by God had come. He did, in fact, no further miracle in Jerusalem.

How far Isaiah liii. may have contributed to suggest the conception of such a death being a necessary part of Messiah's work, it is impossible to discover. In the popular expectation there was no thought of the Messiah as suffering. The thought was conceived by Jesus independently, through His deep and penetrating spiritual insight. Without any external suggestion whatever He announces to His disciples that He is to die at Jerusalem, and that He is going thither with that end in view. He journeyed, not to the Passover, but to His death. The fact that it took place at the time of the Feast was, so far as Jesus was concerned, accidental. The circumstances of His entry were such as to suggest anything rather than the fulfilment of His predictions; but though the jubilant multitude surrounded Him day by day, as with a wall of defence, He did not let that make Him falter in His purpose; rather He forced the authorities to arrest Him; He preserved silence [pg 133] before Pilate with the deliberate purpose of rendering His death inevitable. The theory of later defenders of the Marcan hypothesis that Jesus, giving up His cause in Galilee for lost, went up to Jerusalem to conquer or die, is foreign to Weisse's conception. In his view, Jesus, breaking off His Galilaean work while the tide of success was still flowing strongly, journeyed to Jerusalem, in the scorn of consequence, with the sole purpose of dying there.

It is true there are some premonitions of the later course of Marcan exegesis. The Second Gospel mentions no Passover journeys as falling in the course of the public ministry of Jesus; consequently the most natural conclusion would be that no Passover journeys fall within that period; that is, that Jesus' ministry began after one Passover and closed with the next, thus lasting less than a full year. Weisse thinks, however, that it is impossible to understand the success of His teaching unless we assume a ministry of several years, of more than three years, indeed. Mark does not mention the Feasts simply because Jesus did not go up to Jerusalem. "Intrinsic probability is, in our opinion, so strongly in favour of a duration of a considerable number of years, that we are at a loss to explain how it is that at least a few unprejudiced investigators have not found in this a sufficient reason for departing from the traditional opinion."

The account of the mission of the Twelve is also, on the ground of "intrinsic probability," explained in a way which is not in accordance with the plain sense of the words. "We do not think," says Weisse, "that it is necessary to understand this in the sense that He sent all the twelve out at one time, two and two, remaining alone in the meantime; it is much more natural to suppose that He only sent them out two at a time, keeping the others about Him. The object of this mission was less the immediate spreading abroad of His teaching than the preparation of the disciples themselves for the independent activity which they would have to exercise after His death." These are, however, the only serious liberties which he takes with the statements of Mark.

When did Jesus begin to think of Himself as the Messiah? The baptism seems to have marked an epoch in regard to His Messianic consciousness, but that does not mean that He had not previously begun to have such thoughts about Himself. In any case He did not on that occasion arrive all at once at that point of His inward journey which He had reached at the time of His first public appearance. We must assume a period of some duration between the baptism and the beginning of His ministry—a longer period than we should suppose from the Synoptists—during which Jesus cast off the Messianic ideas of Judaism and attained to a spiritual conception of the Messiahship. When He began to [pg 134] teach, His "development" was already closed. Later interpreters of Mark have generally differed from Weisse in assuming a development in the thought of Jesus during His public ministry.

His conception of the Messiahship was therefore fully formed when He began to teach in Capernaum; but He did not allow the people to see that He held Himself to be the Messiah until His triumphal entry. It was in order to avoid declaring His Messiahship that He kept away from Jerusalem. "It was only in Galilee and not in the Jewish capital that an extended period of teaching and work was possible for Him without being obliged to make an explicit declaration whether He were the Messiah or no. In Jerusalem itself the High Priests and Scribes would soon have put this question to Him in such a way that He could not have avoided answering it, whereas in Galilee He doubtless on more than one occasion cut short such attempts to question Him too closely by the incisiveness of His replies." Like Strauss, Weisse recognises that the key to the explanation of the Messianic consciousness of Jesus lies in the self-designation "Son of Man." "We are most certainly justified," he says, with almost prophetic insight, in his "Problem of the Gospels," published in 1856, "in regarding the question, what sense the Divine Saviour desired to attach to this predicate?—what, in fact, He intended to make known about Himself by using the title Son of Man—as an essential question for the right understanding of His teaching, and not of His teaching only, but also of the very heart and inmost essence of His personality."

But at this point Weisse lets in the cloven hoof of that fatal method of interpretation, by the aid of which the defenders of the Marcan hypothesis who succeeded him were to wage war, with a kind of dull and dogged determination, against eschatology, in the interests of an original and "spiritual" conception of the Messiahship supposed to be held by Jesus. Under the obsession of the fixed idea that it was their mission to defend the "originality" of Jesus by ascribing to Him a modernising transformation and spiritualisation of the eschatological system of ideas, the defenders of the Marcan hypothesis have impeded the historical study of the Life of Jesus to an almost unbelievable extent.

The explanation of the name Son of Man had, Weisse explains, hitherto oscillated between two extremes. Some had held the expression to be, even in the mouth of Jesus, equivalent to "man" in general, an interpretation which cannot be carried through; others had connected it with the Son of Man in Daniel, and supposed that in using the term Jesus was employing a Messianic title understood by and current among the Jews. But how came He to employ only this unusual periphrastic name for the Messiah? Further, if this name were really a Messianic title, how could He [pg 135] repeatedly have refused Messianic salutations, and not until the triumphal entry suffered the people to hail Him as Messiah?

The questions are rightly asked; it is therefore the more pity that they are wrongly answered. It follows, Weisse says, from the above considerations that Jesus did not assume an acquaintance on the part of His hearers with the Old Testament Messianic significance of the expression. "It was therefore incontestably the intention of Jesus—and any one who considers it unworthy betrays thereby his own want of insight—that the designation should have something mysterious about it, something which would compel His hearers to reflect upon His meaning." The expression Son of Man was calculated to lead them on to higher conceptions of His nature and origin, and therefore sums up in itself the whole spiritualisation of the Messiahship.

Weisse, therefore, passionately rejects any suggestion, however modest, that Jesus' self-designation, Son of Man, implies any measure of acceptance of the Jewish apocalyptic system of ideas. Ewald had furnished forth his Life of Jesus[88] with a wealth of Old Testament learning, and had made some half-hearted attempts to show the connexion of Jesus' system of thought with that of post-canonical Judaism, but without taking the matter seriously and without having any suspicion of the real character of the eschatology of Jesus. But even these parade-ground tactics excite Weisse's indignation; in his book, published in 1856, he reproaches Ewald with failing to understand his task.

The real duty of criticism is, according to Weisse, to show that Jesus had no part in those fantastic errors which are falsely attributed to Him when a literal Jewish interpretation is given to His great sayings about the future of the Son of Man, and to remove all the obstacles which seem to have prevented hitherto the recognition of the novel character and special significance of the expression, Son of Man, in the mouth of Him who, of His own free choice, applied this name to Himself. "How long will it be," he cries, "before theology at last becomes aware of the deep importance of its task? Historical criticism, exercised with all the thoroughness and impartiality which alone can produce a genuine conviction, must free the Master's own teaching from the imputation that lies upon it—the imputation of sharing the errors and false expectations in which, as we cannot deny, owing to imperfect or mistaken understanding of the suggestions of the Master, the Apostles, and with them the whole early Christian Church, became involved."

This fundamental position determines the remainder of Weisse's views. Jesus cannot have shared the Jewish particularism. He [pg 136] did not hold the Law to be binding. It was for this reason that He did not go up to the Feasts. He distinctly and repeatedly expressed the conviction that His doctrine was destined for the whole world. In speaking of the parousia of the Son of Man He was using a figure—a figure which includes in a mysterious fashion all His predictions of the future. He did not speak to His disciples of His resurrection, His ascension, and His parousia as three distinct acts, since the event to which He looked forward is not identical with any of the three, but is composed of them all. The resurrection is, at the same time, the ascension and parousia, and in the parousia the resurrection and the ascension are also included. "The one conclusion to which we believe we can point with certainty is that Jesus spoke of the future of His work and His teaching in a way that implied the consciousness of an influence to be continued after His death, whether unbrokenly or intermittently, and the consciousness that by this influence His work and teaching would be preserved from destruction and the final victory assured to it."

The personal presence of Jesus which the disciples experienced after His death was in their view only a partial fulfilment of that general promise. The parousia appeared to them as still awaiting fulfilment. Thought of thus, as an isolated event, they could only conceive it from the Jewish apocalyptic standpoint, and they finally came to suppose that they had derived these fantastic ideas from the Master Himself.

In his determined opposition to the recognition of eschatology in Strauss's first Life of Jesus, Weisse here lays down the lines which were to be followed by the "liberal" Lives of Jesus of the 'sixties and following years, which only differ from him, not always to their advantage, in their more elaborate interpretation of the detail of Mark. The only work, therefore, which was a conscious continuation of Strauss's, takes, in spite of its just appreciation of the character of the sources, a wrong path, led astray by the mistaken idea of the "originality" of Jesus, which it exalts into a canon of historical criticism. Only after long and devious wanderings did the study of the subject find the right road again. The whole struggle over eschatology is nothing else than a gradual elimination of Weisse's ideas. It was only with Johannes Weiss that theology escaped from the influence of Christian Hermann Weisse.
[pg 137]

XI. Bruno Bauer. The First Sceptical Life Of Jesus

Kritik der evangelischen Geschichte des Johannes. (Criticism of the Gospel History of John.) Bremen, 1840. 435 pp.

Kritik der evangelischen Geschichte der Synoptiker. (Criticism of the Gospel History of the Synoptics.) 3 vols., Leipzig, 1841-1842; vol. i. 416 pp.; vol. ii. 392 pp.; vol. iii. 341 pp.

Kritik der Evangelien. (Criticism of the Gospels.) 2 vols., 1850-1851, Berlin.

Kritik der Apostelgeschichte. (Criticism of Acts.) 1850.

Kritik der Paulinischen Briefe. Berlin, 1850-1852. In three parts.

Philo, Strauss, Renan und das Urchristentum. (P., S., R., and Primitive Christianity.) Berlin, 1874. 155 pp.

Christus und die Cäsaren. Der Ursprung des Christentums aus dem römischen Griechentum. (The Origin of Christianity from Graeco-Roman Civilisation.) Berlin, 1877. 387 pp.

Bruno Bauer was born in 1809 at Eisenberg, in the duchy of Sachsen-Altenburg. In philosophy, he was at first associated entirely with the Hegelian "right." Like Strauss, he received a strong impulse from Vatke. At this stage of his development he reviewed, in 1835 and 1836, Strauss's Life of Jesus in the *Jahrbücher für wissenschaftliche Kritik*, and wrote in 1838 a "Criticism of the History of Revelation."[89]

In 1834 he had become Privat-Docent in Berlin, but in 1839 he removed to Bonn. He was then in the midst of that intellectual crisis of which the evidence appeared in his critical works on John and the Synoptics. In August 1841 the Minister, Eichhorn, requested the Faculties of the Prussian Universities to report on the question whether Bauer should be allowed to retain the *venia docendi*. Most of them returned an evasive answer, Königsberg replied in the affirmative, and Bonn in the negative. In March 1842 Bauer was obliged to cease lecturing, and retired to Rixdorf near Berlin. In the first heat of his furious indignation over this treatment he wrote a work with the title "Christianity [pg 138] Exposed,"[90] which, however, was cancelled before publication at Zurich in 1843.

He then turned his attention to secular history and wrote on the French Revolution, on Napoleon, on the Illuminism of the Eighteenth Century, and on the party struggles in Germany during the years 1842-1846. At the beginning of the 'fifties he returned to theological subjects, but failed to exercise any influence. His work was simply ignored.

Radical though he was in spirit, Bauer found himself fighting, at the end of the 'fifties and beginning of the 'sixties, in the ranks of the Prussian Conservatives—we are reminded how Strauss in the Würtemberg Chamber was similarly forced to side with the reactionaries. He died in 1882. His was a pure, modest, and lofty character.

At the time of his removal from Berlin to Bonn he was just at the end of the twenties, that critical age when pupils often surprise their teachers, when men begin to find themselves and show what they are, not merely what they have been taught.

In approaching the investigation of the Gospel history, Bauer saw, as he himself tells us, two ways open to him. He might take as his starting-point the Jewish Messianic conception, and endeavour to answer the question how the intuitive prophetic idea of the Messiah became a fixed reflective conception. That was the historical method; he chose, however, the other, the literary method. This starts from the opposite side of the question, from the end instead of the beginning of the Gospel history. Taking first the Gospel of John, in which it is obvious that reflective thought has fitted the life of the Jewish Messiah into the frame of the Logos conception, he then, starting as it were from the embouchure of the stream, works his way upwards to the high ground in which the Gospel tradition takes its rise. The decision in favour of the latter view determined the character of Bauer's life-work; it was his task to follow out, to its ultimate consequences, the literary solution of the problem of the life of Jesus.

How far this path would lead him he did not at first suspect. But he did suspect how strong was the influence upon the formation of history of a dominant idea which moulds and shapes it with a definite artistic purpose. His interest was especially arrested by Philo, who, without knowing or intending it, contributed to the fulfilment of a higher task than that with which he was immediately engaged. Bauer's view is that a speculative principle such as Philo's, when it begins to take possession of men's minds, influences them in the first glow of enthusiasm which it evokes [pg 139] with such overmastering power that the just claims of that which is actual and historical cannot always secure the attention which is their due. In Philo's pupil, John, we must look, not for history, but for art.

The Fourth Gospel is in fact a work of art. This was now for the first time appreciated by one who was himself an artist. Schleiermacher, indeed, had at an earlier period taken up the aesthetic standpoint in considering this Gospel. But he had used it as an apologist, proceeding to exalt the artistic truth which he rightly recognised into historic reality, and his critical sense failed him, precisely because he was an aesthete and an apologist, when he came to deal with the Fourth Gospel. Now, however, there comes forward a true artist, who shows that the depth of religious and intellectual insight which Tholuck and Neander, in opposing Strauss, had urged on behalf of the Fourth Gospel, is—Christian art.

In Bauer, however, the aesthete is at the same time a critic. Although much in the Fourth Gospel is finely "felt," like the opening scenes referring to the Baptist and to Jesus, which Bauer groups together under the heading "The Circle of the Expectant," yet his art is by no means always perfect. The author who conceived those discourses, of which the movement consists in a kind of tautological return upon itself, and who makes the parables trail out into dragging allegories, is no perfect artist. "The parable of the Good Shepherd," says Bauer, "is neither simple, nor natural, nor a true parable, but a metaphor, which is, nevertheless, much too elaborate for a metaphor, is not clearly conceived, and, finally, in places shows much too clearly the skeleton of reflection over which it is stretched."

Bauer treats, in his work of 1840,[91] the Fourth Gospel only. The Synoptics he deals with only in a quite incidental fashion, "as opposing armies make demonstrations in order to provoke the enemy to a decisive conflict."

He breaks off at the beginning of the story of the passion, because here it would be necessary to bring in the Synoptic parallels. "From the distant heights on which the Synoptic forces have taken up a menacing position, we must now draw them down into the plain; now comes the pitched battle between them and the Fourth Gospel, and the question regarding the historical character of that which we have found to be the ultimate basis of the last Gospel, can now at length be decided."

If, in the Gospel of John, no smallest particle could be found which was unaffected by the creative reflection of the author, how will it stand with the Synoptists?

When Bauer broke off his work upon John in this abrupt way—for [pg 140] he had not originally intended to conclude it at this point—how far did he still retain a belief in the historical character of the Synoptics? It looks as if he had intended to treat then as the solid foundation, in contrast with the fantastic structure raised upon it by the Fourth Gospel. But when he began to use his pick upon the rock, it crumbled away. Instead of a difference of kind he found only a difference of degree. The "Criticism of the Gospel History of the Synoptists" of 1841 is built on the site which Strauss had levelled. "The abiding influence of Strauss," says Bauer, "consists in the fact that he has removed from the path of subsequent criticism the danger and trouble of a collision with the earlier orthodox system."

Bauer finds his material laid ready to his hand by Weisse and Wilke. Weisse had divined in Mark the source from which criticism—becoming barren in the work of Strauss—might draw a new spring of vigorous life; and Wilke, whom Bauer places above Weisse, had raised this happy conjecture to the level of a scientifically assured result. The Marcan hypothesis was no longer on its trial.

But its bearing upon the history of Jesus had still to be determined. What position do Weisse and Wilke take up towards the hypothesis of a tradition lying behind the Gospel of Mark? If it be once admitted that the whole Gospel tradition, so far as concerns its plan, goes back to a single writer, who has created the connexion between the different events—for neither Weisse nor Wilke regards the connexion of the sections as historical—does not the possibility naturally suggest itself that the narrative of the events themselves, not merely the connexion in which they appear in Mark, is to be set down to the account of the author of the Gospel? Weisse and Wilke had not suspected how great a danger arises when, of the three witnesses who represent the tradition, only one is allowed to stand, and the tradition is recognised and allowed to exist in this one written form only. The triple embankment held; will a single one bear the strain?

The following considerations have to be taken into account. The criticism of the Fourth Gospel compels us to recognise that a Gospel *may* have a purely literary origin. This discovery dawned upon Bauer at a time when he was still disinclined to accept Wilke's conclusions regarding Mark.

But when he had recognised the truth of the latter he felt compelled by the combination of the two to accept the idea that Mark also might be of purely literary origin. For Weisse and Wilke the Marcan hypothesis had not implied this result, because they continued to combine with it the wider hypothesis of a general tradition, holding that Matthew and Luke used the collection of "Logia," [pg 141] and also owed part of their supplementary matter to a free use of floating tradition, so that Mark, it might almost be said, merely supplied them with the formative principle by means of which they might order their material.

But what if Papias's statement about the collection of "Logia" were worthless, and could be shown to be so by the literary data? In that case Matthew and Luke would be purely literary expansions of Mark, and like him, purely literary inventions.

In this connexion Bauer attaches decisive importance to the phenomena of the birth-stories. If these had been derived from tradition they could not differ from each other as they do. If it is suggested that tradition had produced a large number of independent, though mutually consistent, stories of the childhood, out of which the Evangelists composed their opening narratives, this also is found to be untenable, for these narratives are not composite structures. The separate stories of which each of these two histories of the childhood consists could not have been formed independently of one another; none of them existed by itself; each points to the others and is informed by a view which implies the whole. The histories of the childhood are therefore not literary versions of a tradition, but literary inventions.

If we go on to examine the discourse and narrative material, additional to that of Mark, which is found in Matthew and Luke, a similar result appears. The same standpoint is regulative throughout, showing that the additions do not consist of oral or written traditional material which has been worked into the Marcan plan, but of a literary development of certain fundamental ideas and suggestions found in the first author. These developments, as is shown by the accounts of the Sermon on the Mount and the charge to the Twelve, are not carried as far in Luke as in Matthew. The additional material in the latter seems indeed to be worked up from suggestions in the former. Luke thus forms the transition stage between Mark and Matthew. The Marcan hypothesis, accordingly, now takes on the following form. Our knowledge of the Gospel history does not rest upon any basis of tradition, but only upon three literary works. Two of these are not independent, being merely expansions of the first, and the third, Matthew, is also dependent upon the second. Consequently there is no tradition of the Gospel history, but only a single *literary source*.

But, if so, who is to assure us that this Gospel history, with its assertion of the Messiahship of Jesus, was already a matter of common knowledge before it was fixed in writing, and did not first become known in a literary form? In the latter case, one man would have created out of general ideas the definite historical tradition in which these ideas are embodied. [pg 142] The only thing that could be set against this literary possibility, as a historical counter-possibility, would be a proof that at the period when the Gospel history is supposed to take place a Messianic expectation really existed among the Jews, so that a man who claimed to be the Messiah and was recognised as such, as Mark represents Jesus to have been, would be historically conceivable. This presupposition had hitherto been unanimously accepted by all writers, no matter how much opposed in other respects. They were all satisfied "that before the appearance of Jesus the expectation of a Messiah prevailed among the Jews"; and were even able to explain its precise character.

But where—apart from the Gospels—did they get their information from? Where is the documentary evidence of the Jewish Messianic doctrine on which that of the Gospels is supposed to be based? Daniel was the last of the prophets. Everything tends to suggest that the mysterious content of his work remained without influence in the subsequent period. Jewish literature ends with the Wisdom writings, in which there is no mention of a Messiah. In the LXX there is no attempt to translate in accordance with a preconceived picture of the Messiah. In the Apocalypses, which are of small importance, there is reference to a Messianic Kingdom; the Messiah Himself, however, plays a quite subordinate part, and is, indeed, scarcely mentioned. For Philo He has no existence; the Alexandrian does not dream of connecting Him with his Logos speculation. There remain, therefore, as witnesses for the Jewish Messianic expectations in the time of Tiberius, only Mark and his imitators. This evidence, however, is of such a character that in certain points it contradicts itself.

In the first place, if at the time when the Christian community was forming its view of history and the religious ideas which we find in the Gospels, the Jews had already possessed a doctrine of the Messiah, there would have been already a fixed type of interpretation of the Messianic passages in the Old Testament, and it would have been impossible for the same passages to be interpreted in a totally different way, as referring to Jesus and His work, as we find them interpreted in the New Testament. Next, consider the representation of the Baptist's work. We should have expected him to connect his baptism with the preaching of "Him who was to come"—if this were really the Messiah—by baptizing in the name of this "Coming One." He, however, keeps them separate, baptizing in preparation for the Kingdom, though referring in his discourses to "Him who was to come."

The earliest Evangelist did not venture openly to carry back into the history the idea that Jesus had claimed to be the [pg 143] Messiah, because he was aware that in the time of Jesus no general expectation of the Messiah had prevailed among the people. When the disciples in Mark viii. 28 report the opinions of the people concerning Jesus they cannot mention any who hold Him to be the Messiah. Peter is the first to attain to the recognition of His Messiahship. But as soon as the confession is made the Evangelist makes Jesus forbid His disciples to tell the people who He is. Why is the attribution of the Messiahship to Jesus made in this surreptitious and inconsistent way? It is because the writer who gave the history its form well knew that no one had ever come forward publicly on Palestinian soil to claim the Messiahship, or had been recognised by the people as Messiah.

The "reflective conception of the Messiah" was not, therefore, taken over ready-made from Judaism; that dogma first arose along with the Christian community, or rather the moment in which it arose was the same in which the Christian community had its birth.

Moreover, how unhistorical, even on a priori grounds, is the mechanical way in which Jesus at this first appearance at once sets Himself up as the Messiah and says, "Behold I am He whom ye have expected." In essence, Bauer thinks, there is not so much difference between Strauss and Hengstenberg. For Hengstenberg the whole life of Jesus is the living embodiment of the Old Testament picture of the Messiah; Strauss, a less reverent counterpart of Hengstenberg, made the image of the Messiah into a mask which Jesus Himself was obliged to assume, and which legend afterwards substituted for His real features.

"We save the honour of Jesus," says Bauer, "when we restore His Person to life from the state of inanition to which the apologists have reduced it, and give it once more a living relation to history, which it certainly possessed—that can no longer be denied. If a conception was to become dominant which should unite heaven and earth, God and man, nothing more and nothing less was necessary as a preliminary condition, than that a Man should appear, the very essence of whose consciousness should be the reconciliation of these antitheses, and who should manifest this consciousness to the world, and lead the religious mind to the sole point from which its difficulties can be solved. Jesus accomplished this mighty work, but not by prematurely pointing to His own Person. Instead He gradually made known to the people the thoughts which filled and entered into the very essence of His mind. It was only in this indirect way that His Person—which He freely offered up in the cause of His historical vocation and of the idea for which He lived—continued to live on in so far as this idea was accepted. When, in the belief of His followers, He rose again and lived on in the [pg 144] Christian community, it was as the Son of God who had overcome and reconciled the great antithesis. He was that in which alone the religious consciousness found rest and peace, apart from which there was nothing firm, trustworthy, and enduring."

"It was only now that the vague, ill-defined, prophetic representations were focused into a point; were not only fulfilled, but were also united together by a common bond which strengthened and gave greater value to each of them. With His appearance and the rise of belief in Him, a clear conception, a definite mental picture of the Messiah became possible; and thus it was that a Christology[92] first arose."

While, therefore, at the close of Bauer's first work it might have seemed that it was only the Gospel of John which he held to be a literary creation, here the same thing is said of the original Gospel. The only difference is that we find more primitive reflection in the Synoptics, and later work in the representation given by the Fourth Evangelist; the former is of a more practical character, the latter more dogmatic.

Nevertheless it is false to assert that according to Bauer the earliest Evangelist invented the Gospel history and the personality of Jesus. That is to carry back the ideas of a later period and a further stage of development into the original form of his view. At the moment when, having disposed of preliminaries, he enters on his investigation, he still assumes that a great, a unique Personality, who so impressed men by His character that it lived on among them in an ideal form, had awakened into life the Messianic idea; and that what the original Evangelist really did was to portray the life of this Jesus—the Christ of the community which He founded—in accordance with the Messianic view of Him, just as the Fourth Evangelist portrayed it in accordance with the presupposition that Jesus was the revealer of the Logos. It was only in the course of his investigations that Bauer's opinion became more radical. As he goes on, his writing becomes ill-tempered, and takes the form of controversial dialogues with "the theologians," whom he apostrophises in a biting and injurious fashion, and whom he continually reproaches with not daring, owing to their apologetic prejudices, to see things as they really are, and with declining to face the ultimate results of criticism from fear that the tradition might suffer more loss of historic value than religion could bear. In spite of this hatred of the theologians, which is pathological in character, like his meaningless punctuation, his critical analyses are always exceedingly acute. One has the impression of walking alongside a man who is reasoning quite intelligently, but who talks [pg 145] to himself as though possessed by a fixed idea. What if the whole thing should turn out to be nothing but a literary invention—not only the incidents and discourses, but even the Personality which is assumed as the starting-point of the whole movement? What if the Gospel history were only a late imaginary embodiment of a set of exalted ideas, and these were the only historical reality from first to last? This is the idea which obsesses his mind more and more completely, and moves him to contemptuous laughter. What, he mocks, will these apologists, who are so sure of everything, do then with the shreds and tatters which will be all that is left to them?

But at the outset of his investigations Bauer was far from holding such views. His purpose was really only to continue the work of Strauss. The conception of myth and legend of which the latter made use is, Bauer thinks, much too vague to explain this deliberate "transformation" of a personality. In the place of myth Bauer therefore sets "reflection." The life which pulses in the Gospel history is too vigorous to be explained as created by legend; it is real "experience," only not the experience of Jesus, but of the Church. The representation of this experience of the Church in the Life of a Person is not the work of a number of persons, but of a single author. It is in this twofold aspect—as the composition of one man, embodying the experience of many—that the Gospel history is to be regarded. As religious art it has a profound truth. When it is regarded from this point of view the difficulties which are encountered in the endeavour to conceive it as real immediately disappear.

We must take as our point of departure the belief in the sacrificial death and the resurrection of Jesus. Everything else attaches itself to this as to its centre. When the need arose to fix definitely the beginning of the manifestation of Jesus as the Saviour—to determine the point of time at which the Lord issued forth from obscurity—it was natural to connect this with the work of the Baptist; and Jesus comes to his baptism. While this is sufficient for the earliest Evangelist, Matthew and Luke feel it to be necessary, in view of the important consequences involved in the connexion of Jesus with the Baptist, to bring them into relation once more by means of the question addressed by the Baptist to Jesus, although this addition is quite inconsistent with the assumptions of the earliest Evangelist. If he had conceived the story of the baptism with the idea of introducing the Baptist again on a later occasion, and this time, moreover, as a doubter, he would have given it a different form. This is a just observation of Bauer's; the story of the baptism with the miracle which took place at it, and the Baptist's question, understood as implying a doubt of the Messiahship of Jesus, mutually exclude one another.

[pg 146]

The story of the temptation embodies an experience of the early Church. This narrative represents her inner conflicts under the form of a conflict of the Redeemer. On her march through the wilderness of this world she has to fight with temptations of the devil, and in the story composed by Mark and Luke, and artistically finished by Matthew, she records a vow to build only on the inner strength of her constitutive principle. In the sermon on the mount also, Matthew has carried out with greater completeness that which was more vaguely conceived by Luke. It is only when we understand the words of Jesus as embodying experiences of the early Church that their deeper sense becomes clear and what would otherwise seem offensive disappears. The saying, "Let the dead bury their dead," would not have been fitting for Jesus to speak, and had He been a real man, it could never have entered into His mind to create so unreal and cruel a collision of duties; for no command, Divine or human, could have sufficed to make it right for a man to contravene the ethical obligations of family life. So here again, the obvious conclusion is that the saying originated in the early Church, and was intended to inculcate renunciation of a world which was felt to belong to the kingdom of the dead, and to illustrate this by an extreme example.

The mission of the Twelve, too, is, as an historical occurrence, simply inconceivable. It would have been different if Jesus had given them a definite teaching, or form of belief, or positive conception of any kind, to take with them as their message. But how ill the charge to the Twelve fulfils its purpose as a discourse of instruction! What the disciples needed to learn, namely, what and how they were to teach, they are not told; and the discourse which Matthew has composed, working on the basis of Luke, implies quite a different set of circumstances. It is concerned with the struggles of the Church with the world and the sufferings which it must endure. This is the explanation of the references to suffering which constantly recur in the discourses of Jesus, in spite of the fact that His disciples were not enduring any sufferings, and that the Evangelist cannot even make it conceivable as a possibility that those before whose eyes Jesus holds up the way of the Cross could ever come into such a position. The Twelve, at any rate, had no sufferings to encounter during their mission, and if they were merely being sent by Jesus into the surrounding districts they were not very likely to meet with kings and rulers there.

That it is a case of invented history is also shown by the fact that nothing is said about the doings of the disciples, and they seem to come back again immediately, though the earliest Evangelist, it is true, to prevent this from being too apparent, inserts at this point the story of the execution of the Baptist.

All this is just and acute criticism. The charge to the Twelve [pg 147] is not a discourse of instruction. What Jesus there sets before the disciples they could not at that time have understood, and the promises which He makes to them are not appropriate to their circumstances.

Many of the discourses are mere bundles of heterogeneous sayings, though this is not so much the case in Mark as in the others. He has not forgotten that effective polemic consists of short, pointed, incisive arguments. The others, as advanced theologians, are of opinion that it is fitting to indulge in arguments which have nothing to do with the matter in hand, or only the most distant connexion with it. They form the transition to the discourses of the Fourth Gospel, which usually degenerate into an aimless wrangle. In the same connexion it is rightly observed that the discourses of Jesus do not advance from point to point by the logical development of an idea, the thoughts are merely strung together one after another, the only connexion, if connexion there is, being due to a kind of conventional mould in which the discourse is cast.

The parables, Bauer continues, present difficulties no less great. It is an ineptitude on the part of the apologists to suggest that the parables are intended to make things clear. Jesus Himself contradicts this view by saying bluntly and unambiguously to His disciples that to them it was given to know the mysteries of the Kingdom of God, but to the people all His teaching must be spoken as parables, that "seeing they might see and not perceive, and hearing they might hear and not understand." The parables were therefore intended only to exercise the intelligence of the disciples; and so far from being understood by the people, mystified and repelled them; as if it would not have been much better to exercise the minds of the disciples in this way when He was alone with them. The disciples, however, do not even understand the simple parable of the

Sower, but need to have it interpreted to them, so that the Evangelist once more stultifies his own theory.

Bruno Bauer is right in his observation that the parables offer a serious problem, seeing that they were intended to conceal and not to make plain, and that Jesus nevertheless taught only in parables. The character of the difficulty, however, is such that even literary criticism has no explanation ready. Bruno Bauer admits that he does not know what was in the mind of the Evangelist when he composed these parables, and thinks that he had no very definite purpose, or at least that the suggestions which were floating in his mind were not worked up into a clearly ordered whole.

Here, therefore, Bauer's method broke down. He did not, however, allow this to shake his confidence in his reading of the facts, and he continued to maintain it in the face of a new difficulty [pg 148] which he himself brought clearly to light. Mark, according to him, is an artistic unity, the offspring of a single mind. How then is it to be explained that in addition to other less important doublets it contains two accounts of the feeding of the multitude? Here Bauer has recourse to the aid of Wilke, who distinguishes our Mark from an Ur-Markus,[93] and ascribes these doublets to later interpolation. Later on he became more and more doubtful about the artistic unity of Mark, despite the fact that this was the fundamental assumption of his theory, and in the second edition of his "Criticism of the Gospels," of 1851, he carried through the distinction between the canonical Mark and the Ur-Markus.

But even supposing the assumption of a redaction were justified, how could the redactor have conceived the idea of adding to the first account of the feeding of the multitude a second which is identical with it almost to the very wording? In any case, on what principle can Mark be distinguished from Ur-Markus? There are no fundamental differences to afford a ready criterion. The distinction is purely one of subjective feeling, that is to say, it is arbitrary. As soon as Bauer admits that the artistic unity of Mark, on which he lays so much stress, has been tampered with, he cannot maintain his position except by shutting his eyes to the fact that it can only be a question of the weaving in of fragments of tradition, not of the inventions of an imitator. But if he once admits the presence of traditional materials, his whole theory of the earliest Evangelist's having created the Gospel falls to the ground.

For the moment he succeeds in laying the spectre again, and continues to think of Mark as a work of art, in which the interpolation alters nothing.

Bauer discusses with great thoroughness those sayings of Jesus in which He forbids those whom He had healed to noise abroad their cure. In the form in which they appear these cannot, he argues, be historical, for Jesus imposes this prohibition in some cases where it is quite meaningless, since the healing had taken place in the presence of a multitude. It must therefore be derived from the Evangelist. Only when it is recognised as a free creation can its meaning be discerned. It finds its explanation in the inconsistent views regarding miracle which were held side by side in the early Church. No doubt was felt that Jesus had performed miracles, and by these miracles had given evidence of His Divine mission. On the other hand, by the introduction of the Christian principle, the Jewish demand for a sign had been so far limited, and the other, the spiritual line of evidence, had become so important, or at least so indispensable, that it was no longer possible to build on the miracles only, or to regard Jesus merely as a [pg 149] wonder-worker; so in some way or other the importance ascribed to miracle must be reduced. In the graphic symbolism of the Gospel history this antithesis takes the form that Jesus did miracles—there was no getting away from that—but on the other hand Himself declared that He did not wish to lay any stress upon such acts. As there are times when miracles must hide their light under a bushel, Jesus, on occasion, forbids that they should be made known. The other Synoptists no longer understood this theory of the first Evangelist, and introduced the prohibition in passages where it was absurd.

The way in which Jesus makes known His Messiahship is based on another theory of the original Evangelist. The order of Mark can give us no information regarding the chronology of the life of Jesus, since this Gospel is anything rather than a chronicle. We cannot even assert that there is a deliberate logic in the way in which the sections are connected. But there is one fundamental principle of arrangement which comes quite clearly to light, viz. that it was only at Caesarea Philippi, in the closing period of His life, that Jesus made Himself known as the Messiah, and that, therefore, He was not previously held to be so either by His disciples or by the people. This is clearly shown in the answers of the disciples when Jesus asked them whom men took Him to be. The implied course of events, however, is determined by art, not history—as history it would be inconceivable.

Could there indeed be a more absurd impossibility? "Jesus," says Bauer, "must perform these innumerable, these astounding miracles because, according to the view which the Gospels represent, He is the Messiah; He must perform them in order to prove Himself to be the Messiah—and yet no one recognises Him as the Messiah! That is the greatest miracle of all, that the people had not long ago recognised the Messiah in this wonder-worker. Jesus could only be held to be the Messiah in consequence of doing miracles; but He only began to do miracles when, in the faith of the early Church, He rose from the dead as Messiah, and the facts that He rose as Messiah and that He did miracles, are one and the same fact."

Mark, however, represents a Jesus who does miracles and who nevertheless does not thereby reveal Himself to be the Messiah. He was obliged so to represent Him, because he was conscious that Jesus was not recognised and acknowledged as Messiah by the people, nor even by His immediate followers, in the unhesitating fashion in which those of later times imagined Him to have been recognised. Mark's conception and representation of the matter carried back into the past the later developments by which there finally arose a Christian community for which Jesus had become the Messiah. "Mark is also influenced by an artistic instinct which [pg 150] leads him to develop the main interest, the origin of the faith, gradually. It is only after the ministry of Jesus has extended over a considerable period, and is, indeed, drawing towards its close, that faith arises in the circle of the disciples; and it is only later still, when, in the person of the blind man at Jericho, a prototype of the great company of believers that was to be has hailed the Lord with a Messianic salutation, that, at the triumphal entry into Jerusalem, the faith of the people suddenly ripens and finds expression."

It is true, this artistic design is completely marred when Jesus does miracles which must have made Him known to every child as the Messiah. We cannot, therefore, blame Matthew very much if, while he retains this plan in its external outlines in a kind of mechanical way, he contradicts it somewhat awkwardly by making Jesus at an earlier point clearly designate Himself as Messiah and many recognise Him as such. And the Fourth Evangelist cannot be said to be destroying any very wonderful work of art when he gives the impression that from the very first any one who wished could recognise Jesus as the Messiah.

Mark himself does not keep strictly to his own plan. He makes Jesus forbid His disciples to make known His Messiahship; how then does the multitude at Jerusalem recognise it so suddenly, after a single miracle which they had not even witnessed, and which was in no way different from others which He had done before? If that "chance multitude" in Jerusalem was capable of such sudden enlightenment it must have fallen from heaven!

The following remarks of Bauer, too, are nothing less than classical. The incident at Caesarea Philippi is the central fact of the Gospel history; it gives us a fixed point from which to group and criticise the other statements of the Gospel. At the same time it introduces a complication into the plan of the life of Jesus, because it necessitates the carrying through of the theory—often in the face of the text—that previously Jesus had never been regarded as the Messiah; and lays upon us the necessity of showing not only how Peter had come to recognise His Messiahship, but also how He subsequently became Messiah for the multitude—if indeed He ever did become Messiah for them. But the very fact that it does introduce this complication is in itself a proof that in this scene at Caesarea Philippi we have the one ray of light which history sheds upon the life of Jesus. It is impossible to explain how any one could come to reject the simple and natural idea that Jesus claimed from the first to be the Messiah, if that had been the fact, and accept this complicated representation in its place. The latter, therefore, must be the original version. In pointing this out, Bauer gave for the first time the real proof, from internal evidence, of the priority of Mark.

[pg 151]

The difficulty involved in the conception of miracle as a proof of the Messiahship of Jesus is another discovery of Bauer's. Only here, instead of probing the question to the bottom, he stops half-way. How do we know, he should have gone on to ask, that the Messiah was expected to appear as an earthly wonder-worker? There is nothing to that effect in Jewish writings. And do not the Gospels themselves prove that any one might do miracles without suggesting to a single person the idea that he might be the Messiah? Accordingly the only inference to be drawn from the Marcan representation is that miracles were not among the characteristic marks of the Messiah, and that it was only later, in the Christian community, which made Jesus the miracle-worker into Jesus the Messiah, that this connexion between miracles and Messiahship was established. In dealing with the question of the triumphal entry, too, Bauer halts half-way. Where do we read that Jesus was hailed as Messiah upon that occasion? If He had been taken by the people to be the Messiah, the controversy in Jerusalem must have turned on this personal question; but it did not even touch upon it, and the Sanhedrin never thinks of setting up witnesses to Jesus' claim to be the Messiah. When once Bauer had exposed the historical and literary impossibility of Jesus' being hailed by the people as Messiah, he ought to have gone on to draw the conclusion that Jesus did not, according to Mark, make a Messianic entry into Jerusalem.

It was, however, a remarkable achievement on Bauer's part to have thus set forth clearly the historical difficulties of the life of Jesus. One might suppose that between the work of Strauss and that of Bauer there lay not five, but fifty years—the critical work of a whole generation.

The stereotyped character of the thrice-repeated prediction of the passion, which, according to Bauer, betrays a certain poverty and feebleness of imagination on the part of the earliest Evangelist, shows clearly, he thinks, the unhistorical character of the utterance recorded. The fact that the prediction occurs three times, its definiteness increasing upon each occasion, proves its literary origin.

It is the same with the transfiguration. The group in which the heroic representatives of the Law and the Prophets stand as supporters of the Saviour, was modelled by the earliest Evangelist. In order to place it in the proper light and to give becoming splendour to its great subject, he has introduced a number of traits taken from the story of Moses.

Bauer pitilessly exposes the difficulties of the journey of Jesus from Galilee to Jerusalem, and exults over the perplexities of the "apologists." "The theologian," he says, "must not boggle at this journey, he must just believe it. He must in faith follow the footsteps of his Lord! Through the midst of Galilee and Samaria—and [pg 152] at the same time, for Matthew also claims a hearing, through Judaea on the farther side of Jordan! I wish him *Bon voyage!*"

The eschatological discourses are not history, but are merely an expansion of those explanations of the sufferings of the Church of which we have had a previous example in the charge to the Twelve. An Evangelist who wrote before the destruction of Jerusalem would have referred to the Temple, to Jerusalem, and to the Jewish people, in a very different way.

The story of Lazarus deserves special attention. Did not Spinoza say that he would break his system in pieces if he could be convinced of the reality of this event? This is the decisive point for the question of the relation between the Synoptists and John. Vain are all the efforts of the apologists to explain why the Synoptists do not mention this miracle. The reason they ignore it is that it originated after their time in the mind of the Fourth Evangelist, and they were unacquainted with his Gospel. And yet it is the most valuable of all, because it shows clearly the concentric circles of progressive intensification by which the development of the Gospel history proceeds. "The Fourth Gospel," remarks Bauer, "represents a dead man as having been restored to life after having been four days under the power of death, and having consequently become a prey to corruption; Luke represents the young man at Nain as being restored to life when his body was being carried to the grave; Mark, the earliest Evangelist, can only tell us of the restoration of a dead person who had the moment before succumbed to an illness. The theologians have a great deal to say about the contrast between the canonical and the apocryphal writings, but they might have found a similar contrast even within the four Gospels, if the light had not been so directly in their eyes."

The treachery of Judas, as described in the Gospels, is inexplicable.

The Lord's Supper, considered as an historic scene, is revolting and inconceivable. Jesus can no more have instituted it than He can have uttered the saying, "Let the dead bury their dead." In both cases the objectionableness arises from the fact that a tenet of the early Church has been cast into the form of an historical saying of Jesus. A man who was present in person, corporeally present, could not entertain the idea of offering others his flesh and blood to eat. To demand from others that they should, while he was actually present, imagine the bread and wine which they were eating to be his body and blood, would be for an actual man wholly impossible. It was only when Jesus' actual bodily presence had been removed, and only when the Christian community had existed for some time, that such a conception as is expressed in that formula could have arisen. A point which clearly betrays the [pg 153] later composition of the narrative is that the Lord does not turn to the disciples sitting with Him at table and say, "This is my blood which is shed for you," but, since the words were invented by the early Church, speaks of the "many" for whom He gives Himself. The only historical fact is that the Jewish Passover was gradually transformed by the Christian community into a feast which had reference to Jesus.

As regards the scene in Gethsemane, Mark, according to Bauer, held it necessary that in the moment when the last conflict and final catastrophe were coming upon Jesus, He should show clearly by His actions that He met this fate of His own free will. The reality of His choice could only be made clear by showing Him first engaged in an inner struggle against the acceptance of His vocation, before showing how He freely submitted to His fate.

The last words ascribed to Jesus by Mark, "My God, my God, why hast Thou forsaken me?" were written without thinking of the inferences that might be drawn from them, merely with the purpose of showing that even to the last moment of His passion Jesus fulfilled the rôle of the Messiah, the picture of whose sufferings had been revealed to the Psalmist so long beforehand by the Holy Spirit.

It is scarcely necessary now, Bauer thinks, to go into the contradictions in the story of the resurrection, for "the doughty Reimarus, with his thorough-going honesty, has already fully exposed them, and no one has refuted him."

The results of Bauer's analysis may be summed up as follows:—

The Fourth Evangelist has betrayed the secret of the original Gospel, namely, that it too can be explained on purely literary grounds. Mark has "loosed us from the theological lie." "Thanks to the kindly fate," cries Bauer, "which has preserved to us this writing of Mark by which we have been delivered from the web of deceit of this hellish pseudo-science!"

In order to tear this web of falsehood the critic and historian must, despite his repugnance, once more take up the pretended arguments of the theologians in favour of the historicity of the Gospel narratives and set them on their feet, only to knock them down again. In the end Bauer's only feeling towards the theologians was one of contempt. "The expression of his contempt," he declares, "is the last weapon which the critic, after refuting the arguments of the theologians, has at his disposal for their discomfiture; it is his right to use it; that puts the finishing touch upon his task and points forward to the happy time when the arguments of the theologians shall no more be heard of."

These outbreaks of bitterness are to be explained by the feeling of repulsion which German apologetic theology inspired in every genuinely honest and thoughtful man by the methods which it adopted in opposing Strauss. Hence the fiendish joy with which [pg 154] he snatches away the crutches of this pseudo-science, hurls them to a distance, and makes merry over its helplessness. A furious hatred, a fierce desire to strip the theologians absolutely bare, carried Bauer much farther than his critical acumen would have led him in cold blood.

Bauer hated the theologians for still holding fast to the barbarous conception that a great man had forced himself into a stereotyped and unspiritual system, and in that way had set in motion great ideas, whereas he held that that would have signified the death of both the personality and the ideas; but this hatred is only the surface symptom of another hatred, which goes deeper than theology, going down, indeed, to the very depths of the Christian conception of the world. Bruno Bauer hates not only the theologians, but Christianity, and hates it because it expresses a truth in a wrong way. It is a religion which has become petrified in a transitional form. A religion which ought to have led on to the true religion has usurped the place of the true religion, and in this petrified form it holds prisoner all the real forces of religion.

Religion is the victory over the world of the self-conscious ego. It is only when the ego grasps itself in its antithesis to the world as a whole, and is no longer content to play the part of a mere "walking gentleman" in the world-drama, but faces the world with independence and reserve, that the necessary conditions of universal religion are present. These conditions came into being with the rise of the Roman Empire, in which the individual suddenly found himself helpless and unarmed in face of a world in which he could no longer find free play for his activities, but must stand prepared at any moment to be ground to powder by it.

The self-conscious ego, recognising this position, found itself faced by the necessity of breaking loose from the world and standing alone, in order in this way to overcome the world. Victory over the world by alienation from the world—these were the ideas out of which Christianity was born. But it was not the true victory over the world; Christianity remained at the stage of violent opposition to the world.

Miracle, to which the Christian religion has always appealed, and to which it gives a quite fundamental importance, is the appropriate symbol of this false victory over the world. There are some wonderfully deep thoughts scattered through Bauer's critical investigations. "Man's realisation of his personality," he says, "is the death of Nature, but in the sense that he can only bring about this death by the knowledge of Nature and its laws, that is to say from within, being himself essentially the annihilation and negation of Nature.... Spirit honours and recognises the worth of the very thing which it negates.... Spirit does not fume and bluster, and rage and rave against Nature, as it is supposed to do [pg 155] in miracle, for that would be the denial of its inner law, but quietly works its way through the antithesis. In short the death of Nature implied in the conscious realisation of personality is the resurrection of Nature in a nobler form, not the maltreatment, mockery, and insult to which it would be exposed by miracle." Not only miracle, however, but the portrait of Jesus Christ as drawn in the Gospels, is a stereotyping of that false idea of victory over the world. The Christ of the Gospel history, thought of as a really historic figure, would be a figure at which humanity would shudder, a figure which could only inspire dismay and horror. The historical Jesus, if He really existed, can only have been One who reconciled in His own consciousness the antithesis which obsessed the Jewish mind, namely the separation between God and Man; He cannot in the process of removing this antithesis have called into existence a new principle of religious division and alienation; nor can He have shown the way of escape, by the principle of inwardness, from the bondage of the Law only to impose a new set of legal fetters.

The Christ of the Gospel history, on the other hand, is Man exalted by the religious consciousness to heaven, who, even if He comes down to earth to do miracles, to teach, and to suffer, is no longer true man. The Son of Man of religion, even though His mission be to reconcile, is man as alienated from himself. This Christ of the Gospel history, the ego exalted to heaven and become God, overthrew antiquity, and conquered the world in the sense that He exhausted it of all its vitality. This magnified ego would have fulfilled its historical vocation if, by means of the terrible disorganisation into which it threw the real spirit of mankind, it had compelled the latter to come to a knowledge of itself, to become self-conscious with a thoroughness and decisiveness which had not been possible to the simple spirit of antiquity. It was disastrous that the figure which stood for the first emancipation of the ego, remained alive. That transformation of the human spirit which was brought about by the encounter of the world-power of Rome with philosophy was represented by the Gospels, under the influence of the Old Testament, as realised in a single historic Personality; and the strength of the spirit of mankind was swallowed up by the omnipotence of the pure absolute ego, an ego which was alien from actual humanity. The self-consciousness of humanity finds itself reflected in the Gospels, a self, indeed, in alienation from itself, and therefore a grotesque parody of itself, but, after all, in some sense, itself; hence the magical charm which attracted mankind and enchained it, and, so long as it had not truly found itself, urged it to sacrifice everything to grasp the image of itself, to prefer it to all other and all else, counting all, as the apostle says, but "dung" in comparison with it.

Even when the Roman world was no more, and a new world [pg 156] had come into being, the Christ so created did not die. The magic of His enchantment became only more terrible, and as new strength came flooding into the old world, the time arrived when it was to accomplish its greatest work of destruction. Spirit, in its abstraction, became a vampire, the destroyer of the world. Sap and strength, blood and life, it sucked, to the last drop, out of humanity. Nature and art, family, nation, state, all were destroyed by it; and in the ruins of the fallen world the ego, exhausted by its efforts, remained the only surviving power.

Having made a desert all about it, the ego could not immediately create anew, out of the depths of its inner consciousness, nature and art, nation and state; the awful process which now went on, the only activity of which it was now capable, was the absorption into itself of all that had hitherto had life in the world. The ego was now everything; and yet it was a void. It had become the universal power, and yet as it brooded over the ruins of the world it was filled with horror at itself and with despair at all that it had lost. The ego which had devoured all things and was still a void now shuddered at itself.

Under the oppression of this awful power the education of mankind has been going on; under this grim task-master it has been preparing for true freedom, preparing to rouse itself from the depths of its distress, to escape from its opposition to itself and cast out that alien ego which is wasting its substance. Odysseus has now returned to his home, not by favour of the gods, not laid on the shore in sleep, but awake, by his own thought and his own strength. Perchance, as of yore, he will have need to fight with the suitors who have devoured his substance and sought to rob him of all he holds most dear. Odysseus must string the bow once more.

The baleful charm of the self-alienated ego is broken the moment any one proves to the religious sense of mankind that the Jesus Christ of the Gospels is its creation and ceases to exist as soon as this is recognised. The formation of the Church and the arising of the idea that the Jesus of the Gospels is the Messiah are not two different things, they are one and the same thing, they coincide and synchronise; but the idea was only the imaginative conception of the Church, the first movement of its life, the religious expression of its experience.

The question which has so much exercised the minds of men—whether Jesus was the historic Christ (= Messiah)—is answered in the sense that everything that the historical Christ is, everything that is said of Him, everything that is known of Him, belongs to the world of imagination, that is, of the imagination of the Christian community, and therefore has nothing to do with any man who belongs to the real world.

[pg 157]

The world is now free, and ripe for a higher religion in which the ego will overcome nature, not by self-alienation, but by penetrating it and ennobling it. To the theologian we may fling as a gift the shreds of his former science, when we have torn it to pieces; that will be something to occupy himself with, that time may not hang heavy upon his hands in the new world whose advent is steadily drawing nearer.

Thus the task which Bauer had set himself at the beginning of his criticism of the Gospel history, turned, before he had finished, into something different. When he began, he thought to save the honour of Jesus and to restore His Person from the state of inanition to which the apologists had reduced it, and hoped by furnishing a proof that the historical Jesus could not have been the Jesus Christ of the Gospels, to bring Him into a living relation with history. This task, however, was given up in favour of the larger one of freeing the world from the domination of the Judaeo-Roman idol, Jesus the Messiah, and in carrying out this endeavour the thesis that Jesus Christ is a product of the imagination of the early Church is formulated in such a way that the existence of a historic Jesus becomes problematical, or, at any rate, quite indifferent.

At the end of his study of the Gospels, Bauer is inclined to make the decision of the question whether there ever was a historic Jesus depend on the result of a further investigation which he proposed to make into the Pauline Epistles. It was not until ten years later (1850-1851) that he accomplished this task,[94] and applied the result in his new edition of the "Criticism of the Gospel History."[95] The result is negative: there never was any historical Jesus. While criticising the four great Pauline Epistles, which the Tübingen school fondly imagined to be beyond the reach of criticism, Bauer shows, however, his inability to lay a positive historic foundation for his view of the origin of Christianity. The transference of the Epistles to the second century is effected in so arbitrary a fashion that it refutes itself. However, this work professes to be only a preliminary study for a larger one in which the new theory was to be fully worked out. This did not appear until 1877; it was entitled "Christ and the Caesars; How Christianity originated from Graeco-Roman Civilisation."[96] The historical basis for his theory, which he here offers, is even more unsatisfactory than that suggested in the preliminary work on the Pauline Epistles. There is no longer any pretence of following [pg 158] an historical method, the whole thing works out into an imaginary picture of the life of Seneca. Nero's tutor had, Bauer thinks, already in his inmost consciousness fully attained to inner opposition to the world. There are expressions in his works which, in their mystical emancipation from the world, prelude the utterances of Paul. The same thoughts, since they belong not to Seneca only, but to his time, are found also in the works of the three poets of the Neronian period, Persius, Lucan, and Petronius. Though they had but a feeble breath of the divine afflatus, they are interesting witnesses to the spiritual condition of the time. They, too, contributed to the making of Christianity.

But Seneca, in spite of his inner alienation from the world, remained in active relations with the world. He desired to found a kingdom of virtue upon earth. At the courts of Claudius and Nero he used the arts of intrigue to further his ends, and even quietly approved deeds of violence which he thought likely to serve his cause. Finally, he grasped at the supreme power; and paid the supreme penalty. Stoicism had made an attempt to reform the world, and had failed. The great thinkers began to despair of exercising any influence upon history, the Senate was powerless, all public bodies were deprived of their rights. Then a spirit of resignation came over the world. The alienation from the world, which in Seneca had still been only half serious, was come in earnest. The time of Nero and Domitian was a great epoch in that hidden spiritual history which goes silently forward side by side with the noisy outward history of the world. When Stoicism, in this development, had been deepened by the introduction of neo-Platonic ideas, it was on its way to become the Gospel.

But by itself it would not have given birth to that new thing. It attached itself as a formative principle to Judaism, which was then just breaking loose from the limitations of nationality. Bauer points to Josephus as a type of this new Roman Judaism. This "neo-Roman" lived in the conviction that his God, who had withdrawn from His Temple, would take possession of the world, and make the Roman Empire submit to His law. Josephus realised in his life that for which the way had been spiritually prepared by Philo. The latter did not merely effect a fusion of Jewish ideas with Greek speculations; he took advantage of the universal dominion established by the Romans to found upon it his spiritual world. Bauer had already pictured him in this rôle in his work "Philo, Strauss, and Renan, and Primitive Christianity."

Thus was the new religion formed. The spirit of it came from the west, the outward frame was furnished by Judaism. The new movement had two foci, Rome and Alexandria. Philo's "Therapeutae" were real people; they were the forerunners of Christianity. Under Trajan the new religion began to be known. [pg 159] Pliny's letter asking for instructions as to how to deal with the new movement is its certificate of birth—the original form of the letter, it must be understood, not the present form, which has undergone editing at the hands of Christians.

The literary process by which the origin of the movement was thrown back to an earlier date in history lasted about fifty years.

When this latest work of Bauer's appeared he had long been regarded by theologians as an extinct force; nay, more, had been forgotten. And he had not even kept his promise. He had not succeeded in showing what that higher form of victory over the world was, which he declared superior to Christianity; and in place of the personality of Jesus he had finally set up a hybrid thing, laboriously compounded out of two personalities of so little substance as those of Seneca and Josephus. That was the end of his great undertaking.

But it was a mistake to bury, along with the Bauer of the second period, also the Bauer of the first period, the critic—for the latter was not dead. It was, indeed, nothing less than a misfortune that Strauss and Bauer appeared within so short a time of one another. Bauer passed practically unnoticed, because every one was preoccupied with Strauss. Another unfortunate thing was that Bauer overthrew with his powerful criticism the hypothesis which attributed real historical value to Mark, so that it lay for a long time disregarded, and there ensued a barren period of twenty years in the critical study of the Life of Jesus.

The only critic with whom Bauer can be compared is Reimarus. Each exercised a terrifying and disabling influence upon his time. No one else had been so keenly conscious as they of the extreme complexity of the problem offered by the life of Jesus. In view of this complexity they found themselves compelled to seek a solution outside the confines of verifiable history. Reimarus, by finding the basis of the story of Jesus in a deliberate imposture on the part of the disciples; Bauer, by postulating an original Evangelist who invented the history. On this ground it was just that they should lose their case. But in dismissing the solutions which they offered, their contemporaries also dismissed the problems which had necessitated such solutions; they dismissed them because they were as little able to grasp as to remove these difficulties.

But the time is past for pronouncing judgment upon Lives of Christ on the ground of the solutions which they offer. For us the great men are not those who solved the problems, but those who discovered them. Bauer's "Criticism of the Gospel History" is worth a good dozen Lives of Jesus, because his work, as we are only now coming to recognise, after half a century, is the ablest and most complete collection of the difficulties of the Life of Jesus which is anywhere to be found.

[pg 160]

Unfortunately, by the independent, the too loftily independent way in which he developed his ideas, he destroyed the possibility of their influencing contemporary theology. The shaft which he had driven into the mountain broke down behind him, so that it needed the work of a whole generation to lay bare once more the veins of ore which he had struck. His contemporaries could not suspect that the abnormality of his solutions was due to the intensity with which he grasped the problems as problems, and that he had become blind to history by examining it too microscopically. Thus for his contemporaries he was a mere eccentric.

But his eccentricity concealed a penetrating insight. No one else had as yet grasped with the same completeness the idea that primitive Christianity and early Christianity were not merely the direct outcome of the preaching of Jesus, not merely a teaching put into practice, but more, much more, since to the experience of which Jesus was the subject there allied itself the experience of the world-soul at a time when its body—humanity under the Roman Empire—lay in the throes of death. Since Paul, no one had apprehended so powerfully the mystic idea of the super-sensible σῶμα Χριστοῦ. Bauer transferred it to the historical plane and found the "body of Christ" in the Roman Empire.

[pg 161]

XII. Further Imaginative Lives Of Jesus

Charles Christian Hennell. Untersuchungen über den Ursprung des Christentums. (An Inquiry concerning the Origin of Christianity.) 1840. With a preface by David Friedrich Strauss. English edition, 1838.

Wichtige Enthüllungen über die wirkliche Todesart Jesu. Nach einem alten zu Alexandria gefundenen Manuskripte von einem Zeitgenossen Jesu aus dem heiligen Orden der Essäer. (Important Disclosures concerning the Manner of Jesus' Death. From an ancient MS. found at Alexandria, written by a contemporary of Jesus belonging to the sacred Order of the Essenes.) 1849. 5th ed., Leipzig. (Anonymous.)

Historische Enthüllungen über die wirklichen Ereignisse der Geburt und Jugend Jesu. Als Fortsetzung der zu Alexandria aufgefundenen alten Urkunden aus dem Essäerorden. (Historical Disclosures concerning the real circumstances of the Birth and Youth of Jesus. A Continuation of the ancient Essene MS. discovered at Alexandria.) 1849. 2nd ed., Leipzig.

August Friedrich Gfrörer. Kritische Geschichte des Urchristentums. (Critical History of Primitive Christianity.)

Vol. i. 1st ed., 1831; 2nd, 1835. Part i. 543 pp.; Part ii. 406 pp. Vol. ii. 1838. Part i. 452 pp.; Part ii. 417 pp.

Richard von der Alm. (Pseudonym of *Friedrich Wilhelm Ghillany*.) Theologische Briefe an die Gebildeten der deutschen Nation, 1863. (Theological Letters to the Cultured Classes of the German People, 1863.) Vol. i. 929 pp.; Vol. ii. 656 pp.; Vol. iii. 802 pp.

Ludwig Noack. Die Geschichte Jesu auf Grund freier geschichtlicher Untersuchungen über das Evangelium und die Evangelien. (The History of Jesus on the Basis of a free Historical Inquiry regarding the Gospel and the Gospels.) 2nd ed., 1876, Mannheim. Book i. 251 pp.; Book ii. 187 pp.; Book iii. 386 pp.; Book iv. 285 pp.

Strauss can hardly be said to have done himself honour by contributing a preface to the translation of Hennell's work, which is nothing more than Venturini's "Non-miraculous History of the Great Prophet of Nazareth" tricked out with a fantastic paraphernalia of learning.[97]

The two series of "Important Disclosures" also are really "conveyed" with no particular ability from that classic romance of [pg 162] the Life of Jesus, but that did not prevent their making something of a sensation at the time when they appeared.[98] Jesus, according to his narrative, was the son of a member of the Essene Order. The child was watched over by the Order and prepared for His future mission. He entered on His public ministry as a tool of the Essenes, who after the crucifixion took Him down from the cross and resuscitated Him.

These "Disclosures" only preserve the more external features of Venturini's representation. His Life of Jesus had been more than a mere romance, it had been an imaginative solution of problems which he had intuitively perceived. It may be regarded as the Forerunner of rationalistic criticism. The problems which Venturini had intuitively perceived were not solved either by the rationalists, or by Strauss, or by Weisse. These writers had not succeeded in providing that of which Venturini had dreamed—a living purposeful connexion between the events of the life of Jesus—or in explaining His Person and Work as having a relation, either positive or negative, to the circumstances of Late Judaism. Venturini's plan, however fantastic, connects the life of Jesus with Jewish history and contemporary thought much more closely than any other Life of Jesus, for that connexion is of course vital to the plot of the romance. In Weisse's "Gospel History" criticism had deliberately renounced the attempt to explain Jesus directly from Judaism, finding itself unable to establish any connexion between His teachings and contemporary Jewish ideas. The way was therefore once more open to the imagination. Accordingly several imaginative Lives preluded a new era in the study of the subject, in so far as they endeavoured to understand Jesus on the basis of purely Jewish ideas, in some cases as affirming these, in others as opposing them in favour of a more spiritual conception. In Gfrörer, Richard von der Alm, and Noack, begins the skirmishing preparatory to the future battle over eschatology.[99]

[pg 163]

August Friedrich Gfrörer, born in 1803 at Calw, was "Repetent" at the Tübingen theological seminary at the time when Strauss was studying there. After being curate at the principal church in Stuttgart for a year he gave up, in 1830, the clerical profession in order to devote himself wholly to his clerical studies.

By that time he had abandoned Christianity. In the preface to the first edition of the first volume of his work, he describes Christianity as a system which now only maintains itself by the force of custom, after having commended itself to antiquity "by the hope of the mystic Kingdom of the future world and having ruled the middle ages by the fear of the same future." By enunciating this view he has made an end, he thinks, of all high-flying Hegelian ideas, and being thus freed from all speculative prejudices he feels himself in a position to approach his task from a purely historical standpoint, with a view to showing how much of Christianity is the creation of one exceptional Personality, and how much belongs to the time in which it arose. In the first volume he describes how the transformation of Jewish theology in Alexandria reacted upon Palestinian theology, and how it came to its climax in Philo. The great Alexandrian anticipated, according to Gfrörer, the ideas of Paul. His "Therapeutae" are identical with the Essenes. At the same period Judaea was kept in a ferment by a series of risings, to all of which the incentive was found in Messianic expectations. Then Jesus appeared. The three points to be investigated in His history are: what end He had in view; why He died; and what modifications His work underwent at the hands of the Apostles.

The second volume, entitled "The Sacred Legend," does not, however, carry out this plan. The works of Strauss and Weisse necessitated a new method of treatment. The fame of Strauss's achievement stirred Gfrörer to emulation, and Weisse, with his priority of Mark and rejection of John, must be refuted. The work is therefore almost a polemic against Weisse for his "want of historic sense," and ends in setting up views which had not entered into Gfrörer's mind at the time when he wrote his first volume.

The statements of Papias regarding the Synoptists, which Weisse followed, are not deserving of credence. For a whole generation and more the tradition about Jesus had passed from mouth to mouth, and it had absorbed much that was legendary. Luke was the first—as his preface shows—who checked that process, and undertook to separate what was genuine from what was not. He is the most trustworthy of the Evangelists, for he keeps closely to his sources and adds nothing of his own, in contrast with Matthew who, writing at a later date, used sources of less value and invented matter of his own, which Gfrörer finds especially in the story of the passion in this Gospel. The lateness of Matthew is also evident [pg 164] from his tendency to carry over the Old Testament into the New. In Luke, on the other hand, the sources are so conscientiously treated that Gfrörer finds no difficulty in analysing the narrative into its component parts, especially as he always has a purely instinctive feeling "whenever a different wind begins to blow."

Both Gospels, however, were written long after the destruction of the holy city, since they do not draw their material from the Jerusalem tradition, but "from the Christian legends which had grown up in the neighbourhood of the Sea of Tiberias," and in consequence "mistakenly transferred the scene of Jesus' ministry to Galilee." For this reason it is not surprising "that even down into the second century many Christians had doubts about the truth of the Synoptics and ventured to express their doubts." Such doubts only ceased when the Church became firmly established and began to use its authority to suppress the objections of individuals. Mark is the earliest witness to doubts within the primitive Christian community regarding the credibility of his predecessors. Luke and Matthew are for him not yet sacred books; he desires to reconcile their inconsistencies, and at the same time to produce "a Gospel composed of materials of which the authenticity could be maintained even against the doubters." For this reason he omits most of the discourses, ignores the birth-story, and of the miracles retains only those which were most deeply embedded in the tradition. His Gospel was probably produced between 110 and 120. The "non-genuine" conclusion was a later addition, but by the Evangelist himself. Thus Mark proves that the Synoptists contain legendary matter even though they are separated from the events which they relate only by a generation and a half, or at most two generations. To show that there is nothing strange in this, Gfrörer gives a long catalogue of miracles found in historians who were contemporaries of the events which they describe, and in some cases were concerned in them—in this connexion Cortez affords him a rich storehouse of material. On the other hand, all objections against the genuineness of the Fourth Gospel collapse miserably. It is true that, like the others, it offers no historically accurate report of the discourses of Jesus. It pictures Him as the Logos-Christ and makes Him speak in this character; which Jesus certainly did not do. Inadvertently the author makes John the Baptist speak in the same way. That does not matter, however, for the historical conditions are rightly represented; rightly, because Jerusalem was the scene of the greater part of the ministry, and the five Johannine miracles are to be retained. The healing of the nobleman's son, that of the lame man at the pool of Bethesda, and that of the man blind from birth happened just as they are told. The story of the miracle at Cana rests on a misunderstanding, for the wine which Jesus provided was really the wedding-gift which He had brought [pg 165] with Him. In the raising of Lazarus a real case of apparent death is combined with a polemical exaggeration of it, the restoration to life becoming, in the course of controversy with the Jews, an actual resurrection. Having thus won free, dragging John along with him, from the toils of the Hegelian denial of miracle—only, it is true, by the aid of Venturini—and being prepared to explain the feeding of the multitude on the most commonplace rationalistic lines, he may well boast that he has "driven the doubt concerning the Fourth Gospel into a very small corner."

"The miserable era of negation," cries Gfrörer, "is now at an end; affirmation begins. We are ascending the eastern mountains from which the pure airs of heaven breathe upon the spirit. Our guide shall be historical mathematics, a science which is as yet known to few, and has not been applied by any one to the New Testament." This "mathematic" of Gfrörer's consists in developing his whole argument out of a single postulate. Let it be granted to him that all other claimants of the Messiahship—Gfrörer, in defiance of the evidence of Josephus, makes all the leaders of revolt in Palestine claimants of the Messiahship—were put to death by the Romans, whereas Jesus was crucified by His own people: it follows that the Messiahship of Jesus was not political, but spiritual. He had declared Himself to be in a certain sense the longed-for Messiah, but in another sense He was not so. His preaching moved in the sphere of Philonian ideas; although He did not as yet explicitly apply the Logos doctrine, it was implicit in His thought, so that the discourses of the Fourth Gospel have an essential truth. All Messianic conceptions, the Kingdom of God, the judgment, the future world, are sublimated into the spiritual region. The resurrection of the dead becomes a present eternal life. The saying in John v. 24, "He that heareth my word, and believeth on Him that sent me, hath eternal life and cometh not into judgment; but is passed from death into life," is the only authentic part of that discourse. The reference which follows to the coming judgment and the resurrection of the dead is a Jewish interpolation. Jesus did not believe that He Himself was to rise from the dead. Nevertheless, the "resurrection" is historic; Joseph of Arimathea, a member of the Essene Order, whose tool Jesus unconsciously was, had bribed the Romans to make the crucifixion of Jesus only a pretence, and to crucify two others with Him in order to distract attention from Him. After He was taken down from the cross, Joseph removed Him to a tomb of his own which had been hewn out for the purpose in the neighbourhood of the cross, and succeeded in resuscitating Him. The Christian Church grew out of the Essene Order by giving a further development to its ideas, and it is impossible to explain the organisation of the Church without taking account of the regulations of the Order. [pg 166] The work closes with a rhapsody on the Church and its development into the Papal system.

Gfrörer thus works into Venturini's plan a quantity of material drawn from Philo. His first volume would have led one to expect a more original and scientific result. But the author is one of those "epileptics of criticism" for whom criticism is not a natural and healthy means of arriving at a result, but who, in consequence of the fits of criticism to which they are subject, and which they even endeavour to intensify, fall into a condition of exhaustion, in which the need for some fixed point becomes so imperative that they create it for themselves by self-suggestion—as they previously did their criticism—and then flatter themselves that they have really found it.

This need for a fixed point carried the former rival of Strauss into Catholicism, for which his "General History of the Church" (1841-1846) already shows a strong admiration. After the appearance of this work Gfrörer became Professor of History in the University of Freiburg. In 1848 he was active in the German Parliament in endeavouring to promote a reunion of the Protestants with the Catholics. In 1853 he went over to the Roman Church. His family had already gone over, at Strassburg, during the revolutionary period. In the conflict of the church with the Baden Government he vehemently supported the claims of the Pope. He died in 1861.

Incomparably better and more thorough is the attempt to write a Life of Jesus embodied in the "Theological Letters to the Cultured Classes of the German Nation." Their writer takes Gfrörer's studies as his starting-point, but instead of spiritualising unjustifiably he ventures to conceive the Jewish world of thought in which Jesus lived in its simple realism. He was the first to place the eschatology recognised by Strauss and Reimarus in an historical setting—that of Venturini's plan—and to write a Life of Jesus entirely governed by the idea of eschatology.

The author, Friedrich Wilhelm Ghillany, was born in 1807 at Erlangen. His first studies were in theology. His rationalistic views, however, compelled him to abandon the clerical profession. He became librarian at Nuremberg in 1841 and engaged in controversial writing of an anti-orthodox character, but distinguished himself also by historical work of outstanding merit. A year after the publication of the "Theological Letters," which he issued under the pseudonym of Richard von der Alm, he published a collection of "The Opinions of Heathen and Christian Writers of the first Christian Centuries about Jesus Christ" (1864), a work which gives evidence of a remarkable range of reading. In 1855 he removed to Munich in the hope of obtaining a post in the diplomatic [pg 167] service, but in spite of his solid acquirements he did not succeed. No one would venture to appoint a man of such outspoken anti-ecclesiastical views. He died in 1876.

As regards the question of the sources, Ghillany occupies very nearly the Tübingen standpoint, except that he holds Matthew to be later than Luke, and Mark to be extracted, not from these Gospels in their present form, but from their sources. John is not authentic.

The worship offered to Jesus after His death by the Christian community is, according to Ghillany, not derived from pure Judaism, but from a Judaism influenced by oriental religions. The influence of the cult of Mithra, for example, is unmistakable. In it, as in Christianity, we find the virgin-birth, the star, the wise men, the cross, and the resurrection. Were it not for the human sacrifice of the Mithra cult, the idea which is operative in the Supper, of eating and drinking the flesh and blood of the Son of Man, would be inexplicable.

The whole Eastern world was at that time impregnated with Gnostic ideas, which centred in the revelation of the Divine in the human. In this way there arose, for example, a Samaritan Gnosis, independent of the Christian. Christianity itself is a species of Gnosis. In any case the metaphysical conception of the Divine Sonship of Jesus is of secondary origin. If He was in any sense the Son of God for the disciples, they can only have thought of this sonship in a Gnostic fashion, and supposed that the "highest angel," the Son of God, had taken up His abode in Him.

John the Baptist had probably come forth from among the Essenes, and he preached a spiritualised Kingdom of Heaven. He held himself to be Elias. Jesus' aims were originally similar; He came forward "in the cause of sound religious teaching for the people." He made no claim to Davidic descent; that is to be credited to dogmatic theology. Similarly Papias is wrong in ascribing to Jesus the crude eschatological expectations implied in the saying about the miraculous vine in the Messianic Kingdom.

It is certain, however, that Jesus held Himself to be Messiah and expected the early coming of the Kingdom. His teaching is Rabbinic; all His ideas have their source in contemporary Judaism, whose world of thought we can reconstruct from the Rabbinic writings; for even if these only became fixed at a later period, the thoughts on which they are based were already current in the time of Jesus. Another source of great importance is Justin's "Dialogue with the Jew Trypho."

The starting-point in interpreting the teaching of Jesus is the idea of repentance. In the tractate "Sanhedrin" we find: "The set time of the Messiah is already here; His coming depends now upon repentance and good works. Rabbi Eleazer says, 'When the [pg 168] Jews repent they shall be redeemed.'" The Targum of Jonathan observes, on Zech. x. 3, 4,[100] "The Messiah is already born, but remains in concealment because of the sins of the Hebrews." We find the same thoughts put into the mouth of Trypho in Justin. In the same Targum of Jonathan, Isa. liii. is interpreted with reference to the sufferings of the Messiah. Judaism, therefore, was not unacquainted with the idea of a suffering Messiah. He was not identified, however, with the heavenly Messiah of Daniel. The Rabbis distinguished two Messiahs, one of Israel and one of Judah. First the Messiah of the Kingdom of Israel, denominated the Son of Joseph, was to come from Galilee to suffer death at the hands of the Gentiles in order to make atonement for the sins of the Hebrew nation. Only after that would the Messiah predicted by Daniel, the son of David, of the tribe of Judah, appear in glory upon the clouds of heaven. Finally, He also, after two-and-sixty weeks of years, should be taken away, since the Messianic Kingdom, even as conceived by Paul, was only a temporary supernatural condition of the world.

The Messianic expectation, being directed to supernatural events, had no political character, and one who knew Himself to be the Messiah could never dream of using earthly means for the attainment of His ends; He would expect all things to be brought about by the Divine intervention. In this respect Ghillany grasps clearly the character of the eschatology of Jesus—more clearly than any one had ever done before.

The rôle of the Messiah, who prior to His supernatural manifestation remains in concealment upon earth, is therefore passive. He who is conscious of a Messianic vocation does not seek to found a Kingdom among men. He waits with confidence. He issues forth from His passivity with the sole purpose of making atonement, by vicarious suffering, for the sins of the people, in order that it may be possible for God to bring about the new condition of things. If, in spite of the repentance of the people and the occurrence of the signs which pointed to its being at hand, the coming of the Kingdom should be delayed, the man who is conscious of a Messianic vocation must, by His death, compel the intervention of God. His vocation in this world is to die.

Brought within the lines of these reflections the Life of Jesus shapes itself as follows.

Jesus was the tool of a mystical sect allied to the Essenes, the head of which was doubtless that Joseph of Arimathea who makes so sudden and striking an appearance in the Gospel narrative. This party desired to bring about the coming of the Kingdom of Heaven by mystical means, whereas the mass of the people, led astray by the Pharisees, thought to force on its coming by means [pg 169] of a rising. In the preacher of a spiritual Kingdom of Heaven, who was resolved to go to death for His cause, the mystical party discovered Messiah the son of Joseph, and they recognised that His death was necessary to make possible the coming of the heavenly Messiah predicted by Daniel. That Jesus Himself was the Messiah of Daniel, that He would immediately rise again in order to ascend to His heavenly throne, and would come thence with the hosts of heaven to establish the Kingdom of Heaven, these people did not themselves believe. But they encouraged Him in this belief, thinking that He would hardly commit Himself to a sacrificial death from which there was to be no resurrection. It was left uncertain to His mind whether Jehovah would be content with the repentance of the people, in so far as it had taken place, as realising the necessary condition for the bringing in of the Kingdom of Heaven, or whether an atonement by blood, offered by the death of Messiah the son of Joseph, would be needful. It had been explained to Him that when the calculated year of grace arrived, He must go up to Jerusalem and endeavour to rouse the Jews to Messianic enthusiasm in order to compel Jehovah to come to their aid with His heavenly hosts. From the action of Jehovah it could then be discovered whether the preaching of repentance and baptism would suffice to make atonement for the people before God or not. If Jehovah did not appear, a deeper atonement must be made; Jesus must pay the penalty of death for the sins of the Jews, but on the third day would rise again from the dead and ascend to the throne of God and come again thence to found the Kingdom of Heaven. "Any one can see," concludes Ghillany, "that our view affords a very natural explanation of the anxiety of the disciples, the suspense of Jesus Himself, and the prayer, 'If it be possible let this cup pass from me.' "

"It was apparently only towards the close of His life that Jesus revealed to the disciples the possibility that the Son of Man might have to suffer and die before He could found the Messianic Kingdom."

With this possibility before Him, He came to Jerusalem and there awaited the Divine intervention. Meanwhile Joseph of Arimathea lent his aid towards securing His condemnation in the Sanhedrin. He must die on the day of the Passover; on the day of the Preparation He must be at hand and ready in Jerusalem. He held, with His disciples, a love-feast after the Essene custom, not a Paschal meal, and in doing so associated thoughts of His death with the breaking of bread and the pouring out of the wine. "He did not lay upon His disciples any injunction to continue the celebration of a feast of this kind until the time of His return, because He thought of His resurrection and His heavenly glory as about to take place after three days. But when His return was [pg 170] delayed the early Christians attached these sayings of His about the bread and wine to their Essene love-feast, and explained this common meal of the community as a commemoration of the Last Supper of Jesus and His disciples, a memorial Feast in honour of their Saviour, the celebration of which must be continued until His coming."

When the armed band came to arrest Him, Jesus surrendered to His fate. Pilate almost set Him free, holding Him to be a mere enthusiast who placed His hopes only in the Divine intervention. Joseph of Arimathea, however, succeeded in averting this danger. "Even on the cross Jesus seems to have continued to hope for the Divine intervention, as is evidenced by the cry, 'My God! My God! why hast thou forsaken me?' " Joseph of Arimathea provided for His burial.

The belief in His resurrection rests upon the visions of the disciples, which are to be explained by their intense desire for the Parousia, of which He had given them the promise. After setting their affairs in order in Galilee they returned at the Feast of Pentecost to Jerusalem, which they had left in alarm, in order there to await the Parousia in company with other Galilaean believers.

The confession of faith of the primitive Christian community was the simplest conceivable: Jesus the Messiah had come, not as a temporal conqueror, but as the Son of Man foretold by Daniel, and had died for the sins of the people. In other respects they were strict Jews, kept the Law, and were constantly in the Temple. Only the community of goods and the brotherhood-meal are of an Essene character.

"The Christianity of the original community in Jerusalem was thus a mixture of Zealotism and Mysticism which did not include any wholly new element, and even in its conception of the Messiah had nothing peculiar to itself except the belief that the Son of Man predicted by Daniel had already come in the person of Jesus of Nazareth ... that He was now enthroned at the right hand of God, and would again appear as the expected Son of Man upon the clouds of heaven according to Daniel's prophecy." Jesus, therefore, had triumphed over the mystical party who desired to make use of Him in the character of Messiah the son of Joseph—their Messiah, the heavenly Son of Man, had not come. Jesus, in virtue of what He had done, had taken His place both in heaven and in earth.

How much of Venturini's plan is here retained? Only the "mystical part" which serves the purpose of setting the action of the drama in motion. All the rest of it, the rationalistic part, has been transmuted into an historical conception. Miracle and trickery, along with the stage-play resurrection, have been purged [pg 171] away in the fires of Strauss's criticism. There remains only a fundamental conception which has a certain greatness—a brotherhood which looks for the coming of the Kingdom of Heaven appoints one of its members to undergo as Messiah an atoning death, that the coming of the Kingdom, for which the time is at hand, may not be delayed. This brotherhood is the only fictitious element in the whole construction—much as in the primitive steam-engine the valves were still worked by hand while the rest of the machinery was actuated by its own motive-power. So in this Life of Jesus the motive-power is drawn entirely from historical sources, and the want of an automatic starting arrangement is a mere anachronism. Strike out the superfluous rôle of Joseph of Arimathea, and the distinction of the two Messiahs, which is not clear even in the Rabbis, and substitute the simple hypothesis that Jesus, in the course of His Messianic vocation, when He thinks the time for the coming of the Kingdom has arrived, goes freely to Jerusalem, and, as it were, compels the secular power to put Him to death, in order by this act of atonement to win for the world the immediate coming of the Kingdom, and for Himself the glory of the Son of Man—make these changes, and you have a life of Jesus in which the motive-power is a purely historical force. It is impossible to indicate briefly all the parts of which the seemingly complicated, but in reality impressively simple, mechanism of this Life of Jesus is composed. The conduct of Jesus, alike in its resolution and in its hesitation, becomes clear, and not less so that of the disciples. All far-fetched historical ingenuity is dispensed with. Jesus acts "because His hour is come." This decisive placing of the Life of Jesus in the "last time" (*cf.* 1 Peter i. 20 φανερωθέντος δὲ ἐπ' ἐσχάτων τῶν χρόνων δἰ ὑμᾶς) is an historical achievement without parallel. Not less so is the placing of the thought of the passion in its proper eschatological setting as an act of atonement. Where had the character and origin of the primitive community ever been brought into such clear connexion with the death of Jesus? Who had ever before so earnestly considered the problem why the Christian community arose in Jerusalem and not in Galilee? "But the solution is too simple, and, moreover, is not founded on a severely scientific chain of reasoning, but on historical intuition and experiment, the simple experiment of introducing the Life of Jesus into the Jewish eschatological world of thought"—so the theologians replied, or so, at least, they might have replied if they had taken this curious work seriously, if, indeed, they had read it at all. But how were they to suspect that in a book which seemed to aim at founding a new Deistic Church, and which went out with the Wolfenbüttel Fragmentist into the desert of the most barren natural religion, a valuable historical conception might be found? It is true that [pg 172] no one suspected at that time that in the forgotten work of Reimarus there lay a dangerous historical discovery, a kind of explosive material such as can only be collected by those who stand free from every responsibility towards historical Christianity, who have abandoned every prejudice, in the good sense as well as in the bad—and whose one desire in regard to the Gospel history is to be "spirits that constantly deny."[101] Such thinkers, if they have historical gifts, destroy artificial history in the cause of true history and, willing evil, do good—if it be admitted that the discovery of truth is good. If this negative work is a good thing, the author of the "Letters to the German People" performed a distinguished service, for his negation is radical. The new Church which was to be founded on this historic overcoming of historic Christianity was to combine "only what was according to reason in Judaism and Christianity." From Judaism it was to take the belief in one sole, spiritual, perfect God; from Christianity the requirement of brotherly love to all men. On the other hand, it was to eliminate what was contrary to reason in each: from Judaism the ritual system and the sacrifices; from Christianity the deification of Jesus and the teaching of redemption through His blood. How comes so completely unhistorical a temperament to be combined with so historical an intellect? His Jesus, after all, has no individuality; He is a mere eschatological machine.

In accordance with the confession of faith of the new Church of which Ghillany dreamed, the calendar of the Feasts is to be transformed as follows:—

1. Feast of the Deity, the first and second of January.

2. Feast of the Dignity of Man and Brotherly Love, first and second of April.

3. Feast of the Divine Blessing in Nature, first and second of July.

4. Feast of Immortality, first and second of October.

Apart from these eight Feast days, and the Sundays, all the other days of the year are working days.

From the order of divine service we may note the following: "The sermon, which should begin with instruction and exhortation and close with consolation and encouragement, must not last longer than half an hour."

The series of Lives of Jesus which combine criticism with fiction is closed by Noack's Story of Jesus. A freethinker like Ghillany, but lacking the financial independence which a kindly fate had conferred upon the latter, Noack led a life which may properly be described as a constant martyrdom, lightened only by his intense love of theological studies, which nevertheless were [pg 173] responsible for all his troubles. Born in 1819, of a clerical family in Hesse, he became in 1842 Pastor's assistant and teacher of religion at Worms in the Hessian Palatinate. The Darmstadt reactionaries drove him out of this position in 1844 without his having given any ground of offence. In 1849 he became "Repetent" in Philosophy at the University of Giessen at a salary of four hundred gulden. In 1855 he was promoted to be Professor Extraordinary without having his salary raised. In 1870, at the age of 51, he was appointed assistant at the University Library and received at the same time the title of Ordinary Professor. He died in 1885. He was an extremely prolific writer, always ingenious, and possessed of wide knowledge, but he never did anything of real permanent value either in philosophy or theology. He was not without critical acumen, but there was too much of the poet in him; a critical discovery was an incitement to an imaginative reconstruction of the history. In 1870-1871 he published, after many preliminary studies, his chief work, "From the Jordan Uplands to Golgotha; four books on the Gospel and the Gospels."[102] It passed unnoticed. Attributing its failure to the excitement aroused by the war, which ousted all other interests, he issued a revised edition in 1876 under the title "The History of Jesus, on the Basis of Free Historical Inquiry concerning the Gospel and the Gospels,"[103] but with hardly greater success.

And yet the fundamental critical ideas which can be detected beneath this narrative, in spite of its having the form of fiction, give this work a significance such as the contemporary Lives of Jesus which won the applause of theologians did not possess. It is the only Life of Jesus hitherto produced which is written consistently from the Johannine point of view from beginning to end. Strauss had not, after all, in Noack's opinion, conclusively shown the absolute incompatibility of the Synoptics with the Fourth Gospel; neither he nor any other critic had felt the full difficulty of the question why the Fourth Evangelist should be at pains to invent the numerous journeys to the Feasts, seeing that the development of the Logos Christology did not necessarily involve any alteration of the scene of the ministry; on the contrary, it would, one might think, have been the first care of the Evangelist to inweave his novel theory with the familiar tradition in order to avoid discrediting his narrative in advance by his innovations. Noack's conclusion is that the inconsistency is not due to a single author; it is the result of a long process of redaction in which various divergent tendencies have been at work. But as the Fourth Gospel is not the logical terminus of the process of [pg 174] alteration, the only alternative is to place it at the beginning. What we have to seek in it is the original Gospel from which the process of transforming the tradition started.

There is also another line of argument based on the contradictions in the Gospel tradition which leads to the hypothesis that we have to do with redactions of the Gospels. Either Jesus was the Jewish Messiah of the Synoptics, or a Son of God in the Greek, spiritual sense, whose self-consciousness must be interpreted by means of the Logos doctrine: He cannot have been both at the same time. But it is inconceivable that a Jewish claimant of the Messiahship would have been left unmolested up to the last, and have had virtually to force the authorities to put him to death. On the other hand, if He were a simple enthusiast claiming to be a Son of God, a man who lived only for his own "self-consciousness," He might from the beginning have taken up this attitude without being in any way molested, except by the scorn of men. In this respect also, therefore, the primitive Gospel which we can recover from John has the advantage. It was only later that this "Son of God" became the Jewish Messiah.

We arrive at the primitive Johannine writing when we cancel in the Fourth Gospel all Jewish doctrine and all miracles.[104] Its date is the year 60 and it was composed by—Judas, the beloved disciple. This primitive Gospel received little modification and still shows clearly "the wonderful reality of its history." It aims only at giving a section of Jesus' history, a representation of His attitude of mind and spirit. With "simple ingenuousness" it gives, "along with the kernel of the historical material of the Gospel, Jesus' thoughts about His own Person in the mysterious oracular sayings and deeply thoughtful and moving discourses by which the Nazarene stirred rather than enlightened the world." Events of a striking character were, however, absent from it. The feeding of the multitude was represented in it as effected by natural means. It was a philanthropic feeding of a multitude which certainly did not number thousands, the numbers are a later insertion; Jesus fed them with bread and fish which He purchased from a "sutler-lad." The healing of the lame man at the pool of Bethesda was the unmasking of a malingerer, whom the Lord exposed and ordered to depart. As He had bidden him carry his bed, and it was on the Sabbath, this brought Him into conflict with the authorities. His only "acts" were acts of self-revelation—mystical sayings which He threw out to the people. "The problem which meets us in

His history is in truth a psychological problem, how, namely, His exalted view of Himself came to be accepted as the purest and highest truth—in His lifetime, it is true, only by a limited circle of disciples, but after His departure by a constantly growing [pg 175] multitude of believing followers." The gospel of the beloved disciple Judas made its way quietly into the world, understood by few, even as Jesus Himself had been understood by a few only.

About ten years later, according to Noack, appeared the original form of Luke, which we can reconstruct from what is known of Marcion's Luke.[105] This Evangelist is under Pauline influence, and writes with an apologetic purpose. He desires to refute the calumny that Jesus was "possessed of a devil," and he does this by making Him cast out devils. It was in this way that miracle forced itself into the Gospel history.

But this primitive Luke, as Noack reconstructs it by combining the statements of the Fathers regarding Marcion's Gospel, knows nothing of Jesus' journey to Jerusalem to die. This circumstance is of capital importance to Noack, because in the course of his attempt to bring the topography of the Fourth Gospel into harmony with that of the Synoptics he had arrived at the remarkable result that the Johannine Christ worked in Galilee, not in Judaea. On the basis of the *Onomasticon* of Eusebius—which Noack, with the aid of topographical traditions derived from the Crusaders and statements of Mohammedan writers, interprets with a recklessness which is nothing short of criminal—Cana and Bethany (Bethabara) were not in the latitude of Jerusalem, but "near the head-waters of the Jordan in the upper part of the Jordan valley before it flows into the lake of Huleh. There, in Coele-Syria, on the southern slope of Hermon, was the scene of John the Baptist's labours; there Jesus began His ministry; thither He returned to die." "It is in the Galilaean district which forms the scene of the Song of Solomon that the reader of this book must be prepared to find the Golgotha of the cross." That is the sentence with which Noack's account of the Life of Jesus opens. This alludes to an idea which had already been worked out in his "Studies on the Song of Solomon,"[106] namely, that the mountain country surrounding the upper Jordan was the pre-exilic Judaea, and that the "city of David" was situated there. The Jews on their return from exile had at first endeavoured to rebuild that Coele-Syrian city of David with the ruins of Solomon's Temple, but had been driven away from it and had then taken the desperate resolution to build the temple of Zerubbabel upon the high plateau lying far to the south of ancient Israel. Ezra the Scribe interpolated the forgery on the ground of which this site began to be accepted as the former city of David. Under the Syrian oppression all remembrance of the ancient city of David entirely disappeared.

This fantastic edifice, in the construction of which the wildest [pg 176] etymologies play a part, is founded on the just recognition that a reconciliation of John with the Synoptists can only be effected by transferring some of the Johannine localities to the North; but this involves not only finding Bethany, Arimathea and the other places, but even the scene of Jesus' death in this district. The brook Kedron conveniently becomes the "brook of Cedars."

For fifty years the two earliest Evangelists, in spite of their poverty of incident, sufficed for the needs of the Christians. The "fire of Jesus" was fed chiefly by the Pauline Gospel. The original form of the Gospel of Luke accordingly became the starting-point of the next stage of development. Thus arose the Gospel of Mark. Mark was not a native of Palestine, but a man of Roman extraction living in Decapolis, who had not the slightest knowledge of the localities in which the life of Jesus was really passed. He undertook, about the year 130, "in the interest of the new Christian settlement at Jerusalem in Hadrian's time, deliberately and consciously to transform the original plan of the Gospel history and to represent the Lord as crucified at Jerusalem." The man who from the year 132 onward, as Mark the Bishop, preached the word of the Crucified to a Gentile Christian community amid the ruins of the holy city, had previously, as Mark the Evangelist, taken care that a prophet should not perish out of Jerusalem. In composing his Gospel he made use, in addition to Luke, of a traditional source which he found in Decapolis. He deliberately omitted the frequent journeys to Jerusalem which were still found in the original Luke, and inserted instead Jesus' journey to His death. He it was, also, who made the Nazarite into the Nazarene, laying the scene of Jesus' youth in Nazareth. To the cures of demoniacs he added magical acts such as the feeding of the multitude and the resurrection.

In Matthew, who appeared about 135, legend and fiction riot unchecked. In addition, Jewish parables and sayings are put into the mouth of Jesus, whereas He really had nothing to do with the Jewish world of ideas. For if anything is certain, it is that the moral maxims of the latest Gospel are of a distinctively Jewish origin. About the middle of the second century the originals of John and Luke underwent redaction. The redaction of the Logos Gospel was completed by the addition of the twenty-first chapter; the last redaction of Luke was perhaps carried out by Justin Martyr, fresh from completing his "Dialogue with Trypho"! Thus John and Luke are, in this final form, which is full of contradictions, the latest Gospels, and the saying is fulfilled about the first being last, and the last first.

Arbitrary as these suggestions are, there is nevertheless something impressive in the attempt to explain the remarkable inconsistencies which are found within the Gospel tradition by [pg 177] considerations relating to its origin and development. Despite all his far-fetched ideas, Noack really stands higher than some of his contemporaries who showed more prudence in their theological enterprises, and about that time were earning the applause of the faculty, and quieting the minds of the laity, by performing once more the old conjuring trick—assisted by some new feats of legerdemain—of harmonising John with the Synoptists in such a way as to produce a Life of Jesus which could be turned to the service of ecclesiastical theology.

The outline of the public Life of Jesus, as reconstructed by Noack, is as follows. It lasted from early in the year 35 to the 14th Nisan of the year 37, and began in the moment when Jesus revealed His consciousness of what He was. We do not know how long previously He had cherished it in secret. It is certain that the Baptist helped to bring about this revelation. This is the only part which he plays in the Gospel of John. He was neither a preacher of repentance, nor an Elias, nor the forerunner of Jesus, nor a mere signpost pointing to the Messiah, such as the secondary tradition makes him out to be.

Similarly everything that is Messianic in the consciousness of Jesus is secondary. The lines of His thought were guided by the Greek ideas about sons of God, for the soil of northern Galilee was saturated with these ideas. Other sources which contributed something were the personification of the Divine Wisdom in the "Wisdom Literature" and some of Philo's doctrines. Jesus became the son of God in an ecstatic trance! Had not Philo recognised ecstasy as the last and highest means of rising to union with the Divine?

Jesus' temperament, according to Noack, was pre-disposed to ecstasy, since He was born out of wedlock. One who had this burden upon His spirit may well have early taken refuge in His own thoughts, above the clouds, in the presence of the God of His fathers. Assailed in a thousand ways by the cruelty of the world, it would seem to Him as though His Heavenly Father, though unseen, was stretching out to Him the arms of consolation. Imagination, which ever mercifully lightens for men the yoke of misery, charmed the fatherless child out of His earthly sufferings and put into His hand a coloured glass through which He saw the world and life in a false light. Ecstatic enthusiasm had carried Him up to the dizzy height of spiritual union with the Father in Heaven. A hundred times He was cast down out of His dreams into the hard world of reality, to experience once more His earthly distresses, but ever anew He won His way by fasting, vigil, and prayer to the starry heaven of ecstasy.

"Jesus," Noack explains, "had in thought projected Himself beyond His earthly nativity and risen to the conception that His [pg 178] ego had been in existence before this earthly body in which He stood visibly upon the stage of the world. He felt that His ego had had being and life before He became incarnate upon earth.... This new conception of Himself, born of His solitary musings, was incorporated into the very substance of His natural personal ego. A new ego had superseded the old natural, corporeally conditioned ego."

Ambition, too, came into play—the high ambition to do God a service by the offering up of Himself. The passion of self-sacrifice is characteristic of a consciousness such as this. According to the document which underlies the Johannine Gospel it was not in consequence of outward events that Jesus took His resolve to die. "It was the later Gospel tradition which exhibited His fate as an inevitable consequence of His conflict with a world impervious to spiritual impression." In the original Gospel that fate was freely embraced from the outset as belonging to the vocation of the Son of God. Only by the constant presence of the thought of death could a life which for two years walked the razor edge of such dizzy dreams have been preserved from falling. The conviction, or perhaps rather the instinctive feeling, that the rôle of a Son of God upon earth was not one to be maintained for decades was the necessary counterpoise to the enthusiasm of Jesus' spirit. From the first He was as much at home with the thought of death as with His Heavenly Father.

This Son of Man—according to Noack's interpretation the title is equivalent to Son of Hope—requires of the multitude that they shall take His lofty dream for solid reality. "He revealed His message from heaven to the world at the Paschal Feast of the year 35, by throwing out a challenge to the Sadducaean hierarchy in Jerusalem." In the time between John's removal from the scene and John's death, there falls the visit of Jesus to Samaria and a sojourn in the neighbourhood of His Galilaean home. At the Feast of Tabernacles in Jerusalem in the autumn of that year, the healing of the lame man at the pool of Bethesda led to a breach with the Sabbatic regulations of the Pharisees. Later on, in consequence of His generous feeding of the multitude in the Gaulonite table-land, there is an attempt to make Him into a Messianic King; which He, however, repudiates. At the time of the Passover in Galilee in the year 36, in the synagogue at Capernaum, He tests the spiritual insight of those who may, He hopes, be ripe for the higher teaching concerning the Son of God made flesh, by the touchstone of His mystical words about the bread of life. At the next Feast of Tabernacles, in the city of Zion, He makes a last desperate attempt to move men's hearts by the parable of the Good Shepherd who is ready to lay down His life for His sheep, the people of Israel.

[pg 179]

But His adversaries are remorseless; they wound Him to the very depths of His spirit by bringing to Him the woman taken in adultery, and asking Him what they are to do with her. When this question was sprung upon Him, He saw in a moment the public humiliation designed by His adversaries. All eyes were turned upon Him, and for a few moments the embarrassment of One who was usually so self-possessed was patent to all. He stooped as though He desired to write with His finger upon the ground. Was it shame at His dishonourable birth that compelled Him thus to lower His gaze? But the painful silence of expectation among the spectators did not last long. His adversaries repeated their question, He raised His head and spoke the undying words: "Let him that is without sin among you cast the first stone at her."

Incensed by His constant references to His heavenly Sonship, they endeavour at last to stone Him. He flees from the Temple and takes refuge in the Jordan uplands. His purpose is, at the next Passover, that of the year 37, here in the mountains which were blessed as Joseph's portion, to offer His atoning death as that of the true paschal lamb, and with this act to quit the stage of the world's history. He remained in hiding in order to avoid the risk of assassination by the emissaries of the Pharisees. In Bethany He receives the mysterious visit of the Greeks, who doubtless desired to tempt Him to raise the standard of revolt as a claimant of the Messiahship, but He refuses to be shaken in His determination to die. The washing of the disciples' feet signifies their baptism with water, that they might thereafter receive the baptism of the Holy Spirit.

Judas, the disciple whom Jesus loved, who was a man of much resource, helped Him to avoid being arrested as a disturber of the peace by arranging that the "betrayal" should take place on the evening before the Passover, in order that Jesus might die, as He desired, on the day of the Passover. For this service of love he was, in the secondary tradition, torn from the bosom of the Lord and branded as a traitor.
[pg 180]

XIII. Renan

Ernest Renan. La Vie de Jésus. 1863. Paris, Michel Lévy Frères. 462 pp.

E. de Pressensé. Jésus-Christ, son temps, sa vie, son œuvre. Paris, 1865. 684 pp.

Ernest Renan was born in 1823 at Tréguier in Brittany. Intended for the priesthood, he entered the seminary of St. Sulpice in Paris, but there, in consequence of reading the German critical theology, he began to doubt the truth of Christianity and of its history. In October 1845, shortly before the time arrived for him to be ordained a sub-deacon, he left the seminary and began to work for his living as a private teacher. In 1849 he received a government grant to enable him to make a journey to Italy for the prosecution of his studies, the fruits of which appeared in his *Averroès et l'Averroïsme* (Paris, 1852); in 1856 he was made a member of the Académie des Inscriptions; in 1860 he received from Napoléon III. the means to make a journey to Phoenicia and Syria. After his return in 1862 he obtained the professorship of Semitic Languages at the Collège de France. But the widespread indignation aroused by his Life of Jesus, which appeared in the following year, forced the Government to remove him from his office. He refused a post as Librarian of the Imperial Library, and lived in retirement until the Republic of 1871 restored him to his professorship. In politics, as in religion, his position was somewhat indefinite. In religion he was no longer a Catholic; avowed free-thought was too plebeian for his taste, and in Protestantism the multiplicity of sects repelled him. Similarly in politics, in the period immediately following the fall of the Empire, he was in turn Royalist, Republican, and Bonapartist. At bottom he was a sceptic. He died in 1892, already half-forgotten by the public; until his imposing funeral and interment in the Panthéon recalled him to its memory.

Like Strauss, Renan designed his Life of Jesus to form part of a complete account of the history and dogma of the early Church. His purpose, however, was purely historical; it was no part of his [pg 181] project to set up, on the basis of the history, a new system of dogma, as Strauss had desired to do. This plan was not only conceived, but carried out. *Les Apôtres* appeared in 1866; *St. Paul* in 1869; *L'Anté-Christ* in 1873; *Les Évangiles* in 1877; *L'Église chrétienne* in 1879; *Marc-Aurèle et la fin du monde antique* in 1881. Several of these works were more valuable than the one which opened the series, but for the world Renan continued to be the author of the *Vie de Jésus*, and of that alone.

He planned the work at Gaza, and he dedicated it to his sister Henriette, who died soon after, in Syria, and lies buried at Byblus.

This was the first Life of Jesus for the Catholic world, which had scarcely been touched—the Latin peoples least of all—by the two and a half generations of critical study which had been devoted to the subject. It is true, Strauss's work had been translated into French,[107] but it had made only a passing stir, and that only among a little circle of intellectuals. Now came a writer with the characteristic French mental accent, who gave to the Latin world in a single book the result of the whole process of German criticism.

But Renan's work marked an epoch, not for the Catholic world only, but for general literature. He laid the problem which had hitherto occupied only theologians before the whole cultured world. And not as a problem, but as a question of which he, by means of his historical science and aesthetic power of reviving the past, could provide a solution. He offered his readers a Jesus who was alive, whom he, with his artistic imagination, had met under the blue heaven of Galilee, and whose lineaments his inspired pencil had seized. Men's attention was arrested, and they thought to see Jesus, because Renan had the skill to make them see blue skies, seas of waving corn, distant mountains, gleaming lilies, in a landscape with the Lake of Gennesareth for its centre, and to hear with him in the whispering of the reeds the eternal melody of the Sermon on the Mount.

Yet the aesthetic feeling for nature which gave birth to this Life of Jesus was, it must be confessed, neither pure nor profound. It is a standing enigma why French art, which in painting grasps nature with a directness and vigour, with an objectivity in the best sense of the word, such as is scarcely to be found in the art of any other nation, has in poetry treated it in a fashion which scarcely ever goes beyond the lyrical and sentimental, the artificial, the subjective, in the worst sense of the word. Renan is no exception to this rule, any more than Lamartine or Pierre Loti. He looks at the landscape with the eye of a decorative painter seeking a *motif* for a lyrical composition upon which he is engaged. But that was not noticed by the many, because they, after all, were accustomed to have [pg 182] nature dressed up for them, and had had their taste so corrupted by a certain kind of lyricism that they had lost the power of distinguishing between truth and artificiality. Even those who might have noticed it were so astonished and delighted at being shown Jesus in the Galilaean landscape that they were content to yield to the enchantment.

Along with this artificial feeling for nature a good many other things were accepted without question. There is scarcely any other work on the subject which so abounds in lapses of taste— and those of the most distressing kind—as Renan's *Vie de Jésus*. It is Christian art in the worst sense of the term—the art of the wax image. The gentle Jesus, the beautiful Mary, the fair Galilaeans who formed the retinue of the "amiable carpenter," might have been taken over in a body from the shop-window of an ecclesiastical art emporium in the Place St. Sulpice. Nevertheless, there is something magical about the work. It offends and yet it attracts. It will never be quite forgotten, nor is it ever likely to be surpassed in its own line, for nature is not prodigal of masters of style, and rarely is a book so directly born of enthusiasm as that which Renan planned among the Galilaean hills.

The essay on the sources of the Life of Jesus with which it opens is itself a literary masterpiece. With a kind of effortless ease he makes his readers acquainted with the criticism of Strauss, of Baur, of Reuss, of Colani. He does not argue, but simply sets the result vividly before the reader, who finds himself at once at home in the new world of ideas. He avoids any hard or glaring effects; by means of that skilful transition from point to point which Wagner in one of his letters praises as the highest art, everything is surrounded with atmosphere. But how much trickery and illusion there is in this art! In a few strokes he indicates the relation of John to the Synoptists; the dilemma is made clear, it seems as if one horn or the other must be chosen. Then he begins by artful touches to soften down the contrast. The discourses of John are not authentic; the historical Jesus cannot have spoken thus. But what about the statements of fact? Here Renan declares himself convinced by the graphic presentment of the passion story. Touches like "it was night," "they had lighted a fire of coals," "the coat was without seam," cannot have been invented. Therefore the Gospel must in some way go back to the disciple whom Jesus loved. It is possible, nay certain, that when as an old man he read the other Gospels, he was displeased by certain inaccuracies, and perhaps vexed that he was given so small a place in the history. He began to dictate a number of things which he had better means of knowing than the others; partly, too, with the purpose of showing that in many cases where Peter only had been mentioned he also had played a part, and indeed the principal part. [pg 183] Sometimes his recollection was quite fresh, sometimes it had been modified by time. When he wrote down the discourses, he had forgotten the Lake of Gennesareth and the winsome words which he had listened to upon its shores. He was now living in quite a different world. The events of the year 70 destroyed his hopes of the return of his Master. His Jewish prejudices fell away, and as he was still young, he adapted himself to the syncretistic, philosophic, gnostic environment amid which he found himself in Ephesus. Thus even Jesus' world of thought took on a new shape for him; although the discourses are perhaps rather to be referred to his school than to himself. But, when all is said, John remains the best biographer. Or, to put it more accurately, while all the Gospels are biographies, they are legendary biographies, even though they come down from the first century. Their texts need interpretation, and the clue to the interpretation can be supplied by aesthetic feeling. They must be subjected to a gentle pressure to bring them together, and make them coalesce into a unity in which all the data are happily combined.

How this is to be done Renan shows later in his description of the death of Jesus. "Suddenly," he says, "Jesus gave a terrible cry in which some thought they heard 'Father, into thy hands I commend my spirit,' but which others, whose thoughts were running on the fulfilment of prophecy, reported as 'It is finished.' "

The authentic sayings of Jesus are more or less self-evidencing. Coming in contact with one of them amid the welter of heterogeneous traditions, you feel a thrill of recognition. They leap forth and take their proper place, where their vivid power becomes apparent. For one who writes the life of Jesus on His native soil, the Gospels are not so much sources of information as incentives to revelation. "I had," Renan avows, "a fifth Gospel before my eyes, mutilated in parts, but still legible, and taking it for my guide I saw behind the narratives of Matthew and Mark, instead of an ideal Being of whom it might be maintained that He had never existed, a glorious human countenance full of life and movement." It is this Jesus of the fifth Gospel that he desires to portray.

In looking at the picture, the reader must not allow the vexed question of miracle to distract him and disturb the proper frame of mind. The author refuses to assert either the possibility or the impossibility of miracle, but speaks only as an historian. "We do not say miracle is impossible, we say only that there has never been a satisfactorily authenticated miracle."

In view of the method of treatment adopted by Renan there can, of course, be no question of an historical plan. He brings in each saying at the point where it seems most appropriate. None of them is passed over, but none of them appears in its historical setting. He shifts individual incidents hither and thither in the [pg 184] most arbitrary fashion. For example, the coming of Jesus' mother to seek Him (in the belief that He is beside Himself) must belong to the later part of Jesus' life, since it is out of tone with the happy innocence of the earlier period. Certain scenes are transposed from the later period to the earlier, because they are not gloomy enough for the later time. Others again are made the basis of an unwarranted generalisation. It is not enough that Jesus once rode upon an ass while the disciples in the intoxication of joy cast their garments in the way; according to Renan, He constantly rode about, even in Galilee, upon a mule, "that favourite riding-animal of the East, which is so docile and sure-footed and whose great dark eyes, shaded by long lashes, are full of gentleness." Sometimes the disciples surrounded Him with rustic pomp, using their garments by way of carpeting. They laid them upon the mule which carried Him, or spread them before Him on the way.

Scenes of little significance are sometimes elaborately described by Renan while more important ones are barely touched on. "One day, indeed," he remarks in describing the first visit to Jerusalem, "anger seems to have, as the saying goes, overmastered Him; He struck some of the miserable chafferers with the scourge, and overthrew their tables." Such is the incidental fashion in which the cleansing of the temple was brought in. In this way it is possible to smuggle in a miracle without giving any further explanation of it. The miracle at Cana is brought, by means of the following unobtrusive turn of phrase, into the account of the period of success in Galilee. "One of His miracles was done by Jesus for the sole purpose of increasing the happiness of a wedding-party in a little country town."

This Life of Jesus is introduced by a kind of prelude. Jesus had been living in Galilee before He came to the Baptist; when He heard of the latter's success He went to him with His little company of followers. They were both young, and Jesus became the imitator of the Baptist. Fortunately the latter soon disappeared from the scene, for his influence on Jesus was in some respects injurious. The Galilaean teacher was on the verge of losing the sunny religion which He had learned from His only teacher, the glorious natural scenery which surrounded His home, and of becoming a gloomy Jewish fanatic. But this influence fell away from Him again; when He returned to Galilee He became Himself once more. The only thing which He had gained from John was some knowledge of the art of preaching. He had learned from him how to influence masses of men. From that time forward He preached with much more power and gained greater ascendancy over the people.

With the return to Galilee begins the first act of the piece. The story of the rise of Christianity is a pastoral play. Bauer, in [pg 185] his "Philo, Strauss, and Renan," writes with biting sarcasm: "Renan, who is at once the author of the play, the stage-manager, and the director of the theatre, gives the signal to begin, and at a sign from him the electric lights are put on full power, the Bengal fires flare up, the footlights are turned higher, and while the flutes and shawms of the orchestra strike up the overture, the people enter and take their places among the bushes and by the shore of the Lake." And how confiding they were, this gentle and peaceful company of Galilaean fisher folk! And He, the young carpenter, conjured the Kingdom of Heaven down to earth for a year, by the spell of the infinite tenderness which radiated from Him. A company of men and women, all of the same youthful integrity and simple innocence, became His followers and constantly repeated "Thou art the Messiah." By the women He was more beloved than He Himself liked, but from His passion for the glory of His Father He was content to attract these "fair creatures" (*belles créatures*) and suffered them to serve Him, and God through Him. Three or four devoted Galilaean women constantly accompanied Him and strove with one another for the pleasure (*le plaisir*) of listening to His teaching and attending to His comfort. Some of them were wealthy and used their means to enable the "amiable" (*charmant*) prophet to live without needing to practise His handicraft. The most devoted of all was Mary Magdalene, whose disordered mind had been healed by the influence of the pure and gracious beauty (*par la beauté pure et douce*) of the young Rabbi.

Thus He rode, on His long-eyelashed gentle mule, from village to village, from town to town. The sweet theology of love (*la délicieuse théologie de l'amour*) won Him all hearts. His preaching was gentle and mild (*suave et douce*), full of nature and the fragrance of the country. Wherever He went the people kept festival. At marriages He was a welcome guest; to the feasts which He gave He invited women who were sinners, and publicans like the good Zacchaeus.

"The Frenchman," remarks Noack, "takes the mummied figure of the Galilaean Rabbi, which criticism has exhumed, endows it with life and energy, and brings Him upon the stage, first amid the lustre of the earthly happiness which it was His pleasure to bestow, and then in the moving aspect of one doomed to suffer."

When Jesus goes up to the Passover at the end of this first year, He comes into conflict with the Rabbis of the capital. The "winsome teacher, who offered forgiveness to all on the sole condition of loving Him," found in the capital people upon whom His charm had no effect. When He returned to Galilee He had entirely abandoned His Jewish beliefs, and a revolutionary ardour glowed in His heart. The second act begins. "The action becomes more serious and gloomy, and the pupil of Strauss turns [pg 186] down the footlights of his stage."[108] The erstwhile "winsome moralist" has become a transcendental revolutionary. Up to this point He had thought to bring about the triumph of the Kingdom of God by natural means, by teaching and influencing men. The Jewish eschatology stood vaguely in the background. Now it becomes prominent. The tension set up between His purely ethical ideas and these eschatological expectations gives His words from this time forward a special force. The period of joyous simplicity is past.

Even the character of the hero loses its simplicity. In the furtherance of His cause He becomes a wonder-worker. It is true that even before He had sometimes practised innocent arts such as Joan of Arc made use of later.[109] He had, for instance, pretended to know the unspoken thoughts of one whom He desired to win, had reminded him, perhaps, of some experience of which he cherished the memory. He allowed the people to believe that He received knowledge of certain matters through a kind of revelation. Finally, it came to be whispered that He had spoken with Moses and Elias upon the mountains. But He now finds Himself compelled to adopt in earnest the rôle which He had formerly taken, as it were, in play. Against His will He is compelled to found His work upon miracle. He must face the alternative of either renouncing His mission or becoming a thaumaturge. He consented, therefore, to play an active part in many miracles. In this astute friends gave Him their aid. At Bethany something happened which could be regarded as a raising of the dead. Perhaps this miracle was arranged by Lazarus himself. When very ill he had allowed himself to be wrapped in the cerements of the dead and laid in the grave. His sisters sent for Jesus and brought Him to the tomb. He desired to look once more upon His friend, and when, overcome with grief, He cried his name aloud, Lazarus came forth from the grave. Why should the brother and sisters have hesitated to provide a miracle for the Master, in whose miracle-working power they, indeed, believed? Where, then, was Renan's allegiance to his "honoured master" Strauss, when he thus enrolled himself among the rationalists?

On these lines Jesus played His part for eighteen months, from the Easter of 31 to the Feast of Tabernacles of 32. How great is the change from the gentle teacher of the Sermon on the Mount! His discourse takes on a certain hardness of tone. In the synagogue at Capernaum He drives many from Him, offended by the saying about eating and drinking His flesh and blood. The "extreme materialism of the expression," which in Him had always been the natural counterpoise to the "extreme idealism of the [pg 187] thought," becomes more and more pronounced. His "Kingdom of God" was indeed still essentially the kingdom of the poor, the kingdom of the soul, the great spiritual kingdom; but He now preached it as the kingdom of the apocalyptic writings. And yet in the very moment when He seems to be staking everything upon a supernatural fulfilment of His hopes, He provides with remarkable prescience the basis of a permanent Church. He appoints the Twelve Apostles and institutes the fellowship-meal. It is certain, Renan thinks, that the "Supper" was not first instituted on that last evening; even in the second Galilaean period He must have practised with His followers the mystic rite of the Breaking of Bread, which in some way symbolised His death.

By the end of this period He had cast off all earthly ambitions. Nothing of earth existed for Him any more. A strange longing for persecution and martyrdom had taken possession of Him. It was not, however, the resolve to offer an atonement for the sins of His people which familiarised Him with the thought of death; it was forced upon Him by the knowledge that He had entered upon a path in which it was impossible for Him to sustain His rôle for more than a few months, or perhaps even weeks. So He sets out for Jerusalem, outwardly a hero, inwardly half in despair because He has turned aside from His true path. The gentle, faithful, long-eyelashed mule bears Him, amid the acclamations of the multitude, through the gate of the capital.

The third act begins: the stage is dark and becomes constantly darker, until at last, through the darkness of the scene, there is faintly visible only the figure of a woman—of her who in her deep grief beside the grave was by her vision to call to life again Him whom she loved. There was darkness, too, in the souls of the disciples, and in that of the Master. The bitter jealousy between Judas and John made one of them a traitor. As for Jesus, He had His hour of gloom to fight through in Gethsemane. For a moment His human nature awakened in Him; all that He thought He had slain and put behind Him for ever rose up and confronted Him as He knelt there upon the ground. "Did He remember the clear brooks of Galilee at which He might have slaked His thirst—the vine and the fig-tree beneath which He might have rested—the maidens who would perhaps have been willing to love Him? Did He regret His too exalted nature? Did He, a martyr to His own greatness, weep that He had not remained the simple carpenter of Nazareth? We do not know!"

He is dead. Renan, as though he stood in Père Lachaise, commissioned to pronounce the final allocution over a member of the Academy, apostrophises Him thus: "Rest now, amid Thy glory, noble pioneer. Thou conqueror of death, take the sceptre of Thy Kingdom, into which so many centuries of Thy [pg 188] worshippers shall follow Thee, by the highway which Thou hast opened up."

The bell rings; the curtain begins to fall; the swing-seats tilt. The epilogue is scarcely heard: "Jesus will never have a rival. His religion will again and again renew itself; His story will call forth endless tears: His sufferings will soften the hearts of the best; every successive century will proclaim that among the sons of men there hath not arisen a greater than Jesus."

The book passed through eight editions in three months. The writings of those who opposed it had an equal vogue. That of Freppel had reached its twelfth edition in 1864.[110] Their name was legion. Whatever wore a soutane and could wield a pen charged against Renan, the bishops leading the van. The tone of these attacks was not always very elevated, nor their logic very profound. In most cases the writers were only concerned to defend the Deity of Christ,[111] and the miracles, and are satisfied that they have done so when they have pointed out some of the glaring inconsistencies in Renan's work. Here and there, however, among these refutations we catch the tone of a loftier ethical spirit which has recognised the fundamental weakness of the work, the lack of any definite ethical principles in the writer's outlook upon life.[112] There were some indeed who were not content with a refutation; they would gladly have seen active measures taken against Renan. One of his most embittered adversaries, Amadée Nicolas,[113] reckons up in an appendix to his work the maximum penalties authorised by the existing enactments against free-thought, and would welcome the application of the law of the 25th of March 1822, according to which five years' imprisonment could be imposed for the crime of "insulting or making ridiculous a religion recognised by the state."

Renan was defended by the *Siècle*, the *Débats*, at that time the leading French newspaper, and the *Temps*, in which Scherer published five articles upon the book. Even the *Revue des deux mondes*, which had formerly raised a warning voice against Strauss, allowed itself to go with the stream, and published in its August [pg 189] number of 1863 a critical analysis by Havet[114] who hailed Renan's work as a great achievement, and criticised only the inconsistencies by which he had endeavoured to soften down the radical character of his undertaking. Later on the *Revue* changed its attitude and sided with Renan's opponents. In the Protestant camp there was an even keener sense of distaste than in the Catholic for the sentimental gloss which Renan had spread over his work to make it attractive to the multitude by its iridescent colours. In four remarkable letters Athanase Coquerel the younger took the author to task for this.[115] From the standpoint of orthodox scholarship E. de Pressensé condemned him;[116] and proceeded without loss of time to refute him in a large-scale Life of Jesus.[117] He was answered by Albert Réville,[118] who claims recognition for Renan's services to criticism.

In general, however, the rising French school of critical theology was disappointed in Renan. Their spokesman was Colani. "This is not the Christ of history, the Christ of the Synoptics," he writes in 1864 in the *Revue de théologie*, "but the Christ of the Fourth Gospel, though without His metaphysical halo, and painted over with a brush which has been dipped in the melancholy blue of modern poetry, in the rose of the eighteenth-century idyll, and in the grey of a moral philosophy which seems to be derived from La Rochefoucauld." "In expressing this opinion," he adds, "I believe I am speaking in the name of those who belong to what is known as the new Protestant theology, or the Strassburg school. We opened M. Renan's book with sympathetic interest; we closed it with deep disappointment."[119]

The Strassburg school had good cause to complain of Renan, for he had trampled their growing crops. They had just begun to arouse some interest, and slowly and surely to exercise an influence upon the whole spiritual life of France. Sainte-Beuve had called attention to the work of Reuss, Colani, Réville, and Scherer. [pg 190] Others of the school were Michel Nicolas of Montauban and Gustave d'Eichthal. Nefftzer, the editor of the *Temps*, who was at the same time a prophet of coming political events, defended their cause in the Parisian literary world. The *Revue germanique* of that period, the influence of which upon French literature can hardly be over-estimated, was their sworn ally. Then came Renan and threw public opinion into a ferment of excitement. Everything in the nature of criticism, and of progress in religious thought, was associated with his name, and was thereby discredited. By his untimely and over-easy popularisation of the ideas of the critical school he ruined their quiet work. The excitement roused by his book swept away all that had been done by those noble and lofty spirits, who now found themselves involved in a struggle with the outraged orthodoxy of Paris, and were hard put to it to defend themselves. Even down to the present day Renan's work forms the greatest hindrance to any serious advance in French religious thought.

The excitement aroused upon the other side of the Rhine was scarcely less than in Paris. Within a year there appeared five different German translations, and many of the French criticisms of Renan were also translated.[120] The German Catholic press was wildly excited;[121] the Protestant press was more restrained, more inclined to give the author a fair hearing, and even ventured to express admiration of the historical merits of his performance. Beyschlag[122] saw in Renan an advance upon Strauss, inasmuch as for him the life of Jesus as narrated in the Gospels, while not, indeed, in any sense supernatural, is nevertheless historical. For a certain school of theology, therefore, Renan was a deliverer from Strauss; they were especially grateful to him for his defence, sophistical though it was, of the Fourth Gospel. Weizsäcker expressed his admiration. Strauss, far from directing his "Life of Jesus for the German People," with which he was then occupied, [pg 191] against the superficial and frivolous French treatment of the subject—as has sometimes been alleged—hailed Renan in his preface as a kindred spirit and ally, and "shook hands with him across the Rhine." Luthardt,[123] however, remained inexorable. "What is there lacking in Renan's work?" he asks. And he replies, "It lacks conscience."

That is a just judgment. From this lack of conscience, Renan has not been scrupulous where he ought to have been so. There is a kind of insincerity in the book from beginning to end. Renan professes to depict the Christ of the Fourth Gospel, though he does not believe in the authenticity or the miracles of that Gospel. He professes to write a scientific work, and is always thinking of the great public and how to interest it. He has thus fused together two works of disparate character. The historian finds it hard to forgive him for not going more deeply into the problem of the development in the thought of Jesus, with which he was brought face to face by the emphasis which he laid on eschatology, and for offering in place of a solution the highly-coloured phrases of the novelist.

Nevertheless, this work will always retain a certain interest, both for Frenchmen and for Germans. The German is often so completely fascinated by it as to lose his power of criticism, because he finds in it German thought in a novel and piquant form. Conversely the Frenchman discovers in it, behind the familiar form, which is here handled in such a masterly fashion, ideas belonging to a world which is foreign to him, ideas which he can never completely assimilate, but which yet continually attract him. In this double character of the work lies its imperishable charm.

[pg 192]

And its weakness? That it is written by one to whom the New Testament was to the last something foreign, who had not read it from his youth up in the mother-tongue, who was not accustomed to breathe freely in its simple and pure world, but must perfume it with sentimentality in order to feel himself at home in it.
[pg 193]

XIV. The "Liberal" Lives Of Jesus

David Friedrich Strauss. Das Leben Jesu für das deutsche Volk bearbeitet. (A Life of Jesus for the German People.) Leipzig, 1864. 631 pp.

Der Christus des Glaubens und der Jesus der Geschichte. Eine Kritik des Schleiermacher'schen Lebens Jesu. (The Christ of Faith and the Jesus of History, a Criticism of Schleiermacher's Life of Jesus.) Berlin, 1865. 223 pp. Appendix, pp. 224-240.

Der Schenkel'sche Handel in Baden. (The Schenkel Affair in Baden.) A corrected reprint from No. 441 of the *National-Zeitung*, of the 21st September 1864.

Die Halben und die Ganzen. (The Half-way-ers and the Whole-way-ers.) 1865.

Daniel Schenkel. Das Charakterbild Jesu. (The Portrait of Jesus.) Wiesbaden, 1864 (ed. 1 and 2). 405 pp. Fourth edition, with a preface opposing Strauss's "Der alte und der neue Glaube" (The Old Faith and the New), 1873.

Karl Heinrich Weizsäcker. Untersuchungen über die evangelische Geschichte, ihre Quellen und den Gang ihrer Entwicklung. (Studies in the Gospel History, its Sources and the Progress of its Development.) Gotha, 1864. 580 pp.

Heinrich Julius Holtzmann. Die synoptischen Evangelien. Ihr Ursprung und geschichtlicher Charakter. (The Synoptic Gospels. Their Origin and Historical Character.) Leipzig, 1863. 514 pp.

Theodor Keim. Die Geschichte Jesu von Nazara. (The History of Jesus of Nazara.) 3 vols., Zurich; vol. i., 1867, 446 pp.; vol. ii., 1871, 616 pp.; vol. iii., 1872, 667 pp.

Die Geschichte Jesu. Zurich, 1872. 398 pp.

Karl Hase. Geschichte Jesu. Nach akademischen Vorlesungen. (The History of Jesus. Academic Lectures, revised.) Leipzig, 1876. 612 pp.

Willibald Beyschlag. Das Leben Jesu. First Part: Preliminary Investigations, 1885, 450 pp. Second Part: Narrative, 1886, 495 pp.; 2nd ed., 1887-1888.

Bernhard Weiss. Das Leben Jesu. 1st ed., 2 vols., 1882; 2nd ed., 1884. First vol., down to the Baptist's question, 556 pp. Second vol., 617 pp.

"My hope is," writes Strauss in concluding the preface of his new Life of Jesus, "that I have written a book as thoroughly well adapted for Germans as Renan's is for Frenchmen." He was mistaken; in spite of its title the book was not a book for the people. It had nothing new to offer, and what it did offer was not in a form calculated to become popular. It is true Strauss, like Renan, was an artist, but he did not write, like an imaginative novelist, with a constant eye to effect. His art was unpretentious, [pg 194] even austere, appealing to the few, not to the many. The people demand a complete and vivid picture. Renan had given them a figure which was theatrical no doubt, but full of life and movement, and they had been grateful to him for it. Strauss could not do that.

Even the arrangement of the work is thoroughly unfortunate. In the first part, which bears the title "The Life of Jesus," he attempts to combine into a harmonious portrait such of the historical data as have some claim to be considered historical; in the second part he traces the "Origin and Growth of the Mythical History of Jesus." First, therefore, he tears down from the tree the ivy and the rich growth of creepers, laying bare the worn and corroded bark; then he fastens the faded growths to the stem again, and describes the nature, origin, and characteristics of each distinct species.

How vastly different, how much more full of life, had been the work of 1835! There Strauss had not divided the creepers from the stem. The straining strength which upheld this wealth of creepers was but vaguely suspected. Behind the billowy mists of legend we caught from time to time a momentary glimpse of the gigantic figure of Jesus, as though lit up by a lightning-flash. It was no complete and harmonious picture, but it was full of suggestions, rich in thoughts thrown out carelessly, rich in contradictions even, out of which the imagination could create a portrait of Jesus. It is just this wealth of suggestion that is lacking in the second picture. Strauss is trying now to give a definite portrait. In the inevitable process of harmonising and modelling to scale he is obliged to reject the finest thoughts of the previous work because they will not fit in exactly; some of them are altered out of recognition, some are filed away.

There is wanting, too, that perfect freshness as of the spring which is only found when thoughts have but newly come into flower. The writing is no longer spontaneous; one feels that Strauss is setting forth thoughts which have ripened with his mind and grown old with it, and now along with their definiteness of form have taken on a certain stiffness. There are now no hinted possibilities, full of promise, to dance gaily through the movement of his dialectic; all is sober reason—a thought too sober. Renan had one advantage over Strauss in that he wrote when the material was fresh to him—one might almost say strange to him—and was capable of calling up in him the response of vivid feeling.

For a popular book, too, it lacks that living interplay of reflection with narration without which the ordinary reader fails to get a grip of the history. The first Life of Jesus had been rich in this respect, since it had been steeped in the Hegelian theory regarding the realisation of the Idea. In the meantime Strauss [pg 195] had seen the Hegelian philosophy fall from its high estate, and himself had found no way of reconciling history and idea, so that his present Life of Jesus was a mere objective presentment of the history. It was, therefore, not adapted to make any impression upon the popular mind.

In reality it is merely an exposition, in more or less popular form, of the writer's estimate of what had been done in the study of the subject during the past thirty years, and shows what he had learnt and what he had failed to learn.

As regards the Synoptic question he had learnt nothing. In his opinion the criticism of the Gospels has "run to seed." He treats with a pitying contempt both the earlier and the more recent defenders of the Marcan hypothesis. Weisse is a dilettante; Wilke had failed to make any impression on him; Holtzmann's work was as yet unknown to him. But in the following year he discharged the vials of his wrath upon the man who had both strengthened the foundations and put on the coping-stone of the new hypothesis. "Our lions of St. Mark, older and younger," he says in the appendix to his criticism of Schleiermacher's Life of Jesus, "may roar as loud as they like, so long as there are six solid reasons against the priority of Mark to set against every one of their flimsy arguments in its favour—and they themselves supply us with a store of counter-arguments in the shape of admissions of later editing and so forth. The whole theory appears to me a temporary aberration, like the 'music of the future' or the anti-vaccination movement; and I seriously believe that it is the same order of mind which, in different circumstances, falls a victim to the one delusion or the other." But he must not be supposed, he says, to take the critical mole-hills thrown up by Holtzmann for veritable mountains.

Against such opponents he does not scruple to seek aid from Schleiermacher, whose unbiased but decided opinion had ascribed a tertiary character to Mark. Even Gfrörer's view that Mark adapted his Gospel to the needs of the Church by leaving out everything which was open to objection in Matthew and Luke, is good enough to be brought to bear against the bat-eyed partisans of Mark. F. C. Baur is reproached for having given too much weight to the "tendency" theory in his criticism of the Gospels; and also for having taken suggestions of Strauss's and worked them out, supposing that he was offering something new when he was really only amplifying. In the end he had only given a criticism of the Gospels, not of the Gospel history.

But this irritation against his old teacher is immediately allayed when he comes to speak of the Fourth Gospel. Here the teacher has carried to a successful issue the campaign which the pupil had begun. Strauss feels compelled to "express his gratitude for the work done by the Tübingen school on the Johannine question." [pg 196] He himself had only been able to deal with the negative side of the question—to show that the Fourth Gospel was not an historical source, but a theological invention; they had dealt with it positively, and had assigned the document to its proper place in the evolution of Christian thought. There is only one point with which he quarrels. Baur had made the Fourth Gospel too completely spiritual, "whereas the fact is," says Strauss, "that it is the most material of all." It is true, Strauss explains, that the Evangelist starts out to interpret miracle and eschatology symbolically; but he halts half-way and falls back upon the miraculous, enhancing the professed fact in proportion as he makes it spiritually more significant. Beside the spiritual return of Jesus in the Paraclete he places His return in a material body, bearing the marks of the wounds; beside the inward present judgment, a future outward judgment; and the fact that he sees the one in the other, finds the one present and visible in the other, is just what constitutes the mystical character of his Gospel. This mysticism attracts the modern world. "The Johannine Christ, who in His descriptions of Himself seems to be always out-doing Himself, is the counterpart of the modern believer, who in order to remain a believer must continually out-do himself; the Johannine miracles which are always being interpreted spiritually, and at the same time raised to a higher pitch of the miraculous, which are counted and documented in every possible way, and yet must not be considered the true ground of faith, are at once miracles and no miracles. We must believe them, and yet can believe without them; in short they exactly meet the taste of the present day, which delights to involve itself in contradictions and is too lethargic and wanting in courage for any clear insight or decided opinion on religious matters."

Strictly speaking, however, the Strauss of the second Life of Jesus has no right to criticise the Fourth Gospel for sublimating the history, for he himself gives what is nothing else than a spiritualisation of the Jesus of the Synoptics. And he does it in such an arbitrary fashion that one is compelled to ask how far he does it with a good conscience. A typical case is the exposition of Jesus' answer to the Baptist's message. "Is it possible," Jesus means, "that you fail to find in Me the miracles which you expect from the Messiah? And yet I daily open the eyes of the spiritually blind and the ears of the spiritually deaf, make the lame walk erect and vigorous, and even give new life to those who are morally dead. Any one who understands how much greater these spiritual miracles are, will not be offended at the absence of bodily miracles; only such an one can receive, and is worthy of, the salvation which I am bringing to mankind."

Here the fundamental weakness of his method is clearly shown. [pg 197] The vaunted apparatus for the evaporation of the mythical does not work quite satisfactorily. The ultimate product of this process was expected to be a Jesus who should be essential man; the actual product, however, is Jesus the historical man, a being whose looks and sayings are strange and unfamiliar. Strauss is too purely a critic, too little of the creative historian, to recognise this strange being. That Jesus really lived in a world of Jewish ideas and held Himself to be Messiah in the Jewish sense is for the writer of the Life of Jesus an impossibility. The deposit which resists the chemical process for the elimination of myth, he must therefore break up with the hammer.

How different from the Strauss of 1835! He had then recognised eschatology as the most important element in Jesus' world of thought, and in some incidental remarks had made striking applications of it. He had, for example, proposed to regard the Last Supper not as the institution of a feast for coming generations, but as a Paschal meal, at which Jesus declared that He would next partake of the Paschal bread and Paschal wine along with His disciples in the heavenly kingdom. In the second Life of Jesus this view is given up; Jesus did found a feast. "In order to give a living centre of unity to the society which it was His purpose to found, Jesus desired to institute this distribution of bread and wine as a feast to be constantly repeated." One might be reading Renan. This change of attitude is typical of much else.

Strauss is not in the least disquieted by finding himself at one with Schleiermacher in these attempts to spiritualise. On the contrary, he appeals to him. He shares, he says, Schleiermacher's conviction "that the unique self-consciousness of Jesus did not develop as a consequence of His conviction that He was the Messiah; on the contrary, it was a consequence of His self-consciousness that He arrived at the view that the Messianic prophecies could point to no one but Himself." The moment eschatology entered into the consciousness of Jesus it came in contact with a higher principle which over-mastered it and gradually dissolved it. "Had Jesus applied the Messianic idea to Himself before He had had a profound religious consciousness to which to relate it, doubtless it would have taken possession of Him so powerfully that He could never have escaped from its influence." We must suppose the ideality, the concentration upon that which was inward, the determination to separate religion, on the one hand, from politics, and on the other, from ritual, the serene consciousness of being able to attain to peace with God and with Himself by purely spiritual means—all this we must suppose to have reached a certain ripeness, a certain security, in the mind of Jesus, before He permitted Himself to entertain the thought of His Messiahship, and this we may believe is the reason why He grasped [pg 198] it in so independent and individual a fashion. In this, therefore, Strauss has become the pupil of Weisse.

Even in the Old Testament prophecies, he explains, we find two conceptions, a more ideal and a more practical. Jesus holds consistently to the first, He describes Himself as the Son of Man because this designation "contains the suggestion of humility and lowliness, of the human and natural." At Jerusalem, Jesus, in giving His interpretation of Psalm cx., "made merry over the Davidic descent of the Messiah." He desired "to be Messiah in the sense of a patient teacher exercising a quiet influence." As the opposition of the people grew more intense, He took up some of the features of Isaiah liii. into His conception of the Messiah.

Of His resurrection, Jesus can only have spoken in a metaphorical sense. It is hardly credible that one who was pure man could have arrogated to himself the position of judge of the world. Strauss would like best to ascribe all the eschatology to the distorting medium of early Christianity, but he does not venture to carry this through with logical consistency. He takes it as certain, however, that Jesus, even though it sometimes seems as if He did not expect the Kingdom to be realised in the present, but in a future, world-era, and to be brought about by God in a supernatural fashion, nevertheless sets about the establishment of the Kingdom by purely spiritual influence.

With this end in view He leaves Galilee, when He judges the time to be ripe, in order to work on a larger scale. "In case of an unfavourable issue, He reckons on the influence which a martyr-death has never failed to exercise in giving momentum to a lofty idea." How far He had advanced, when He entered on the fateful journey to Jerusalem, in shaping His plan, and especially in organising the company of adherents who had gathered about Him, it is impossible to determine with any exactness. He permitted the triumphal entry because He did not desire to decline the role of the Messiah in every aspect of it.

Owing to this arbitrary spiritualisation of the Synoptic Jesus, Strauss's picture is in essence much more unhistorical than Renan's. The latter had not needed to deny that Jesus had done miracles, and he had been able to suggest an explanation of how Jesus came in the end to fall back upon the eschatological system of ideas. But at what a price! By portraying Jesus as at variance with Himself, a hero broken in spirit. This price is too high for Strauss. Arbitrary as his treatment of history is, he never loses the intuitive feeling that in Jesus' self-consciousness there is a unique absence of struggle; that He does not bear the scars which are found in those natures which win their way to freedom and purity through strife and conflict, that in Him there is no trace of the hardness, harshness, and gloom which cleave to such natures [pg 199] throughout life, but that He "is manifestly a beautiful nature from the first." Thus, for all Strauss's awkward, arbitrary handling of the history he is greater than the rival[124] who could manufacture history with such skill.

Nevertheless, from the point of view of theological science, this work marks a standstill. That was the net result of the thirty years of critical study of the life of Jesus for the man who had inaugurated it so impressively. This was the only fruit which followed those blossoms so full of promise of the first Life of Jesus.

It is significant that in the same year there appeared Schleiermacher's lectures on the Life of Jesus, which had not seen the light for forty years, because, as Strauss himself remarked in his criticism of the resurrected work, it had neither anodyne nor dressing for the wounds which his first Life of Jesus had made.[125] The wounds, however, had cicatrised in the meantime. It is true Strauss is a just judge, and makes ample acknowledgment of the greatness of Schleiermacher's achievement.[126] He blames Schleiermacher for setting up his "presuppositions in regard to Christ" as an historical canon, and considering it a proof that a statement is unhistorical if it does not square with those presuppositions. But does not the purely human, but to a certain extent unhistorical, man, who is to be the ultimate product of the process of eliminating myth, serve Strauss as his "theoretic Christ" who determines the presentment of his historical Jesus? Does he not share with Schleiermacher the erroneous, artificial, "double" construction of the consciousness of Jesus? And what about their views of Mark? What fundamental difference is there, when all is said, between Schleiermacher's de-rationalised Life of Jesus and Strauss's? Certainly this second Life of Jesus would not have frightened Schleiermacher's away into hiding for thirty years.

So Schleiermacher's Life of Jesus might now safely venture [pg 200] forth into the light. There was no reason why it should feel itself a stranger at this period, and it had no need to be ashamed of itself. Its rationalistic birth-marks were concealed by its brilliant dialectic.[127] And the only real advance in the meantime was the general recognition that the Life of Jesus was not to be interpreted on rationalistic, but on historical lines. All other, more definite, historical results had proved more or less illusory; there is no vitality in them. The works of Renan, Strauss, Schenkel, Weizsäcker, and Keim are in essence only different ways of carrying out a single ground-plan. To read them one after another is to be simply appalled at the stereotyped uniformity of the world of thought in which they move. You feel that you have read exactly the same thing in the others, almost in identical phrases. To obtain the works of Schenkel and Weizsäcker you only need to weaken down in Strauss the sharp discrimination between John and the Synoptists so far as to allow of the Fourth Gospel being used to some extent as an historical source "in the higher sense," and to put the hypothesis of the priority of Mark in place of the Tübingen view adopted by Strauss. The latter is an external operation and does not essentially modify the view of the Life of Jesus, since by admitting the Johannine scheme the Marcan plan is again disturbed, and Strauss's arbitrary spiritualisation of the Synoptics comes to something not very different from the acceptance of that "in a higher sense historical Gospel" alongside of them. The whole discussion regarding the sources is only loosely connected with the process of arriving at the portrait of Jesus, since this portrait is fixed from the first, being determined by the mental atmosphere and religious horizon of the 'sixties. They all portray the Jesus of liberal theology; the only difference is that one is a little more conscientious in his colouring than another, and one perhaps has a little more taste than another, or is less concerned about the consequences.

The desire to escape in some way from the alternative between the Synoptists and John was native to the Marcan hypothesis. Weisse had endeavoured to effect this by distinguishing between the sources in the Fourth Gospel.[128] Schenkel and Weizsäcker are [pg 201] more modest. They do not feel the need of any clear literary view of the Fourth Gospel, of any critical discrimination between original and secondary elements in it; they are content to use as historical whatever their instinct leads them to accept. "Apart from the fourth Gospel," says Schenkel, "we should miss in the portrait of the Redeemer the unfathomable depths and the inaccessible heights." "Jesus," to quote his aphorism, "was not always thus in reality, but He was so in truth." Since when have historians had the right to distinguish between reality and truth? That was one of the bad habits which the author of this characterisation of Jesus brought with him from his earlier dogmatic training.

Weizsäcker[129] expresses himself with more circumspection. "We possess," he says, "in the Fourth Gospel genuine apostolic reminiscences as much as in any part of the first three Gospels; but between the facts on which the reminiscences are based and their reproduction in literary form there lies the development of their possessor into a great mystic, and the influence of a philosophy which here for the first time united itself in this way with the Gospel; they need, therefore, to be critically examined; and the historical truth of this gospel, great as it is, must not be measured with a painful literality."

One wonders why both these writers appeal to Holtzmann, seeing that they practically abandon the Marcan plan which he had worked out at the end of his very thorough examination of this Gospel. They do not accept as sufficient the controversy regarding the ceremonial regulations in Mark vii. which, with the rejection at Nazareth, constitute, in Holtzmann's view, the turning-point of the Galilaean ministry, but find the cause of the change of attitude on the part of the people rather in the Johannine discourse about eating and drinking the flesh and blood of the Son of Man. The section Mark x.-xv., which has a certain unity, they interpret in the light of the Johannine tradition, finding in it traces of a previous ministry of Jesus in Jerusalem and interweaving with it the Johannine story of the Passion. According to Schenkel the last visit to Jerusalem must have been of considerable duration. When confronted with John, the admission may be wrung from the Synoptists that Jesus did not travel straight through Jericho to the capital, but worked first for a considerable time in Judaea. Strauss [pg 202] tartly observes that he cannot see what the author of the "characterisation" stood to gain by underwriting Holtzmann's Marcan hypothesis.[130]

Weizsäcker is still bolder in making interpolations from the Johannine tradition. He places the cleansing of the Temple, in contradiction to Mark, in the early period of Jesus' ministry, on the ground that "it bears the character of a first appearance, a bold deed with which to open His career." He fails to observe, however, that if this act really took place at this point of time, the whole development of the life of Jesus which Holtzmann had so ingeniously traced in Mark, is at once thrown into confusion. In describing the last visit to Jerusalem, Weizsäcker is not content to insert the Marcan stones into the Johannine cement; he goes farther and expressly states that the great farewell discourses of Jesus to His disciples agree with the Synoptic discourses to the disciples spoken during the last days, however completely they of all others bear the peculiar stamp of the Johannine diction.

Thus in the second period of the Marcan hypothesis the same spectacle meets us as in the earlier. The hypothesis has a literary existence, indeed it is carried by Holtzmann to such a degree of demonstration that it can no longer be called a mere hypothesis, but it does not succeed in winning an assured position in the critical study of the Life of Jesus. It is common-land not yet taken into cultivation.

That is due in no small measure to the fact that Holtzmann did not work out the hypothesis from the historical side, but rather on literary lines, recalling Wilke—as a kind of problem in Synoptic arithmetic—and in his preface expresses dissent from the Tübingen school, who desired to leave no alternative between John on the one side and the Synoptics on the other, whereas he approves the attempt to evade the dilemma in some way or other, and thinks he can find in the didactic narrative of the Fourth Gospel the traces of a development of Jesus similar to that portrayed in the Synoptics, and has therefore no fundamental objection to the use of John alongside of the Synoptics. In taking up this position, however, he does not desire to be understood as meaning that "it would be to the interests of science to throw Synoptic and Johannine passages together indiscriminately and thus construct a life of Jesus out of them." "It would be much better first to reconstruct separately the Synoptic and Johannine pictures of Christ, composing each of its own distinctive material. It is only when this has been done that it is possible to make a fruitful comparison of the two." Exactly the same position had been taken up sixty-seven years [pg 203] before by Herder. In Holtzmann's case, however, the principle was stated with so many qualifications that the adherents of his view read into it the permission to combine, in a picture treated "in the grand style," Synoptic with Johannine passages.

In addition to this, the plan which Holtzmann finally evolved out of Mark was much too fine-drawn to bear the weight of the remainder of the Synoptic material. He distinguishes seven stages in the Galilaean ministry,[131] of which the really decisive one is the sixth, in which Jesus leaves Galilee and goes northward, so that Schenkel and Weizsäcker are justified in distinguishing practically only two great Galilaean periods, the first of which—down to the controversy about ceremonial purity—they distinguish as the period of success, the second—down to the departure from Judaea—as the period of decline. What attracted these writers to the Marcan hypothesis was not so much the authentification which it gave to the detail of Mark, though they were willing enough to accept that, but the way in which this Gospel lent itself to the a priori view of the course of the life of Jesus which they unconsciously brought with them. They appealed to Holtzmann because he showed such wonderful skill in extracting from the Marcan narrative the view which commended itself to the spirit of the age as manifested in the 'sixties.

Holtzmann read into this Gospel that Jesus had endeavoured in Galilee to found the Kingdom of God in an ideal sense; that He concealed His consciousness of being the Messiah, which was constantly growing more assured, until His followers should have attained by inner enlightenment to a higher view of the Kingdom of God and of the Messiah; that almost at the end of His Galilaean ministry He declared Himself to them as the Messiah at Caesarea Philippi; that on the same occasion He at once began to picture to them a suffering Messiah, whose lineaments gradually became more and more distinct in His mind amid the growing opposition which He encountered, until finally, He communicated to His disciples His decision to put the Messianic cause to the test in the capital, and that they followed Him thither and saw how His fate fulfilled itself. It was this fundamental view which made the success of the hypothesis. Holtzmann, not less than his followers, believed that he had discovered it in the Gospel itself, although Strauss, the passionate opponent of the Marcan hypothesis, took essentially the same view of the development of Jesus' thought. But the way in which Holtzmann exhibited this characteristic view of the 'sixties as arising naturally out of the detail of Mark, was so perfect, so artistically charming, that this view appeared henceforward to be inseparably bound up with the [pg 204] Marcan tradition. Scarcely ever has a description of the life of Jesus exercised so irresistible an influence as that short outline—it embraces scarcely twenty pages—with which Holtzmann closes his examination of the Synoptic Gospels. This chapter became the creed and catechism of all who handled the subject during the following decades. The treatment of the life of Jesus had to follow the lines here laid down until the Marcan hypothesis was delivered from its bondage to that a priori view of the development of Jesus. Until then any one might appeal to the Marcan hypothesis, meaning thereby only that general view of the inward and outward course of development in the life of Jesus, and might treat the remainder of the Synoptic material how he chose, combining with it, at his pleasure, material drawn from John. The victory, therefore, belonged, not to the Marcan hypothesis pure and simple, but to the Marcan hypothesis as psychologically interpreted by a liberal theology.

The points of distinction between the Weissian and the new interpretation are as follows:— Weisse is sceptical as regards the detail; the new Marcan hypothesis ventures to base conclusions even upon incidental remarks in the text. According to Weisse there were not distinct periods of success and failure in the ministry of Jesus; the new Marcan hypothesis confidently affirms this distinction, and goes so far as to place the sojourn of Jesus in the parts beyond Galilee under the heading "Flights and Retirements."[132] The earlier Marcan hypothesis expressly denies that outward circumstances influenced the resolve of Jesus to die; according to the later, it was the opposition of the people, and the impossibility of carrying out His mission on other lines which forced Him to enter on the path of suffering.[133] The Jesus of Weisse's view has [pg 205] completed His development at the time of His appearance; the Jesus of the new interpretation of Mark continues to develop in the course of His public ministry.

There is complete agreement, however, in the rejection of eschatology. For Holtzmann, Schenkel, and Weizsäcker, as for Weisse, Jesus desires "to found an inward kingdom of repentance."[134] It was Israel's duty, according to Schenkel, to believe in the presence of the Kingdom which Jesus proclaimed. John the Baptist was unable to believe in it, and it was for this reason that Jesus censured him—for it is in this sense that Schenkel understands the saying about the greatest among those born of women who is nevertheless the least in the Kingdom of Heaven. "So near the light and yet shutting his eyes to its beams—is there not some blame here, an undeniable lack of spiritual and moral receptivity?"

Jesus makes Messianic claims only in a spiritual sense. He does not grasp at super-human glory; it is His purpose to bear the sin of the whole people, and He undergoes baptism "as a humble member of the national community."

His whole teaching consists, when once He Himself has attained to clear consciousness of His vocation, in a constant struggle to root out from the hearts of His disciples their theocratic hopes and to effect a transformation of their traditional Messianic ideas. When, on Simon's hailing Him as the Messiah, He declares that flesh and blood has not revealed it to him, He means, according to Schenkel, "that Simon has at this moment overcome the false Messianic ideas, and has recognised in Him the ethical and spiritual deliverer of Israel."

"That Jesus predicted a personal, bodily, Second Coming, in the brightness of His heavenly splendour and surrounded by the heavenly hosts, to establish an earthly kingdom, is not only not proved, it is absolutely impossible." His purpose is to establish a community of which His disciples are to be the foundation, and by means of this community to bring about the coming of the Kingdom of God. He can, therefore, only have spoken of His return as an impersonal return in the Spirit. The later exponents of the Marcan view were no doubt generally inclined to regard the return as personal and corporeal. For Schenkel, however, it is historically certain that the real meaning of the eschatological [pg 206] discourses is more faithfully preserved in the Fourth Gospel than in the Synoptics.

In his anxiety to eliminate any enthusiastic elements from the representation of Jesus, he ends by drawing a bourgeois Messiah whom he might have extracted from the old-fashioned rationalistic work of the worthy Reinhard. He feels bound to save the credit of Jesus by showing that the entry into Jerusalem was not intended as a provocation to the government. "It is only by making this supposition," he explains, "that we avoid casting a slur upon the character of Jesus. It was certainly a constant trait in His character that He never unnecessarily exposed Himself to danger, and never, except for the most pressing reasons, did He give any support to the suspicions which were arising against Him; He avoided provoking His opponents to drastic measures by any overt act directed against them." Even the cleansing of the Temple was not an act of violence but merely an attempt at reform.

Schenkel is able to give these explanations because he knows the most secret thoughts of Jesus and is therefore no longer bound to the text. He knows, for example, that immediately after His baptism He attained to the knowledge "that the way of the Law was no longer the way of salvation for His people." Jesus cannot therefore have uttered the saying about the permanence of the Law in Mark v. 18. In the controversies about the Sabbath "He proclaims freedom of worship."

As time went on, He began to take the heathen world into the scope of His purpose. "The hard saying addressed to the Canaanite woman represents rather the proud and exclusive spirit of Pharisaism than the spirit of Jesus." It was a test of faith, the success of which had a decisive influence upon Jesus' attitude towards the heathen. Henceforth it is obvious that He is favourably disposed towards them. He travels through Samaria and establishes a community there. In Jerusalem He openly calls the heathen to Him. At certain feasts which they had arranged for that purpose, some of the leaders of the people set a trap for Him, and betrayed Him into liberal sayings in regard to the Gentiles which sealed His fate.

This was the course of development of the Master, who, according to Schenkel, "saw with a clear eye into the future history of the world," and knew that the fall of Jerusalem must take place in order to close the theocratic era and give the Gentiles free access to the universal community of Christians which He was to found. "This period He described as the period of His coming, as in a sense His Second Advent upon earth."

The same general procedure is followed by Weizsäcker in his "Gospel History," though his work is of a much higher quality [pg 207] than Schenkel's. His account of the sources is one of the clearest that has ever been written. In the description of the life of Jesus, however, the unhesitating combination of material from the Fourth Gospel with that of the Synoptics rather confuses the picture. And whereas Renan only offers the results of the completed process, Weizsäcker works out his, it might almost be said, under the eyes of the reader, which makes the arbitrary character of the proceeding only the more obvious. But in his attitude towards the sources Weizsäcker is wholly free from the irresponsible caprice in which Schenkel indulges. From time to time, too, he gives a hint of unsolved problems in the background. For example, in treating of the declaration of Jesus to His judges that He would come as the Son of Man upon the clouds of heaven, he remarks how surprising it is that Jesus could so often have used the designation Son of Man on earlier occasions without being accused of claiming the Messiahship. It is true that this is a mere scraping of the keel upon a sandbank, by which the steersman does not allow himself to be turned from his course, for Weizsäcker concludes that the name Son of Man, in spite of its use in Daniel, "had not become a generally current or really popular designation of the Messiah." But even this faint suspicion of the difficulty is a welcome sign. Much emphasis, in fact, in practice rather too much emphasis, is laid on the principle that in the great discourses of Jesus the structure is not historical; they are only collections of sayings formed to meet the needs of the Christian community in later times. In this Weizsäcker is sometimes not less arbitrary than Schenkel, who represents the Lord's Prayer as given by Jesus to the disciples only in the last days at Jerusalem. It was an axiom of the school that Jesus could not have delivered discourses such as the Evangelists record.

If Schenkel's picture of Jesus' character attracted much more attention than Weizsäcker's work, that is mainly due to the art of lively popular presentation by which it is distinguished. The writer knows well how to keep the reader's interest awake by the use of exciting headlines. Catchwords abound, and arrest the ear, for they are the catchwords about which the religious controversies of the time revolved. There is never far to look for the moral of the history, and the Jesus here portrayed can be imagined plunging into the midst of the debates in any ministerial conference. The moralising, it must be admitted, sometimes becomes the occasion of the feeblest ineptitudes. Jesus sent out His disciples two and two; this is for Schenkel a marvellous exhibition of wisdom. The Lord designed, thereby, to show that in His opinion "nothing is more inimical to the interests of the Kingdom of God than individualism, self-will, self-pleasing." Schenkel entirely fails to recognise the superb irony of the saying that in this life all that a [pg 208] man gives up for the sake of the Kingdom of God is repaid a hundredfold in persecutions, in order that in the Coming Age he may receive eternal life as his reward. He interpreted it as meaning that the sufferer shall be compensated by love; his fellow-Christians will endeavour to make it up to him, and will offer him their own possessions so freely that, in consequence of this brotherly love, he will soon have, for the house which he has lost, a hundred houses, for the lost sisters, brothers, and so forth, a hundred sisters, a hundred brothers, a hundred fathers, a hundred mothers, a hundred farms. Schenkel forgets to add that, if this is to be the interpretation of the saying, the persecuted man must also receive through this compensating love, a hundred wives.[135]

This want of insight into the largeness, the startling originality, the self-contradictoriness, and the terrible irony in the thought of Jesus, is not a peculiarity of Schenkel's; it is characteristic of all the liberal Lives of Jesus from Strauss's down to Oskar Holtzmann's.[136] How could it be otherwise? They had to transpose a way of envisaging the world which belonged to a hero and a dreamer to the plane of thought of a rational bourgeois religion. But in Schenkel's representation, with its popular appeal, this banality is particularly obtrusive.

In the end, however, what made the success of the book was not its popular characteristics, whether good or bad, but the enmity which it drew down upon the author. The Basle Privat-Docent who, in his work of 1839, had congratulated the Zurichers on having rejected Strauss, now, as Professor and Director of the Seminary at Heidelberg, came very near being adjudged worthy of the martyr's crown himself. He had been at Heidelberg since 1851, after holding for a short time De Wette's chair at Basle. At his first coming a mildly reactionary theology might have claimed him as its own. He gave it a right to do so by the way in which he worked against the philosopher, Kuno Fischer, in the Higher Consistory. But in the struggles over the constitution of the Church he changed his position. As a defender of the rights of the laity he ranged himself on the more liberal side. After his great victory in the General Synod of 1861, in which the new constitution of the Church was established, he called a German Protestant assembly at Frankfort, in order to set on foot a general movement for Church reform. This assembly met in 1863, and led to the formation of the Protestant Association.

When the *Charakterbild Jesu* appeared, friend and foe were alike surprised at the thoroughness with which Schenkel advocated the more liberal views. "Schenkel's book," complained Luthardt, [pg 209] in a lecture at Leipzig,[137] "has aroused a painful interest. We had learnt to know him in many aspects; we were not prepared for such an apostasy from his own past. How long is it since he brought about the dismissal of Kuno Fischer from Heidelberg because he saw in the pantheism of this philosopher a danger to Church and State? It is still fresh in our memory that it was he who in the year 1852 drew up the report of the Theological Faculty of Heidelberg upon the ecclesiastical controversy raised by Pastor Dülon at Bremen, in which he denied Dülon's Christianity on the ground that he had assailed the doctrines of original sin, of justification by faith, of a living and personal God, of the eternal Divine Sonship of Christ, of the Kingdom of God, and of the credibility of the holy Scriptures." And now this same Schenkel was misusing the Life of Jesus as a weapon in "party polemics"!

The agitation against him was engineered from Berlin, where his successful attack upon the illiberal constitution of the Church had not been forgiven. One hundred and seventeen Baden clerics signed a protest declaring the author unfitted to hold office as a theological teacher in the Baden Church. Throughout the whole of Germany the pastors agitated against him. It was especially demanded that he should be immediately removed from his post as Director of the Seminary. A counter-protest was issued by the Durlach Conference in the July of 1864, in which Bluntschli and Holtzmann vigorously defended him. The Ecclesiastical Council supported him, and the storm gradually died away, especially when Schenkel in two "Defences" skilfully softened down the impression made by his work, and endeavoured to quiet the public mind by pointing out that he had only attempted to set forth one side of the truth.[138]

The position of the prospective martyr was not rendered any more easy by Strauss. In an appendix to his criticism of Schleiermacher's Life of Jesus he settled accounts with his old antagonist.[139] He recognises no scientific value whatever in the work. None of the ideas developed in it are new. One might [pg 210] fairly say, he thinks, "that the conclusions which have given offence had been carried down the Neckar from Tübingen to Heidelberg, and had there been salvaged by Herr Schenkel—in a somewhat sodden and deteriorated condition, it must be admitted—and incorporated into the edifice which he was constructing." Further, Strauss censures the book for its want of frankness, its half-and-half character, which manifests itself especially in the way in which the author clings to orthodox phraseology. "Over and over again he gives criticism with one hand all that it can possibly ask, and then takes back with the other whatever the interests of faith seem to demand; with the constant result that what is taken back is far too much for criticism and not nearly enough for faith." "In the future," he concludes, "it will be said of the seven hundred Durlachers that they fought like paladins to prevent the enemy from capturing a standard which was really nothing but a patched dish-clout."

Schenkel died in 1885 after severe sufferings. As a critic he lacked independence, and was, therefore, always inclined to compromises; in controversy he was vehement. Though he did nothing remarkable in theology, German Protestantism owes him a vast debt for acting as its tribune in the 'sixties.

That was the last time that any popular excitement was aroused in connexion with the critical study of the life of Jesus; and it was a mere storm in a tea-cup. Moreover, it was the man and not his work that aroused the excitement. Henceforth public opinion was almost entirely indifferent to anything which appeared in this department. The great fundamental question whether historical criticism was to be applied to the life of Jesus had been decided in connexion with Strauss's first work on the subject. If here and there indignation aroused by a Life of Jesus brought inconveniences to the author and profit to the publisher, that was connected in every case with purely external and incidental circumstances. Public opinion was not disquieted for a moment by Volkmar and Wrede, although they are much more extreme than Schenkel.

Most of the Lives of Jesus which followed had, it is true, nothing very exciting about them. They were mere variants of the type established during the 'sixties, variants of which the minute differences were only discernible by theologians, and which were otherwise exactly alike in arrangement and result. As a contribution to criticism, Keim's[140] "History of Jesus of Nazara" [pg 211] was the most important Life of Jesus which appeared in a long period.

It is not of much consequence that he believes in the priority of Matthew, since his presentment of the history follows the general lines of the Marcan plan, which is preserved also in Matthew. He gives it as his opinion that the life of Jesus is to be reconstructed from the Synoptics, whether Matthew has the first place or Mark. He sketches the development of Jesus in bold lines. As early as his inaugural address at Zurich, delivered on the 17th of December 1860, which, short as it was, made a powerful impression upon Holtzmann as well as upon others, he had set up the thesis that the Synoptics "artlessly, almost against their will, show us unconsciously in incidental, unobtrusive traits the progressive development of Jesus as youth and man."[141] His later works are the development of this sketch.

His grandiose style gave the keynote for the artistic treatment of the portrait of Jesus in the 'sixties. His phrases and expressions became classical. Every one follows him in speaking of the "Galilaean spring-tide" in the ministry of Jesus.

On the Johannine question he takes up a clearly defined position, denying the possibility of using the Fourth Gospel side by side with the Synoptics as an historical source. He goes very far in finding special significance in the details of the Synoptists, especially when he is anxious to discover traces of want of success in the second period of Jesus' ministry, since the plan of his Life of Jesus depends on the sharp antithesis between the periods of success and failure. The whole of the second half of the Galilaean period consists for him in "flights and retirements." "Beset by constantly renewed alarms and hindrances, Jesus left the scene of His earlier work, left His dwelling-place at Capernaum, and accompanied only by a few faithful followers, in the end only by the Twelve, sought in all directions for places of refuge for longer or shorter periods, in order to avoid and elude His enemies." Keim frankly admits, indeed, that there is not a syllable in the Gospels to suggest that these journeys are the journeys of a fugitive. But instead of allowing that to shake his conviction, he abuses the narrators and suggests that they desired to conceal the truth. "These flights," he says, "were no doubt inconvenient to the Evangelists. Matthew is here the frankest, but in order to restore the impression of Jesus' greatness he transfers to this [pg 212] period the greatest miracles. The later Evangelists are almost completely silent about these retirements, and leave us to suppose that Jesus made His journeys to Caesarea Philippi and the neighbourhood of Tyre and Sidon in the middle of winter from mere pleasure in travel, or for the extension of the Gospel, and that He made His last journey to Jerusalem without any external necessity, entirely in consequence of His free decision, even though the expectation of death which they ascribe to Him goes far to counteract the impression of complete freedom." Why do they thus correct the history? "The motive was the same difficulty which draws from us also the question, 'Is it possible that Jesus should flee?' " Keim answers "Yes." Here the liberal psychology comes clearly to light. "Jesus fled," he explains, "because He desired to preserve Himself for God and man, to secure the continuance of His ministry to Israel, to defeat as long as possible the dark designs of His enemies, to carry His cause to Jerusalem, and there, while acting, as it was His duty to do, with prudence and foresight in his relations with men, to recognise clearly, by the Divine silence or the Divine action, what the Divine purpose really was, which could not be recognised in a moment. He acts like a man who knows the duty both of examination and action, who knows His own worth and what is due to Him and His obligations towards God and man."[142]

In regard to the question of eschatology, however, Keim does justice to the texts.[143] He admits that eschatology, "a Kingdom of God clothed with material splendours," forms an integral part of the preaching of Jesus from the first; "that He never rejected it, and therefore never by a so-called advance transformed the sensuous Messianic idea into a purely spiritual one." "Jesus does not uproot from the minds of the sons of Zebedee their belief in the thrones on His right hand and His left; He does not hesitate to make His entry into Jerusalem in the character of the Messiah; He acknowledges His Messiahship before the Council without making any careful reservations; upon the cross His title is The King of the Jews; He consoles Himself and His followers with the thought of His return as an earthly ruler, and leaves with His disciples, without making any attempt to check it, the belief, which long survived, in a future establishment or restoration of the Kingdom in an Israel delivered from bondage." Keim remarks with much justice "that Strauss had been wrong in rejecting his own earlier and more correct formula," which combined the eschatological [pg 213] and spiritual elements as operating side by side in the plan of Jesus.

Keim, however, himself in the end allows the spiritual elements practically to cancel the eschatological. He admits, it is true, that the expression Son of Man which Jesus uses designated the Messiah in the sense of Daniel's prophecy, but he thinks that these pictorial representations in Daniel did not repel Jesus because He interpreted them spiritually, and "intended to describe Himself as belonging to mankind even in His Messianic office." To solve the difficulty Keim assumes a development. Jesus' consciousness of His vocation had been strengthened both by success and by disappointment. As time went on He preached the Kingdom not as a future Kingdom, as at first, but as one which was present in Him and with Him, and He declares His Messiahship more and more openly before the world. He thinks of the Kingdom as undergoing development, but not with an unlimited, infinite horizon as the moderns suppose; the horizon is bounded by the eschatology. "For however easy it may be to read modern ideas into the parables of the draught of fishes, the mustard seed and the leaven, which, taken by themselves, seem to suggest the duration contemplated by the modern view, it is nevertheless indubitable that Jesus, like Paul, by no means looks forward to so protracted an earthly development; on the contrary, nothing appears more clearly from the sources than that He thought of its term as rapidly approaching, and of His victory as nigh at hand; and looked to the last decisive events, even to the day of judgment, as about to occur during the lifetime of the existing generation, including Himself and His apostles." "It was the overmastering pressure of circumstances which held Him prisoner within the limitations of this obsolete belief." When His confidence in the development of His Kingdom came into collision with barriers which He could not pass, when His belief in the presence of the Kingdom of God grew dim, the purely eschatological ideas won the upper hand, "and if we may suppose that it was precisely this thought of the imminent decisive action of God, taking possession of His mind with renewed force at this point, which steeled His human courage, and roused Him to a passion of self-sacrifice with the hope of saving from the judgment whatever might still be saved, we may welcome His adoption of these narrower ideas as in accordance with the goodwill of God, which could only by this means maintain the failing strength of its human instrument and secure the spoils of the Divine warfare—the souls of men subdued and conquered by Him."

The thought which had hovered before the mind of Renan, but which in his hands had become only the motive of a romance—*une ficelle dé roman* as the French express it—was realised by [pg 214] Keim. Nothing deeper or more beautiful has since been written about the development of Jesus.

Less critical in character is Hase's "History of Jesus,"[144] which superseded in 1876 the various editions of the Handbook on the Life of Jesus which had first appeared in 1829.

The question of the use of John's Gospel side by side with the Synoptics he leaves in suspense, and speaks his last word on the subject in the form of a parable. "If I may be allowed to use an avowedly parabolic form of speech, the relation of Jesus to the two streams of Gospel tradition may be illustrated as follows. Once there appeared upon earth a heavenly Being. According to His first three biographers He goes about more or less incognito, in the long garment of a Rabbi, a forceful popular figure, somewhat Judaic in speech, only occasionally, almost unmarked by His biographers, pointing with a smile beyond this brief interlude to His home. In the description left by His favourite disciple, He has thrown off the *talar* of the Rabbi, and stands before us in His native character, but in bitter and angry strife with those who took offence at His magnificent simplicity, and then later—it must be confessed, more attractively—in deep emotion at parting with those whom, during His pilgrimage on earth, He had made His friends, though they did not rightly understand His strange, unearthly speech."

This is Hase's way, always to avoid a final decision. The fifty years of critical study of the subject which he had witnessed and taken part in had made him circumspect, sometimes almost sceptical. But his notes of interrogation do not represent a covert supernaturalism like those in the Life of Jesus of 1829. Hase had been penetrated by the influence of Strauss and had adopted from him the belief that the true life of Jesus lies beyond the reach of criticism. "It is not my business," he says to his students in an introductory lecture, "to recoil in horror from this or that thought, or to express it with embarrassment as being dangerous; I would not forbid even the enthusiasm of doubt and destruction which makes Strauss so strong and Renan so seductive."

It is left uncertain whether Jesus' consciousness of His Messiahship reaches back to the days of His childhood, or whether it arose in the ethical development of His ripening manhood. The concealment of His Messianic claims is ascribed, [pg 215] as by Schenkel and others, to paedagogic motives; it was necessary that Jesus should first educate the people and the disciples up to a higher ethical view of His office. In the stress which he lays upon the eschatology Hase has points of affinity with Keim, for whom he had prepared the way in his Life of Jesus of 1829, in which he had been the first to assert a development in Jesus in the course of which He at first fully shared the Jewish eschatological views, but later advanced to a more spiritual conception. In his Life of Jesus of 1876 he is prepared to make the eschatology the dominant feature in the last period also, and does not hesitate to represent Jesus as dying in the enthusiastic expectation of returning upon the clouds of heaven. He feels himself driven to this by the eschatological ideas in the last discourses. "Jesus' clear and definite sayings," he declares, "with the whole context of the circumstances in which they were spoken and understood, have been forcing me to this conclusion for years past."

"That lofty Messianic dream must therefore continue to hold its place, since Jesus, influenced as much by the idea of the Messianic glories taken over from the beliefs of His people as by His own religious exaltation, could not think of the victory of His Kingdom except as closely connected with His own personal action. But that was only a misunderstanding due to the unconscious poesy of a high-ranging religious imagination, the ethical meaning of which could only be realised by a long historical development. Christ certainly came again as the greatest power on earth, and His power, along with His word, is constantly judging the world. He faced the sufferings which lay immediately before Him with His eyes fixed upon this great future."

The chief excellence of Beyschlag's Life of Jesus consists in its arrangement.[145] He first, in the volume of preliminary investigations, discusses the problems, so that the narrative is disencumbered of all explanations, and by virtue of the author's admirable style becomes a pure work of art, which rivets the interest of the reader and almost causes the want of a consistent historical conception to be overlooked. The fact is, however, that in regard to the two decisive questions Beyschlag is deliberately inconsistent. Although he recognises that the Gospel [pg 216] of John has not the character of an essentially historical source, "being, rather, a brilliant subjective portrait," "a didactic, quite as much as an historical work," he produces his Life of Jesus by "combining and mortising together Synoptic and Johannine elements." The same uncertainty prevails in regard to the recognition of the definitely eschatological character of Jesus' system of ideas. Beyschlag gives a very large place to eschatology, so that in order to combine the spiritual with the eschatological view his Jesus has to pass through three stages of development. In the first He preaches the Kingdom as something future, a supernatural event which was to be looked forward to, much as the Baptist preached it. Then the response which was called forth on all hands by His preaching led Him to believe that the Kingdom was in some sense already present, "that the Father, while He delays the outward manifestation of the Kingdom, is causing it to come even now in quiet and unnoticed ways by a humble gradual growth, and the great thought of His parables, which dominates the whole middle period of His public life, the resemblance of the Kingdom to mustard seed or leaven, comes to birth in His mind." As His failure becomes more and more certain, "the centre of gravity of His thought is shifted to the world beyond the grave, and the picture of a glorious return to conquer and to judge the world rises before Him."

The peculiar interweaving of Synoptic and Johannine ideas leads to the result that, between the two, Beyschlag in the end forms no clear conception of the eschatology, and makes Jesus think in a half-Johannine, half-Synoptic fashion. "It is a consequence of Jesus' profound conception of the Kingdom of God as something essentially growing that He regards its final perfection not as a state of rest, but rather as a living movement, as a process of becoming, and since He regards this process as a cosmic and supernatural process in which history finds its consummation, and yet as arising entirely out of the ethical and historical process, He combines elements from each into the same prophetic conception." An eschatology of this kind is not matter for history.

In the acceptance of the "miracles" Beyschlag goes to the utmost limits allowed by criticism; in considering the possibility of one or another of the recorded raisings from the dead he even finds himself within the borders of rationalist territory.

Whether Bernhard Weiss's[146] is to be numbered with the liberal [pg 217] Lives of Jesus is a question to which we may answer "Yes; but along with the faults of these it has some others in addition." Weiss shares with the authors of the liberal "Lives" the assumption that Mark designed to set forth a definite "view of the course of development of the public ministry of Jesus," and on the strength of that believes himself justified in giving a very far-reaching significance to the details offered by this Evangelist. The arbitrariness with which he carries out this theory is quite as unbounded as Schenkel's, and in his fondness for the "argument from silence" he even surpasses him. Although Mark never allows a single word to escape him about the motives of the northern journeys, Weiss is so clever at reading between the lines that the motives are "quite sufficiently" clear to him. The object of these journeys was, according to his explanation, "that the people might have an opportunity, undistracted by the immediate impression of His words and actions, to make up their minds in regard to the questions which they had put to Him so pressingly and inescapably in the last days of His public ministry; they must themselves draw their own conclusions alike from the declarations and from the conduct of Jesus. Only by Jesus' removing Himself for a time from their midst could they come to a clear decision as to their attitude to Jesus." This modern psychologising, however, is closely combined with a dialectic which seeks to show that there is no irreconcilable opposition between the belief in the Son of [pg 218] God and Son of Man which the Church of Christ has always confessed, and a critical investigation of the question how far the details of His life have been accurately preserved by tradition, and how they are to be historically interpreted. That means that Weiss is going to cover up the difficulties and stumbling-blocks with the mantle of Christian charity which he has woven out of the most plausible of the traditional sophistries. As a dialectical performance on these lines his Life of Jesus rivals in importance any except Schleiermacher's. On points of detail there are many interesting historical observations. When all is said, one can only regret that so much knowledge and so much ability have been expended in the service of so hopeless a cause.

What was the net result of these liberal Lives of Jesus? In the first place the clearing up of the relation between John and the Synoptics. That seems surprising, since the chief representatives of this school, Holtzmann, Schenkel, Weizsäcker, and Hase, took up a mediating position on this question, not to speak of Beyschlag and Weiss, for whom the possibility of reconciliation between the two lines of tradition is an accepted datum for ecclesiastical and apologetic reasons. But the very attempt to hold the position made clear its inherent untenability. The defence of the combination of the two traditions exhausted itself in the efforts of these its critical champions, just as the acceptance of the supernatural in history exhausted itself in the—to judge from the approval of the many—victorious struggle against Strauss. In the course of time Weizsäcker, like Holtzmann,[147] advanced to the rejection of any possibility of reconciliation, and gave up the Fourth Gospel as an historical source. The second demand of Strauss's first Life of Jesus was now—at last—conceded by scientific criticism.

That does not mean, of course, that no further attempts at reconciliation appeared thenceforward. Was ever a street so closed by a cordon that one or two isolated individuals did not get through? And to dodge through needs, after all, no special [pg 219] intelligence, or special courage. Must we never speak of a victory so long as a single enemy remains alive? Individual attempts to combine John with the Synoptics which appeared after this decisive point are in some cases deserving of special attention, as for example, Wendt's[148] acute study of the "Teaching of Jesus," which has all the importance of a full treatment of the "Life." But the very way in which Wendt grapples with his task shows that the main issue is already decided. All he can do is to fight a skilful and determined rearguard action. It is not the Fourth Gospel as it stands, but only a "ground-document" on which it is based, which he, in common with Weiss, Alexander Schweizer, and Renan, would have to be recognised "alongside of the Gospel of Mark and the Logia of Matthew as an historically trustworthy tradition regarding the teaching of Jesus," and which may be used along with those two writings in forming a picture of the Life of Jesus. For Wendt there is no longer any question of an interweaving and working up together of the individual sections of John and the Synoptists. He takes up much the same standpoint as Holtzmann occupied in 1863, but he provides a much more comprehensive and well-tested basis for it.

In the end there is no such very great difference between Wendt and the writers who had advanced to the conviction of the irreconcilability of the two traditions. Wendt refuses to give up the Fourth Gospel altogether; they, on their part, won only a half victory because they did not as a matter of fact escape from the Johannine interpretation of the Synoptics. By means of their psychological interpretation of the first three Gospels they make for themselves an ideal Fourth Gospel, in the interests of which they reject the existing Fourth Gospel. They will hear nothing of the spiritualised Johannine Christ, and refuse to acknowledge even to themselves that they have only deposed Him in order to put in His place a spiritualised Synoptic Jesus Christ, that is, a man who claimed to be the Messiah, but in a spiritual sense. All the development which they discover in Jesus is in the last analysis only an evidence of the tension between the Synoptics, in their natural literal sense, and the "Fourth Gospel" which is extracted from them by an artificial interpretation.

The fact is, the separation between the Synoptics and the Fourth Gospel is only the first step to a larger result which [pg 220] necessarily follows from it—the complete recognition of the fundamentally eschatological character of the teaching and influence of the Marcan and Matthaean Jesus. Inasmuch as they suppressed this consequence, Holtzmann, Schenkel, Hase, and Weizsäcker, even after their critical conversion, still lay under the spell of the Fourth Gospel, of a modern, ideal Fourth Gospel. It is only when the eschatological question is decided that the problem of the relation of John to the Synoptics is finally laid to rest. The liberal Lives of Jesus grasped their incompatibility only from a literary point of view, not in its full historical significance.

There is another result in the acceptance of which the critical school had stopped half-way. If the Marcan plan be accepted, it follows that, setting aside the references to the Son of Man in Mark ii. 10 and 28, Jesus had never, previous to the incident at Caesarea Philippi, given Himself out to be the Messiah or been recognised as such. The perception of this fact marks one of the greatest advances in the study of the subject. This result, once accepted, ought necessarily to have suggested two questions: in the first place, why Jesus down to that moment had made a secret of His Messiahship even to His disciples; in the second place, whether at any time, and, if so, when and how, the people were made acquainted with His Messianic claims. As a fact, however, by the application of that ill-starred psychologising both questions were smothered;

that is to say, a sham answer was given to them. It was regarded as self-evident that Jesus had concealed His Messiahship from His disciples for so long in order in the meantime to bring them, without their being aware of it, to a higher spiritual conception of the Messiah; it was regarded as equally self-evident that in the last weeks the Messianic claims of Jesus could no longer be hidden from the people, but that He did not openly avow them, but merely allowed them to be divined, in order to lead up the multitude to the recognition of the higher spiritual character of the office which He claimed for Himself. These ingenious psychologists never seemed to perceive that there is not a word of all this in Mark; but that they had read it all into some of the most contradictory and inexplicable facts in the Gospels, and had thus created a Messiah who both wished to be Messiah and did not wish it, and who in the end, so far as the people were concerned, both was and was not the Messiah. Thus these writers had only recognised the importance of the scene at Caesarea Philippi, they had not ventured to attack the general problem of Jesus' attitude in regard to the Messiahship, and had not reflected further on the mutually contradictory facts that Jesus purposed to be the Messiah and yet did not come forward publicly in that character.

Thus they had side-tracked the study of the subject, and based all their hopes of progress on an intensive exegesis of the detail of [pg 221] Mark. They thought they had nothing to do but to occupy a conquered territory, and never suspected that along the whole line they had only won a half victory, never having thought out to the end either the eschatological question or the fundamental historical question of the attitude of Jesus to the Messiahship.

They were not disquieted by the obstinate persistence of the discussion on the eschatological question. They thought it was merely a skirmish with a few unorganised guerrillas; in reality it was the advance-guard of the army with which Reimarus was threatening their flank, and which under the leadership of Johannes Weiss was to bring them to so dangerous a pass. And while they were endeavouring to avoid this turning movement they fell into the ambush which Bruno Bauer had laid in their rear: Wrede held up the Marcan hypothesis and demanded the pass-word for the theory of the Messianic consciousness and claims of Jesus to which it was acting as convoy.

The eschatological and the literary school, finding themselves thus opposed to a common enemy, naturally formed an alliance. The object of their combined attack was not the Marcan outline of the life of Jesus, which, in fact, they both accept, but the modern "psychological" method of reading between the lines of the Marcan narrative. Under the cross fire of these allies that idea of development which had been the strongest entrenchment of the liberal critical Lives of Jesus, and which they had been desperately endeavouring to strengthen down to the very last, was finally blown to atoms.

But the striking thing about these liberal critical Lives of Jesus was that they unconsciously prepared the way for a deeper historical view which could not have been reached apart from them. A deeper understanding of a subject is only brought to pass when a theory is carried to its utmost limit and finally proves its own inadequacy.

There is this in common between rationalism and the liberal critical method, that each had followed out a theory to its ultimate consequences. The liberal critical school had carried to its limit the explanation of the connexion of the actions of Jesus, and of the events of His life, by a "natural" psychology; and the conclusions to which they had been driven had prepared the way for the recognition that the natural psychology is not here the historical psychology, but that the latter must be deduced from certain historical data. Thus through the meritorious and magnificently sincere work of the liberal critical school the a priori "natural" psychology gave way to the eschatological. That is the net result, from the historical point of view, of the study of the life of Jesus in the post-Straussian period.

XV. The Eschatological Question

Timothée Colani. Jésus-Christ et les croyances messianiques de son temps. Strassburg, 1864. 255 pp.

Gustav Volkmar. Jesus Nazarenus und die erste christliche Zeit, mit den beiden ersten Erzählern. (Jesus the Nazarene and the Beginnings of Christianity, with the two earliest narrators of His life.) Zurich, 1882. 403 pp.

Wilhelm Weiffenbach. Der Wiederkunftsgedanke Jesu. (Jesus' Conception of His Second Coming.) 1873. 424 pp.

W. Baldensperger. Das Selbstbewusstsein Jesu im Lichte der messianischen Hoffnungen seiner Zeit. (The Self-consciousness of Jesus in the Light of the Messianic Hopes of His time.) Strassburg, 1888. 2nd ed., 1892, 282 pp.; 3rd ed. pt. i. 240 pp.

Johannes Weiss. Die Predigt Jesu vom Reiche Gottes. (The Preaching of Jesus concerning the Kingdom of God.) 1892. Göttingen. 67 pp. Second revised and enlarged edition, 1900, 210 pp.

So long as it was merely a question of establishing the distinctive character of the thought of Jesus as compared with the ancient prophetic and Danielic conceptions, and so long as the only available storehouse of Rabbinic and Late-Jewish ideas was Lightfoot's *Horae Hebraicae et Talmudicae in quatuor Evangelistas*,[149] it was still possible to cherish the belief that the preaching of Jesus could be conceived as something which was, in the last analysis, independent of all contemporary ideas. But after the studies of Hilgenfeld and Dillmann[150] had made known the Jewish apocalyptic in its fundamental characteristics, and the Jewish pseudepigrapha were no longer looked on as "forgeries," but as representative documents of the last stage of Jewish thought, the necessity of taking account of them in interpreting the thought of Jesus became more and more emphatic. Almost two decades [pg 223] were to pass, however, before the full significance of this material was realised.

It might almost have seemed as if it was to meet this attack by anticipation that Colani wrote in 1864 his work, *Jésus-Christ et les croyances messianiques de son temps*.

Timothée Colani was born in 1824 at Lemé (Aisne), studied in Strassburg and became pastor there in 1851. In the year 1864 he was appointed Professor of Pastoral Theology in Strassburg in spite of some attempted opposition to the appointment on the part of the orthodox party in Paris, which was then growing in strength. The events of the year 1870 left him without a post. As he had no prospect of being called to a pastorate in France, he became a merchant. In consequence of some unfortunate business operations he lost all his property. In 1875 he obtained a post as librarian at the Sorbonne. He died in 1888.

How far was Jesus a Jew? That was the starting-point of Colani's study. According to him there was a complete lack of homogeneity in the Messianic hopes cherished by the Jewish people in the time of Jesus, since the prophetic conception, according to which the Kingdom of the Messiah belonged to the present world-order, and the apocalyptic, which transferred it to the future age, had not yet been brought into any kind of unity. The general expectation was focused rather upon the Forerunner than upon the Messiah. Jesus Himself in the first period of His public ministry, up to Mark viii., had never designated Himself as the Messiah, for the expression Son of Man carried no Messianic associations for the multitude. His fundamental thought was that of perfect communion with God; only little by little, as the success of the preaching of the Kingdom more and more impressed His mind, did His consciousness take on a Messianic colouring. In face of the undisciplined expectations of the people He constantly repeats in His parables of the growth of the Kingdom, the word "patience." By revealing Himself as the Lord of this spiritual kingdom He makes an end of the oscillation between the sensuous and the spiritual in the current expectations of the future blessedness. He points to mankind as a whole, not merely to the chosen people, as the people of the Kingdom, and substitutes for the apocalyptic catastrophe an organic development. By His interpretation of Psalm cx., in Mark xii. 35-37, He makes known that the Messiah has nothing whatever to do with the Davidic kingship. It was only with difficulty that He came to resolve to accept the title of Messiah; He knew what a weight of national prejudices and national hopes hung upon it.

But He is "Messiah the Son of Man"; He created this expression in order thereby to make known His lowliness. In the moment in which He accepted the office He registered the resolve [pg 224] to suffer. His purpose is, to be the suffering, not the triumphant, Messiah. It is to the influence which His Passion exercises upon the souls of men that He looks for the firm establishment of His Kingdom.

This spiritual conception of the Kingdom cannot possibly be combined with the thought of a glorious Second Coming, for if Jesus had held this latter view He must necessarily have thought of the present life as only a kind of prologue to that second existence. Neither the Jewish, nor the Jewish-Christian eschatology as represented in the eschatological discourses in the Gospels, can, therefore, in Colani's opinion, belong to the preaching of Jesus. That He should sometimes have made use of the imagery associated with the Jewish expectations of the future is, of course, only natural. But the eschatology occupies far too important a place in the tradition of the preaching of Jesus to be explained as a mere symbolical mode of expression. It forms a substantial element of that preaching. A spiritualisation of it will not meet the case. Therefore, if the conviction has been arrived at on other grounds that Jesus' preaching did not follow the lines of Jewish eschatology, there is only one possible way of dealing with it, and that is by excising it from the text on critical grounds.

The only element in the preaching of Jesus which can, in Colani's opinion, be called in any sense "eschatological" was the conviction that there would be a wide extension of the Gospel even within the existing generation, that Gentiles should be admitted to the Kingdom, and that in consequence of the general want of receptivity towards the message of salvation, judgment should come upon the nations.

These views of Colani furnish him with a basis upon which to decide on the genuineness or otherwise of the eschatological discourses. Among the sayings put into the mouth of Jesus which must be rejected as impossible are: the promise, in the discourse at the sending forth of the Twelve, of the imminent coming of the Son of Man, Matt. x. 23; the promise to the disciples that they should sit upon twelve thrones judging the tribes of Israel, Matt. xix. 28; the saying about His return in Matt. xxiii. 39; the final eschatological saying at the Last Supper, Matt. xxvi. 29, "the Papias-like Chiliasm of which is unworthy of Jesus"; and the prediction of His coming on the clouds of heaven with which He closes His Messianic confession before the Council. The apocalyptic discourses in Mark xiii., Matt. xxiv., and Luke xxi. are interpolated. A Jewish-Christian apocalypse of the first century, probably composed before the destruction of Jerusalem, has been interwoven with a short exhortation which Jesus gave on the occasion when He predicted the destruction of the temple.

According to Colani, therefore, Jesus did not expect to come [pg 225] again from Heaven to complete His work. It was completed by His death, and the purpose of the coming of the Spirit was to make manifest its completion. Strauss and Renan had entered upon the path of explaining Jesus' preaching from the history of the time by the assumption of an intermixture in it of Jewish ideas, but it was now recognised "that this path is a cul-de-sac, and that criticism must turn round and get out of it as quickly as possible."

The new feature of Colani's view was not so much the uncompromising rejection of eschatology as the clear recognition that its rejection was not a matter to be disposed of in a phrase or two, but necessitated a critical analysis of the text.

The systematic investigation of the Synoptic apocalypse was a contribution to criticism of the utmost importance.

In the year 1882 Volkmar took up this attempt afresh, at least in its main features.[151] His construction rests upon two main points of support; upon his view of the sources and his conception of the eschatology of the time of Jesus. In his view the sole source for the Life of Jesus is the Gospel of Mark, which was "probably written exactly in the year 73," five years after the Johannine apocalypse.

The other two of the first three Gospels belong to the second century, and can only be used by way of supplement. Luke dates from the beginning of the first decade of the century; while Matthew is regarded by Volkmar, as by Wilke, as being a combination of Mark and Luke, and is relegated to the end of this first decade. The work is in his opinion a revision of the Gospel tradition "in the spirit of that primitive Christianity which, while constantly opposing the tendency of the apostle of the Gentiles to make light of the Law, was nevertheless so far universalistic that, starting from the old legal ground, it made the first steps towards a catholic unity." Once Matthew has been set aside in this way, the literary elimination of the eschatology follows as a matter of course; the much smaller element of discourse in Mark can offer no serious resistance.

As regards the Messianic expectations of the time, they were, in Volkmar's opinion, such that Jesus could not possibly have come [pg 226] forward with Messianic claims. The Messianic Son of Man, whose aim was to found a super-earthly Kingdom, only arose in Judaism under the influence of Christian dogma. The contemporaries of Jesus knew only the political ideal of the Messianic King. And woe to any one who conjured up these hopes! The Baptist had done so by his too fervent preaching about repentance and the Kingdom, and had been promptly put out of the way by the Tetrarch. The version found even in Mark, which represents that it was on Herodias' account, and at her daughter's petition, that John was beheaded, is a later interpretation which, according to Volkmar, is evidently false on chronological grounds, since the Baptist was dead before Herod took Herodias as his wife. Had Jesus desired the Messiahship, He could only have claimed it in this political sense. The alternative is to suppose that He did not desire it.

Volkmar's contribution to the subject consists in the formulating of this clean-cut alternative. Colani had indeed recognised the alternative, but had not taken up a consistent attitude in regard to it. Here, that way of escape from the difficulty is barred, which suggests that Jesus set Himself up as Messiah, but in another than the popular sense. What may be called Jesus' Messianic consciousness consisted solely "in knowing Himself to be first-born among many brethren, the Son of God after the Spirit, and consequently feeling Himself enabled and impelled to bring about that regeneration of His people which alone could make it worthy of deliverance." It is in any case clearly evident from Paul, from the Apocalypse, and from Mark, "the three documentary witnesses emanating from the circle of the followers of Jesus during the first century, that it was only after His crucifixion that Jesus was hailed as the Christ; never during His earthly life." The elimination of the eschatology thus leads also to the elimination of the Messiahship of Jesus.

If we are told in Mark viii. 29 that Simon Peter was the first among men to hail Jesus as the Messiah, it is to be noticed, Volkmar points out, that the Evangelist places this confession at a time when Jesus' work was over and the thought of His Passion first appears; and if we desire fully to understand the author's purpose we must fix our attention on the Lord's command not to make known His Messiahship until after His resurrection (Mark viii. 30, ix. 9 and 10), which is a hint that we are to date Jesus' Messiahship from His death. For Mark is no mere naïve chronicler, but a conscious artist interpreting the history; sometimes, indeed, a powerful epic writer in whose work the historical and the poetic are intermingled.

Thus the conclusion is that Mark, in agreement with Paul, represents Jesus as becoming the Messiah only as a consequence of His resurrection. He really appeared, and His first appearance [pg 227] was to Peter. When Peter on that night of terror fled from Jerusalem to take refuge in Galilee, Jesus, according to the mystic prediction of Mark xiv. 28 and xvi. 7, went before him. "He was constantly present to his spirit, until on the third day He manifested Himself before his eyes, in the heavenly appearance which was also vouchsafed to the last of the apostles 'as he was in the way'—and Peter, enraptured, gave expression to the clear conviction with which the whole life of Jesus had inspired him in the cry 'Thou art the Christ.'"

The historical Jesus therefore founded a community of followers without advancing any claims to the Messiahship. He desired only to be a reformer, the spiritual deliverer of the people of God, to realise upon earth the Kingdom of God which they were all seeking in the beyond, and to extend the reign of God over all nations. "The Kingdom of God is doubtless to win its final and decisive victory by the almighty aid of God; our duty is to see to its beginnings"—that is, according to Volkmar, the lesson which Jesus teaches us in the parable of the Sower. The ethic of this Kingdom was not yet confused by any eschatological ideas. It was only when, as the years went on, the expectation of the Parousia rose to a high pitch of intensity that "marriage and the bringing up of children came to be regarded as superfluous, and were consequently thought of as signs of an absorption in earthly interests which was out of harmony with the near approach to the goal of these hopes." Jesus had renewed the foundations on which "the family" was based and had made it, in turn, a corner stone of the Kingdom of God, even as He had consecrated the common meal by making it a love feast.

In most things Jesus was conservative. The ritual worship of the God of Israel remained for Him always a sacred thing. But in spite of that He withdrew more and more from the synagogue, the scene of His earliest preaching, and taught in the houses of His disciples. "He had learned to fulfil the law as implicit in one highest commandment and supreme principle, therefore 'in spirit and in truth'; but He never, as appears from all the evidence, declared it to be abolished." "We may be equally certain, however, that Jesus, while He asserted the abiding validity of the Ten Commandments, never explicitly declared that of the Mosaic Law as a whole. The absence of any such saying from the tradition regarding Jesus made it possible for Paul to take his decisive step forward."

As regards the Gospel discourses about the Parousia, it is easy to recognise that, even in Mark, these "are one and all the work of the narrator, whose purpose is edification. He connects his work as closely as possible with the Apocalypse, which had appeared some five years earlier, in order to emphasise, in contrast to it, the [pg 228] higher truth." Jesus' own hope, in all its clearness and complete originality, is recorded in the parables of the seed growing secretly and the grain of mustard seed, and in the saying about the immortality of His words. Nothing beyond this is in any way certain, however remarkable the saying in Mark ix. 1 may be, that the looked-for consummation is to take place during the lifetime of the existing generation.

"It is only the fact that Mark is preceded by 'the book of the Birth (and History) of Christ according to Matthew'—not only in the Scriptures, but also in men's minds, which were dominated by it as the 'first Gospel'—which has caused it to be taken as self-evident that Jesus, knowing Himself from the first to be the Messiah, expected His Parousia solely from heaven, and therefore with, or in, the clouds of heaven.... But since He who was thought of as by birth the Son of God, is now thought of as the Son of Man, born an Israelite, and becoming the Son of God after the spirit only at His baptism, the hope that looks to the clouds of heaven cannot be, or at least ought not to be, any longer explained otherwise than as an enthusiastic dream."

If, even at the beginning of the 'eighties, a so extreme theory on the other side could, without opposition, occupy all the points of vantage, it is evident that the theory which gave eschatology its due place was making but slow progress. It was not that any one had been disputing the ground with it, but that all its operations were characterised by a nervous timidity. And these hesitations are not to be laid to the account of those who did not perceive the approach of the decisive conflict, or refused to accept battle, like the followers of Reuss, for instance, who were satisfied with the hypothesis that thoughts about the Last Judgment had forced their way into the authentic discourses of Jesus about the destruction of the city;[152] even those who like Weiffenbach are fully convinced that "the eschatological question, and in particular the question of the Second Coming, which in many quarters has up to the present been treated as a *noli me tangere*, must sooner or later become the battle-ground of the greatest and most decisive of theological controversies"—even those who shared this conviction stopped half-way on the road on which they had entered.

Weiffenbach's[153] work, "Jesus' Conception of His Second Coming," published in 1873, sums up the results of the previous discussions of the subject. He names as among those who ascribe the [pg 229] expectation of the Parousia, in the sensuous form in which it meets us in the documents, to a misunderstanding of the teaching of Jesus on the part of the disciples and the writers who were dependent upon them—Schleiermacher, Bleek, Holtzmann, Schenkel, Colani, Baur, Hase, and Meyer. Among those who maintained that the Parousia formed an integral part of Jesus' teaching, he cites Keim, Weizsäcker, Strauss, and Renan. He considers that the readiest way to advance the discussion will be by undertaking a critical review of the attempt to analyse the great Synoptic discourse about the future in which Colani had led the way.

The question of the Parousia is like, Weiffenbach suggests, a vessel which has become firmly wedged between rocks. Any attempt to get it afloat again will be useless until a new channel is found for it. His detailed discussions are devoted to endeavouring to discover the relation between the declarations regarding the Second Coming and the predictions of the Passion. In the course of his analysis of the great prophetic discourse he rejects the suggestion made by Weisse in his *Evangelienfrage* of 1856, that the eschatological character of the discourse results from the way in which it is put together; that while the sayings in their present mosaic-like combination certainly have a reference to the last things, each of them individually in its original context might well bear a natural sense. In Colani's hypothesis of conflation the suggestion was to be rejected that it was not "Ur-Markus," but the author of the Synoptic apocalypse who was responsible for the working in of the "Little Apocalypse."[154] It was an unsatisfactory feature of Weizsäcker's position[155] that he insisted on regarding the "Little Apocalypse" as Jewish, not Jewish-Christian; Pfleiderer had distinguished sharply what belongs to the Evangelist from the "Little Apocalypse," and had sought to prove that the purpose of the Evangelist in thus breaking up the latter and working it into a discourse of Jesus was to tone down the eschatological hopes expressed in the discourse, because they had remained unfulfilled even at the fall of Jerusalem, and to retard the rapid development of the apocalyptic process by inserting between its successive phases passages from a different discourse.[156] Weiffenbach carries this series of tentative suggestions to its logical conclusion, advancing the view that the link of connexion between [pg 230] the Jewish-Christian Apocalypse and the Gospel material in which it is embedded is the thought of the Second Coming. This was the thought which gave the impulse from without towards the transmutation of Jewish into Jewish-Christian eschatology. Jesus must have given expression to the thought of His near return; and Jewish-Christianity subsequently painted it over with the colours of Jewish eschatology.

In developing this theory, Weiffenbach thought that he had succeeded in solving the problem which had been first critically formulated by Keim, who is constantly emphasising the idea that the eschatological hopes of the disciples could not be explained merely from their Judaic pre-suppositions, but that some incentive to the formation of these hopes must be sought in the preaching of Jesus; otherwise primitive Christianity and the life of Jesus would stand side by side unconnected and unexplained, and in that case we must give up all hope "of distinguishing the sure word of the Lord from Israel's restless speculations about the future."

When the Jewish-Christian Apocalypse has been eliminated, we arrive at a discourse, spoken on the Mount of Olives, in which Jesus exhorted His disciples to watchfulness, in view of the near, but nevertheless undefined, hour of the return of "the Master of the House."

In this discourse, therefore, we have a standard by which criticism may test all the eschatological sayings and discourses. Weiffenbach has the merit of having gathered together all the eschatological material of the Synoptics and examined it in the light of a definite principle. In Colani the material was incomplete, and instead of a critical principle he offered only an arbitrary exegesis which permitted him, for example, to conceive the watchfulness on which the eschatological parables constantly insist as only a vivid expression for the sense of responsibility "which weighs upon the life of man."

And yet the outcome of this attempt of Weiffenbach's, which begins with so much real promise, is in the end wholly unsatisfactory. The "authentic thought of the return" which he takes as his standard has for its sole content the expectation of a visible personal return in the near future "free from all more or less fantastic apocalyptic and Jewish-Christian speculations about the future." That is to say, the whole of the eschatological discourses of Jesus are to be judged by the standard of a colourless, unreal figment of theology. Whatever cannot be squared with that is to be declared spurious and cut away! Accordingly the eschatological closing saying at the Last Supper is stigmatised as a "Chiliastic-Capernaitic"[157] distortion of a "normal" promise of the Second Coming; the idea of the παλιγγενεσία, Matt. xix. 28, is said to be [pg 231] wholly foreign to Jesus' world of thought; it is impossible, too, that Jesus can have thought of Himself as the Judge of the world, for the Jewish and Jewish-Christian eschatology does not ascribe the conduct of the Last Judgment to the Messiah; that is first done by Gentile Christians, and especially by Paul. It was, therefore, the later eschatology which set the Son of Man on the throne of His glory and prepared "the twelve thrones of judgment for the disciples." The historian ought only to admit such of the sayings about bearing rule in the Messianic Kingdom as can be interpreted in a spiritual, non-sensuous fashion.

In the end Weiffenbach's critical principle proves to be merely a bludgeon with which he goes seal-hunting and clubs the defenceless Synoptic sayings right and left. When his work is done you see before you a desert island strewn with quivering corpses. Nevertheless the slaughter was not aimless, or at least it was not without result.

In the first place, it did really appear, as a by-product of the critical processes, that Jesus' discourses about the future had nothing to do with an historical prevision of the destruction of Jerusalem, whereas the supposition that they had, had hitherto been taken as self-evident, the prediction of the destruction of Jerusalem being regarded as the historic nucleus of Jesus' discourses regarding the future, to which the idea of the Last Judgment had subsequently attached itself.

Here, then, we have the introduction of the converse opinion, which was subsequently established as correct; namely, that Jesus foresaw, indeed, the Last Judgment, but not the historical destruction of Jerusalem.

In the next place, in the course of his critical examination of the eschatological material, Weiffenbach stumbles upon the discourse at the sending forth of the Twelve in Matt. x., and finds himself face to face with the fact that the discourse which he was expected to regard as a discourse of instruction was really nothing of the kind, but a collection of eschatological sayings. As he had taken over along with the Marcan hypothesis the closely connected view of the composite character of the Synoptic discourses, he does not allow himself to be misled, but regards this inappropriate charge to the Twelve as nothing else than an impossible anticipation and a bold anachronism. He knows that he is at one in this with Holtzmann, Colani, Bleek, Scholten, Meyer, and Keim, who also made the discourse of instruction end at the point beyond which they find it impossible to explain it, and regard the predictions of persecution as only possible in the later period of the life of Jesus. "For these predictions," to express Weiffenbach's view in the words of Keim, "are too much at variance with the essentially gracious and happy mood which suggested the sending [pg 232] forth of the disciples, and reflect instead the lurid gloom of the fierce conflicts of the later period and the sadness of the farewell discourses."

It was a good thing that Bruno Bauer did not hear this chorus. If he had, he would have asked Weiffenbach and his allies whether the poor fragment that remained after the critical dissection of the "charge to the Twelve" was "a discourse of instruction," and if in view of these difficulties they could not realise why he had refused, thirty years before, to believe in the "discourse of instruction." But Bruno Bauer heard nothing: and so their blissful unconsciousness lasted for nearly a generation longer.

The expectation of His Second Coming, repeatedly expressed by Jesus towards the close of His life, is on this hypothesis authentic; it was painted over by the primitive Christian community with the colours of its own eschatology, in consequence of the delay of the Parousia; and in view of the mission to the Gentiles a more cautious conception of the nearness of the time commended itself; nay, when Jerusalem had fallen and the "signs of the end" which had been supposed to be discovered in the horrors of the years 68 and 69 had passed without result, the return of Jesus was relegated to a distant future by the aid of the doctrine that the Gospel must first be preached to all the heathen. Thus the Parousia, which according to the Jewish-Christian eschatology belonged to the present age, was transferred to the future. "With this combination and making coincident—they were not so at the first—of the Second Coming, the end of the world, and the final Judgment, the idea of the Second Coming reached the last and highest stage of its development."

Weiffenbach's view, as we have seen, empties Jesus' expectation of His return of almost all its content, and to that is due the fact that his investigation did not prove so useful as it might have done. His purpose is, following suggestions thrown out by Schleiermacher and Weisse, to prove the identity of the predictions of the Second Coming and of the Resurrection, and he takes as his starting-point the observation that the conduct of the disciples after the death of Jesus forbids us to suppose that the Resurrection had been predicted in clear and unambiguous sayings, and that, on the other hand, the announcement of the Second Coming coincides in point of time with the predictions of the Resurrection, and the predictions both of the Second Coming and of the Resurrection stand in organic connexion with the announcement of His approaching death. The two are therefore identical.

It was only after the death of their Master that the disciples differentiated the thought of the Resurrection from that of the Second Coming. The Resurrection did not bring them that which the Second Coming had promised; but it produced the result that the eschatological hopes, which Jesus had with difficulty succeeded [pg 233] in damping, flamed up again in the hearts of His disciples. The spiritual presence of the Deliverer who had manifested Himself to them did not seem to them to be the fulfilment of the promise of the Second Coming; but the expectation of the latter, being brought into contact with the flame of eschatological hope with which their hearts were a-fire, was fused, and cast into a form quite different from that in which it had been derived from the words of Jesus.

That is all finely observed. For the first time it had dawned upon historical criticism that the great question is that concerning the identity or difference of the Parousia and the Resurrection. But the man who had been the first to grasp that thought, and who had undertaken his whole study with the special purpose of working it out, was too much under the influence of the spiritualised eschatology of Schleiermacher and Weisse to be able to assign the right values in the solution of his equation. And, withal, he is too much inclined to play the apologist as a subsidiary rôle. He is not content merely to render the history intelligible; he is, by his own confession, urged on by the hope that perhaps a way may be found of causing that "error" of Jesus to disappear and proving it to be an illusion due to the want of a sufficiently close study of His discourses. But the historian simply must not be an apologist; he must leave that to those who come after him and he may do so with a quiet mind, for the apologists, as we learn from the history of the Lives of Jesus, can get the better of any historical result whatever. It is, therefore, quite unnecessary that the historian should allow himself to be led astray by following an apologetic will-o'-the-wisp.

Technically regarded, the mistake on which Weiffenbach's investigation made shipwreck was the failure to bring the Jewish apocalyptic material into relation with the Synoptic data. If he had done this, it would have been impossible for him to extract an absolutely unreal and unhistorical conception of the Second Coming out of the discourses of Jesus.

The task which Weiffenbach had neglected remained undone—to the detriment of theology—until Baldensperger[158] repaired the omission. His book, "The Self-consciousness of Jesus in the Light of the Messianic Hopes of His Time,"[159] published in 1888, made its impression by reason of the fullness of its material. Whereas Colani and Volkmar had still been able to deny the existence of [pg 234] a fully formed Messianic expectation in the time of Jesus, the genesis of the expectation was now fully traced out, and it was shown that the world of thought which meets us in Daniel had won the victory, that the "Son of Man" Messiah of the Similitudes of Enoch was the last product of the Messianic hope prior to the time of Jesus; and that therefore the fully developed Danielic scheme with its unbridgeable chasm between the present and the future world furnished the outline within which all further and more detailed traits were inserted. The honour of having effectively pioneered the way for this discovery belongs to Schürer.[160] Baldensperger adopts his ideas, but sets them forth in a much more direct way, because he, in contrast with Schürer, gives no *system* of Messianic expectation—and there never in reality was a system—but is content to picture its many-sided growth.

He does not, it is true, escape some minor inconsistencies. For example, the idea of a "political Messiahship," which is really set aside by his historical treatment, crops up here and there, as though the author had not entirely got rid of it himself. But the impression made by the book as a whole was overpowering.

Nevertheless this book does not exactly fulfil the promise of its title, any more than Weiffenbach's. The reader expects that now at last Jesus' sayings about Himself will be consistently explained in the light of the Jewish Messianic ideas, but that is not done. For Baldensperger, instead of tracing down and working out the conception of the Kingdom of God held by Jesus as a product of the Jewish eschatology, at least by way of trying whether that method would suffice, takes it over direct from modern historical theology. He assumes as self-evident that Jesus' conception of the Kingdom of God had a double character, that the eschatological and spiritual elements were equally represented in it and mutually conditioned one another, and that Jesus therefore began, in pursuance of this conception, to found a spiritual invisible Kingdom, although He expected its fulfilment to be effected by supernatural means. Consequently there must also have been a [pg 235] duality in His religious consciousness, in which these two conceptions had to be combined. Jesus' Messianic consciousness sprang, according to Baldensperger, "from a religious root"; that is to say, the Messianic consciousness was a special modification of a self-consciousness in which a pure, spiritual, unique relation to God was the fundamental element; and from this arises the possibility of a spiritual transformation of the Jewish-Messianic self-consciousness. In making these assumptions, Baldensperger does not ask himself whether it is not possible that for Jesus the purely Jewish consciousness of a transcendental Messiahship may itself have been religious, nay even spiritual, just as well as the Messiahship resting on a vague, indefinite, colourless sense of union with God which modern theologians arbitrarily attribute to Him.

Again, instead of arriving at the two conceptions, Kingdom of God and Messianic consciousness, purely empirically, by an unbiased comparison of the Synoptic passages with the Late-Jewish conceptions, Baldensperger, in this following Holtzmann, brings them into his theory in the dual form in which contemporary theology, now becoming faintly tinged with eschatology, offered them to him. Consequently, everything has to be adapted to this duality. Jesus, for example, in applying to Himself the title Son of Man, thinks not only of the transcendental significance which it has in the Jewish apocalyptic, but gives it at the same time an ethico-religious colouring.

Finally, the duality is explained by an application of the genetic method, in which the "course of the development of the self-consciousness of Jesus" is traced out. The historical psychology of the Marcan hypothesis here shows its power of adapting itself to eschatology. From the first, to follow the course of Baldensperger's exposition, the eschatological view influenced Jesus' expectation of the Kingdom and His Messianic consciousness. In the wilderness, after the dawn of His Messianic consciousness at His baptism, He had rejected the ideal of the Messianic king of David's line and put away all warlike thoughts. Then He began to found the Kingdom of God by preaching. For a time the spiritualised idea of the Kingdom was dominant in His mind, the Messianic eschatological idea falling rather into the background.

But His silence regarding His Messianic office was partly due to paedagogic reasons, "since He desired to lead His hearers to a more spiritual conception of the Kingdom and so to obviate a possible political movement on their part and the consequent intervention of the Roman government." In addition to this He had also personal reasons for not revealing Himself which only disappeared in the moment when His death and Second Coming became part of His plan; previous to that He did not know how and when the Kingdom was to come. Prior to the confession at [pg 236] Caesarea Philippi, the disciples "had only a faint and vague suspicion of the Messianic dignity of their Master."

This was "rather the preparatory stage of His Messianic work." Objectively, it may be described "as the period of growing emphasis upon the spiritual characteristics of the Kingdom, and of resigned waiting and watching for its outward manifestation in glory; subjectively, from the point of view of the self-consciousness of Jesus, it may be characterised as the period of the struggle between His religious conviction of His Messiahship and the traditional rationalistic Messianic belief."

This first period opens out into a second in which He had attained to perfect clearness of vision and complete inner harmony. By the acceptance of the idea of suffering, Jesus' inner peace is enhanced to the highest degree conceivable. "By throwing Himself upon the thought of death He escaped the lingering uncertainty as to when and how God would fulfil His promise...." "The coming of the Kingdom was fixed down to the Second Coming of the Messiah. Now He ventured to regard Himself as the Son of Man who was to be the future Judge of the world, for the suffering and dying Son of Man was closely associated with the Son of Man surrounded by the host of heaven. Would the people accept Him as Messiah? He now, in Jerusalem, put the question to them in all its sharpness and burning actuality; and the people were moved to enthusiasm. But so soon as they saw that He whom they had hailed with such acclamation was neither able nor willing to fulfil their ambitious dreams, a reaction set in."

Thus, according to Baldensperger, there was an interaction between the historical and the psychological events. And that is right!—if only the machinery were not so complicated, and a "development" had not to be ground out of it at whatever cost. But this, and the whole manner of treatment in the second part, encumbered as it is with parenthetic qualifications, was rendered inevitable by the adoption of the two aforesaid not purely historical conceptions. Sometimes, too, one gets the impression that the author felt that he owed it to the school to which he belonged to advance no assertion without adding the limitations which scientifically secure it against attack. Thus on every page he digs himself into an entrenched position, with palisades of footnotes—in fact the book actually ends with a footnote. But the conception which underlay the whole was so full of vigour that in spite of the thoughts not being always completely worked out, it produced a powerful impression. Baldensperger had persuaded theology at least to admit the hypothesis—whether it took up a positive or negative position in regard to it—that Jesus possessed a fully-developed eschatology. He thus provided a new basis for discussion and gave an impulse to the study of the subject such as it had not received [pg 237] since the 'sixties, at least not in the same degree of energy. Perhaps the very limitations of the work, due as they were to its introduction of modern ideas, rendered it better adapted to the spirit of the age, and consequently more influential, than if it had been characterised by that rigorous maintenance of a single point of view which was abstractly requisite for the proper treatment of the subject. It was precisely the rejection of this rigorous consistency which enabled it to gain ground for the cause of eschatology.

But the consistent treatment from a single point of view was bound to come; and it came four years later. In passing from Weiffenbach and Baldensperger to Johannes Weiss[161] the reader feels like an explorer who after weary wanderings through billowy seas of reed-grass at length reaches a wooded tract, and instead of swamp feels firm ground beneath his feet, instead of yielding rushes sees around him the steadfast trees. At last there is an end of "qualifying clause" theology, of the "and yet," the "on the other hand," the "notwithstanding"! The reader had to follow the others step by step, making his way over every footbridge and gang-plank which they laid down, following all the meanderings in which they indulged, and must never let go their hands if he wished to come safely through the labyrinth of spiritual and eschatological ideas which they supposed to be found in the thought of Jesus.

In Weiss there are none of these devious paths: "behold the land lies before thee."

His "Preaching of Jesus concerning the Kingdom of God,"[162] published in 1892, has, on its own lines, an importance equal to that of Strauss's first Life of Jesus. He lays down the third great alternative which the study of the life of Jesus had to meet. The first was laid down by Strauss: *either* purely historical *or* purely supernatural. The second had been worked out by the Tübingen school and Holtzmann: *either* Synoptic *or* Johannine. Now came the third: *either* eschatological *or* non-eschatological!

Progress always consists in taking one or other of two alternatives, in abandoning the attempt to combine them. The pioneers of progress have therefore always to reckon with the law of mental inertia which manifests itself in the majority—who always go on believing that it is possible to combine that which can no longer be combined, and in fact claim it as a special merit that they, in contrast with the "one-sided" writers, can do justice to the other side of the question. One must just let them be, till their time is over, [pg 238] and resign oneself not to see the end of it, since it is found by experience that the complete victory of one of two historical alternatives is a matter of two full theological generations.

This remark is made in order to explain why the work of Johannes Weiss did not immediately make an end of the mediating views. Another reason perhaps was that, according to the usual canons of theological authorship, the book was much too short—only sixty-seven pages—and too simple to allow its full significance to be realised. And yet it is precisely this simplicity which makes it one of the most important works in historical theology. It seems to break a spell. It closes one epoch and begins another.

Weiffenbach had failed to solve the problem of the Second Coming, Baldensperger that of the Messianic consciousness of Jesus, because both of them allowed a false conception of the Kingdom of God to keep its place among the data. The general conception of the Kingdom was first rightly grasped by Johannes Weiss. All modern ideas, he insists, even in their subtlest forms, must be eliminated from it; when this is done, we arrive at a Kingdom of God which is wholly future; as is indeed implied by the petition in the Lord's prayer, "Thy Kingdom come." Being still to come, it is at present purely supra-mundane. It is present only as a cloud may be said to be present which throws its shadow upon the earth; its nearness, that is to say, is recognised by the paralysis of the Kingdom of Satan. In the fact that Jesus casts out the demons, the Pharisees are bidden to recognise, according to Matt. xii. 25-28, that the Kingdom of God is already come upon them.

This is the only sense in which Jesus thinks of the Kingdom as present. He does not "establish it," He only proclaims its coming. He exercises no "Messianic functions," but waits, like others, for God to bring about the coming of the Kingdom by supernatural means. He does not even know the day and hour when this shall come to pass. The missionary journey of the disciples was not designed for the extension of the Kingdom of God, but only as a means of rapidly and widely making known its nearness. But it was not so near as Jesus thought. The impenitence and hardness of heart of a great part of the people, and the implacable enmity of His opponents, at length convinced Him that the establishment of the Kingdom of God could not yet take place, that such penitence as had been shown hitherto was not sufficient, and that a mighty obstacle, the guilt of the people, must first be put away. It becomes clear to Him that His own death must be the ransom-price. He dies, not for the community of His followers only, but for the nation; that is why He always speaks of His atoning death as "for many," not "for you." After His death He would come again in all the splendour and glory with which, since the days of [pg 239]

Daniel, men's imaginations had surrounded the Messiah, and He was to come, moreover, within the lifetime of the generation to which He had proclaimed the nearness of the Kingdom of God.

The setting up of the Kingdom was to be preceded by the Day of Judgment. In describing the Messianic glory Jesus makes use of the traditional picture, but He does so with modesty, restraint, and sobriety. Therein consists His greatness.

With political expectations this Kingdom has nothing whatever to do. "To hope for the Kingdom of God in the transcendental sense which Jesus attaches to it, and to raise a revolution, are two things as different as fire and water." The transcendental character of the expectation consists precisely in this, that the State and all earthly institutions, conditions, and benefits, as belonging to the present age, shall either not exist at all in the coming Kingdom, or shall exist only in a sublimated form. Hence Jesus cannot preach to men a special ethic of the Kingdom of God, but only an ethic which in this world makes men free from the world and prepared to enter unimpeded into the Kingdom. That is why His ethic is of so completely negative a character; it is, in fact, not so much an ethic as a penitential discipline.

The ministry of Jesus is therefore not in principle different from that of John the Baptist: there can be no question of a founding and development of the Kingdom within the hearts of men. What distinguishes the work of Jesus from that of the Baptist is only His consciousness of being the Messiah. He awoke to this consciousness at His baptism. But the Messiahship which He claims is not a present office; its exercise belongs to the future. On earth He is only a man, a prophet, as in the view implied in the speeches in the Acts of the Apostles. "Son of Man" is therefore, in the passages where it is authentic, a purely eschatological designation of the Messiah, though we cannot tell whether His hearers understood Him as speaking of Himself in His future rank and dignity, or whether they thought of the Son of Man as a being quite distinct from Himself, whose coming He was only proclaiming in advance.

"The sole object of this argument is to prove that the Messianic self-consciousness of Jesus, as expressed in the title 'Son of Man,' shares in the transcendental apocalyptic character of Jesus' idea of the Kingdom of God, and cannot be separated from that idea." The only partially correct evaluation of the factors in the problem of the Life of Jesus which Baldensperger had taken over from contemporary theology, and which had hitherto prevented historical science from obtaining a solution of that problem, had now been corrected from the history itself, and it was now only necessary to insert the corrected data into the calculation.

Here is the point at which it is fitting to recall Reimarus. He [pg 240] was the first, and indeed, before Johannes Weiss, the only writer who recognised and pointed out that the preaching of Jesus was purely eschatological. It is true that his conception of the eschatology was primitive, and that he applied it not as a constructive, but as a destructive principle of criticism. But read his statement of the problem "with the signs changed," and with the necessary deduction for the primitive character of the eschatology, and you have the view of Weiss.

Ghillany, too, has a claim to be remembered. When Weiss asserts that the part played by Jesus was not the active rôle of establishing the Kingdom, but the passive rôle of waiting for the coming of the Kingdom; and that it was, in a sense, only by the acceptance of His sufferings that He emerged from that passivity; he is only asserting what Ghillany had maintained thirty years before with the same arguments and with the same decisiveness. But Weiss places the assertion on a scientifically unassailable basis.

XVI. The Struggle Against Eschatology

Wilhelm Bousset. Jesu Predigt in ihrem Gegensatz zum Judentum. Ein religionsgeschichtlicher Vergleich. (The Antithesis between Jesus' Preaching and Judaism. A Religious-Historical Comparison.) Göttingen, 1892. 130 pp.

Erich Haupt. Die eschatologischen Aussagen Jesu in den synoptischen Evangelien. (The Eschatological Sayings of Jesus in the Synoptic Gospels.) 1895. 167 pp.

Paul Wernle. Die Anfänge unserer Religion. Tübingen-Leipzig, 1901; 2nd ed., 1904, 410 pp.

Emil Schürer. Das messianische Selbstbewusstsein Jesu-Christi. 1903. Akademische Festrede. (The Messianic Self-consciousness of Jesus Christ.) 24 pp.

Wilhelm Brandt. Die evangelische Geschichte und der Ursprung des Christentums auf Grund einer Kritik der Berichte über das Leiden und die Auferstehung Jesu. (The Gospel History and the Origin of Christianity. Based upon a Critical Study of the Narratives of the Sufferings and Resurrection of Jesus.) Leipzig, 1893. 591 pp.

Adolf Jülicher. Die Gleichnisreden Jesu. (The Parables of Jesus.) Vol. i., 1888, 291 pp.; vol. ii., 1899, 643 pp.

In this period the important books are short. The sixty-seven pages of Johannes Weiss are answered by Bousset[163] in a bare hundred and thirty. People began to see that the elaborate Lives of Jesus which had hitherto held the field, and enjoyed an immortality of revised editions, only masked the fact that the study of the subject was at a standstill; and that the tedious re-handling of problems which had been solved so far as they were capable of solution only served as an excuse for not grappling with those which still remained unsolved.

This conviction is expressed by Bousset at the beginning of his work. The criticism of the sources, he says, is finished, and its results may be regarded, so far as the Life of Jesus is concerned, as provisionally complete. The separation between John and the Synoptists has been secured. For the Synoptists, the two-document hypothesis has been established, according to which the sources are a primitive form of Mark, and a collection of "logia." A certain interest might still attach to the attempt to arrive at the primitive kernel of Mark; but the attempt has a priori so little [pg 242] prospect of success that it was almost a waste of time to continue to work at it. It would be a much more important thing to get rid of the feeling of uncertainty and artificiality in the Lives of Jesus. What is now chiefly wanted, Bousset thinks, is "a firmly-drawn and life-like portrait which, with a few bold strokes, should bring out clearly the originality, the force, the personality of Jesus."

It is evident that the centre of the problem has now been reached. That is why the writing becomes so terse. The masses of thought can only be manœuvred here in a close formation such as Weiss gives them. The loose order of discursive exegetical discussions of separate passages is now no longer in place. The first step towards further progress was the simple one of marshalling the passages in such a way as to gain a single consistent impression from them.

In the first instance Bousset is as ready as Johannes Weiss to admit the importance for the mind of Jesus of the eschatological "then" and "now." The realistic school, he thinks, are perfectly right in endeavouring to relate Jesus, without apologetic or theological inconsistencies, to the background of contemporary ideas. Later, in 1901, he was to make it a reproach against Harnack's "What is Christianity?" (*Das Wesen des Christentums*) that it did not give sufficient importance to the background of contemporary thought in its account of the preaching of Jesus.[164]

He goes on to ask, however, whether the first enthusiasm over the discovery of this genuinely historical way of looking at things should not be followed by some "second thoughts" of a deeper character. Accepting the position laid down by Johannes Weiss, we must ask, he thinks, whether this purely historical criticism, by the exclusive emphasis which it has laid upon eschatology, has not allowed the "essential originality and power of the personality of Jesus to slip through its fingers," and closed its grasp instead upon contemporary conceptions and imaginations which are often of a quite special character.

The Late-Jewish eschatology was, according to Bousset, by no means a homogeneous system of thought. Realistic and transcendental elements stand side by side in it, unreconciled. The genuine popular belief of Late Judaism still clung quite naively to the earthly realistic hopes of former times, and had never been able to rise to the purely transcendental regions which are the characteristic habitat of apocalyptic. The rejection of the world is never carried out consistently; something of the Jewish national ideal always remains. And for this reason Late Judaism made no progress towards the overcoming of particularism.

Probably, Bousset holds, this Apocalyptic thought is not even genuinely Jewish; as he ably argued in another work, there [pg 243] was a considerable strain of Persian influence in it.[165] The dualism, the transference to the transcendental region of the future hope, the conception of the world which appears in Jewish apocalyptic, are of Iranian rather than Jewish origin.

Two thoughts are especially characteristic of Bousset's position; first, that this transcendentalising of the future implied a spiritualisation of it; secondly, that in post-exilic Judaism there was always an undercurrent of a purer and more spontaneous piety, the presence of which is especially to be traced in the Psalms.

Into a dead world, where a kind of incubus seems to stifle all naturalness and spontaneity, there comes a living Man. According to the formulae of His preaching and the designations which He applies to Himself, He seems at first sight to identify Himself with this world rather than to oppose it. But these conceptions and titles, especially the Kingdom of God and the Son of Man, must be provisionally left in the background, since they, as being conceptions taken over from the past, conceal rather than reveal what is most essential in His personality. The primary need is to discover, behind the phenomenal, the real character of the personality and preaching of Jesus. The starting-point must therefore be the simple fact that Jesus came as a living Man into a dead world. He is living, because in contrast with His contemporaries He has a living idea of God. His faith in the Fatherhood of God is Jesus' most essential act. It signifies a breach with the transcendental Jewish idea of God, and an unconscious inner negation of the Jewish eschatology. Jesus, therefore, walks through a world which denies His own eschatology like a man who has firm ground under his feet.

That which on a superficial view appears to be eschatological preaching turns out to be essentially a renewal of the old prophetic preaching with its positive ethical emphasis. Jesus is a manifestation of that ancient spontaneous piety of which Bousset had shown the existence in Late Judaism.

The most characteristic thing in the character of Jesus, according to Bousset, is His joy in life. It is true that if, in endeavouring to understand Him, we take primitive Christianity as our starting-point, we might conceive of this joy in life as the complement of the eschatological mood, as the extreme expression of indifference to the world, which can as well enjoy the world as flee it. But the purely eschatological attitude, though it reappears [pg 244] in early Christianity, does not give the right clue for the interpretation of the character of Jesus as a whole. His joy in the world was real, a genuine outcome of His new type of piety. It prevented the eudaemonistic eschatological idea of reward, which some think they find in Jesus' preaching, from ever really becoming an element in it.

Jesus is best understood by contrasting Him with the Baptist. John was a preacher of repentance whose eyes were fixed upon the future. Jesus did not allow the thought of the nearness of the end to rob Him of His simplicity and spontaneity, and was not crippled by the reflection that everything was transitory, preparatory, a mere means to an end. His preaching of repentance was not gloomy and forbidding; it was the proclamation of a new righteousness, of which the watchword was, "Ye shall be perfect as your Father in Heaven is perfect." He desires to communicate this personal piety by personal influence. In contrast with the Baptist He never aims at influencing masses of men, but rather avoids it. His work was accomplished mainly among little groups and individuals. He left the task of carrying the Gospel far and wide as a legacy to the community of His followers. The mission of the Twelve, conceived as a mission for the rapid and widespread extension of the Gospel, is not to be used to explain Jesus' methods of teaching; the narrative of it rests on an "obscure and unintelligible tradition."

This genuine joy in life was not unnoticed by the contemporaries of Jesus who contrasted Him as "a gluttonous man and a wine-bibber," with the Baptist. They were vaguely conscious that the whole life of Jesus was "sustained by the feeling of an absolute antithesis between Himself and His times." He lived not in anxious expectation, but in cheerful gladness, because by the native strength of His piety He had brought present and future into one. Free from all extravagant Jewish delusions about the future, He was not paralysed by the conditions which must be fulfilled to make this future present. He has a peculiar conviction of its coming which gives Him courage to "marry" the present with the future. The present as contrasted with the beyond is for Him no mere shadow, but truth and reality; life is not for Him a mere illusion, but is charged with a real and valuable meaning. His own time is the Messianic time, as His answer to the Baptist's question shows. "And it is among the most certain things in the Gospel that Jesus in His earthly life acknowledged Himself as Messiah both to His disciples and to the High-Priest, and made His entry into Jerusalem as such."

He can, therefore, fully recognise the worth of the present. It is not true that He taught that this world's goods were in themselves bad; what He said was only that they must not be put first. [pg 245] Indeed He gives a new value to life by teaching that man cannot be righteous in isolation, but only in the fellowship of love. And as, moreover, the righteousness which He preaches is one of the goods of the Kingdom of God, He cannot have thought of the Kingdom as wholly transcendental. The Reign of God begins for Him in the present era. His consciousness of being able to cast out demons in the spirit of God because Satan's kingdom on earth is at an end is only the supernaturalistic expression for something of which He also possesses an ethical consciousness, namely, that in the new social righteousness the Kingdom of God is already present.

This presence of the Kingdom was not, however, clearly explained by Jesus, but was set forth in paradoxes and parables, especially in the parables of Mark iv. When we find the Evangelist, in immediate connexion with these parables, asserting that the aim of the parables was to mystify and conceal, we may conclude that the basis of this theory is the fact that these parables concerning the presence of the Kingdom of God were not understood.

In effecting this tacit transformation Jesus is acting in accordance with a tendency of the time. Apocalyptic is itself a spiritualisation of the ancient Israelitish hopes of the future, and Jesus only carries this process to its completion. He raises Late Judaism above the limitations in which it was involved, separates out the remnant of national, political, and sensuous ideas which still clung to the expectation of the future in spite of its having been spiritualised by apocalyptic, and breaks with the Jewish particularism, though without providing a theoretical basis for this step.

Thus, in spite of, nay even because of, His opposition to it, Jesus was the fulfiller of Judaism. In Him were united the ancient and vigorous prophetic religion and the impulse which Judaism itself had begun to feel towards the spiritualisation of the future hope. The transcendental and the actual meet in a unity which is full of life and strength, creative not reflective, and therefore not needing to set aside the ancient traditional ideas by didactic explanations, but overcoming them almost unconsciously by the truth which lies in this paradoxical union. The historical formula embodied in Bousset's closing sentence runs thus: "The Gospel develops some of the deeper-lying *motifs* of the Old Testament, but it protests against the prevailing tendency of Judaism."

Such of the underlying assumptions of this construction as invite challenge lie open to inspection, and do not need to be painfully disentangled from a web of exegesis; that is one of the merits of the book. The chief points to be queried are as follows:—

Is it the case that the apocalypses mark the introduction of a process of spiritualisation applied to the ancient Israelitish hopes? [pg 246] A picture of the future is not spiritualised simply by being projected upon the clouds. This elevation to the transcendental region signifies, on the contrary, the transference to a place of safety of the eudaemonistic aspirations which have not been fulfilled in the present, and which are expected, by way of compensation, from the other world. The apocalyptic conception is so far from being a spiritualisation of the future expectations, that it represents on the contrary the last desperate effort of a strongly eudaemonistic popular religion to raise to heaven the earthly goods from which it cannot make up its mind to part.

Next we must ask: Is it really necessary to assume the existence of so wide reaching a Persian influence in Jewish eschatology? The Jewish dualism and the sublimation of its hope have become historical just because, owing to the fate of the nation, the religious life of the present and the fair future which was logically bound up with it became more and more widely separated, temporally and locally, until at last only its dualism and the sublimation of its hope enabled the nation to survive its disappointment.

Again, is it historically permissible to treat the leading ideas of the preaching of Jesus, which bear so clearly the marks of the contemporary mould of thought, as of secondary importance for the investigation, and to endeavour to trace Jesus' thoughts from within outwards and not from without inwards?

Further, is there really in Judaism no tendency towards the overcoming of particularism? Has not its eschatology, as shaped by the deutero-prophetic literature, a universalistic outlook? Did Jesus overcome particularism in principle otherwise than it is overcome in Jewish eschatology, that is to say, with reference to the future?

What is there to prove that Jesus' distinctive faith in the Fatherhood of God ever existed independently, and not as an alternative form of the historically-conditioned Messianic consciousness? In other words, what is there to show that the "religious attitude" of Jesus and His Messianic consciousness are anything else than identical, temporally and conceptually, so that the first must always be understood as conditioned by the second?

Again, is the saying about the gluttonous man and wine-bibber a sufficient basis for the contrast between Jesus and the Baptist? Is not Jesus' preaching of repentance gloomy as well as the Baptist's? Where do we read that He, in contrast with the Baptist, avoided dealing with masses of men? Where did He give "the community of His disciples" marching orders to go far and wide in the sense required by Bousset's argument? Where is there a word to tell us that He thought of His work among individuals and little groups of men as the most important feature [pg 247] of His ministry? Are we not told the exact contrary, that He "taught" His disciples as little as He did the people? Is there any justification for characterising the missionary journey of the Twelve, just because it directly contradicts this view, as "an obscure and unintelligible tradition?"

Is it so certain that Jesus made a Messianic entry into Jerusalem, and that, accordingly, He declared Himself to the disciples and to the High Priest as Messiah in the present, and not in a purely future sense?

What are the sayings which justify us in making the attitude of opposition which He took up towards the Rabbinic legalism into a "sense of the absolute opposition between Himself and His people"? The very "absolute," with its ring of Schleiermacher, is suspicious.

All these, however, are subsidiary positions. The decisive point is: Can Bousset make good the assertion that Jesus' joy in life was a more or less unconscious inner protest against the purely eschatological world-renouncing religious attitude, the primal expression of that "absolute" antithesis to Judaism? Is it not the case that His attitude towards earthly goods was wholly conditioned by eschatology? That is to say, were not earthly goods emptied of any essential value in such a way that joy in the world and indifference to the world were simply the final expression of an ironic attitude which had been sublimated into pure serenity. That is the question upon the answer to which depends the decision whether Bousset's position is tenable or not.

It is not in fact tenable, for the opposite view has at its disposal inexhaustible reserves of world-renouncing, world-contemning sayings, and the few utterances which might possibly be interpreted as expressing a purely positive joy in the world, desert and go over to the enemy, because they textually and logically belong to the other set of sayings. Finally, the promise of earthly happiness as a reward, to which Bousset had denied a position in the teaching of Jesus, also falls upon his rear, and that in the very moment when he is seeking to prove from the saying, "Seek ye first the Kingdom of God and His righteousness, and all these things shall be added unto you," that for Jesus this world's goods are not in themselves evil, but are only to be given a secondary place. Here the eudaemonism is written on the forehead of the saying, since the receiving of these things—we must remember, too, the "hundredfold" in another passage—is future, not present, and will only "come" at the same time as the Kingdom of God. All present goods, on the other hand, serve only to support life and render possible an undistracted attitude of waiting in pious hope for that future, and therefore are not thought of as gains, but purely as a gift of God, to be cheerfully and freely enjoyed as a foretaste [pg 248] of those blessings which the elect are to enjoy in the future Divine dispensation.

The loss of this position decides the further point that if there is any suggestion in the teaching of Jesus that the future Kingdom of God is in some sense present, it is not to be understood as implying an anti-eschatological acceptance of the world, but merely as a phenomenon indicative of the extreme tension of the eschatological consciousness, just in the same way as His joy in the world. Bousset has a kind of indirect recognition of this in his remark that the presence of the Kingdom of God is only asserted by Jesus as a kind of paradox. If the assertion of its presence indicated that acceptance of the world formed part of Jesus' system of thought, it would be at variance with His eschatology. But the paradoxical character of the assertion is due precisely to the fact that His acceptance of the world is but the last expression of the completeness with which He rejects it.

But what do critical cavils matter in the case of a book of which the force, the influence, the greatness, depends upon its spirit? It is great because it recognises—what is so rarely recognised in theological works—the point where the main issue really lies; in the question, namely, whether Jesus preached and worked as Messiah, or whether, as follows if a prominent place is given to eschatology, as Colani had long ago recognised, His career, historically regarded, was only the career of a prophet with an undercurrent of Messianic consciousness.

As a consequence of grasping the question in its full significance, Bousset rejects all the little devices by which previous writers had endeavoured to relate Jesus' ministry to His times, each one prescribing at what point He was to connect Himself with it, and of course proceeding in his book to represent Him as connecting Himself with it in precisely that way. Bousset recognises that the supreme importance of eschatology in the teaching of Jesus is not to be got rid of by whittling away a little point here and there, and rubbing it smooth with critical sandpaper until it is capable of reflecting a different thought, but only by fully admitting it, while at the same time counteracting it by asserting a mysterious element of world-acceptance in the thought of Jesus, and conceiving His whole teaching as a kind of alternating current between positive and negative poles.

This is the last possible sincere attempt to limit the exclusive importance of eschatology in the preaching of Jesus, an attempt so gallant, so brilliant, that its failure is almost tragic; one could have wished success to the book, to which Carlyle might have stood sponsor. That it is inspired by the spirit of Carlyle, that it vindicates the original force of a great Personality against the attempt to dissolve it into a congeries of contemporary conceptions, [pg 249] therein lies at once its greatness and its weakness. Bousset vindicates Jesus, not for history, but for Protestantism, by making Him the heroic representative of a deeply religious acceptance of the goods of life amid an apocalyptic world. His study is not unhistorical, but supra-historical. The spirit of Jesus was in fact world-accepting in the sense that through the experience of centuries it advanced historically to the acceptance of the world, since nothing can appear phenomenally which is not in some sense ideally present from the first. But the teaching of the historical Jesus was purely and exclusively world-renouncing. If, therefore, the problem which Bousset has put on the blackboard for the eschatological school to solve is to be successfully solved, the solution is to be sought on other, more objectively historical, lines.

That the decision of the question whether Jesus' preaching of the Kingdom of God is wholly eschatological or only partly eschatological, is primarily to be sought in His ethical teaching, is recognised by all the critics of Baldensperger and Weiss. They differ only in the importance which they assign to eschatology. But no other writer has grasped the problem as clearly as Bousset.

The Parisian Ehrhardt emphasises eschatology very strongly in his work "The Fundamental Character of the Preaching of Jesus in Relation to the Messianic Hopes of His People and His own Messianic Consciousness."[166] Nevertheless he asserts the presence of a twofold ethic in Jesus' teaching: eschatology did not attempt to evacuate everything else of all value, but allowed the natural and ethical goods of this world to hold their place, as belonging to a world of thought which resisted its encroachments.

A much more negative attitude is taken up by Albert Réville in his *Jésus de Nazareth*.[167] According to him both Apocalyptic and Messianism are foreign bodies in the teaching of Jesus which have been forced into it by the pressure of contemporary thought. Jesus would never of His own motion have taken up the rôle of Messiah.

Wendt, too, in the second edition of his *Lehre Jesu*, which appeared in 1903, held in the main to the fundamental idea of the first, the 1890, edition; namely, that Jesus in view of His purely religious relation to God could not do otherwise than transform, from within outwards, the traditional conceptions, even though [pg 250] they seem to be traceable in their actual contemporary form on the surface of His teaching. He had already, in 1893, in the *Christliche Welt* clearly expounded, and defended against Weiss, his view of the Kingdom of God as already present for the thought of Jesus.

The effect which Baldensperger and Weiss had upon Weiffenbach[168] was to cause him to bring out in full strength the apologetic aspect which had been somewhat held in check in his work of 1873 by the thoroughness of his exegesis. The apocalyptic of this younger school, which was no longer willing to believe that in the mouth of Jesus the Parousia meant nothing more than an issuing from death clothed with power, is on all grounds to be rejected. It assumes, since this expectation was not fulfilled, an error on the part of Jesus. It is better to rest content with not being able to see quite clearly.

Protected by a similar armour, the successive editions of Bernhard Weiss's Life of Jesus went their way unmolested down to 1902.

Not with an apologetic purpose, but on the basis of an original religious view, Titius, in his work on the New Testament doctrine of blessedness, develops the teaching of Jesus concerning the Kingdom of God as a present good.[169]

In the same year, 1895, appeared E. Haupt's work on "The Eschatological Sayings of Jesus in the Synoptic Gospels."[170] In contradistinction to Bousset he takes as his starting-point the eschatological passages, examining each separately and modulating them back to the Johannine key. It is so delicately and ingeniously done that the reading of the book is an aesthetic pleasure which makes one in the end quite forget the apologetic *motif* in order to surrender oneself completely to the author's mystical system of religious thought.

It is, indeed, not the least service of the eschatological school that it compels modern theology, which is so much preoccupied with history, to reveal what is its own as its own. Eschatology makes it impossible to attribute modern ideas to Jesus and then by way of "New Testament Theology" take them back from Him as a loan, as even Ritschl not so long ago did with such *naïveté*. Johannes Weiss, in cutting himself loose, as an historian, from Ritschl, and recognising that "the real roots of Ritschl's ideas [pg 251] are to be found in Kant and the illuminist theology,"[171] introduced the last decisive phase of the process of separation between historical and "modern" theology. Before the advent of eschatology, critical theology was, in the last resort, without a principle of discrimination, since it possessed no reagent capable of infallibly separating out modern ideas on the one hand and genuinely ancient New Testament ideas on the other. The application of the criterion has now begun. What will be the issue, the future alone can show.

But even now we can recognise that the separation was not only of advantage to historical theology; for modern theology, the manifestation of the modern spirit as it really is, was still more important. Only when it became conscious of its own inmost essence and of its right to exist, only when it freed itself from its illegitimate historical justification, which, leaping over the centuries, appealed directly to an historical exposition of the New Testament, only then could it unfold its full wealth of ideas, which had been hitherto root-bound by a false historicity. It was not by chance that in Bousset's reply a certain affirmation of life, something expressive of the genius of Protestantism, cries aloud as never before in any theological work of this generation, or that in Haupt's work German mysticism interweaves its mysterious harmonies with the Johannine *motif*. The contribution of Protestantism to the interpretation of the world had never been made so manifest in any work prior to Weiss's. The modern spirit is here breaking in wreaths of foam upon the sharp cliffs of the rock-bound eschatological world-view of Jesus. To put it more prosaically, modern theology is at last about to become sincere. But this is so far only a prophecy of the future.

If we are to speak of the present it must be fully admitted that even historical science, when it desires to continue the history of Christianity beyond the life of Jesus, cannot help protesting against the one-sidedness of the eschatological world of thought of the "Founder." It finds itself obliged to distinguish in the thought of Jesus "permanent elements and transitory elements" which, being interpreted, means eschatological and not essentially eschatological materials; otherwise it can get no farther. For if Jesus' world of thought was wholly and exclusively eschatological, there can only have arisen out of it, as Reimarus long ago maintained, an exclusively eschatological primitive Christianity. But how a community of that kind could give birth to the Greek non-eschatological theology no Church history and no history of dogma has so far shown. Instead of that they all—Harnack, with the most consummate historical ability—lay down from the very first, alongside [pg 252] of the main line intended for "contemporary views" traffic, a relief line for the accommodation of through trains of "non-temporally limited ideas"; and at the point where primitive Christian eschatology becomes of less importance they switch off the train to the relief line, after slipping the carriages which are not intended to go beyond that station.

This procedure has now been rendered impossible for them by Weiss, who leaves no place in the teaching of Jesus for anything but the single-line traffic of eschatology. If, during the last fifteen years, any one had attempted to carry out in a work on a large scale the plan of Strauss and Renan, linking up the history of the life of Jesus with the history of early Christianity, and New Testament theology with the early history of dogma, the immense difficulties which Weiss had raised without suspecting it, in the course of his sixty-seven pages, would have become clearly apparent. The problem of the Hellenisation of Christianity took on quite a new aspect when the trestle bridge of modern ideas connecting the eschatological early Christianity with Greek theology broke down under the weight of the newly-discovered material, and it became necessary to seek within the history itself an explanation of the way in which an exclusively eschatological system of ideas came to admit Greek influences, and—what is much more difficult to explain—how Hellenism, on its part, found any point of contact with an eschatological sect.

The new problem is as yet hardly recognised, much less grappled with. The few who since Weiss's time have sought to pass over from the life of Jesus to early Christianity, have acted like men who find themselves on an ice-floe which is slowly dividing into two pieces, and who leap from one to the other before the cleft grows too wide. Harnack, in his "What is Christianity?" almost entirely ignores the contemporary limitations of Jesus' teaching, and starts out with a Gospel which carries him down without difficulty to the year 1899. The anti-historical violence of this procedure is, if possible, still more pronounced in Wernle. The "Beginnings of our Religion"[172] begins by putting the Jewish eschatology in a convenient posture for the coming operation by urging that the idea of the Messiah, since there was no appropriate place for it in connexion with the Kingdom of God or the new Earth, had become obsolete for the Jews themselves.

The inadequateness of the Messianic idea for the purposes of Jesus is therefore self-evident. "His whole life long"—as if we knew any more of it than the few months of His public ministry!—"He laboured to give a new and higher content to the Messianic title which He had adopted." In the course of this endeavour He [pg 253] discarded "the Messiah of the Zealots"—by that is meant the political non-transcendent Messianic ideal. As if we had any knowledge of the existence of such an ideal in the time of Jesus! The statements of Josephus suggest, and the conduct of Pilate at the trial of Jesus confirms the conclusion, that in none of the risings did a claimant of the Messiahship come forward, and this should be proof enough that there did not exist at that time a political eschatology alongside of the transcendental, and indeed it could not on inner grounds subsist alongside of it. That was, after all, the thing which Weiss had shown most clearly!

Jesus, therefore, had dismissed the Messiah of the Zealots; He had now to turn Himself into the "waiting" Messiah of the Rabbis. Yet He does not altogether accept this rôle, for He works actively as Messiah. His struggle with the Messianic conception could not but end in transforming it. This transformed conception is introduced by Jesus to the people at His entry into Jerusalem, since His choice of the ass to bear Him inscribed as a motto, so to speak, over the demonstration the prophecy of the Messiah who should be a bringer of peace. A few days later He gives the Scribes to understand by His enigmatic words with reference to Mark xii. 37, that His Messiahship has nothing to do with Davidic descent and all that that implied.

The Kingdom of God was not, of course, for Him, according to Wernle, a purely eschatological entity; He saw in many events evidence that it had already dawned. Wernle's only real concession to the eschatological school is the admission that the Kingdom always remained for Jesus a supernatural entity.

The belief in the presence of the Kingdom was, it seems, only a phase in the development of Jesus. When confronted with growing opposition He abandoned this belief again, and the super-earthly future character of the Kingdom was all that remained. At the end of His career Jesus establishes a connexion between the Messianic conception, in its final transformation, and the Kingdom, which had retained its eschatological character; He goes to His death for the Messiahship in its new significance, but He goes on believing in His speedy return as the Son of Man. This expectation of His Parousia as Son of Man, which only emerges immediately before His exit from the world—when it can no longer embarrass the author in his account of the preaching of Jesus—is the only point in which Jesus does not overcome the inadequacy of the Messianic idea with which He had to deal. "At this point the fantastic conception of Late Judaism, the magically transformed world of the ancient popular belief, thrusts itself incongruously into Jesus' great and simple consciousness of His vocation."

Thus Wernle takes with him only so much of Apocalyptic as he can safely carry over into early Christianity. Once he has got [pg 254] safely across, he drags the rest over after him. He shows that in and with the titles and expressions borrowed from apocalyptic thought, Messiah, Son of God, Son of Man, which were all at bottom so inappropriate to Jesus, early Christianity slipped in again "either the old ideas or new ones misunderstood." In pointing this out he cannot refrain from the customary sigh of regret—these apocalyptic titles and expressions "were from the first a misfortune for the new religion." One may well ask how Wernle has discovered in the preaching of Jesus anything that can be called, historically, a new religion, and what would have become of this new religion apart from its apocalyptic hopes and its apocalyptic dogma? We answer: without its intense eschatological hope the Gospel would have perished from the earth, crushed by the weight of historic catastrophes. But, as it was, by the mighty power of evoking faith which lay in it, eschatology made good in the darkest times Jesus' sayings about the imperishability of His words, and died as soon as these sayings had brought forth new life upon a new soil. Why then make such a complaint against it?

The tragedy does not consist in the modification of primitive Christianity by eschatology, but in the fate of eschatology itself, which has preserved for us all that is most precious in Jesus, but must itself wither, because He died upon the cross with a loud cry, despairing of bringing in the new heaven and the new earth—that is the real tragedy. And not a tragedy to be dismissed with a theologian's sigh, but a liberating and life-giving influence, like every great tragedy. For in its death-pangs eschatology bore to the Greek genius a wonder-child, the mystic, sensuous, Early-Christian doctrine of immortality, and consecrated Christianity as the religion of immortality to take the place of the slowly dying civilisation of the ancient world.

But it is not only those who want to find a way from the preaching of Jesus to early Christianity who are conscious of the peculiar difficulties raised by the recognition of its purely Jewish eschatological character, but also those who wish to reconstruct the connexion backwards from Jesus to Judaism. For example, Wellhausen and Schürer repudiate the results arrived at by the eschatological school, which, on its part, bases itself upon their researches into Late Judaism. Wellhausen, in his "Israelitish and Jewish History,"[173] gives a picture of Jesus which lifts Him out of the Jewish frame altogether. The Kingdom which He desires to found becomes a present spiritual entity. To the Jewish eschatology [pg 255] His preaching stands in a quite external relation, for what was in His mind was rather a fellowship of spiritual men engaged in seeking a higher righteousness. He did not really desire to be the Messiah, and in His inmost heart had renounced the hopes of His people. If He called Himself Messiah, it was in view of a higher Messianic ideal. For the people His acceptance of the Messiahship denoted the supersession of their own very differently coloured expectation. The transcendental events become immanent. In regard to the apocalyptic Judgment of the World, he retains only the sermon preserved by John about the inward and constant process of separation.

Although not to the same extent, Schürer also, in his view of the teaching of Jesus, is strongly influenced by the Fourth Gospel. In an inaugural discourse of 1903[174] he declares that in his opinion there is a certain opposition between Judaism and the preaching of Jesus, since the latter contains something absolutely new. His Messiahship is only the temporally limited expression of a unique, generally ethical, consciousness of being a child of God, which has a certain analogy with the relation of all God's children to their Heavenly Father. The reason for His reserve in regard to His Messiahship was, according to Schürer, Jesus' fear of kindling "political enthusiasm"; from the same motive He repudiates in Mark xii. 37 all claim to be the Messiah of David's line. The ideas of the Messiah and the Kingdom of God at least underwent a transformation in His use of them. If in His earlier preaching He only announces the Kingdom as something future, in His later preaching He emphasises the thought that in its beginnings it is already present.

That it is precisely the representatives of the study of Late Judaism who lift Jesus out of the Late-Jewish world of thought, is not in itself a surprising phenomenon. It is only an expression of the fact that here something new and creative enters into an uncreative age, and of the clear consciousness that this Personality cannot be resolved into a complex of contemporary ideas. The problem of which they are conscious is the same as Bousset's. But the question cannot be avoided whether the violent separation of Jesus from Late Judaism is a real solution, or whether the very essence of Jesus' creative power does not consist, not in taking out one or other of the parts of the eschatological machinery, but in doing what no one had previously done, namely, in setting the whole machinery in motion by the application of an ethico-religious motive power. To perceive the unsatisfactoriness of the transformation hypothesis it is only necessary to think of all the [pg 256] conditions which would have to be realised in order to make it possible to trace, even in general outline, the evidence of such a transformation in the Gospel narrative.

All these solutions of the eschatological question start from the teaching of Jesus, and it was, indeed, from this point of view that Johannes Weiss had stated the problem. The final decision of the question is not, however, to be found here, but in the examination of the whole course of Jesus' life. On which of the two presuppositions, the assumption that His life was completely dominated by eschatology, or the assumption that He repudiated it, do we find it easiest to understand the connexion of events in the life of Jesus, His fate, and the emergence of the expectation of the Parousia in the community of His disciples?

The works which in the examination of the connexion of events follow a critical procedure are few and far between. The average "Life of Jesus" shows in this respect an inconceivable stupidity. The first, after Bruno Bauer, to apply critical methods to this point was Volkmar; between Volkmar and Wrede the only writer who here showed himself critical, that is sceptical, was W. Brandt. His work on the "Gospel History"[175] appeared in 1893, a year after Johannes Weiss's work and in the same year as Bousset's reply. In this book the question of the absolute, or only partial, dominance of eschatology is answered on the ground of the general course of Jesus' life.

Brandt goes to work with a truly Cartesian scepticism. He first examines all the possibilities that the reported event did not happen in the way in which it is reported before he is satisfied that it really did happen in that way. Before he can accept the statement that Jesus died with a loud outcry, he has to satisfy his critical conscience by the following consideration: "The statement regarding this cry, is, so far as I can see, to be best explained by supposing that it was really uttered." The burial of Jesus owes its acceptance as history to the following reflection. "We hold Joseph of Arimathea to be an historical person; but the only reason which the narrative has for preserving his name is that he buried Jesus. Therefore the name guarantees the fact."

But the moment the slightest possibility presents itself that the event happened in a different way, Brandt declines to be held by any seductions of the text, and makes his own "probably" into an [pg 257] historical fact. For instance, he thinks it unlikely that Peter was the only one to smite with the sword; so the history is immediately rectified by the phrase "that sword-stroke was doubtless not the only one, other disciples also must have pressed to the front." That Jesus was first condemned by the Sanhedrin at a night-sitting, and that Pilate in the morning confirmed the sentence, seems to him on various grounds impossible. It is therefore decided that we have here to do only with a combination devised by "a Christian from among the Gentiles." In this way the "must have been's" and "may have been's" exercise a veritable reign of terror throughout the book.

Yet that does not prevent the general contribution of the book to criticism from being a very remarkable one. Especially in regard to the trial of Jesus, it brings to light a whole series of previously unsuspected problems. Brandt is the first writer since Bauer who dares to assert that it is an historical absurdity to suppose that Pilate, when the people demanded from him the *condemnation* of Jesus, answered: "No, but I will *release* you another instead of Him."

As his starting-point he takes the complete contrast between the Johannine and Synoptic traditions, and the inherent impossibility of the former is proved in detail. The Synoptic tradition goes back to Mark alone. His Gospel is, as was also held by Bruno Bauer, and afterwards by Wrede, a sufficient basis for the whole tradition. But this Gospel is not a purely historical source, it is also, and in a very much larger degree, poetic invention. Of the real history of Jesus but little is preserved in the Gospels. Many of the so-called sayings of the Lord are certainly to be pronounced spurious, a few are probably to be recognised as genuine. But the theory of the "poetic invention" of the earliest Evangelist is not consistently carried out, because Brandt does not take as his criterion, as Wrede did later, a definite principle on which Mark is supposed to have constructed his Gospel, but decides each case separately. Consequently the most important feature of the work lies in the examination of detail.

Jesus died and was believed to have risen again: this is the only absolutely certain information that we have regarding His "Life." And accordingly this is the crucial instance for testing the worth of the Gospel tradition. It is only on the basis of an elaborate criticism of the accounts of the suffering and resurrection of Jesus that Brandt undertakes to give a sketch of the life of Jesus as it really was.

What was, then, so far as appears from His life, Jesus' attitude towards eschatology? It was, according to Brandt, a self-contradictory attitude. "He believed in the near approach of the Kingdom of God, and yet, as though its time were still far distant, [pg 258] He undertakes the training of disciples. He was a teacher and yet is said to have held Himself to be the Messiah." The duality lies not so much in the teaching itself; it is rather a cleavage between His conviction and consciousness on the one hand, and His public attitude on the other.

To this observation we have to add a second, namely, that Jesus cannot possibly during the last few days at Jerusalem have come forward as Messiah. Critics, with the exception, of course, of Bruno Bauer, had only cursorily touched on this question. The course of events in the last few days in Jerusalem does not at all suggest a Messianic claim on the part of Jesus, indeed it directly contradicts it. Only imagine what would have happened if Jesus had come before the people with such claims, or even if such thoughts had been so much as attributed to Him! On the other side, of course, we have the report of the Messianic entry, in which Jesus not only accepted the homage offered to Him as Messiah, but went out of His way to invite it; and the people must therefore from that point onwards have regarded him as Messiah. In consequence of this contradiction in the narrative, all Lives of Jesus slur over the passage, and seem to represent that the people sometimes suspected Jesus' Messiahship, sometimes did not suspect it, or they adopt some other similar expedient. Brandt, however, rigorously drew the logical inference. Since Jesus did not stand and preach in the temple as Messiah, He cannot have entered Jerusalem as Messiah. Therefore "the well-known Messianic entry is not historical." That is also implied by the manner of His arrest. If Jesus had come forward as a Messianic claimant, He would not simply have been arrested by the civil police; Pilate would have had to suppress a revolt by military force.

This admission implies the surrender of one of the most cherished prejudices of the anti-eschatological school, namely, that Jesus raised the thoughts of the people to a higher conception of His Messiahship, and consequently to a spiritual view of the Kingdom of God, or at least tried so to raise them. But we cannot assume this to have been His intention, since He does not allow the multitude to suspect His Messiahship. Thus the conception of a "transformation" becomes untenable as a means of reconciling eschatological and non-eschatological elements. And as a matter of fact—that is the stroke of critical genius in the book—Brandt lets the two go forward side by side without any attempt at reconciliation; for the reconciliation which would be possible if one had only to deal with the teaching of Jesus becomes impossible when one has to take in His life as well. For Brandt the life of Jesus is the life of a Galilaean teacher who, in consequence of the eschatology with which the period was so fully charged, was for a time and to a certain extent set at variance with [pg 259] Himself and who met His fate for that reason. This conception is at bottom identical with Renan's. But the stroke of genius in leaving the gap between eschatological and non-eschatological elements unbridged sets this work, as regards its critical foundation and historical presentment, high above the smooth romance of the latter.

The course of Jesus' life, according to Brandt, was therefore as follows: Jesus was a teacher; not only so, but He took disciples in order to train them to be teachers. "This is in itself sufficient to show there was a period in His life in which His work was not determined by the thought of the immediate nearness of the decisive moment. He sought men, therefore, who might become His fellow-workers. He began to train disciples who, if He did not Himself live to see the Day of the Lord, would be able after His death to carry on the work of educating the people along the lines which He had laid down." "Then there occurred in Judaea an event of which the rumour spread like wildfire throughout Palestine. A prophet arose—a thing which had not happened for centuries—a man who came forward as an envoy of God; and this prophet proclaimed the immediate coming of the reign of God: 'Repent that ye may escape the wrath of God.' " The Baptist's great sermon on repentance falls, according to Brandt, in the last period of the life of Jesus. We must assume, he thinks, that before John came forward in this dramatic fashion he had been a teacher, and at that period of his life had numbered Jesus among his pupils. Nevertheless his life previous to his public appearance must have been a rather obscure one. When he suddenly launched out into this eschatological preaching of repentance "he seemed like an Elijah who had long ago been rapt away from the earth and now appeared once more."

From this point onwards Jesus had to concentrate His activity, for the time was short. If He desired to effect anything and so far as possible to make the people, before the coming of the end, obedient to the will of God, He must make Jerusalem the starting-point of His work. "Only from this central position, and only with the help of an authority which had at its disposal the whole synagogal system, could He effect within a short time much, perhaps all, of what was needful. So He determined on journeying to Jerusalem with this end in view, and with the fixed resolve there to carry into effect the will of God."

The journey to Jerusalem was not therefore a pilgrimage of death. "So long as we are obliged to take the Gospels as a true reflection of the history of Jesus we must recognise with Weizsäcker that Jesus did not go to Jerusalem in order to be put to death there, nor did He go to keep the Feast. Both suppositions are excluded by the vigour of his action in Jerusalem, and the bright colours of hope with which the picture of that period was painted [pg 260] in the recollection of those who had witnessed it." We cannot therefore regard the predictions of the Passion as historical, or "at most we might perhaps suppose that Jesus in the consciousness of His innocence may have said to His disciples: 'If I should die, may God for the sake of My blood be merciful to you and to the people.'"

He went to Jerusalem, then, to fulfil the will of God. "It was God's will that the preaching by which alone the people could be inwardly renewed and made into a real people of God should be recognised and organised by the national and religious authorities. To effect this through the existing authorities, or to realise it in some other way, such was the task which Jesus felt Himself called on to perform." With his eyes upon this goal, behind which lay the near approach of the Kingdom of God, He set His face towards Jerusalem.

"But nothing could be more natural than that out of the belief that He was engaged in a work which God had willed, there should arise an ever stronger belief in His personal vocation." It was thus that the Messianic consciousness entered into Jesus' thoughts. His conviction of His vocation had nothing to do with a political Messiahship, it was only gradually from the development of events that He was able to draw the inference that He was destined to the Messianic sovereignty, "it may have become more and more clear to Him, but it did not become a matter of absolute certainty." It was only amid opposition, in deep dejection, in consequence of a powerful inner reaction against circumstances, that He came to recognise Himself with full conviction as the anointed of God.

When it began to be bruited about that He was the Messiah, the rulers had Him arrested and handed Him over to the Procurator. Judas the traitor "had only been a short time among His followers, and only in those unquiet days at Jerusalem when the Master had scarcely any opportunity for private intercourse with him and for learning really to know him. He had not been with Jesus during the Galilaean days, and Jesus was consequently nothing more to him than the future ruler of the Kingdom of God."

After His death the disciples "could not, unless something occurred to restore their faith, continue to believe in His Messiahship." Jesus had taken away with Him in His death the hopes which they had set upon Him, especially as He had not foretold His death, much less His resurrection. "At first, therefore, it would be all in favour of His memory if the disciples remembered that He Himself had never openly and definitely declared Himself to be the Messiah." They returned to Galilee. "Simon Peter, and perhaps the son of Zebedee, who afterwards ranked along with him as a pillar of the Church, resolved to continue that preparation for their work which [pg 261] had been interrupted by their journey to Jerusalem. It seemed to them that if they were once more on Galilaean soil the days which they had spent in the inhospitable Jerusalem would cease to oppress their spirits with the leaden weight of sorrowful recollection.... One might almost say that they had to make up their minds to give up Jesus the author of the attempt to take Jerusalem by storm; but for Jesus the gracious gentle Galilaean teacher they kept a warm place in their hearts." So love watched over the dead until hope was rekindled by the Old Testament promises and came to reawaken Him. "The first who, in an enthusiastic vision, saw this wish fulfilled was Simon Peter." This "resurrection" has nothing to do with the empty grave, which, like the whole narrative of the Jerusalem appearances, only came into the tradition later. The first appearances took place in Galilee. It was there that the Church was founded.

This attempt to grasp the connexion of events in the life of Jesus from a purely historical point of view is one of the most important that have ever been made in this department of study. If it had been put in a purely constructive form, this criticism would have made an impression unequalled by any other Life of Jesus since Renan's. But in that case it would have lost that free play of ideas which the critical recognition of the unbridged gap admits. The eschatological question is not, it is true, decided by this investigation. It shows the impossibility of the previous attempts to establish a present Messiahship of Jesus, but it shows, too, that the questions, which are really historical questions, concerning the public attitude of Jesus, are far from being solved by asserting the exclusively eschatological character of His preaching, but that new difficulties are always presenting themselves.

It was perhaps not so much through these general ethico-religious historical discussions as in consequence of certain exegetical problems which unexpectedly came to light that theologians became conscious that the old conception of the teaching of Jesus was not tenable, or was only tenable by violent means. On the assumption of the modified eschatological character of His teaching, Jesus is still a teacher; that is to say, He speaks in order to be understood, in order to explain, and has no secrets. But if His teaching is throughout eschatological, then He is a prophet, who points in mysterious speech to a coming age, whose words conceal secrets and offer enigmas, and are not intended to be understood always and by everybody. Attention was now turned to a number of passages in which the question arises whether Jesus had any secrets to keep or not.

This question presents itself in connexion with the very earliest of the parables. In Mark iv. 11, 12 it is distinctly stated that the parables spoken in the immediate context embody the mystery of the [pg 262] Kingdom of God in an obscure and unintelligible form, in order that those for whom it is not intended may hear without understanding. But this is not borne out by the character of the parables themselves, since *we* at least find in them the thought of the constant and victorious development of the Kingdom from small beginnings to its perfect development. After the passage had had to suffer many things from constantly renewed attempts to weaken down or explain away the statement, Jülicher, in his work upon the Parables,[176] released it from these tortures, left Jesus the parables in their natural meaning, and put down this unintelligible saying about the purpose of the parabolic form of discourse to the account of the Evangelist. He would rather, to use his own expression, remove a little stone from the masonry of tradition than a diamond from the imperishable crown of honour which belongs to Jesus. Yes, but, for all that, it is an arbitrary assumption which damages the Marcan hypothesis more than will be readily admitted. What was the reason, or what was the mistake which led the earliest Evangelist to form so repellent a theory regarding the purpose of the parables? Is the progressive exaggeration of the contrast between veiled and open speech, to which Jülicher often appeals, sufficient to account for it? How can the Evangelist have invented such a theory, when he immediately proceeds to invalidate it by the rationalising, rather commonplace explanation of the parable of the Sower?

Bernhard Weiss, not being so much under the influence of modern theology as to feel bound to recognise the paedagogic purpose in Jesus, gives the text its due, and admits that Jesus intended to use the parabolic form of discourse as a means of separating receptive from unreceptive hearers. He does not say, however, what kind of secret, intelligible only to the predestined, was concealed in these parables which seem clear as daylight.

That was before Johannes Weiss had stated the eschatological question. Bousset, in his criticism of the eschatological theory,[177] is obliged to fall back upon Jülicher's method in order to justify the rationalising modern way of explaining these parables as pointing to a Kingdom of God actually present. It is true Jülicher's explanation of the way in which the theory arose does not satisfy him; he prefers to assume that the basis of this false theory of Mark's is to be found in the fact that the parables concerning the presence of the Kingdom remained unintelligible to the contemporaries of Jesus. But we may fairly ask that he should point out the connecting link between that failure to understand and [pg 263] the invention of a saying like this, which implies so very much more!

If there are no better grounds than that for calling in question Mark's theory of the parables, then the parables of Mark iv., the only ones from which it is possible to extract the admission of a present Kingdom of God, remain what they were before, namely, mysteries.

The second volume of Jülicher's "Parables"[178] found the eschatological question already in possession of the field. And, as a matter of fact, Jülicher does abandon "the heretofore current method of modernising the parables," which finds in one after another of them only its own favourite conception of the slow and gradual development of the Kingdom of God. The Kingdom of Heaven is for Jülicher a completely supernatural idea; it is to be realised without human help and independently of the attitude of men, by the sole power of God. The parables of the mustard seed and the leaven are not intended to teach the disciples the necessity and wisdom of a development occupying a considerable time, but are designed to make clear and vivid to them the idea that the period of perfecting and fulfilment will follow with super-earthly necessity upon that of imperfection.

But in general the new problem plays no very special part in Jülicher's exposition. He takes up, it might almost be said, in relation to the parables, too independent a position as a religious thinker to care to understand them against the background of a wholly different world-view, and does not hesitate to exclude from the authentic discourses of Jesus whatever does not suit him. This is the fate, for instance, of the parable of the wicked husbandmen in Mark xii. He finds in it traits which read like *vaticinia ex eventu*, and sees therefore in the whole thing only a prophetically expressed "view of the history as it presented itself to an average man who had been present at the crucifixion of Jesus and nevertheless believed in Him as the Son of God."

But this absolute method of explanation, independent of any traditional order of time or events, makes it impossible for the author to draw from the parables any general system of teaching. He makes no distinction between the Galilaean mystical parables and the polemical, menacing Jerusalem parables. For instance, he supposes the parable of the Sower, which according to Mark was the very first of Jesus' parabolic discourses, to have been spoken as the result of a melancholy review of a preceding period [pg 264] of work, and as expressing the conviction, stamped upon His mind by the facts, "that it was in accordance with higher laws that the word of God should have to reckon with defeats as well as victories." Accordingly he adopts in the main the explanation which the Evangelist gives in Mark iv. 13-20. The parable of the seed growing secretly is turned to account in favour of the "present" Kingdom of God.

Jülicher has an incomparable power of striking fire out of every one of the parables, but the flame is of a different colour from that which it showed when Jesus pronounced the parables before the enchanted multitude. The problem posed by Johannes Weiss in connexion with the teaching of Jesus is treated by Jülicher only so far as it has a direct interest for the creative independence of his own religious thought.

Alongside of the parabolic discourses of Mark iv. we have now to place, as a newly discovered problem, the discourse at the sending out of the Twelve in Matt. x. Up to the time of Johannes Weiss it had been possible to rest content with transplanting the gloomy sayings regarding persecutions to the last period of Jesus' life; but now there was the further difficulty to be met that while so hasty a proclamation of the Kingdom of God is quite reconcilable with an exclusively eschatological character of the preaching of the Kingdom, the moment this is at all minimised it becomes unintelligible, not to mention the fact that in this case nothing can be made of the saying about the immediate coming of the Son of Man in Matt. x. 23. As though he felt the stern eye of old Reimarus upon him, Bousset hastens in a footnote to throw overboard the whole report of the mission of the Twelve as an "obscure and unintelligible tradition." Not content with that, he adds: "Perhaps the whole narrative is merely an expansion of some direction about missionising given by Jesus to the disciples in view of a later time." Before, it was only the discourse which was unhistorical; now it is the whole account of the mission—at least if we may assume that here, as is usual with theologians of all times, the author's real opinion is expressed in the footnote, and his most cherished opinion of all introduced with "perhaps." But how much historical material will remain to modern theologians in the Gospels if they are forced to abandon it wholesale from their objection to pure eschatology? If all the pronouncements of this kind to which the representatives of the Marcan hypothesis have committed themselves were collected together, they would make a book which would be much more damaging even than that book of Wrede's which dropped a bomb into their midst.

A third problem is offered by the saying in Matt. xi. 12, about "the violent" who, since the time of John the Baptist, "take the Kingdom of Heaven by force," which raises fresh difficulties for the [pg 265] exegetical art. It is true that if art sufficed, we should not have long to wait for the solution in this case. We should be asked to content ourselves with one or other of the artificial solutions with which exegetes have been accustomed from of old to find a way round this difficulty. Usually the saying is claimed as supporting the "presence" of the Kingdom. This is the line taken by Wendt, Wernle, and Arnold Meyer.[179] According to the last named it means: "From the days of John the Baptist it has been possible to get possession of the Kingdom of God; yea, the righteous are every day earning it for their own." But no explanation has heretofore succeeded in making it in any degree intelligible how Jesus could date the presence of the Kingdom from the Baptist, whom in the same breath He places outside of the Kingdom, or why, in order to express so simple an idea, He uses such entirely unnatural and inappropriate expressions as "rape" and "wrest to themselves."

The full difficulties of the passage are first exhibited by Johannes Weiss.[180] He restores it to its natural sense, according to which it means that since that time the Kingdom suffers, or is subjected to, violence, and in order to be able to understand it literally he has to take it in a condemnatory sense. Following Alexander Schweizer,[181] he sums up his interpretation in the following sentence: Jesus describes, and in the form of the description shows His condemnation of, a violent Zealotistic Messianic movement which has been in progress since the days of the Baptist.[182] But this explanation again makes Jesus express a very simple meaning in a very obscure phrase. And what indication is there that the sense is condemnatory? Where do we hear anything more about a Zealotic Messianic movement, of which the Baptist formed the starting-point? His preaching certainly offered no incentive to such a movement, and Jesus' attitude towards the Baptist is elsewhere, even in Jerusalem, entirely one of approval. Moreover, a condemnatory saying of this kind would not have been closed with the distinctive formula: "He that hath ears to hear let him hear" (Matt. xi. 15), which elsewhere, cf. Mark iv. 9, indicates a mystery.

We must, therefore, accept the conclusion that we really do not understand the saying, that we "have not ears to hear it," that we do not know sufficiently well the essential character of the Kingdom of God, to understand why Jesus describes the coming of the [pg 266] Kingdom as a doing-violence-to-it, which has been in progress since the days of the Baptist, especially as the hearers themselves do not seem to have cared, or been able, to understand what was the connexion of the coming with the violence; nor do we know why He expects them to understand how the Baptist is identical with Elias.

But the problem which became most prominent of all the new problems raised by eschatology, was the question concerning the Son of Man. It had become a dogma of theology that Jesus used the term Son of Man to veil His Messiahship; that is to say, every theologian found in this term whatever meaning he attached to the Messiahship of Jesus, the human, humble, ethical, unpolitical, unapocalyptic, or whatever other character was held to be appropriate to the orthodox "transformed" Messiahship. The Danielic Son of Man entered into the conception only so far as it could do so without endangering the other characteristics. Confronted with the Similitudes of Enoch, theologians fell back upon the expedient of assuming them to be spurious, or at least worked-over in a Christian sense in the Son of Man passages, just as the older history of dogma got rid of the Ignatian letters, of which it could make nothing, by denying their genuineness. But once the Jewish eschatology was seriously applied to the explanation of the Son of Man conception, all was changed. A new dilemma presented itself; either Jesus used the expression, and used it in a purely Jewish apocalyptic sense, or He did not use it at all.

Although Baldensperger did not state the dilemma in its full trenchancy, Hilgenfeld thought it necessary to defend Jesus against the suspicion of having borrowed His system of thought and His self-designation from Jewish Apocalypses.[183] Orello Cone, too, will not admit that the expression Son of Man has only apocalyptic suggestion in the mouth of Jesus, but will have it interpreted according to Mark ii. 10 and 28, where His pure humanity is the idea which is emphasised.[184] Oort holds, more logically, that Jesus did not use it, but that the disciples took the expression from "the Gospel" and put it into the mouth of Jesus.[185]

Johannes Weiss formulated the problem clearly, and proposed that, with the exception of the two passages where Son of Man means man in general, only those should be recognised in which the significance attached to the term in Daniel and the Apocalypses is demanded by the context. By so doing he set theology a problem calculated to keep it occupied for many years. Not many indeed at first recognised the problem. Charles, however, meets it [pg 267] in a bold fashion, proposing to regard the Son of Man, in Jesus' usage of the title, as a conception in which the Messiah of the Book of Enoch and the Servant of the Lord in Isaiah are united into one.[186] Most writers, however, did not free themselves from inconsistencies. They wanted at one and the same time to make the apocalyptic element dominant in the expression, and to hold that Jesus could not have taken the conception over unaltered, but must have transformed it in some way. These inconsistencies necessarily result from the assumption of Weiss's opponents that Jesus intended to designate Himself as Messiah in the actual present. For since the expression Son of Man has in itself only an apocalyptic sense referring to the future, they had to invent another sense applicable to the present, which Jesus might have inserted into it. In all these learned discussions of the title Son of Man this operation is assumed to have been performed.

According to Bousset, Jesus created, and embodied in this term, a new form of the Messianic ideal which united the super-earthly with the human and lowly. In any case, he thinks, the term has a meaning applicable in this present world. Jesus uses it at once to conceal and to suggest His Messianic dignity. How conscious Bousset, nevertheless, is of the difficulty is evident from the fact that in discussing the meaning of the title he remarks that the Messianic significance must have been of subordinate importance in the estimation of Jesus, and cannot have formed the basis of His actions, otherwise He would have laid more stress upon it in His preaching. As if the term Son of Man had not meant for His contemporaries all He needed to say!

Bousset's essay on Jewish Apocalyptic,[187] published in 1903, seeks the solution in a rather different direction, by postponing, namely, to the very last possible moment the adoption of this self-designation. "In all probability Jesus in a few isolated sayings towards the close of His life hit upon this title Son of Man as a means of expressing, in the face of the thought of defeat and death, which forced itself upon Him, His confidence in the abiding victory of His person and His cause." If this is so, the emphasis must be principally on the triumphant apocalyptic aspects of the title.

Even this belated adoption of the title Son of Man is more [pg 268] than Brandt is willing to admit, and he holds it to be improbable that Jesus used the expression at all. It would be more natural, he thinks, to suppose that the Evangelist Mark introduced this self-designation, as he introduced so much else, into the Gospel on the ground of the figurative apocalyptic discourses in the Gospel.

Just when ingenuity appeared to have exhausted itself in attempts to solve the most difficult of the problems raised by the eschatological school, the historical discussion suddenly seemed about to be rendered objectless. Philology entered a *caveat*. In 1896 appeared Lietzmann's essay upon "The Son of Man," which consisted of an investigation of the linguistic basis of the enigmatic self-designation.

# XVII. Questions Regarding The Aramaic Language, Rabbinic Parallels, And Buddhistic Influence

Arnold Meyer. Jesu Muttersprache. (The Mother Tongue of Jesus.) Leipzig, 1896. 166 pp.

Hans Lietzmann. Der Menschensohn. Ein Beitrag zur neutestamentlichen Theologie. (The Son of Man. A Contribution to New Testament Theology.) Freiburg, 1896. 95 pp.

J. Wellhausen. Israelitische und jüdische Geschichte. (History of Israel and the Jews.) 3rd ed., 1897; 4th ed., 1901. 394 pp.

Gustaf Dalman. Grammatik des jüdisch-palästinensischen Aramäisch. (Grammar of Jewish-Palestinian Aramaic.) Leipzig, 1894. Die Worte Jesu. Mit Berücksichtigung des nachkanonischen jüdischen Schrifttums und der aramäischen Sprache. (The Sayings of Jesus considered in connexion with the post-canonical Jewish writings and the Aramaic Language.) I. Introduction and certain leading conceptions: with an appendix on Messianic texts. Leipzig, 1898. 309 pp.

A. Wünsche. Neue Beiträge zur Erläuterung der Evangelien aus Talmud und Midrasch. (New Contributions to the Explanation of the Gospels, from Talmud and Midrash.) Göttingen, 1878. 566 pp.

Ferdinand Weber. System der altsynagogalen palästinensischen Theologie. (System of Theology of the Ancient Palestinian Synagogue.) Leipzig, 1880. 399 pp. 2nd ed., 1897.

Rudolf Seydel. Das Evangelium Jesu in seinen Verhältnissen zur Buddha-Sage und Buddha-Lehre. (The Gospel of Jesus in its relations to the Buddha-Legend and the Teaching of Buddha.) Leipzig, 1882. 337 pp. Die Buddha-Legende und das Leben Jesu nach den Evangelien. Erneute Prüfung ihres gegenseitigen Verhältnisses. (The Buddha-Legend and the Life of Jesus in the Gospels. A New Examination of their Mutual Relations.) 2nd ed., 1897. 129 pp.

Only since the appearance of Dalman's Grammar of Jewish Palestinian Aramaic in 1894 have we really known what was the dialect in which the Beatitudes of the Sermon on the Mount were spoken. This work closes a discussion which had been proceeding for centuries on a line parallel to that of theology proper, and which, according to the clear description of Arnold Meyer, ran its course somewhat as follows.[188]

[pg 270]

The question regarding the language spoken by Jesus had been vigorously discussed in the sixteenth century. Up till that time no one had known what to make of the tradition recorded by Eusebius that the speech of the apostles had been "Syrian" since the distinction between Syrian, Hebrew, and "Chaldee" was not understood and all three designations were used indiscriminately. Light was first thrown upon the question by Joseph Justus Scaliger († 1609). In the year 1555, Joh. Alb. Widmanstadt, Chancellor of Ferdinand I., had published the Syriac translation of the Bible in fulfilment of the wishes of an old scholar of Bologna, Theseus Ambrosius, who had left him the manuscript as a sacred legacy. He himself and his contemporaries believed that in this they had the Gospel in the mother-tongue of Jesus, until Scaliger, in one of his letters, gave a clear sketch of the Syrian dialects, distinguished Syriac from Chaldee, and further drew a distinction between the Babylonian Chaldee and Jewish Chaldee of the Targums, and in the language of the Targums itself distinguished an earlier from a later stratum. The apostles spoke, according to Scaliger, a Galilaean dialect of Chaldaic, or according to the more correct nomenclature introduced later, following a suggestion of Scaliger's, a dialect of Aramaic, and, in addition to that, the Syriac of Antioch. Next, Hugo Grotius put in a strong plea for a distinction between Jewish and Antiochian Syriac. Into the confusion caused at that time by the use of the term "Hebrew" some order was introduced by the Leyden Calvinistic professor Claude Saumaise, who, writing in French, emphasised the point that the New Testament, and the Early Fathers, when they speak of Hebrew, mean Syriac, since Hebrew had become completely unknown to the Jews of that period. Brian Walton, the editor of the London polyglot, which was completed in 1657, supposed that the dialect of Onkelos and Jonathan was the language of Jesus, being under the impression that both these Targums were written in the time of Jesus.

The growing knowledge of the distinction between Hebrew and Aramaic did not prevent the Vienna Jesuit Inchofer († 1648) from maintaining that Jesus spoke—Latin! The Lord cannot have used any other language upon earth, since this is the language of the saints in heaven. On the Protestant side, Vossius, opposing Richard Simon, endeavoured to establish the thesis that Greek was the language of Jesus, being partly inspired by the apologetic purpose of preventing the authenticity of the discourses and sayings of Jesus from being weakened by supposing them to have been translated from Aramaic into Greek, but also rightly recognising the importance which the Greek language must have assumed at that time in northern Palestine, through which there passed such important trade routes.

This view was brought up again by the Neapolitan legal scholar, [pg 271] Dominicus Diodati, in his book *De Christo Graece loquente*, 1767, who added some interesting material concerning the importance of the Greek language at the period and in the native district of Jesus. But five years later, in 1772, this view was thoroughly refuted by Giambernardo de Rossi,[189] who argued convincingly that among a people so separate and so conservative as the Jews the native language cannot possibly have been wholly driven out. The apostles wrote Greek for the sake of foreign readers. In the year 1792, Johann Adrian Bolten, "first collegiate pastor at the principal church in Altona" († 1807), made the first attempt to re-translate the sayings of Jesus into the original tongue.[190]

The certainly original Greek of the Epistles and the Johannine literature was a strong argument against the attempt to recognise no language save Aramaic as known to Jesus and His disciples. Paulus the rationalist, therefore, sought a middle path, and explained that while the Aramaic dialect was indeed the native language of Jesus, Greek had become so generally current among the population of Galilee, and still more of Jerusalem, that the founders of Christianity could use this language when they found it needful to do so. His Catholic contemporary, Hug, came to a similar conclusion.

In the course of the nineteenth century Aramaic—known down to the time of Michaelis as "Chaldee"[191]—was more thoroughly studied. The various branches of this language and the history of its progress became more or less clearly recognisable. Kautzsch's grammar of Biblical Aramaic[192] (1884) and Dalman's[193] work embody the result of these studies. "The Aramaic language," explains Meyer, "is a branch of the North Semitic, the linguistic stock to which also belong the Assyrio-Babylonian language in the East, and the Canaanitish languages, including Hebrew, in the West, while the South Semitic languages—the Arabic and Aethiopic—form a group by themselves." The users of these languages, the [pg 272] Aramaeans, were seated in historic times between the Babylonians and Canaanites, the area of their distribution extending from the foot of Lebanon and Hermon in a north-easterly direction as far as Mesopotamia, where "Aram of the two rivers" forms their easternmost province. Their immigration into these regions forms the third epoch of the Semitic migrations, which probably lasted from 1600 B.C. down to 600.

The Aramaic states had no great stability. The most important of them was the kingdom of Damascus, which at a certain period was so dangerous an enemy to northern Israel. In the end, however, the Aramaean dynasties were crushed, like the two Israelitish kingdoms, between the upper and nether millstones of Babylon and Egypt. In the time of the successors of Alexander, there arose in these regions the Syrian kingdom; which in turn gave place to the Roman power.

But linguistically the Aramaeans conquered the whole of Western Asia. In the course of the first millennium B.C. Aramaic became the language of commerce and diplomacy, as Babylonian had been during the second. It was only the rise of Greek as a universal language which put a term to these conquests of the Aramaic.

In the year 701 B.C. Aramaic had not yet penetrated to Judaea. When the *rabshakeh* (officer) sent by Sennacherib addressed the envoys of Hezekiah in Hebrew, they begged him to speak Aramaic in order that the men upon the wall might not understand.[194] For the post-exilic period the Aramaic edicts in the Book of Ezra and inscriptions on Persian coins show that throughout wide districts of the new empire Aramaic had made good its position as the language of common intercourse. Its domain extended from the Euxine southwards as far as Egypt, and even into Egypt itself. Samaria and the Hauran adopted it. Only the Greek towns and Phoenicia resisted.

The influence of Aramaic upon Jewish literature begins to be noticeable about the year 600. Jeremiah and Ezekiel, writing in a foreign land in an Aramaic environment, are the first witnesses to its supremacy. In the northern part of the country, owing to the immigration of foreign colonists after the destruction of the northern kingdom, it had already gained a hold upon the common people. In the Book of Daniel, written in the year 167 B.C., the Hebrew and Aramaic languages alternate. Perhaps, indeed, we ought to assume an Aramaic ground-document as the basis of this work.

At what time Aramaic became the common popular speech in the post-exilic community we cannot exactly discover. Under Nehemiah "Judaean," that is to say, Hebrew, was still spoken in

Jerusalem; in the time of the Maccabees Aramaic seems to have [pg 273] wholly driven out the ancient national language. Evidence for this is to be found in the occurrence of Aramaic passages in the Talmud, from which it is evident that the Rabbis used this language in the religious instruction of the people. The provision that the text, after being read in Hebrew, should be interpreted to the people, may quite well reach back into the time of Jesus. The first evidence for the practice is in the Mishna, about A.D. 150.

In the time of Jesus three languages met in Galilee—Hebrew, Aramaic, and Greek. In what relation they stood to each other we do not know, since Josephus, the only writer who could have told us, fails us in this point, as he so often does elsewhere. He informs us that when acting as an envoy of Titus he spoke to the people of Jerusalem in the ancestral language, and the word he uses is ἑβραΐζων. But the very thing we should like to know—whether, namely, this language was Aramaic or Hebrew, he does not tell us. We are left in the same uncertainty by the passage in Acts (xxii. 2) which says that Paul spoke to the people Ἑβραΐδι διαλέκτῳ, thereby gaining their attention, for there is no indication whether the language was Aramaic or Hebrew. For the writers of that period "Hebrew" simply means Jewish.

We cannot, therefore, be sure in what relation the ancient Hebrew sacred language and the Aramaic of ordinary intercourse stood to one another as regards religious writings and religious instruction. Did the ordinary man merely learn by heart a few verses, prayers, and psalms? Or was Hebrew, as the language of the cultus, also current in wider circles?

Dalman gives a number of examples of works written in Hebrew in the century which witnessed the birth of Christ: "A Hebrew original," he says, "must be assumed in the case of the main part of the Aethiopic book of Enoch, the Assumption of Moses, the Apocalypse of Baruch, Fourth Ezra, the Book of Jubilees, and for the Jewish ground-document of the Testament of the Twelve Patriarchs, of which M. Gaster has discovered a Hebrew manuscript." The first Book of Maccabees, too, seems to him to go back to a Hebrew original. Nevertheless, he holds it to be impossible that synagogue discourses intended for the people can have been delivered in Hebrew, or that Jesus taught otherwise than in Aramaic.

Franz Delitzsch's view, on the other hand, is that Jesus and the disciples taught in Hebrew; and that is the opinion of Resch also. Adolf Neubauer,[195] Reader in Rabbinical Hebrew at Oxford, attempted a compromise. It was certainly the case, he thought, [pg 274] that in the time of Jesus Aramaic was spoken throughout Palestine; but whereas in Galilee this language had an exclusive dominance, and the knowledge of Hebrew was confined to texts learned by heart, in Jerusalem Hebrew had renewed itself by the adoption of Aramaic elements, and a kind of Neo-Hebraic language had arisen. This solution at least testifies to the difficulty of the question. The fact is that from the language of the New Testament it is often difficult to make out whether the underlying words are Hebrew or Aramaic. Thus, for instance, Dalman remarks—with reference to the question whether the statement of Papias refers to a Hebrew or an Aramaic "primitive Matthew"—that it is difficult "to produce proof of an Aramaic as distinct from a Hebrew source, because it is often the case in Biblical Hebrew, and still more often in the idiom of the Mishna, that the same expressions and forms of phrase are possible as in Aramaic." Delitzsch's[196] "retranslation" of the New Testament into Hebrew is therefore historically justified.

But the question about the language of Jesus must not be confused with the problem of the original language of the primitive form of Matthew's Gospel. In reference to the latter, Dalman thinks that the tradition of the Early Church regarding an earlier Aramaic form of the Gospel must be considered as lacking confirmation. "It is only in the case of Jesus' own words that an Aramaic original form is undeniable, and it is only for these that Early Church tradition asserted the existence of a Semitic documentary source. It is, therefore, the right and duty of Biblical scholarship to investigate the form which the sayings of Jesus must have taken in the original and the sense which in this form they must have conveyed to Jewish hearers."

That Jesus spoke Aramaic, Meyer has shown by collecting all the Aramaic expressions which occur in His preaching.[197] He considers the "Abba" in Gethsemane decisive, for this means that Jesus prayed in Aramaic in His hour of bitterest need. Again the cry from the cross was, according to Mark xv. 34, also Aramaic: Ἐλωΐ, ἐλωΐ, λαμὰ σαβαχθανεί. The Old Testament was therefore most familiar to Him in an Aramaic translation, otherwise this form of the Psalm passage would not have come to His lips at the moment of death.

It is a quite independent question whether Jesus could speak, [pg 275] or at least understand, Greek. According to Josephus the knowledge of Greek in Palestine at that time, even among educated Jews, can only have been of a quite elementary character. He himself had to learn it laboriously in order to be able to write in it. His "Jewish War" was first written in Aramaic for his fellow-countrymen; the Greek edition was, by his own avowal, not intended for them. In another passage, it is true, he seems to imply a knowledge of, and interest in, foreign languages even among people in humble life.[198]

An analogy, which is in many respects very close, to the linguistic conditions in Palestine was offered by Alsace under French rule in the 'sixties of the nineteenth century. Here, too, three languages met in the same district. The High-German of Luther's translation of the Bible was the language of the Church, the Alemannic dialect was the usual speech of the people, while French was the language of culture and of government administration. This remarkable analogy would be rather in favour—if analogy can be admitted to have any weight in the question—of Delitzsch and Resch, since the Biblical High-German, although never spoken in social intercourse, strongly influenced the Alemannic dialect—although this was, on the other hand, quite uninfluenced by Modern High-German—but did not allow it to penetrate into Church or school, there maintaining for itself an undivided sway. French made some progress, but only in certain circles, and remained entirely excluded from the religious sphere. The Alsatians of the poorer classes who could at that time have repeated the Lord's Prayer or the Beatitudes in French would not have been difficult to count. The Lutheran translation still holds its own to some extent against the French translation with the older generation of the Alsatian community in Paris, which has in other respects become completely French—so strong is the influence of a former ecclesiastical language even among those who have left their native home. There is one factor, however, which is not represented in the analogy; the influence of the Greek-speaking Jews of the Diaspora, who gathered to the Feasts at Jerusalem, upon the extension of the Greek language in the mother-country.

Jesus, then, spoke Galilaean Aramaic, which is known to us as a separate dialect from writings of the fourth to the seventh century. For the Judaean dialect we have more and earlier evidence. We have literary monuments in it from the first to the third century. "It is very probable," Dalman thinks, "that the popular dialect of Northern Palestine, after the final fall of the Judaean centre of the Aramaic-Jewish culture, which followed on the Bar-Cochba rising, spread over almost the whole of Palestine."

The retranslations into Aramaic are therefore justified. After [pg 276] J. A. Bolten's attempt had remained for nearly a hundred years the only one of its kind, the experiment has been renewed in our own time by J. T. Marshall, E. Nestle, J. Wellhausen, Arnold Meyer, and Gustaf Dalman; in the case of Marshall and Nestle with the subsidiary purpose of endeavouring to prove the existence of an Aramaic documentary source. These retranslations first attracted their due meed of attention from theologians in connexion with the Son-of-Man question. Rarely, if ever, have theologians experienced such a surprise as was sprung upon them by Hans Lietzmann's essay in 1896.[199] Jesus had never, so ran the thesis of the Bonn candidate in theology, applied to Himself the title Son of Man, because in the Aramaic the title did not exist, and on linguistic grounds could not have existed. In the language which He used, בן אנש was merely a periphrasis for "a man." That Jesus meant Himself when He spoke of the Son of Man, none of His hearers could have suspected.

Lietzmann had not been without predecessors.[200] Gilbert Génébrard, who died Archbishop of Aix as long ago as 1597, had emphasised the point that the term Son of Man should not be interpreted with reference solely to Christ, but to the race of mankind. Hugo Grotius maintained the same position even more emphatically. With a quite modern one-sidedness, Paulus the rationalist maintained in his commentaries and in his Life of Jesus that according to Ezek. ii. 1 "Barnash" meant man in general. Jesus, he thought, whenever He used the expression the Son of Man, pointed to Himself and thus gave it the sense of "this man." In taking this line he gives up the general reference to mankind as a whole for which Mark ii. 28 is generally cited as the classical passage. The suggestion that the term Son of Man in its apocalyptic signification was first attributed to Jesus at a later time and that the passages where it occurs in this sense are therefore suspicious, was first put forward by Fr. Aug. Fritzsche. He hoped in this way to get rid of Matt. x. 23. De Lagarde, like Paulus, emphatically asserted that Son of Man only meant man. But instead of the clumsy explanation of the rationalist he gave another and a more pleasing one, namely, that Jesus by choosing this title designed to ennoble mankind. Wellhausen, in his "History of Israel and of the Jews" (1894), remarked on it as strange that Jesus should have called Himself "the Man." B. D. Eerdmans, taking the apocalyptic significance of the term as his starting-point, attempted to carry out consistently the theory of the later interpolation of this title into the sayings of Jesus.[201]

[pg 277]

Thus Lietzmann had predecessors; but they were not so in any real sense. They had either started out from the Marcan passage where the Son of Man is described as the Lord of the Sabbath, and endeavoured arbitrarily to interpret all the Son-of-Man passages in the same sense; or they assumed without sufficient grounds that the title Son of Man was a later interpolation. The new idea consisted in combining the two attempts, and declaring the passages about the Son of Man to be linguistically and historically impossible, seeing that, on linguistic grounds, "son of man" means "man."

Arnold Meyer and Wellhausen expressed themselves in the same sense as Lietzmann. The passages where Jesus uses the expression in an unmistakably Messianic sense are, according to them, to be put down to the account of Early Christian theology. The only passages which in their opinion are historically tenable are the two or three in which the expression denotes man in general, or is equivalent to the simple "I." These latter were felt to be a difficulty by the Church when it came to think in Greek, since this way of speaking of oneself was strange to them; consequently the expression appeared to them deliberately enigmatic and only capable of being interpreted in the sense which it bears in Daniel. The Son-of-Man conception, argued Lietzmann, when he again approached the question two years later, had arisen in a Hellenistic environment,[202] on the basis of Dan. vii. 13; N. Schmidt,[203] too, saw in the apocalyptic Bar-Nasha passages which follow the revelation of the Messiahship at Caesarea Philippi an interpolation from the later apocalyptic theology. On the other hand, P. Schmiedel still wished to make it a Messianic designation, and to take it as being historical in this sense even in passages in which the term man "gave a possible sense."[204] H. Gunkel thought that it was possible to translate Bar-Nasha simply by "man," and nevertheless hold to the historicity of the expression as a self-designation of Jesus. Jesus, he suggests, had borrowed this enigmatic term, which goes back to Dan. vii. 13, from the mystical apocalyptic literature, meaning thereby to indicate that He was the Man of God in contrast to the Man of Sin.[205]

Holtzmann felt a kind of relief in handing over to the philologists the obstinate problem which since the time of Baldensperger and [pg 278] Weiss had caused so much trouble to theologians, and wanted to postpone the historical discussion until the Aramaic experts had settled the linguistic question. That happened sooner than was expected. In 1898 Dalman declared in his epoch-making work (*Die Worte Jesu*) that he could not admit the linguistic objections to the use of the expression Son of Man by Jesus. "Biblical Aramaic," he says, "does not differ in this respect from Hebrew. The simple אנש and not בן אנש is the term for man."... It was only later that the Jewish-Galilaean dialect, like the Palestinian-Christian dialect, used בן אנש for man, though in both idioms the simple אנש occurs in the sense of "some one." "In view of the whole facts of the case," he continues, "what has to be said is that Jewish-Palestinian Aramaic of the earlier period used אנש for 'man,' and occasionally to designate a plurality of men makes use of the expression בני אנשא. The singular בן אנש was not current, and was only used in imitation of the Hebrew text of the Bible, where בן אדם belongs to the poetic diction, and is, moreover, not of very frequent occurrence." "It is," he says elsewhere, "by no means a sign of a sound historical method, instead of working patiently at the solution of the problem, to hasten like Oort and Lietzmann to the conclusion that the absence of the expression in the New Testament Epistles is a proof that Jesus did not use it either, but that there was somewhere or other a Hellenistic community in the Early Church which had a predilection for this name, and often made Jesus speak of Himself in the Gospel narrative in the third person, in order to find an opportunity of bringing it in."

So the oxen turned back with the ark into the land of the Philistines. It was a case of returning to the starting-point and deciding on historical grounds in what sense Jesus had used the expression.[206] But the possibilities were reduced by the way in which Lietzmann had posed the problem, since the interpretations according to which Jesus had used it in a veiled ethical Messianic sense, to indicate the ethical and spiritual transformation of all the eschatological conceptions, were now manifestly incapable of offering any convincing argument against the radical denial of the use of the expression. Baldensperger rightly remarked in a review of the whole discussion that the question which was ultimately at stake in [pg 279] the combat over the title Son of Man was the question whether Jesus was the Messiah or no, and that Dalman, by his proof of its linguistic possibility, had saved the Messiahship of Jesus.[207]

But what kind of Messiahship? Is it any other kind than the future Messiahship of the apocalyptic Son of Man which Johannes Weiss had asserted? Did Jesus mean anything different by the Son of Man from that which was meant by the apocalyptic writers? To put it otherwise:

behind the Son-of-Man problem there lies the general question whether Jesus can have described Himself as a present Messiah; for the fundamental difficulty is that He, a man upon earth, should give Himself out to be the Son of Man, and at the same time apparently give to that title a quite different sense from that which it previously possessed.

The champion of the linguistic possibility of this self-designation made the last serious attempt to render the transformation of the conception historically conceivable. He argues that Jesus cannot have used it as a mere meaningless expression, a periphrasis for the simple I.[208] On the other hand, the term cannot have been understood by the disciples as an exalted title, or at least only in the sense that the title indicative of exaltation is paradoxically connected with the title indicative of humility. "We shall be justified in saying, that, for the Synoptic Evangelists, 'Man's Son' was no title of honour for the Messiah, but—as it must necessarily appear to a Hellenist—a veiling of His Messiahship under a name which emphasises the humanity of its bearer." For them it was not the references to the sufferings of "Man's Son" that were paradoxical, but the references to His exaltation: that "Man's Son" should be put to death is not wonderful; what is wonderful is His "coming again upon the clouds of heaven."

If Jesus called Himself the Son of Man, the only conclusion which could be drawn by those that heard Him was, "that for some reason or other He desired to describe Himself as a Man *par excellence*." There is no reason to think of the Heavenly Son of Man of the Similitudes of Enoch and Fourth Ezra; that conception could hardly be present to the minds of His auditors.

[pg 280]

"How was one who was now walking upon earth, to come from heaven? He would have needed first to be translated thither. One who had died or been rapt away from earth might be brought back to earth again in this way, or a being who had never before been upon earth, might be conceived as descending thither."

But if, on the one hand, the title Son of Man was not to be understood apart from the reference to the passage in Daniel, while on the other Jesus so designated Himself as a man actually present upon earth, "what was really implied was that He was the man in whom Daniel's vision of 'one like unto a Son of Man' was being fulfilled." He could not certainly expect from His hearers a complete understanding of the self-designation. "We are doubtless justified in saying that in using it, He intentionally offered them an enigma which challenged further reflection upon His Person."

According to Peter's confession the name was intelligible to the disciples as coming from Dan. vii. 13, and obviously indicating Him who was destined to the sovereignty of the world. Jesus calls Himself the Son of Man, "not as meaning the lowly one, but as a scion of the human race with its human weakness, whom nevertheless God will make Lord of the world; and it is very probable that Jesus found the Son of Man of Dan. vii. in Ps. viii. 5 ff. also." Sayings regarding humiliation and suffering could be attached to the title just as well as references to exaltation. For since the "Child of Man" has placed Himself upon the throne of God, He is in reality no longer a mere man, but ruler over heaven and earth, "the Lord."

This attempt of Dalman's has the same significance in regard to the question of the Messiahship as Bousset's had for the ethical question. Just as in Bousset's view the Kingdom of God was, in a paradoxical way, after all proclaimed as present, so here the self-designation "Son of Man" is retained by a paradox as conveying the sense of a present Messiahship. But the documents do not give any support to this assumption; on the contrary they contradict it at every point. According to Dalman it was not the predictions of the passion of the Son of Man which sounded paradoxical to the disciples, but the predictions of His exaltation. But we are distinctly told that when He spoke of His passion they did not understand the saying. The predictions of His exaltation, however, they understood so well that without troubling themselves further about the predictions of the sufferings, they began to dispute who should be greatest in the Kingdom of Heaven, and who should have his throne closest to the Son of Man. And if it is once admitted that Jesus took the designation from Daniel, what ground is there for asserting that the [pg 281] purely eschatological transcendental significance which the term had taken on in the Similitudes of Enoch and retains in Fourth Ezra had no existence for Jesus? Thus, by a long round-about, criticism has come back to Johannes Weiss.[209] His eschatological solution of the Son-of-Man question—the elements of which are to be found in Strauss's first Life of Jesus—is the only possible one. Dalman expresses the same idea in the form of a question. "How could one who was actually walking the earth come down from heaven? He would have needed first to be translated thither. One who had died or been rapt away from earth might possibly be brought back to earth in this way." Having reached this point we have only to observe further that Jesus, from the "confession of Peter" onwards, always speaks of the Son of Man in connexion with death and resurrection. That is to say, that once the disciples know in what relation He stands to the Son of Man, He uses this title to suggest the manner of His return: as the sequel to His death and resurrection He will return to the world again as a superhuman Personality. Thus the purely transcendental use of the term suggested by Dalman as a possibility turns out to be the historical reality.

Broadly speaking, therefore, the Son-of-Man problem is both historically solvable and has been solved. The authentic passages are those in which the expression is used in that apocalyptic sense which goes back to Daniel. But we have to distinguish two different uses of the term according to the degree of knowledge assumed in the hearers. If the secret of Jesus is unknown to them, then in that case they understand simply that Jesus is speaking of the "Son of Man" and His coming without having any suspicion that He and the Son of Man have any connexion. It would be thus, for instance, when in sending out the disciples in Matt. x. 23, He announced the imminence of the appearing of the Son of Man; or when He pictured the judgment which the Son of Man would hold (Matt. xxv. 31-46), if we may imagine [pg 282] it to have been spoken to the people at Jerusalem. Or, on the other hand, the secret is known to the hearers. In that case they understand that the term Son of Man points to the position to which He Himself is to be exalted when the present era passes into the age to come. It was thus, no doubt, in the case of the disciples at Caesarea Philippi, and of the High Priest to whom Jesus, after answering his demand with the simple "Yea" (Mark xiv. 62), goes on immediately to speak of the exaltation of the Son of Man to the right hand of God, and of His coming upon the clouds of heaven.

Jesus did not, therefore, veil His Messiahship by using the expression Son of Man, much less did He transform it, but He used the expression to refer, in the only possible way, to His Messianic office as destined to be realised at His "coming," and did so in such a manner that only the initiated understood that He was speaking of His own coming, while others understood Him as referring to the coming of a Son of Man who was other than Himself.

The passages where the title has not this apocalyptic reference, or where, previous to the incident at Caesarea Philippi, Jesus in speaking to the disciples equates the Son of Man with His own "ego," are to be explained as of literary origin. This set of secondary occurrences of the title has nothing to do with "Early Church theology"; it is merely a question of phenomena of translation and tradition. In the saying about the Sabbath in Mark ii. 28, and perhaps also in the saying about the right to forgive sins in Mark ii. 10, Son of Man doubtless stood in the original in the general sense of "man," but was later, certainly by our Evangelists, understood as referring to Jesus as the Son of Man. In other passages tradition, following the analogy of those passages in which the title is authentic, put in place of the simple I—expressed in the Aramaic by "the man"—the self-designation "Son of Man," as we can clearly show by comparing Matt. xvi. 13, "Who do men say that the Son of Man is?" with Mark viii. 27, "Who do men say that I am?"

Three passages call for special discussion. In the statement that a man may be forgiven for blasphemy against the Son of Man, but not for blasphemy against the Holy Spirit, in Matt. xii. 32, the "Son of Man" may be authentic. But of course it would not, even in that case, give any hint that "Son of Man designates the Messiah in His humiliation" as Dalman wished to infer from the passage, but would mean that Jesus was speaking of the Son of Man, here as elsewhere, in the third person without reference to Himself, and was thinking of a contemptuous denial of the Parousia such as might have been uttered by a Sadducee. But if we take into account the parallel in Mark iii. 28 and 29, where blasphemy against the Holy Ghost is spoken of without any mention of [pg 283] blasphemy against the Son of Man, it seems more natural to take the mention of the Son of Man as a secondary interpolation, derived from the same line of tradition, perhaps from the same hand, as the "Son of Man" in the question to the disciples at Caesarea Philippi.

The two other sayings, the one about the Son of Man "who hath not where to lay His head," Matt. viii. 20, and that about the Son of Man who must submit to the reproach of being a glutton and a wine-bibber, Matt. xi. 19, belong together. If we assume it to be possible, in conformity with the saying about the purpose of the parables in Mark iv. 11 and 12, that Jesus sometimes spoke words which He did not intend to be understood, we may—if we are unwilling to accept the supposition of a later periphrasis for the ego, which would certainly be the most natural explanation—recognise in these sayings two obscure declarations regarding the Son of Man. They would then be supposed to have meant in the original form, which is no longer clearly recognisable, that the Son of Man would in some way justify the conduct of Jesus of Nazareth. But the way in which this idea is expressed was not such as to make it easy for His hearers to identify Him with the Son of Man. Moreover, it was for them a conception impossible to realise, since Jesus was a natural, and the Son of Man a supernatural, being; and the eschatological scheme of things had not provided for a man who at the end of the existing era should hint to others that at the great transformation of all things He would be manifested as the Son of Man. This case presented itself only in the course of history, and it created a preparatory stage of eschatology which does not answer to any traditional scheme.

That act of the self-consciousness of Jesus by which He recognised Himself in His earthly existence as the future Messiah is the act in which eschatology supremely affirms itself. At the same time, since it brings, spiritually, that which is to come, into the unaltered present, into the existing era, it is the end of eschatology. For it is its "spiritualisation," a spiritualisation of which the ultimate consequence was to be that all its "supersensuous" elements were to be realised only spiritually in the present earthly conditions, and all that is affirmed as supersensuous in the transcendental sense was to be regarded as only the ruined remains of an eschatological world-view. The Messianic secret of Jesus is the basis of Christianity, since it involves the de-nationalising and the spiritualisation of Jewish eschatology.

Yet more. It is the primal fact, the starting-point, of a process which manifests itself, indeed, in Christianity, but cannot fully work itself out even here, of a movement in the direction of inwardness which brings all religious magnitudes into the one indivisible spiritual present, and which Christian dogmatic has not [pg 284] ventured to carry to its completion. The Messianic consciousness of the uniquely great Man of Nazareth sets up a struggle between the present and the beyond, and introduces that resolute absorption of the beyond by the present, which in looking back we recognise as the history of Christianity, and of which we are conscious in ourselves as the essence of religious progress and experience—a process of which the end is not yet in sight.

In this sense Jesus did "accept the world" and did stand in conflict with Judaism. Protestantism was a step—a step on which hung weighty consequences—in the progress of that "acceptance of the world" which was constantly developing itself from within. By a mighty revolution which was in harmony with the spirit of that great primal act of the consciousness of Jesus, though in opposition to some of the most certain of His sayings, ethics became world-accepting. But it will be a mightier revolution still when the last remaining ruins of the supersensuous other-worldly system of thought are swept away in order to clear the site for a new spiritual, purely real and present world. All the inconsistent compromises and constructions of modern theology are merely an attempt to stave off the final expulsion of eschatology from religion, an inevitable but a hopeless attempt. That proleptic Messianic consciousness of Jesus, which was in reality the only possible actualisation of the Messianic idea, carries these consequences with it inexorably and unfailingly. At that last cry upon the cross the whole eschatological supersensuous world fell in upon itself in ruins, and there remained as a spiritual reality only that present spiritual world, bound as it is to sense, which Jesus by His all-powerful word had called into being within the world which He contemned. That last cry, with its despairing abandonment of the eschatological future, is His real acceptance of the world. The "Son of Man" was buried in the ruins of the falling eschatological world; there remained alive only Jesus "the Man." Thus these two Aramaic synonyms include in themselves, as in a symbol of reality, all that was to come.

If theology has found it so hard a task to arrive at an historical comprehension of the secret of this self-designation, this is due to the fact that the question is not a purely historical one. In this word there lies the transformation of a whole system of thought, the inexorable consequence of the elimination of eschatology from religion. It was only in this future form, not as actual, that Jesus spoke of His Messiahship. Modern theology keeps on endeavouring to discover in the title of Son of Man, which is bound up with the future, a humanised present Messiahship. It does so in the conviction that the recognition of a purely future reference in the Messianic consciousness of Jesus would lead in the last result to a modification of the historic basis of our faith, which has itself become [pg 285] historical, and therefore true and self-justifying. The recognition of the claims of eschatology signifies for our dogmatic a burning of the boats by which it felt itself able to return at any moment from the time of Jesus direct to the present.

One point that is worthy of notice in this connexion is the trustworthiness of the tradition. The Evangelists, writing in Greek, and the Greek-speaking Early Church, can hardly have retained an understanding of the purely eschatological character of that self-designation of Jesus. It had become for them merely an indirect method of self-designation. And nevertheless the Evangelists, especially Mark, record the sayings of Jesus in such a way that the original significance and application of the designation in His mouth is still clearly recognisable, and we are able to determine with certainty the isolated cases in which this self-designation in His discourses is of a secondary origin.

Thus the use of the term Son of Man—which, if we admitted the sweeping proposal of Lietzmann and Wellhausen to cancel it everywhere as an interpolation of Greek Early Church theology, would throw doubt on the whole of the Gospel tradition—becomes a proof of the certainty and trustworthiness of that tradition. We may, in fact, say that the progressive recognition of the eschatological character of the teaching and action of Jesus carries with it a progressive justification of the Gospel tradition. A series of passages and discourses which had been endangered because from the modern theological point of view which had been made the criterion of the tradition they appeared to be without meaning, are now secured. The stone which the critics rejected has become the corner-stone of the tradition.

If Aramaic scholarship appears in regard to the Son-of-Man question among the opponents of the thorough-going eschatological view, it takes no other position in connexion with the retranslations and in the application of illustrative parallels from the Rabbinic literature.

In looking at the earlier works in this department, one is struck with the smallness of the result in proportion to the labour expended. The names that call for mention here are those of John Lightfoot, Christian Schöttgen, Joh. Gerh. Meuschen, J. Jak. Wettstein, F. Nork, Franz Delitzsch, Carl Siegfried, and A. Wünsche.[210] But even a work like F. Weber's *System der altsynagogalen* [pg 286]*palästinensischen Theologie*,[211] which does not confine itself to single sayings and thoughts, but aims at exhibiting the Rabbinic system of thought as a whole, throws, in the main, but little light on the thoughts of Jesus. The Rabbinic parables supply, according to Jülicher, but little of value for the explanation of the parables of Jesus.[212] In this method of discourse, Jesus is so pre-eminently original, that any other productions of the Jewish parabolic literature are like stunted undergrowth beside a great tree; though that has not prevented His originality from being challenged in this very department, both in earlier times and at the present. As early as 1648, Robert Sheringham, of Cambridge,[213] suggested that the parables in Matt. xx. 1 ff., xxv. 1 ff., and Luke xvi., were derived from Talmudic sources, an opinion against which J. B. Carpzov, the younger, raised a protest; in 1839, F. Nork asserted, in his work on "Rabbinic Sources and Parallels for the New Testament Writings," that the best thoughts in the discourses of Jesus are to be attributed to His Jewish teachers; in 1880 the Dutch Rabbi, T. Tal, maintained the thesis that the parables of the New Testament are all borrowed from the Talmud.[214] Theories of this kind cannot be refuted, because they lack the foundation necessary to any theory which is to be capable of being rationally discussed—that of plain common sense.[215]

We possess, however, really scientific attempts to define more closely the thoughts of Jesus by the aid of the Rabbinic language and Rabbinic ideas in the works of Arnold Meyer and Dalman. It cannot indeed be said that the obscure sayings which form the problem of present-day exegesis are in all cases made clearer by them, much as we may admire the comprehensive knowledge of [pg 287] these scholars. Sometimes, indeed, they become more obscure than before. According to Meyer, for instance, the question of Jesus whether His disciples can drink of His cup, and be baptized with His baptism means, if put back into Aramaic, "Can you drink as bitter a drink as I; can you eat as sharply salted meat as I?"[216] Nor does Dalman's Aramaic retranslation help us much with the saying about the violent who take the Kingdom of Heaven by force. According to him, it is not spoken of the faithful, but of the rulers of this world, and refers to the epoch of the Divine rule which has been introduced by the imprisonment of the Baptist. No one can violently possess himself of the Divine reign, and Jesus can therefore only mean that violence is done to it in the person of its subjects.

On this it must be remarked, that if the saying really means this, it is about as appropriate to its setting as a rock in the sky. Jesus is not speaking of the imprisonment of the Baptist. By the days of John the Baptist He means the time of his public ministry.

It is equally open to question whether in putting that crucial question regarding the Messiah in Mark xii. 37 He really intended to show, as Dalman thinks, "that physical descent from David was not of decisive importance—it did not belong to the essence of the Messiahship."

But a point in regard to which Dalman's remarks are of great value for the reconstruction of the life of Jesus is the entry into Jerusalem. Dalman thinks that the simple "Hosanna, blessed be he that cometh in the name of the Lord" (Mark xi. 9) was what the people really shouted in acclamation, and that the additional words in Mark and Matthew are simply an interpretative expansion. This acclamation did not itself contain any Messianic reference. This explains "why the entry into Jerusalem was not made a count in the charge urged against Him before Pilate." The events of "Palm Sunday" only received their distinctively Messianic colour later. It was not the Messiah, but the prophet and wonder-worker of Galilee whom the people hailed with rejoicing and accompanied with invocations of blessing.[217]

Generally speaking, the value of Dalman's work lies less in the solutions which it offers than in the problems which it raises. By its very thorough discussions it challenges historical theology to test its most cherished assumptions regarding the teaching of Jesus, and make sure whether they are really so certain and self-evident. Thus, in opposition to Schürer, he denies that the thought of the [pg 288] pre-existence in heaven of all the good things belonging to the Kingdom of God was at all generally current in the Late-Jewish world of ideas, and thinks that the occasional references[218] to a pre-existing Jerusalem, which shall finally be brought down to the earth, do not suffice to establish the theory. Similarly, he thinks it doubtful whether Jesus used the terms "this world (age)," "the world (age) to come" in the eschatological sense which is generally attached to them, and doubts, on linguistic grounds, whether they can have been used at all. Even the use of עלם or עולם for "world" cannot be proved. In the pre-Christian period there is much reason to doubt its occurrence, though in later Jewish literature it is frequent. The expression ἐν τῇ παλιγγενεσίᾳ in Matt. xix. 28, is specifically Greek and cannot be reproduced in either Hebrew or Aramaic. It is very strange that the use which Jesus makes of *Amen* is unknown in the whole of Jewish literature. According to the proper idiom of the language "אמן is never used to emphasise one's own speech, but always with reference to the speech, prayer, benediction, oath, or curse of another." Jesus, therefore, if He used the expression in this sense, must have given it a new meaning as a formula of asseveration, in place of the oath which He forbade.

All these acute observations are marked by the general tendency which was observable in the interpretation of the term Son of Man, that is, by the endeavour so to weaken down the eschatological conceptions of the Kingdom and the Messiah, that the hypothesis of a making-present and spiritualising of these conceptions in the teaching of Jesus might appear inherently and linguistically possible and natural. The polemic against the pre-existent realities of the Kingdom of God is intended to show that for Jesus the Reign of God is a present benefit, which can be sought after, given, possessed, and taken. Even before the time of Jesus, according to Dalman, a tendency had shown itself to lay less emphasis, in connexion with the hope of the future, upon the national Jewish element. Jesus forced this element still farther into the background, and gave a more decided prominence to the purely religious element. "For Him the reign of God was the Divine power, which from this time onward was steadily to carry forward the renewal of the world, and also the renewed world, into which men shall one day enter, which even now offers itself, and therefore can be grasped and received as a present good." The supernatural coming of the Kingdom is only the final stage of the coming which is now being inwardly spiritually brought about by the preaching of Jesus. Though He may perhaps have spoken of "this" world and the "world to come," these expressions had in His use of them no very special importance. It is for Him less a question of an antithesis between "then" and [pg 289] "now," than of establishing a connexion between them by which the transition from one to the other is to be effected.

It is the same in regard to Jesus' consciousness of His Messiahship. "In Jesus' view," says Dalman, "the period before the commencement of the Reign of God was organically connected with the actual period of His Reign." He was the Messiah because He knew Himself to stand in a unique ethico-religious relation to God. His Messiahship was not something wholly incomprehensible to those about Him. If redemption was regarded as being close at hand, the Messiah must be assumed to be in some sense already present. Therefore Jesus is both directly and indirectly spoken of as Messiah.

Thus the most important work in the department of Aramaic scholarship shows clearly the anti-eschatological tendency which characterised it from the beginning. The work of Lietzmann, Meyer, Wellhausen, and Dalman, forms a distinct episode in the general resistance to eschatology. That Aramaic scholarship should have taken up a hostile attitude towards the eschatological system of thought of Jesus lies in the nature of things. The thoughts which it takes as its standard of comparison were only reduced to writing long after the period of Jesus, and, moreover, in a lifeless and distorted form, at a time when the apocalyptic temper no longer existed as the living counterpoise to the legal righteousness, and this legal righteousness had allowed only so much of Apocalyptic to survive as could be brought into direct connexion with it. In fact, the distance between Jesus' world of thought and this form of Judaism is as great as that which separates it from modern ideas. Thus in Dalman modernising tendencies and Aramaic scholarship were able to combine in conducting a criticism of the eschatology in the teaching of Jesus in which the modern man thought the thoughts and the expert in Aramaic formulated and supported them, yet without being able in the end to make any impression upon the well-rounded whole formed by Jesus' eschatological preaching of the Kingdom.

Whether Aramaic scholarship will contribute to the investigation of the life and teaching of Jesus along other lines and in a direct and positive fashion, only the future can show. But certainly if theologians will give heed to the question-marks so acutely placed by Dalman, and recognise it as one of their first duties to test carefully whether a thought or a connexion of thought is linguistically or inherently Greek, and only Greek, in character, they will derive a notable advantage from what has already been done in the department of Aramaic study.

But if the service rendered by Aramaic studies has been hitherto mainly indirect, no success whatever has attended, or seems likely [pg 290] to attend, the attempt to apply Buddhist ideas to the explanation of the thoughts of Jesus. It could only indeed appear to have some prospect of success if we could make up our minds to follow the example of the author of one of the most recent of fictitious lives of Christ in putting Jesus to school to the Buddhist priests; in which case the six years which Monsieur Nicolas Notowitsch allots to this purpose, would certainly be none too much for the completion of the course.[219] If imagination boggles at this, there remains no possibility of showing that Buddhist ideas exercised any direct influence upon Jesus. That Buddhism may have had some kind of influence upon Late Judaism and thus indirectly upon Jesus is not inherently impossible, if we are prepared to recognise Buddhistic influence on the Babylonian and Persian civilisations. But it is unproved, unprovable, and unthinkable, that Jesus derived the suggestion of the new and creative ideas which emerge in His teaching from Buddhism. The most that can be done in this direction is to point to certain analogies. For the parables of Jesus, Buddhist parallels were suggested by Renan and Havet.[220]

How little these analogies mean in the eyes of a cautious observer is evident from the attitude which Max Müller took up towards the question. "That there are startling coincidences between Buddhism and Christianity," he remarks in one passage,[221] "cannot be denied; and it must likewise be admitted that Buddhism existed at least four hundred years before Christianity. I go even further and say that I should be extremely grateful if anybody would point out to me the historical channels through which Buddhism had influenced early Christianity. I have been looking for such channels all my life, but hitherto I have found none. What I have found is that for some of the most startling coincidences there are historical antecedents on both sides; and if we once know these antecedents the coincidences become far less startling."

A year before Max Müller formulated his impression in these terms, Rudolf Seydel[222] had endeavoured to explain the analogies [pg 291] which had been noticed by supposing Christianity to have been influenced by Buddhism. He distinguishes three distinct classes of analogies:

1. Those of which the points of resemblance can without difficulty be explained as due to the influence of similar sources and motives in the two cases.

2. Those which show a so special and unexpected agreement that it appears artificial to explain it from the action of similar causes, and the dependence of one upon the other commends itself as the most natural explanation.

3. Those in which there exists a reason for the occurrence of the idea only within the sphere of one of the two religions, or in which at least it can very much more easily be conceived as originating within the one than within the other, so that the inexplicability of the phenomenon within the one domain gives ground for seeking its source within the other.

This last class demands a literary explanation of the analogy. Seydel therefore postulates, alongside of primitive forms of Matthew and Luke, a third source, "a poetic-apocalyptic Gospel of very early date which fitted its Christian material into the frame of a Buddhist type of Gospel, transforming, purifying, and ennobling the material taken from the foreign but related literature by a kind of rebirth inspired by the Christian Spirit." Matthew and Luke, especially Luke, follow this poetic Gospel up to the point where historic sources become more abundant, and the primitive form of Mark begins to dominate their narrative. But even in later parts the influence of this poetical source, which as an independent document was subsequently lost, continued to make itself felt.

The strongest point of support for this hypothesis, if a mere conjecture can be described as such, is found by Seydel in the introductory narratives in Luke. Now it is not inherently impossible that Buddhist legends, which in one form or another were widely current in the East, may have contributed more or less to the formation of the mythical preliminary history. Who knows the laws of the formation of legend? Who can follow the course of the wind which carries the seed over land and sea? But in general it may be said that Seydel actually refutes the hypothesis which he is defending. If the material which he brings forward is all that there is to suggest a relation between Buddhism and Christianity, we are justified in waiting until new discoveries are made in that quarter before asserting the necessity of a Buddhist primitive Gospel. That will not prevent a succession of theosophic Lives of Jesus from finding their account in Seydel's classical work. Seydel indeed delivered himself into their hands, because he did not [pg 292] entirely avoid the rash assumption of theosophic "historical science" that Jewish eschatology can be equated with Buddhistic.

Eduard von Hartmann, in the second edition of his work, "The Christianity of the New Testament,"[223] roundly asserts that there can be no question of any relation of Jesus to Buddha, nor of any indebtedness either in His teaching or in the later moulding of the story of His life, but only of a parallel formation of myth.

XVIII. The Position Of The Subject At The Close Of The Nineteenth Century

Oskar Holtzmann. Das Leben Jesu. Tübingen, 1901. 417 pp.

Das Messianitätsbewusstsein Jesu und seine neueste Bestreitung. Vortrag. (The Messianic Consciousness of Jesus and the most recent denial of it. A Lecture.) 1902. 26 pp. (Against Wrede.)

War Jesus Ekstatiker? (Was Jesus an ecstatic?) Tübingen, 1903. 139 pp.

Paul Wilhelm Schmidt. Die Geschichte Jesu. (The History of Jesus.) Freiburg. 1899. 175 pp. (4th impression.)

Die Geschichte Jesu. Erläutert. Mit drei Karten von Prof. K. Furrer (Zürich). (The History of Jesus. Preliminary Discussions. With three maps by Prof. K. Furrer of Zurich.) Tübingen, 1904. 414 pp.

Otto Schmiedel. Die Hauptprobleme der Leben-Jesu-Forschung. (The main Problems in the Study of the Life of Jesus.) Tübingen, 1902. 71 pp. 2nd ed., 1906.

Hermann Freiherr von Soden. Die wichtigsten Fragen im Leben Jesu. (The most important Questions about the Life of Jesus.) Vacation Lectures. Berlin, 1904. 111 pp.

Gustav Frenssen. Hilligenlei. Berlin, 1905, pp. 462-593: "Die Handschrift."("The Manuscript"—in which a Life of Jesus, written by one of the characters of the story, is given in full.)

Otto Pfleiderer. Das Urchristentum, seine Schriften und Lehren in geschichtlichem Zusammenhang beschrieben. (Primitive Christianity. Its Documents and Doctrines in their Historical Context.) 2nd ed. Berlin, 1902. Vol. i., 696 pp.

Die Entstehung des Urchristentums. (How Primitive Christianity arose.) Munich, 1905. 255 pp.

Albert Kalthoff. Das Christus-Problem. Grundlinien zu einer Sozialtheologie. (The Christ-problem. The Ground-plan of a Social Theology.) Leipzig, 1902. 87 pp.

Die Entstehung des Christentums. Neue Beiträge zum Christus-Problem. (How Christianity arose. New contributions to the Christ-problem.) Leipzig, 1904. 155 pp.

Eduard von Hartmann. Das Christentum des Neuen Testaments. (The Christianity of the New Testament.) 2nd revised edition of "Letters on the Christian Religion." Sachsa-in-the-Harz, 1905. 311 pp.

De Jonge. Jeschua. Der klassische jüdische Mann. Zerstörung des kirchlichen, Enthüllung des jüdischen Jesus-Bildes. Berlin, 1904. 112 pp. (Jeshua. The Classical Jewish Man. In which the Jewish picture of Jesus is unveiled, and the ecclesiastical picture destroyed.)

[pg 294]

Wolfgang Kirchbach. Was lehrte Jesus? Zwei Urevangelien. (What was the teaching of Jesus? Two Primitive Gospels.) Berlin, 1897. 248 pp. 2nd revised and greatly enlarged edition, 1902, 339 pp.

Albert Dulk. Der Irrgang des Lebens Jesu. In geschichtlicher Auffassung dargestellt. (The Error of the Life of Jesus. An Historical View.) 1st part, 1884, 395 pp.; 2nd part, 1885, 302 pp.

Paul de Régla. Jesus von Nazareth. German by A. Just. Leipzig, 1894. 435 pp.

Ernest Bosc. La Vie ésotérique de Jésus de Nazareth et les origines orientales du christianisme. (The secret Life of Jesus of Nazareth, and the Oriental Origins of Christianity.) Paris, 1902.

The ideal Life of Jesus of the close of the nineteenth century is the Life which Heinrich Julius Holtzmann did not write—but which can be pieced together from his commentary on the Synoptic Gospels and his New Testament Theology.[224] It is ideal because, for one thing, it is unwritten, and arises only in the idea of the reader by the aid of his own imagination, and, for another, because it is traced only in the most general outline. What Holtzmann gives us is a sketch of the public ministry, a critical examination of details, and a full account of the teaching of Jesus. He provides, therefore, the plan and the prepared building material, so that any one can carry out the construction in his own way and on his own responsibility. The cement and the mortar are not provided by Holtzmann; every one must decide for himself how he will combine the teaching and the life, and arrange the details within each.

We may recall the fact that Weisse, too, the other founder of the Marcan hypothesis, avoided writing a Life of Jesus, because the difficulty of fitting the details into the ground-plan appeared to him so great, not to say insuperable. It is just this modesty which constitutes his greatness and Holtzmann's. Thus the Marcan hypothesis ends, as it had begun, with a certain historical scepticism.[225]

[pg 295]

The subordinates, it is true, do not allow themselves to be disturbed by the change of attitude at head-quarters. They keep busily at work. That is their right, and therein consists their significance. By keeping on trying to take the positions, and constantly failing, they furnish a practical proof that the plan of operations worked out by the general staff is not capable of being carried out, and show why it is so, and what kind of new tactics will have to be evolved.

The credit of having written a life of Christ which is strictly scientific, in its own way very remarkable, and yet foredoomed to failure, belongs to Oskar Holtzmann.[226] He has complete confidence in the Marcan plan, and makes it his task to fit all the sayings of Jesus into this framework, to show "what can belong to each period of the preaching of Jesus, and what cannot." His method is to give free play to the magnetic power of the most important passages in the Marcan text, making other sayings of similar import detach themselves from their present connexion and come and group themselves round the main passages.

[pg 296]

For example, the controversy with the scribes at Jerusalem regarding the charge of doing miracles by the help of Satan (Mark iii. 22-30) belongs, according to Holtzmann, as regards content and chronology, to the same period as the controversy, in Mark vii., about the ordinances of men which results in Jesus being "obliged to take to flight"; the woes pronounced upon Chorazin, Bethsaida, and Capernaum, which now follow on the eulogy upon the Baptist (Matt. xi. 21-23), and are accordingly represented as having been spoken at the time of the sending forth of the Twelve, are drawn by the same kind of magnetic force into the neighbourhood of Mark vii., and "express very clearly the attitude of Jesus at the time of His withdrawal from the scene of His earlier ministry." The saying in Matt. vii. 6 about not giving that which is holy to the dogs or casting pearls before swine, does not belong to the Sermon on the Mount, but to the time when Jesus, after Caesarea Philippi, forbids the disciples to reveal the secret of His Messiahship to the multitude; Jesus' action in cursing the fig-tree so that it should henceforth bring no fruit to its owner, who was perhaps a poor man, is to be brought into relation with the words spoken on the evening before, with reference to the lavish expenditure involved in His anointing, "The poor ye have always with you," the point being that Jesus now, "in the clear consciousness of His approaching death, feels His own worth," and dismisses "the contingency of even the poor having to lose something for His sake" with the words "it does not matter."[227]

All these transpositions and new connexions mean, it is clear, a great deal of internal and external violence to the text.

A further service rendered by this very thorough work of Oskar Holtzmann's, is that of showing how much reading between the lines is necessary in order to construct a Life of Jesus on the basis of the Marcan hypothesis in its modern interpretation. It is thus, for instance, that the author must have acquired the knowledge that the controversy about the ordinances of purification in Mark vii. forced the people "to choose between the old and the new religion"—in which case it is no wonder that many "turned back from following Jesus."

Where are we told that there was any question of an old and a new "religion"? The disciples certainly did not think of things in this way, as is shown by their conduct at the time of His death [pg 297] and the discourses of Peter in Acts. Where do we read that the people turned away from Jesus? In Mark vii. 17 and 24 all that is said is, that Jesus left the people, and in Mark vii. 33 the same multitude is still assembled when Jesus returns from the "banishment" into which Holtzmann relegates Him.

Oskar Holtzmann declares that we cannot tell what was the size of the following which accompanied Jesus in His journey northwards, and is inclined to assume that others besides the Twelve shared His exile. The Evangelists, however, say clearly that it was only the μαθηταί, that is, the Twelve, who were with Him. The value which this special knowledge, independent of the text, has for the author, becomes evident a little farther on. After Peter's confession Jesus calls the "multitude" to Him (Mark viii. 34) and speaks to them of His sufferings and of taking up the cross and following Him. This "multitude" Holtzmann wants to make "the whole company of Jesus' followers," "to which belonged, not only the Twelve whom Jesus had formerly sent out to preach, but many others also." The knowledge drawn from outside the text is therefore required to solve a difficulty in the text.

But how did His companions in exile, the remnant of the previous multitude, themselves become a multitude, the same multitude as before? Would it not be better to admit that we do not know how, in a Gentile country, a multitude could suddenly rise out of the ground as it were, continue with Him until Mark ix. 30, and then disappear into the earth as suddenly as they came, leaving Him to pursue His journey towards Galilee and Jerusalem alone?

Another thing which Oskar Holtzmann knows is that it required a good deal of courage for Peter to hail Jesus as Messiah, since the "exile wandering about with his small following in a Gentile country" answered "so badly to the general picture which people had formed of the coming of the Messiah." He knows too, that in the moment of Peter's confession, "Christianity was complete" in the sense that "a community separate from Judaism and centring about a new ideal, then arose." This "community" frequently appears from this point onwards. There is nothing about it in the narratives, which know only the Twelve and the people.

Oskar Holtzmann's knowledge even extends to dialogues which are not reported in the Gospels. After the incident at Caesarea Philippi, the minds of the disciples were, according to him, preoccupied by two questions. "How did Jesus know that He was the Messiah?" and "What will be the future fate of this Messiah?" The Lord answered both questions. He spoke to them of His baptism, and "doubtless in close connexion with that" He told them the story of His temptation, during which He had laid down the lines which He was determined to follow as Messiah.

[pg 298]

Of the transfiguration, Oskar Holtzmann can state with confidence, "that it merely represents the inner experience of the disciples at the moment of Peter's confession." How is it then that Mark expressly dates that scene, placing it (ix. 2) six days after the discourse of Jesus about taking up the cross and following Him? The fact is that the time-indications of the text are treated as non-existent whenever the Marcan hypothesis requires an order determined by inner connexion. The statement of Luke that the transfiguration took place eight days after, is dismissed in the remark "the motive of this indication of time is doubtless to be found in the use of the Gospel narratives for reading in public worship; the idea was that the section about the transfiguration should be read on the Sunday following that on which the confession of Peter formed the lesson." Where did Oskar Holtzmann suddenly discover this information about the order of the "Sunday lessons" at the time when Luke's Gospel was written?

It was doubtless from the same private source of information that the author derived his knowledge regarding the gradual development of the thought of the Passion in the consciousness of Jesus. "After the confession of Peter at Caesarea Philippi," he explains, "Jesus' death became for Him only the necessary point of transition to the glory beyond. In the discourse of Jesus to which the request of Salome gave occasion, the death of Jesus already appears as the means of saving many from death, because His death makes possible the coming of the Kingdom of God. At the institution of the Supper, Jesus regards His imminent death as the meritorious deed by which the blessings of the New Covenant, the forgiveness of sins and victory over sin, are permanently secured to His 'community.' We see Jesus constantly becoming more and more at home with the idea of His death and constantly giving it a deeper interpretation."

Any one who is less skilled in reading the thoughts of Jesus, and more simple and natural in his reading of the text of Mark, cannot fail to observe that Jesus speaks in Mark x. 45 of His death as an expiation, not as a means of saving others from death, and that at the Lord's Supper there was no reference to His "community," but only to the inexplicable "many," which is also the word in Mark x. 45. We ought to admit freely that we do not know what the thoughts of Jesus about His death were at the time of the first prediction of the Passion after Peter's confession; and to be on our guard against the "original sin" of theology, that of exalting the argument from silence, when it happens to be useful, to the rank of positive realities.

Is there not a certain irony in the fact that the application of "natural" psychology to the explanation of the thoughts of Jesus compels the assumption of supra-historical private information [pg 299] such as this? Bahrdt and Venturini hardly read more subjective interpretations into the text than many modern Lives of Jesus; and the hypothesis of the secret society, which after all did recognise and do justice to the inexplicability from an external standpoint of the relation of events and of the conduct of Jesus, was in many respects more historical than the psychological links of connexion which our modernising historians discover without having any foundation for them in the text.

In the end this supplementary knowledge destroys the historicity of the simplest sections. Oskar Holtzmann ventures to conjecture that the healing of the blind man at Jericho "is to be understood as a symbolical representation of the conversion of Zacchaeus," which, of course, is found only in Luke. Here then the defender of the Marcan hypothesis rejects the incident by which the Evangelist explains the enthusiasm of the entry into Jerusalem, not to mention that Luke tells us nothing whatever about a conversion of Zacchaeus, but only that Jesus was invited to his house and graciously accepted the invitation.

It would be something if this almost Alexandrian symbolical exegesis contributed in some way to the removal of difficulties and to the solution of the main question, that, namely, of the present or future Messiah, the present or future Kingdom. Oskar Holtzmann lays great stress upon the eschatological character of the preaching of Jesus regarding the Kingdom, and assumes that, at least at the beginning, it would not have been natural for His hearers to understand that Jesus, the herald of the Messiah, was Himself the Messiah. Nevertheless, he is of opinion that, in a certain sense, the presence of Jesus implied the presence of the Kingdom, that Peter and the rest of the disciples, advancing beyond the ideas of the multitude, recognised Him as Messiah, that this recognition ought to have been possible for the people also, and, in that case, would have been "the strongest incentive to abandon evil ways," and "that Jesus at the time of His entry into Jerusalem seems to have felt that in Isa. lxii. 11[228] there was a direct command not to withhold the knowledge of His Messiahship from the inhabitants of Jerusalem."

But if Jesus made a Messianic entry He must thereafter have given Himself out as Messiah, and the whole controversy would necessarily have turned upon this claim. This, however, was not the case. According to Holtzmann, all that the hearers could make out of that crucial question for the Messiahship in Mark xii. 35-37 was only "that Jesus clearly showed from the Scriptures that the Messiah was not in reality the son of David."[229]

[pg 300]

But how was it that the Messianic enthusiasm on the part of the people did not lead to a Messianic controversy, in spite of the fact that Jesus "from the first came forward in Jerusalem as Messiah"? This difficulty O. Holtzmann seems to be trying to provide against when he remarks in a footnote: "We have no evidence that Jesus, even during the last sojourn in Jerusalem, was recognised as Messiah except by those who belonged to the inner circle of disciples. The repetition by the children of the acclamations of the disciples (Matt. xxi. 15 and 16) can hardly be considered of much importance in this connexion." According to this, Jesus entered Jerusalem as Messiah, but except for the disciples and a few children no one recognised His entry as having a Messianic significance! But Mark states that many spread their garments upon the way, and others plucked down branches from the trees and strewed them in the way, and that those that went before and those that followed after, cried "Hosanna!" The Marcan narrative must therefore be kept out of sight for the moment in order that the Life of Jesus as conceived by the modern Marcan hypothesis may not be endangered.

We should not, however, regard the evidence of supernatural knowledge and the self-contradictions of this Life of Jesus as a matter for censure, but rather as a proof of the merits of O. Holtzmann's work.[230] He has written the last large-scale Life of Jesus, the only one which the Marcan hypothesis has produced, and aims at providing a scientific basis for the assumptions which the general lines of that hypothesis compel him to make; and in [pg 301] this process it becomes clearly apparent that the connexion of events can only be carried through at the decisive passages by violent treatment, or even by rejection of the Marcan text in the interests of the Marcan hypothesis.

These merits do not belong in the same measure to the other modern Lives of Jesus, which follow more or less the same lines. They are short sketches, in some cases based on lectures, and their brevity makes them perhaps more lively and convincing than Holtzmann's work; but they take for granted just what he felt it necessary to prove. P. W. Schmidt's[231] *Geschichte Jesu* (1899), which as a work of literary art has few rivals among theological works of recent years, confines itself to pure narrative. The volume of prolegomena which appeared in 1904, and is intended to exhibit the foundations of the narrative, treats of the sources, of the Kingdom of God, of the Son of Man, and of the Law. It makes the most of the weakening of the eschatological standpoint which is manifested in the second edition of Johannes Weiss's "Preaching of Jesus," but it does not give sufficient prominence to the difficulties of reconstructing the public ministry of Jesus.

Neither Otto Schmiedel's "The Principal Problems of the Study of the Life of Jesus," nor von Soden's "Vacation Lectures" on "The Principal Questions in the Life of Jesus" fulfils the promise of its title.[232] They both aim rather at solving new problems proposed by themselves than at restating the old ones and adding new. They hope to meet the views of Johannes Weiss by strongly emphasising the eschatology, and think they can escape the critical scepticism of writers like Volkmar and Brand by assuming an "Ur-Markus." Their view is, therefore, that with a few modifications dictated by the eschatological and sceptical school, the traditional conception of the Life of Jesus is still tenable, whereas it is just the a priori presuppositions of this conception, hitherto held to be self-evident, which constitute the main problems.

[pg 302]

"It is self-evident," says von Soden in one passage, "in view of the inner connexion in which the Kingdom of God and the Messiah stood in the thoughts of the people ... that in all classes the question must have been discussed, so that Jesus could not permanently have avoided their question, 'What of the Messiah? Art thou not He?' " Where, in the Synoptics, is there a word to show that this is "self-evident"? When the disciples in Mark viii. tell Jesus "whom men held Him to be," none of them suggests that any one had been tempted to regard Him as the Messiah. And that was shortly before Jesus set out for Jerusalem.

From the day when the envoys of the Scribes from Jerusalem first appeared in the north, the easily influenced Galilaean multitude began, according to von Soden, "to waver." How does he know that the Galilaeans were easily influenced? How does he know they "wavered"? The Gospels tell us neither one nor the other. The demand for a sign was, to quote von Soden again, a demand for a proof of His Messiahship. "Yet another indication," adds the author, "that later Christianity, in putting so high a value on the miracles of Jesus as a proof of His Messiahship, departed widely from the thoughts of Jesus."

Before levelling reproaches of this kind against later Christianity, it would be well to point to some passage of Mark or Matthew in which there is mention of a demand for a sign as a proof of His Messiahship.

When the appearance of Jesus in the south—we are still following von Soden—aroused the Messianic expectations of the people, as they had formerly been aroused in His native country, "they once more failed to understand the correction of them which Jesus had made by the manner of His entry and His conduct in Jerusalem." They are unable to understand this "transvaluation of values," and as often as the impression made by His personality suggested the thought that He was the Messiah, they became doubtful again. Wherein consisted the correction of the Messianic expectation given at the triumphal entry? Was it that He rode upon an ass? Would it not be better if modern historical theology, instead of always making the people "grow doubtful," were to grow a little doubtful of itself, and begin to look for the evidence of that "transvaluation of values" which, according to them, the contemporaries of Jesus were not able to follow?

Von Soden also possesses special information about the "peculiar history of the origin" of the Messianic consciousness of Jesus. He knows that it was subsidiary to a primary general religious consciousness of Sonship. The rise of this Messianic consciousness implies, in its turn, the "transformation of the conception of the Kingdom of God, and explains how in the mind of Jesus this conception was both present and future." The greatness [pg 303] of Jesus is, he thinks, to be found in the fact that for Him this Kingdom of God was only a "limiting conception"—the ultimate goal of a gradual process of approximation. "To the question whether it was to be realised here or in the beyond Jesus would have answered, as He answered a similar question, 'That, no man knoweth; no, not the Son.' "

As if He had not answered that question in the petition "Thy Kingdom come"—supposing that such a question could ever have occurred to a contemporary—in the sense that the Kingdom was to pass from the beyond into the present!

This modern historical theology will not allow Jesus to have formed a "theory" to explain His thoughts about His passion. "For Him the certainty was amply sufficient; 'My death will effect what My life has not been able to accomplish.'"

Is there then no theory implied in the saying about the "ransom for many," and in that about "My blood which is shed for many for the forgiveness of sins," although Jesus does not explain it? How does von Soden know what was "amply sufficient" for Jesus or what was not?

Otto Schmiedel goes so far as to deny that Jesus gave distinct expression to an expectation of suffering; the most He can have done—and this is only a "perhaps"—is to have hinted at it in His discourses.

In strong contrast with this confidence in committing themselves to historical conjectures stands the scepticism with which von Soden and Schmiedel approach the Gospels. "It is at once evident," says Schmiedel, "that the great groups of discourses in Matthew, such as the Sermon on the Mount, the Seven Parables of the Kingdom, and so forth, were not arranged in this order in the source (the *Logia*), still less by Jesus Himself. The order is, doubtless, due to the Evangelist. But what is the answer to the question, 'On what grounds is this "at once" clear?'"[233]

Von Soden's pronouncement is even more radical. "In the composition of the discourses," he says, "no regard is paid in Matthew, any more than in John, to the supposed audience, or to the point of time in the life of Jesus to which they are attributed." As early as the Sermon on the Mount we find references to persecutions, and warnings against false prophets. Similarly, in the charge to the Twelve, there are also warnings, which undoubtedly [pg 304] belong to a later time. Intimate sayings, evidently intended for the inner circle of disciples, have the widest publicity given to them.

But why should whatever is incomprehensible to us be unhistorical? Would it not be better simply to admit that we do not understand certain connexions of ideas and turns of expression in the discourses of Jesus?

But instead even of making an analytical examination of the apparent connexions, and stating them as problems, the discourses of Jesus and the sections of the Gospels are tricked out with ingenious headings which have nothing to do with them. Thus, for instance, von Soden heads the Beatitudes (Matt. v. 3-12), "What Jesus brings to men," the following verses (Matt. v. 13-16), "What He makes of men." P. W. Schmidt, in his "History of Jesus," shows himself a past master in this art. "The rights of the wife" is the title of the dialogue about divorce, as if the question at stake had been for Jesus the equality of the sexes, and not simply and solely the sanctity of marriage. "Sunshine for the children" is his heading for the scene where Jesus takes the children in His arms—as if the purpose of Jesus had been to protest against severity in the upbringing of children. Again, he brings together the stories of the man who must first bury his father, of the rich young man, of the dispute about precedence, of Zacchaeus, and others which have equally little connexion under the heading "Discipline for Jesus' followers." These often brilliant creations of artificial connexions of thought give a curious attractiveness to the works of Schmidt and von Soden. The latter's survey of the Gospels is a really delightful performance. But this kind of thing is not consistent with pure objective history.

Disposing in this lofty fashion of the connexion of events, Schmiedel and von Soden do not find it difficult to distinguish between Mark and "Ur-Markus"; that is, to retain just so much of the Gospel as will fit in to their construction. Schmiedel feels sure that Mark was a skilful writer, and that the redactor was "a Christian of Pauline sympathies." According to "Ur-Markus," to which Mark iv. 33 belongs, the Lord speaks in parables in order that the people may understand Him the better; "it was only by the redactor that the Pauline theory about hardening their hearts (Rom. ix.-xi.) was interpolated, in Mark iv. 10 ff., and the meaning of Mark iv. 33 was thus obscured."

It is high time that instead of merely asserting Pauline influences in Mark some proof of the assertion should be given. What kind of appearance would Mark have presented if it had really passed through the hands of a Pauline Christian?

Von Soden's analysis is no less confident. The three outstanding miracles, the stilling of the storm, the casting out of the legion of devils, the overcoming of death (Mark iv. 35-v. 43), the [pg 305] romantically told story of the death of the Baptist (Mark vi. 17-29), the story of the feeding of the multitudes in the desert, of Jesus' walking on the water, and of the transfiguration upon an high mountain, and the healing of the lunatic boy—all these are dashed in with a broad brush, and offer many analogies to Old Testament stories, and some suggestions of Pauline conceptions, and reflections of experiences of individual believers and of the Christian community. "All these passages were, doubtless, first written down by the compiler of our Gospel."

But how can Schmiedel and von Soden fail to see that they are heading straight for Bruno Bauer's position? They assert that there is no distinction of principle between the way in which the Johannine and the Synoptic discourses are composed: the recognition of this was Bruno Bauer's starting-point. They propose to find experiences of the Christian community and Pauline teaching reflected in the Gospel of Mark; Bruno Bauer asserted the same. The only difference is that he was consistent, and extended his criticism to those portions of the Gospel which do not present the stumbling-block of the supernatural. Why should these not also contain the theology and the experiences of the community transformed into history? Is it only because they remain within the limits of the natural?

The real difficulty consists in the fact that all the passages which von Soden ascribes to the redactor stand, in spite of their mythical colouring, in a closely-knit historical connexion; in fact, the historical connexion is nowhere so close. How can any one cut out the feeding of the multitudes and the transfiguration as narratives of secondary origin without destroying the whole of the historical fabric of the Gospel of Mark? Or was it the redactor who created the plan of the Gospel of Mark, as von Soden seems to imply?[234]

[pg 306]

But in that case how can a modern Life of Jesus be founded on the Marcan plan? How much of Mark is, in the end, historical? Why should not Peter's confession at Caesarea Philippi have been derived from the theology of the primitive Church, just as well as the transfiguration? The only difference is that the incident at Caesarea Philippi is more within the limits of the possible, whereas the scene upon the mountain has a supernatural colouring. But is the incident at Philippi so entirely natural? Whence does Peter know that Jesus is the Messiah?

This semi-scepticism is therefore quite unjustifiable, since in Mark natural and supernatural both stand in an equally good and close historical connexion. Either, then, one must be completely sceptical like Bruno Bauer, and challenge without exception all the facts and connexions of events asserted by Mark; or, if one means to found an historical Life of Jesus upon Mark, one must take the Gospel as a whole because of the plan which runs right through it, accepting it as historical and then endeavouring to explain why certain narratives, like the feeding of the multitude and the transfiguration, are bathed in a supernatural light, and what is the historical basis which underlies them. A division between the natural and supernatural in Mark is purely arbitrary, because the supernatural is an essential part of the history. The mere fact that he has not adopted the mythical material of the childhood stories and the post-resurrection scenes ought to have been accepted as evidence that the supernatural material which he does embody belongs to a category of its own and cannot be simply rejected as due to the invention of the primitive Christian community. It must belong in some way to the original tradition.

Oskar Holtzmann realises that to a certain extent. According to him Mark is a writer "who embodied the materials which he received from the tradition more faithfully than discriminatingly." "That which was related as a symbol of inner events, he takes as history—in the case, for example, of the temptation, the walking on the sea, the transfiguration of Jesus." "Again in other cases he has made a remarkable occurrence into a supernatural miracle, [pg 307] as in the case of the feeding of the multitude, where Jesus' courageous love and ready organising skill overcame a momentary difficulty, whereas the Evangelist represents it as an amazing miracle of Divine omnipotence."

Oskar Holtzmann is thus more cautious than von Soden. He is inclined to see in the material which he wishes to exclude from the history, not so much inventions of the Church as mistaken shaping of history by Mark, and in this way he gets back to genuine old-fashioned rationalism. In the feeding of the multitude Jesus showed "the confidence of a courageous housewife who knows how to provide skilfully for a great crowd of children from small resources." Perhaps in a future work Oskar Holtzmann will be less reserved, not for the sake of theology, but of national well-being, and will inform his contemporaries what kind of domestic economy it was which made it possible for the Lord to satisfy with five loaves and two fishes several thousand hungry men.

Modern historical theology, therefore, with its three-quarters scepticism, is left at last with only a torn and tattered Gospel of Mark in its hands. One would naturally suppose that these preliminary operations upon the source would lead to the production of a Life of Jesus of a similarly fragmentary character. Nothing of the kind. The outline is still the same as in Schenkel's day, and the confidence with which the construction is carried out is not less complete. Only the catch-words with which the narrative is enlivened have been changed, being now taken in part from Nietzsche. The liberal Jesus has given place to the Germanic Jesus. This is a figure which has as little to do with the Marcan hypothesis as the "liberal" Jesus had which preceded it; otherwise it could not so easily have survived the downfall of the Gospel of Mark as an historical source. It is evident, therefore, that this professedly historical Jesus is not a purely historical figure, but one which has been artificially transplanted into history. As formerly in Renan the romantic spirit created the personality of Jesus in its own image, so at the present day the Germanic spirit is making a Jesus after its own likeness. What is admitted as historic is just what the Spirit of the time can take out of the records in order to assimilate it to itself and bring out of it a living form.

Frenssen betrays the secret of his teachers when in *Hilligenlei* he confidently superscribes the narrative drawn from the "latest critical investigations" with the title "The Life of the Saviour portrayed according to German research as the basis for a spiritual re-birth of the German nation."[235]

[pg 308]

As a matter of fact the Life of Jesus of the "Manuscript"[236] is unsatisfactory both scientifically and artistically, just because it aims at being at once scientific and artistic. If only Frenssen, with his strongly life-accepting instinct, which gives to his thinking, at least in his earliest writings where he reveals himself without artificiality, such a wonderful simplicity and force, had dared to read his Jesus boldly from the original records, without following modern historical theology in all its meanderings! He would have been able to force his way through the underwood well enough if only he had been content to break the branches that got in his way, instead of always waiting until some one went in front to disentwine them for him. The dependence to which he surrenders himself is really distressing. In reading almost every paragraph one can tell whether Kai Jans was looking, as he wrote it, into Oskar Holtzmann or P. W. Schmidt or von Soden. Frenssen resigns the dramatic scene of the healing of the blind man at Jericho. Why? Because at this point he was listening to Holtzmann, who proposes to regard the healing of the blind man as only a symbolical representation of the "conversion of Zacchaeus." Frenssen's masters have robbed him of all creative spontaneity. He does not permit himself to discover *motifs* for himself, but confines himself to working over and treating in cruder colours those which he finds in his teachers.

And since he cannot veil his assumptions in the cautious, carefully modulated language of the theologians, the faults of the modern treatment of the life of Jesus appear in him exaggerated an hundredfold. The violent dislocation of narratives from their connexion, and the forcing upon them of a modern interpretation, becomes a mania with the writer and a torture to the reader. The range of knowledge not drawn from the text is infinitely increased. Kai Jans sees Jesus after the temptation cowering beneath the brow of the hill "a poor lonely man, torn by fearful doubts, a man in the deepest distress." He knows too that there was often great danger that Jesus would "betray the 'Father in heaven' and go back to His village to take up His handicraft again, but now as a man with a torn and distracted soul and a conscience tortured by the gnawings of remorse."

The pupil is not content, as his teachers had been, merely to make the people sometimes believe in Jesus and sometimes doubt [pg 309] Him; he makes the enthusiastic earthly Messianic belief of the people "tug and tear" at Jesus Himself. Sometimes one is tempted to ask whether the author in his zeal "to use conscientiously the results of the whole range of scientific criticism" has not forgotten the main thing, the study of the Gospels themselves.

And is all this science supposed to be new?[237] Is this picture of Jesus really the outcome of the latest criticism? Has it not been in existence since the beginning of the 'forties, since Weisse's criticism of the Gospel history? Is it not in principle the same as Renan's, only that Germanic lapses of taste here take the place of Gallic, and "German art for German people,"[238] here quite out of place, has done its best to remove from the picture every trace of fidelity?

Kai Jans' "Manuscript" represents the limit of the process of diminishing the personality of Jesus. Weisse left Him still some greatness, something unexplained, and did not venture to apply to everything the petty standards of inquisitive modern psychology. In the 'sixties psychology became more confident and Jesus smaller; at the close of the century the confidence of psychology is at its greatest and the figure of Jesus at its smallest—so small, that Frenssen ventures to let His life be projected and written by one who is in the midst of a love affair!

This human life of Jesus is to be "heart-stirring" from beginning to end, and "in no respect to go beyond human standards"! And this Jesus who "racks His brains and shapes His plans" is to contribute to bring about a re-birth of the German people. How could He? He is Himself only a phantom created by the Germanic mind in pursuit of a religious will-o'-the-wisp.

It is possible, however, to do injustice to Frenssen's presentation, and to the whole of the confident, unconsciously modernising criticism of which he here acts as the mouthpiece. These writers have the great merit of having brought certain cultured circles nearer to Jesus and made them more sympathetic towards Him. Their fault lies in their confidence, which has blinded them to what Jesus is and is not, what He can and cannot do, so that in the end they fail to understand "the signs of the times" either as historians or as men of the present.

[pg 310]

If the Jesus who owes His birth to the Marcan hypothesis and modern psychology were capable of regenerating the world He would have done it long ago, for He is nearly sixty years old and his latest portraits are much less life-like than those drawn by Weisse, Schenkel, and Renan, or by Keim, the most brilliant painter of them all.

For the last ten years modern historical theology has more and more adapted itself to the needs of the man in the street. More and more, even in the best class of works, it makes use of attractive head-lines as a means of presenting its results in a lively form to the masses. Intoxicated with its own ingenuity in inventing these, it becomes more and more confident in its cause, and has come to believe that the world's salvation depends in no small measure upon the spreading of its own "assured results" broad-cast among the people. It is time that it should begin to doubt itself, to doubt its "historical" Jesus, to doubt the confidence with which it has looked to its own construction for the moral and religious regeneration of our time. Its Jesus is not alive, however Germanic they may make Him.

It was no accident that the chief priest of "German art for German people" found himself at one with the modern theologians and offered them his alliance. Since the 'sixties the critical study of the Life of Jesus in Germany has been unconsciously under the influence of an imposing modern-religious nationalism in art. It has been deflected by it as by an underground magnetic current. It was in vain that a few purely historical investigators uplifted their voices in protest. The process had to work itself out. For historical criticism had become, in the hands of most of those who practised it, a secret struggle to reconcile the Germanic religious spirit with the Spirit of Jesus of Nazareth.[239] It was concerned for the religious interests of the present. Therefore its error had a kind of greatness, it was in fact the greatest thing about it; and the severity with which the pure historian treats it is in proportion to his respect for its spirit. For this German critical study of the Life of Jesus is an essential part of German religion. As of old Jacob wrestled with the angel, so German theology wrestles with Jesus of Nazareth and will not let Him go until

He bless it—that is, until He will consent to serve it and will suffer Himself to be drawn by the Germanic spirit into the midst of our time and our civilisation. But when the day breaks, the wrestler must let Him go. He will not cross the ford with us. Jesus of Nazareth will not suffer Himself to be modernised. As an historic figure He refuses to be detached from His own time. He has no answer [pg 311] for the question, "Tell us Thy name in our speech and for our day!" But He does bless those who have wrestled with Him, so that, though they cannot take Him with them, yet, like men who have seen God face to face and received strength in their souls, they go on their way with renewed courage, ready to do battle with the world and its powers.

But the historic Jesus and the Germanic spirit cannot be brought together except by an act of historic violence which in the end injures both religion and history. A time will come when our theology, with its pride in its historical character, will get rid of its rationalistic bias. This bias leads it to project back into history what belongs to our own time, the eager struggle of the modern religious spirit with the Spirit of Jesus, and seek in history justification and authority for its beginning. The consequence is that it creates the historical Jesus in its own image, so that it is not the modern spirit influenced by the Spirit of Jesus, but the Jesus of Nazareth constructed by modern historical theology, that is set to work upon our race.

Therefore both the theology and its picture of Jesus are poor and weak. Its Jesus, because He has been measured by the petty standard of the modern man, at variance with himself, not to say of the modern candidate in theology who has made shipwreck; the theologians themselves, because instead of seeking, for themselves and others, how they may best bring the Spirit of Jesus in living power into our world, they keep continually forging new portraits of the historical Jesus, and think they have accomplished something great when they have drawn an Oh! of astonishment from the multitude, such as the crowds of a great city emit on catching sight of a new advertisement in coloured lights.

Anyone who, admiring the force and authority of genuine rationalism, has got rid of the naïve self-satisfaction of modern theology, which is in essence only the degenerate offspring of rationalism with a tincture of history, rejoices in the feebleness and smallness of its professedly historical Jesus, rejoices in all those who are beginning to doubt the truth of this portrait, rejoices in the over-severity with which it is attacked, rejoices to take a share in its destruction.

Those who have begun to doubt are many, but most of them only make known their doubts by their silence. There is one, however, who has spoken out, and one of the greatest—Otto Pfleiderer.[240]

In the first edition of his *Urchristentum*, published in 1887, he still shared the current conceptions and constructions, except that he held the credibility of Mark to be more affected than was [pg 312] usually supposed by hypothetical Pauline influences. In the second edition[241] his positive knowledge has been ground down in the struggle with the sceptics—it is Brandt who has especially affected him—and with the partisans of eschatology. This is the first advance-guard action of modern theology coming into touch with the troops of Reimarus and Bruno Bauer.

Pfleiderer accepts the purely eschatological conception of the Kingdom of God and holds also that the ethics of Jesus were wholly conditioned by eschatology. But in regard to the question of the Messiahship of Jesus he takes his stand with the sceptics. He rejects the hypothesis of a

Messiah who, as being a "spiritual Messiah," conceals His claim, but on the other hand, he cannot accept the eschatological Son-of-Man Messiahship having reference to the future, which the eschatological school finds in the utterances of Jesus, since it implies prophecies of His suffering, death, and resurrection which criticism cannot admit. "Instead of finding the explanation of how the Messianic title arose in the reflections of Jesus about the death which lay before Him," he is inclined to find it "rather in the reflection of the Christian community upon the catastrophic death and exaltation of its Lord after this had actually taken place."

Even the Marcan narrative is not history. The scepticism in regard to the main source, with which writers like Oskar Holtzmann, Schmiedel, and von Soden conduct a kind of intellectual flirtation, is here erected into a principle. "It must be recognised," says Pfleiderer, "that in respect of the recasting of the history under theological influences, the whole of our Gospels stand in principle on the same footing. The distinction between Mark, the other two Synoptists, and John is only relative—a distinction of degree corresponding to different stages of theological reflection and the development of the ecclesiastical consciousness." If only Bruno Bauer could have lived to see this triumph of his opinions!

Pfleiderer, however, is conscious that scepticism, too, has its difficulties. He wishes, indeed, to reject the confession of Jesus before the Sanhedrin "because its historicity is not well established (none of the disciples were present to hear it, and the apocalyptic prophecy which is added, Mark xiv. 62, is certainly derived from the ideas of the primitive Church)"; on the other hand, he is inclined to admit as possibilities—though marking them with a note of interrogation—that Jesus may have accepted the homage of the Passover pilgrims, and that the controversy with the Scribes [pg 313] about the Son of David had some kind of reference to Jesus Himself.

On the other hand, he takes it for granted that Jesus did not prophesy His death, on the ground that the arrest, trial, and betrayal must have lain outside all possibility of calculation even for Him. All these, he thinks, came upon Jesus quite unexpectedly. The only thing that He might have apprehended was "an attack by hired assassins," and it is to this that He refers in the saying about the two swords in Luke xxii. 36 and 38, seeing that two swords would have sufficed as a protection against such an attack as that, though hardly for anything further. When, however, he remarks in this connexion that "this has been constantly overlooked" in the romances dealing with the Life of Jesus, he does injustice to Bahrdt and Venturini, since according to them the chief concern of the secret society in the later period of the life of Jesus was to protect Jesus from the assassination with which He was menaced, and to secure His formal arrest and trial by the Sanhedrin. Their view of the historical situation is therefore identical with Pfleiderer's, viz. that assassination was possible, but that administrative action was unexpected and is inexplicable.

But how is this Jesus to be connected with primitive Christianity? How did the primitive Church's belief in the Messiahship of Jesus arise? To that question Pfleiderer can give no other answer than that of Volkmar and Brandt, that is to say, none. He laboriously brings together wood, straw, and stubble, but where he gets the fire from to kindle the whole into the ardent faith of primitive Christianity he is unable to make clear.

According to Albert Kalthoff,[242] the fire lighted itself—Christianity arose—by spontaneous combustion, when the inflammable material, religious and social, which had collected together in the Roman Empire, came in contact with the Jewish Messianic expectations. Jesus of Nazareth never existed; and even supposing He had been one of the numerous Jewish Messiahs who were put to death by crucifixion, He certainly did not found Christianity. The story of Jesus which lies before us in the Gospels is in reality only the story of the way in which the picture of Christ arose, that is to say, the story of the growth of the Christian community. There is therefore no problem of the Life of Jesus, but only a problem of the Christ.

[pg 314]

Kalthoff has not indeed always been so negative. When in the year 1880 he gave a series of lectures on the Life of Jesus he felt himself justified "in taking as his basis without further argument the generally accepted results of modern theology." Afterwards he became so completely doubtful about the Christ after the flesh whom he had at that time depicted before his hearers that he wished to exclude Him even from the register of theological literature, and omitted to enter these lectures in the list of his writings, although they had appeared in print.[243]

His quarrel with the historical Jesus of modern theology was that he could find no connecting link between the Life of Jesus constructed by the latter and primitive Christianity. Modern theology, he remarks in one passage, with great justice, finds itself obliged to assume, at the point where the history of the Church begins, "an immediate declension from, and falsification of, a pure original principle," and that in so doing "it is deserting the recognised methods of historical science." If then we cannot trace the path from its beginning onwards, we had better try to work backwards, endeavouring first to define in the theology of the primitive Church the values which we shall look to find again in the Life of Jesus.

In that he is right. Modern historical theology will not have refuted him until it has explained how Christianity arose out of the life of Jesus without calling in that theory of an initial "Fall" of which Harnack, Wernle, and all the rest make use. Until this modern theology has made it in some measure intelligible how, under the influence of the Jewish Messiah-sect, in the twinkling of an eye, in every direction at once, Graeco-Roman popular Christianity arose; until at least it has described the popular Christianity of the first three generations, it must concede to all hypotheses which fairly face this problem and endeavour to solve it their formal right of existence.

The criticism which Kalthoff directs against the "positive" accounts of the Life of Jesus is, in part, very much to the point. "Jesus," he says in one place, "has been made the receptacle into which every theologian pours his own ideas." He rightly remarks that if we follow "the Christ" backwards from the Epistles and Gospels of the New Testament right to the apocalyptic vision of Daniel, we always find in Him superhuman traits alongside of the human. "Never and nowhere," he insists, "is He that which critical theology has endeavoured to make out of Him, a purely natural man, an indivisible historical unit." "The title of 'Christ' had been raised by the Messianic apocalyptic writings so completely into the sphere of the heroic that it had become impossible to [pg 315] apply it to a mere historical man." Bruno Bauer had urged the same considerations upon the theology of his time, declaring it to be unthinkable that a man could have arisen among the Jews and declared "I am the Messiah."

But the unfortunate thing is that Kalthoff has not worked through Bruno Bauer's criticism, and does not appear to assume it as a basis, but remains standing half-way instead of thinking the questions through to the end as that keen critic did. According to Kalthoff it would appear that, year in year out, there was a constant succession of Messianic disturbances among the Jews and of crucified claimants of the Messiahship. "There had been many a 'Christ,'" he says in one place, "before there was any question of a Jesus in connexion with this title."

How does Kalthoff know that? If he had fairly considered and felt the force of Bruno Bauer's arguments, he would never have ventured on this assertion; he would have learned that it is not only historically unproved, but intrinsically impossible.

But Kalthoff was in far too great a hurry to present to his readers a description of the growth of Christianity, and therewith of the picture of the Christ, to absorb thoroughly the criticism of his great predecessor. He soon leads his reader away from the high road of criticism into a morass of speculation, in order to arrive by a short cut at Graeco-Roman primitive Christianity. But the trouble is that while the guide walks lightly and safely, the ordinary man, weighed down by the pressure of historical considerations, sinks to rise no more.

The conjectural argument which Kalthoff follows out is in itself acute, and forms a suitable pendant to Bauer's reconstruction of the course of events. Bauer proposed to derive Christianity from the Graeco-Roman philosophy; Kalthoff, recognising that the origin of popular Christianity constitutes the main question, takes as his starting-point the social movements of the time.

In the Roman Empire, so runs his argument, among the oppressed masses of the slaves and the populace, eruptive forces were concentrated under high tension. A communistic movement arose, to which the influence of the Jewish element in the proletariat gave a Messianic-Apocalyptic colouring. The Jewish synagogue influenced Roman social conditions so that "the crude social ferment at work in the Roman Empire amalgamated itself with the religious and philosophical forces of the time to form the new Christian social movement." Early Christian writers had learned in the synagogue to construct "personifications." The whole Late-Jewish literature rests upon this principle. Thus "the Christ" became the ideal hero of the Christian community, "from the socio-religious standpoint the figure of Christ is the [pg 316] sublimated religious expression for the sum of the social and ethical forces which were at work at a certain period." The Lord's Supper was the memorial feast of this ideal hero.

"As the Christ to whose Parousia the community looks forward this Hero-god of the community bears within Himself the capacity for expansion into the God of the universe, into the Christ of the Church, who is identical in essential nature with God the Father. Thus the belief in the Christ brought the Messianic hope of the future into the minds of the masses, who had already a certain organisation, and by directing their thoughts towards the future it won all those who were sick of the past and despairing about the present."

The death and resurrection of Jesus represent experiences of the community. "For a Jew crucified under Pontius Pilate there was certainly no resurrection. All that is possible is a vague hypothesis of a vision lacking all historical reality, or an escape into the vaguenesses of theological phraseology. But for the Christian community the resurrection was something real, a matter of fact. For the community as such was not annihilated in that persecution: it drew from it, rather, new strength and life."

But what about the foundations of this imposing structure?

For what he has to tell us about the condition of the Roman Empire and the social organisation of the proletariat in the time of Trajan—for it was then that the Church first came out into the light—we may leave the responsibility with Kalthoff. But we must inquire more closely how he brings the Jewish apocalyptic into contact with the Roman proletariat.

Communism, he says, was common to both. It was the bond which united the apocalyptic "other-worldliness" with reality. The only difficulty is that Kalthoff omits to produce any proof out of the Jewish apocalypses that communism was "the fundamental economic idea of the apocalyptic writers." He operates from the first with a special preparation of apocalyptic thought, of a socialistic or Hellenistic character. Messianism is supposed to have taken its rise from the Deuteronomic reform as "a social theory which strives to realise itself in practice." The apocalyptic of Daniel arose, according to him, under Platonic influence. "The figure of the Messiah thus became a human figure; it lost its specifically Jewish traits." He is the heavenly proto-typal ideal man. Along with this thought, and similarly derived from Plato, the conception of immortality makes its appearance in apocalyptic.[244] This Platonic apocalyptic never had any existence, or at least, [pg 317] to speak with the utmost possible caution, its existence must not be asserted in the absence of all proof.

But, supposing it were admitted that Jewish apocalyptic had some affinity for the Hellenic world, that it was Platonic and communistic, how are we to explain the fact that the Gospels, which describe the genesis of Christ and Christianity, imply a Galilaean and not a Roman environment?

As a matter of fact, Kalthoff says, they do imply a Roman environment. The scene of the Gospel history is laid in Palestine, but it is drawn in Rome. The agrarian conditions implied in the narratives and parables are Roman. A vineyard with a wine-press of its own could only be found, according to Kalthoff, on the large Roman estates. So, too, the legal conditions. The right of the creditor to sell the debtor, with his wife and children, is a feature of Roman, not of Jewish law.

Peter everywhere symbolises the Church at Rome. The confession of Peter had to be transferred to Caesarea Philippi because this town, "as the seat of the Roman administration," symbolised for Palestine the political presence of Rome.

The woman with the issue was perhaps Poppaea Sabina, the wife of Nero, "who in view of her strong leaning towards Judaism might well be described in the symbolical style of the apocalyptic writings as the woman who touched the hem of Jesus' garment."

The story of the unfaithful steward alludes to Pope Callixtus, who, when the slave of a Christian in high position, was condemned to the mines for the crime of embezzlement; that of the woman who was a sinner refers to Marcia, the powerful mistress of Commodus, at whose intercession Callixtus was released, to be advanced soon afterwards to the bishopric of Rome. "These two narratives, therefore," Kalthoff suggests, "which very clearly allude to events well known at that time, and doubtless much discussed in the Christian community, were admitted into the Gospel to express the views of the Church regarding the life-story of a Roman bishop which had run its course under the eyes of the community, and thereby to give to the events themselves the Church's sanction and interpretation."

Kalthoff does not, unfortunately, mention whether this is a case of simple, ingenuous, or of conscious, didactic, Early Christian imagination.

That kind of criticism is a casting out of Satan by the aid of Beelzebub. If he was going to invent on this scale, Kalthoff need not have found any difficulty in accepting the figure of Jesus evolved by modern theology. One feels annoyed with him because, while his thesis is ingenious, and, as against "modern theology" has a considerable measure of justification, he has worked it out in so uninteresting a fashion. He has no one but himself to blame [pg 318] for the fact that instead of leading to the right explanation, it only introduced a wearisome and unproductive controversy.[245]

In the end there remains scarcely a shade of distinction between Kalthoff and his opponents. They want to bring their "historical Jesus" into the midst of our time. He wants to do the same with his "Christ." "A secularised Christ," he says, "as the type of the self-determined man who amid strife and suffering carries through victoriously, and fully realises, His own personality in order to give the infinite fullness of love which He bears within Himself as a blessing to mankind—a Christ such as that can awaken to new life the antique Christ-type of the Church. He is no longer the Christ of the scholar, of the abstract theological thinker with his scholastic rules and methods. He is the people's Christ, the Christ of the ordinary man, the figure in which all those powers of the human soul which are most natural and simple—and therefore most exalted and divine—find an expression at once sensible and spiritual." But that is precisely the description of the Jesus of modern historical theology; why, then, make this long roundabout through scepticism? The Christ of Kalthoff is nothing else than the Jesus of those whom he combats in such a lofty fashion; the only difference is that he draws his figure of Christ in red ink on blotting-paper, and because it is red in colour and smudgy in outline, wants to make out that it is something new.

It is on ethical grounds that Eduard von Hartmann[246] refuses to accept the Jesus of modern theology. He finds fault with it because in its anxiety to retain a personality which would be of value to religion it does not sufficiently distinguish between the authentic and the "historical" Jesus. When criticism has removed the paintings-over and retouchings to which this authentic portrait of Jesus has been subjected, it reaches, according to him, an unrecognisable painting below, in which it is impossible to discover any clear likeness, least of all one of any religious use and value.

Were it not for the tenacity and the simple fidelity of the epic tradition, nothing whatever would have remained of the historic Jesus. What has remained is merely of historical and psychological interest.

At His first appearance the historic Jesus was, according to [pg 319] Eduard von Hartmann, almost "an impersonal being," since He regarded Himself so exclusively as the vehicle of His message that His personality hardly came into the question. As time went on, however, He developed a taste for glory and for wonderful deeds, and fell at last into a condition of "abnormal exaltation of personality." In the end He declares Himself to His disciples and before the council as Messiah. "When He felt His death drawing nigh He struck the balance of His life, found His mission a failure, His person and His cause abandoned by God, and died with the unanswered question on His lips, 'My God, why hast thou forsaken me?' "

It is significant that Eduard von Hartmann has not fallen into the mistake of Schopenhauer and many other philosophers, of identifying the pessimism of Jesus with the Indian speculative pessimism of Buddha. The pessimism of Jesus, he says, is not metaphysical, it is "a pessimism of indignation," born of the intolerable social and political conditions of the time. Von Hartmann also clearly recognises the significance of eschatology, but he does not define its character quite correctly, since he bases his impressions solely on the Talmud, hardly making any use of the Old Testament, of Enoch, the Psalms of Solomon, Baruch, or Fourth Ezra. He has an irritating way of still using the name "Jehovah."

Like Reimarus—von Hartmann's positions are simply modernised Reimarus—he is anxious to show that Christian theology has lost the right "to treat the ideal Kingdom of God as belonging to itself." Jesus and His teaching, so far as they have been preserved, belong to Judaism. His ethic is for us strange and full of stumbling-blocks. He despises work, property, and the duties of family life. His gospel is fundamentally plebeian, and completely excludes the idea of any aristocracy except in so far as it consents to plebeianise itself, and this is true not only as regards the aristocracy of rank, property, and fortune, but also the aristocracy of intellect. Von Hartmann cannot resist the temptation to accuse Jesus of "Semitic harshness," finding the evidence of this chiefly in Mark iv. 12, where Jesus declares that the purpose of His parables was to obscure His teaching and cause the hearts of the people to be hardened.

His judgment upon Jesus is: "He had no genius, but a certain talent which, in the complete absence of any sound education, produced in general only moderate results, and was not sufficient to preserve Him from numerous weaknesses and serious errors; at heart a fanatic and a transcendental enthusiast, who in spite of an inborn kindliness of disposition hates and despises the world and everything it contains, and holds any interest in it to be injurious to the sole true, transcendental interest; an amiable and modest youth who, through a remarkable concatenation of circumstances [pg 320] arrived at the idea, which was at that time epidemic,[247] that He was Himself the expected Messiah, and in consequence of this met His fate."

It is to be regretted that a mind like Eduard von Hartmann's should not have got beyond the externals of the history, and made an effort to grasp the simple and impressive greatness of the figure of Jesus in its eschatological setting; and that he should imagine he has disposed of the strangeness which he finds in Jesus when he has made it as small as possible. And yet in another respect there is something satisfactory about his book. It is the open struggle of the Germanic spirit with Jesus. In this battle the victory will rest with true greatness. Others wanted to make peace before the struggle, or thought that theologians could fight the battle alone, and spare their contemporaries the doubts about the historical Jesus through which it was necessary to pass in order to reach the eternal Jesus—and to this end they kept preaching reconciliation while fighting the battle. They could only preach it on a basis of postulates, and postulates make poor preaching! Thus, Jülicher, for example, in his latest sketches of the Life of Jesus[248] distinguishes between "Jewish and supra-Jewish" in Jesus, and holds that Jesus transferred the ideal of the Kingdom of God "to the solid ground of the present, bringing it into the course of historical events," and further "associated with the Kingdom of God" the idea of development which was utterly opposed to all Jewish ideas about the Kingdom. Jülicher also desires to raise "the strongest protest against the poor little definition of His preaching which makes it consist in nothing further than an announcement of the nearness of the Kingdom, and an exhortation to the repentance necessary as a condition for attaining the Kingdom."

But when has a protest against the pure truth of history ever been of any avail? Why proclaim peace where there is no peace, and attempt to put back the clock of time? Is it not enough that Schleiermacher and Ritschl succeeded again and again in making theology send on earth peace instead of a sword, and does not the [pg 321] weakness of Christian thought as compared with the general culture of our time result from the fact that it did not face the battle when it ought to have faced it, but persisted in appealing to a court of arbitration on which all the sciences were represented, but which it had successfully bribed in advance?

Now there comes to join the philosophers a jurist. Herr Doctor jur. De Jonge lends his aid to Eduard von Hartmann in "destroying the ecclesiastical," and "unveiling the Jewish picture of Jesus."[249]

De Jonge is a Jew by birth, baptized in 1889, who on the 22nd of November 1902 again separated himself from the Christian communion and was desirous of being received back "with certain evangelical reservations" into the Jewish community. In spite of his faithful observance of the Law, this was refused. Now he is waiting "until in the Synagogue of the twentieth century a freedom of conscience is accorded to him equal to that which in the first century was enjoyed by John, the beloved disciple of Jeschua of Nazareth." In the meantime he beguiles the period of waiting by describing Jesus and His earliest followers in the character of pattern Jews, and sets them to work in the interest of his "Jewish views with evangelical reservations."

It is the colourless, characterless Jesus of the Superintendents and Konsistorialrats which especially arouses his enmity. With this figure he contrasts his own Jesus, the man of holy anger, the man of holy calm, the man of holy melancholy, the master of dialectic, the imperious ruler, the man of high gifts and practical ability, the man of inexorable consistency and reforming vigour.

Jesus was, according to De Jonge, a pupil of Hillel. He demanded voluntary poverty only in special cases, not as a general principle. In the case of the rich young man, He knew "that the property which he had inherited was derived in this particular case from impure sources which must be cut off at once and for ever."

But how does De Jonge know that Jesus knew this?

A writer who is attacking the common theological picture of Jesus, and who displays in the process, as De Jonge does, not only [pg 322] wit and address, but historical intuition, ought not to fall into the error of the theology with which he is at feud; he ought to use sober history as his weapon against the supplementary knowledge which his opponents seem to find between the lines, instead of meeting it with an esoteric historical knowledge of his own.

De Jonge knows that Jesus possessed property inherited from His father: "One proof may serve where many might be given—the hasty flight into Egypt with his whole family to escape from Herod, and the long sojourn in that country."

De Jonge knows—he is here, however, following the Gospel of John, to which he everywhere gives the preference—that Jesus was between forty and fifty years old at the time of His first coming forward publicly. The statement in Luke iii. 23, that He was ὡσεί thirty years old, can only mislead those who do not remember that Luke was a portrait painter and only meant that "Jeschua, in consequence of His glorious beauty and His ever-youthful appearance, looked ten years younger than He really was."

De Jonge knows also that Jesus, at the time when He first emerged from obscurity, was a widower and had a little son—the "lad" of John vi. 9, who had the five barley loaves and two fishes, was in fact His son. This and many other things the author finds in "the glorious John." According to De Jonge too we ought to think of Jesus as the aristocratic Jew, more accustomed to a dress coat than to a workman's blouse, something of an expert, as appears from some of the parables, in matters of the table, and conning the menu with interest when He dined with "privy-finance-councillor" Zacchaeus.

But this is to modernise more distressingly than even the theologians!

De Jonge's one-sided preference for the Fourth Gospel is shared by Kirchbach's book, "What did Jesus teach?"[250] but here everything, instead of being judaised, is spiritualised. Kirchbach does not seem to have been acquainted with Noack's "History of Jesus," otherwise he would hardly have ventured to repeat the same experiment without the latter's touch of genius and with much less skill and knowledge.

The teaching of Jesus is interpreted on the lines of the Kantian philosophy. The saying, "No man hath seen God at any time," is to be understood as if it were derived from the same system of thought as the "Critique of Pure Reason." Jesus always used the [pg 323] words "death" and "life" in a purely metaphorical sense. Eternal life is for Him not a life in another world, but in the present. He speaks of Himself as the Son of God, not as the Jewish Messiah. Son of Man is only the ethical explanation of Son of God. The only reason why a Son-of-Man problem has arisen, is because Matthew translated the ancient term Son of Man in the original collection of Logia "with extreme literality."

The great discourse of Matt. xxiii. with its warnings and threatenings is, according to Kirchbach, merely "a patriotic oration in which Jesus gives expression in moving words to His opposition to the Pharisees and His inborn love of His native land."

The teaching of Jesus is not ascetic, it closely resembles the real teaching of Epicurus, "that is, the rejection of all false metaphysics, and the resulting condition of blessedness, of *makaria*." The only purpose of the demand addressed to the rich young man was to try him. "If the youth, instead of slinking away dejectedly because he was called upon to sell all his goods, had replied, confident in the possession of a rich fund of courage, energy, ability, and knowledge, 'Right gladly. It will not go to my heart to part with my little bit of property; if I'm not to have it, why then I can do without it,' the Rabbi would probably in that case not have taken him at his word, but would have said, 'Young man, I like you. You have a good chance before you, you may do something in the Kingdom of God, and in any case for My sake you may attach yourself to Me by way of trial. We can talk about your stocks and bonds later.'"

Finally, Kirchbach succeeds, though only, it must be admitted, by the aid of some rather awkward phraseology, in spiritualising John vi. "It is not the body," he explains, "of the long departed thinker, who apparently attached no importance whatever to the question of personal survival, that we, who understand Him in the right Greek sense, 'eat'; in the sense which He intended, we eat and drink, and absorb into ourselves, His teaching, His spirit, His sublime conception of life, by constantly recalling them in connexion with the symbol of bread and flesh, the symbol of blood, the symbol of water."[251]

Worthless as Kirchbach's Life of Jesus is from an historical point of view, it is quite comprehensible as a phase in the struggle between the modern view of the world and Jesus. The aim of the [pg 324] work is to retain His significance for a metaphysical and non-ascetic time; and since it is not possible to do this in the case of the historical Jesus, the author denies His existence in favour of an apocryphal Jesus.

It is, in fact, the characteristic feature of the Life-of-Jesus literature on the threshold of the new century even in the productions of professedly historical and scientific theology, to subordinate the historical interest to the interest of the general world-view. And those who "wrest the Kingdom of Heaven" are beginning to wrest Jesus Himself along with it. Men who have no qualifications for the task, whose ignorance is nothing less than criminal, who loftily anathematise scientific theology instead of making themselves in some measure acquainted with the researches which it has carried out, feel impelled to write a Life of Jesus, in order to set forth their general religious view in a portrait of Jesus which has not the faintest claim to be historical, and the most far-fetched of these find favour, and are eagerly absorbed by the multitude.

It would be something to be thankful for if all these Lives of Jesus were based on as definite an idea and as acute historical observation as we find in Albert Dulk's "The Error of the Life of Jesus."[252] In Dulk the story of the fate of Jesus is also the story of the fate of religion. The Galilaean teacher, whose true character was marked by deep religious inwardness, was doomed to destruction from the moment when He set Himself upon the dizzy heights of the divine sonship and the eschatological expectation. He died in despair, having vainly expected, down to the very last, a "telegram from heaven." Religion as a whole can only avoid the same fate by renouncing all transcendental elements.

The vast numbers of imaginative Lives of Jesus shrink into remarkably small compass on a close examination. When one knows two or three of them, one knows them all. They have scarcely altered since Venturini's time, except that some of the cures performed by Jesus are handled in the modern Lives from the point of view of the recent investigations in hypnotism and suggestion.[253]

[pg 325]

According to Paul de Régla[254] Jesus was born out of wedlock. Joseph, however, gave shelter and protection to the mother. De Régla dwells on the beauty of the child. "His eyes were not exceptionally large, but were well-opened, and were shaded by long, silky, dark-brown eyelashes, and rather deep-set. They were of a blue-grey colour, which changed with changing emotions, taking on various shades, especially blue and brownish-grey."

He and His disciples were Essenes, as was also the Baptist. That implies that He was no longer a Jew in the strict sense. His preaching dealt with the rights of man, and put forward socialistic and communistic demands: His religion in the pure consciousness of communion with God. With eschatology He had nothing whatever to do, it was first interpolated into His teaching by Matthew.

The miracles are all to be explained by suggestion and hypnotism. At the marriage at Cana, Jesus noticed that the guests were taking too much, and therefore secretly bade the servants pour out water instead of wine while He Himself said, "Drink, this is better wine." In this way He succeeded in suggesting to a part of the company that they were really drinking wine. The feeding of the multitude is explained by striking out a couple of noughts from the numbers; the raising of Lazarus by supposing it a case of premature burial. Jesus Himself when taken down from the cross was not dead, and the Essenes succeeded in reanimating Him. His work is inspired with hatred against Catholicism, but with a real reverence for Jesus.

Another mere variant of the plan of Venturini is the fictitious Life of Jesus of Pierre Nahor.[255] The sentimental descriptions of nature and the long dialogues characteristic of the Lives of Jesus of a hundred years ago are here again in full force. After John had already begun to preach in the neighbourhood of the Dead Sea, Jesus, in company with a distinguished Brahmin who possessed property at Nazareth and had an influential following in Jerusalem, made a journey to Egypt and was there indoctrinated into all kinds of Egyptian, Essene, and Indian philosophy, thus giving the author, [pg 326] or rather the authoress, an opportunity to develop her ideas on the philosophy of religion in didactic dialogues. When He soon afterwards begins to work in Galilee the young teacher is much aided by the fact that, at the instance of His fellow-traveller, He had acquired from Egyptian mendicants a practical acquaintance with the secrets of hypnotism. By His skill He healed Mary of Magdala, a distinguished courtesan of Tiberias. They had met before at Alexandria. After being cured she left Tiberias and went to live in a small house, inherited from her mother, at Magdala.

Jesus Himself never went to Tiberias, but the social world of that place took an interest in Him, and often had itself rowed to the beach when He was preaching. Rich and pious ladies used to inquire of Him where He thought of preaching to the people on a given day, and sent baskets of bread and dried fish to the spot which He indicated, that the multitude might not suffer hunger. This is the explanation of the stories about the feeding of the multitudes; the people had no idea whence Jesus suddenly obtained the supplies which He caused His disciples to distribute.

When he became aware that the priests had resolved upon His death, He made His friend Joseph of Arimathea, a leading man among the Essenes, promise that he would take Him down from the cross as soon as possible and lay Him in the grave without other witnesses. Only Nicodemus was to be present. On the cross He put Himself into a cataleptic trance; He was taken down from the cross seemingly dead, and came to Himself again in the grave. After appearing several times to His disciples he set out for Nazareth and dragged His way painfully thither. With a last effort He reaches the house of His mysterious old Indian teacher. At the door He falls helpless, just as the morning dawns. The old slave-woman recognises Him and carries

Him into the house, where He dies. "The serene solemn night withdrew and day broke in blinding splendour behind Tiberias."

Nikolas Notowitsch[256] finds in Luke i. 80 ("And the child grew [pg 327] ... and was in the deserts until the day of his shewing unto Israel") a "gap in the life of Jesus," in spite of the fact that this passage refers to the Baptist, and proposes to fill it by putting Jesus to school with the Brahmins and Buddhists from His thirteenth to His twenty-ninth year. As evidence for this he refers to statements about Buddhist worship of a certain Issa which he professes to have found in the monasteries of Little Thibet. The whole thing is, as was shown by the experts, a barefaced swindle and an impudent invention.

To the fictitious Lives of Jesus belong also in the main the theosophical "Lives," which equally play fast and loose with the history, though here with a view to proving that Jesus had absorbed the Egyptian and Indian theosophy, and had been indoctrinated with "occult science." The theosophists, however, have the advantage of escaping the dilemma between reanimation after a trance and resurrection, since they are convinced that it was possible for Jesus to reassume His body after He had really died. But in the touching up and embellishment of the Gospel narratives they out-do even the romancers.

Ernest Bosc,[257] writing as a theosophist, makes it the chief aim of his work to describe the oriental origin of Christianity, and ventures to assert that Jesus was not a Semite, but an Aryan. The Fourth Gospel is, of course, the basis of his representation. He does not hesitate, however, to appeal also to the anonymous "Revelations" published in 1849, which are a mere plagiarism from Venturini.

A work which is written with some ability and with much out-of-the-way learning is "Did Jesus live 100 B.C.?"[258] The author compares the Christian tradition with the Jewish, and finds in the latter a reminiscence of a Jesus who lived in the time of Alexander Jannaeus (104-76 B.C.). This person was transferred by the earliest Evangelist to the later period, the attempt being facilitated by the fact that during the procuratorship of Pilate a false prophet had attracted some attention. The author, however, only professes to offer it as a hypothesis, and apologises in advance for the offence which it is likely to cause.

XIX. Thoroughgoing Scepticism And Thoroughgoing Eschatology

W. Wrede. Das Messiasgeheimnis in den Evangelien. Zugleich ein Beitrag zum Verständnis des Markusevangeliums. (The Messianic Secret in the Gospels. Forming a contribution also to the understanding of the Gospel of Mark.) Göttingen, 1901. 286 pp.

Albert Schweitzer. Das Messianitäts- und Leidensgeheimnis. Eine Skizze des Lebens Jesu. (The Secret of the Messiahship and the Passion. A Sketch of the Life of Jesus.) Tübingen and Leipzig, 1901. 109 pp.

The coincidence between the work of Wrede[259] and the "Sketch of the Life of Jesus" is not more surprising in regard to the time of their appearance than in regard to the character of their contents. They appeared upon the self-same day, their titles are almost identical, and their agreement in the criticism of the modern historical conception of the life of Jesus extends sometimes to the very phraseology. And yet they are written from quite different standpoints, one from the point of view of literary criticism, the other from that of the historical recognition of eschatology. It seems to be the fate of the Marcan hypothesis that at the decisive periods its problems should always be attacked simultaneously and independently from the literary and the historical sides, and the results declared in two different forms which corroborate each other. So it was in the case of Weisse and Wilke; so it is again now, when, retaining the assumption of the priority of Mark, the historicity of the hitherto accepted view of the life of Jesus, based upon the Marcan narrative, is called in question.

[pg 329]

The meaning of that is that the literary and the eschatological view, which have hitherto been marching parallel, on either flank, to the advance of modern theology, have now united their forces, brought theology to a halt, surrounded it, and compelled it to give battle.

That in the last three or four years so much has been written in which this enveloping movement has been ignored does not alter the real position of modern historical theology in the least. The fact is deserving of notice that during this period the study of the subject has not made a step in advance, but has kept moving to and fro upon the old lines with wearisome iteration, and has thrown itself with excessive zeal into the work of popularisation, simply because it was incapable of advancing.

And even if it professes gratitude to Wrede for the very interesting historical point which he has brought into the discussion, and is also willing to admit that thoroughgoing eschatology has advanced the solution of many problems, these are mere demonstrations which are quite inadequate to raise the blockade of modern theology by the allied forces. Supposing that only a half—nay, only a third—of the critical arguments which are common to Wrede and the "Sketch of the Life of Jesus" are sound, then the modern historical view of the history is wholly ruined.

The reader of Wrede's book cannot help feeling that here no quarter is given; and any one who goes carefully through the present writer's "Sketch" must come to see that between the modern historical and the eschatological Life of Jesus no compromise is possible.

Thoroughgoing scepticism and thoroughgoing eschatology may, in their union, either destroy, or be destroyed by modern historical theology; but they cannot combine with it and enable it to advance, any more than they can be advanced by it.

We are confronted with a decisive issue. As with Strauss's "Life of Jesus," so with the surprising agreement in the critical basis of these two schools—we are not here considering the respective solutions which they offer—there has entered into the domain of the theology of the day a force with which it cannot possibly ally itself. Its whole territory is threatened. It must either reconquer it step by step or else surrender it. It has no longer the right to advance a single assertion until it has taken up a definite position in regard to the fundamental questions raised by the new criticism.

Modern historical theology is no doubt still far from recognising this. It is warned that the dyke is letting in water and sends a couple of masons to repair the leak; as if the leak did not mean that the whole masonry is undermined, and must be rebuilt from the foundation.

[pg 330]

To vary the metaphor, theology comes home to find the broker's marks on all the furniture and goes on as before quite comfortably, ignoring the fact it will lose everything if it does not pay its debts.

The critical objections which Wrede and the "Sketch" agree in bringing against the modern treatment of the subject are as follows.

In order to find in Mark the Life of Jesus of which it is in search, modern theology is obliged to read between the lines a whole host of things, and those often the most important, and then to foist them upon the text by means of psychological conjecture. It is determined to find evidence in Mark of a development of Jesus, a development of the disciples, and a development of the outer circumstances; and professes in so doing to be only reproducing the views and indications of the Evangelist. In reality, however, there is not a word of all this in the Evangelist, and when his interpreters are asked what are the hints and indications on which they base their assertions they have nothing to offer save *argumenta e silentio*.

Mark knows nothing of any development in Jesus; he knows nothing of any paedagogic considerations which are supposed to have determined the conduct of Jesus towards the disciples and the people; he knows nothing of any conflict in the mind of Jesus between a spiritual and a popular, political Messianic ideal; he does not know, either, that in this respect there was any difference between the view of Jesus and that of the people; he knows nothing of the idea that the use of the ass at the triumphal entry symbolised a non-political Messiahship; he knows nothing of the idea that the question about the Messiah's being the Son of David had something to do with this alternative between political and non-political; he does not know, either, that Jesus explained the secret of the passion to the disciples, nor that they had any understanding of it; he only knows that from first to last they were in all respects equally wanting in understanding; he does not know that the first period was a period of success and the second a period of failure; he represents the Pharisees and Herodians as (from iii. 6 onwards) resolved upon the death of Jesus, while the people, down to the very last day when He preached in the temple, are enthusiastically loyal to Him.

All these things of which the Evangelist says nothing—and they are the foundations of the modern view—should first be proved, if proved they can be; they ought not to be simply read into the text as something self-evident. For it is just those things which appear so self-evident to the prevailing critical temper which are in reality the least evident of all.

Another hitherto self-evident point—the "historical kernel" which it has been customary to extract from the narratives—must [pg 331] be given up, until it is proved, if it is capable of proof, that we can and ought to distinguish between the kernel and the husk. We may take all that is reported as either historical or unhistorical, but, in respect of the definite predictions of the passion, death, and resurrection, we ought to give up taking the reference to the passion as historical and letting the rest go; we may accept the idea of the atoning death, or we may reject it, but we ought not to ascribe to Jesus a feeble, anaemic version of this idea, while setting down to the account of the Pauline theology the interpretation of the passion which we actually find in Mark.

Whatever the results obtained by the aid of the historical kernel, the method pursued is the same; "it is detached from its context and transformed into something different." "It finally comes to this," says Wrede, "that each critic retains whatever portion of the traditional sayings can be fitted into his construction of the facts and his conception of historical possibility and rejects the rest." The psychological explanation of motive, and the psychological connexion of the events and actions which such critics have proposed to find in Mark, simply do not exist. That being so, nothing is to be made out of his account by the application of a priori psychology. A vast quantity of treasures of scholarship and erudition, of art and artifice, which the Marcan hypothesis has gathered into its storehouse in the two generations of its existence to aid it in constructing its life of Jesus has become worthless, and can be of no further service to true historical research. Theology has been simplified. What would become of it if that did not happen every hundred years or so? And the simplification was badly needed, for no one since Strauss had cleared away its impedimenta.

Thoroughgoing scepticism and thoroughgoing eschatology, between them, are compelling theology to read the Marcan text again with simplicity of mind. The simplicity consists in dispensing with the connecting links which it has been accustomed to discover between the sections of the narrative (*pericopes*), in looking at each one separately, and recognising that it is difficult to pass from one to the other.

The material with which it has hitherto been usual to solder the sections together into a life of Jesus will not stand the temperature test. Exposed to the cold air of critical scepticism it cracks;

when the furnace of eschatology is heated to a certain point the solderings melt. In both cases the sections all fall apart.

Formerly it was possible to book through-tickets at the supplementary-psychological-knowledge office which enabled those travelling in the interests of Life-of-Jesus construction to use express trains, thus avoiding the inconvenience of having to stop at every little station, change, and run the risk of missing their [pg 332] connexion. This ticket office is now closed. There is a station at the end of each section of the narrative, and the connexions are not guaranteed.

The fact is, it is not simply that there is no very obvious psychological connexion between the sections; in almost every case there is a positive break in the connexion. And there is a great deal in the Marcan narrative which is inexplicable and even self-contradictory.

In their statement of the problems raised by this want of connexion Wrede and the "Sketch" are in the most exact agreement. That these difficulties are not artificially constructed has been shown by our survey of the history of the attempts to write the Life of Jesus, in the course of which these problems emerge one after another, after Bruno Bauer had by anticipation grasped them all in their complexity.

How do the demoniacs know that Jesus is the Son of God? Why does the blind man at Jericho address Him as the Son of David, when no one else knows His Messianic dignity? How was it that these occurrences did not give a new direction to the thoughts of the people in regard to Jesus? How did the Messianic entry come about? How was it possible without provoking the interference of the Roman garrison of occupation? Why is it as completely ignored in the subsequent controversies as if had never taken place? Why was it not brought up at the trial of Jesus? "The Messianic acclamation at the entry into Jerusalem," says Wrede, "is in Mark quite an isolated incident. It has no sequel, neither is there any preparation for it beforehand."

Why does Jesus in Mark iv. 10-12 speak of the parabolic form of discourse as designed to conceal the mystery of the Kingdom of God, whereas the explanation which He proceeds to give to the disciples has nothing mysterious about it? What is the mystery of the Kingdom of God? Why does Jesus forbid His miracles to be made known even in cases where there is no apparent purpose for the prohibition? Why is His Messiahship a secret and yet no secret, since it is known, not only to the disciples, but to the demoniacs, the blind man at Jericho, the multitude at Jerusalem—which must, as Bruno Bauer expresses it, "have fallen from heaven"—and to the High Priest?

Why does Jesus first reveal His Messiahship to the disciples at Caesarea Philippi, not at the moment when He sends them forth to preach? How does Peter know without having been told by Jesus that the Messiahship belongs to his Master? Why must it remain a secret until the "resurrection"? Why does Jesus indicate His Messiahship only by the title Son of Man? And why is it that this title is so far from prominent in primitive Christian theology?

[pg 333]

What is the meaning of the statement that Jesus at Jerusalem discovered a difficulty in the fact that the Messiah was described as at once David's son and David's Lord? How are we to explain the fact that Jesus had to open the eyes of the people to the greatness of the Baptist's office, subsequently to the mission of the Twelve, and to enlighten the disciples themselves in regard to it during the descent from the mount of transfiguration? Why should this be described in Matt. xi. 14 and 15 as a mystery difficult to grasp ("If ye can receive it" … "He that hath ears to hear, let him hear")? What is the meaning of the saying that he that is least in the Kingdom of Heaven is greater than the Baptist? Does the Baptist, then, not enter into the Kingdom of Heaven? How is the Kingdom of Heaven subjected to violence since the days of the Baptist? Who are the violent? What is the Baptist intended to understand from the answer of Jesus?

What importance was attached to the miracles by Jesus Himself? What office must they have caused the people to attribute to Him? Why is the discourse at the sending out of the Twelve filled with predictions of persecutions which experience had given no reason to anticipate, and which did not, as a matter of fact, occur? What is the meaning of the saying in Matt. x. 23 about the imminent coming of the Son of Man, seeing that the disciples after all returned to Jesus without its being fulfilled? Why does Jesus leave the people just when His work among them is most successful, and journey northwards? Why had He, immediately after the sending forth of the Twelve, manifested a desire to withdraw Himself from the multitude who were longing for salvation?

How does the multitude mentioned in Mark viii. 34 suddenly appear at Caesarea Philippi? Why is its presence no longer implied in Mark ix. 30? How could Jesus possibly have travelled unrecognised through Galilee, and how could He have avoided being thronged in Capernaum although He stayed at "the house"?

How came He so suddenly to speak to His disciples of His suffering and dying and rising again, without, moreover, explaining to them either the natural or the moral "wherefore"? "There is no trace of any attempt on the part of Jesus," says Wrede, "to break this strange thought gradually to His disciples … the prediction is always flung down before the disciples without preparation, it is, in fact, a characteristic feature of these sayings that all attempt to aid the understanding of the disciples is lacking."

Did Jesus journey to Jerusalem with the purpose of working there, or of dying there? How comes it that in Mark x. 39, He holds out to the sons of Zebedee the prospect of drinking His [pg 334] cup and being baptized with His baptism? And how can He, after speaking so decidedly of the necessity of His death, think it possible in Gethsemane that the cup might yet pass from Him? Who are the undefined "many," for whom, according to Mark x. 45 and xiv. 24, His death shall serve as a ransom?[260]

How came it that Jesus alone was arrested? Why were no witnesses called at His trial to testify that He had given Himself out to be the Messiah? How is it that on the morning after His arrest the temper of the multitude seems to be completely changed, so that no one stirs a finger to help Him?

In what form does Jesus conceive the resurrection, which He promises to His disciples, to be combined with the coming on the clouds of heaven, to which He points His judge? In what relation do these predictions stand to the prospect held out at the time of the sending forth of the Twelve, but not realized, of the immediate appearance of the Son of Man?

What is the meaning of the further prediction on the way to Gethsemane (Mark xiv. 28) that after His resurrection He will go before the disciples into Galilee? How is the other version of this saying (Mark xvi. 7) to be explained, according to which it means, as spoken by the angel, that the disciples are to journey to Galilee to have their first meeting with the risen Jesus there, whereas, on the lips of Jesus, it betokened that, just as now as a sufferer He was going before them from Galilee to Jerusalem, so, after His resurrection, He would go before them from Jerusalem to Galilee? And what was to happen there?

These problems were covered up by the naturalistic psychology as by a light snow-drift. The snow has melted, and they now stand out from the narratives like black points of rock. It is no longer allowable to avoid these questions, or to solve them, each by itself, by softening them down and giving them an interpretation by which the reported facts acquire a quite different significance from that which they bear for the Evangelist. Either the Marcan text as it stands is historical, and therefore to be retained, or it is not, and then it should be given up. What is really unhistorical is any softening down of the wording, and the meaning which it naturally bears.

The sceptical and eschatological schools, however, go still farther in company. If the connexion in Mark is really no connexion, it is important to try to discover whether any principle can be discovered in this want of connexion. Can any order be brought into the chaos? To this the answer is in the affirmative.

The complete want of connexion, with all its self-contradictions, is ultimately due to the fact that two representations of the life of [pg 335] Jesus, or, to speak more accurately, of His public ministry, are here crushed into one; a natural and a deliberately supernatural representation. A dogmatic element has intruded itself into the description of this Life—something which has no concern with the events which form the outward course of that Life. This dogmatic element is the Messianic secret of Jesus and all the secrets and concealments which go along with it.

Hence the irrational and self-contradictory features of the presentation of Jesus, out of which a rational psychology can make only something which is unhistorical and does violence to the text, since it must necessarily get rid of the constant want of connexion and self-contradiction which belongs to the essence of the narrative, and portray a Jesus who was the Messiah, not one who at once was and was not Messiah, as the Evangelist depicts Him. When rational psychology conceives Him as one who was Messiah, but not in the sense expected by the people, that is a concession to the self-contradictions of the Marcan representation; which, however, does justice neither to the text nor to the history which it records, since the Gospel does not contain the faintest hint that the contradiction was of this nature.

Up to this point—up to the complete reconstruction of the system which runs through the disconnectedness, and the tracing back of the dogmatic element to the Messianic secret—there extends a close agreement between thoroughgoing scepticism and thoroughgoing eschatology. The critical arguments are identical, the construction is analogous and based on the same principle. The defenders of the modern psychological view cannot, therefore, play off one school against the other, as one of them proposed to do, but must deal with them both at once. They differ only when they explain whence the system that runs through the disconnectedness comes. Here the ways divide, as Bauer saw long ago. The inconsistency between the public life of Jesus and His Messianic claim lies either in the nature of the Jewish Messianic conception, or in the representation of the Evangelist. There is, on the one hand, the eschatological solution, which at one stroke raises the Marcan account as it stands, with all its disconnectedness and inconsistencies, into genuine history; and there is, on the other hand, the literary solution, which regards the incongruous dogmatic element as interpolated by the earliest Evangelist into the tradition and therefore strikes out the Messianic claim altogether from the historical Life of Jesus. *Tertium non datur.*

But in some respects it really hardly matters which of the two "solutions" one adopts. They are both merely wooden towers erected upon the solid main building of the consentient critical induction which offers the enigmas detailed above to modern historical theology. It is interesting in this connexion that Wrede's [pg 336] scepticism is just as constructive as the eschatological outline of the Life of Jesus in the "Sketch."

Bruno Bauer chose the literary solution because he thought that we had no evidence for an eschatological expectation existing in the time of Christ. Wrede, though he follows Johannes Weiss in assuming the existence of a Jewish eschatological Messianic expectation, finds in the Gospel only the Christian conception of the Messiah. "If Jesus," he thinks, "really knew Himself to be the Messiah and designated Himself as such, the genuine tradition is so closely interwoven with later accretions that it is not easy to recognise it." In any case, Jesus cannot, according to Wrede, have spoken of His Messianic Coming in the way which the Synoptists report. The Messiahship of Jesus, as we find it in the Gospels, is a product of Early Christian theology correcting history according to its own conceptions.

It is therefore necessary to distinguish in Mark between the reported events which constitute the outward course of the history of Jesus, and the dogmatic idea which claims to lay down the lines of its inward course. The principle of division is found in the contradictions.

The recorded events form, according to Wrede, the following picture. Jesus came forward as a teacher,[261] first and principally in Galilee. He was surrounded by a company of disciples, went about with them, and gave them instruction. To some of them He accorded a special confidence. A larger multitude sometimes attached itself to Him, in addition to the disciples. He is fond of discoursing in parables. Besides the teaching there are the miracles. These make a stir, and He is thronged by the multitudes. He gives special attention to the cases of demoniacs. He is in such close touch with the people that He does not hesitate to associate even with publicans and sinners. Towards the Law He takes up an attitude of some freedom. He encounters the opposition of the Pharisees and the Jewish authorities. They set traps for Him and endeavour to bring about His fall. Finally they succeed, when He ventures to show Himself not only on Judaean soil, but in Jerusalem. He remains passive and is condemned to death. The Roman administration supports the Jewish authorities.

"The texture of the Marcan narrative as we know it," continues Wrede, "is not complete until to the warp of these general historical notions there is added a strong weft of ideas of a dogmatic character," the substance of which is that "Jesus, the bearer of a special office to which He was appointed by God," becomes "a higher, superhuman being." If this is the case, however, then the motives of His conduct are not derived from human characteristics, human aims and necessities. "The one [pg 337] motive which runs throughout is rather a Divine decree which lies beyond human understanding. This He seeks to fulfil alike in His actions and His sufferings. The teaching of Jesus is accordingly supernatural." On this assumption the want of understanding of the disciples to whom He communicates, without commentary, unconnected portions of this supernatural knowledge becomes natural and explicable. The people are, moreover, essentially "non-receptive of revelation."

"It is these *motifs* and not those which are inherently historical which give movement and direction to the Marcan narrative. It is they that give the general colour. On them naturally depends the main interest, it is to them that the thought of the writer is really directed. The consequence is that the general picture offered by the Gospel is not an historical representation of the Life of Jesus. Only some faded remnants of such an impression have been taken over into a supra-historical religious view. In this sense the Gospel of Mark belongs to the history of dogma."

The two conceptions of the Life of Jesus, the natural and the supernatural, are brought, not without inconsistencies, into a kind of harmony by means of the idea of intentional secrecy. The Messiahship of Jesus is concealed in His life as in a closed dark lantern, which, however, is not quite closed—otherwise one could not see that it was there—and allows a few bright beams to escape.

The idea of a secret which must remain a secret until the resurrection of Jesus could only arise at a time when nothing was known of a Messianic claim of Jesus during His life upon earth: that is to say, at a time when the Messiahship of Jesus was thought of as beginning with the resurrection. But that is a weighty piece of indirect historical evidence that Jesus did not really profess to be the Messiah at all.

The positive fact which is to be inferred from this is that the appearances of the risen Jesus produced a sudden revolution in His disciples' conception of Him. "The resurrection" is for Wrede the real Messianic event in the Life of Jesus.

Who is responsible, then, for introducing this singular feature, so destructive of the real historical connexion, into the life of Jesus, which was in reality that of a teacher? It is quite impossible, Wrede argues, that the idea of the Messianic secret is the invention of Mark. "A thing like that is not done by a single individual. It must, therefore, have been a view which was current in certain circles, and was held by a considerable number, though not necessarily perhaps by a very great number of persons. To say this is not to deny that Mark had a share and perhaps a considerable share in the creation of the view which he sets forth ... the *motifs* themselves are doubtless not, in part at least, [pg 338] peculiar to the Evangelist, but the concrete embodiment of them is certainly his own work; and to this extent we may speak of a special Marcan point of view which manifests itself here and there. Where the line is to be drawn between what is traditional and what is individual cannot always be determined even by a careful examination directed to this end. We must leave it commingled, as we find it."

The Marcan narrative has therefore arisen from the impulse to give a Messianic form to the earthly life of Jesus. This impulse was, however, restrained by the impression and tradition of the non-Messianic character of the life of Jesus, which were still strong and vivid, and it was therefore not able wholly to recast the material, but could only bore its way into it and force it apart, as the roots of the bramble disintegrate a rock. In the Gospel literature which arose on the basis of Mark the Messianic secret becomes gradually of more subordinate importance and the life of Jesus more Messianic in character, until in the Fourth Gospel He openly comes before the people with Messianic claims.

In estimating the value of this construction we must not attach too much importance to its a priori assumptions and difficulties. In this respect Wrede's position is much more precarious than that of his precursor Bruno Bauer. According to the latter the interpolation of the Messianic secret is the personal, absolutely original act of the Evangelist. Wrede thinks of it as a collective act, representing the new conception as moulded by the tradition before it was fixed by the Evangelist. That is very much more difficult to carry through. Tradition alters its materials in a different way from that in which we find them altered in Mark. Tradition transforms from without. Mark's way of drawing secret threads of a different material through the texture of the tradition, without otherwise altering it, is purely literary, and could only be the work of an individual person.

A creative tradition would have carried out the theory of the Messianic secret in the life of Jesus much more boldly and logically, that is to say, at once more arbitrarily and more consistently.

The only alternative is to distinguish two stages of tradition in early Christianity, a naive, freely-working, earlier stage, and a more artificial later stage confined to a smaller circle of a more literary character. Wrede does, as a matter of fact, propose to find in Mark traces of a simpler and bolder transformation which, leaving aside the Messianic secret, makes Jesus an openly-professed Messiah, and is therefore of a distinct origin from the conception of the secret Christ. To this tradition may belong, he thinks, the entry into Jerusalem and the confession before the High Priest, since these narratives "naively" imply an openly avowed Messiahship.

[pg 339]

The word "naively" is out of place here; a really naive tradition which intended to represent the entry of Jesus as Messianic would have done so in quite a different way from Mark, and would not have stultified itself so curiously as we find done even in Matthew, where the Galilaean Passover pilgrims, after the "Messianic entry," answer the question of the people of Jerusalem as to who it was whom they were acclaiming, with the words "This is the Prophet Jesus from Nazareth of Galilee" (Matt. xxi. 11).

The tradition, too, which makes Jesus acknowledge His Messiahship before His judges is not "naive" in Wrede's sense, for, if it were, it would not represent the High Priest's knowledge of Jesus' Messiahship as something so extraordinary and peculiar to himself that he can cite witnesses only for the saying about the Temple, not with reference to Jesus' Messianic claim, and bases his condemnation only on the fact that Jesus in answer to his question acknowledges Himself as Messiah—and Jesus does so, it should be remarked, as in other passages, with an appeal to a future justification of His claim. The confession before the council is therefore anything but a "naive representation of an openly avowed Messiahship."

The Messianic statements in these two passages present precisely the same remarkable character as in all the other cases to which Wrede draws attention. We have not here to do with a different tradition, with a clear Messianic light streaming in through the window-pane, but, just as elsewhere, with the rays of a dark lantern. The real point is that Wrede cannot bring these two passages within the lines of the theory of secrecy, and practically admits this by assuming the existence of a second and rather divergent line of tradition. What concerns us is to note that this theory does not suffice to explain the two facts in question, the knowledge of

Jesus' Messiahship shown by the Galilaean Passover pilgrims at the time of the entry into Jerusalem, and the knowledge of the High Priest at His trial.

We can only touch on the question whether any one who wished to date back in some way or other the Messiahship into the life of Jesus could not have done it much more simply by making Jesus give His closest followers some hints regarding it. Why does the re-moulder of the history, instead of doing that, have recourse to a supernatural knowledge on the part of the demoniacs and the disciples? For Wrede rightly remarks, as Bruno Bauer and the "Sketch" also do, that the incident of Caesarea Philippi, as represented by Mark, involves a miracle, since Jesus does not, as is generally supposed, reveal His Messiahship to Peter; it is Peter who reveals it to Jesus (Mark viii. 29). This fact, however, makes nonsense of the whole theory about the disciples' want of understanding. It will not therefore fit into the concealment theory, [pg 340] and Wrede, as a matter of fact, feels obliged to give up that theory as regards this incident. "This scene," he remarks, "can hardly have been created by Mark himself." It also, therefore, belongs to another tradition.

Here, then, is a third Messianic fact which cannot be brought within the lines of Wrede's "literary" theory of the Messianic secret. And these three facts are precisely the most important of all: Peter's confession, the Entry into Jerusalem, and the High Priest's knowledge of Jesus' Messiahship! In each case Wrede finds himself obliged to refer these to tradition instead of to the literary conception of Mark.[262] This tradition undermines his literary hypothesis, for the conception of a tradition always involves the possibility of genuine historical elements.

How greatly this inescapable intrusion of tradition weakens the theory of the literary interpolation of the Messiahship into the history, becomes evident when we consider the story of the passion. The representation that Jesus was publicly put to death as Messiah because He had publicly acknowledged Himself to be so, must, like the High Priest's knowledge of His claim, be referred to the other tradition which has nothing to do with the Messianic secret, but boldly antedates the Messiahship without employing any finesse of that kind. But that strongly tends to confirm the historicity of this tradition, and throws the burden of proof upon those who deny it. It is wholly independent of the hypothesis of secrecy, and in fact directly opposed to it. If, on the other hand, in spite of all the difficulties, the representation that Jesus was condemned to death on account of His Messianic claims is dragged by main force into the theory of secrecy, the question arises: What interest had the persons who set up the literary theory of secrecy, in representing Jesus as having been openly put to death as Messiah and in consequence of His Messianic claims? And the answer is: "None whatever: quite the contrary." For in doing so the theory of secrecy stultifies itself. As though one were to develop a photographic plate with painful care and, just when one had finished, fling open the shutters, so, on this hypothesis, the natural Messianic light suddenly shines into the room which ought to be lighted only by the rays of the dark lantern.

Here, therefore, the theory of secrecy abandoned the method which it had hitherto followed in regard to the traditional material. For if Jesus was not condemned and crucified at Jerusalem as [pg 341] Messiah, a tradition must have existed which preserved the truth about the last conflicts, and the motives of the condemnation. This is supposed to have been here completely set aside by the theory of the secret Messiahship, which, instead of drawing its delicate threads through the older tradition, has simply substituted its own representation of events. But in that case why not do away with the remainder of the public ministry? Why not at least get rid of the public appearance at Jerusalem? How can the crudeness of method shown in the case of the passion be harmonised with the skilful conservatism towards the non-Messianic tradition which it is obvious that the "Marcan circle" has scrupulously observed elsewhere?

If according to the original tradition, of which Wrede admits the existence, Jesus went to Jerusalem not to die, but to work there, the dogmatic view, according to which He went to Jerusalem to die, must have struck out the whole account of His sojourn in Jerusalem and His death, in order to put something else in its place. What we now read in the Gospels concerning those last days in Jerusalem cannot be derived from the original tradition, for one who came to work, and, according to Wrede, "to work with decisive effect," would not have cast all His preaching into the form of obscure parables of judgment and minatory discourses. That is a style of speech which could be adopted only by one who was determined to force his adversaries to put him to death. Therefore the narrative of the last days of Jesus must be, from beginning to end, a creation of the dogmatic idea. And, as a matter of fact, Wrede, here in agreement with Weisse, "sees grounds for asserting that the sojourn at Jerusalem is presented to us in the Gospels in a very much abridged and weakened version." That is a euphemistic expression, for if it was really the dogmatic idea which was responsible for representing Jesus as being condemned as Messiah, it is not a mere case of "abridging and weakening down," but of displacing the tradition in favour of a new one.

But if Jesus was not condemned as Messiah, on what grounds was He condemned? And, again, what interest had those whose concern was to make the Messiahship a secret of His earthly life, in making Him die as Messiah, contrary to the received tradition? And what interest could the tradition have had in falsifying history in that way? Even admitting that the prediction of the passion to the disciples is of a dogmatic character, and is to be regarded as a creation of primitive Christian theology, the historic fact that He died would have been a sufficient fulfilment of those sayings. That He was publicly condemned and crucified as Messiah has nothing to do with the fulfilment of those predictions, and goes far beyond it.

To take a more general point: what interest had primitive [pg 342] theology in dating back the Messiahship of Jesus to the time of His earthly ministry? None whatever. Paul shows us with what complete indifference the earthly life of Jesus was regarded by primitive Christianity. The discourses in Acts show an equal indifference, since in them also Jesus first becomes the Messiah by virtue of His exaltation. To date the Messiahship earlier was not an undertaking which offered any advantage to primitive theology, in fact it would only have raised difficulties for it, since it involved the hypothesis of a dual Messiahship, one of earthly humiliation and one of future glory. The fact is, if one reads through the early literature one becomes aware that so long as theology had an eschatological orientation and was dominated by the expectation of the Parousia the question of how Jesus of Nazareth "had been" the Messiah not only did not exist, but was impossible. Primitive theology is simply a theology of the future, with no interest in history! It was only with the decline of eschatological interest and the change in the orientation of Christianity which was connected therewith that an interest in the life of Jesus and the "historical Messiahship" arose.

That is to say, the Gnostics, who were the first to assert the Messiahship of the historical Jesus, and who were obliged to assert it precisely because they denied the eschatological conceptions, forced this view upon the theology of the Early Church, and compelled it to create in the Logos Christology an un-Gnostic mould in which to cast the speculative conception of the historical

Messiahship of Jesus; and that is what we find in the Fourth Gospel. Prior to the anti-Gnostic controversies we find in the early Christian literature no conscious dating back of the Messiahship of Jesus to His earthly life, and no theological interest at work upon the dogmatic recasting of His history.[263] It is therefore difficult to suppose that the Messianic secret in Mark, that is to say, in the very earliest tradition, was derived from primitive theology. The assertion of the Messiahship of Jesus was wholly independent of the latter. The instinct which led Bruno Bauer to explain the Messianic secret as the literary invention of Mark himself was therefore quite correct. Once suppose that tradition and primitive theology have anything to do with the matter, and the theory of the interpolation of the Messiahship into the history becomes almost impossible to carry through. But Wrede's greatness consists precisely in the fact that he was compelled by his acute perception of the significance of the critical data to set aside the purely literary version of the hypothesis and make Mark, so to speak, the instrument of the [pg 343] literary realisation of the ideas of a definite intellectual circle within the sphere of primitive theology.

The positive difficulty which confronts the sceptical theory is to explain how the Messianic beliefs of the first generation arose, if Jesus, throughout His life, was for all, even for the disciples, merely a "teacher," and gave even His intimates no hint of the dignity which He claimed for Himself. It is difficult to eliminate the Messiahship from the "Life of Jesus," especially from the narrative of the passion; it is more difficult still, as Keim saw long ago, to bring it back again after its elimination from the "Life" into the theology of the primitive Church. In Wrede's acute and logical thinking this difficulty seems to leap to light.

Since the Messianic secret in Mark is always connected with the resurrection, the date at which the Messianic belief of the disciples arose must be the resurrection of Jesus. "But the idea of dating the Messiahship from the resurrection is certainly not a thought of Jesus, but of the primitive Church. It presupposes the Church's experience of the appearance of the risen Jesus."

The psychologist will say that the "resurrection experiences," however they may be conceived, are only intelligible as based upon the expectation of the resurrection, and this again as based on references of Jesus to the resurrection. But leaving psychology aside, let us accept the resurrection experiences of the disciples as a pure psychological miracle. Even so, how can the appearances of the risen Jesus have suggested to the disciples the idea that Jesus, the crucified teacher, was the Messiah? Apart from any expectations, how can this conclusion have resulted for them from the mere "fact of the resurrection"? The fact of the appearance did not by any means imply it. In certain circles, indeed, according to Mark vi. 14-16, in the very highest quarters, the resurrection of the Baptist was believed in; but that did not make John the Baptist the Messiah. The inexplicable thing is that, according to Wrede, the disciples began at once to assert confidently and unanimously that He was the Messiah and would before long appear in glory.

But how did the appearance of the risen Jesus suddenly become for them a proof of His Messiahship and the basis of their eschatology? That Wrede fails to explain, and so makes this "event" an "historical" miracle which in reality is harder to believe than the supernatural event.

Any one who holds "historical" miracles to be just as impossible as any other kind, even when they occur in a critical and sceptical work, will be forced to the conclusion that the Messianic eschatological significance attached to the "resurrection experience" by the disciples implies some kind of Messianic eschatological references on the part of the historical Jesus which gave to the [pg 344] "resurrection" its Messianic eschatological significance. Here Wrede himself, though without admitting it, postulates some Messianic hints on the part of Jesus, since he conceives the judgment of the disciples upon the resurrection to have been not analytical, but synthetic, inasmuch as they add something to it, and that, indeed, the main thing, which was not implied in the conception of the event as such.

Here again the merit of Wrede's contribution to criticism consists in the fact that he takes the position as it is and does not try to improve it artificially. Bruno Bauer and others supposed that the belief in the Messiahship of Jesus had slowly solidified out of a kind of gaseous state, or had been forced into primitive theology by the literary invention of Mark. Wrede, however, feels himself obliged to base it upon an historical fact, and, moreover, the same historical fact which is pointed to by the sayings in the Synoptics and the Pauline theology. But in so doing he creates an almost insurmountable difficulty for his hypothesis.

We can only briefly refer to the question what form the accounts of the resurrection must have taken if the historic fact which underlay them was the first surprised apprehension and recognition of the Messiahship of Jesus on the part of the disciples. The Messianic teaching would necessarily in that case have been somehow or other put into the mouth of the risen Jesus. It is, however, completely absent, because it was already contained in the teaching of Jesus during His earthly life. The theory of Messianic secrecy must therefore have re-moulded not merely the story of the passion, but also that of the resurrection, removing the revelation of the Messiahship to the disciples from the latter in order to insert it into the public ministry!

Wrede, moreover, will only take account of the Marcan text as it stands, not of the historical possibility that the "futuristic Messiahship" which meets us in the mysterious utterances of Jesus goes back in some form to a sound tradition. Further he does not take the eschatological character of the teaching of Jesus into his calculations, but works on the false assumption that he can analyse the Marcan text in and by itself and so discover the principle on which it is composed. He carries out experiments on the law of crystallisation of the narrative material in this Gospel, but instead of doing so in the natural and historical atmosphere he does it in an atmosphere artificially neutralised, which contains no trace of contemporary conceptions.[264] Consequently the conclusion [pg 345] based on the sum of his observations has in it something arbitrary. Everything which conflicts with the rational construction of the course of the history is referred directly to the theory of the concealment of the Messianic secret. But in the carrying out of that theory a number of self-contradictions, without which it could not subsist, must be recognised and noted.

Thus, for example, all the prohibitions,[265] whatever they may refer to, even including the command not to make known His miracles, are referred to the same category as the injunction not to reveal the Messianic secret. But what justification is there for that? It presupposes that according to Mark the miracles could be taken as proofs of the Messiahship, an idea of which there is no hint whatever in Mark. "The miracles," Wrede argues, "are certainly used by the earliest Christians as evidence of the nature and significance of Christ.... I need hardly point to the fact that Mark, not less than Matthew, Luke, and John, must have held the opinion that the miracles of Jesus encountered a widespread and ardent Messianic expectation."

In John this Messianic significance of the miracles is certainly assumed; but then the really eschatological view of things has here fallen into the background. It seems indeed as if genuine eschatology excluded the Messianic interpretation of the miracles. In Matthew the miracles of Jesus have nothing whatever to do with the proof of the Messiahship, but, as is evident from the saying about Chorazin and Bethsaida, Matt. xi. 20-24, are only an exhibition of mercy intended to awaken repentance, or, according to Matt. xii. 28, an indication of the nearness of the Kingdom of God. They have as little to do with the Messianic office as in the Acts of the Apostles.[266] In Mark, from first to last, there is [pg 346] not a single syllable to suggest that the miracles have a Messianic significance. Even admitting the possibility that the "miracles of Jesus encountered an ardent Messianic expectation," that does not necessarily imply a Messianic significance in them. To justify that conclusion requires the pre-supposition that the Messiah was expected to be some kind of an earthly man who should do miracles. This is presupposed by Wrede, by Bruno Bauer, and by modern theology in general, but it has not been proved, and it is at variance with eschatology, which pictured the Messiah to itself as a heavenly being in a world which was already being transformed into something supra-mundane.

The assumption that the clue to the explanation of the command not to make known the miracles is to be found in the necessity of guarding the secret of the Messiahship is, therefore, not justified. The miracles are connected with the Kingdom and the nearness of the Kingdom, not with the Messiah. But Wrede is obliged to refer everything to the Messianic secret, because he leaves the preaching of the Kingdom out of account.

The same process is repeated in the discussion of the veiling of the mystery of the Kingdom of God in the parables of Mark iv. The mystery of the Kingdom is for Wrede the secret of Jesus' Messiahship. "We have learned in the meantime," he says, "that one main element in this mystery is that Jesus is the Messiah, the Son of God. If Jesus, according to Mark, conceals his Messiahship, we are justified in interpreting the μυστήριον τῆς βασιλείας τοῦ θεοῦ in the light of this fact."

That is one of the weakest points in Wrede's whole theory. Where is there any hint of this in these parables? And why should the secret of the Kingdom of God contain within it as one of its principal features the secret of the Messiahship of Jesus?

"Mark's account of Jesus' parabolic teaching," he concludes, "is completely unhistorical," because it is directly opposed to the essential nature of the parables. The ultimate reason, according to Wrede, why this whole view of the parables arose, was simply "because the general opinion was already in existence that Jesus had revealed Himself to the disciples, but concealed Himself from the multitude."

Instead of simply admitting that we are unable to discover what the mystery of the Kingdom in Mark iv. is, any more than we can understand why it must be veiled, and numbering it among the unsolved problems of Jesus' preaching of the Kingdom, Wrede forces this chapter inside the lines of his theory of the veiled Messiahship.

The desire of Jesus to be alone, too, and remain unrecognised (Mark vii. 24 and ix. 30 ff.) is supposed to have some kind of connexion with the veiling of the Messiahship. He even brings [pg 347] the multitude, which in Mark x. 47 ff. rebukes the blind beggar at Jericho who cried out to Jesus, into the service of his theory ... on the ground that the beggar had addressed Him as

Son of David. But all the narrative says is that they told him to hold his peace—to cease making an outcry—not that they did so because of his addressing Jesus as "Son of David."

In an equally arbitrary fashion the surprising introduction of the "multitude" in Mark viii. 34, after the incident of Caesarea Philippi, is dragged into the theory of secrecy.[267] Wrede does not feel the possibility or impossibility of the sudden appearance of the multitude in this locality as an historical problem, any more than he grasps the sudden withdrawal of Jesus from His public ministry as primarily an historical question. Mark is for him a writer who is to be judged from a pathological point of view, a writer who, dominated by the fixed idea of introducing everywhere the Messianic secret of Jesus, is always creating mysterious and unintelligible situations, even when these do not directly serve the interests of his theory, and who in some of his descriptions, writes in a rather "fairy-tale" style. When all is said, his treatment of the history scarcely differs from that of the fourth Evangelist.

The absence of historical prepossessions which Wrede skilfully assumes in his examination of the connexion in Mark is not really complete. He is bound to refer everything inexplicable to the principle of the concealment of the Messiahship, which is the only principle that he recognises in the dogmatic stratum of the narrative, and is consequently obliged to deny the historicity of such passages, whereas in reality the veiling of the Messiahship is only involved in a few places and is there indicated in clear and simple words. He is unwilling to recognise that there is a second, wider circle of mystery which has to do, not with Jesus' Messiahship, but with His preaching of the Kingdom, with the mystery of the Kingdom of God in the wider sense, and that within this second circle there lie a number of historical problems, above all the mission of the Twelve and the inexplicable abandonment of public activity on the part of Jesus which followed soon afterwards. His mistake consists in endeavouring by violent methods to subsume the more general, the mystery of the Kingdom of God, under the more special, the mystery of the Messiahship, instead of inserting the latter as the smaller circle, within the wider, the secret of the Kingdom of God.

As he does not deal with the teaching of Jesus, he has no occasion to take account of the secret of the Kingdom of God. That is the more remarkable because corresponding to one fundamental idea of the Messianic secret there is a parallel, [pg 348] more general dogmatic conception in Jesus' preaching of the Kingdom. For if Jesus in Matt. x. gives the disciples nothing to take with them on their mission but predictions of suffering; if at the very beginning of His ministry He closes the Beatitudes with a blessing upon the persecuted; if in Mark viii. 34 ff. He warns the people that they will have to choose between life and life, between death and death; if, in short, from the first, He loses no opportunity of preaching about suffering and following Him in His sufferings; that is just as much a matter of dogma as His own sufferings and predictions of sufferings. For in both cases the necessity of suffering, the necessity of facing death, is not "a necessity of the historical situation," not a necessity which arises out of the circumstances; it is an assertion put forth without empirical basis, a prophecy of storm while the sky is blue, since neither Jesus nor the people to whom He spoke were undergoing any persecution; and when His fate overtook Him not even the disciples were involved in it. It is distinctly remarkable that, except for a few meagre references, the enigmatic character of Jesus' constant predictions of suffering has not been discussed in the Life-of-Jesus literature.[268]

What has now to be done, therefore, is, in contradistinction to Wrede, to make a critical examination of the dogmatic element in the life of Jesus on the assumption that the atmosphere of the time was saturated with eschatology, that is, to keep in even closer touch with the facts than Wrede does, and moreover, to proceed, not from the particular to the general, but from the general to the particular, carefully considering whether the dogmatic element is not precisely the historical element. For, after all, why should not Jesus think in terms of doctrine, and make history in action, just as well as a poor Evangelist can do it on paper, under the pressure of the theological interests of the primitive community.

Once again, however, we must repeat that the critical analysis and the assertion of a system running through the disorder are the same in the eschatological as in the sceptical hypothesis, only that in the eschatological analysis a number of problems come more clearly to light. The two constructions are related like the bones and cartilage of the body. The general structure is the same, only that in the case of the one a solid substance, lime, is distributed even in the minutest portions, giving it firmness and solidity, while in the other case this is lacking. This reinforcing substance is the eschatological world-view.

How is it to be explained that Wrede, in spite of the eschatological school, in spite of Johannes Weiss, could, in critically [pg 349] investigating the connecting principle of the life of Jesus, simply leave eschatology out of account? The blame rests with the eschatological school itself, for it applied the eschatological explanation only to the preaching of Jesus, and not even to the whole of this, but only to the Messianic secret, instead of using it also to throw light upon the whole public work of Jesus, the connexion and want of connexion between the events. It represented Jesus as thinking and speaking eschatologically in some of the most important passages of His teaching, but for the rest gave as uneschatological a presentation of His life as modern historical theology had done. The teaching of Jesus and the history of Jesus were set in different keys. Instead of destroying the modern-historical scheme of the life of Jesus, or subjecting it to a rigorous examination, and thereby undertaking the performance of a highly valuable service to criticism, the eschatological theory confined itself within the limits of New Testament Theology, and left it to Wrede to reveal one after another by a laborious purely critical method the difficulties which from its point of view it might have grasped historically at a single glance. It inevitably follows that Wrede is unjust to Johannes Weiss and Johannes Weiss towards Wrede.[269]

It is quite inexplicable that the eschatological school, with its clear perception of the eschatological element in the preaching of the Kingdom of God, did not also hit upon the thought of the "dogmatic" element in the history of Jesus. Eschatology is simply "dogmatic history"—history as moulded by theological beliefs—which breaks in upon the natural course of history and abrogates. it. Is it not even a priori the only conceivable view that the conduct of one who looked forward to His Messianic "Parousia" in the near future should be determined, not by the natural course of events, but by that expectation? The chaotic confusion of the narratives ought to have suggested the thought that the events had been thrown into this confusion by the volcanic force of an incalculable personality, not by some kind of carelessness or freak of the tradition.

[pg 350]

A very little consideration suffices to show that there is something quite incomprehensible in the public ministry of Jesus taken as a whole. According to Mark it lasted less than a year, for since he speaks of only one Passover-journey we may conclude that no other Passover fell within the period of Jesus' activity as a teacher. If it is proposed to assume that He allowed a Passover to go by without going up to Jerusalem, His adversaries, who took Him to task about hand-washings and about rubbing the ears of corn on the Sabbath, would certainly have made a most serious matter of this, and we should have to suppose that the Evangelist for some reason or other thought fit to suppress the fact. That is to say, the burden of proof lies upon those who assert a longer duration for the ministry of Jesus.

Until they have succeeded in proving it, we may assume something like the following course of events. Jesus, in going up to a Passover, came in contact with the movement initiated by John the Baptist in Judaea, and, after the lapse of a little time—if we bring into the reckoning the forty days' sojourn in the wilderness mentioned in Mark i. 13, a few weeks later—appeared in Galilee proclaiming the near approach of the Kingdom of God. According to Mark He had known Himself since His baptism to be the Messiah, but from the historical point of view that does not matter, since history is concerned with the first announcement of the Messiahship, not with inward psychological processes.[270]

This work of preaching the Kingdom was continued until the sending forth of the Twelve; that is to say, at the most for a few weeks. Perhaps in the saying "the harvest is great but the labourers are few," with which Jesus closes His work prior to sending forth the disciples, there lies an allusion to the actual state of the natural fields. The flocking of the people to Him after the Mission of the Twelve, when a great multitude thronged about Him for several days during His journey along the northern shore of the lake, can be more naturally explained if the harvest had just been brought in.

However that may be, it is certain that Jesus, in the midst of His initial success, left Galilee, journeyed northwards, and only resumed His work as a teacher in Judaea on the way to Jerusalem! Of His "public ministry," therefore, a large section falls out, being cancelled by a period of inexplicable concealment; it dwindles to [pg 351] a few weeks of preaching here and there in Galilee and the few days of His sojourn in Jerusalem.[271]

But in that case the public life of Jesus becomes practically unintelligible. The explanation that His cause in Galilee was lost, and that He was obliged to flee, has not the slightest foundation in the text.[272] That was recognised even by Keim, the inventor of the successful and unsuccessful periods in the life of Jesus, as is shown by his suggestion that the Evangelists had intentionally removed the traces of failure from the decisive period which led up to the northern journey. The controversy over the washing of hands in Mark vii. 1-23, to which appeal is always made, is really a defeat for the Pharisees. The theory of the "desertion of the Galilaeans," which appears with more or less artistic variations in all modern Lives of Jesus, owes its existence not to any other confirmatory fact, but simply to the circumstance that Mark makes the simple statement: "And Jesus departed and went into the region of Tyre" (vii. 24) without offering any explanation of this decision.

The only conclusion which the text warrants is that Mark mentioned no reason because he knew of none. The decision of Jesus did not rest upon the recorded facts, since it ignores these, but upon considerations lying outside the history. His life at this period was dominated by a "dogmatic idea" which rendered Him indifferent to all else ... even to the happy and successful work as a teacher which was opening before Him. How could Jesus the "teacher" abandon at that moment a people so anxious to learn and so eager for salvation? His action suggests a doubt whether He really felt Himself to be a "teacher." If all the controversial discourses and sayings and answers to questions, which were so to speak wrung from Him, were subtracted from the sum of His utterances, how much of the didactic preaching of Jesus would be left over?

But even the supposed didactic preaching is not really that of a "teacher," since the purpose of His parables was, according to Mark iv. 10-12, not to reveal, but to conceal, and of the Kingdom of God He spoke only in parables (Mark iv. 34).

Perhaps, however, we are not justified in extending the theory [pg 352] of concealment, simply because it is mentioned in connexion with the first parable, to all the parables which He ever spoke, for it is never mentioned again. It could hardly indeed be applied to the parables with a moral, like that, for instance, of the pearl of great price. It is equally inapplicable to the parables of coming judgment uttered at Jerusalem, in which He explicitly exhorts the people to be prepared and watchful in view of the coming of judgment and of the Kingdom. But here too it is deserving of notice that Jesus, whenever He desires to make known anything further concerning the Kingdom of God than just its near approach, seems to be confined, as it were by a higher law, to the parabolic form of discourse. It is as though, for reasons which we cannot grasp, His teaching lay under certain limitations. It appears as a kind of accessory aspect of His vocation. Thus it was possible for Him to give up His work as a teacher even at the moment when it promised the greatest success.

Accordingly the fact of His always speaking in parables and of His taking this inexplicable resolution both point back to a mysterious pre-supposition which greatly reduces the importance of Jesus' work as a teacher.

One reason for this limitation is distinctly stated in Mark iv. 10-12, viz. predestination! Jesus knows that the truth which He offers is exclusively for those who have been definitely chosen, that the general and public announcement of His message could only thwart the plans of God, since the chosen are already winning their salvation from God. Only the phrase, "Repent for the Kingdom of God is at hand" and its variants belong to the public preaching. And this, therefore, is the only message which He commits to His disciples when sending them forth. What this repentance, supplementary to the law, the special ethic of the interval before the coming of the Kingdom (*Interimsethik*) is, in its positive acceptation, He explains in the Sermon on the Mount. But all that goes beyond that simple phrase must be publicly presented only in parables, in order that those only, who are shown to possess predestination by having the initial knowledge which enables them to understand the parables, may receive a more advanced knowledge, which is imparted to them in a measure corresponding to their original degree of knowledge: "Unto him that hath shall be given, and from him that hath not shall be taken away even that which he hath" (Mark iv. 24-25).

The predestinarian view goes along with the eschatology. It is pushed to its utmost consequences in the closing incident of the parable of the marriage of the King's son (Matt. xxii. 1-14) where the man who, in response to a publicly issued invitation, sits down at the table of the King, but is recognised from his appearance as not called, is thrown out into perdition. "Many are called but few are chosen." [pg 353] The ethical idea of salvation and the predestinarian limitation of acceptance to the elect are constantly in conflict in the mind of Jesus. In one case, however, He finds relief in the thought of predestination. When the rich young man turned away, not having strength to give up his possessions for the sake of following

Jesus as he had been commanded to do, Jesus and His disciples were forced to draw the conclusion that he, like other rich men, was lost, and could not enter into the Kingdom of God. But immediately afterwards Jesus makes the suggestion, "With men it is impossible, but not with God, for with God all things are possible" (Mark x. 17-27). That is, He will not give up the hope that the young man, in spite of appearances, which are against him, will be found to have belonged to the Kingdom of God, solely in virtue of the secret all-powerful will of God. Of a "conversion" of the young man there is no question.

In the Beatitudes, on the other hand, the argument is reversed; the predestination is inferred from its outward manifestation. It may seem to us inconceivable, but they are really predestinarian in form. Blessed are the poor in spirit! Blessed are the meek! Blessed are the peacemakers!—that does not mean that by virtue of their being poor in spirit, meek, peace-loving, they deserve the Kingdom. Jesus does not intend the saying as an injunction or exhortation, but as a simple statement of fact: in their being poor in spirit, in their meekness, in their love of peace, it is made manifest that they are predestined to the Kingdom. By the possession of these qualities they are marked as belonging to it. In the case of others (Matt. v. 10-12) the predestination to the Kingdom is made manifest by the persecutions which befall them in this world. These are the light of the world, which already shines among men for the glory of God (Matt. v. 14-15).

The kingdom cannot be "earned"; what happens is that men are called to it, and show themselves to be called to it. On careful examination it appears that the idea of reward in the sayings of Jesus is not really an idea of reward, because it is relieved against a background of predestination. For the present it is sufficient to note the fact that the eschatologico-predestinarian view brings a mysterious element of dogma not merely into the teaching, but also into the public ministry of Jesus.

To take another point, what is the mystery of the Kingdom of God? It must consist of something more than merely its near approach, and something of extreme importance; otherwise Jesus would be here indulging in mere mystery-mongering. The saying about the candle which He puts upon the stand, in order that what was hidden may be revealed to those who have ears to hear, implies that He is making a tremendous revelation to those who understand the parables about the growth of the seed. The mystery must [pg 354] therefore contain the explanation why the Kingdom must now come, and how men are to know how near it is. For the general fact that it is very near had already been openly proclaimed both by the Baptist and by Jesus. The mystery, therefore, must consist of something more than that.

In these parables it is not the idea of development, but of the apparent absence of causation which occupies the foremost place. The description aims at suggesting the question, how, and by what power, incomparably great and glorious results can be infallibly produced by an insignificant fact without human aid. A man sowed seed. Much of it was lost, but the little that fell into good ground brought forth a harvest—thirty, sixty, an hundredfold—which left no trace of the loss in the sowing. How did that come about?

A man sows seed and does not trouble any further about it—cannot indeed do anything to help it, but he knows that after a definite time the glorious harvest which arises out of the seed will stand before him. By what power is that effected?

An extremely minute grain of mustard seed is planted in the earth and there necessarily arises out of it a great bush, which cannot certainly have been contained in the grain of seed. How was that?

What the parables emphasise is, therefore, so to speak, the in itself negative, inadequate, character of the initial fact, upon which, as by a miracle, there follows in the appointed time, through the power of God, some great thing. They lay stress not upon the natural, but upon the miraculous character of such occurrences.

But what is the initial fact of the parables? It is the sowing.

It is not said that by the man who sows the seed Jesus means Himself. The man has no importance. In the parable of the mustard seed he is not even mentioned. All that is asserted is that the initial fact is already present, as certainly present as the time of the sowing is past at the moment when Jesus speaks. That being so, the Kingdom of God must follow as certainly as harvest follows seed-sowing. As a man believes in the harvest, without being able to explain it, simply because the seed has been sown; so with the same absolute confidence he may believe in the Kingdom of God.

And the initial fact which is symbolised? Jesus can only mean a fact which was actually in existence—the movement of repentance evoked by the Baptist and now intensified by His own preaching. That necessarily involves the bringing in of the Kingdom by the power of God; as man's sowing necessitates the giving of the harvest by the same Infinite Power. Any one who knows this sees with different eyes the corn growing in the fields [pg 355] and the harvest ripening, for he sees the one fact in the other, and awaits along with the earthly harvest the heavenly, the revelation of the Kingdom of God.

If we look into the thought more closely we see that the coming of the Kingdom of God is not only symbolically or analogically, but also really and temporally connected with the harvest. The harvest ripening upon earth is the last! With it comes also the Kingdom of God which brings in the new age. When the reapers are sent into the fields, the Lord in Heaven will cause His harvest to be reaped by the holy angels.

If the three parables of Mark iv. contain the mystery of the Kingdom of God, and are therefore capable of being summed up in a single formula, this can be nothing else than the joyful exhortation: "Ye who have eyes to see, read, in the harvest which is ripening upon earth, what is being prepared in heaven!" The eager eschatological hope was to regard the natural process as the last of its kind, and to see in it a special significance in view of the event of which it was to give the signal.

The analogical and temporal parallelism becomes complete if we assume that the movement initiated by the Baptist began in the spring, and notice that Jesus, according to Matt. ix. 37 and 38, before sending out the disciples to make a speedy proclamation of the nearness of the Kingdom of God, uttered the remarkable saying about the rich harvest. It seems like a final expression of the thought contained in the parables about the seed and its promise, and finds its most natural explanation in the supposition that the harvest was actually at hand.

Whatever may be thought of this attempt to divine historically the secret of the Kingdom of God, there is one thing that cannot be got away from, viz. that the initial fact to which Jesus points, under the figure of the sowing, is somehow or other connected with the eschatological preaching of repentance, which had been begun by the Baptist.

That may be the more confidently asserted because Jesus in another mysterious saying describes the days of the Baptist as a time which makes preparation for the coming of the Kingdom of God. "From the days of John the Baptist," He says in Matt. xi. 12, "even until now, the Kingdom of Heaven is subjected to violence, and the violent wrest it to themselves." The saying has nothing to do with the entering of individuals into the Kingdom; it simply asserts, that since the coming of the Baptist a certain number of persons are engaged in forcing on and compelling the coming of the Kingdom. Jesus' expectation of the Kingdom is an expectation based upon a fact which exercises an active influence upon the Kingdom of God. It was not He, and not the Baptist who "were working at the coming of the Kingdom"; it is the host [pg 356] of penitents which is wringing it from God, so that it may now come at any moment.

The eschatological insight of Johannes Weiss made an end of the modern view that Jesus founded the Kingdom. It did away with all activity, as exercised upon the Kingdom of God, and made the part of Jesus purely a waiting one. Now the activity comes back into the preaching of the Kingdom, but this time eschatologically conditioned. The secret of the Kingdom of God which Jesus unveils in the parables about confident expectation in Mark iv., and declares in so many words in the eulogy on the Baptist (Matt. xi.), amounts to this, that in the movement to which the Baptist gave the first impulse, and which still continued, there was an initial fact which was drawing after it the coming of the Kingdom, in a fashion which was miraculous, unintelligible, but unfailingly certain, since the sufficient cause for it lay in the power and purpose of God.

It should be observed that Jesus in these parables, as well as in the related saying at the sending forth of the Twelve, uses the formula, "He that hath ears to hear, let him hear" (Mark iv. 23 and Matt. xi. 15), thereby signifying that in this utterance there lies concealed a supernatural knowledge concerning the plans of God, which only those who have ears to hear—that is, the foreordained—can detect. For others these sayings are unintelligible.

If this genuinely "historical" interpretation of the mystery of the Kingdom of God is correct, Jesus must have expected the coming of the Kingdom at harvest time. And that is just what He did expect. It is for that reason that He sends out His disciples to make known in Israel, as speedily as may be, what is about to happen. That in this He is actuated by a dogmatic idea, becomes clear when we notice that, according to Mark, the mission of the Twelve followed immediately on the rejection at Nazareth. The unreceptiveness of the Nazarenes had made no impression upon Him; He was only astonished at their unbelief (Mark vi. 6). This passage is often interpreted to mean that He was astonished to find His miracle-working power fail Him. There is no hint of that in the text. What He is astonished at is, that in His native town there were so few believers, that is, elect, knowing as He does that the Kingdom of God may appear at any moment. But that fact makes no difference whatever to the nearness of the coming of the Kingdom.

The Evangelist, therefore, places the rejection at Nazareth and the mission of the Twelve side by side, simply because he found them in this temporal connexion in the tradition. If he had been working by "association of ideas," he would not have arrived at this order. The want of connexion, the impossibility of applying any natural explanation, is just what is historical, because the course of [pg 357] the history was determined, not by outward events, but by the decisions of Jesus, and these were determined by dogmatic, eschatological considerations.

To how great an extent this was the case in regard to the mission of the Twelve is clearly seen from the "charge" which Jesus gave them. He tells them in plain words (Matt. x. 23), that He does not expect to see them back in the present age. The Parousia of the Son of Man, which is logically and temporally identical with the dawn of the Kingdom, will take place before they shall have completed a hasty journey through the cities of Israel to announce it. That the words mean this and nothing else, that they ought not to be in any way weakened down, should be sufficiently evident. This is the form in which Jesus reveals to them the secret of the Kingdom of God. A few days later, He utters the saying about the violent who, since the days of John the Baptist, are forcing on the coming of the Kingdom.

It is equally clear, and here the dogmatic considerations which guided the resolutions of Jesus become still more prominent, that this prediction was not fulfilled. The disciples returned to Him; and the appearing of the Son of Man had not taken place. The actual history disavowed the dogmatic history on which the action of Jesus had been based. An event of supernatural history which must take place, and must take place at that particular point of time, failed to come about. That was for Jesus, who lived wholly in the dogmatic history, the first "historical" occurrence, the central event which closed the former period of His activity and gave the coming period a new character. To this extent modern theology is justified when it distinguishes two periods in the Life of Jesus; an earlier, in which He is surrounded by the people, a later in which He is "deserted" by them, and travels about with the Twelve only. It is a sound observation that the two periods are sharply distinguished by the attitude of Jesus. To explain this difference of attitude, which they thought themselves bound to account for on natural historical grounds, theologians of the modern historical school invented the theory of growing opposition and waning support. Weisse, no doubt, had expressed himself in direct opposition to this theory.[273] Keim, who gave it its place in theology, was aware that in setting it up he was going against the plain sense of the texts. Later writers lost this consciousness, just as in the first and third Gospel the significance of the Messianic secret in [pg 358] Mark gradually faded away; they imagined that they could find the basis of fact for the theory in the texts, and did not realise that they only believed in the desertion of the multitude and the "flights and retirements" of Jesus because they could not otherwise explain historically the alteration in His conduct, His withdrawal from public work, and His resolve to die.

The thoroughgoing eschatological school makes better work of it. They recognise in the non-occurrence of the Parousia promised in Matt. x. 23, the "historic fact," in the estimation of Jesus, which in some way determined the alteration in His plans, and His attitude towards the multitude.

The whole history of "Christianity" down to the present day, that is to say, the real inner history of it, is based on the delay of the Parousia, the non-occurrence of the Parousia, the abandonment of eschatology, the progress and completion of the "de-eschatologising" of religion which has been connected therewith. It should be noted that the non-fulfilment of Matt. x. 23 is the first postponement of the Parousia. We have therefore here the first significant date in the "history of Christianity"; it gives to the work of Jesus a new direction, otherwise inexplicable.

Here we recognise also why the Marcan hypothesis, in constructing its view of the Life of Jesus, found itself obliged to have recourse more and more to the help of modern psychology, and thus necessarily became more and more unhistorical. The fact which alone makes possible an understanding of the whole, is lacking in this Gospel. Without Matt. x. and xi. everything remains enigmatic. For this reason Bruno Bauer and Wrede are in their own way the only consistent representatives of the Marcan hypothesis from the point of view of historical criticism, when they arrive at the result that the Marcan account is inherently unintelligible. Keim, with his strong sense of historical reality, rightly felt that the plan of the Life of Jesus should not be constructed exclusively on the basis of Mark.

The recognition that Mark alone gives an inadequate basis, is more important than any "Ur-Markus" theories, for which it is impossible to discover a literary foundation, or find an historical use. A simple induction from the "facts" takes us beyond Mark. In the discourse-material of Matthew, which the modern-historical school thought they could sift in here and there, wherever there seemed to be room for it, there lie hidden certain facts—facts which never happened but are all the more important for that.

Why Mark describes the events and discourses in the neighbourhood of the mission of the Twelve with such careful authentication is a literary question which the historical study of the life of Jesus may leave open; the more so since, even as a literary question, it is insoluble.

[pg 359]

The prediction of the Parousia of the Son of Man is not the only one which remained unfulfilled. There is the prediction of sufferings which is connected with it. To put it more accurately, the prediction of the appearing of the Son of Man in Matt. x. 23 runs up into a prediction of sufferings, which, working up to a climax, forms the remainder of the discourse at the sending forth of the disciples. This prediction of sufferings has as little to do with objective history as the prediction of the Parousia. Consequently, none of the Lives of Jesus, which follow the lines of a natural psychology, from Weisse down to Oskar Holtzmann, can make anything of it.[274] They either strike it out, or transfer it to the last "gloomy epoch" of the life of Jesus, regard it as an unintelligible anticipation, or put it down to the account of "primitive theology," which serves as a scrap-heap for everything for which they cannot find a place in the "historical life of Jesus."

In the texts it is quite evident that Jesus is not speaking of sufferings after His death, but of sufferings which will befall them as soon as they have gone forth from Him. The death of Jesus is not here pre-supposed, but only the Parousia of the Son of Man, and it is implied that this will occur just after these sufferings and bring them to a close. If the theology of the primitive Church had remoulded the tradition, as is always being asserted, it would have made Jesus give His followers directions for their conduct after His death. That we do not find anything of this kind is the best proof that there can be no question of a remoulding of the Life of Jesus by primitive theology. How easy it would have been for the Early Church to scatter here and there through the discourses of Jesus directions which were only to be applied after His death! But the simple fact is that it did not do so.

The sufferings of which the prospect is held out at the sending forth are doubly, trebly, nay four times over, unhistorical. In the first place—and this is the only point which modern historical theology has noticed—because there is not a shadow of a suggestion in the outward circumstances of anything which could form a natural occasion for such predictions of, and exhortations relating to, sufferings. In the second place—and this has been overlooked by modern theology because it had already declared them to be unhistorical in its own characteristic fashion, viz. by striking them out—because they were not fulfilled. In the third place—and this has not entered into the mind of modern theology at all—because these sayings were spoken in the closest connexion [pg 360] with the promise of the Parousia and are placed in the closest connexion with that event. In the fourth place, because the description of that which is to befall the disciples is quite without any basis in experience. A time of general dissension will begin, in which brothers will rise up against brothers, and fathers against sons and children against their parents to cause them to be put to death (Matt. x. 21). And the disciples "shall be hated of all men for His name's sake." Let them strive to hold out to the "end," that is, to the coming of the Son of Man, in order that they may be saved (Matt. x. 22).

But why should they suddenly be hated and persecuted for the name of Jesus, seeing that this name played no part whatever in their preaching? That is simply inconceivable. The relation of Jesus to the Son of Man, the fact, that is to say, that it is He who is to be manifested as Son of Man, must therefore in some way or other become known in the interval; not, however, through the disciples, but by some other means of revelation. A kind of supernatural illumination will suddenly make known all that Jesus has been keeping secret regarding the Kingdom of God and His position in the Kingdom. This illumination will arise as suddenly and without preparation as the spirit of strife.

And as a matter of fact Jesus predicts to the disciples in the same discourse that to their own surprise a supernatural wisdom will suddenly speak from their lips, so that it will be not they but the Spirit of God who will answer the great ones of the earth. As the Spirit is for Jesus and early Christian theology something concrete which is to descend upon the elect among mankind only in consequence of a definite event—the outpouring of the Spirit which, according to the prophecy of Joel, should precede the day of judgment—Jesus must have anticipated that this would occur during the absence of the disciples, in the midst of the time of strife and confusion.

To put it differently; the whole of the discourse at the sending forth of the Twelve, taken in the clear sense of the words, is a prediction of the events of the "time of the end," events which are immediately at hand, in which the supernatural eschatological course of history will break through into the natural course. The expectation of sufferings is therefore doctrinal and unhistorical, as is, precisely in the same way, the expectation of the pouring forth of the Spirit uttered at the same time. The Parousia of the Son of Man is to be preceded according to the Messianic dogma by a time of strife and confusion—as it were, the birth-throes of the Messiah—and the outpouring of the Spirit. It should be noticed that according to Joel iii. and iv. the outpouring of the Spirit, along with the miraculous signs, forms the prelude to the judgment; and also, that in the same context, Joel iii. 13, the judgment [pg 361] is described as the harvest-day of God.[275] Here we have a remarkable parallel to the saying about the harvest in Matt. ix. 38, which forms the introduction to the discourse at the sending forth of the disciples.

There is only one point in which the predicted course of eschatological events is incomplete: the appearance of Elias is not mentioned.

Jesus could not prophesy to the disciples the Parousia of the Son of Man without pointing them, at the same time, to the pre-eschatological events which must first occur. He must open to them a part of the secret of the Kingdom of God, viz. the nearness of the harvest, that they might not be taken by surprise and caused to doubt by these events.

Thus this discourse is historical as a whole and down to the smallest detail precisely because, according to the view of modern theology, it must be judged unhistorical. It is, in fact, full of eschatological dogma. Jesus had no need to instruct the disciples as to what they were to teach; for they had only to utter a cry. But concerning the events which should supervene, it was necessary that He should give them information. Therefore the discourse does not consist of instruction, but of predictions of sufferings and of the Parousia.

That being so, we may judge with what right the modern psychological theology dismisses the great Matthaean discourses off-hand as mere "composite structures." Just let any one try to show how the Evangelist when he was racking his brains over the task of making a "discourse at the sending forth of the disciples," [pg 362] half by the method of piecing it together out of traditional sayings and "primitive theology," and half by inventing it, lighted on the curious idea of making Jesus speak entirely of inopportune and unpractical matters; and of then going on to provide the evidence that they never happened.

The foretelling of the sufferings that belong to the eschatological distress is part and parcel of the preaching of the approach of the Kingdom of God, it embodies the secret of the Kingdom. It is for that reason that the thought of suffering appears at the end of the Beatitudes and in the closing petition of the Lord's Prayer. For the πειρασμός which is there in view is not an individual psychological temptation, but the general eschatological time of tribulation, from which God is besought to exempt those who pray so earnestly for the coming of the Kingdom, and not to expose them to that tribulation by way of putting them to the test.

There followed neither the sufferings, nor the outpouring of the Spirit, nor the Parousia of the Son of Man. The disciples returned safe and sound and full of a proud satisfaction; for one promise had been realised—the power which had been given them over the demons.

But from the moment when they rejoined Him, all His thoughts and efforts were devoted to getting rid of the people in order to be alone with them (Mark vi. 30-33). Previously, during their absence, He had, almost in open speech, taught the multitude concerning the Baptist, concerning that which was to precede the coming of the Kingdom, and concerning the judgment which should come upon the impenitent, even upon whole towns of them (Matt. xi. 20-24), because, in spite of the miracles which they had witnessed, they had not recognised the day of grace and diligently used it for repentance. At the same time He had rejoiced before them over all those whom God had enlightened that they might see what was going forward; and had called them to His side (Matt. xi. 25-30).

And now suddenly, the moment the disciples return, His one thought is to get away from the people. They, however, follow Him and overtake Him on the shores of the lake. He puts the Jordan between Himself and them by crossing to Bethsaida. They also come to Bethsaida. He returns to Capernaum. They do the same. Since in Galilee it is impossible for Him to be alone, and He absolutely must be alone, He "slips away" to the north. Once more modern theology was right: He really does flee; not, however, from hostile Scribes, but from the people, who dog

His footsteps in order to await in His company the appearing of the Kingdom of God and of the Son of Man—to await it in vain.[276]

[pg 363]

In Strauss's first Life of Jesus the question is thrown out whether, in view of Matt. x. 23, Jesus did not think of His Parousia as a transformation which should take place during His lifetime. Ghillany bases his work on this possibility as on an established historical fact. Dalman takes this hypothesis to be the necessary correlative of the interpretation of the self-designation Son of Man on the basis of Daniel and the Apocalypses.

If Jesus, he argues, designated Himself in this futuristic sense as the Son of Man who comes from Heaven, He must have assumed that He would first be transported thither. "A man who had died or been rapt away from the earth might perhaps be brought into the world again in this way, or one who had never been on earth might so descend thither." But as this conception of transformation and removal seems to Dalman untenable in the case of Jesus, he treats it as a *reductio ad absurdum* of the eschatological interpretation of the title.

But why? If Jesus as a man walking in a natural body upon earth, predicts to His disciples the Parousia of the Son of Man in the immediate future, with the secret conviction that He Himself was to be revealed as the Son of Man, He must have made precisely this assumption that He would first be supernaturally removed and transformed. He thought of Himself as any one must who believes in the immediate coming of the last things, as living in two different conditions: the present, and the future condition into which He is to be transferred at the coming of the new supernatural world. We learn later that the disciples on the way up to Jerusalem were entirely possessed by the thought of what they should be when this transformation took place. They contend as to who shall have the highest position (Mark ix. 33); James and John wish Jesus to promise them in advance the thrones on His right hand and on His left (Mark x. 35-37).

He, moreover, does not rebuke them for indulging such thoughts, but only tells them how much, in the present age, of service, humiliation, and suffering is necessary to constitute a claim to such places in the future age, and that it does not in the last resort belong to Him to allot the places on His left and on His right, but that they shall be given to those for whom they are prepared; therefore, perhaps not to any of the disciples (Mark x. 40). At this point, therefore, the knowledge and will of Jesus are thwarted and limited by the predestinarianism which is bound up with eschatology.

[pg 364]

It is quite mistaken, however, to speak as modern theology does, of the "service" here required as belonging to the "new ethic of the Kingdom of God." There is for Jesus no ethic of the Kingdom of God, for in the Kingdom of God all natural relationships, even, for example, the distinction of sex (Mark xii. 25 and 26), are abolished. Temptation and sin no longer exist. All is "reign," a "reign" which has gradations—Jesus speaks of the "least in the Kingdom of God"—according as it has been determined in each individual case from all eternity, and according as each by his self-humiliation and refusal to rule in the present age has proved his fitness for bearing rule in the future Kingdom.

For the loftier stations, however, it is necessary to have proved oneself in persecution and suffering. Accordingly, Jesus asks the sons of Zebedee whether, since they claim these thrones on His right hand and on His left, they feel themselves strong enough to drink of His cup and be baptized with His baptism (Mark x. 38). To serve, to humble oneself, to incur persecution and death, belong to "the ethic of the interim" just as much as does penitence. They are indeed only a higher form of penitence.

A vivid eschatological expectation is therefore impossible to conceive apart from the idea of a metamorphosis. The resurrection is only a special case of this metamorphosis, the form in which the new condition of things is realised in the case of those who are already dead. The resurrection, the metamorphosis, and the Parousia of the Son of Man take place simultaneously, and are one and the same act.[277] It is therefore quite indifferent whether a man loses his life shortly before the Parousia in order to "find his life," if that is what is ordained for him; that signifies only that he will undergo the eschatological metamorphosis with the dead instead of with the living.

The Pauline eschatology recognises both conceptions side by side, in such a way, however, that the resurrection is subordinated to the metamorphosis. "Behold, I shew you a mystery," he says in 1 Cor. xv. 51 ff.; "we shall not all sleep, but we shall all be changed. In a moment, in the twinkling of an eye, at the last trump: for the trumpet shall sound, and the dead shall be raised incorruptible, and we shall be changed."

The apostle himself desires to be one of those who live to experience the metamorphosis and to be clothed with the heavenly mode of existence (2 Cor. v. 1 ff.). The metamorphosis, however, and the resurrection are, for those who are "in Christ," connected [pg 365] with a being caught up into the clouds of heaven (1 Thess. iv. 15 ff.). Therefore Paul also makes one and the same event of the metamorphosis, resurrection, and translation.

In seeking clues to the eschatology of Jesus, scholars have passed over the eschatology which lies closest to it, that of Paul. But why? Is it not identical with that of Jesus, at least in so far that both are "Jewish eschatology"? Did not Reimarus long ago declare that the eschatology of the primitive Christian community was identical with the Jewish, and only went beyond it in claiming a definite knowledge on a single point which was unessential to the nature and course of the expected events, in knowing, that is, who the Son of Man should be? That Christians drew no distinction between their own eschatology and the Jewish is evident from the whole character of the earlier apocalyptic literature, and not least from the Apocalypse of John! After all, what alteration did the belief that Jesus was the Son of Man who was to be revealed make in the general scheme of the course of apocalyptic events?

From the Rabbinic literature little help is to be derived towards the understanding of the world of thought in which Jesus lived, and His view of His own Person. The latest researches may be said to have made that clear. A few moral maxims, a few halting parables—that is all that can be produced in the way of parallels. Even the conception which is there suggested of the hidden coming and work of the Messiah is of little importance. We find the same ideas in the mouth of Trypho in Justin's dialogue, and that makes their Jewish character doubtful. That Jesus of Nazareth knew Himself to be the Son of Man who was to be revealed is for us the great fact of His self-consciousness, which is not to be further explained, whether there had been any kind of preparation for it in contemporary theology or not.

The self-consciousness of Jesus cannot in fact be illustrated or explained; all that can be explained is the eschatological view, in which the Man who possessed that self-consciousness saw reflected in advance the coming events, both those of a more general character, and those which especially related to Himself.[278]

The eschatology of Jesus can therefore only be interpreted by the aid of the curiously intermittent Jewish apocalyptic literature of the period between Daniel and the Bar-Cochba rising. What else, indeed, are the Synoptic Gospels, the Pauline letters, the Christian apocalypses than products of Jewish apocalyptic, belonging, [pg 366] moreover, to its greatest and most flourishing period? Historically regarded, the Baptist, Jesus, and Paul are simply the culminating manifestations of Jewish apocalyptic thought. The usual representation is the exact converse of the truth. Writers describe Jewish eschatology in order to illustrate the ideas of Jesus. But what is this "Jewish eschatology" after all? It is an eschatology with a great gap in it, because the culminating period, with the documents which relate to it, has been left out. The true historian will describe the eschatology of the Baptist, of Jesus, and of Paul in order to explain Jewish eschatology. It is nothing less than a misfortune for the science of New Testament Theology that no real attempt has hitherto been made to write the history of Jewish eschatology as it really was; that is, with the inclusion of the Baptist, of Jesus, and of Paul.[279]

All this has had to be said in order to justify the apparently self-evident assertion that Mark, Matthew, and Paul are the best sources for the Jewish eschatology of the time of Jesus. They represent a phase, which even in detail is self-explanatory, of that Jewish apocalyptic hope which manifested itself from time to time. We are, therefore, justified in first reconstructing the Jewish apocalyptic of the time independently out of these documents, that is to say, in bringing the details of the discourses of Jesus into an eschatological system, and then on the basis of this system endeavouring to explain the apparently disconnected events in the history of His public life.

The lines of connection which run backwards towards the Psalms of Solomon, Enoch, and Daniel, and forwards towards the apocalypses of Baruch and Enoch, are extremely important for the understanding of certain general conceptions. On the other hand, it is impossible to over-emphasise the uniqueness of the point of view from which the eschatology of the time of the Baptist, of Jesus, and of Paul presents itself to us.

In the first place, men feel themselves so close to the coming events that they only see what lies nearest to them, the imaginative development of detail entirely ceases. In the second place, it appears to us as though seen, so to speak, from within, passed through the medium of powerful minds like those of the Baptist and Jesus. That is why it is so great and simple. On the other hand, a certain complication arises from the fact that it now intersects actual history. All these are original features of it, which are not found in the Jewish apocalyptic writings of the preceding and following periods, and that is why these documents [pg 367] give us so little help in regard to the characteristic detail of the eschatology of Jesus and His contemporaries.

A further point to be noticed is that the eschatology of the time of Jesus shows the influence of the eschatology of the ancient prophets in a way which is not paralleled either before or after. Compare the Synoptic eschatology with that of the Psalms of Solomon. In place of the legal righteousness, which, since the return from the exile, had formed the link of connexion between the present and the future, we find the prophetic ethic, the demand for a general repentance, even in the case of the Baptist. In the Apocalypses of Baruch and Ezra we see, especially in the theological character of the latter, the persistent traces of this ethical deepening of apocalyptic.

But even in individual conceptions the apocalyptic of the Baptist, and of the period which he introduces, reaches back to the eschatology of the prophetic writings. The pouring forth of the spirit, and the figure of Elias, who comes again to earth, play a great rôle in it. The difficulty is, indeed, consciously felt of combining the two eschatologies, and bringing the prophetic within the Danielic. How, it is asked, can the Son of David be at the same time the Danielic Son-of-Man Messiah, at once David's son and David's Lord?

It is inadequate to speak of a synthesis of the two eschatologies. What has happened is nothing less than the remoulding, the elevation, of the Daniel-Enoch apocalyptic by the spirit and conceptions belonging to the ancient prophetic hope.

A great simplification and deepening of eschatology begins to show itself even in the Psalms of Solomon. The conception of righteousness which the writer applies is, in spite of its legal aspect, of an ethical, prophetic character. It is an eschatology associated with great historical events, the eschatology of a Pharisaism which is fighting for a cause, and has therefore a certain inward greatness.[280] Between the Psalms of Solomon and the appearance of the Baptist there lies the decadence of Pharisaism. At this point there suddenly appears an eschatological movement detached from Pharisaism, which was declining into an external legalism, a movement resting on a basis of its own, and thoroughly penetrated with the spirit of the ancient prophets.

The ultimate *differentia* of this eschatology is that it was not, like the other apocalyptic movements, called into existence by [pg 368] historical events. The Apocalypse of Daniel was called forth by the religious oppression of Antiochus;[281] the Psalms of Solomon by the civil strife at Jerusalem and the first appearance of the Roman power under Pompey;[282] Fourth Ezra and Baruch by the destruction of Jerusalem.[283] The apocalyptic movement in the time of Jesus is not connected with any historical event. It cannot be said, as Bruno Bauer rightly perceived, that we know anything about the Messianic expectations of the Jewish people at that time.[284] On the contrary, the indifference shown by the Roman administration towards the movement proves that the Romans knew nothing of a condition of great and general Messianic excitement among the Jewish people. The conduct of the Pharisaic party also, and the indifference of the great mass of the people, show that there can have been no question at that time of a national movement. What is really remarkable about this wave of apocalyptic enthusiasm is the fact that it was called forth not by external events, but solely by the appearance of two great personalities, and subsides with their disappearance, without leaving among the people generally any trace, except a feeling of hatred towards the new sect.

The Baptist and Jesus are not, therefore, borne upon the current of a general eschatological movement. The period offers no events calculated to give an impulse to eschatological enthusiasm. They themselves set the times in motion by acting, by creating eschatological facts. It is this mighty creative force which constitutes the difficulty in grasping historically the eschatology of Jesus and the Baptist. Instead of literary artifice speaking out of a distant imaginary past, there now enter into the field of eschatology men, living, acting men. It was the only time when that ever happened in Jewish eschatology.

There is silence all around. The Baptist appears, and cries: "Repent, for the Kingdom of Heaven is at hand." Soon after that comes Jesus, and in the knowledge that He is the coming [pg 369] Son of Man lays hold of the wheel of the world to set it moving on that last revolution which is to bring all ordinary history to a close. It refuses to turn, and He throws Himself upon it. Then it does turn; and crushes Him. Instead of bringing in the eschatological conditions, He has destroyed them. The wheel rolls onward, and the mangled body of the one immeasurably great Man, who was strong enough to think of Himself as the spiritual ruler of mankind and to bend history to His purpose, is hanging upon it still. That is His victory and His reign.

These considerations regarding the distinctive character of the Synoptic eschatology were necessary in order to explain the significance of the sending forth of the disciples and the discourse which Jesus uttered upon that occasion. Jesus' purpose is to set in motion the eschatological development of history, to let loose the final woes, the confusion and strife, from which shall issue the Parousia, and so to introduce the supra-mundane phase of the eschatological drama. That is His task, for which He has authority here below. That is why He says in the same discourse, "Think not that I am come to send peace on the earth; I am not come to send peace, but a sword" (Matt. x. 34).

It was with a view to this initial movement that He chose His disciples. They are not His helpers in the work of teaching; we never see them in that capacity, and He did not prepare them to carry on that work after His death. The very fact that He chooses just twelve shows that it is a dogmatic idea which He has in mind. He chooses them as those who are destined to hurl the firebrand into the world, and are afterwards, as those who have been the comrades of the unrecognised Messiah, before He came to His Kingdom, to be His associates in ruling and judging it.[285]

But what was to be the fate of the future Son of Man during the Messianic woes of the last times? It appears as if it was appointed for Him to share the persecution and the suffering. He [pg 370] says that those who shall be saved must take their cross and follow Him (Matt. x. 38), that His followers must be willing to lose their lives for His sake, and that only those who in this time of terror confess their allegiance to Him, shall be confessed by Him before His heavenly Father (Matt. x. 32). Similarly, in the last of the Beatitudes, He had pronounced those blessed who were despised and persecuted for His sake (Matt. v. 11, 12). As the future bearer of the supreme rule He must go through the deepest humiliation. There is danger that His followers may doubt Him. Therefore, the last words of His message to the Baptist, just at the time when He had sent forth the Twelve, is, "Blessed is he whosoever shall not be offended in me" (Matt. xi. 6).

If He makes a point of familiarising others with the thought that in the time of tribulation they may even lose their lives, He must have recognised that this possibility was still more strongly present in His own case. It is possible that in the enigmatic saying about the disciples fasting "when the bridegroom is taken away from them" (Mark ii. 20), there is a hint of what Jesus expected. In that case suffering, death, and resurrection must have been closely united in the Messianic consciousness from the first. So much, however, is certain, viz. that the thought of suffering formed part, at the time of the sending forth the disciples, of the mystery of the Kingdom of God and of the Messiahship of Jesus, and that in the form that Jesus and all the elect were to be brought low in the πειρασμός at the time of the death-struggle against the evil world-power which would arise against them; brought down, it might be, even to death. It mattered as little in His own case as in that of others whether at the time of the Parousia He should be one of those who should be metamorphosed, or one who had died and risen again. The question arises, however, how this self-consciousness of Jesus could remain concealed. It is true the miracles had nothing to do with the Messiahship, since no one expected the Messiah to come as an earthly miracle-worker in the present age. On the contrary, it would have been the greatest of miracles if any one had recognised the Messiah in an earthly miracle-worker. How far the cries of the demoniacs who addressed Him as Messiah were intelligible by the people must remain an open question. What is clear is that His Messiahship did not become known in this way even to His disciples.

And yet in all His speech and action the Messianic consciousness shines forth. One might, indeed, speak of the acts of His Messianic consciousness. The Beatitudes, nay, the whole of the Sermon on the Mount, with the authoritative "I" for ever breaking through, bear witness to the high dignity which He ascribed to Himself. Did not this "I" set the people thinking?

[pg 371]

What must they have thought when, at the close of this discourse, He spoke of people who, at the Day of Judgment, would call upon Him as Lord, and appeal to the works that they had done in His name, and who yet were destined to be rejected because He would not recognise them (Matt. vii. 21-23)?

What must they have thought of Him when He pronounced those blessed who were persecuted and despised for His sake (Matt. v. 11, 12)? By what authority did this man forgive sins (Mark ii. 5 ff.)?

In the discourse at the sending forth of the disciples the "I" is still more prominent. He demands of men that in the trials to come they shall confess Him, that they shall love Him more than father or mother, bear their cross after Him, and follow Him to the death, since it is only for such that He can entreat His Heavenly Father (Matt. x. 32 ff.). Admitting that the expression "Heavenly Father" contained no riddle for the listening disciples, since He had taught them to pray "Our Father which art in Heaven," we have still to ask who was He whose yea or nay should prevail with God to determine the fate of men at the Judgment?

And yet they found it hard, nay impossible, to think of Him as Messiah. They guessed Him to be a prophet; some thought of Elias, some of John the Baptist risen from the dead, as appears clearly from the answer of the disciples at Caesarea Philippi.[286] The Messiah was a supernatural personality who was to appear in the last times, and who was not expected upon earth before that.

At this point a difficulty presents itself. How could Jesus be Elias for the people? Did they not hold John the Baptist to be Elias? Not in the least! Jesus was the first and the only person who attributed this office to him. And, moreover, He declares it to the people as something mysterious, difficult to understand—"If ye can receive it, this is Elias, which was for to come. He that hath ears to hear, let him hear" (Matt. xi. 14, 15). In making this revelation He is communicating to them a piece of supernatural knowledge, opening up a part of the mystery of the Kingdom of God. Therefore He uses the same formula of emphasis as when making known in parables the mystery of the Kingdom of God (Mark iv.).

The disciples were not with Him at this time, and therefore did not learn what was the rôle of John the Baptist. When a little later, in descending from the mount of transfiguration He [pg 372] predicted to the three who formed the inner circle of His followers the resurrection of the Son of Man, they came to Him with difficulties about the rising from the dead—how could this be possible when, according to the Pharisees and Scribes, Elias must first come?—whereupon Jesus explains to them that the preacher of repentance whom Herod had put to death had been Elias (Mark ix. 11-13).

Why did not the people take the Baptist to be Elias? In the first place no doubt because he did not describe himself as such. In the next place because he did no miracle! He was only a natural man without any evidence of supernatural power, only a prophet. In the third place, and that was the decisive point, he had himself pointed forward to the coming of Elias. He who was to come, he whom he preached, was not the Messiah, but Elias.

He describes him, not as a supernatural personality, not as a judge, not as one who will be manifested at the unveiling of the heavenly world, but as one who in his work shall resemble himself, only much greater—one who, like himself, baptizes, though with the Holy Spirit. Had it ever been represented as the work of the Messiah to baptize?

Before the Last Judgment, so it was inferred from Joel, the great outpouring of the Spirit was to take place; before the Last Judgment, so taught Malachi, Elias was to come. Until these events had occurred the manifestation of the Son of Man was not to be looked for. Men's thoughts were fixed, therefore, not on the Messiah, but upon Elias and the outpouring of the Spirit.[287] The Baptist in his preaching combines both ideas, and predicts the coming of the Great One who shall "baptize with the Holy Spirit," *i.e.* who brings about the outpouring of the Spirit. His own preaching was only designed to secure that at His coming that Great One should find a community sanctified and prepared to receive the Spirit.

When he heard in the prison of one who did great wonders and signs, he desired to learn with certainty whether this was "he who was to come." If this question is taken as referring to the Messiahship the whole narrative loses its meaning, and it upsets the theory of the Messianic secret, since in this case at least one person had become aware, independently, of the office which belonged to Jesus, not to mention all the ineptitudes involved in making the Baptist here speak in doubt and confusion. Moreover, on this false interpretation of the question the point of Jesus' discourse is lost, for in this case it is not clear why He says to the people afterwards, "If ye can receive it, John himself is Elias." This revelation presupposes that Jesus and the people, who had [pg 373] heard the question which had been addressed to Him, also gave it its only natural meaning, referring it to Jesus as the bearer of the office of Elias.

That even the first Evangelist gives the episode a Messianic setting by introducing it with the words "When John heard in the prison of the works of the Christ" does not alter the facts of the body of the narrative. The sequel directly contradicts the introduction. And this interpretation fully explains the evasive answer of Jesus, in which exegesis has always recognised a certain reserve without ever being able to make it intelligible why Jesus did not simply send him the message, "Yes, I am he"—whereto, however, according to modern theology, He would have needed to add, "but another kind of Messiah from him whom you expect."

The fact was, the Baptist had put Him in an extremely difficult position. He could not answer that He was Elias if He held Himself to be the Messiah; on the other hand He could not, and would not, disclose to him, and still less to the messengers and the listening multitude, the secret of His Messiahship. Therefore He sends this obscure message, which only contains a confirmation of the facts which John had already heard and closes with a warning, come what may, not to be offended in Him. Of this the Baptist was to make what he could.

It mattered, in fact, little how John understood the message. The time was much more advanced than he supposed; the hammer of the world's clock had risen to strike the last hour. All that he needed to know was that he had no cause to doubt.

In revealing to the people the true office of the Baptist, Jesus unveiled to them almost the whole mystery of the Kingdom of God, and nearly disclosed the secret of His Messiahship. For if Elias was already present, was not the coming of the Kingdom close at hand? And if John was Elias, who was Jesus?... There could only be one answer: the Messiah. But this seemed impossible, because Messiah was expected as a supernatural personality. The eulogy on the Baptist is, historically regarded, identical in content with the prediction of the Parousia in the discourse at the sending forth of the disciples. For after the coming of Elias there must follow immediately the judgment and the other events belonging to the last time. Now we can understand why in the enumeration of the events of the last time in the discourse to the Twelve the coming of Elias is not mentioned.

We see here, too, how, in the thought of Jesus, Messianic doctrine forces its way into history and simply abolishes the historic aspect of the events. The Baptist had not held himself to be Elias, the people had not thought of attributing this office to him; the description of Elias did not fit him at all, since he had [pg 374] done none of those things which Elias was to do: and yet Jesus makes him Elias, simply because He expected His own manifestation as Son of Man, and before that it was necessary that Elias must first have come. And even when John was dead Jesus still told the disciples that in him Elias had come, although the death of Elias was not contemplated in the eschatological doctrine, and was in fact unthinkable, But Jesus must somehow drag or force the eschatological events into the framework of the actual occurrences.

Thus the conception of the "dogmatic element" in the narrative widens in an unsuspected fashion. And even what before seemed natural becomes on a closer examination doctrinal. The Baptist is made into Elias solely by the force of Jesus' Messianic consciousness.

A short time afterwards, immediately upon the return of the disciples, He spoke and acted before their eyes in a way which presupposed the Messianic secret. The people had been dogging his steps; at a lonely spot on the shores of the lake they surrounded Him, and He "taught them about many things" (Mark vi. 30-34). The day was drawing to a close, but they held closely to Him without troubling about food. In the evening, before sending them away, He fed them.

Weisse, long ago, had constantly emphasised the fact that the feeding of the multitude was one of the greatest historical problems, because this narrative, like that of the transfiguration, is very firmly riveted to its historical setting and, therefore, imperatively demands explanation. How is the historical element in it to be got at? Certainly not by seeking to explain the apparently miraculous in it on natural lines, by representing that at the bidding of Jesus people brought out the baskets of provisions which they had been concealing, and, thus importing into the tradition a natural fact which, so far from being hinted at in the narrative, is actually excluded by it.

Our solution is that the whole is historical, except the closing remark that they were all filled. Jesus distributed the provisions which He and His disciples had with them among the multitude so that each received a very little, after He had first offered thanks. The significance lies in the giving of thanks and in the fact that they had received from Him consecrated food. Because He is the future Messiah, this meal becomes without their knowledge the Messianic feast. With the morsel of bread which He gives His disciples to distribute to the people He consecrates them as partakers in the coming Messianic feast, and gives them the guarantee that they, who had shared His table in the time of His obscurity, would also share it in the time of His glory. In the prayer He gave thanks not only for the food, but also for the coming Kingdom and all its blessings. It is the counterpart of [pg 375] the Lord's prayer, where He so strangely inserts the petition for daily bread between the petitions for the coming of the Kingdom and for deliverance from the πειρασμός.

The feeding of the multitude was more than a love-feast, a fellowship-meal. It was from the point of view of Jesus a sacrament of salvation.

We never realise sufficiently that in a period when the judgment and the glory were expected as close at hand, one thought arising out of this expectation must have acquired special prominence—how, namely, in the present time a man could obtain a guarantee of coming scatheless through the judgment, of being saved and received into the Kingdom, of being signed and sealed for deliverance amid the coming trial, as the Chosen People in Egypt had a sign revealed to them from God by means of which they might be manifest as those who were to be spared. But once we do realise this, we can understand why the thought of signing and sealing runs through the whole of the apocalyptic literature. It is found as early as the ninth chapter of Ezekiel. There, God is making preparation for judgment. The day of visitation of the city is at hand. But first the Lord calls unto "the man clothed with linen who had the writer's ink-horn by his side" and said unto him, "Go through the midst of the city, through the midst of Jerusalem, and set a mark upon the foreheads of the men that sigh and that cry for all the abominations that be done in the midst thereof." Only after that does He give command to those who are charged with the judgment to begin, adding, "But come not near any man upon whom is the mark" (Ezek. ix. 4 and 6).

In the fifteenth of the Psalms of Solomon,[288] the last eschatological writing before the movement initiated by the Baptist, it is expressly said in the description of the judgment that "the saints of God bear a sign upon them which saves them."

In the Pauline theology very striking prominence is given to the thought of being sealed unto salvation. The apostle is conscious of bearing about with him in his body "the marks of Jesus" (Gal. vi. 17), the "dying" of Jesus (2 Cor. iv. 10). This sign is received in baptism, since it is a baptism "into the death of Christ"; in this act the recipient is in a certain sense really buried with Him, and thenceforth walks among men as one who belongs, even here below, to risen humanity (Rom. vi. 1 ff.). Baptism is the seal, the earnest of the spirit, the pledge of that which is to come (2 Cor i. 22; Eph. i. 13, 14, iv. 30).

This conception of baptism as a "salvation" in view of that which was to come goes down through the whole of ancient theology. Its preaching might really be summed up in the words, "Keep your baptism holy and without blemish."

[pg 376]

In the Shepherd of Hermas even the spirits of the men of the past must receive "the seal, which is the water" in order that they may "bear the name of God upon them." That is why the tower is built over the water, and the stones which are brought up out of the deep are rolled through the water (Vis. iii. and Sim. ix. 16).

In the Apocalypse of John the thought of the sealing stands prominently in the foreground. The locusts receive power to hurt those only who have not the seal of God on their foreheads (Rev. ix. 4, 5). The beast (Rev. xiii. 16 ff.) compels men to bear his mark; only those who will not accept it are to reign with Christ (Rev. xx. 4). The chosen hundred and forty-four thousand bear the name of God and the name of the Lamb upon their foreheads (Rev. xiv. 1).

"Assurance of salvation" in a time of eschatological expectation demanded some kind of security for the future of which the earnest could be possessed in the present. And with this the predestinarian thought of election was in complete accord. If we find the thought of being sealed unto salvation previously in the Psalms of Solomon, and subsequently in the same signification in Paul, in the Apocalypse of John, and down to the Shepherd of Hermas, it may be assumed in advance that it will be found in some form or other in the so strongly eschatological teaching of Jesus and the Baptist.

It may be said, indeed, to dominate completely the eschatological preaching of the Baptist, for this preaching does not confine itself to the declaration of the nearness of the Kingdom, and the demand for repentance, but leads up to an act to which it gives a special reference in relation to the forgiveness of sins and the outpouring of the spirit. It is a mistake to regard baptism with water as a "symbolic act" in the modern sense, and make the Baptist decry his own wares by saying, "I baptize only with water, but the other can baptize with the Holy Spirit." He is not contrasting the two baptisms, but connecting them—he who is baptized by him has the certainty that he will share in the outpouring of the Spirit which shall precede the judgment, and at the judgment shall receive forgiveness of sins, as one who is signed with the mark of repentance. The object of being baptized by him is to secure baptism with the Spirit later. The forgiveness of sins associated with baptism is proleptic; it is to be realised at the judgment. The Baptist himself did not forgive sin.[289] If he had done so, how could [pg 377] such offence have been taken when Jesus claimed for Himself the right to forgive sins in the present (Mark ii. 10).

The baptism of John was therefore an eschatological sacrament pointing forward to the pouring forth of the spirit and to the judgment, a provision for "salvation." Hence the wrath of the Baptist when he saw Pharisees and Sadducees crowding to his baptism: "Ye generation of vipers, who hath warned you to flee from the wrath to come? Bring forth now fruits meet for repentance" (Matt. iii. 7, 8). By the reception of baptism, that is, they are saved from the judgment.

As a cleansing unto salvation it is a divine institution, a revealed means of grace. That is why the question of Jesus, whether the baptism of John was from heaven or from men, placed the Scribes at Jerusalem in so awkward a dilemma (Mark xi. 30).

The authority of Jesus, however, goes farther than that of the Baptist. As the Messiah who is to come He can give even here below to those who gather about Him a right to partake in the Messianic feast, by this distribution of food to them; only, they do not know what is happening to them and He cannot solve the riddle for them. The supper at the Lake of Gennesareth was a veiled eschatological sacrament. Neither the disciples nor the multitude understood what was happening, since they did not know who He was who thus made them His guests.[290] This meal must [pg 378] have been transformed by tradition into a miracle, a result which may have been in part due to the references to the wonders of the Messianic feast which were doubtless contained in the prayers, not to speak of the eschatological enthusiasm which then prevailed universally. Did not the disciples believe that on the same evening, when they had been commanded to take Jesus into their ship at the mouth of the Jordan, to which point He had walked along the shore—did they not believe that they saw Him come walking towards them upon the waves of the sea? The impulse to the introduction of the miraculous into the narrative came from the unintelligible element with which the men who surrounded Jesus were at this time confronted.[291]

The Last Supper at Jerusalem had the same sacramental significance as that at the lake. Towards the end of the meal Jesus, after giving thanks, distributes the bread and wine. This had as little to do with the satisfaction of hunger as the distribution to the Galilaean believers. The act of Jesus is an end in itself, and the significance of the celebration consists in the fact that it is He Himself who makes the distribution. In Jerusalem, however, they understood what was meant, and He explained it to them explicitly by telling them that He would drink no more of the fruit of the vine until He drank it new in the Kingdom of God. The mysterious images which He used at the time of the distribution concerning the atoning significance of His death do not touch the essence of the celebration, they are only discourses accompanying it.

On this interpretation, therefore, we may think of Baptism and the Lord's Supper as from the first eschatological sacraments in the eschatological movement which later detached itself from Judaism under the name of Christianity. That explains why we find them both in Paul and in the earliest theology as sacramental acts, not as symbolic ceremonies, and find them dominating the whole Christian doctrine. Apart from the assumption of the eschatological sacraments, we can only make the history of dogma begin with a "fall" from the earlier purer theology into the sacramental magical, without being able to adduce a single syllable in support of the idea that after the death of Jesus Baptism and the Lord's Supper existed even for an hour as symbolical actions—Paul, indeed, makes this supposition wholly impossible.

In any case the adoption of the baptism of John in Christian practice cannot be explained except on the assumption that it was [pg 379] the sacrament of the eschatological community, a revealed means of securing "salvation" which was not altered in the slightest by the Messiahship of Jesus. How else could we explain the fact that baptism, without any commandment of Jesus, and without Jesus' ever having baptized, was taken over, as a matter of course, into Christianity, and was given a special reference to the receiving of the Spirit?

It is no use proposing to explain it as having been instituted as a symbolical repetition of the baptism of Jesus, thought of as "an anointing to the Messiahship." There is not a single passage in ancient theology to support such a theory. And we may point also to the fact that Paul never refers to the baptism of Jesus in explaining the character of Christian baptism, never, in fact, makes any distinct reference to it. And how could baptism, if it had been a symbolical repetition of the baptism of Jesus, ever have acquired this magic-sacramental sense of "salvation"?

Nothing shows more clearly than the dual character of ancient baptism, which makes it the guarantee both of the reception of the Spirit and of deliverance from the judgment, that it is nothing else than the eschatological baptism of John with a single difference. Baptism with water and baptism with the Spirit are now connected not only logically, but also in point of time, seeing that since the day of Pentecost the period of the outpouring of the Spirit is present. The two portions of the eschatological sacrament which in the Baptist's preaching were distinguished in point of time—because he did not expect the outpouring of the Spirit until some future period—are now brought together, since one eschatological condition—the baptism with the Spirit—is now present. The "Christianising" of baptism consisted in this and in nothing else; though Paul carried it a stage farther when he formed the conception of baptism as a mystic partaking in the death and resurrection of Jesus.

Thus the thoroughgoing eschatological interpretation of the Life of Jesus puts into the hands of those who are reconstructing the history of dogma in the earliest times an explanation of the conception of the sacraments, of which they had been able hitherto only to note the presence as an *x* of which the origin was undiscoverable, and for which they possessed no equation by which it could be evaluated. If Christianity as the religion of historically revealed mysteries was able to lay hold upon Hellenism and overcome it, the reason of this was that it was already in its purely eschatological beginnings a religion of sacraments, a religion of eschatological sacraments, since Jesus had recognised a Divine institution in the baptism of John, and had Himself performed a sacramental action in the distribution of food at the Lake of Gennesareth and at the Last Supper.

[pg 380]

This being so, the feeding of the multitude also belongs to the dogmatic element in the history. But no one had previously recognised it as what it really was, an indirect disclosure of the Messianic secret, just as no one had understood the full significance of Jesus' description of the Baptist as Elias.

But how does Peter at Caesarea Philippi know the secret of his Master? What he there declares is not a conviction which had gradually dawned on him, and slowly grown through various stages of probability and certainty.

The real character of this incident has been interpreted with remarkable penetration by Wrede. The incident itself, he says, is to be understood in quite as supernatural a fashion in Mark as in Matthew. But on the other hand one does not receive the impression that the writer intends to represent the confession as a merit or a discovery of Peter. "For according to the text of Mark, Jesus shows no trace of joy or surprise at this confession. His only answer consists of the command to say nothing about His Messiahship." Keim, whom Wrede quotes, had received a similar impression from the Marcan account, and had supposed that Jesus had actually found the confession of Peter inopportune.

How is all this to be explained—the supernatural knowledge of Peter and the rather curt fashion in which Jesus receives his declaration?

It might be worth while to put the story of the transfiguration side by side with the incident at Caesarea Philippi, since there the Divine Sonship of Jesus is "a second time" revealed to the "three," Peter, James, and John, and the revelation is made supernaturally by a voice from heaven. It is rather striking that Mark does not seem to be conscious that he is reporting something which the disciples knew already. At the beginning of the actual transfiguration Peter still addresses Jesus simply as Rabbi (Mark ix. 5). And what does it mean when Jesus, during the descent from the mountain, forbids them to speak to any man concerning that which they have seen until after the resurrection of the Son of Man? That would exclude even the other disciples who knew only the secret of His Messiahship. But why should they not be told of the Divine confirmation of that which Peter had declared at Caesarea Philippi and Jesus had "admitted"?

What has the transfiguration to do with the resurrection of the dead? And why are the thoughts of the disciples suddenly busied, not with what they have seen, not with the fact that the Son of Man shall rise from the dead, but simply with the possibility of the rising from the dead, the difficulty being that Elias was not yet present? Those who see in the transfiguration a projection backwards of the Pauline theology into the Gospel history do not realise what are the principal points and difficulties of the [pg 381] narrative. The problem lies in the conversation during the descent. Against the Messiahship of Jesus, against His rising from the dead, they have only one objection to suggest: Elias had not yet come.

We see here, in the first place, the importance of the revelation which Jesus had made to the people in declaring to them the secret that the Baptist is Elias. From the standpoint of the eschatological expectation no one could recognise Elias in the Baptist, unless he knew of the Messiahship of Jesus. And no one could believe in the Messiahship and "resurrection" of Jesus, that is, in His Parousia, without presupposing that Elias had in some way or other already come. This was therefore the primary difficulty of the disciples, the stumbling-block which Jesus must remove for them by making the same revelation concerning the Baptist to them as to the people. It is also once more abundantly clear that expectation was directed at that time primarily to the coming of Elias.[292] But since the whole eschatological movement arose out of the Baptist's preaching, the natural conclusion is that by "him who was to come after" and baptize with the Holy Spirit John meant, not the Messiah, but Elias.

But if the non-appearance of Elias was the primary difficulty of the disciples in connexion with the Messiahship of Jesus and all that it implied, why does it only strike the "three," and moreover, all three of them together, now, and not at Caesarea Philippi?[293] How could Peter there have declared it and here be still labouring with the rest over the difficulty which stood in the way of his own declaration? To make the narrative coherent, the transfiguration, as being a revelation of the Messiahship, ought to precede the incident at Caesarea Philippi. Now let us look at the connexion in which it actually occurs. It falls in that inexplicable section Mark viii. 34-ix. 30 in which the multitude suddenly appears in the company of Jesus who is sojourning in a Gentile district, only to disappear again, equally enigmatically, afterwards, when He sets out for Galilee, instead of accompanying Him back to their own country.

In this section everything points to the situation during the days at Bethsaida after the return of the disciples from their mission. Jesus is surrounded by the people, while what He desires is to be alone with His immediate followers. The disciples make use of the healing powers which He had bestowed upon them when sending them forth, and have the experience of finding that they are not in all cases adequate (Mark ix. 14-29). The [pg 382] mountain to which He takes the "three" is not a mountain in the north, or as some have suggested, an imaginary mountain of the Evangelist, but the same to which Jesus went up to pray and to be alone on the evening of the feeding of the multitude (Mark vi. 46 and ix. 2). The house to which He goes after His return from the transfiguration is therefore to be placed at Bethsaida.

Another thing which points to a sojourn at Bethsaida after the feeding of the multitude is the story of the healing of the blind man at Bethsaida (Mark viii. 22-26).

The circumstances, therefore, which we have to presuppose are that Jesus is surrounded and thronged by the people at Bethsaida. In order to be alone He once more puts the Jordan between Himself and the multitude, and goes with the "three" to the mountain where He had prayed after the feeding of the five thousand. This is the only way in which we can understand how the people failed to follow Him, and He was able really to carry out His plan.

But how could this story be torn out of its natural context and its scene removed to Caesarea Philippi, where it is both on external and internal grounds impossible? What we need to notice is the Marcan account of the events which followed the sending forth of the disciples. We have two stories of the feeding of the multitude with a crossing of the lake after each (Mark vi. 31-56, Mark viii. 1-22), two stories of Jesus going away towards the north with the same motive, that of being alone and unrecognised. The first time, after the controversy about the washing of hands, His course is directed towards Tyre (Mark vii. 24-30), the second time, after the demand for a sign, he goes into the district of Caesarea Philippi (Mark viii. 27). The scene of the controversy about the washing of hands is some locality in the plain of Gennesareth (Mark vi. 53 ff); Dalmanutha is named as the place where the sign was demanded (Mark viii. 10 ff.).

The most natural conclusion is to identify the two cases of feeding the multitude, and the two journeys northwards. In that case we should have in the section Mark vi. 31-ix. 30, two sets of narratives worked into one another, both recounting how Jesus, after the disciples came back to Him, went with them from Capernaum to the northern shore of the lake, was there surprised by the multitude, and after the meal which He gave them, crossed the Jordan by boat to Bethsaida, stayed there for a while, and then returned again by ship to the country of Gennesareth, and was there again overtaken and surrounded by the people; then after some controversial encounters with the Scribes, who at the report of His miracles had come down from Jerusalem (Mark vii. 1), left Galilee and again went northwards.[294]

[pg 383]

The seams at the joining of the narratives can be recognised in Mark vii. 31, where Jesus is suddenly transferred from the north to Decapolis, and in the saying in Mark viii. 14 ff., which makes explicit reference to the two miracles of feeding the multitude. Whether the Evangelist himself worked these two sets of narratives together, or whether he found them already united, cannot be determined, and is not of any direct historical interest. The disorder is in any case so complete that we cannot fully reconstruct each of the separate sets of narratives.

The external reasons why the narratives of Mark viii. 34-ix. 30, of which the scene is on the northern shore of the lake, are placed in this way after the incident of Caesarea Philippi are not difficult to grasp. The section contains an impressive discourse to the people on following Jesus in His sufferings, crucifixion, and death (Mark viii. 34-ix. 1). For this reason the whole series of scenes is attached to the revelation of the secret of the suffering of the Son of Man; and the redactor did not stop to think how the people could suddenly appear, and as suddenly disappear again. The statement, too, "He called the people with the disciples" (Mark viii. 34), helped to mislead him into inserting the section at this point, although this very remark points to the circumstances of the time just after the return of the disciples, when Jesus was sometimes alone with the disciples, and sometimes calls the eager multitude about Him.

The whole scene belongs, therefore, to the days which He spent at Bethsaida, and originally followed immediately upon the crossing of the lake, after the feeding of the multitude. It was after Jesus had been six days surrounded by the people, not six days after the revelation at Caesarea Philippi, that the "transfiguration" took place (Mark ix. 2). On this assumption, all the difficulties of the incident at Caesarea Philippi are cleared up in a moment; there is no longer anything strange in the fact that Peter declares to Jesus who He really is, while Jesus appears neither surprised nor especially rejoiced at the insight of His disciple. The transfiguration had, in fact, been the revelation of the secret of the Messiahship to the three who constituted the inner circle of the disciples.[295] And Jesus had not Himself revealed it to them; what had happened was, that [pg 384] in a state of rapture common to them all, in which they had seen the Master in a glorious transfiguration, they had seen Him talking with Moses and Elias and had heard a voice from heaven saying, "This is my beloved Son, hear ye Him."

We must always make a fresh effort to realise to ourselves, that Jesus and His immediate followers were, at that time, in an enthusiastic state of intense eschatological expectation. We must picture them among the people, who were filled with penitence for their sins, and with faith in the Kingdom, hourly expecting the coming of the Kingdom, and the revelation of Jesus as the Son of Man, seeing in the eager multitude itself a sign that their reckoning of the time was correct; thus the psychological conditions were present for a common ecstatic experience such as is described in the account of the transfiguration.

In this ecstasy the "three" heard the voice from heaven saying who He was. Therefore, the Matthaean report, according to which Jesus praises Simon "because flesh and blood have not revealed it to him, but the Father who is in heaven," is not really at variance with the briefer Marcan account, since it rightly indicates the source of Peter's knowledge.

Nevertheless Jesus was astonished. For Peter here disregarded the command given during the descent from the mount of transfiguration. He had "betrayed" to the Twelve Jesus' consciousness of His Messiahship. One receives the impression that Jesus did not put the question to the disciples in order to reveal Himself to them as Messiah, and that by the impulsive speech of Peter, upon whose silence He had counted because of His command, and to whom He had not specially addressed the question, He was forced to take a different line of action in regard to the Twelve from what He had intended. It is probable that He had never had the intention of revealing the secret of His Messiahship to the disciples. Otherwise He would not have kept it from them at the time of their mission, when He did not expect them to return before the Parousia. Even at the transfiguration the "three" do not learn it from His lips, but in a state of ecstasy, an ecstasy which He shared with them. At Caesarea Philippi it is not He, but

Peter, who reveals His Messiahship. We may say, therefore, that Jesus did not voluntarily give up His Messianic secret; it was wrung from Him by the pressure of events.

However that may be, from Caesarea Philippi onwards it was known to the other disciples through Peter; what Jesus Himself revealed to them, was the secret of his sufferings.

Pfleiderer and Wrede were quite right in pointing to the clear and definite predictions of the suffering, death, and resurrection as the historically inexplicable element in our reports, since the necessity of Jesus' death, by which modern theology endeavours [pg 385] to make His resolve and His predictions intelligible, is not a necessity which arises out of the historical course of events. There was not present any natural ground for such a resolve on the part of Jesus. Had He returned to Galilee, He would immediately have had the multitudes flocking after Him again.

In order to make the historical possibility of the resolve to suffer and the prediction of the sufferings in some measure intelligible, modern theology has to ignore the prediction of the resurrection which is bound up with them, for this is "dogmatic." That is, however, not permissible. We must, as Wrede insists, take the words as they are, and must not even indulge in ingenious explanations of the "three days." Therefore, the resolve to suffer and to die are dogmatic; therefore, according to him, they are unhistorical, and only to be explained by a literary hypothesis.

But the thoroughgoing eschatological school says they are dogmatic, and therefore historical; because they find their explanation in eschatological conceptions.

Wrede held that the Messianic conception implied in the Marcan narrative is not the Jewish Messianic conception, just because of the thought of suffering and death which it involves. No stress must be laid on the fact that in Fourth Ezra vii. 29 the Christ dies and rises again, because His death takes place at the end of the Messianic Kingdom.[296] The Jewish Messiah is essentially a glorious being who shall appear in the last time. True, but the case in which the Messiah should be present, prior to the Parousia, should cause the final tribulations to come upon the earth, and should Himself undergo them, does not arise in the Jewish eschatology as described from without. It first arises with the self-consciousness of Jesus. Therefore, the Jewish conception of the Messiah has no information to give us upon this point.

In order to understand Jesus' resolve to suffer, we must first recognise that the mystery of this suffering is involved in the mystery of the Kingdom of God, since the Kingdom cannot come until the πειρασμός has taken place. This certainty of suffering is quite independent of the historic circumstances, as the beatitude on the persecuted in the sermon on the mount, and the predictions in the discourse at the sending forth of the Twelve, clearly show. Jesus' prediction of His own sufferings at Caesarea Philippi is precisely as unintelligible, precisely as dogmatic, and therefore precisely as historical as the prediction to the disciples at the time of their mission. The "must be" of the sufferings is the same—the coming of the Kingdom, and of the Parousia, which are dependent upon the πειρασμός having first taken place.

[pg 386]

In the first period Jesus' thoughts concerning His own sufferings were included in the more general thought of the sufferings which formed part of the mystery of the Kingdom of God. The exhortations to hold steadfastly to Him in the time of trial, and not to lose faith in Him, certainly tended to suggest that He thought of Himself as the central point amid these conflicts and confusions, and reckoned on the possibility of His own death as much as on that of others. Upon this point nothing more definite can be said, since the mystery of Jesus' own sufferings does not detach itself from the mystery of the sufferings connected with the Kingdom of God until after the Messianic secret is made known at Caesarea Philippi. What is certain is that, for Him, suffering was always associated with the Messianic secret, since He placed His Parousia at the end of the pre-Messianic tribulations in which He was to have His part.

The suffering, death, and resurrection of which the secret was revealed at Caesarea Philippi are not therefore in themselves new or surprising.[297] The novelty lies in the form in which they are conceived. The tribulation, so far as Jesus is concerned, is now connected with an historic event: He will go to Jerusalem, there to suffer death at the hands of the authorities.

For the future, however, He no longer speaks of the general tribulation which He is to bring upon the earth, nor of the sufferings which await His followers, nor of the sufferings in which they must rally round Him. In the predictions of the passion there is no word of that; at Jerusalem there is no word of that. This thought disappears once for all.

In the secret of His passion which Jesus reveals to the disciples at Caesarea Philippi the pre-Messianic tribulation is for others set aside, abolished, concentrated upon Himself alone, and that in the [pg 387] form that they are fulfilled in His own passion and death at Jerusalem. That was the new conviction that had dawned upon Him. He must suffer for others ... that the Kingdom might come.

This change was due to the non-fulfilment of the promises made in the discourse at the sending forth of the Twelve. He had thought then to let loose the final tribulation and so compel the coming of the Kingdom. And the cataclysm had not occurred. He had expected it also after the return of the disciples. In Bethsaida, in speaking to the multitude which He had consecrated by the foretaste of the Messianic feast, as also to the disciples at the time of their mission, He had turned their thoughts to things to come and had adjured them to be prepared to suffer with Him, to give up their lives, not to be ashamed of Him in His humiliation, since otherwise the Son of Man would be ashamed of them when He came in glory (Mark viii. 34-ix. 1).[298]

In leaving Galilee He abandoned the hope that the final tribulation would begin of itself. If it delays, that means that there is still something to be done, and yet another of the violent must lay violent hands upon the Kingdom of God. The movement of repentance had not been sufficient. When, in accordance with His commission, by sending forth the disciples with their message, he hurled the fire-brand which should kindle the fiery trials of the Last Time, the flame went out. He had not succeeded in sending the sword on earth and stirring up the conflict. And until the time of trial had come, the coming of the Kingdom and His own manifestation as Son of Man were impossible.

That meant—not that the Kingdom was not near at hand—but that God had appointed otherwise in regard to the time of trial. He had heard the Lord's Prayer in which Jesus and His followers prayed for the coming of the Kingdom—and at the same time, for deliverance from the πειρασμός. The time of trial was not come; therefore God in His mercy and omnipotence had eliminated it from the series of eschatological events, and appointed to Him whose commission had been to bring it about, instead to accomplish it in His own person. As He who was to rule over the members of the Kingdom in the future age, He was appointed to serve them in the present, to give His life for them, the many (Mark x. 45 and xiv. 24), and to make in His own blood the atonement which they would have had to render in the tribulation.

The Kingdom could not come until the debt which weighed upon the world was discharged. Until then, not only the now living believers, but the chosen of all generations since the beginning [pg 388] of the world wait for their manifestation in glory—Abraham, Isaac, and Jacob and all the countless unknown who should come from the East and from the West to sit at tables with them at the Messianic feast (Matt. viii. 11). The enigmatic πολλοί for whom Jesus dies are those predestined to the Kingdom, since His death must at last compel the Coming of the Kingdom.[299]

This thought Jesus found in the prophecies of Isaiah, which spoke of the suffering Servant of the Lord. The mysterious description of Him who in His humiliation was despised and misunderstood, who, nevertheless bears the guilt of others and afterwards is made manifest in what He has done for them, points, He feels, to Himself.

And since He found it there set down that He must suffer unrecognised, and that those for whom He suffered should doubt Him, His suffering should, nay must, remain a mystery. In that case those who doubted Him would not bring condemnation upon themselves. He no longer needs to adjure them for their own sakes to be faithful to Him and to stand by Him even amid reproach and humiliation; He can calmly predict to His disciples that they shall all be offended in Him and shall flee (Mark xiv. 26, 27); He can tell Peter, who boasts that he will die with Him, that before the dawn he shall deny Him thrice (Mark xiv. 29-31); all that is so set down in the Scripture. They must doubt Him. But now they shall not lose their blessedness, for He bears all sins and transgressions. That, too, is buried in the atonement which He offers.

[pg 389]

Therefore, also, there is no need for them to understand His secret. He spoke of it to them without any explanation. It is sufficient that they should know why He goes up to Jerusalem. They, on their part, are thinking only of the coming transformation of all things, as their conversation shows. The prospect which He has opened up to them is clear enough; the only thing that they do not understand is why He must first die at Jerusalem. The first time that Peter ventured to speak to Him about it, He had turned on him with cruel harshness, had almost cursed him (Mark viii. 32, 33); from that time forward they no longer dared to ask Him anything about it. The new thought of His own passion has its basis therefore in the authority with which Jesus was armed to bring about the beginning of the final tribulation. Ethically regarded, His taking the suffering upon Himself is an act of mercy and compassion towards those who would otherwise have had to bear these tribulations, and perhaps would not have stood the test. Historically regarded, the thought of His sufferings involves the same lofty treatment both of history and eschatology as was manifested in the identification of the Baptist with Elias. For now He identifies His condemnation and execution, which are to take place on natural lines, with the predicted pre-Messianic tribulations. This imperious forcing of eschatology into history is also its destruction; its assertion and abandonment at the same time.

Towards Passover, therefore, Jesus sets out for Jerusalem, solely in order to die there.[300] "It is," says Wrede, "beyond question the opinion of Mark that Jesus went to Jerusalem because He had decided to die; that is obvious even from the details of the story." It is therefore a mistake to speak of Jesus as "teaching" in Jerusalem. He has no intention of doing so. As a prophet He foretells in veiled parabolic form the offence which must come (Mark xii. 1-12), exhorts men to watch for the Parousia, pictures the nature of the judgment which the Son of Man shall hold, and, for the rest, thinks only how He can so provoke the Pharisees and the rulers that they will be compelled to get rid of Him. That is why He violently cleanses the Temple, and attacks the Pharisees, in the presence of the people, with passionate invective.

From the revelation at Caesarea Philippi onward, all that belongs to the history of Jesus, in the strict sense, are the events which lead up to His death; or, to put it more accurately, the events in which He Himself is the sole actor. The other things which happen, the questions which are laid before Him for decision, the episodic incidents which occur in those days, have nothing to [pg 390] do with the real "Life of Jesus," since they contribute nothing to the decisive issue, but merely form the anecdotic fringes of the real outward and inward event, the deliberate bringing down of death upon Himself.

It is in truth surprising that He succeeded in transforming into history this resolve which had its roots in dogma, and really dying alone. Is it not almost unintelligible that His disciples were not involved in His fate? Not even the disciple who smote with the sword was arrested along with Him (Mark xiv. 47); Peter, recognised in the courtyard of the High Priest's house as one who had been with Jesus the Nazarene, is allowed to go free.

For a moment indeed, Jesus believes that the "three" are destined to share His fate, not from any outward necessity, but because they had professed themselves able to suffer the last extremities with Him. The sons of Zebedee, when He asked them whether, in order to sit at His right hand and His left, they are prepared to drink His cup and be baptized with His baptism, had declared that they were, and thereupon He had predicted that they should do so (Mark x. 38, 39). Peter again had that very night, in spite of the warning of Jesus, sworn that he would go even unto death with Him (Mark xiv. 30, 31). Hence He is conscious of a higher possibility that these three are to go through the trial with Him. He takes them with Him to Gethsemane and bids them remain near Him and watch with Him. And since they do not perceive the danger of the hour, He adjures them to watch and pray. They are to pray that they may not have to pass through the trial (ἵνα μὴ ἔλθητε εἰς πειρασμόν) since, though the spirit is willing, the flesh is weak. Amid His own sore distress He is anxious about them and their capacity to share His trial as they had declared their willingness to do.[301]

Here also it is once more made clear that for Jesus the necessity of His death is grounded in dogma, not in external historical facts. Above the dogmatic eschatological necessity, however, there stands the omnipotence of God, which is bound by no limitations. As Jesus in the Lord's Prayer had taught His followers to pray for deliverance from the πειρασμός, and as in His fears for the three He bids them pray for the same thing, so now He Himself prays for deliverance, even in this last moment when He knows that the armed band which is coming to arrest Him is already on the way. Literal history does not exist for Him, only the will of God; and this is exalted even above eschatological necessity.

But how did this exact agreement between the fate of Jesus and His predictions come about? Why did the authorities strike at Him only, not at His whole following, not even at the disciples? [pg 391] He was arrested and condemned on account of His Messianic claims. But how did the High Priest know that Jesus claimed to be the Messiah? And why does he put the accusation as a direct question without calling witnesses in support of it? Why was the attempt first made to bring up a saying about the Temple which could be interpreted as blasphemy in order to condemn Him on this ground (Mark xiv. 57-59)? Before that again, as is evident from Mark's account, they had brought up a whole crowd of witnesses in the hope of securing evidence sufficient to justify His condemnation; and the attempt had not succeeded.

It was only after all these attempts had failed that the High Priest brought his accusation concerning the Messianic claim, and he did so without citing the three necessary witnesses. Why so? Because he had not got them. The condemnation of Jesus depended on His own admission. That was why they had endeavoured to convict Him upon other charges.[302]

This wholly unintelligible feature of the trial confirms what is evident also from the discourses and attitude of Jesus at Jerusalem, viz. that He had not been held by the multitude to be the Messiah, that the idea of His making such claims had not for a moment occurred to them—lay in fact for them quite beyond the range of possibility. Therefore He cannot have made a Messianic entry.

According to Havet, Brandt, Wellhausen, Dalman, and Wrede the ovation at the entry had no Messianic character whatever. It is wholly mistaken, as Wrede quite rightly remarks, to represent matters as if the Messianic ovation was forced upon Jesus—that He accepted it with inner repugnance and in silent passivity. For that would involve the supposition that the people had for a moment regarded Him as Messiah and then afterwards had shown themselves as completely without any suspicion of His Messiahship as though they had in the interval drunk of the waters of Lethe. The exact opposite is true: Jesus Himself made the preparations for the Messianic entry. Its Messianic features were due to His arrangements. He made a point of riding upon the ass, not because He was weary, but because He desired that the Messianic prophecy of Zech. ix. 9 should be secretly fulfilled.

The entry is therefore a Messianic act on the part of Jesus, an action in which His consciousness of His office breaks through, as it did at the sending forth of the disciples, in the explanation that [pg 392] the Baptist was Elias, and in the feeding of the multitude. But others can have had no suspicion of the Messianic significance of that which was going on before their eyes. The entry into Jerusalem was therefore Messianic for Jesus, but not Messianic for the people.

But what was He for the people? Here Wrede's theory that He was a teacher again refutes itself. In the triumphal entry there is more than the ovation offered to a teacher. The jubilations have reference to "Him who is to come"; it is to Him that the acclamations are offered and because of Him that the people rejoice in the nearness of the Kingdom, as in Mark, the cries of jubilation show; for here, as Dalman rightly remarks, there is actually no mention of the Messiah.

Jesus therefore made His entry into Jerusalem as the Prophet, as Elias. That is confirmed by Matthew (xxi. 11), although Matthew gives a Messianic colouring to the entry itself by bringing in the acclamation in which He was designated the Son of David, just as, conversely, he reports the Baptist's question rightly, and introduces it wrongly, by making the Baptist hear of the "works of the Christ."

Was Mark conscious, one wonders, that it was not a Messianic entry that he was reporting? We do not know. It is not inherently impossible that, as Wrede asserts, "he had no real view concerning the historical life of Jesus," did not know whether Jesus was recognised as Messiah, and took no interest in the question from an historical point of view. Fortunately for us! For that is why he simply hands on tradition and does not write a Life of Jesus.

The Marcan hypothesis went astray in conceiving this Gospel as a Life of Jesus written with either complete or partial historical consciousness, and interpreting it on these lines, on the sole ground that it only brings in the name Son of Man twice prior to the incident at Caesarea Philippi. The Life of Jesus cannot be arrived at by following the arrangement of a single Gospel, but only on the basis of the tradition which is preserved more or less faithfully in the earliest pair of Synoptic Gospels.

Questions of literary priority, indeed literary questions in general, have in the last resort, as Keim remarked long ago, nothing to do with the gaining of a clear idea of the course of events, since the Evangelists had not themselves a clear idea of it before their minds; it can only be arrived at hypothetically by an experimental reconstruction based on the necessary inner connexion of the incidents.

But who could possibly have had in early times a clear conception of the Life of Jesus? Even its most critical moments were totally unintelligible to the disciples who had themselves shared in the experiences, and who were the only sources for the tradition.

[pg 393]

They were simply swept through these events by the momentum of the purpose of Jesus. That is why the tradition is incoherent. The reality had been incoherent too, since it was only the secret Messianic self-consciousness of Jesus which created alike the events and their connexion. Every Life of Jesus remains therefore a reconstruction on the basis of a more or less accurate insight into the nature of the dynamic self-consciousness of Jesus which created the history.

The people, whatever Mark may have thought, did not offer Jesus a Messianic ovation at all; it was He who, in the conviction that they were wholly unable to recognise it, played with His Messianic self-consciousness before their eyes, just as He did at the time after the sending forth of the disciples, when, as now, He thought the end at hand. It was in the same way, too, that He closed the invective against the Pharisees with the words "I say unto you, ye shall see me no more until ye shall say, Blessed is he that cometh in the name of the Lord" (Matt. xxiii. 39). This saying implies His Parousia.

Similarly He is playing with His secret in that crucial question regarding the Messiahship in Mark xii. 35-37.[303] There is no question of dissociating the Davidic Sonship from the Messiahship. He asks only how can the Christ in virtue of His descent from David be, as his son, inferior to David, and yet be addressed by David in the Psalm as his Lord? The answer is; by reason of the metamorphosis and Parousia in which natural relationships are abolished and the scion of David's line who is the predestined Son of Man shall take possession of His unique glory.

Far from rejecting the Davidic Sonship in this saying, Jesus, on the contrary, presupposes His possession of it. That raises the question whether He did not really during His lifetime regard Himself as a descendant of David and whether He was not regarded as such. Paul, who otherwise shows no interest in the earthly phase of the existence of the Lord, certainly implies His descent from David.

The blind man at Jericho, too, cries out to the Nazarene prophet as "Son of David" (Mark x. 47). But in doing so he does not mean to address Jesus as Messiah, for afterwards, when he is brought to Him he simply calls Him "Rabbi" (Mark x. 51). And the people thought nothing further about what he had said. When the expectant people bid him keep silence they do not do so because the expression Son of David offends them, but because his clamour annoys them. Jesus, however, was struck by this cry, stood still and caused him, as he was standing timidly behind the [pg 394] eager multitude, to be brought to Him. It is possible, of course, that this address is a mere mistake in the tradition, the same tradition which unsuspectingly brought in the expression Son of Man at the wrong place.

So much, however, is certain: the people were not made aware of the Messiahship of Jesus by the cry of the blind man any more than by the outcries of the demoniacs. The entry into Jerusalem was not a Messianic ovation. All that history is concerned with is that this fact should be admitted on all hands. Except Jesus and the disciples, therefore, no one knew the secret of His Messiahship even in those days at Jerusalem. But the High Priest suddenly showed himself in possession of it. How? Through the betrayal of Judas.

For a hundred and fifty years the question has been historically discussed why Judas betrayed his Master. That the main question for history was *what he betrayed* was suspected by few and they touched on it only in a timid kind of way—indeed the problems of the trial of Jesus may be said to have been non-existent for criticism.

The traitorous act of Judas cannot have consisted in informing the Sanhedrin where Jesus was to be found at a suitable place for an arrest. They could have had that information more cheaply by causing Jesus to be watched by spies. But Mark expressly says that Judas when he betrayed Jesus did not yet know of a favourable opportunity for the arrest, but was seeking such an opportunity. Mark xiv. 10, 11, "And Judas Iscariot, one of the twelve, went unto the chief priests, to betray him unto them. And when they heard it, they were glad, and promised to give him money. And he sought how he might conveniently betray him."

In the betrayal, therefore, there were two points, a more general and a more special: the general fact by which he gave Jesus into their power, and the undertaking to let them know of the next opportunity when they could arrest Him quietly, without publicity. The betrayal by which he brought his Master to death, in consequence of which the rulers decided upon the arrest, knowing that their cause was safe in any case, was the betrayal of the Messianic secret. Jesus died because two of His disciples had broken His command of silence: Peter when he made known the secret of the Messiahship to the Twelve at Caesarea Philippi; Judas Iscariot by communicating it to the High Priest. But the difficulty was that Judas was the sole witness. Therefore the betrayal was useless so far as the actual trial was concerned unless Jesus admitted the charge. So they first tried to secure His condemnation on other grounds, and only when these attempts broke down did the High Priest put, in the form of a question, the charge in support of which he could have brought no witnesses.

[pg 395]

But Jesus immediately admitted it, and strengthened the admission by an allusion to His Parousia in the near future as Son of Man.

The betrayal and the trial can only be rightly understood when it is realised that the public knew nothing whatever of the secret of the Messiahship.[304]

It is the same in regard to the scene in the presence of Pilate. The people on that morning knew nothing of the trial of Jesus, but came to Pilate with the sole object of asking the release of a prisoner, as was the custom at the feast (Mark xv. 6-8). The idea then occurs to Pilate, who was just about to hand over, willingly enough, this troublesome fellow and prophet to the priestly faction, to play off the people against the priests and work on the multitude to petition for the release of Jesus. In this way he would have secured himself on both sides. He would have condemned Jesus to please the priests, and after condemning Him would have released Him to please the people. The priests are greatly embarrassed by the presence of the multitude. They had done everything so quickly and quietly that they might well have hoped to get Jesus crucified before any one knew what was happening or had had time to wonder at His non-appearance in the Temple.

The priests therefore go among the people and induce them not to agree to the Procurator's proposal. How? By telling them why He was condemned, by revealing to them the Messianic secret. That makes Him at once from a prophet worthy of honour into a deluded enthusiast and blasphemer. That was the explanation of the "fickleness" of the Jerusalem mob which is always so eloquently described, without any evidence for it except this single inexplicable case.

At midday of the same day—it was the 14th Nisan, and in the evening the Paschal lamb would be eaten—Jesus cried aloud and expired. He had chosen to remain fully conscious to the last.

XX. Results

Those who are fond of talking about negative theology can find their account here. There is nothing more negative than the result of the critical study of the Life of Jesus.

The Jesus of Nazareth who came forward publicly as the Messiah, who preached the ethic of the Kingdom of God, who founded the Kingdom of Heaven upon earth, and died to give His work its final consecration, never had any existence. He is a figure designed by rationalism, endowed with life by liberalism, and clothed by modern theology in an historical garb.

This image has not been destroyed from without, it has fallen to pieces, cleft and disintegrated by the concrete historical problems which came to the surface one after another, and in spite of all the artifice, art, artificiality, and violence which was applied to them, refused to be planed down to fit the design on which the Jesus of the theology of the last hundred and thirty years had been constructed, and were no sooner covered over than they appeared again in a new form. The thoroughgoing sceptical and the thoroughgoing eschatological school have only completed the work of destruction by linking the problems into a system and so making an end of the *Divide et impera* of modern theology, which undertook to solve each of them separately, that is, in a less difficult form. Henceforth it is no longer permissible to take one problem out of the series and dispose of it by itself, since the weight of the whole hangs upon each.

Whatever the ultimate solution may be, the historical Jesus of whom the criticism of the future, taking as its starting-point the problems which have been recognised and admitted, will draw the portrait, can never render modern theology the services which it claimed from its own half-historical, half-modern, Jesus. He will be a Jesus, who was Messiah, and lived as such, either on the ground of a literary fiction of the earliest Evangelist, or on the ground of a purely eschatological Messianic conception.

In either case, He will not be a Jesus Christ to whom the [pg 397] religion of the present can ascribe, according to its long-cherished custom, its own thoughts and ideas, as it did with the Jesus of its own making. Nor will He be a figure which can be made by a popular historical treatment so sympathetic and universally intelligible to the multitude. The historical Jesus will be to our time a stranger and an enigma.

The study of the Life of Jesus has had a curious history. It set out in quest of the historical Jesus, believing that when it had found Him it could bring Him straight into our time as a Teacher and Saviour. It loosed the bands by which He had been riveted for centuries to the stony rocks of ecclesiastical doctrine, and rejoiced to see life and movement coming into the figure once more, and the historical Jesus advancing, as it seemed, to meet it. But He does not stay; He passes by our time and returns to His own. What surprised and dismayed the theology of the last forty years was that, despite all forced and arbitrary interpretations, it could not keep Him in our time, but had to let Him go. He returned to His own time, not owing to the application of any historical ingenuity, but by the same inevitable necessity by which the liberated pendulum returns to its original position.

The historical foundation of Christianity as built up by rationalistic, by liberal, and by modern theology no longer exists; but that does not mean that Christianity has lost its historical foundation. The work which historical theology thought itself bound to carry out, and which fell to pieces just as it was nearing completion, was only the brick facing of the real immovable historical foundation which is independent of any historical confirmation or justification.

Jesus means something to our world because a mighty spiritual force streams forth from Him and flows through our time also. This fact can neither be shaken nor confirmed by any historical discovery. It is the solid foundation of Christianity.

The mistake was to suppose that Jesus could come to mean more to our time by entering into it as a man like ourselves. That is not possible. First because such a Jesus never existed. Secondly because, although historical knowledge can no doubt introduce greater clearness into an existing spiritual life, it cannot call spiritual life into existence. History can destroy the present; it can reconcile the present with the past; can even to a certain extent transport the present into the past; but to contribute to the making of the present is not given unto it.

But it is impossible to over-estimate the value of what German research upon the Life of Jesus has accomplished. It is a uniquely great expression of sincerity, one of the most significant events in the whole mental and spiritual life of humanity. What has been done for the religious life of the present and the [pg 398] immediate future by scholars such as P. W. Schmidt, Bousset, Jülicher, Weinel, Wernle—and their pupil Frenssen—and the others who have been called to the task of bringing to the knowledge of wider circles, in a form which is popular without being superficial, the results of religious-historical study, only becomes evident when one examines the literature and social culture of the Latin nations, who have been scarcely if at all touched by the influence of these thinkers.

And yet the time of doubt was bound to come. We modern theologians are too proud of our historical method, too proud of our historical Jesus, too confident in our belief in the spiritual gains which our historical theology can bring to the world. The thought that we could build up by the increase of historical knowledge a new and vigorous Christianity and set free new spiritual forces, rules us like a fixed idea, and prevents us from seeing that the task which we have grappled with and in some measure discharged is only one of the intellectual preliminaries of the great religious task. We thought that it was for us to lead our time by a roundabout way through the historical Jesus, as we understood Him, in order to bring it to the Jesus who is a spiritual power in the present. This roundabout way has now been closed by genuine history.

There was a danger of our thrusting ourselves between men and the Gospels, and refusing to leave the individual man alone with the sayings of Jesus.

There was a danger that we should offer them a Jesus who was too small, because we had forced Him into conformity with our human standards and human psychology. To see that, one need only read the Lives of Jesus written since the 'sixties, and notice what they have made of the great imperious sayings of the Lord, how they have weakened down His imperative world-contemning demands upon individuals, that He might not come into conflict with our ethical ideals, and might tune His denial of the world to our acceptance of it. Many of the greatest sayings are found lying in a corner like explosive shells from which the charges have been removed. No small portion of elemental religious power needed to be drawn off from His sayings to prevent them from conflicting with our system of religious world-acceptance. We have made Jesus hold another language with our time from that which He really held.

In the process we ourselves have been enfeebled, and have robbed our own thoughts of their vigour in order to project them back into history and make them speak to us out of the past. It is nothing less than a misfortune for modern theology that it mixes history with everything and ends by being proud of the skill with which it finds its own thoughts—even to its beggarly pseudo-metaphysic [pg 399] with which it has banished genuine speculative metaphysic from the sphere of religion—in Jesus, and represents Him as expressing them. It had almost deserved the reproach: "he who putteth his hand to the plough, and looketh back, is not fit for the Kingdom of God."

It was no small matter, therefore, that in the course of the critical study of the Life of Jesus, after a resistance lasting for two generations, during which first one expedient was tried and then another, theology was forced by genuine history to begin to doubt the artificial history with which it had thought to give new life to our Christianity, and to yield to the facts, which, as Wrede strikingly said, are sometimes the most radical critics of all. History will force it to find a way to transcend history, and to fight for the lordship and rule of Jesus over this world with weapons tempered in a different forge.

We are experiencing what Paul experienced. In the very moment when we were coming nearer to the historical Jesus than men had ever come before, and were already stretching out our hands to draw Him into our own time, we have been obliged to give up the attempt and acknowledge our failure in that paradoxical saying: "If we have known Christ after the flesh yet henceforth know we Him no more." And further we must be prepared to find that the historical knowledge of the personality and life of Jesus will not be a help, but perhaps even an offence to religion.

But the truth is, it is not Jesus as historically known, but Jesus as spiritually arisen within men, who is significant for our time and can help it. Not the historical Jesus, but the spirit which goes forth from Him and in the spirits of men strives for new influence and rule, is that which overcomes the world.

It is not given to history to disengage that which is abiding and eternal in the being of Jesus from the historical forms in which it worked itself out, and to introduce it into our world as a living influence. It has toiled in vain at this undertaking. As a water-plant is beautiful so long as it is growing in the water, but once torn from its roots, withers and becomes unrecognisable, so it is with the historical Jesus when He is wrenched loose from the soil of eschatology, and the attempt is made to conceive Him "historically" as a Being not subject to temporal conditions. The abiding and eternal in Jesus is absolutely independent of historical knowledge and can only be understood by contact with His spirit which is still at work in the world. In proportion as we have the Spirit of Jesus we have the true knowledge of Jesus.

Jesus as a concrete historical personality remains a stranger to our time, but His spirit, which lies hidden in His words, is known in simplicity, and its influence is direct. Every saying contains in its own way the whole Jesus. The very strangeness and [pg 400] unconditionedness in which He stands before us makes it easier for individuals to find their own personal standpoint in regard to Him.

Men feared that to admit the claims of eschatology would abolish the significance of His words for our time; and hence there was a feverish eagerness to discover in them any elements that might be considered not eschatologically conditioned. When any sayings were found of which the wording did not absolutely imply an eschatological connexion there was great jubilation—these at least had been saved uninjured from the coming *débâcle*.

But in reality that which is eternal in the words of Jesus is due to the very fact that they are based on an eschatological world-view, and contain the expression of a mind for which the contemporary world with its historical and social circumstances no longer had any existence. They are appropriate, therefore, to any world, for in every world they raise the man who dares to meet their challenge, and does not turn and twist them into meaninglessness, above his world and his time, making him inwardly free, so that he is fitted to be, in his own world and in his own time, a simple channel of the power of Jesus.

Modern Lives of Jesus are too general in their scope. They aim at influencing, by giving a complete impression of the life of Jesus, a whole community. But the historical Jesus, as He is depicted in the Gospels, influenced individuals by the individual word. They understood Him so far as it was necessary for them to understand, without forming any conception of His life as a whole, since this in its ultimate aims remained a mystery even for the disciples.

Because it is thus preoccupied with the general, the universal, modern theology is determined to find its world-accepting ethic in the teaching of Jesus. Therein lies its weakness. The world affirms itself automatically; the modern spirit cannot but affirm it. But why on that account abolish the conflict between modern life, with the world-affirming spirit which inspires it as a whole, and the world-negating spirit of Jesus? Why spare the spirit of the individual man its appointed task of fighting its way through the world-negation of Jesus, of contending with Him at every step over the value of material and intellectual goods—a conflict in which it may never rest? For the general, for the institutions of society, the rule is: affirmation of the world, in conscious opposition to the view of Jesus, on the ground that the world has affirmed itself! This general affirmation of the world, however, if it is to be Christian, must in the individual spirit be Christianised and transfigured by the personal rejection of the world which is preached in the sayings of Jesus. It is only by means of the tension thus set up that religious energy can be communicated to our time. There [pg 401] was a danger that modern theology, for the sake of peace, would deny the world-negation in the sayings of Jesus, with which Protestantism was out of sympathy, and thus unstring the bow and make Protestantism a mere sociological instead of a religious force. There was perhaps also a danger of inward insincerity, in the fact that it refused to admit to itself and others that it maintained its affirmation of the world in opposition to the sayings of Jesus, simply because it could not do otherwise.

For that reason it is a good thing that the true historical Jesus should overthrow the modern Jesus, should rise up against the modern spirit and send upon earth, not peace, but a sword. He was not teacher, not a casuist; He was an imperious ruler. It was because He was so in His inmost being that He could think of Himself as the Son of Man. That was only the temporally conditioned expression of the fact that He was an authoritative ruler. The names in which men expressed their recognition of Him as such, Messiah, Son of Man, Son of God, have become for us historical parables. We can find no designation which expresses what He is for us.

He comes to us as One unknown, without a name, as of old, by the lake-side, He came to those men who knew Him not. He speaks to us the same word: "Follow thou me!" and sets us to the tasks which He has to fulfil for our time. He commands. And to those who obey Him, whether they be wise or simple, He will reveal Himself in the toils, the conflicts, the sufferings which they shall pass through in His fellowship, and, as an ineffable mystery, they shall learn in their own experience Who He is.

Index Of Authors And Works

(Including Reference To English Translations)

Ammon, Christoph Friedrich von. Fortbildung des Christentums (Leipzig, 1840);
Die Geschichte des Lebens Jesu mit steter Rücksicht auf die vorhandenen Quellen (1842-1847), 11, 97, 104 f., 117 f.
Anonymous Works—
Das Leben Napoleons kritisch geprüft. Aus dem Englischen (see under Whateley) nebst einigen Nutzanwendungen auf das Leben-Jesu von Strauss (1836), 112
Did Jesus live 100 B.C.? (London and Benares, Theosophical Publishing Society, 1903), 327
Dr. Strauss und die Züricher Kirche (Basle, 1839), 103
Wichtige Enthüllungen über die wirkliche Todesart Jesu (5th ed., Leipzig, 1849);
Historische Enthüllungen über die wirklichen Ereignisse der Geburt und Jugend Jesu (2nd ed., Leipzig, 1849), 161 f.
Zwei Gespräche über die Ansicht des Herrn Dr. Strauss von der evangelischen Geschichte (Jena, 1839), 100
Baader, Franz. Über das Leben-Jesu von Strauss (Munich, 1836), 100
Bahrdt, Karl Friedrich. Briefe über die Bibel im Volkston (1782);
Ausführung des Plans und Zwecks Jesu (1784-1792);
Die sämtlichen Reden Jesu aus den Evangelien ausgezogen (1786), 4, 5, 38, 39 f., 46, 53, 59, 299, 313
Baldensperger, Wilhelm. Das Selbstbewusstsein Jesu im Lichte der messianischen Hoffnungen seiner Zeit (Strassburg, 1888, 2nd ed. 1892, 3rd ed. pt. i. 1903), 12, 233-237, 250, 266, 278 f., 365, 366
Barth, Fritz. Die Hauptprobleme des Lebens Jesu (1st ed. 1899, 2nd ed. 1903), 301
Bauer, Bruno. Kritik der evangelischen Geschichte des Johannes (Bremen, 1840);
Kritik der evangelischen Geschichte der Synoptiker (Leipzig, 1841-1842);
Kritik der Evangelien und Geschichte ihres Ursprungs (Berlin, 1850-1851);
Kritik der Apostelgeschichte (1850);
Kritik der Paulinischen Briefe (Berlin, 1850-1852);
Philo, Strauss, Renan und das Urchristentum (Berlin, 1874);
Christus und die Cäsaren (Berlin, 1877);
Die gute Sache der Freiheit und meine eigene Angelegenheit (Zurich, 1843), 5, 9, 10, 12, 137-160, 186 f., 221, 231, 256-258, 305 f., 312, 315, 328, 332, 335 f., 338, 342, 346, 358, 368, 388
Baumer, Friedrich. Schwarz, Strauss, Renan (Leipzig, 1864), 191
Baur, Ferdinand Christian. Kritische Untersuchungen über die kanonischen Evangelien (Tübingen, 1847), 25, 58, 68, 87, 89, 124, 182, 195, 201, 229
Bergh van Eysinga, Van den. Indische Einflüsse auf evangelische Erzählungen (Göttingen, 1904), 290
Bernhard ter Haar (Utrecht). Zehn Vorlesungen über Renans "Leben-Jesu" (German by H. Doermer, Gotha, 1864), 191
Beyschlag, Willibald. Über das Leben-Jesu von Renan (Berlin, 1864);
Das Leben-Jesu (pt. i. 1885, pt. ii. 1886, 2nd ed. 1887-1888), 6, 10, 190, 215 f., 218

Binder, 68, 69

Bleby, H. W. The Trial of Jesus of Nazareth considered as a Judicial Act (1880), 391

Bleek, 229, 231

[pg 404]

Böklen, E. Die Verwandtschaft der jüdisch-christlichen und der parsischen Eschatologie (1902), 287

Bolten, Johann Adrian. Der Bericht des Matthäus von Jesu dem Messias (Altona, 1792), 271, 276

Bosc, Ernest. La Vie ésotérique de Jésus de Nazareth et les origines orientales du christianisme (Paris, 1902), 294, 327

Bousset, Wilhelm. Jesu Predigt in ihrem Gegensatz zum Judentum. Ein religionsgeschichtlicher Vergleich (Göttingen, 1892);

Die jüdische Apokalyptik in ihrer religionsgeschichtlichen Herkunft und ihrer Bedeutung für das Neue Testament (Berlin, 1903);

Die Religion des Judentums im neutestamentlichen Zeitalter (1902);

Was wissen wir von Jesus? Vorträge im Protestantenverein zu Bremen (Halle, 1904);

Jesus (Religionsgeschichtliche Volksbücher, herausgegeben von Schiele, Halle, 1904) (English translation, *Jesus*, by J. P. Trevelyan, London, 1906), 241-249, 255 f., 262, 264, 267, 280, 300, 359, 398

Brandt, Wilhelm. Die evangelische Geschichte und der Ursprung des Christentums auf Grund einer Kritik der Berichte über das Leiden und die Auferstehung Jesu (Leipzig, 1893), 241, 256-261, 267, 301, 309, 312, 313, 391

Bretschneider, Karl Gottlob, 85, 118

Brunner, Sebastian. Der Atheist Renan und sein Evangelium (Regensburg, 1864), 190

Bugge, Chr. A. Die Hauptparabeln Jesu. (From the Norwegian) (Giessen, 1903), 263

Bunsen, Christian Karl Josias, Ritter von. Das Leben Jesu, vol. ix. of Bunsen's "Bibelwerk" (published by Holtzmann, 1865), 200

Cairns, John. Falsche Christi und der wahre Christus, oder Verteidigung der evangelischen Geschichte gegen Strauss und Renan. Aus dem Englischen übersetzt (Hamburg, 1864) (*False Christ and the True*, A sermon delivered before the National Bible Society of Scotland, Edinburgh, 1864), 191

Capitaine, W. Jesus von Nazareth (Regensburg, 1905), 294

Cassel, Paulus. Bericht über Renans Leben-Jesu (Berlin, 1864), 191

"Casuar." Das Leben Luthers kritisch bearbeitet. Herausgegeben von Jul. Ferd. Wurm ("Mexiko, 2836"), 112

Chamberlain, H. S. Worte Christi (1901), 310

Charles, R. H. "The Son of Man" (Expos. Times, 1893), 267

Colani, Timothée. Examen de la vie de Jésus de M. Renan (Strassburg, 1864);

Jésus-Christ et les croyances messianiques de son temps (Strassburg, 1864), 182, 189, 209, 221 f., 226, 229, 233, 248, 372

Cone, Orello. "Jesus' Self-designation in the Synoptic Gospels" (The New World, 1893), 266

Coquerel, Athanase (jun.), 189, 209

Credner, 89

Dalman, Gustaf. Grammatik des jüdisch-palästinensischen Aramäisch (Leipzig, 1894);

Die Worte Jesu. Mit Berücksichtigung des nachkanonischen Schrifttums und der aramäischen Sprache, I. (Leipzig, 1898) (authorised English translation by D. M. Kay, *The Words of Jesus*, Edinburgh, 1902), 269, 271, 273-275, 278, 279-281, 286-289, 363, 391 f.

Darboy, Georges. Lettre pastorale de Monseigneur l'Archevêque de Paris sur la divinité de Jésus-Christ, et mandement pour le carême de 1864, 188

Delff, Hugo. Geschichte des Rabbi Jesus von Nazareth (Leipzig, 1889), 11, 323

Delitzsch, Franz, 273, 285

Deutlinger, Martin. Renan und das Wunder. Ein Beitrag zur christlichen Apologetik (Munich, 1864), 190

Didon, Le Père, de l'ordre des frères prêcheurs. Jésus Christ (Paris, 1891, 2 vols., German, 1895) (English translation, *Jesus Christ*, 2 vols., 1891), 295

Dieu, Louis de, 14

Dillmann, 223

Diodati, Dominicus, 271

Döderlein. Fragmente und Antifragmente (Nuremberg, 1778), 25

Dulk, Albert. Der Irrgang des Lebens Jesu. In geschichtlicher Auffassung dargestellt (pt. i. 1884, pt. ii. 1885), 294, 324

Dupanloup, Félix Antoine Philibert, Évêque d'Orléans. Avertissement à la jeunesse et aux pères de famille sur les attaques dirigées contre la religion par quelques écrivains de nos jours (Paris, 1864), 188

Ebrard, August. Wissenschaftliche Kritik der evangelischen Geschichte (Frankfort, 1842), 97, 116 f.

[pg 405]

Edersheim, Alfred. The Life and Times of Jesus the Messiah (London, 1st ed. 1883, 3rd ed. 1886, 2 vols.), 233

Eerdmanns, B. E. "De Oorsprong van de uitdrukking 'Zoon des Menschen' als evangelische Messiastitel" (Theol. Tijdschr., 1894), 276

Ehrhardt. Der Grundcharakter der Ethik Jesu in Verhältnis zu den messianischen Hoffnungen seines Volkes und zu seinem eigenen Messiasbewusstsein (Freiburg, 1895);

Le Principe de la morale de Jésus (Paris, 1896), 249

Eichhorn, Johann Gottfried, 78, 89

Emmerich, Anna Katharina. Das bittere Leiden unseres Herrn Jesu Christi. Herausgegeben von Brentano (1858-1860, new ed. 1895) (English translation, *The Dolorous Passion of Our Lord Jesus Christ*, London, 1862);

Das Leben Jesu, 3 vols. (1858-1860), 109 f., 295

Ewald, Georg Heinrich August. "Geschichte Christus' und seiner Zeit," vol. v. of the "Geschichte des Volkes Israel" (Göttingen, 1855, 2nd ed. 1857), English translation of the *Life of Jesus Christ*, by Octavius Glover (London, 1865);

Die drei ersten Evangelien (1850), 97, 117, 124, 135

Fiebig, Paul. Der Menschensohn (Tübingen, 1901);

Altjüdische Gleichnisse und die Gleichnisse Jesu (Tübingen, 1904), 278, 286

Frantzen, Wilhelm. Die "Leben-Jesu-" Bewegung seit Strauss (Dorpat, 1898), 12

Frenssen, Gustav. Hilligenlei (Berlin, 1905), pp. 462-593: "Die Handschrift" (English translation, *Holy Land*, by M. A. Hamilton, London, 1906), 293, 307-309, 398

Freppel, Charles Emile. Examen critique de la vie de Jesus de M. Renan (Paris, 1864) (German by Kollmus, Vienna, 1864), 188, 190

Frick, Otto. Mythus und Evangelium (Heilbronn, 1879), 112

Furrer, Konrad. Vorträge über das Leben Jesu Christi (1902), 301

Gabler, 78

Gardner, P. Exploratio Evangelica. A Brief Examination of the Basis and Origin of Christian Belief (1899, 2nd ed. 1907), 217

Gerlach, Hermann. Gegen Renans Leben-Jesu 1864 (Berlin), 191

Gfrörer, August Friedrich. Kritische Geschichte des Urchristentums (vol. i. 1st ed. 1831, 2nd ed. 1835, vol. ii. 1838), 161, 163-166, 195

Ghillany, Friedrich Wilhelm ("Richard von der Alm"). Theologische Briefe an die Gebildeten der deutschen Nation (3 vols. 1863);

Die Urteile heidnischer und christlicher Schriftsteller der vier ersten christlichen Jahrhunderte über Jesus (1864), 161, 166-172, 240, 363

Godet, F. Das Leben Jesu vor seinem öffentlichen Auftreten (German by M. Reineck, Hanover, 1897), 217

Gratz, 89

Greiling. Das Leben Jesu von Nazareth (1813), 50

Gressman, Hugo, 234

Griesbach, Johann Jakob, 13, 89

Grimm, Eduard. Die Ethik Jesu (Hamburg, 1903), 320

Grimm, Joseph. Das Leben Jesu (Würzburg, 6 vols., 2nd ed. 1890-1903), 294

Grotius, Hugo, 270

Gunkel, Hermann, 277

Hagel, Maurus. Dr. Strauss' Leben-Jesu aus dens Standpunkt des Katholicismus betrachtet (1839), 108

Hahn, Werner. Leben-Jesu (Berlin, 1844), 118

Haneberg, Daniel Bonifacius. Ernest Renans Leben-Jesu (Regensburg, 1864), 190

Hanson, Sir Richard. The Jesus of History (1869), 202

Harless, Adolf. Die kritische Bearbeitung des Lebens Jesu von David Friedrich Strauss nach ihrem wissenschaftlichen Werte beleuchtet (Erlangen, 1836), 98 f.

Harnack, Adolf, 242, 252, 314

Hartmann, Eduard von. Das Christentum des Neuen Testaments, 2nd ed. of the "Briefe über die christliche Religion" (Sachsa-in-the-Harz, 1905), 292, 318-320

Hartmann, Julius. Leben Jesu (2 vols., 1837-1839), 101

Hase, Karl August von. Das Leben Jesu (1st ed. 1829);

Geschichte Jesu (Leipzig, 1876), 4, 5, 10, 11, 12, 28, 58 f., 65, 72, 81, 88, 99, 106, 116, 120, 162, 193, 214 f., 218, 220, 229

Haupt, Erich. Die eschatologischen Aussagen Jesu in den synoptischen Evangelien (1895), 241, 250 f.

Hausrath, Adolf. Neutestamentliche Zeitgeschichte (1st ed., Munich, 1868 ff., 3rd ed., vol. i. 1879) (English translation, *A History of the* [pg 406]*New Testament Times, The Time of Jesus*, by C. T. Poynting and P. Quenzer, London, 1878), 214

Havet, Ernest. Jésus dans l'histoire. Examen de la vie de Jésus par M. Renan. Extrait de la Revue des deux mondes (Paris, 1863);

Le Christianisme et ses origines, 3me p^{tie}, Le Nouveau Testament (1884), 189, 290, 328, 391

Hegel, Georg Friedrich Wilhelm, 49, 68 f., 79 f., 107, 111, 114 f., 122, 137, 163, 165, 194

Hengstenberg, Ernst Wilhelm, 106 f., 111, 115, 143

Hennell, Charles Christian. An Inquiry concerning the Origin of Christianity (London, 1838) (Untersuchungen über den Ursprung des Christentums. Vorrede von David Friedrich Strauss, 1840), 161

Herder, Johann Gottfried. Vom Erlöser der Menschen. Nach unsern drei ersten Evangelien (1796);

Von Gottes Sohn, der Welt Heiland. Nach Johannes Evangelium (1797), 27, 29, 34, 89, 203

Hess, Johann Jakob. Geschichte der drei letzten Lebensjahre Jesu (1768 ff.), 4, 14, 27-31

Hilgenfeld, Adolf, 124, 222, 266

Hoekstra. "De Christologie van het canonieke Marcus-Evangelie, vergeleken met die van de beide andere synoptische Evangelien" (Theol. Tijdschrift, v., 1871), 328

Hoffmann, Wilhelm. Das Leben-Jesu kritisch bearbeitet von Dr. David Fried. Strauss. Geprüft für Theologen und Nicht-Theologen (1836), 99

Holtzmann, Heinrich Julius, 10, 61, 125, 195, 200, 202-205, 209, 218, 220, 229, 231, 235, 237, 277, 294

Holtzmann, Oskar. Das Leben Jesu, (1901) (English translation, *The Life of Jesus*, by J. T. Bealby and Maurice A. Canney, London, 1904);

Das Messianitätsbewusstsein Jesu und seine neueste Bestreitung. Vortrag (1902);

War Jesus Ekstatiker? (Tübingen, 1903), 208, 293, 295-300, 306 f., 308, 312, 359

Hug, Leonhard. Gutachten über das Leben-Jesu, kritisch bearbeitet von D. Fr. Strauss (Freiburg, 1840), 97, 108, 109, 271

Ingraham, J. H. The Prince of the House of David (London, 1859) (Der Fürst aus Davids Hause, new ed., 1896, Brunswick), 326

Inchofer, 270

Issel, 237

Jacobi, Johann Adolf. Die Geschichte Jesu für denkende und gemütvolle Leser (1816), 27, 34

Jonge, De. Jeschua. Der klassische jüdische Mann. Zerstörung des kirchlichen, Enthüllung des jüdischen Jesus-Bildes (Berlin, 1904), 293, 321 f.

Jülicher, Adolf. Die Gleichnisreden Jesu (pt. i. 1888, pt. ii. 1899);

Die Kultur der Gegenwart (Teubner, Berlin, 1905), pp. 40-69;

"Jesus," 241, 262-264, 286, 290, 320, 398

Kalthoff, Albert. Das Christus-Problem. Grundlinien zu einer Sozialtheologie (Leipzig, 1902);

Die Entstehung des Christentums. Neue Beiträge zum Christus-Problem (Leipzig, 1904) (English translation, *The Rise of Christianity*, by Joseph M'Cabe, London, 1907);

Das Leben Jesu. Reden gehalten im prot. Reformverein zu Berlin (1880);

Was wissen wir von Jesus? Eine Abrechnung mit Professor Bousset in Göttingen (Berlin, 1904), 293, 314-318

Kant, Emmanuel, 50, 105, 322

Kapp, W. Das Christus-und Christentum-Problem bei Kalthoff (Strassburg, 1905), 318

Kautzsch, Emil Friedrich, 271

Keim, Theodor. Die Geschichte Jesu von Nazara (3 vols., Zurich, pt. i. 1867, pt. ii. 1871, pt. iii. 1872);

Die Geschichte Jesu. Nach den Ergebnissen heutiger Wissenschaft für weitere Kreise übersichtlich erzählt (Zurich, 1872) (English translation of the larger work, *The History of Jesus of Nazara*, by E. M. Geldart and A. Ransom, 6 vols., London, 1873-1883), 11, 61, 193, 200, 209, 211-214, 231 f., 310, 343, 351, 357, 380, 392

Kienlen, 228

Kirchbach, Wolfgang. Was lehrte Jesus? (Berlin, 1897, 2nd ed. 1902);

Das Buch Jesus (Berlin, 1897), 294, 322-324

Koppe, 89

Köstlin, Karl Reinhold, 124

Krabbe. Vorlesungen über das Leben Jesu für Theologen und Nicht-Theologen (Hamburg, 1839), 100

Kralik, Richard von. Jesu Leben und Werk (Kempten-Nürnberg, 1904), 294

Krauss, S. Das Leben Jesu nach jüdischen Quellen (1902), 327

[pg 407]

Krüger-Velthusen, W. Leben Jesu. (Elberfeld, 1872), 217

Kuhn, Johannes von. Leben Jesu (Tübingen, 1840), 108

Kunz, K. Christus medicus (Freiburg, 1905), 325

Lachmann, 89

Lamy. Renans Leben-Jesu vor dem Richterstuhle der Kritik. Übersetzt von Aug. Rohling (Münster, 1864), 190

Lange, Johann Peter. Das Leben Jesu, 5 vols. (1844-1847) (English translation, *The Life of the Lord Jesus Christ*, by Sophia Taylor, Edinburgh, 1864), 117

Längin, G. Der Christus der Geschichte und sein Christentum (2 vols., 1897-1898), 217

Langsdorf, Karl von. Wohlgeprüfte Darstellung des Lebens Jesu (Mannheim, 1831), 162

Lasserre, Henri. L'Évangile selon Renan (1864, 12 editions, German, Munich, 1864), 188, 190

Lehmann. Renan wider Renan (Zwickau, 1864), 191

Lessing, Gotthold Ephraim, 5, 14-16, 75

Levi, Giuseppe. Parabeln, Legenden und Gedanken aus Talmud und Midrasch (2nd ed., Leipzig, 1877), 286

Lichtenstein, Wilhelm Jakob. Leben des Herrn Jesu Christi (Erlangen, 1856), 101

Lietzmann, Hans. Der Menschensohn (Freiburg, 1896);
Zur Menschensohnfrage (1898), 265, 276 f., 285, 289

Lightfoot, John. Horae Hebraicae et Talmudicae in quatuor Evangelistas. Herausgegeben von J. B. Carpzov (Leipzig, 1684), 222, 285

Lillie, A. The Influence of Buddhism on Primitive Christianity (London, 1893), 326

Littré, M., 181

Loisy, Alfred. Le Quatrième Évangile (Paris, 1903);
Les Évangiles synoptiques, 2 vols. (Paris, 1907);
L'Évangile et l'Église (Paris, 1903) (translated by C. Home, *The Gospel and the Church*, new ed. with a preface by G. Tyrrell, 1908), 295

Lücke, 106

Luthardt, Christoph Ernst. Die modernen Darstellungen des Lebens Jesu. Vortrag (Leipzig, 1864), 191, 209

Luther, 13

Mack, Joseph. Bericht über des Herrn Dr. Strauss' historische Bearbeitung des Lebens Jesu (1837), 108

Manen, van, 286

Marius, Emmanuel. Die Persönlichkeit Jesu mit besonderer Rücksicht auf die Mythologien und Mysterien der alten Völker (Leipzig, 1879), 112

Meinhold, J. Jesus und das Alte Testament (1896), 255

Meuschen, Johann Gerhardt, 285

Meyer, Arnold. Jesu Muttersprache (Leipzig, 1896), 229, 231, 265, 269, 271, 274, 276, 286, 287, 289

Michaelis, 49, 271

Michelis. Renans Roman vom Leben-Jesu (Münster, 1864), 190

Müller, A. Jesus ein Arier (Leipzig, 1904), 327

Müller, Max, 290

Mussard, Eugène. Du système mythique appliqué à l'histoire de la vie de Jésus (1838), 112

Nahor, Pierre (Émilie Lerou), Jésus. (German by Walther Bloch, Berlin, 1905), 325

Neander, August Wilhelm. Das Leben Jesu Christi (Hamburg, 1837) (English translation, *The Life of Jesus Christ*, by J. M'Clintock and C. E. Blumenthal, London, 1851);
Gutachten über das Buch des Dr. Strauss', Leben-Jesu (1836), 72, 97, 101-103, 116, 139

Nestle, 276

Neubauer, Adolf, 273

Neumann, Arno. Jesus wie er geschichtlich war (Freiburg, 1904), 320

Nicolas, Amadée. Renan et sa vie de Jésus sous les rapports moral, légal et littéraire (Paris-Marseille, 1864), 188

Nippold, Friedrich. Der Entwicklungsgang des Lebens Jesu im Wortlaut der drei ersten Evangelien (Hamburg, 1895);
Die psychiatrische Seite der Heilstätigkeit Jesu (1889), 301, 324

Noack, Ludwig. Die Geschichte Jesu (2nd ed., Mannheim, 1876);
Aus der Jordanwiege nach Golgatha (1870-1871), 161 f., 172-179, 185, 322

Nork, J., 285, 286

Notowitsch, Nicolas. La Vie inconnue de Jésus-Christ (Paris, 1894) (German, Stuttgart, 1894), 290, 326

Oort, H. L. Die Uitdrukking ὁ υἱὸς τοῦ ἀνθρώπου in het Nieuwe Testament (Leiden, 1893), 266, 278, 286

Opitz, Ernst August. Geschichte und Characterzüge Jesu (1812), 27, 34

[pg 408]

Osiander, Andreas, 13

Osiander, Johann Ernst. Apologie des Lebens Jesu gegenüber dem neuesten Versuch, es in Mythen aufzulösen (1837), 100

Osterzee, J. J. van (Utrecht). Geschichte oder Roman? Das Leben-Jesu von Ernest Renan vorläufig beleuchtet. (From the Dutch) (Hamburg, 1864), 191

Otto, Rudolf. Leben und Wirken Jesu nach historisch-kritischer Auffassung. Vortrag (Göttingen, 1902), 301

Paul, Ludwig. Die Vorstellung vom Messias und vom Gottesreich bei den Synoptikern (Bonn, 1895), 265

Paulus, Heinrich Eberhard Gottlob. Das Leben Jesu als Grundlage einer reinen Geschichte des Urchristentums (1828), 4, 28, 37, 48 f., 104, 271, 276, 303

Pfleiderer, Otto. Das Urchristentum, seine Schriften und Lehren in geschichtlichem Zusammenhang beschrieben (2nd ed., Berlin, 1902, 2 vols.) (English translation, *Primitive Christianity*, vols. i. and ii. (vol. i. of original), London, 1906, 1909);
Die Entstehung des Urchristentums (Munich, 1905) (English translation, *Christian Origins*, by D. A. Huebsch, London, 1905), 229, 293, 309, 311-313, 384

Plank. Geschichte des Christentums (Göttingen, 1818), 34

Pressel, Theodor. Leben Jesu Christi (1857), 101

Pressensé, Edmond Dehoult de. Jésus-Christ, son temps, sa vie, son œuvre (Paris, 1865) (English translation, *Jesus Christ, His Times, His Life, His Work*, by A. Harwood, 3rd ed., London, 1869);
L'École critique et Jésus-Christ, à propos de la vie de Jésus de M. Renan, 180, 189

Quinet, Edgar, 108

Rauch, C. Jeschua ben Joseph (Deichert, 1899), 326

Régla, Paul de. Jesus von Nazareth, (German by A. Just, Leipzig, 1894), 294, 325

Reimarus, Hermann Samuel. Von dem Zwecke Jesu und seiner Jünger (published by Lessing, Brunswick, 1778) (English translation, *The Object of Jesus and His disciples, as seen in the New Testament*, edited by A. Voysey, 1879), 4, 9, 10, 13-26, 75, 94, 107, 120, 159, 166, 172, 221, 239, 264, 303, 312, 319, 345, 365

Reinhard, Franz Volkmar. Versuch über den Plan, welchen der Stifter der christlichen Religion zum Besten der Menschheit entwarf (1798), 4, 31 f., 48, 206

Renan, Ernest. La Vie de Jésus (Paris, 1863), German, 1895 (English translation, *The Life of Jesus*, London, 1864; translated with an introduction by W. G. Hutchison, London, 1898), 11, 75, 108, 180-192, 193 f., 197, 200, 207, 213 f., 219, 225, 229, 252, 259, 290, 295, 303, 309, 310

Resch, 273

Reuss, Eduard, 124, 182, 189, 228

Réville, Albert. La Vie de Jésus de Renan devant les orthodoxes et devant la critique (1864), 125, 189, 249

Ritschl, Albrecht, 1, 124 f., 250, 320

Robertson, J. M. Christianity and Mythology (London, 1900), 290 f.

Rogers, A. K. The Life and Teachings of Jesus: a critical analysis, etc. (London and New York, 1894), 249

Rosegger, Peter. Frohe Botschaft eines armen Sünders (Leipzig, 1906), 326

Rossi, Giambernardo de. Dissertazione della lingua propria di Christo e degli Ebrei nazionali della Palestina da' tempi de' Maccabei in disamina del sentimento di un recente scrittore italiano (Parma, 1772), 271

Salvator. Jésus-Christ et sa doctrine (Paris, 1838, 2 vols.), 162

Sanday, 90

Saumaise, Claude, 270

Scaliger, Justus, 270

Schegg, Peter. Sechs Bücher des Lebens Jesu (Freiburg, 1874-1875), 294

Schell, Hermann. Christus (Mainz, 1903), 294 f.

Schenkel, Daniel. Das Charakterbild Jesu (Wiesbaden, 1st and 2nd ed. 1864, 4th ed. 1873) (English translation, *A Sketch of the Character of Jesus*, London, 1869), 11, 103, 131, 193, 200, 203, 205-210, 215, 218, 220, 229, 310

Scherer, Edmond, 189, 191, 209

Scherer, Edmond, und Athanase Coquerel (jun.). Zwei französische Stimmen über Renans Leben-Jesu (Regensburg, 1864), 189

Schleiermacher, Friedrich Ernst Daniel. Das Leben Jesu (1864), 49, 58, 62 f., 70, 73, 80, 81, 85, 88, 89, 101 f., [pg 409] 108, 116, 127, 139, 195, 197, 218, 233, 320

Schmiedel, Otto. Die Hauptprobleme der Leben-Jesu-Forschung (Tübingen, 1902), 12, 22, 293, 301, 303, 305, 312

Schmiedel, P., 277

Schmidt, N. "Was בן נשא a Messianic Title?" (Journal of the Society for Biblical Literature, xv., 1896), 277

Schmidt, Paul Wilhelm. Die Geschichte Jesu, i. (Freiburg, 1899), ii. (Tübingen, 1904), 265, 278, 293, 301, 304, 308, 398

Schmoller. Über die Lehre vom Reiche Gottes im Neuen Testament, 237

Scholten, 231

Schöttgen, Christian, 285

Schürer, Emil. Geschichte des jüdischen Volkes ins Zeitalter Jesu Christi (2nd ed., 2nd pt., 1886) (English translation, *History of Jewish People in time of Jesus Christ*, Edinburgh, 1885); Das messianische Selbstbewusstsein Jesu Christi (1903), 234, 241, 254 f., 287

Schwartzkopff. Die Weissagungen Jesu Christi von seinem Tode, seiner Auferstehung und Wiederkunft und ihre Erfüllung (1895), 267

Schweitzer, Albert. Das Messianitätsund Leidensgeheimnis. Eine Skizze des Lebens Jesu (Tübingen, 1901), 281, 287, 328-330, 332 f., 336, 339 f., 351, 382 f.

Schweizer, Alexander, 118, 127 f., 200, 219, 265

Semler, Johann Salomo. Beantwortung der Fragmente eines Ungenannten, insbesondere vom Zweck Jesu und seiner Jünger (Halle, 1779), 13, 15, 25 f., 49

Sepp, Johann Nepomuk. Das Leben Jesu Christi (Regensburg, 7 vols., 1st ed. 1843-1846, 2nd ed. 1853-1862), 108, 294

Seydel, Rudolf. Das Evangelium Jesu in seinen Verhältnissen zur Buddha-Saga und Buddha-Lehre (Leipzig, 1882);

Die Buddha-Legende und das Leben Jesu nach den Evangelien (2nd ed. 1897);

Buddha und Christus (Breslau, 1884), 269, 290-292

Siegfried, Carl, 285

Simon, Richard, 270

Soden, Hermann Freiherr von. Die wichtigsten Fragen im Leben Jesu (Berlin, 1904), 12, 293, 301-308, 312

Stalker, J. The Life of Jesus Christ (Edinburgh, 1880) (German, Tübingen, 1898), 217

Stapfer, E. La Vie de Jésus (pt. i. 1896, pt. ii. 1897, pt. iii. 1898) (English translation, *Jesus Christ before His Ministry*, by L. S. Houghton, 1897, *Jesus Christ during His Ministry*, by L. S. Houghton, 1897), 217

Stave, 243

Storr, 89

Strauss, David Friedrich. Der Christus des Glaubens und der Jesus der Geschichte. Eine Kritik des Schleiermacher'schen Lebens Jesu (Berlin, 1865);

Das Leben Jesu (1st ed. 1835 and 1836, 2 vols., 3rd ed., revised, 1838 and 1839, 4th ed. 1840) (*The Life of Jesus Critically Examined*, translated from the 4th German ed. by George Eliot, London, 1846, 3rd ed. with a preface by Otto Pfleiderer, 1898);

Das Leben Jesu für das deutsche Volk bearbeitet (Leipzig, 1864, 8th ed.) (English translation, *A New Life of Jesus*, London, 1865), 4, 5, 10, 11, 12, 14, 24, 28, 35-37, 58, 60, 62, 65, 79 f., 97 f., 68-121, 125, 129 f., 136, 138, 140, 145, 151, 153, 158, 159, 161, 162, 163, 166, 171, 173, 180 f., 182, 185, 188, 190, 193-199, 200, 201, 209 f., 214, 218, 221, 225, 229, 237, 252, 281, 294, 303, 309, 329, 331, 363

Stricker. Jesus von Nazareth (1868), 202

Tal, T., 286

Tholuck, August. Die Glaubwürdigkeit der evangelischen Geschichte, zugleich eine Kritik des Lebens Jesu von Strauss (Hamburg, 1837) (English translation, *The Credibility of the Evangelical History, illustrated with reference to the "Leben-Jesu" of Dr. Strauss*, London, 1844), 70, 97, 100 f., 116, 119, 122, 139

Titius, Arthur, 250

Uhlhorn, Johann Gerhard Wilhelm. Das Leben Jesu in seinen neueren Darstellungen. Vorträge (1892), 5, 11

Ullmann, 100

Usteri, 78

Venturini, Karl Heinrich. Natürliche Geschichte des grossen Propheten von Nazareth (1st ed. 1800-1802, 2nd ed. 1806), 4, 38, 44, 45, 50, 59, 82, 162, 170, 299, 303, 313, 325, 327

Veuillot, Louis. La Vie de notre Seigneur Jésus-Christ (Paris, 1863), (German by Waldener, Köln-Neuss, 1864), 295

[pg 410]

Volkmar, Gustav. Jesus Nazarenus und die erste christliche Zeit, mit den beiden ersten Erzählern (Zurich, 1882), 11, 210, 225-228, 233, 256, 301, 309, 313, 328

Volz, Paul. Die jüdische Eschatologie von Daniel bis Akiba (Tübingen, 1903), 234

Vossius, 270

Wallon, H. Vie de notre Seigneur Jésus-Christ (Paris, 1865), 295

Walton, Brian, 270

Weber, Ferdinand. System der altsynagogalen palästinensischen Theologie (Leipzig, 1880, 2nd ed. 1897), 269, 285 f.

Weiffenbach, Wilhelm. Der Wiederkunftsgedanke Jesu (1873), 222, 228-233, 237, 250

Weinel, Heinrich. Jesus im neunzehnten Jahrhundert (1904), 12, 398

Weiss, Bernhard. Das Leben Jesu (1st ed. 2 vols. 1882, 2nd ed. 1884) (English translation, *The Life of Jesus*, by J. W. Hope, Edinburgh, 1883), 10, 193, 216-218, 250, 262

Weiss, Johannes. Die Predigt Jesu vom Reiche Gottes (1st ed. 1892, 2nd ed. 1900), 9, 10, 11, 23, 61, 91, 92, 136, 221, 222, 237-240, 249 f., 256, 262, 265-267, 278, 301, 309, 336, 349, 383, 388

Weisse, Christian Hermann. Die evangelische Geschichte kritisch und philosophisch bearbeitet (2 vols., Leipzig, 1838);

Die Evangelienfrage in ihrem gegenwärtigen Stadium (Leipzig, 1856), 12, 118, 120, 121-136, 140, 162, 195, 198, 200, 204 f., 218, 229, 232, 294, 309, 328, 341, 357, 374, 378, 389

Weitbrecht, M. G. Das Leben Jesu nach den vier Evangelien (1881), 217

Weizsäcker, Karl Heinrich. Untersuchungen über die evangelische Geschichte, ihre Quellen und den Gang ihrer Entwicklung (Gotha, 1864), 190, 193, 200-202, 205, 207, 218, 229, 259

Wellhausen, Julius. Israelitische und jüdische Geschichte (3rd ed. 1897, 4th ed. 1902);

Das Evangelium Marci (1903);

Das Evangelium Matthäi (1904);

Das Evangelium Lucae (1904);

Skizzen und Vorarbeiten (1899), 254, 269, 276, 277, 285, 287, 289, 391

Wendt, Hans Heinrich. Die Lehre Jesu (Göttingen, pt. i. 1886, pt. ii. 1890) (English translation, *The Teaching of Jesus*, by J. Wilson, Edinburgh, 1892) (2nd German ed. 1902, 3rd ed. 1903), 219, 249, 265

Wernle, Paul. Die Anfänge unserer Religion (Tübingen-Leipzig, 1901, 2nd ed. 1904) (English translation, *The Beginnings of Christianity*, by G. A. Bienemann, London, 1903);

Die Reichgotteshoffnung in den ältesten christlichen Dokumenten und bei Jesus (1903), 241, 252-254, 265, 267, 314, 398

Wette, Wilhelm Martin Leberecht de, 72, 78, 86, 103, 119, 208

Wettstein, Johann Jakob, 285

Whateley, Richard. Historic Doubts relative to Napoleon Bonaparte (London, 1819) (adapted as Das Leben Napoleons kritisch geprüft), 112

Wieseler, Karl Georg. Chronologische Synopse der vier Evangelien (Hamburg, 1843), 117

Wiesinger, Albert. Aphorismen gegen Renans Leben-Jesu (Vienna, 1864), 117, 190

Widmanstadt, Joh. Alb., 270

Wilke, Christian Gottlob. Tradition und Mythe (Leipzig, 1837);

Der Urevangelist (Dresden and Leipzig, 1838), 97, 112-114, 119, 121, 124, 140 f., 148, 195, 202, 225, 328

Wittichen, Karl. Leben Jesu (Jena, 1876), 218

Wrede, Wilhelm. Das Messiasgeheimnis in den Evangelien (Göttingen, 1901), 9, 11, 25, 131, 210, 221, 256, 257, 264, 309, 328-349, 350, 358, 380, 384 f., 389, 391 f., 399

Wünsche, August. Neue Beiträge zur Erläuterung der Evangelien aus Talmud und Midrasch (Göttingen, 1878);

Jesus in seiner Stellung zu den Frauen (1876), 269, 285 f.

Xavier, Hieronymus. Historia Christi persice conscripta (Lugd. 1639), 14

Ziegler, Heinrich. Der geschichtliche Christus (1891), 217

Ziegler, Theobald, 69

Footnotes

1. *Quoted by Dr. Inge in the Hibbert Journal for Jan. 1910, p. 438 (from "Jesus or Christ," p. 32).*

2. *"Quest," p. 4.*

3. An order founded in 1776 by Professor Adam Weishaupt of Ingolstadt in Bavaria. Its aim was the furtherance of rational religion as opposed to orthodox dogma; its organisation was largely modelled on that of the Jesuits. At its most flourishing period it numbered over 2000 members, including the rulers of several German States.—TRANSLATOR.

4. D. Fr. Strauss, *Gespräche von Ulrich von Hutten*. Leipzig, 1860.

5. W. Wrede, *Das Messiasgeheimnis in den Evangelien*. (The Messianic Secret in the Gospels.) Göttingen, 1901, pp. 280-282.

6. In the author's usage "the Marcan hypothesis" means the theory that the Gospel of Mark is not only the earliest and most valuable source for the facts, but differs from the other Gospels in embodying a more or less clear and historically intelligible view of the connexion of events. See Chaps. X. and XIV. below.—TRANSLATOR.

7. Dr. Christoph Friedrich von Ammon, *Fortbildung des Christentums*, Leipzig, 1840, vol. iv. p. 156 ff.

8. Hase, *Geschichte Jesu*, Leipzig, 1876, pp. 110-162. The second edition, published in 1891, carries the survey no further than the first.

9. *Das Leben Jesu in seinen neueren Darstellungen*, 1892, five lectures.

10. W. Frantzen, *Die "Leben-Jesu" Bewegung seit Strauss*, Dorpat, 1898.

11. *Theol. Rundschau*, ii. 59-67 (1899); iii. 9-19 (1900).

12. Von Soden's study, *Die wichtigsten Fragen im Leben Jesu*, 1904, belongs here only in a very limited sense, since it does not seek to show how the problems have gradually emerged in the various Lives of Jesus.

13. Hase, *Geschichte Jesu*, 1876, pp. 112, 113.

14. *Historia Christi persice conscripta simulque multis modis contaminata a Hieronymo Xavier, lat. reddita et animadd, notata a Ludovico de Dieu.* Lugd. 1639.

15.

Johann Jakob Hess, *Geschichte der drei letzten Lebensjahre Jesu.* (History of the Last Three Years of the Life of Jesus.) 3 vols. 1768 ff.

16.

D. F. Strauss, *Hermann Samuel Reimarus und seine Schutzschrift für die vernünftigen Verehrer Gottes.* (Reimarus and his Apology for the Rational Worshippers of God.) 1862.

17.

The quotations inserted without special introduction are, of course, from Reimarus. It is Dr. Schweitzer's method to lead up by a paragraph of exposition to one of these characteristic phrases.—TRANSLATOR.

18.

Otto Schmiedel, *Die Hauptprobleme der Leben-Jesu-Forschung.* Tübingen, 1902.

19.

Döderlein also wrote a defence of Jesus against the Fragmentist: *Fragmente und Antifragmente.* Nuremberg, 1778.

20.

This is perhaps the place to mention the account of the life of Jesus which is given in the first part of Plank's *Geschichte des Christentums.* Göttingen, 1818.

21.

Briefe das Studium der Theologie betreffend, 1st ed., 1780-1781; 2nd ed., 1785-1786; *Werke*, ed. Suphan, vol. x.

22.

A Life of Jesus which is completely dependent on the Commentaries of Paulus is that of Greiling, superintendent at Aschersleben, *Das Leben Jesu von Nazareth Ein religiöses Handbuch für Geist und Herz der Freunde Jesu unter den Gebildeten.* (The Life of Jesus of Nazareth, a religious Handbook for the Minds and Hearts of the Friends of Jesus among the Cultured.) Halle, 1813.

23.

Paulus prided himself on a very exact acquaintance with the physical and geographical conditions of Palestine. He had a wide knowledge of the literature of Eastern travel.—TRANSLATOR.

24.

This interpretation, it ought to be remarked, seems to be implied by the ancient reading. "Few things are needful, or one," given in the margin of the Revised Version.—TRANSLATOR.

25.

Associations of students, at that time of a political character.—TRANSLATOR.

26.

The ground of the inference is that, according to this theory, they did not attach much importance to the keeping of the Feasts at Jerusalem. Dr. Schweitzer reminds us in a footnote that a certain want of clearness is due to the fact of this work having been compiled from lecture-notes.

27.

See Theobald Ziegler, "Zur Biographie von David Friedrich Strauss" (Materials for the Biography of D. F. S.), in the *Deutsche Revue*, May, June, July 1905. The hitherto unpublished letters to Binder throw some light on the development of Strauss during the formative years before the publication of the Life of Jesus.

Binder, later Director of the Board of Studies at Stuttgart, was the friend who delivered the funeral allocution at the grave of Strauss. This last act of friendship exposed him to enmity and calumny of all kinds. For the text of his short address, see the *Deutsche Revue*, 1905, p. 107.

28.

Deutsche Revue, May 1905, p. 199.

29.

Ibid. p. 201.

30.

Deutsche Revue, p. 203.

31.

Assistant lecturer.

32.

Ibid., June 1905, p. 343 ff.

33.

See Hase, *Leben Jesu*, 1876, p. 124. The "text-book" referred to is Hase's first Life of Jesus.

34.

He to whom my plaint is
Knows I shed no tear;
She to whom I say this
Feels I have no fear.

Time has come for fading,
Like a glimmering ray,
Or a sense-evading
Strain that floats away.

May, though fainter, dimmer,
Only, clear and pure,
To the last the glimmer
And the strain endure.

The persons alluded to in the first verse are his son, who, as a physician, attended him in his illness, and to whom he was deeply attached, and a very old friend to whom the verses were addressed.—TRANSLATOR.

35.

2 Kings iv. 42-44.

36.

Probabilia de evangelii et epistolarum Ioannis Apostoli indole et origine eruditorum iudiciis modeste subjecit C. Th. Bretschneider. Leipzig, 1820.

37.

Dr. Fr. Schleiermacher, *Über die Schriften des Lukas. Ein kritischer Versuch.* (The Writings of Luke. A critical essay.) C. Reimer, Berlin, 1817.

38.

39. Koppe, *Marcus non epitomator Matthäi*, 1782.

40. Storr, *De Fontibus Evangeliorum Mt. et Lc.*, 1794.

41. Gratz, *Neuer Versuch, die Entstehung der drei ersten Evangelien zu erklären*, 1812.

42. *V. sup.* p. 35 f. For the earlier history of the question see F. C. Baur, *Krit. Untersuch. über die kanonischen Evangelien*, Tübingen, 1847, pp. 1-76.

43. So called because largely based on the reference in Luke i. 1, to the "many" who had "taken in hand to draw up a narrative (δεήγησις)."—TRANSLATOR.

44. We take the translation of this striking image from Sanday's "Survey of the Synoptic Question," *The Expositor*, 4th ser. vol. 3, p. 307.

45. For general title see above. First part: "Herr Dr. Steudel, or the Self-deception of the Intellectual Supernaturalism of our Time." 182 pp. Second part: "Die Herren Eschenmayer und Menzel." 247 pp. Third part: "*Die evangelische Kirchenzeitung, die Jahrbücher für wissenschaftliche Kritik* und *Die theologischen Studien und Kritiken* in ihrer Stellung zu meiner Kritik des Lebens Jesu.*" (The attitude taken up by ... in regard to my critical Life of Jesus.) 179 pp. In the *Studien und Kritiken* two reviews had appeared: a critical review by Dr. Ullmann (vol. for 1836, pp. 770-816) and that of Müller, written from the standpoint of the "common faith" (vol. for 1836, pp. 816-890). In the *Evangelische Kirchenzeitung* the articles referred to are the following: *Vorwort* (Editorial Survey), 1836, pp. 1-6, 9-14, 17-23, 25-31, 33-38, 41-45; "The Future of our Theology" (1836, pp. 281 ff.); "Thoughts suggested by Dr. Strauss's essay on 'The Relation of Theological Criticism and Speculation to the Church' " (1836, pp. 382 ff.); Strauss's essay had appeared in the *Allgemeine Kirchenzeitung* for 1836, No. 39. "*Die kritische Bearbeitung des Lebens Jesu von D. F. Strauss nach ihrem wissenschaftlichen Werte beleuchtet*" (An Inquiry into the Scientific Value of D. F. Strauss's Critical Study of the Life of Jesus.) By Prof. Dr. Harless. Erlangen, 1836.

46. "Everything turns to the advantage of the elect, even to the obscurities of scripture, for they treat them with reverence because of its perspicuities; everything turns to the disadvantage of the reprobate, even to the perspicuities of scripture, for they blaspheme them because they cannot understand its obscurities." For the title of Harless's essay, see end of previous note.

47. *Das Leben-Jesu kritisch bearbeitet von Dr. D. F. Strauss. Geprüft für Theologen und Nicht-Theologen*, von Wilhelm Hoffmann. 1836. (Strauss's Critical Study of the Life of Jesus examined for the Benefit of Theologians and non-Theologians.)

48. *Apologie des Lebens Jesu gegenüber dem neuesten Versuch, es in Mythen aufzulösen.* (Defence of the Life of Jesus against the latest attempt to resolve it into myth.) By Joh. Ernst Osiander, Professor at the Evangelical Seminary at Maulbronn.

Über das Leben-Jesu von Strauss, von Franz Baader, 1836. Here may be mentioned also the lectures which Krabbe (subsequently Professor at Rostock) delivered against Strauss:

Vorlesungen über das Leben-Jesu für Theologen und Nicht-Theologen (Lectures on the Life of Jesus for Theologians and non-Theologians), Hamburg, 1839. They are more tolerable to non-theologians than to theologians. The author at a later period distinguished himself by the fanatical zeal with which he urged on the deposition of his colleague, Michael Baumgarten, whose *Geschichte Jesu*, published in 1859, though fully accepting the miracles, was weighed in the balance by Krabbe and found light-weight by the Rostock standard.

49.

For the title, see head of chapter. Tholuck was born in 1799 at Breslau, and became in 1826 Professor at Halle, where he worked until his death in 1877. With the possible exception of Neander, he was the most distinguished representative of the mediating theology. His piety was deep and his learning was wide, but his judgment went astray in the effort to steer his freight of pietism safely between the rocks of rationalism and the shoals of orthodoxy.

50.

Stud. u. Krit., 1836, p. 777. In his "Open letter to Dr. Ullmann," Strauss examines this suggestion in a serious and dignified fashion, and shows that nothing would be gained by such expedients.—*Streitschriften*, 3rd pt., p. 129 ff.

51.

Das Leben Jesu-Christi. Hamburg, 1837. Aug. Wilhelm Neander was born in 1789 at Göttingen, of Jewish parents, his real name being David Mendel. He was baptized in 1806, studied theology, and in 1813 was appointed to a professorship in Berlin, where he displayed a many-sided activity and exercised a beneficent influence. He died in 1850. The best-known of his writings is the *Geschichte der Pflanzung und Leitung der christlichen Kirche durch die Apostel* (History of the Propagation and Administration of the Christian Church by the Apostles), Hamburg, 1832-1833, of which a reprint appeared as late as 1890. Neander was a man not only of deep piety, but also of great solidity of character.

Strauss, in his Life of Jesus of 1864, passes the following judgment upon Neander's work: "A book such as in these circumstances Neander's Life of Jesus was bound to be calls forth our sympathy; the author himself acknowledges in his preface that it bears upon it only too clearly the marks of the time of crisis, division, pain, and distress in which it was produced."

Of the innumerable "positive" Lives of Jesus which appeared about the end of the 'thirties we may mention that of Julius Hartmann (2 vols., 1837-1839). Among the later Lives of Jesus of the mediating theology may be mentioned that of Theodore Pressel of Tübingen, which was much read at the time of its appearance (1857, 592 pp.). It aims primarily at edification. We may also mention the *Leben des Herrn Jesu Christi* by Wil. Jak. Lichtenstein (Erlangen, 1856), which reflects the ideas of von Hofmann.

52.

For title see head of chapter.

53.

Aphorismen zur Apologie des Dr. Strauss und seines Werkes. Grimma, 1838.

54.

307

55. From the *Xame Xenien*, p. 259 of Goethe's Works, ed. Hempel.

56. *Die Wissenschaft und die Kirche. Zur Verständigung über die Straussische Angelegenheit.* (A contribution to the adjustment of opinion regarding the Strauss affair.) By Daniel Schenkel, Licentiate in Theology and Privat-Docent of the University of Basle, with a dedicatory letter to Herr Dr. Lücke, Konsistorialrat. Basle, 1839.

57. *Dr. Strauss und die Züricher Kirche. Eine Stimme aus Norddeutschland. Mit einer Vorrede von Dr. W. M. L. de Wette.* (A voice from North Germany. With an introduction by Dr. W. M. L. de Wette.) Basle, 1839.

58. *Über theologische Lehrfreiheit und Lehrerwahl für Hochschulen.* Zurich, 1839.

59. For full title see head of chapter. Reference may also be made to the same author's *Fortbildung des Christentums zur Weltreligion.* (Development of Christianity into a World-religion.) Leipzig, 1833-1835. 4 vols. Ammon was born in 1766 at Bayreuth; became Professor of theology at Erlangen in 1790; was Professor in Göttingen from 1794 to 1804, and, after being back in Erlangen in the meantime, became in 1813 Senior Court Chaplain and "Oberkonsistorialrat" at Dresden, where he died in 1850. He was the most distinguished representative of historico-critical rationalism.

60. He is at one with Strauss in rejecting the explanation of this miracle on the analogy of an expedited natural process, to which Hase had pointed, and which was first suggested by Augustine in *Tract viii. in Ioann.*: "That Christ changed water into wine is nothing wonderful to those who consider the works of God. What was there done in the water-pots, God does yearly in the vine." [Augustine's words are: Miraculum quidem Domini nostri Jesu Christi, quo de aqua vinum fecit, non est mirum eis qui noverunt quia Deus fecit (*i.e.* that He who did it was God). Ipse enim fecit vinum illo die ... in sex hydriis, qui omni anno facit hoc in vitibus.] Nevertheless the poorest naturalistic explanation is at least better than the resignation of Lücke, who is content to wait "until it please God through the further progress of Christian thought and life to bring about the solution of this riddle in its natural and historical aspects." Lücke, *Johannes-Kommentar*, p. 474 ff.

61. Ernst Wilhelm Hengstenberg was born in 1802 at Fröndenberg in the "county" (*Grafschaft*) of Mark, became Professor of Theology in Berlin in 1826, and died there in 1869. He founded the *Evangelische Kirchenzeitung* in 1827.

62. *Bericht über des Herrn Dr. Strauss' historische Bearbeitung des Lebens Jesu.*

63. *Dr. Strauss' Leben-Jesu aus dem Standpunkt des Catholicismus betrachtet.*

64. Johann Leonhard Hug was born in 1765 at Constance, and had been since 1791 Professor of New Testament Theology at Freiburg, where he died in 1846. He had a wide knowledge of his own department of theology, and his Introduction to the New Testament Writings won him some reputation among Protestant theologians also.

Among the Catholic "Leben-Jesu," of which the authors found their incentive in the desire to oppose Strauss, the first place belongs to that of Kuhn of Tübingen.

Unfortunately only the first volume appeared (1838, 488 pp.). Here there is a serious and scholarly attempt to grapple with the problems raised by Strauss. Of less importance is the work of the same title in seven volumes, by the Munich Priest and Professor of History, Nepomuk Sepp (1843-1846; 2nd ed. 1853-1862).

65.

Über das Leben-Jesu von Doctor Strauss. By Edgar Quinet. Translated from the French by Georg Kleine. Published by J. Erdmann and C. C. Müller, 1839. In 1840 Strauss's book was translated into French by M. Littré. It failed, however, to exercise any influence upon French theology or literature. Strauss is one of those German thinkers who always remain foreign and unintelligible to the French mind. Could Renan have written his Life of Jesus as he did if he had had even a partial understanding of Strauss?

66.

Anna Katharina Emmerich was born in 1774 at Flamske near Coesfeld. Her parents were peasants. In 1803 she took up her abode with the Augustinian nuns of the convent of Agnetenberg at Dülmen. After the dissolution of the convent, she lived in a single room in Dülmen itself. The "stigmata" showed themselves first in 1812. She died on the 9th of February 1824. Brentano had been in her neighbourhood since 1819. *Das bittere Leiden unseres Herrn Jesu Christi* (The Bitter Sufferings of Our Lord Jesus Christ) was issued by Brentano himself in 1834. The *Life of Jesus* was published on the basis of notes left by him—he died in 1842—in three volumes, 1858-1860, at Regensburg, under the sanction of the Bishop of Limberg.

First volume.—From the death of St. Joseph to the end of the first year after the Baptism of Jesus in Jordan. Communicated between May 1, 1821, and October 1, 1822.

Second volume.—From the beginning of the second year after the Baptism in Jordan to the close of the second Passover in Jerusalem. Communicated between October 1, 1822, and April 30, 1823.

Third volume.—From the close of the second Passover in Jerusalem to the Mission of the Holy Spirit. Communicated between October 21, 1823, and January 8, 1824, and from July 29, 1820, to May 1821.

Both works have been frequently reissued, the "Bitter Sufferings" as late as 1894.

67.

Auszüge aus der Schrift "Das Leben Luthers kritisch bearbeitet." (Extracts from a work entitled "A Critical Study of the Life of Luther.") By Dr. Casuar ("Cassowary"; Strauss = Ostrich). Mexico, 1836. Edited by Julius Ferdinand Wurm.

68.

Das Leben Napoleons kritisch geprüft. (A Critical Examination of the Life of Napoleon.) From the English, with some pertinent applications to Strauss's Life of Jesus, 1836. [The English original referred to seems to have been Whateley's *Historic Doubts relative to Napoleon Bonaparte*, published in 1819, and primarily directed against Hume's *Essay on Miracles*.—Translator.]

69.

La Vie de Strauss. Écrite en l'an 1839. Paris, 1839.

70.

Ch. G. Wilke, *Tradition und Mythe*. A contribution to the historical criticism of the Gospels in general, and in particular to the appreciation of the treatment of myth and idealism in Strauss's "Life of Jesus." Leipzig, 1837.

Christian Gottlob Wilke was born in 1786 at Werm, near Zeitz, studied theology and became pastor of Hermannsdorf in the Erzgebirge. He resigned this office in 1837 in order to devote himself to his studies, perhaps also because he had become conscious of an inner unrest. In 1845 he prepared the way for his conversion to Catholicism by publishing a work entitled "Can a Protestant go over to the Roman Church with a good conscience?" He took the decisive step in August 1846. Later he removed to Würzburg. Subsequently he recast his famous *Clavis Novi Testamenti Philologica*—which had appeared in 1840-1841—in the form of a lexicon for Catholic students of theology. His *Hermeneutik des Neuen Testaments*, published in 1843-1844, appeared in 1853 as *Biblische Hermeneutik nach katholischen Grundsätzen* (The Science of Biblical Interpretation according to Catholic principles). He was engaged in recasting his Clavis when he died in 1854.

Of later works dealing with the question of myth, we may refer to Emanuel Marius, *Die Persönlichkeit Jesu mit besonderer Rücksicht auf die Mythologien und Mysterien der alten Völker* (The Personality of Jesus, with special reference to the Mythologies and Mysteries of Ancient Nations), Leipzig, 1879, 395 pp.; and Otto Frick, *Mythus und Evangelium* (Myth and Gospel), Heilbronn, 1879, 44 pp.

71.

See p. 89 above.

72.

Streitschriften. Drittes Heft, pp. 55-126: *Die Jahrbücher für wissenschaftliche Kritik*: i. *Allgemeines Verhältnis der Hegel'schen Philosophie zur theologischen Kritik*: ii. *Hegels Ansicht über den historischen Wert der evangelischen Geschichte* (Hegel's View of the Historical Value of the Gospel History); iii. *Verschiedene Richtungen innerhalb der Hegel'schen Schule in Betreff der Christologie* (Various Tendencies within the Hegelian School in regard to Christology). 1837.

73.

Wissenschaftliche Kritik der evangelischen Geschichte. (Scientific Criticism of the Gospel History.) August Ebrard. Frankfort, 1842; 3rd ed., 1868.

Johannes Heinrich Aug. Ebrard was born in 1818 at Erlangen, was, first, Professor of Reformed Theology at Zurich and Erlangen, afterwards (1853) went to Speyer as "Konsistorialrat," but was unable to cope with the Liberal opposition there, and returned in 1861 to Erlangen, where he died in 1888.

A characteristic example of Ebrard's way of treating the subject is his method of meeting the objection that a fish with a piece of money in its jaws could not have taken the hook. "The fish might very well," he explains, "have thrown up the piece of money from its belly into the opening of the jaws in the moment in which Peter opened its mouth."

Upon this Strauss remarks: "The inventor of this argument tosses it down before us as who should say, 'I know very well it is bad, but it is good enough for you, at any rate so long as the Church has livings to distribute and we Konsistorialrats have to examine the theological candidates.'" Strauss, therefore, characterises Ebrard's Life of Jesus as "Orthodoxy restored on a basis of impudence." The pettifogging character of this work made a bad impression even in Conservative quarters.

74.

Chronologische Synopse der vier Evangelien. (Chronological Synopsis of the four Gospels.) By Karl Georg Wieseler. Hamburg, 1843. Wieseler was born in 1813 at Altencelle (Hanover), and was Professor successively at Göttingen, Kiel, and Greifswald. He died in 1883.

75.

Johann Peter Lange, Pastor in Duisburg, afterwards Professor at Zurich in place of Strauss. *Das Leben Jesu.* 5 vols., 1844-1847.

76.

Georg Heinrich August Ewald, *Geschichte des Volkes Israel.* (History of the People of Israel.) 7 vols. Göttingen, 1843-1859; 3rd ed., 1864-1870. Fifth vol., *Geschichte Christus' und seiner Zeit.* (History of Christ and His Times.) 1855; 2nd ed., 1857.

Ewald was born in 1803 at Göttingen, where in 1827 he was appointed Professor of Oriental Languages. Having made a protest against the repeal of the fundamental law of the Hanoverian Constitution he was removed from his office and went to Tübingen, first as Professor of philology; in 1841 he was transferred to the theological faculty. In 1848 he returned to Göttingen. When, in 1866, he refused to take the oath of allegiance to the King of Prussia, he was compulsorily retired, and, in consequence of imprudent expressions of opinion, was also deprived of the right to lecture. The town of Hanover chose him as its representative in the North German and in the German Reichstag, where he sat among the Guelph opposition, in the middle of the centre party. He died in 1875 at Göttingen. His contributions to New Testament studies were much inferior to his Oriental and Old Testament researches. His Life of Jesus, in particular, is worthless, in spite of the Old Testament and Oriental learning with which it was furnished forth. He lays great stress upon making the genitive of "Christus" not "Christi," but, according to German inflection, "Christus'."

77.

Ammon, *Johannem evangelii auctorem ab editore huius libri fuisse diversum*, Erlangen, 1811.

78.

No value whatever can be ascribed to the Life of Jesus by Werner Hahn, Berlin, 1844, 196 pp. The "didactic presentation of the history" which the author offers is not designed to meet the demands of historical criticism. He finds in the Gospels no bare history, but, above all, the inculcation of the principle of love. He casts to the winds all attempt to draw the portrait of Jesus as a true historian, being only concerned with its inner truth and "idealises artistically and scientifically" the actual course of the outward life of Jesus. "It is never the business of a history," he explains, "to relate only the bare truth. It belongs to a mere planless and aimless chronicle to relate everything that

79. happened in such a way that its words are a mere slavish reflection of the outward course of events."

80. Hase, *Geschichte Jesu*, 1876, p. 128.

81. *Philosophische Dogmatik oder Philosophie des Christentums.* Leipzig, 1855-1862.

At the end of his preface he makes the striking remark: "I confess I cannot conceive of any possible way by which Christianity can take on a form which will make it once more the truth for our time, without having recourse to the aid of philosophy; and I rejoice to believe that this opinion is shared by many of the ablest and most respected of present-day theologians."

82. Vol. ii. pp. 438-543. *Philosophische Schlussbetrachtung über die religiöse Bedeutung der Persönlichkeit Christi und der evangelischen Überlieferung.* (Concluding Philosophical Estimate of the Significance of the Person of Christ and of the Gospel Tradition.)

83. Christian Gottlob Wilke, formerly pastor of Hermannsdorf in the Erzgebirge. *Der Urevangelist, oder eine exegetisch-kritische Untersuchung des Verwandschaftsverhältnisses der drei ersten Evangelien.* (The Earliest Evangelist, a Critical and Exegetical Inquiry into the Relationship of the First Three Gospels.) The subsequent course of the discussion of the Marcan hypothesis was as follows:—

In answer to Wilke there appeared a work signed Philosophotos Aletheias, *Die Evangelien, ihr Geist, ihre Verfasser, und ihr Verhältnis zu einander.* (The Gospels, their Spirit, their Authors, and their relation to one another.) Leipzig, 1845, 440 pp. The author sees in Paul the evil genius of early Christianity, and thinks that the work of scientific criticism must be directed to detecting and weeding out the Pauline elements in the Gospels. Luke is in his opinion a party-writing, biased by Paulinism; in fact Paul had a share in its preparation, and this is what Paul alludes to when he speaks in Romans ii. 16, xi. 28, and xvi. 25 of "his" Gospel. His hand is especially recognisable in chapters i.-iii., vii., ix., xi., xviii., xx., xxi., and xxiv. Mark consists of extracts from Matthew and Luke; John presupposes the other three. The Tübingen standpoint was set forth by Baur in his work, *Kritische Untersuchungen über die kanonischen Evangelien*. (A Critical Examination of the Canonical Gospels.) Tübingen, 1847, 622 pp. According to him Mark is based on Matthew and Luke. At the same time, however, the irreconcilability of the Fourth Gospel with the Synoptists is for the first time fully worked out, and the refutation of its historical character is carried into detail.

The order Matthew, Mark, Luke is defended by Adolf Hilgenfeld in his work *Die Evangelien*. Leipzig, 1854, 355 pp.

Karl Reinhold Köstlin's work, *Der Ursprung und die Komposition der synoptischen Evangelien* (Origin and Composition of the Synoptic Gospels), is rendered nugatory by obscurities and compromises. Stuttgart, 1853, 400 pp. The priority of Mark is defended by Edward Reuss, *Die Geschichte der heiligen Schriften des Neuen Testaments* (History of the Sacred Writings of the New Testament), 1842; H. Ewald, *Die drei ersten Evangelien*,

1850; A. Ritschl, *Die Entstehung der altkatholischen Kirche* (Origin of the ancient Catholic Church), 1850; A. Réville, *Études critiques sur l'Évangile selon St. Matthieu*, 1862. In 1863 the foundations of the Marcan hypothesis were relaid, more firmly than before, by Holtzmann's work, *Die synoptischen Evangelien*. Leipzig, 1863, 514 pp.

84.

Alexander Schweizer, *Das Evangelium Johannis nach seinem inneren Werte und seiner Bedeutung für das Leben Jesu kritisch untersucht*. 1841. (A Critical Examination of the Intrinsic Value of the Gospel of John and of its Importance as a Source for the Life of Jesus.) Alexander Schweizer was born in 1808 at Murten, was appointed Professor of Pastoral Theology at Zurich in 1835, and continued to lecture there until his death in 1888, remaining loyal to the ideas of his teacher Schleiermacher, though handling them with a certain freedom. His best-known work is his *Glaubenslehre* (System of Doctrine), 2 vols., 1863-1872; 2nd ed., 1877.

85.

The German is *Mirakeln*, the usual word being *Wunder*, which, though constantly used in the sense of actual "miracles," has, from its obvious derivation, a certain ambiguity.

86.

"And the glory of the Lord abode upon Mount Sinai, and the cloud covered it six days."

87.

We subjoin the titles of the divisions of this work, which are of some interest:

Vol. i. Book i. The Sources of the Gospel History.
Vol. i. Book ii. The Legends of the Childhood.
Vol. i. Book iii. General Sketch of the Gospel History.
Vol. i. Book iv. The Incidents and Discourses according to Mark.
Vol. ii. Book v. The Incidents and Discourses according to Matthew and Luke.
Vol. ii. Book vi. The Incidents and Discourses according to John.
Vol. ii. Book vii. The Resurrection and the Ascension.
Vol. ii. Book viii. Concluding Philosophical Exposition of the Significance of the Person of Christ and of the Gospel Tradition.

88.

Geschichte Christus' und seiner Zeit. (History of Christ and His Times.) By Heinrich Ewald, Göttingen, 1855, 450 pp.

89.

Kritik der Geschichte der Offenbarung.

90.

Das entdeckte Christentum. See also *Die gute Sache der Freiheit und meine eigene Angelegenheit.* (The Good Cause of Freedom, in Connexion with my own Case.) Zurich, 1843.

91.

Kritik der evangelischen Geschichte des Johannes.

92.

Here and elsewhere Bauer seems to use "Christologie" in the sense of Messianic doctrine, rather than in the more general sense which is usual in theology.—TRANSLATOR.

93.

We retain the German phrase, which has naturalised itself in Synoptic criticism as the designation of an assumed primary gospel lying behind the canonical Mark.

94.

Kritik der Paulinischen Briefe. (Criticism of the Pauline Epistles.) Berlin, 1850-1852.

95.

Kritik der Evangelien und Geschichte ihres Ursprungs. (Criticism of the Gospels and History of their Origin.) 2 vols., Berlin, 1850-1851.

96.

Christus und die Cäsaren. Der Ursprung des Christentums aus dem römischen Griechentum. Berlin, 1877.

97.

Hennell, a London merchant, withdrew himself from his business pursuits for two years in order to make the preparatory studies for this Life of Jesus. [He is best known as a friend of George Eliot, who was greatly interested and influenced by the "Inquiry."—TRANSLATOR.] To the same category as Hennell's work belongs the *Wohlgeprüfte Darstellung des Lebens Jesu* (An Account of the Life of Jesus based on the closest Examination) of the Heidelberg mathematician, Karl von Langsdorf, Mannheim, 1831. Supplement, with preface to a future second edition, 1833.

98.

Hase seems not to have recognised that the "Disclosures" were merely a plagiarism from Venturini. He mentions them in connexion with Bruno Bauer and appears to make him responsible for inspiring them; at least that is suggested by his formula of transition when he says: "It was primarily to him that the frivolous apocryphal hypotheses attached themselves." This is quite inaccurate. The anonymous epitomist of Venturini had nothing to do with Bauer, and had probably not read a line of his work. Venturini, whom he had read, he does not name.

99.

One of the most ingenious of the followers of Venturini was the French Jew Salvator. In his *Jésus-Christ et sa doctrine* (Paris, 2 vols., 1838), he seeks to prove that Jesus was the last representative of a mysticism which, drawing its nutriment from the other Oriental religions, was to be traced among the Jews from the time of Solomon onwards. In Jesus this mysticism allied itself with Messianic enthusiasm. After He had lost consciousness upon the cross He was succoured by Joseph of Arimathea and Pilate's wife, contrary to His own expectation and purpose. He ended His days among the Essenes.

Salvator looks to a spiritualised mystical Mosaism as destined to be the successful rival of Christianity.

100.

The reference should be Micah iv. 8.—F. C. B.

101.

"Ich bin der Geist, der stets verneint."—Mephistopheles in *Faust*.

102.

Aus der Jordanwiege nach Golgatha; vier Bücher über das Evangelium und die Evangelien.

103.

104. *Die Geschichte Jesu auf Grund freier geschichtlicher Untersuchungen über das Evangelium and die Evangelien.*

105. For Noack's reconstruction of it see Book iii. pp. 196-225.

106. For the reconstruction see Book iii. pp. 326-386.

107. *Tharraqah und Sunamith.* The Song of Solomon in its historical and topographical setting. 1869.

108. *La Vie de Jésus de D. Fr. Strauss.* Traduite par M. Littré, 1840.

109. Bruno Bauer in *Philo, Strauss, und Renan*.

110. Renan does not hesitate to apply this tasteless parallel.

Charles Émile Freppel (Abbé), Professeur d'éloquence sacrée à la Sorbonne. *Examen critique de la vie de Jésus de M. Renan.* Paris, 1864. 148 pp.

Henri Lasserre's pamphlet, *L'Évangile selon Renan* (The Gospel according to Renan), reached its four-and-twentieth edition in the course of the same year.

111. *Lettre pastorale de Monseigneur l'Archevêque de Paris (Georges Darboy) sur la divinité de Jésus-Christ, et mandement pour le carême de 1864.*

112. See, for example, Félix Antoine Philibert Dupanloup, Bishop of Orléans, *Avertissement à la jeunesse et aux pères de famille sur les attaques dirigées contre la religion par quelques écrivains de nos jours.* (Warning to the Young, and to Fathers of Families, concerning some Attacks directed against Religion by some Writers of our Time.) Paris, 1864. 141 pp.

113. Amadée Nicolas, *Renan et sa vie de Jésus sous les rapports moral, légal, et littéraire. Appel à la raison et la conscience du monde civilisé.* Paris-Marseille, 1864.

114. Ernest Havet, Professeur au Collège de France, *Jésus dans l'histoire. Examen de la vie de Jésus par M. Renan.* Extrait de la *Revue des deux mondes*. Paris, 1863. 71 pp.

115. *Zwei französische Stimmen über Renans Leben-Jesu, von Edmond Scherer und Athanase Coquerel, d.J. Ein Beitrag zur Kenntnis des französischen Protestantismus.* Regensburg, 1864. (Two French utterances in regard to Renan's Life of Jesus, by Edmond Scherer and Athanase Coquerel the younger. A contribution to the understanding of French Protestantism.)

116. E. de Pressensé, *L'École critique et Jésus-Christ, à propos de la vie de Jésus de M. Renan*.

117.

E. de Pressensé, *Jésus-Christ, son temps, sa vie, son œuvre*. Paris, 1865. 684 pp. In general the plan of this work follows Renan's. He divides the Life of Jesus into three periods: i. The Time of Public Favour; ii. The Period of Conflict; iii. The Great Week. Death and Victory. By way of introduction there is a long essay on the supernatural which sets forth the supernaturalistic views of the author.

118.

La Vie de Jésus de Renan devant les orthodoxes et devant la critique. 1864.

119.

T. Colani, Pasteur, "Examen de la vie de Jésus de M. Renan," *Revue de théologie*. Issued separately, Strasbourg-Paris, 1864. 74 pp.

120.

Lasserre, *Das Evangelium nach Renan*. Munich, 1864.

Freppel, *Kritische Beleuchtung der E. Renan'schen Schrift*. Translated by Kallmus. Vienna, 1864.

See also Lamy, Professor of the Theological Faculty of the Catholic University of Louvain, *Renans Leben-Jesu vor dem Richterstuhle der Kritik*. (Renan's Life of Jesus before the Judgment Seat of Criticism.) Translated by August Rohling, Priest. Münster, 1864.

121.

Dr. Michelis, *Renans Roman vom Leben Jesu. Eine deutsche Antwort auf eine französische Blasphemie.* (Renan's Romance on the Life of Jesus. A German answer to a French blasphemy.) Münster, 1864.

Dr. Sebastian Brunner, *Der Atheist Renan und sein Evangelium*. (The Atheist Renan and his Gospel.) Regensburg, 1864.

Albert Wiesinger, *Aphorismen gegen Renans Leben-Jesu*. Vienna, 1864.

Dr. Martin Deutlinger, *Renan und das Wunder*. (Renan and Miracle. A contribution to Christian Apologetic.) Munich, 1864. 159 pp.

Dr. Daniel Bonifacius Haneberg, *Ernest Renans Leben-Jesu*. Regensburg, 1864.

122.

Willibald Beyschlag, Doctor and Professor of Theology, *Über das Leben-Jesu von Renan*. A Lecture delivered at Halle, January 13, 1864. Berlin.

123.

Chr. Ernst Luthardt, Doctor and Professor of Theology, *Die modernen Darstellungen des Lebens Jesu*. (Modern Presentations of the Life of Jesus.) A discussion of the writings of Strauss, Renan, and Schenkel, and of the essays of Coquerel the younger, Scherer, Colani, and Keim. A Lecture. Leipzig, 1864.

Of the remaining Protestant polemics we may name:—

Dr. Hermann Gerlach, *Gegen Renans Leben-Jesu 1864*. Berlin.

Br. Lehmann, *Renan wider Renan*. (Renan *versus* Renan.) A Lecture addressed to cultured Germans. Zwickau, 1864.

Friedrich Baumer, *Schwarz, Strauss, Renan*. A Lecture. Leipzig, 1864.

John Cairns, D. D. (of Berwick). *Falsche Christi und der wahre Christus, oder Verteidigung der evangelischen Geschichte gegen Strauss und Renan*. (False Christs and the True, a Defence of the Gospel History against Strauss and Renan.) A Lecture delivered before the Bible Society. Translated from the English. Hamburg, 1864.

Bernhard ter Haar, Doctor of Theology and Professor at Utrecht, *Zehn Vorlesungen über Renans Leben-Jesu*. (Ten Lectures on Renan's Life of Jesus.) Translated by H. Doermer. Gotha, 1864.

Paulus Cassel, Professor and Licentiate in Theology, *Bericht über Renans Leben-Jesu*. (A Report upon Renan's Life of Jesus.)

J. J. van Oosterzee, Doctor and Professor of Theology at Utrecht, *Geschichte oder Roman? Das Leben-Jesu von Renan vorläufig beleuchtet*. (History or Fiction? A Preliminary Examination of Renan's Life of Jesus.) Hamburg, 1864.

124.
Strauss's second Life of Jesus appeared in French in 1864.

125.
"I can now say without incurring the reproach of self-glorification, and almost without needing to fear contradiction, that if my Life of Jesus had not appeared in the year after Schleiermacher's death, his would not have been withheld for so long. Up to that time it would have been hailed by the theological world as a deliverer; but for the wounds which my work inflicted on the theology of the day, it had neither anodyne nor dressing; nay, it displayed the author as in a measure responsible for the disaster, for the waters which he had admitted drop by drop were now, in defiance of his prudent reservations, pouring in like a flood."—From the Introduction to *The Christ of Faith and the Jesus of History*, 1865.

126.
"Now that Schleiermacher's Life of Jesus at last lies before us in print, all parties can gather about it in heartfelt rejoicing. The appearance of a work by Schleiermacher is always an enrichment to literature. Any product of a mind like his cannot fail to shed light and life on the minds of others. And of works of this kind our theological literature has certainly in these days no superfluity. Where the living are for the most part as it were dead, it is meet that the dead should arise and bear witness. These lectures of Schleiermacher's, when compared with the work of his pupils, show clearly that the great theologian has let fall upon them only his mantle and not his spirit."—*Ibid*.

127.
The lines of Schleiermacher's work were followed by Bunsen. His Life of Jesus forms vol. ix. of his *Bibelwerk*. (Edited by Holtzmann, 1865.) He accepts the Fourth Gospel as an historical source and treats the question of miracle as not yet settled. Christian Karl

Josias von Bunsen, born in 1791 at Korbach in Waldeck, was Prussian ambassador at Rome, Berne, and London, and settled later in Heidelberg. He was well read in theology and philology, and gradually came, in spite of his friendly relations with Friedrich Wilhelm IV., to entertain more liberal views on religion. The issue of his *Bibelwerk für die Gemeinde* was begun in 1858. He died in 1860. (Best known in England as the Chevalier Bunsen.)

128.

Ch. H. Weisse, *Die evangelische Geschichte*, Leipzig, 1838. *Die Evangelienfrage in ihrem gegenwärtigen Stadium.* (The Present Position of the Problem of the Gospels.) Leipzig, 1856. He regarded the discourses as historical, the narrative portions as of secondary origin. Alexander Schweizer, again, wished to distinguish a Jerusalem source and a Galilaean source, the latter being unreliable. *Das Evangelium Johannis nach seinem inneren Werte und seiner Bedeutung für das Leben Jesu*, 1841. (The Gospel of John considered in Relation to its Intrinsic Value and its Importance as a Source for the Life of Jesus.) See p. 127 f. Renan takes the narrative portions as authentic and the discourses as secondary.

129.

Karl Heinrich Weizsäcker was born in 1822 at Öhringen in Würtemberg. He qualified as Privat-Docent in 1847 and, after acting in the meantime as Court-Chaplain and Oberkonsistorialrat at Stuttgart, became in 1861 the successor of Baur at Tübingen. He died in 1899.

130.

The works of a Dutch writer named Stricker, *Jesus von Nazareth* (1868), and of the Englishman Sir Richard Hanson, *The Jesus of History* (1869), were based on Mark without any reference to John.

131.

1, Mark i.; 2, Mark ii. 1-iii. 6; 3, Mark iii. 7-19; 4, Mark iii. 19-iv. 34; 5, Mark iv. 35-vi. 6; 6, Mark vi. 7-vii. 37; 7, Mark viii. 1-ix. 50.

132.

Holtzmann, *Kommentar zu den Synoptikern*, 1889, p. 184. The form of the expression (*Fluchtwege und Reisen*) is derived from Keim.

133.

"Thus the course of Jesus' life hastened forward to its tragic close, a close which was foreseen and predicted by Jesus Himself with ever-growing clearness as the sole possible close, but also that which alone was worthy of Himself, and which was necessary as being foreseen and predetermined in the counsel of God. The hatred of the Pharisees and the indifference of the people left from the first no other prospect open. That hatred could not but be called forth in the fullest measure by the ruthless severity with which Jesus exposed all that it was and implied—a heart in which there was no room for love, a morality inwardly riddled with decay, an outward show of virtue, a hypocritical arrogance. Between two such unyielding opponents—a man who, to all appearance, aimed at using the Messianic expectations of the people for his own ends, and a hierarchy as tenacious of its claims and as sensitive to their infringement as any that has ever existed—it was certain that the breach must soon become irreparable. It was easy to foresee, too, that even in Galilee only a minority of the people would dare to face with Him the danger of such a breach. There was only one thing that could have averted the death sentence which had been early determined upon—a series of vigorous, unambiguous demonstrations on the part of the people. In order to provoke such demonstrations Jesus would have needed, if only for the moment, to take into His service the popular, powerful, inflammatory Messianic ideas, or rather, would have needed to place Himself at their service. His refusal to enter, by so much as a single step, upon this course, which from any ordinary point of view of human policy would have been legitimate, because the only practicable one, was the sole sufficient and all-explaining cause of His destruction."—Holtzmann, *Die synoptischen Evangelien*, 1863, pp. 485, 486.

134.

"Ein innerliches Reich der Sinnesänderung." "Sinnesänderung" corresponds more exactly than "repentance" to the Greek μετάνοια (change of mind, change of attitude), but the *phrase* is no less elliptical in German than in English. The meaning is doubtless "kingdom based upon repentance, consisting of those who have fulfilled this condition."

135.

Omitted in some of the best texts.—F. C. B.

136.

Oskar Holtzmann, *Das Leben Jesu*, 1901.

137.

Die modernen Darstellungen des Lebens Jesu. (Modern Presentments of the Life of Jesus.) A discussion of the works of Strauss, Renan, and Schenkel, and of the Essays of Coquerel the younger, Scherer, Colani, and Keim. A lecture by Chr. Ernest Luthardt, Leipzig. 1st and 2nd editions, 1864. Luthardt was born in 1823 at Maroldsweisach in Lower Franconia, became Docent at Erlangen in 1851, was called to Marburg as Professor Extraordinary in 1854, and to Leipzig as Ordinary Professor in 1856. He died in 1902.

138.

Zur Orientierung über meine Schrift "Das Charakterbild Jesu." (Explanations intended to place my work "A Picture of the Character of Jesus" in the proper light.) 1864. *Die protestantische Freiheit in ihrem gegenwärtigen Kampfe mit der kirchlichen Reaktion.* (Protestant Freedom in its present Struggle with Ecclesiastical Reaction.) 1865.

139.

Der Schenkel'sche Handel in Baden. (The Schenkel Controversy in Baden.) (A corrected reprint from number 441 of the *National-Zeitung* of September 21, 1864.) An appendix to *Der Christus des Glaubens und der Jesus der Geschichte*. 1865.

140.

Theodor Keim, *Die Geschichte Jesu von Nazara, in ihrer Verhaltung mit dem Gesamtleben seines Volkes frei untersucht und ausführlich erzählt*. (The History of Jesus of Nazara in Relation to the General Life of His People, freely examined and fully narrated.) 3 vols. Zurich, 1867-1872. Vol. i. The Day of Preparation; vol. ii. The Year of Teaching in Galilee; vol. iii. The Death-Passover (*Todesostern*) in Jerusalem. A short account in a more popular form appeared in 1872, *Geschichte Jesu nach den Ergebnissen heutiger Wissenschaft für weitere Kreise übersichtlich erzählt*. (The History of Jesus according to the Results of Present-day Criticism, briefly narrated for the General Reader.) 2nd ed., 1875.

Karl Theodor Keim was born in 1825 at Stuttgart, was Repetent at Tübingen from 1851 to 1855, and after he had been five years in the ministry, became Professor at Zurich in 1860. In 1873 he accepted a call to Giessen, where he died in 1878.

141.

Die menschliche Entwicklung Jesu Christi. See Holtzmann, *Die synoptischen Evangelien*, 1863, pp. 7-9. This dissertation was followed by *Der geschichtliche Christus*. 3rd ed., 1866.

142.

Geschichte Jesu. 2nd ed., 1875, pp. 228 and 229.

143.

The ultimate reason why Keim deliberately gives such prominence to the eschatology is that he holds to Matthew, and is therefore more under the direct impression of the masses of discourse in this Gospel, charged, as they are, with eschatological ideas, than those writers who find their primary authority in Mark, where these discourses are lacking.

144.

Geschichte Jesu. Nach akademischen Vorlesungen von Dr. Karl Hase. 1876. Special mention ought also to be made of the fine sketch of the Life of Jesus in A. Hausrath's *Neutestamentliche Zeitgeschichte* (History of New Testament Times), 1st ed., Munich, 1868 ff.; 3rd ed., 1 vol., 1879, pp. 325-515; *Die zeitgeschichtlichen Beziehungen des Lebens Jesu* (The Relations of the Life of Jesus to the History of His time).

Adolf Hausrath was born at Karlsruhe. He was appointed Professor of Theology at Heidelberg in 1867, and died in 1909.

145.

Das Leben Jesu, von Willibald Beyschlag: Pt. i. Preliminary Investigations, 1885, 450 pp.; pt. ii. Narrative, 1886, 495 pp. Joh. Heinr. Christoph Willibald Beyschlag was born in 1823 at Frankfort-on-Main, and went to Halle as Professor in 1860. His splendid eloquence made him one of the chief spokesmen of German Protestantism. As a teacher he exercised a remarkable and salutary influence, although his scientific works are too much under the dominance of an apologetic of the heart. He died in 1900.

146.

Bernhard Weiss, *Das Leben Jesu*. 2 vols. Berlin, 1882. See also *Das Markusevangelium*, 1872; *Das Matthäusevangelium*, 1876; and the *Lehrbuch der neutestamentlichen Theologie*, 5th ed., 1888. Bernhard Weiss was born in 1827 at Königsberg, where he qualified as Privat-Docent in 1852. In 1863 he went as Ordinary Professor to Kiel, and was called to Berlin in the same capacity in 1877.

Among the distinctly liberal Lives of Jesus of an earlier date, that of W. Krüger-Velthusen (Elberfeld, 1872, 271 pp.) might be mentioned if it were not so entirely uncritical. Although the author does not hold the Fourth Gospel to be apostolic he has no hesitation in making use of it as an historical source.

There is more sentiment than science, too, in the work of M. G. Weitbrecht, *Das Leben Jesu nach den vier Evangelien*, 1881.

A weakness in the treatment of the Johannine question and a want of clearness on some other points disfigures the three-volume Life of Jesus of the Paris professor, E.

Stapfer, which is otherwise marked by much acumen and real depth of feeling. Vol. i. *Jésus-Christ avant son ministère* (Fischbacher, Paris, 1896); vol. ii. *Jésus-Christ pendant son ministère* (1897); vol. iii. *La Mort et la résurrection de Jésus-Christ* (1898).

F. Godet writes of "The Life of Jesus before His Public Appearance" (German translation by M. Reineck, *Leben Jesu vor seinem öffentlichen Auftreten*. Hanover, 1897).

G. Längin founds his *Der Christus der Geschichte und sein Christentum* (The Christ of History and His Christianity) on a purely Synoptic basis. 2 vols., 1897-1898.

The English *Life of Jesus Christ*, by James Stalker, D. D. (now Professor of Church History in the United Free Church College, Aberdeen), passed through numberless editions (German, 1898; Tübingen, 4th ed., 1901).

Very pithy and interesting is Dr. Percy Gardner's *Exploratio Evangelica. A Brief Examination of the Basis and Origin of Christian Belief.* 1899; 2nd ed., 1907.

A work which is free from all compromise is H. Ziegler's *Der geschichtliche Christus* (The Historical Christ). 1891. For this reason the five lectures, delivered in Liegnitz, out of which it is composed, attracted such unfavourable attention that the Ecclesiastical Council took proceedings against the author. (See the *Christliche Welt*, 1891, pp. 563-568, 874-877.)

147.

Holtzmann, *Neutestamentliche Einleitung*, 2nd ed., 1886. Weizsäcker declares himself in the *Theologische Literaturzeitung* for 1882, No. 23, and *Das apostolische Zeitalter*, 2nd ed., 1890.

Hase and Schenkel accepted this position in principle, but were careful to keep open a line of retreat.

Towards the end of the 'seventies the rejection of the Fourth Gospel as an historical source was almost universally recognised in the critical camp. It is taken for granted in the Life of Jesus by Karl Wittichen (Jena, 1876, 397 pp.), which might be reckoned one of the most clearly conceived works of this kind based on the Marcan hypothesis if its arrangement were not so bad. It is partly in the form of a commentary, inasmuch as the presentment of the life takes the form of a discussion of sixty-seven sections. The detail is very interesting. It makes an impression of *naïveté* when we find a series of sections grouped under the title, "The establishment of *Christianity* in Galilee." No stress is laid on the significance of Jesus' journey to the north. Wittichen, also, misled by Luke, asserts, just as Weisse had done, that Jesus had worked in Judaea for some time prior to the triumphal entry.

148.

H. H. Wendt, *Die Lehre Jesu*, vol. i. *Die evangelischen Quellenberichte über die Lehre Jesu.* (The Record of the Teaching of Jesus in the Gospel Sources.) 354 pp. Göttingen, 1886; vol. ii., 1890; Eng. trans., 1892. Second German edition in one vol., 626 pp., 1901.

149. See also the same writer's *Das Johannesevangelium. Untersuchung seiner Entstehung und seines geschichtlichen Wertes*, 1900. (The Gospel of John: an Investigation of its Origin and Historical Value.) Hans Heinrich Wendt was born in 1853 at Hamburg, qualified as Privat-Docent in 1877 at Göttingen, was subsequently Extraordinary Professor at Kiel and Heidelberg, and now works at Jena.

150. *Johannis Lightfooti, Doctoris Angli et Collegii S. Catharinae in Cantabrigiensi Academia Praefecti, Horae Hebraicae et Talmudicae in Quatuor Evangelistas ... nunc secundum in Germania junctim cum Indicibus locorum Scripturae rerumque ac verborum necessariis editae e Museo Io. Benedicti Carpzovii. Lipsiae. Anno MDCLXXXIV.*

151. The pioneer works in the study of apocalyptic were Dillmann's *Henoch*, 1851; and Hilgenfeld's *Jüdische Apokalyptik*, 1857.

152. *Jesus Nazarenus und die erste christliche Zeit, mit den beiden ersten Erzählern*, von Gustav Volkmar, Zurich, 1882. To which must be added: *Markus und die Synopse der Evangelien, nach dem urkundlichen Text; und das Geschichtliche vom Leben Jesu.* (Mark and Synoptic Material in the Gospels, according to the original text; and the historical elements in the Life of Jesus.) Zurich, 1869; 2nd edition, 1876, 738 pp. Volkmar was born in 1809, and was living at Fulda as a Gymnasium (High School) teacher, when in 1852 he was arrested by the Hessian Government on account of his political views, and subsequently deprived of his post. In 1853 he went to Zurich, where a new prospect opened to him as a Docent in theology. He died in 1893.

153. Kienlen, "Die eschatologische Rede Jesu Matt. xxiv. cum Parall." (The Eschatological Discourse of Jesus in Matt. xxiv. with the parallel passages), *Jahrbuch für die Theologie*, 1869, pp. 706-709. Analysis of other attempts directed to the same end in Weiffenbach, *Der Wiederkunftsgedanke*, p. 31 ff.

154. Wilhelm Weiffenbach, Director of the Seminary for Theological Students at Friedberg, was born in 1842 at Bornheim in Rhenish Hesse.

155. The English reader will find a constructive analysis of what is known as the "Little Apocalypse" in *Encyclopaedia Biblica*, art. "Gospels," col. 1857. It consists of the verses Matt. xxiv. 6-8, 15-22, 29-31, 34, corresponding to Mark xiii. 7-9a, 14-20, 24-27, 30. According to the theory first sketched by Colani these verses formed an independent Apocalypse which was embedded in the Gospel by the Evangelist.—F. C. B.

156. *Untersuchungen über die evangelische Geschichte*, 1864, pp. 121-126.

157. "Über die Komposition der eschatologischen Rede Matt. xxiv. 4 ff." (The Composition of the Eschatological Discourse in Matt. xxiv. 4 ff.), *Jahrbuch f. d. Theol.* vol. xiii., 1868, pp. 134-149.

158. By "Capernaitic" Weiffenbach apparently means literalistic; cf. John vi. 52 f.

Wilhelm Baldensperger, at present Professor at Giessen, was born in 1856 at Mülhausen in Alsace.

159.

A new edition appeared in 1891. There is no fundamental alteration, but in consequence of the polemic against opponents who had arisen in the meantime it is fuller. The first part of a third edition appeared in 1903 under the title *Die messianisch-apokalyptischen Hoffnungen des Judentums*.

See also the interesting use made of Late-Jewish and Rabbinic ideas in Alfred Edersheim's *The Life and Times of Jesus the Messiah*, 2nd ed., London, 1884, 2 vols.

160.

Emil Schürer, *Geschichte des jüdischen Volkes im Zeitalter Jesu Christi*. (History of the Jewish People in the Time of Christ.) 2nd ed., part second, 1886, pp. 417 ff. Here is to be found also a bibliography of the older literature of the subject. 3rd ed., 1889, vol. ii. pp. 498 ff.

Emil Schürer was born at Augsburg in 1844, and from 1873 onwards was successively Professor at Leipzig, Giessen, and Kiel, and is now (1909) at Göttingen.

The latest presentment of Jewish apocalyptic is *Die jüdische Eschatologie von Daniel bis Akiba*, by Paul Volz, Pastor in Leonberg. Tübingen, 1903. 412 pp. The material is very completely given. Unfortunately the author has chosen the systematic method of treating his subject, instead of tracing the history of its development, the only right way. As a consequence Jesus and Paul occupy far too little space in this survey of Jewish apocalyptic. For a treatment of the origin of Jewish eschatology from the point of view of the history of religion see Hugo Gressmann, now Professor at Berlin, *Der Ursprung der israelitisch-jüdischen Eschatologie* (The Origin of the Israelitish and Jewish Eschatology), Göttingen, 1905. 377 pp.

161.

Johannes Weiss, now Professor at Marburg, was born at Kiel in 1863.

162.

It may be mentioned that this work had been preceded (in 1891) by two Leiden prize dissertations, *Über die Lehre vom Reich Gottes im Neuen Testament* (Concerning the Kingdom of God in the New Testament), one of them by Issel, the other, which lays especially strong emphasis upon the eschatology, by Schmoller.

163.

Wilhelm Bousset, now Professor in Göttingen, born 1865 at Lübeck

164.

Theol. Rundschau (1901), 4, pp. 89-103.

165.

W. Bousset, *Die jüdische Apokalyptik in ihrer religionsgeschichtlichen Herkunft und ihrer Bedeutung für das Neue Testament*. (The Origin of Apocalyptic as indicated by Comparative Religion, and its significance for the understanding of the New Testament.) Berlin, 1903. 67 pp. See also W. Bousset, *Die Religion des Judentums im neutestamentlichen Zeitalter*, 512 pp., 1902. For the assertion of Parsic influences see also Stave, *Der Einfluss des Parsismus auf das Judentum*. Haarlem, 1898.

166.

Der Grundcharakter der Ethik Jesu im Verhältnis zu den messianischen Hoffnungen seines Volkes und zu seinem eigenen Messiasbewusstsein. Freiburg, 1895, 119 pp. See also his inaugural dissertation of 1896, *Le Principe de la morale de Jésus.* Paris, 1896.

A. K. Rogers, *The Life and Teachings of Jesus; a Critical Analysis, etc.* (London and New York, 1894), regards Jesus' teaching as purely ethical, refusing to admit any eschatology at all.

167.

Paris, 2 vols., 500 and 512 pp.

168.

W. Weiffenbach, *Die Frage der Wiederkunst Jesu.* (The Question concerning the Second Coming of Jesus.) Friedberg, 1901.

169.

A. Titius, *Die neutestamentliche Lehre von der Seligkeit und ihre Bedeutung für die Gegenwart.* I. Teil: *Jesu Lehre vom Reich Gottes.* (The New Testament Doctrine of Blessedness and its Significance for the Present. Pt. I., Jesus' Doctrine of the Kingdom of God.) Arthur Titius, now Professor at Kiel, was born in 1864 at Sensburg.

170.

Die eschatologischen Aussagen Jesu in den synoptischen Evangelien, 167 pp. Erich Haupt, now Professor in Halle, was born in 1841 at Stralsund.

171.

Cf. the preface to the 2nd ed. of Joh. Weiss's *Die Predigt Jesu vom Reiche Gottes*. Göttingen, 1900.

172.

Tübingen-Leipzig, 1901, 410 pp.; 2nd ed., 1904. Paul Wernle, now Professor of Church History at Basle, was born in Zurich, 1872.

173.

Israelitische und jüdische Geschichte, 1st ed., 1894, pp. 163-168; 2nd ed., 1895, pp. 198-204; 3rd ed., 1897; 4th ed., 1901, pp. 380-394. See also his *Skizzen* (Sketches), pp. 6, 187 ff.

See also J. Wellhausen, *Das Evangelium Marci*, 1903, 2nd ed., 1909; *Das Evangelium Matthäi*, 1904; *Das Evangelium Lucae*, 1904.

Julius Wellhausen, now Professor at Göttingen, was born in 1844 at Hameln.

174.

Emil Schürer, *Das messianische Selbstbewusstsein Jesu Christi.* (The Messianic Self-consciousness of Jesus Christ.) 1903, 24 pp.

According to J. Meinhold, too, in *Jesus und das alte Testament* (Jesus and the Old Testament), 1896, Jesus did not purpose to be the Messiah of Israel.

175.

Die evangelische Geschichte und der Ursprung des Christentums auf Grund einer Kritik der Berichte über das Leiden und die Auferstehung Jesu. (The Gospel History and the Origin of Christianity considered in the light of a critical investigation of the Reports of the Suffering and Resurrection of Jesus.) By Dr. W. Brandt, Leipzig, 1893, 588 pp.

Wilhelm Brandt was born in 1855 of German parents in Amsterdam and became a pastor of the Dutch Reformed Church. In 1891 he resigned this office and studied in Strassburg and Berlin. In 1893 he was appointed to lecture in General History of Religion as a member of the theological faculty of Amsterdam.

176.

Ad. Jülicher, *Die Gleichnisreden Jesu*. Vol. i., 1888. The substance of it had already been published in a different form. Freiburg, 1886.

Adolf Jülicher, at present Professor in Marburg, was born in 1857 at Falkenberg.

177.

W. Bousset, *Jesu Predigt in ihrem Gegensatz zum Judentum*. Göttingen, 1892.

178.

Ad. Jülicher, *Die Gleichnisreden Jesu*, 2nd pt. (Exposition of the Parables in the first three Gospels.) Freiburg, 1899, 641 pp.

Chr. A. Bugge, *Die Hauptparabeln Jesu* (The most important Parables of Jesus), German, from the Norwegian, Giessen, 1903, rightly remarks on the obscure and inexplicable character of some of the parables, but makes no attempt to deal with it from the historical point of view.

179.

Arnold Meyer, *Jesu Muttersprache*, 1896. P. W. Schmidt, too, in his *Geschichte Jesu* (Freiburg, 1899), defends the same interpretation, and seeks to explain this obscure saying by the other about the "strait gate."

180.

Die Predigt Jesu vom Reiche Gottes, 2nd ed., 1900, p. 192 ff.

181.

Stud. Krit., 1836, pp. 90-122.

182.

See also *Die Vorstellungen vom Messias und vom Gottesreich bei den Synoptikern*. (The Conceptions of the Messiah and the Kingdom of God in the Synoptic Gospels.) By Ludwig Paul. Bonn, 1895. 130 pp. This comprehensive study discusses all the problems which are referred to below. Matt. xi. 12-14 is discussed under the heading "The Hinderers of the Kingdom of God."

183.

A. Hilgenfeld, *Zeitschr. f. wiss. Theol.*, 1888, pp. 488-498; 1892, pp. 445-464.

184.

185. Orello Cone, "Jesus' Self-designation in the Synoptic Gospels," *The New World*, 1893, pp. 492-518.

186. H. L. Oort, *Die uitdrukking ὁ υἱὸς τοῦ ἀνϑρώπου in het Nieuwe Testament*. (The Expression Son of Man in the New Testament.) Leyden, 1893.

187. R. H. Charles, "The Son of Man," *Expos. Times*, 1893.

Die jüdische Apokalyptik in ihrer religionsgeschichtlichen Herkunft und ihrer Bedeutung für das Neue Testament. (Jewish Apocalyptic in its religious-historical origin and in its significance for the New Testament.) 1903.

On the eschatology of Jesus see also Schwartzkoppf, *Die Weissagungen Jesu Christi von seinen Tode, seiner Auferstehung und Wiederkunft und ihre Erfüllung*. (The Predictions of Jesus Christ concerning His Death, His Resurrection, and Second Coming, and their Fulfilment.) 1895.

P. Wernle, *Die Reichgotteshofnung in den ältesten christlichen Dokumenten und bei Jesus*. (The Hope of the Kingdom of God in the most ancient Christian Documents and as held by Jesus.)

188. Arnold Meyer, now Professor of New Testament Theology and Pastoral Theology at Zurich, and formerly at Bonn, was born at Wesel in 1861.

189. Giambern. de Rossi, *Dissertazione della lingua propria di Christo e degli Ebrei nazionali della Palestina da' Tempi de' Maccabei in disamina del sentimento di un recente scrittore Italiano*. Parma, 1772.

190. *Der Bericht des Matthäus von Jesu dem Messias*. (Matthew's account of Jesus the Messiah.) Altona, 1792. According to Meyer, p. 105 ff., this was a very striking performance.

191. The name Chaldee was due to the mistaken belief that the language in which parts of Daniel and Ezra were written was really the vernacular of Babylonia. That vernacular, now known to us from cuneiform tablets and inscriptions, is a Semitic language, but quite different from Aramaic.—F. C. B.

192. Emil Friedrich Kautzsch was born in 1841 at Plauen in Saxony, and studied in Leipzig, where he became Privat-Docent in 1869. In 1872 he was called as Professor to Basle, in 1880 to Tübingen, in 1888 to Halle.

193. Gustaf Dalman, Professor at Leipzig, was born in 1865 at Niesky. In addition to the works of his named above, see also *Der leidende und der sterbende Messias* (The Suffering and Dying Messiah), 1888; and *Was sagt der Talmud über Jesum?* (What does the Talmud say about Jesus?), 1891.

194.

195. 2 Kings xviii. 26 ff.

196. *Studia Biblica* I. *Essays in Biblical Archæology and Criticism and Kindred Subjects by Members of the University of Oxford*. Clarendon Press, 1885, pp. 39-74. See Meyer, p. 29 ff.

197. Franz Delitzsch, *Die Bücher des Neuen Testaments aus dem Griechischen ins Hebräische übersetzt*. 1877. (The Books of the N.T. translated from Greek into Hebrew.) This work has been circulated by thousands among Jews throughout the whole world.

Delitzsch was born in 1813 at Leipzig and became Privat-Docent there in 1842, went to Rostock as Professor in 1846, to Erlangen in 1850, and returned in 1867 to Leipzig. By conviction he was a strict Lutheran in theology. He was one of the leading experts in Late-Jewish and Talmudic literature. He died in 1890.

198. See Meyer, p. 47 ff.

199. See Meyer, p. 61 ff.

200. Hans Lietzmann, now Professor in Jena, was born in 1875 at Düsseldorf. Until his call to Jena he worked as a Privat-Docent at Bonn. He has done some very meritorious work in the publication of Early Christian writings.

201. See Meyer, p. 141 ff.

202. "De Oorsprong van de uitdrukking 'Zoon des Menschen' als evangelische Messiastitel," *Theol. Tijdschr.*, 1894. (The Origin of the Expression "Son of Man" as a Title of the Messiah in the Gospels.)

203. H. Lietzmann, "Zur Menschensohnfrage" (The Son-of-Man Problem), *Theol. Arb. des Rhein. wissenschaftl. Predigervereins*, 1898.

204. N. Schmidt, "Was בן נשא a Messianic title?" *Journal of the Society for Biblical Literature*, xv., 1896.

205. P. Schmiedel, "Der Name Menschensohn und das Messiasbewusstsein Jesu" (The Designation Son of Man and the Messianic Consciousness of Jesus), 1898, *Prot. Monatsh.* 2, pp. 252-267.

206. H. Gunkel, *Z. w. Th.*, 1899, 42, pp. 581-611.

For the last phase of the discussion we may name:

Wellhausen, *Skizzen und Vorarbeiten* (Sketches and Studies), 1899, pp. 187-215, where he throws further light on Dalman's philological objections; and goes on to deny Jesus' use of the expression.

W. Baldensperger, "Die neueste Forschung über den Menschensohn," *Theol. Rundschau*, 1900, 3, pp. 201-210, 243-255.

P. Fiebig, *Der Menschensohn*. Tübingen, 1901.

P. W. Schmiedel, "Die neueste Auffassung des Namens Menschensohn," *Prot. Monatsh.* 5, pp. 333-351, 1901. (The Latest View of the Designation Son of Man.)

P. W. Schmidt, *Die Geschichte Jesu*, ii. (*Erläuterungen*—Explanations). Tübingen, 1904, p. 157 ff.

207.

Dalman's reputation as an authority upon Jewish Aramaic is so deservedly high, that it is necessary to point out that his solution did not, as Dr. Schweitzer seems to say, entirely dispose of the linguistic difficulties raised by Lietzmann as to the meaning and use of *barnâsh* and *barnâshâ* in Aramaic. The English reader will find the linguistic facts well put in sections 4 and 32 of N. Schmidt's article "Son of Man" in *Encyclopædia Biblica* (cols. 4708, 4723), or he may consult Prof. Bevan's review of Dalman's *Worte Jesu* in the *Critical Review* for 1899, p. 148 ff. The main point is that ὁ ἄνθρωπος and ὁ υἱὸς τοῦ ἀνθρώπου are equally legitimate translations of *barnâshâ*. Thus the contrast in the Greek between ὁ ἄνθρωπος and ὁ υἱὸς τοῦ ἀνθρώπου in Mark ii. 27 and 28, or again in Mark viii. 36 and 38, disappears on retranslation into the dialect spoken by Jesus. Whether this linguistic fact makes the sayings in which ὁ υἱὸς τοῦ ἀνθρώπου occurs unhistorical is a further question, upon which scholars can take, and have taken, opposite opinions.—F. C. B.

208.

See *Worte Jesu*, 1898, p. 191 ff. (= E. T. p. 234 ff.).

209.

See the classical discussion in J. Weiss, *Die Predigt Jesus vom Reiche Gottes*, 1892, 1st ed., p. 52 ff.

In the second edition, of 1900, p. 160 ff., he allows himself to be led astray by the "chiefest apostles" of modern theology to indulge in the subtleties of fine-spun psychology, and explain Jesus' way of speaking of Himself in the third person as the Son of Man as due to the "extreme modesty of Jesus," a modesty which did not forsake Him in the presence of His judges. This recent access of psychologising exegesis has not conduced to clearness of presentation, and the preference for the Lucan narrative does not so much contribute to throw light on the facts as to discover in the thoughts of Jesus subtleties of which the historical Jesus never dreamt. If the Lord always used the term Son of Man when speaking of His Messiahship, the reason was that this was the only way in which He could speak of it at all, since the Messiahship was not yet realised, but was only to be so at the appearing of the Son of Man. For a consistent, purely historical, non-psychological exposition of the Son-of-Man passages see Albert Schweitzer, *Das*

Messianitäts- und Leidensgeheimnis. (The Secret of the Messiahship and the Passion.) A sketch of the Life of Jesus. Tübingen, 1901.

210.

See Dalman, p. 60 ff.

John Lightfoot, *Horae Hebraicae et Talmudicae in quatuor Evangelistas*. Edited by J. B. Carpzov. Leipzig, 1684.

Christian Schöttgen, *Horae Hebraicae et Talmudicae in universum Novum Testamentum*. Dresden-Leipzig, 1733.

Joh. Gerh. Meuschen, *Novum Testamentum ex Talmude et antiquitatibus Hebraeorum illustratum*. Leipzig, 1736.

J. Jakob. Wettstein, *Novum Testamentum Graecum*. Amsterdam, 1751 and 1752.

F. Nork, *Rabbinische Quellen und Parallelen zu neutestamentlichen Schriftstellen*, Leipzig, 1839.

Franz Delitzsch, "Horae Hebraicae et Talmudicae," in the *Luth. Zeitsch.*, 1876-1878.

Carl Siegfried, *Analecta Rabbinica*, 1875; "Rabbin. Analekten," *Jahrb. f. prot. Theol.*, 1876.

A. Wünsche, *Neue Beiträge zur Erläuterung der Evangelien aus Talmud und Midrasch*. (Contributions to the Exposition of the Gospels from Talmud and Midrash.) Göttingen, 1878.

211.

Leipzig, 1880; 2nd ed., 1897.

212.

Cf. for what follows, Jülicher, *Die Gleichnisreden Jesu*, i., 1888, p. 164 ff.

213.

Robert Sheringham of Caius College, Cambridge, a royalist divine, published an edition of the Talmudic tractate *Yoma*. London, 1648.—F. C. B.

214.

T. Tal, *Professor Oort und der Talmud*, 1880. See upon this Van Manen, *Jahrb. f. prot. Theol.*, 1884, p. 569. The best collection of Talmudic parables is, according to Jülicher, that of Prof. Guis. Levi, translated by L. Seligman as *Parabeln, Legenden und Gedanken aus Talmud und Midrasch*. Leipzig, 2nd ed., 1877.

215.

The question may be said to have been provisionally settled by Paul Fiebig's work, *Altjüdische Gleichnisse und die Gleichnisse Jesu* (Ancient Jewish Parables and the Parables of Jesus), Tübingen, 1904, in which he gives some fifty Late-Jewish parables, and compares them with those of Jesus, the final result being to show more clearly than ever the uniqueness and absoluteness of His creations.

216.

See the explanation by means of the Aramaic of a selection of the sayings of Jesus in Meyer, pp. 72-90. A Judaism more under Parsee influence is assumed as explaining the origin of Christianity by E. Böklen, *Die Verwandschaft der jüdisch-christlichen mit der parsischen Eschatologie* (The Relation of Jewish-Christian to Persian Eschatology), 1902, 510 ff.

217.

The same view is expressed by Wellhausen, *Israelitische und jüdische Geschichte*, 3rd ed., p. 381, note 2; and by Albert Schweitzer, *Das Messianitäts- und Leidensgeheimnis*, 1901.

218.

See the Apocalypse of Baruch, and Fourth Ezra.

219.

La Vie inconnue de Jésus-Christ, par Nicolas Notowitsch. Paris, 1894.

220.

See Jülicher, *Gleichnisreden Jesu*, i., 1888, p. 172 ff.

221.

Max Müller, *India, What can it teach us?* London, 1883, p. 279.

222.

Rudolf Seydel, Professor in the University of Leipzig, *Das Evangelium von Jesu in seinen Verhältnissen zu Buddha-Sage und Buddha-Lehre mit fortlaufender Rücksicht auf andere Religionskreise*. (The Gospel of Jesus in its relation to the Buddha Legend and the Teaching of Buddha, with constant reference to other religious groups.) Leipzig, 1882, p. 337.

Other works by the same author are *Buddha und Christus*. Deutsche Bücherei No. 33, Breslau, Schottländer, 1884.

Die Buddha-Legende und das Leben Jesu nach den Evangelien. 2nd ed. Weimar, 1897. (Edited by the son of the late author.) 129 pp.

See also on this question Van den Bergh van Eysinga, *Indische Einflüsse auf evangelische Erzählungen*. Göttingen, 1904. 104 pp.

According to J. M. Robertson, *Christianity and Mythology* (London, 1900), the Christ-Myth is merely a form of the Krishna-Myth. The whole Gospel tradition is to be symbolically interpreted.

223.

Das Christentum des Neuen Testaments, 1905.

224.

Heinrich Julius Holtzmann, *Handkommentar. Die Synoptiker*. 1st ed., 1889; 3rd ed., 1901. *Lehrbuch der neutestamentlichen Theologie*, 1896, vol. i.

225.

In the Catholic Church the study of the Life of Jesus has remained down to the present day entirely free from scepticism. The reason of that is, that in principle it has remained at a pre-Straussian standpoint, and does not venture upon an unreserved application of historical considerations either to the miracle question or to the Johannine question, and naturally therefore resigns the attempt to take account of and explain the great historical problems.

We may name the following Lives of Jesus produced by German Catholic writers:—

Joh. Nep. Sepp, *Das Leben Jesu Christi*. Regensburg, 1843-1846. 7 vols., 2nd ed., 1853-1862.

Peter Schegg, *Sechs Bücher des Lebens Jesu*. (The Life of Jesus in Six Books.) Freiburg, 1874-1875. c. 1200 pp.

Joseph Grimm, *Das Leben Jesu*. Würzburg, 2nd ed., 1890-1903. 6 vols.

Richard von Kralik, *Jesu Leben und Werk*. Kempten-Nürnberg, 1904. 481 pp.

W. Capitaine, *Jesus von Nazareth*. Regensburg, 1905. 192 pp.

How narrow are the limits within which the Catholic study of the life of Jesus moves even when it aims at scientific treatment, is illustrated by Hermann Schell's *Christus* (Mainz, 1903. 152 pp.). After reading the forty-two questions with which he introduces his narrative one might suppose that the author was well aware of the bearing of all the historical problems of the life of Jesus, and intended to supply an answer to them. Instead of doing so, however, he adopts as the work proceeds more and more the rôle of an apologist, not facing definitely either the miracle question or the Johannine question, but gliding over the difficulties by the aid of ingenious headings, so that in the end his book almost takes the form of an explanatory text to the eighty-nine illustrations which adorn the book and make it difficult to read.

In France, Renan's work gave the incentive to an extensive Catholic "Life-of-Jesus" literature. We may name the following:—

Louis Veuillot, *La Vie de notre Seigneur Jésus-Christ*. Paris, 1864. 509 pp. German by Waldeyer. Köln-Neuss, 1864. 573 pp.

H. Wallon, *Vie de notre Seigneur Jésus-Christ*. Paris, 1865. 355 pp.

A work which met with a particularly favourable reception was that of Père Didon, the Dominican, *Jésus-Christ*, Paris, 1891, 2 vols., vol. i. 483 pp., vol. ii. 469 pp. The German translation is dated 1895.

In the same year there appeared a new edition of the "Bitter Sufferings of Our Lord Jesus Christ" (see above, p. 109 f.) by Katharina Emmerich; the cheap popular edition of the translation of Renan's "Life of Jesus"; and the eighth edition of Strauss's "Life of Jesus for the German People."

We may quote from the ecclesiastical *Approbation* printed at the beginning of Didon's Life of Jesus. "If the author sometimes seems to speak the language of his opponents, it is at once evident that he has aimed at defeating them on their own ground, and he is particularly successful in doing so when he confronts their irreligious a priori theories with the positive arguments of history."

As a matter of fact the work is skilfully written, but without a spark of understanding of the historical questions.

All honour to Alfred Loisy! (*Le Quatrième Évangile*, Paris, 1903, 960 pp.), who takes a clear view on the Johannine question, and denies the existence of a Johannine historical tradition. But what that means for the Catholic camp may be recognised from the excitement produced by the book and its express condemnation. See also the same writer's *L'Évangile et l'Église* (German translation, Munich, 1904, 189 pp.), in which Loisy here and there makes good historical points against Harnack's "What is Christianity?"

226.

Oskar Holtzmann, Professor of Theology at Giessen, was born in 1859 at Stuttgart.

227.

This suggestion reminds us involuntarily of the old rationalistic Lives of Jesus, which are distressed that Jesus should have injured the good people of the country of the Gesarenes by sacrificing their swine in healing the demoniac. A good deal of old rationalistic material crops up in the very latest Lives of Jesus, as cannot indeed fail to be the case in view of the arbitrary interpretation of detail which is common to both. According to Oskar Holtzmann the barren fig-tree has also a symbolical meaning. "It is a pledge given by God to Jesus that His faith shall not be put to shame in the great work of His life."

228.

Isaiah lxii. 11, "Say ye to the daughter of Zion, Behold, thy salvation cometh."

229.

"For Jesus Himself," Oskar Holtzmann argues, "this discovery"—he means the antinomy which He had discovered in Psalm cx.—"disposed of a doubt which had always haunted him. If He had really known Himself to be descended from the Davidic line, He would certainly not have publicly suggested a doubt as to the Davidic descent of the Messiah."

230.

Oskar Holtzmann's work, *War Jesus Ekstatiker?* (Tübingen, 1903, 139 pp.) is in reality a new reading of the life of Jesus. By emphasising the ecstatic element he breaks with the "natural" conception of the life and teaching of Jesus; and, in so far, approaches the eschatological view. But he gives a very wide significance to the term ecstatic, subsuming under it, it might almost be said, all the eschatological thoughts and utterances of Jesus. He explains, for instance, that "the conviction of the approaching destruction of existing conditions is ecstatic." At the same time, the only purpose served by the hypothesis of ecstasy is to enable the author to attribute to Jesus "The belief that in His own work the Kingdom of God was already beginning, and the promise of the Kingdom to individuals; this can only be considered ecstatic." The opposites which Bousset brings together by the conception of paradox are united by Holtzmann by means of the hypothesis of ecstasy. That is, however, to play fast and loose with the meaning of "ecstasy." An ecstasy is, in the usual understanding of the word, an abnormal, transient condition of excitement in which the subject's natural capacity for thought and feeling, and therewith all impressions from without, are suspended, being superseded by an intense mental excitation and activity. Jesus may possibly have been in an ecstatic state at His baptism and at the transfiguration. What O. Holtzmann represents as a kind of permanent ecstatic state is rather an eschatological fixed idea. With eschatology, ecstasy has no essential connexion. It is possible to be eschatologically minded without being an ecstatic, and vice versa. Philo attributes a great importance to ecstasy in his religious life, but he was scarcely, if at all, interested in eschatology.

231.

P. W. Schmidt, now Professor in Basle, was born in Berlin in 1845.

232.

Otto Schmiedel, Professor at the Gymnasium at Eisenach, *Die Hauptprobleme der Leben-Jesu-Forschung*. Tübingen, 1902. 71 pp. Schmiedel was born in 1858.

Hermann Freiherr von Soden, *Die wichtigsten Fragen im Leben Jesu*. Von Soden, Professor in Berlin, and preacher at the Jerusalem Kirche, was born in 1852.

We may mention also the following works:—

Fritz Barth (born 1856, Professor at Bern), *Die Hauptprobleme des Lebens Jesu*. 1st ed., 1899; 2nd ed., 1903.

Friedrich Nippold's *Der Entwicklungsgang des Lebens Jesu im Wortlaut der drei ersten Evangelien* (The Course of the Life of Jesus in the Words of the First Three Evangelists) (Hamburg, 1895, 213 pp.) is only an arrangement of the sections.

Konrad Furrer's *Vorträge über das Leben Jesu Christi* (Lectures on the Life of Jesus Christ) have a special charm by reason of the author's knowledge of the country and the locality. Furrer, who was born in 1838, is Professor at Zurich.

Another work which should not be forgotten is R. Otto's *Leben und Wirken Jesu nach historisch-kritischer Auffassung* (Life and Work of Jesus from the Point of View of Historical Criticism). A Lecture. Göttingen, 1902. Rudolf Otto, born in 1869, is Privat-Docent at Göttingen.

233.

Schmiedel is not altogether right in making "the Heidelberg Professor Paulus" follow the same lines as Reimarus, "except that his works, of 1804 and 1828, are less malignant, but only the more dull for that." In reality the deistic Life of Jesus by Reimarus, and the rationalistic Life by Paulus have nothing in common. Paulus was perhaps influenced by Venturini, but not by Reimarus. The assertion that Strauss wrote his "Life of Jesus for the German people" because "Renan's fame gave him no peace" is not justified, either by Strauss's character or by the circumstances in which the second Life of Jesus was produced.

234.

Von Soden gives on pp. 24 ff. the passages of Mark which he supposes to be derived from the Petrine tradition in a different order from that in which they occur in Mark, regrouping them freely. He puts together, for instance, Mark i. 16-20, iii. 13-19, vi. 7-16, viii. 27-ix. 1, ix. 33-40, under the title "The formation and training of the band of disciples." He supposes Mark, the pupil of Peter, to have grouped in this way by a kind of association of ideas "what he had heard Peter relate in his missionary journeys, when writing it down after Peter's death, not connectedly, but giving as much as he could remember of it"; this would be in accordance with the statement of Papias that Mark wrote "not in order." Papias's statement, therefore, refers to an "Ur-Markus," which he found lacking in historical order.

But what are we to make of a representative of the early Church thus approaching the Gospels with the demand for historical arrangement? And good, simple old Papias, of all people!

But if the Marcan plan was not laid down in "Ur-Markus," there is nothing for it—since the plan was certainly not given in the collection of Logia—but to ascribe it to the author of our Gospel of Mark, to the man, that is, who wrote down for the first time these "Pauline conceptions," those reflections of experiences of individual believers and of the community, and inserted them into the Gospel. It is proposed, then, to retain the outline which he has given of the life of Jesus, and reject at the same time what he relates. That is to say, he is to be believed where it is convenient to believe him, and silenced where it is inconvenient. No more complete refutation of the Marcan hypothesis could possibly be given than this analysis, for it destroys its very foundation, the confident acceptance of the historicity of the Marcan plan.

If there is to be an analysis of sources in Mark, then the Marcan plan must be ascribed to "Ur-Markus," otherwise the analysis renders the Markan hypothesis historically useless. But if "Ur-Markus" is to be reconstructed on the basis of assigning to it the Marcan plan, then we cannot separate the natural from the supernatural, for the supernatural scenes, like the feeding of the multitude and the transfiguration, are among the main features of the Marcan outline.

No hypothetical analysis of "Ur-Markus" has escaped this dilemma; what it can effect by literary methods is historically useless, and what would be historically useful cannot be attained nor "presented" by literary methods.

235.

Von Soden, for instance, germanises Jesus when he writes, "and this nature is sound to the core. In spite of its inwardness there is no trace of an exaggerated sentimentality. In spite of all the intensity of prayer there is nothing of ecstasy or vision. No apocalyptic dream-pictures find a lodging-place in His soul."

Is a man who teaches a world-renouncing ethic which sometimes soars to the dizzy heights such as that of Matt. xix. 12, according to our conceptions "sound to the core"? And does not the life of Jesus present a number of occasions on which He seems to have been in an ecstasy?

Thus, von Soden has not simply read his Jesus out of the texts, but has added something of his own, and that something is Germanic in colouring.

236.

i.e. the MS. Life of Jesus written by Kai Jans, one of the characters of the novel. The way in which the whole life-experience of this character prepares him for the writing of the Life is strikingly—if not always acceptably—worked out.—TRANSLATOR.

237.

Frenssen's Kai Jans professes to have used the "results of the whole range of critical investigation" in writing his work. Among the books which he enumerates and recommends in the after-word, we miss the works of Strauss, Weisse, Keim, Volkmar, and Brandt, and, generally speaking, the names of those who in the past have done something really great and original. Of the moderns, Johannes Weiss is lacking. Wrede is mentioned, but is virtually ignored. Pfleiderer's remarkable and profound presentation of Jesus in the *Urchristentum* (E. T. "Primitive Christianity," vol. ii., 1909) is non-existent so far as he is concerned.

238.

Heimatkunst, the ideal that every production of German art should be racy of the soil. It has its relative justification as a protest against the long subservience of some departments of German art to French taste.—TRANSLATOR.

239.

The Jesus of H. S. Chamberlain's *Worte Christi*, 1901, 286 pp., is also modern. But the modernity is not so obtrusive, because he describes only the teaching of Jesus, not His life.

240.

Born in 1839 at Stettin. Studied at Tübingen, was appointed Professor in 1870 at Jena and in 1875 at Berlin. (Died 1908.)

241.

Das Urchristentum, seine Schriften und Lehren in geschichtlichem Zusammenhang beschrieben. 2nd ed. Berlin, 1902. Vol. i. (696 pp.), 615 ff.: *Die Predigt Jesu und der Glaube der Urgemeinde* (English Translation, "Primitive Christianity," chap. xvi.). Pfleiderer's latest views are set forth in his work, based on academic lectures, *Die Entstehung des Urchristentums*. (How Christianity arose.) Munich, 1905. 255 pp.

242.

Albert Kalthoff, *Das Christusproblem. Grundlinien zu einer Sozialtheologie.* (The Problem of the Christ: Ground-plan of a Social Theology.) Leipzig, 1902. 87 pp.

Die Entstehung des Christentums. Neue Beiträge zum Christusproblem. (How Christianity arose.) Leipzig, 1904. 155 pp.

Albert Kalthoff was born in 1850 at Barmen, and is engaged in pastoral work in Bremen.

243.

Das Leben Jesu. Lectures delivered before the Protestant Reform Society at Berlin. Berlin, 1880. 173 pp.

244.

If Kalthoff would only have spoken of the conception of the resurrection instead of the conception of immortality! Then his subjective knowledge would have been more or less tolerable.

245.

Against Kalthoff: Wilhelm Bousset, *Was wissen wir von Jesus?* (What do we know about Jesus?) Lectures delivered before the Protestantenverein at Bremen. Halle, 1904. 73 pp. In reply: Albert Kalthoff, *Was wissen wir von Jesus?* A settlement of accounts with Professor Bousset. Berlin, 1904. 43 pp.

A sound historical position is set forth in the clear and trenchant lecture of W. Kapp, *Das Christus- und Christentumsproblem bei Kalthoff*. (The problem of the Christ and of Christianity as handled by Kalthoff.) Strassburg, 1905. 23 pp.

246.

Eduard von Hartmann, *Das Christentum des Neuen Testaments*. (The Christianity of the N.T.) 2nd, revised and altered, edition of the "Letters on the Christian Religion." Sachsa-in-the-Harz, 1905. 311 pp.

247.

Eduard von Hartmann ought, therefore, to have given his assistance to the others who have made this assertion in proving that there really existed Messianic claimants before and at the time of Jesus.

248.

"Jesus," by Jülicher, in *Die Kultur der Gegenwart*. (An encyclopaedic publication which is appearing in parts.) Teubner, Berlin, 1905, pp. 40-69.

See also W. Bousset, "Jesus," *Religionsgeschichtliche Volksbücher*. (A series of religious-historical monographs.) Published by Schiele, Halle, 1904.

Here should be mentioned also the thoughtful book, following very much the lines of Jülicher, by Eduard Grimm, entitled *Die Ethik Jesu*, Hamburg, 1903, 288 pp. The author, born in 1848, is the chief pastor at the Nicolaikirche in Hamburg.

Another work which deserves mention is Arno Neumann, *Jesu wie er geschichtlich war* (Jesus as he historically existed), Freiburg, 1904, 198 pp. (New Paths to the Old God), a Life of Jesus distinguished by a lofty vein of natural poetry and based upon solid theological knowledge. Arno Neumann is headmaster of a school at Apolda.

249.

Jeschua. Der klassische jüdische Mann. Zerstörung des kirchlichen, Enthüllung des jüdischen Jesus-Bildes. Berlin, 1904, 112 pp. Earlier studies of the Life of Jesus from the Jewish point of view had been less ambitious. Dr. Aug. Wünsche had written in 1872 on "Jesus in His attitude towards women" from the Talmudic standpoint (146 pp.), and had described Him from the same standpoint as a Jesus who rejoiced in life, *Der lebensfreudige Jesus der synoptischen Evangelien im Gegensatz zum leidenden Messias der Kirche*. Leipzig, 1876, 444 pp. The basis is so far correct, that the eschatological, world-renouncing ethic which we find in Jesus was due to temporary conditions and is therefore transitory, and had nothing whatever to do with Judaism as such. The spirit of the Law is the opposite of world-renouncing. But the Talmud, be its traditions never so trustworthy, could teach us little about Jesus because it has preserved scarcely a trace of that eschatological phase of Jewish religion and ethics.

250.

Wolfgang Kirchbach, *Was lehrte Jesus? Zwei Urevangelien*. Berlin, 1897, 248 pp.; second greatly enlarged and improved edition, 1902, 339 pp. By the same author, *Das Buch Jesus. Die Urevangelien. Neu nachgewiesen, neu übersetzt, geordnet und aus der Ursprache erklärt.* (The Book of Jesus. The Primitive Gospels. Newly traced, translated, arranged, and explained on the basis of the original.) Berlin, 1897.

251.

Before him, Hugo Delff, in his *History of the Rabbi Jesus of Nazareth* (Leipzig, 1889, 428 pp.), had confined himself to the Fourth Gospel, and even within that Gospel he drew some critical distinctions. His Jesus at first conceals His Messiahship from the fear of arousing the political expectations of the people, and speaks to them of the Son of Man in the third person. At His second visit to Jerusalem He breaks with the rulers, is subsequently compelled, in consequence of the conflict over the Sabbath, to leave Galilee, and then gives up His own people and turns to the heathen. Delff explains the raising of Lazarus by supposing him to have been buried in a state of trance.

252.

Albert Dulk, *Der Irrgang des Lebens Jesu. In geschichtlicher Auffassung dargestellt. Erster Teil: Die historischen Wurzeln und die galiläische Blüte*, 1884. 395 pp. *Zweiter Teil: Der Messiaseinzug und die Erhebung ans Kreuz*, 1885, 302 pp. (The Error of the Life of Jesus. Historically apprehended and set forth. Pt. i., The Historical Roots and the Galilaean Blossom. Pt. ii., The Messianic Entry and the Crucifixion.) The course of Dulk's own life was somewhat erratic. Born in 1819, he came prominently forward in the revolution of 1848, as a political pamphleteer and agitator. Later, though almost without means, he undertook long journeys, even to Sinai and to Lapland. Finally, he worked as a social democratic reformer. He died in 1884.

253.

A scientific treatment of this subject is supplied by Fr. Nippold, *Die psychiatrische Seite der Heilstätigkeit Jesu* (The Psychiatric Side of Jesus' Works of Healing), 1889, in which a luminous review of the medical material is to be found. See also Dr. K. Kunz, *Christus medicus*, Freiburg in Baden, 1905, 74 pp. The scientific value of this work is, however, very much reduced by the fact that the author has no acquaintance with the preliminary questions belonging to the sphere of history and literature, and regards all the miracles of healing as actual events, believing himself able to explain them from the medical point of view. The tendency of the work is mainly apologetic.

254.

Jesus von Nazareth. Described from the Scientific, Historical, and Social Point of View. Translated from the French (into German) by A. Just. Leipzig, 1894. The author, whose real name is P. A. Desjardin, is a practising physician. De Régla, too, makes the Fourth Gospel the basis of his narrative.

255.

Pierre Nahor (Emilie Lerou), *Jesus*. Translated from the French by Walter Bloch. Berlin, 1905. Its motto is: The figure of Jesus belongs, like all mysterious, heroic, or mythical figures, to legend and poetry. In the introduction we find the statement, "This book is a confession of faith." The narrative is based on the Fourth Gospel.

256.

La Vie inconnue de Jésus-Christ. Paris, 1894. 301 pp. German, under the title *Die Lücke im Leben Jesu* (The Gap in the Life of Jesus). Stuttgart, 1894. 186 pp. See Holtzmann in the *Theol. Jahresbericht*, xiv. p. 140.

In a certain limited sense the work of A. Lillie, *The Influence of Buddhism on Primitive Christianity* (London, 1893), is to be numbered among the fictitious works on the life of Jesus. The fictitious element consists in Jesus being made an Essene by the writer, and Essenism equated with Buddhism.

Among "edifying" romances on the life of Jesus intended for family reading, that of the English writer J. H. Ingraham, *The Prince of the House of David*, has had a very long lease of life. It appeared in a German translation as early as 1858, and was reissued in 1906 (Brunswick).

A fictitious life of Jesus of wonderful beauty is Peter Rosegger's *I.N.R.I. Frohe Botschaft eines armen Sünders* (The Glad Tidings of a poor Sinner). Leipzig, 6th-10th thousand, 1906. 293 pp.

A feminine point of view reveals itself in C. Rauch's *Jeschua ben Joseph*. Deichert, 1899.

257.

La Vie ésotérique de Jésu-Christ et les origines orientales du christianisme. Paris, 1902. 445 pp.

That Jesus was of Aryan race is argued by A. Müller, who assumes a Gaulish immigration into Galilee. *Jesus ein Arier.* Leipzig, 1904. 74 pp.

258.

Did Jesus live 100 B.C.? London and Benares. Theosophical Publishing Society, 1903. 440 pp.

A scientific discussion of the "Toledoth Jeshu," with citations from the Talmudic tradition concerning Jesus, is offered by S. Krauss, *Das Leben Jesu nach jüdischen Quellen*, 1902. 309 pp. According to him the *Toledoth Jeshu* was committed to writing in the fifth century, and he is of opinion that the Jewish legend is only a modified version of the Christian tradition.

259.

William Wrede, born in 1859 at Bücken in Hanover, was Professor at Breslau. (He died in 1907.)

Wrede names as his real predecessors on the same lines Bruno Bauer, Volkmar, and the Dutch writer Hoekstra ("De Christologie van het canonieke Marcus-Evangelie, vergeleken met die van de beide andere synoptische Evangelien," *Theol. Tijdschrift*, v., 1871).

In a certain limited degree the work of Ernest Havet (*Le Christianisme et ses origines*) has a claim to be classed in the same category. His scepticism refers principally to the entry into Jerusalem and the story of the passion.

260.

These and the following questions are raised more especially in the *Sketch of the Life of Jesus*.

261.

It would perhaps be more historical to say "as a prophet."

262.

The difficulties which the incident at Caesarea Philippi places in the way of Wrede's construction may be realised by placing two of his statements side by side. P. 101: "From this it is evident that this incident contains no element which cannot be easily understood on the basis of Mark's ideas." P. 238: "But in another aspect this incident stands in direct contradiction to the Marcan view of the disciples. It is inconsistent with their general 'want of understanding,' and can therefore hardly have been created by Mark himself."

263.

The question of the attitude of pre-Origenic theology towards the historical Jesus, and of the influence exercised by dogma upon the evangelical tradition regarding Jesus in the course of the first two centuries, is certainly deserving of a detailed examination.

264.

Certain of the conceptions with which Wrede operates are simply not in accordance with the text, because he gives them a different significance from that which they have in the narrative. Thus, for example, he always takes the "resurrection," when it occurs in the mouth of Jesus, as a reference to that resurrection which as an historical fact became a matter of apprehended experience to the apostles. But Jesus speaks without any distinction of His resurrection and of His Parousia. The conception of the resurrection, therefore, if one is to arrive at it inductively from the Marcan text, is most closely bound up with the Parousia. The Evangelist would thus seem to have made Jesus predict a different kind of resurrection from that which actually happened. The resurrection, according to the Marcan text, is an eschatological event, and has no reference whatever to Wrede's "historical resurrection." Further, if their resurrection experience was the first and fundamental point in the Messianic enlightenment of the disciples, why did they only begin to proclaim it some weeks later? This is a problem which was long ago recognised by Reimarus, and which is not solved by merely assuming that the disciples were afraid.

265.

P. 33 ff. The prohibitions in Mark i. 43 and 44, v. 43, vii. 36, and viii. 26 are put on the same footing with the really Messianic prohibitions in viii. 30 and ix. 9, with which may be associated also the imposition of silence upon the demoniacs who recognise his Messiahship in Mark i. 34 and iii. 12.

266.

The narrative in Matt. xiv. 22-33, according to which the disciples, after seeing Jesus walk upon the sea, hail Him on His coming into the boat as the Son of God, and the description of the deeds of Jesus as "deeds of Christ," in the introduction to the Baptist's question in Matt. xi. 2, do not cancel the old theory even in Matthew, because the Synoptists, differing therein from the fourth Evangelist, do not represent the demand for a sign as a demand for a Messianic sign, nor the cures wrought by Jesus as Messianic proofs of power. The action of the demons in crying out upon Jesus as the Son of God betokens their recognition of Him; it has nothing to do with the miracles of healing as such.

267.

For further examples of the pressing of the theory to its utmost limits, see Wrede, p. 134 ff.

268.

It is always assumed as self-evident that Jesus is speaking of the sufferings and persecutions which would take place after His death, or that the Evangelist, in making Him speak in this way, is thinking of these later persecutions. There is no hint of that in the text.

269.

That the eschatological school showed a certain timidity in drawing the consequences of its recognition of the character of the preaching of Jesus and examining the tradition from the eschatological standpoint can be seen from Johannes Weiss's work, "The Earliest Gospel" (*Das älteste Evangelium*), Göttingen, 1903, 414 pp. Ingenious and interesting as this work is in detail, one is surprised to find the author of the "Preaching of Jesus" here endeavouring to distinguish between Mark and "Ur-Markus," to point to examples of Pauline influence, to exhibit clearly the "tendencies" which guided, respectively, the original Evangelist and the redactor—all this as if he did not possess in his eschatological view of the preaching of Jesus a dominant conception which gives him a clue to quite a different psychology from that which he actually applies. Against Wrede he brings forward many arguments which are worthy of attention, but he can hardly be said to have refuted him, because it is impossible for Weiss to treat the question in the exact form in which it was raised by Wrede.

270.

Wrede certainly goes too far in asserting that even in Mark's version the experience at the baptism is conceived as an open miracle, perceptible to others. The way in which the revelations to the prophets are recounted in the Old Testament does not make in favour of this. Otherwise we should have to suppose that the Evangelist described the incident as a miracle which took place in the presence of a multitude without perceiving that in this case the Messianic secret was a secret no longer. If so, the story of the baptism stands on the same footing as the story of the Messianic entry: it is a revelation of the Messiahship which has absolutely no results.

271.

The statement of Mark that Jesus, coming out of the north, appeared for a moment again in Decapolis and Capernaum, and then started off to the north once more (Mark vii. 31-viii. 27), may here provisionally be left out of account since it stands in relation with the twofold account of the feeding of the multitude. So too the enigmatic appearance and disappearance of the people (Mark viii. 34-ix. 30) may here be passed over. These statements make no difference to the fact that Jesus really broke off his work in Galilee shortly after the Mission of the Twelve, since they imply at most a quite transient contact with the people.

272.

On the theory of the successful and unsuccessful periods in the work of Jesus see the "Sketch," p. 3 ff., "The four Pre-suppositions of the Modern Historical Solution."

273.

Weisse found that there was no hint in the sources of the desertion of the people, since according to these, Jesus was opposed only by the Pharisees, not by the people. The abandonment of the Galilaean work, and the departure to Jerusalem, must, he thought, have been due to some unrecorded fact which revealed to Jesus that the time had come to act in this way. Perhaps, he adds, it was the waning of Jesus' miracle-working power which caused the change in His attitude, since it is remarkable that He performed no further miracles during His sojourn at Jerusalem.

274.

The most logical attitude in regard to it is Bousset's, who proposes to treat the mission and everything connected with it as a "confused and unintelligible" tradition.

275.

Joel iii. 13, "Put in the sickle for the harvest is ripe!" In the Apocalypse of John, too, the Last Judgment is described as the heavenly harvest: "Thrust in thy sickle and reap; for the time is come for thee to reap; for the harvest of the earth is ripe. And he that sat on the cloud thrust in his sickle on the earth; and the earth was reaped" (Rev. xiv. 15 and 16).

The most remarkable parallel to the discourse at the sending forth of the disciples is offered by the Syriac Apocalypse of Baruch: "Behold, the days come, when the time of the world shall be ripe, and the harvest of the sowing of the good and of the evil shall come, when the Almighty shall bring upon the earth and upon its inhabitants and upon their rulers confusion of spirit and terror that makes the heart stand still; and they shall hate one another and provoke one another to war; and the despised shall have power over them of reputation, and the mean shall exalt themselves over them that are highly esteemed. And the many shall be at the mercy of the few ... and all who shall be saved and shall escape the before-mentioned (dangers) ... shall be given into the hands of my servant, the Messiah." (Cap. lxx. 2, 3, 9. Following the translation of E. Kautzsch.)

The connexion between the ideas of harvest and of judgment was therefore one of the stock features of the apocalyptic writings. And as the Apocalypse of Baruch dates from the period about A.D. 70, it may be assumed that this association of ideas was also current in the Jewish apocalyptic of the time of Jesus. Here is a basis for understanding the secret of the Kingdom of God in the parables of sowing and reaping historically and in accordance with the ideas of the time. What Jesus did was to make known to those who understood Him that the coming earthly harvest was the last, and was also the token of the coming heavenly harvest. The eschatological interpretation is immensely strengthened by these parallels.

276.

With what right does modern critical theology tear apart even the discourse in Matt. xi. in order to make the "cry of jubilation" into the cry with which Jesus saluted the return of His disciples, and to find lodgment for the woes upon Chorazin and Bethsaida somewhere else in an appropriately gloomy context? Is not all this apparently disconnected material held together by an inner bond of connexion—the secret of the

Kingdom of God which is imminently impending over Jesus and the people? Or, is Jesus expected to preach like one who has a thesis to maintain and seeks about for the most logical arrangement? Does not a certain lack of orderly connexion belong to the very idea of prophetic speech?

277.

If, therefore, Jesus at a later point predicted to His disciples His resurrection, He means by that, not a single isolated act, but a complex occurrence consisting of His metamorphosis, translation to heaven, and Parousia as the Son of Man. And with this is associated the general eschatological resurrection of the dead. It is, therefore, one and the same thing whether He speaks of His resurrection or of His coming on the clouds of heaven.

278.

The title of Baldensperger's book, *The Self-consciousness of Jesus in the Light of the Messianic Hopes of His Time*, really contains a promise which is impossible of fulfilment. The contemporary "Messianic hopes" can only explain the hopes of Jesus so far as they corresponded thereto, not His view of His own Person, in which He is absolutely original.

279.

Even Baldensperger's book, *Die messianisch-apokalyptischen Hoffnungen des Judentums* (1903), passes at a stride from the Psalms of Solomon to Fourth Ezra. The coming volume is to deal with the eschatology of Jesus. That is a "theological," but not an historical division of the material. The second volume should properly come in the middle of the first.

280.

The fact that in the Psalms of Solomon the Messiah is designated by the ancient prophetic name of the Son of David is significant of the rising influence of the ancient prophetic literature. This designation has nothing whatever to do with a political ideal of a kingly Messiah. This Davidic King and his Kingdom are, in their character and the manner of their coming, every whit as supernatural as the Son of Man and His coming. The same historical fact was read into both Daniel and the prophets.

281.

Enoch is an offshoot of the Danielic apocalyptic writings. The earliest portion, the Apocalypse of the Ten Weeks, is independent of Daniel and of contemporary origin. The Similitudes (capp. xxxvii.-lxix.), which, with their description of the Judgment of the Son of Man, are so important in connexion with the thoughts of Jesus, may be placed in 80-70 B.C. They do not presuppose the taking of Jerusalem by Pompey.

282.

The Psalms of Solomon are therefore a decade later than the Similitudes.

283.

The Apocalypse of Baruch seems to have been composed not very long after the Fall of Jerusalem. Fourth Ezra is twenty to thirty years later.

284.

The Psalms of Solomon form the last document of Jewish eschatology before the coming of the Baptist. For almost a hundred years, from 60 B.C. until A.D. 30, we have no information regarding eschatological movements! And do the Psalms of Solomon really point to a deep eschatological movement at the time of the taking of Jerusalem by Pompey? Hardly, I think. It is to be noticed in studying the times of Jesus that the surrounding circumstances have no eschatological character. The Fall of Jerusalem marks the next turning-point in the history of the apocalyptic hope, as Baruch and Fourth Ezra show.

285.

Jesus promises them expressly that at the appearing of the Son of Man they shall sit upon twelve thrones, judging the twelve tribes of Israel (Matt. xix. 28). It is to their part in the judgment that belong also the authority to bind and to loose which He entrusts to them—first to Peter personally (Matt. xvi. 19) and afterwards to all the Twelve (Matt. xviii. 18)—in such a way, too, that their present decisions will be somehow or other binding at the Judgment. Or does the "upon earth" refer only to the fact that the Messianic Last Judgment will be held on earth? "I give unto thee the Keys of the Kingdom of Heaven, and whatsoever thou shalt bind on earth shall be bound in heaven, and whatsoever thou shalt loose on earth shall be loosed in heaven" (Matt. xvi. 19). Why should these words not be historical? Is it because in the same context Jesus speaks of the "church" which He will found upon the Rock-disciple? But if one has once got a clear idea from Paul, a Clement, the Epistle to the Hebrews, and the Shepherd of Hermas, what the pre-existing "church" was which was to appear in the last times, it will no longer appear impossible that Jesus might have spoken of the church against which the gates of hell shall not prevail. Of course, if the passage is given an uneschatological reference to the Church as we know it, it loses all real meaning and becomes a treasure-trove to the Roman Catholic exegete, and a terror to the Protestant.

286.

That he could be taken for the Baptist risen from the dead shows how short a time before the death of the Baptist His ministry had begun. He only became known, as the Baptist's question shows, at the time of the mission of the disciples; Herod first heard of Him after the death of the Baptist. Had he known anything of Jesus beforehand, it would have been impossible for him suddenly to identify Him with the Baptist risen from the dead. This elementary consideration has been overlooked in all calculations of the length of the public ministry of Jesus.

287.

That had been rightly remarked by Colani. Later, however, theology lost sight of the fact because it did not know how to make any historical use of it.

288.

Psal. Sol. xv. 8.

289.

That the baptism of John was essentially an act which gave a claim to something future may be seen from the fact that Jesus speaks of His sufferings and death as a special baptism, and asks the sons of Zebedee whether they are willing, for the sake of gaining the thrones on His right hand and His left, to undergo this baptism. If the baptism of John had had no real sacramental significance it would be unintelligible that Jesus should use this metaphor.

290.

The thought of the Messianic feast is found in Isaiah lv. 1 ff. and lxv. 12 ff. It is very strongly marked in Isa. xxv. 6-8, a passage which perhaps dates from the time of Alexander the Great, "and Jahweh of Hosts will prepare upon this mountain for all peoples a feast of fat things, a feast of wine on the lees, of fat things prepared with marrow, of wine on the lees well refined. He shall destroy, in this mountain, among all peoples, the veil which has veiled all peoples and the covering which has covered all nations. He shall destroy death for ever, and the Lord Jahweh shall wipe away the tears from off all faces; and the reproach of His people shall disappear from the earth." (The German follows Kautzsch's translation.)

In Enoch xxiv. and xxv. the conception of the Messianic feast is connected with that of the tree of life which shall offer its fruits to the elect upon the mountain of the King. Similarly in the Testament of Levi, cap. xviii. 11.

The decisive passage is in Enoch lxii. 14. After the Parousia of the Son of Man, and after the Judgment, the elect who have been saved "shall eat with the Son of Man, shall sit down and rise up with Him to all eternity."

Jesus' references to the Messianic feast are therefore not merely images, but point to a reality. In Matt. viii. 11 and 12 He prophesies that many shall come from the East and from the West to sit at meat with Abraham, Isaac, and Jacob. In Matt. xxii. 1-14 the Messianic feast is pictured as a royal marriage, in Matt. xxv. 1-13 as a marriage feast.

The Apocalypse is dominated by the thought of the feast in all its forms. In Rev. ii. 7 it appears in connexion with the thought of the tree of life; in ii. 17 it is pictured as a feeding with manna; in iii. 21 it is the feast which the Lord will celebrate with His followers; in vii. 16, 17 there is an allusion to the Lamb who shall feed His own so that they shall no more hunger or thirst; chapter xix. describes the marriage feast of the Lamb.

The Messianic feast therefore played a dominant part in the conception of blessedness from Enoch to the Apocalypse of John. From this we can estimate what sacramental significance a guarantee of taking part in that feast must have had. The meaning of the celebration was obvious in itself, and was made manifest in the conduct of it. The sacramental effect was wholly independent of the apprehension and comprehension of the recipient. Therefore, in this also the meal at the lake-side was a true sacrament.

291.
Weisse rightly remarks that the task of the historian in dealing with Mark must consist in explaining how such "myths" could be accepted by a chronicler who stood so relatively near the events as our Mark does.

292.
It is to be noticed that the cry of Jesus from the cross, "Eli, Eli," was immediately interpreted by the bystanders as referring to Elias.

293.
From this difficulty we can see, too, how impossible it was for any of them to have "arrived gradually at the knowledge of the Messiahship of Jesus."

294.
For the hypothesis of the two sets of narratives which have been worked into one another, see the "Sketch of the Life of Jesus," 1901, p. 52 ff., "After the Mission of the Disciples. Literary and historical problems." A theory resting on the same principle was lately worked out in detail by Johannes Weiss, *Das älteste Evangelium* (The Earliest Gospel), 1903, p. 205 ff.

295.

It is typical of the constant agreement of the critical conclusions in thoroughgoing scepticism and thoroughgoing eschatology that Wrede also observes: "The transfiguration and Peter's confession are closely connected in content" (p. 123). He also clearly perceives the inconsistency in the fact that Peter at Caesarea Philippi gives evidence of possessing a knowledge which he and his fellow-disciples do not show elsewhere (p. 119), but the fact that it is Peter, not Jesus, who reveals the Messianic secret, constitutes a very serious difficulty for Wrede's reading of the facts, since this assumes Jesus to have been the revealer of it.

296.

"After these years shall my Son, the Christ, die, together with all who have the breath of men. Then shall the Age be changed into the primeval silence; seven days, as at the first beginning so that no man shall be left. After seven days shall the Age, which now sleeps, awake, and perishability shall itself perish."

297.

Difficult problems are involved in the prediction of the resurrection in Mark xiv. 28. Jesus there promises His disciples that He will "go before them" into Galilee. That cannot mean that He will go alone into Galilee before them, and that they shall there meet with Him, their risen Master; what He contemplates is that He shall return *with* them, at their head, from Jerusalem to Galilee. Was it that the manifestation of the Son of Man and of the Judgment should take place there? So much is clear: the saying, far from directing the disciples to go away to Galilee, chains them to Jerusalem, there to await Him who should lead them home. It should not therefore be claimed as supporting the tradition of the Galilaean appearances.

We find it "corrected" by the saying of the "young man" at the grave, who says to the women, "Go, tell His disciples and Peter that He goeth before you into Galilee. There shall ye see Him as He said unto you."

Here then the idea of following in point of time is foisted upon the words "he goeth before you," whereas in the original the word has a purely local sense, corresponding to the καὶ ἦν προάγων αὐτοὺς ὁ Ἰησοῦς in Mark x. 32.

But the correction is itself meaningless since the visions took place in Jerusalem. We have therefore in this passage a more detailed indication of the way in which Jesus thought of the events subsequent to His Resurrection. The interpretation of this unfulfilled saying is, however, wholly impossible for us: it was not less so for the earliest tradition, as is shown by the attempt to give it a meaning by the "correction."

298.

Here it is evident also from the form taken by the prophecy of the sufferings that the section Mark viii. 34 ff. cannot possibly come after the revelation at Caesarea Philippi, since in it, it is the thought of the general sufferings which is implied. For the same reason the predictions of suffering and tribulation in the Synoptic Apocalypse in Mark xiii. cannot be derived from Jesus.

299.

Weisse and Bruno Bauer had long ago pointed out how curious it was that Jesus in the sayings about His sufferings spoke of "many" instead of speaking of "His own" or "the believers." Weisse found in the words the thought that Jesus died for the nation as a whole; Bruno Bauer that the "for many" in the words of Jesus was derived from the view of the later theology of the Christian community. This explanation is certainly wrong, for so soon as the words of Jesus come into any kind of contact with early theology the "many" disappear to give place to the "believers." In the Pauline words of institution the form is: My body for you (1 Cor. xi. 24).

Johannes Weiss follows in the footsteps of Weisse when he interprets the "many" as the nation (*Die Predigt Jesu vom Reiche Gottes*, 2nd ed., 1909, p. 201). He gives however, quite a false turn to this interpretation by arguing that the "many" cannot include the disciples, since they "who in faith and penitence have received the tidings of the Kingdom of God no longer need a special means of deliverance such as this." They are the chosen, to them the Kingdom is assured. But a ransom, a special means of salvation, is needful for the mass of the people, who in their blindness have incurred the guilt of rejecting the Messiah. For this grave sin, which is, nevertheless, to some extent excused as due to ignorance, there is a unique atoning sacrifice, the death of the Messiah.

This theory is based on a distinction of which there is no hint in the teaching of Jesus; and it takes no account of the predestinarianism which is an integral part of eschatology, and which, in fact, dominated the thoughts of Jesus. The Lord is conscious that He dies only for the elect. For others His death can avail nothing, nor even their own repentance. Moreover, He does not die in order that this one or that one may come into the Kingdom of God; He provides the atonement in order that the Kingdom itself may come. Until the Kingdom comes even the elect cannot possess it.

300.

One might use it as a principle of division by which to classify the lives of Jesus, whether they make Him go to Jerusalem to work or to die. Here as in so many other places Weisse's clearness of perception is surprising. Jesus' journey was according to him a pilgrimage to death, not to the Passover.

301.

"That ye enter not into temptation" is the content of the prayer that they are to offer while watching with Him.

302.

As long ago as 1880, H. W. Bleby (*The Trial of Jesus considered as a Judicial Act*) had emphasised this circumstance as significant. The injustice in the trial of Jesus consisted, according to him, in the fact that He was condemned on His own admission without any witnesses being called. Dalman, it is true, will not admit that this technical error was very serious.

But the really important point is not whether the condemnation was legal or not; it is the significant fact that the High Priest called no witnesses. Why did he not call any? This question was obscured for Bleby and Dalman by other problems.

303.

That would have been to utter a heresy which would alone have sufficed to secure His condemnation. It would certainly have been brought up as a charge against Him.

304.

When it is assumed that the Messianic claims of Jesus were generally known during those last days at Jerusalem there is a temptation to explain the absence of witnesses in regard to them by supposing that they were too much a matter of common knowledge to require evidence. But in that case why should the High Priest not have fulfilled the prescribed formalities? Why make such efforts first to establish a different charge? Thus the obscure and unintelligible procedure at the trial of Jesus becomes in the end the clearest proof that the public knew nothing of the Messiahship of Jesus.

CPSIA information can be obtained
at www.ICGtesting.com
Printed in the USA
BVOW04s1409290617
488064BV00007B/14/P